FOUNDATIONS OF P

Foundations of Private Law

Property, Tort, Contract, Unjust Enrichment

JAMES GORDLEY

OXFORD

UNIVERSITY PRESS

OXFORD
UNIVERSITY PRESS

Great Clarendon Street, Oxford OX2 6DP

Oxford University Press is a department of the University of Oxford.
It furthers the University's objective of excellence in research, scholarship,
and education by publishing worldwide in

Oxford New York

Auckland   Cape Town Dar es Salaam Hong Kong   Karachi
Kuala Lumpur Madrid Melbourne Mexico City   Nairobi
New Delhi Shanghai Taipei Toronto
With offices in
Argentina Austria Brazil Chile Czech Republic France Greece
Guatemala Hungary Italy Japan South Korea Poland Portugal
Singapore Switzerland Thailand Turkey Ukraine Vietnam

Oxford is a registered trade mark of Oxford University Press
in the UK and in certain other countries

Published in the United States
by Oxford University Press Inc., New York

ISBN 978-0-19-922766-2

To Barbara

Acknowledgements

Many thanks are due to the following publishers for their kind permission to re-use material which has previously appeared, and which has been drawn upon to varying extents in the writing of this book.

Material from 'The Common Law in the Twentieth Century: Some Unfinished Business' © 2000 by the California Law Review, Inc. is reprinted by permission from the *California Law Review* vol. 88, no. 6.

Material from 'Water Rights' by J. Gordley in *Law and Justice in a Multistate World: Essays in Honour of Arthur T. von Mehren* (J. A. R. Nafziger and S. Symeonides, eds., Transnational Publishers, 2002) is reproduced by kind permission of Transnational Publishers, Inc.

Material from 'Servitudes' is reproduced from *Global Jurist* vol. 3, no. 1.; and material from 'The Purpose of Awarding Restitutionary Damages' is reproduced from *Theoretical Inquiries in Law* vol. 1 by kind permission of The Berkeley Electronic Press.

Material from 'Protecting Possession' by J. Gordley and U. Mattei is reproduced from *The American Journal of Comparative Law* vol. 44; material from 'Mistake in Contract Formation' by J. Gordley, *The American Journal of Comparative Law* vol. 52; and material from 'Impossibility and Changed or Unforeseen Circumstances' *The American Journal of Comparative Law* is reproduced here by kind permission.

Material from 'Contract Law in the Aristotelian Tradition' by J. Gordley in *The Theory of Contract Law: New Essays* (P. Benson, ed., Cambridge University Press, 2001); from 'The Universalist Heritage' by J. Gordley in *Comparative Legal Studies: Traditions and Transitions* (P. Legrand and R. Munday, eds., Cambridge University Press, 2003); from 'The Rule against Recovery in Negligence for Pure Economic Loss' by J. Gordley in *Pure Economic Loss in Europe* (M. Bussani and V.V. Palmer, eds., Cambridge University Press, 2003); and from 'Restitution without Enrichment' by J. Gordley in *Unjustified Enrichment: Key Issues in Comparative Perspective* (D. Johnston and R. Zimmermann, eds., Cambridge University Press, 2002) is reproduced by permission of Cambridge University Press.

Material from 'The Principle of Unjust Enrichment?' by J. Gordley in *Gedächtnisschrift für Alexander Lüderitz* (K. Luig, H. Schack, and H. Wiedemann, eds., C.H. Beck Verlag, 2000); and material from 'Immissionsschutz, Nuisance and *Troubles de Voisinage* in Comparative and Historical Perspective' in *Zeitschrift für Europäisches Privatrecht* vol. 13 is reproduced by kind permission of Verlag C.H. Beck.

Contents

V. UNJUST ENRICHMENT

PART I
THE ENTERPRISE

The Enterprise

This book will try to identify the principles that underlie basic fields of private law: property, tort, contract, and unjust enrichment. It will not deal with the law of marriage and inheritance although these fields are often counted as part of private law. They involve much different considerations such as what families should be like and how much control people should have over resources after they have died.

While this work builds on that of other scholars, it is different in two ways. One difference is that I will examine the law of the number of Western countries while most scholars consider their own. Their approach is too narrow if, as we shall see, similar societies face similar problems Moreover, most countries are facing them with common tools forged in the West, at first by the Romans, and now in use throughout the world. Thus they face similar problems as to how these tools should be used.

I wish that time and my own skills enabled me to consider the law of more countries. I have had to concentrate on those which have been the great exporters of ideas: the law of the more prominent common law and civil law jurisdictions. Nevertheless, I am afraid that because I am examining the law of several jurisdictions, this work will be classified, not as one about law, but as one about 'comparative law'. In my view, many scholars who specialize in 'comparative law' have obscured the reason for looking at the law of more than one country. Until late in the 20th century, the idea that dominated comparative legal research was that the law of each jurisdiction constituted a 'system'. One could not compare legal rules without seeing their place within a 'system'.[1] The archetypical work was by René David: *Les Grands Systèmes de droit contemporains*.[2] According to David, 'Each law constitutes in fact a system: it employs a certain vocabulary, corresponding to certain legal concepts; it uses certain methods to interpret them; it is tied to a certain conception of social order which determines the means of application and the function of law'.[3] This approach gave the impression that the law of England or France or Germany formed a coherent whole based on certain general principles or conceptions of law which were the key to understanding its rules. I believe, instead, that the jurists in all these so-called 'systems' were struggling with common problems, guided by similar concepts dimly glimpsed, but not expressed clearly in their national legal systems. If I am right, then we can learn much by seeing how others have faced similar problems. We will feel reassured when solutions are similar. We will understand a problem better when jurists have striven for similar results even at the cost of stretching the formal rules and doctrine of their own systems. We will see that sometimes different rules are different means to obtaining the same results. If so, it is wrong to consider how the jurists of one country deal with a problem without considering the efforts of others. To consider their efforts is not 'comparative law' except in the sense it is 'comparative engineering' for GM to see what Daimler Benz is doing. To do so is integral to the study of the legal problems

---

[1] Marc Ancel, 'Les grandes étapes de la recherche comparative all XXᶜ siècle', in *Studi in memoria di Andrea Torrente* (1968), 21. [2] (7th edn, Paris, 1978).
[3] ibid. 20.

themselves. I will show in Chapter 2 that much of the difference between national laws has little to do with differences in ultimate principles and more to do with how they should be understood and applied.

Another and more fundamental departure from most legal scholarship is my account of where we are in the enterprise of making sense of private law. I have a story to tell which may seem on its face unpersuasive to my contemporaries. I believe the basic principles which can explain private law were once more clearly grasped than they are now. The source of our present confusion is that we lost track of them.

Private law, as we now understand it, was the creation of Roman lawyers. I will show that this is so even in common law jurisdictions. Before the 19th century, English law was organized around writs, with a collage of rules governing when writs could be brought. Order was brought out of chaos in the 19th century when the English, borrowing a huge amount from the civil law, reorganized their thinking around such categories as contract and tort—rather than assumpsit and trespass—and imported continental learning to understand these categories. That says a good deal for the work of the Romans. As will be seen, they developed the legal categories in which we still think, categories which must be of value or they would not have spread across the world. But their thinking was not systematic or theoretical. They considered specific cases or proposed general maxims. They certainly would not have analyzed consent, as a Greek philosopher might have done, by discussing what will or intention means.

I believe, and I have explained in my previous writings,[4] that the first coherent legal theory, in which the particular cases and the maxims were explained by general principles, came from a self-conscious effort to combine Roman law with Greek philosophy, and in particular, the philosophy of Aristotle. Curiously enough, that attempt was not made during the Middle Ages, when the Roman legal texts ruled the law schools and Aristotle much of the rest of the curriculum. The medieval jurists stuck to their Roman texts. The Aristotelians, under the influence of philosophers such as Thomas Aquinas, explored problems of moral philosophy. An attempt to combine the two approaches began in Spain in the 16th century with a group that historians refer to as the 'late scholastics'. The result, I have argued, was a reorganization of Roman law into a systematic doctrinal structure on the basis of Aristotelian philosophical principles. Paradoxically, many of their conclusions were adopted by the northern natural law school of the 17th and 18th centuries just as the Aristotelian premises on which they had been founded were coming under attack by the new school of critical philosophy.

The argument of this book, in essence, is that these older writers in the Aristotelian tradition had it right, or, at least, most of it. They identified the basic principles which best explain not only the Roman law of their times but modern private law as well. True, there were matters they failed to consider—such as what we call the law of nuisance—and matters they failed to explain—such as what we call strict liability. Yet if we consider their basic principles, we can see how to resolve even these problems.

The first chapter of this part will describe their basic principles. It will show that they were relatively simple although they were expressed in a technical vocabulary and

---

[4] Especially, James Gordley, *The Philosophical Origins of Modern Contract Doctrine* (Oxford, 1991).

have often been misunderstood. Indeed, a modern person with no allegiance to any philosophical system might take them as matters of common sense. Chapter 1 will also show that these principles were rejected during the 'Enlightenment' for reasons that do not commend themselves today. They were rejected, not because they contradicted common sense, but rather because common sense was no longer accepted as a proper standard. They were rejected in the hope that new ideas would prove fruitful which in fact have proved sterile. Those contemporaries who take a modern approach are led into inconsistencies. While the first two chapters will deal with these fundamental problems, later chapters will explain how the older principles can best explain private law. If they can, that alone says much about modern attempts. If those principles can explain much of modern law, it is so much the worse for philosophies whose principles cannot.

I will try to show, then, that principles that commend themselves to our own common sense, that were once accepted almost universally long ago, that were discarded for the wrong reasons, still best explain private law. It would be an important objection if these principles were not coherent. I will explain why they are in Chapter 1. It would be an important objection if common principles could not explain laws that differ. I will explain how they can in Chapter 2. The heart of the enterprise, however, to which all but the two introductory chapters are devoted, is to show how these principles can best explain the law of property, tort, contract, and unjust enrichment. If they can, there is something to be said for these principles, whatever one thinks of their philosophical pedigree.

Some scholars may believe I cannot stop there. Historically, those who expounded these principles claimed they were universal and linked them to a coherent metaphysics. Some may think I should preface this book by a larger one considering whether these principles are reflected in the law of every culture or evaluating the truth of Aristotelian metaphysics. Those may be worthy enterprises but I do not think I have to undertake them here. I do believe that the knowledge of each thing is ultimately tied to the knowledge of every other. But it is a poor scholarly method that demands one claim either to know everything or to know nothing. It would be surprising if the principles that govern tort law in England or Germany were not linked to higher principles of moral philosophy which may or may not be universal or linked to the nature of man. That does not mean every book on private law must consider the principles of law in every culture or the nature of man. Each scholar has to work on part of the puzzle. But other scholars should then react to what he has done. Suppose it is right, as we will argue, that Western law, which is now nearly ubiquitous, is best explained by principles of the Aristotelian tradition. Why is that so? Those who are hostile to that tradition should explain why these principles have such explanatory power, how a misguided philosophy gave rise to them, or how they can be defended without recourse to that philosophy. Of course, they might claim instead that these principles do not have the explanatory power with which I credit them. But the point of this book is to show that they do.

1

Basic Principles

I. The Aristotelian Tradition

Writers in the Aristotelian tradition believed there is a distinctively human life to which all one's capacities and abilities contribute. Living such a life is the ultimate end to which all well-chosen actions are a means, either instrumentally or as constituent parts of such a life. Actions which contribute to such a life are right. Those that detract from it are wrong. Unlike other animals, a human being can identify the actions that do contribute. In doing so, a person exercises an acquired ability—a virtue—which these writers called 'prudence'. In following the dictates of prudence, he may need other virtues as well, such as the courage to face pain and danger or the temperance to forego pleasure.

The type of prudence a person exercises in seeing that an action contributes to the sort of life he should live (*nous* for Aristotle, *intellectus* for Thomas Aquinas) has been translated as 'understanding' or 'intuition'.[1] To call this ability 'prudence' does not explain how it works. It is merely to say that somehow, we are able to see that some choices are right and others wrong. Without such an ability we would never be able to act rightly. In any event, this ability is not deductive logic. Prudent people understand things that they cannot demonstrate.

To found ethics on deductive logic might suggest that the same choices are always either right or wrong like the conclusions of mathematics. While prudence indicates that some choices are right or wrong, the same choices are not always right or wrong for everyone. People are different and so are their circumstances. Even if they were not, there still might not be just one right or best choice a person should make. Freedom of the will, according to Aquinas, means not merely that one can choose to do right or wrong but that there can be different ways to choose rightly, no one of which is best.[2] Nevertheless, the choice may matter very much. It matters which of many possible beautiful buildings an architect chooses to build even though one cannot rank order their beauty. For Aquinas, it mattered that God created the universe, but he discussed God's freedom in the same way as that of human beings: there is no best of all possible worlds that God had to create.[3]

The Aristotelian ethical tradition is out of fashion. William James once said, however, without meaning to be complimentary, that much of it could be described as

---

[1] Aristotle, *Nicomachean Ethics* IV.xi; Thomas Aquinas, *Summa theologiae* II-II, Q. 49, a. 2.
[2] Thomas Aquinas, *Summa theologiae* I–II, Q. 10, a. 2; Q. 13, a. 6.   [3] ibid. I, Q. 19, aa. 3, 10.

'common sense made pedantic'. Despite the rise of modern philosophy, I suspect that most people, as a matter of common sense, do believe that some ways a person can live are better than others, and that those people who live in a better way more fully realize what it means to be a human being. They recognize that while there are many good ways to be a human being, there are some that are decidedly bad. They believe that while they are fallible, they have some ability to tell the difference, an ability which is not merely deductive logic.

In any event, for writers in the Aristotelian tradition, living a distinctively human life requires, not only virtues such as prudence, temperance and courage, but external things as well. Moreover, because human life is social, a person should not only want such things for himself but want to help others acquire them as well. They distinguished two fundamental concepts of justice on which the law ultimately rests: distributive and commutative justice. The object of distributive justice is to ensure that each person has the resources he requires. The object of commutative justice is to enable him to obtain them without unfairly diminishing others' ability to do so.

These ideas intertwine. It is good to preserve each person's share of resources because it is good for each person to have what he needs to live as he should. One can speak about how a person should live because there is a distinctively human life to be lived and a distinctively human capacity to understand and to choose what contributes to such a life.

We will consider the concepts of distributive and commutative justice in detail since much of what follows will turn on them. The Aristotelian tradition provided a plausible account of them. Later philosophers, as we will see, did not.

In the case of distributive justice, while the ultimate objective is to provide people with what they need to live well, it does not follow that resources should be allocated by asking what things each person needs and assigning them to him. Hugo Grotius pointed out that such a system could work only if a society is very small and its members are on quite good terms.[4] In any event, each person's own decision about what he most needs would then be subject to the judgment of an allocator rather than left to his own prudence. Most writers in the Aristotelian tradition do not even consider the possibility. For them, distributive justice is concerned with giving each person a proper share of resources.

Ideally, each citizen should receive a share that is proportional to his 'merit' or 'desert'. There is, however, no single principle for appraising merit. Aristotle and Thomas Aquinas mention two different and conflicting ones and hint that there is some truth in both. According to one principle, which would be favored in a democracy, every person ideally should have the same amount. To the extent a society is democratic, greater virtue, meaning a greater capacity to make the right choices, does not entitle a person to make more choices. A society in which greater virtue did entitle one to do so would not be a democracy but an aristocracy, or rule of the virtuous (as distinguished from an oligarchy in which the power to govern would come from wealth or inherited status). According to the principle of distributive justice that an

---

[4] Hugo Grotius, *De iure belli ac pacis libri tres* (B. J. A. de Kanter-van Hetting Tromp, ed., Leiden, 1939), II.ii.2.

aristocracy would favor, those with superior virtue should ideally have a larger share of resources.[5]

Here, equality (or inequality) of resources should not be confused with equality (or inequality) of welfare as a utilitarian or a modern economist would imagine it. True welfare or happiness, in the Aristotelian tradition, is not defined in terms of utility or preference satisfaction but in terms of leading a good life. To say that resources are distributed equally in a democracy does not mean that people are equally able to lead such a life since, democracy or not, the virtuous are better able to make choices and will be able to live better. Equality means equal power to command resources: what we might roughly call equal purchasing power.[6] Ronald Dworkin in an important essay called it 'equality of resources' as opposed to 'equality in welfare'. As an illustration, he imagined shipwrecked sailors on an island dividing its resources equally by auctioning them off, all bids to be made in clam shells, and each sailor to start with an equal number of shells.[7] My image in an earlier article was similar: heirs auctioning the items in an estate among themselves by bidding in poker chips, each starting with an equal number.[8]

Writers in this tradition made it clear that such principles are ideals. A democracy should not confiscate the wealth of rich people, virtuous or otherwise, and divide it up.[9] We can see one reason why they should not if we consider Aristotle's objections—which Aquinas shared—to Plato's proposal to abolish private property. Do so, Aristotle said, and there will be endless quarrels, and people will have no incentive to work or to take care of property.[10]

These conclusions became staples of the Aristotelian tradition. They were accepted in the 16th and early 17th centuries, by a group known to historians as the late scholastics or Spanish natural law school, who self-consciously attempted to synthesize Roman law with the ideas of their intellectual heroes, Aristotle and Aquinas. Few people today are familiar even with the names of its leaders: for example, Domingo de Soto (1494–1560), Luis de Molina (1535–1600) and Leonard Lessius (1554–1623), and yet, as I have shown elsewhere,[11] they were the first to give Roman law a theory and a systematic doctrinal structure. Their work deeply influenced the 17th century

---

[5] Aristotle, *Nicomachean Ethics* V.iv. 1131^b–1132^b; Thomas Aquinas, *Summa theologiae* II-II, Q. 61, a. 2.

[6] Roughly, because people acquire things that are worth more to them than the amount of purchasing power they represent. A person who loses such a thing, and cannot buy another like it, will have lost more than that amount. Consequently, if someone takes or destroys it, he should pay its value to the owner even if that is more than the amount for which the owner could have sold it. If something identical is not available on the market and someone offers to buy it, the owner can sell it for a price that reflects its value to him. See James Gordley, 'Contract Law in the Aristotelian Tradition', in Peter Benson, ed., *The Theory of Contract Law: New Essays* (Cambridge, 2001), 265 at 313.

[7] Ronald Dworkin, 'What is Equality? Part 2: Equality of Resources', *Phil. & Pub. Affairs* 10 (1981), 283–90.   [8] James Gordley, 'Equality in Exchange', *Calif. L. Rev.* 69 (1981), 1587 at 1614–15.

[9] Aristotle, *Politics* V.5. 1304^b; V.9. 1310^a; VI.3. 1318^a, 25–6; VI.5 1319^b–1320^a.

[10] Aristotle, *Politics* II.v; Thomas Aquinas, *Summa theologiae* II-II, Q. 66, a. 2.

[11] James Gordley, *The Philosophical Origins of Modern Contract Doctrine* (Oxford, 1991), 69–111; James Gordley, 'Tort Law in the Aristotelian Tradition', in David Owen, ed., *Philosophical Foundations of Tort Law: A Collection of Essays* (Oxford, 1995), 131; James Gordley, 'The Principle against Unjustified Enrichment', in Klaus Luig, Haimo Schack, and Herbert Wiedemann, eds., *Gedächtnisschrift für Alexander Lüderitz* (Munich, 2000), 213.

founders of the northern natural law school, Hugo Grotius (1583–1645) and Samuel
Pufendorf (1632–94) who disseminated many of their conclusions through northern
Europe, paradoxically, at the very time that Aristotelian and Thomistic philosophy
was falling out of fashion. While these authors developed the ideas just described in
different ways, they all said that by nature, or originally, or in principle, all things
belong to everyone. They all described private ownership as instituted to overcome the
disadvantages of common ownership, usually the ones mentioned by Aristotle and
Aquinas.[12]

Subject to these limitations, however, they agreed that one person could not deprive
another of his property. The owner may have more than he ideally should since an
incentive has to be given to work and to manage. But, by establishing the incentives,
the society has recognized that a person is entitled to the larger share that his work and
good management brings him. The actual distribution of resources in society can only
approximate the ideal.

These writers also accepted the Roman rule, *res pereat domino*—the accidental loss
of a thing is borne by its owner. The late scholastics recognized that not only physical
destruction but fluctuations in prices could change the distribution of purchasing
power. They acknowledged that prices fluctuate, and must do so to reflect what they
called the need, the scarcity and the cost of goods.[13] Modern writers such as Stephen
Perry and Ernest Weinrib have thought it strange that if there is such a thing as a just
distribution, accidents should be allowed to change it.[14] Writers in the Aristotelian
tradition acknowledged that accidents could do so, but still believed, as I think most
people do today, that some distributions of resources are in principle more fair than
others.

While they are not explicit, I doubt if they could imagine a workable society which
did not allow random events and price changes to change the distribution of wealth
anymore than one which did not allow incentives to care for property or to labor.
Indeed, to eliminate chance gains and losses, a society would have to distinguish them
from gains and losses that are the result of labor and care. That may not be possible.
Even if it were, the attempt might lead to so many charges of arbitrariness as to cause
the quarrels that a system of private property is supposed to prevent.

Moreover, some resources are more vulnerable to chance destruction or to price
fluctuation than others. Some decisions about what to produce or consume are more
prone to error. If everyone were fully compensated when his property was destroyed or
his decisions were thwarted by bad luck, those who had chosen to hold more vulnerable

---

[12] Domenicus Soto, *De iustitia et iure libri decem* (Salamanca, 1551), lib. 4, q. 3, a. 1; Ludovicus Molina,
De iustitia et iure tractatus (Venice, 1614), disp. 20; Leonardus Lessius, *De iustitia et iure, ceterisque vir-
tutibus cardinalis libri quatuor* (Paris, 1628), lib. 2, cap. 5, dubs. 1–2; Grotius, *De iure belli ac pacis*, II.ii.2;
Samuel Pufendorf, *De iure naturae et gentium libri octo* (Amsterdam, 1688), II.vi.5; IV.iv.4–7.

[13] Gordley, *Philosophical Origins*, 94–102; Soto, *De iustitia et iure libri*, lib. 6, q. 2, a. 3; Molina, *De iustitia et iure* II, disp. 348; All of these factors had been mentioned, albeit cryptically, by Thomas Aquinas. *In
decem libros ethicorum expositio* (Angeli Pirotta, ed., Matriti, 1934), lib. 5, lec. 9; *Summa theologiae* II-II, Q.
77, a. 3 ad 4. They were discussed by medieval commentators on Aristotle. Odd Langholm, *Price and Value
in the Aristotelian Tradition* (Bergen, 1979), 61–143.

[14] Stephen Perry, 'The Moral Foundations of Tort Law', *Iowa L. Rev.* 77 (1992), 449 at 451; Ernest
Weinrib, 'Corrective Justice', *Iowa L. Rev.* 77 (1992), 403 at 420.

property or to embark on riskier projects would consume more resources than those who did not. A person who chose to live in a glass house, to pick an extreme example, might use up five or ten houses in the same time another person would use up one. If he were compensated, the system would not be conserving a given distribution of wealth but transferring wealth to persons whose property is more vulnerable and whose projects are more adventurous.

Writers in the Aristotelian tradition do not make these arguments expressly. But they may have had an understandable difficulty in seeing how one could eliminate the rule *res pereat domino*. Thus, although they recognized that even commutative justice depended upon distributive justice, they recognized then, that the principle that should ideally govern the distribution of wealth could only be approximated.

If this perspective is correct, the social controversies of modern times can be better understood. While these controversies will not go away, they should turn on questions of feasibility and fairness. It is not helpful to consider property rights without considering fairness and distributive justice. Conversely, it is not helpful to be concerned about justice while failing to look carefully at questions of feasibility.

In any event, in this study, this account of distributive justice will figure in two ways. First, when the question of how property rights should be acquired or defined arises, we will continually return to the reasons why such rights should exist in the first place. Often, the reason may be that there are pragmatic constraints on how they ideally should be. We must identify these constraints and see how they should be limited. That approach is different than one which regards property rights as sacrosanct and unlimited. It is also different than one which identifies pragmatic constraints with 'utility' as a modern economist understands the term. Economists tend to define utility in terms of the ability to satisfy a preference—whatever the preference may be—given the resources one happens to possess—however that distribution may help or hinder others in their pursuit of a good life. The difficulties with this approach will be considered later. Here, we need only note that many writers have seen only these two alternatives: either rights must be sacrosanct or they must depend on utilitarian considerations and so be defeasible when those considerations so dictate.

In contrast, by the older approach, respect for rights and considerations of pragmatism walk hand in hand. Ideally, a person should have a certain share of wealth. Unfortunately, he often cannot if we are to provide others with an incentive to labor and conserve resources. That is a pragmatic consideration which long predated modern economists' notions of utility. If, however, for pragmatic reasons, the law provides such an incentive, then the person who labors and conserves resources thereby acquires a right. The extent of his right is limited by the pragmatic reasons for providing the incentive. But one cannot deprive him of his right without reneging on the commitments which such a system entails. There is no contradiction then, between defining a right in terms of the pragmatic considerations that lead to its recognition, and recognizing that it is a right nonetheless. As we will see, if we overlook that point, we cannot explain most of private law.

One of my critics has claimed that because my approach offers an integral account of both rights and pragmatic considerations, it cannot form an intellectually coherent whole. It must 'disaggregate into a mixture of utilitarian and rights-based justifications'.[15] This critic may be influenced by modern philosophers, who, as we will see, have based their theories either on promoting 'utility' or on preserving rights. But there is no logical inconsistency. Indeed, 'disaggregation' defies common sense. Surely, the law can care both about getting people what they deserve and about the practical difficulties of doing so. Surely, on account of practical difficulties, the law can recognize and delimit certain rights, which are rights even though they owe their origin to practical considerations.

There is a second reason for being concerned about distributive justice when we consider private law. Private law, by the older approach, largely concerns commutative justice. Aristotle distinguished two kinds of commutative justice. In involuntary transactions, where one person took another's resources against his will, commutative justice required that he give them back or their monetary equivalent. In voluntary transactions—what we would call contracts of exchange—each party willed to give up some of his own resources in return for those of another. Commutative justice required that he do so at a price that enriched neither party at the other's expense. As we will see, these distinctions not only resemble the ones we draw between contract and tort but maybe their linear ancestors.[16] As we will see, the late scholastics grounded the law of unjust enrichment on the same principle: that no one should be enriched at another's expense.[17] If this approach is correct, the basic concepts of private law are rooted in the concept of commutative justice, a concept which cannot be divorced from distributive justice.

Two consequences follow. One—which will be pursued throughout this book—is that one cannot define the rules of contract or tort or unjust enrichment without regard to commutative justice, or in other words, without regard to the effect of these rules on the distribution of resources between the parties. The point of contracts of exchange is to allow the parties to exchange resources so that neither party enriches himself at the other's expense. The point of tort is that a party who has enriched himself at another's expense owes compensation. The point of unjust enrichment law is that no one party should be enriched at another's expense without some good reason. In each case fairness—in the sense of commutative justice—shapes the transaction and its rules. One can no more explain contract, tort or unjust enrichment without regard to commutative justice than one could explain the digestive system without regard to the fact that it digests. Fairness, in the sense of commutative justice, is not a sort of limitation on these bodies of law but belongs to their definition.

The other consequence is that concern for justice in private transactions—largely a matter of commutative justice—cannot be divorced from concern for distributive justice. The relation of the two was explained by Thomas Aquinas. Distributive justice governs 'the order of the whole toward the parts, which concerns the order of that which belongs to the community in relation to each single person'. Commutative justice governs 'the order of one part to another, to which corresponds the order of one private individual to another'.[18] It is not the case, then, that at some point, possibly

---

[15] Stephen A. Smith, *Contract Theory* (Oxford, 2004), 52 n. 16 (speaking of my work on contract theory but his point is more general).   [16] Chapter 9 I.
[17] Chapter 19.   [18] *Summa theologiae* II-II, Q. 61, a. 1.

long ago, citizens or their ancestors were given a fair share of societal resources, and everything since has depended on their transactions with each other. Instead, we have to view society as an ongoing enterprise, concerned at the social level with ensuring, so far as possible, that each person has a fair share, and in individual transactions, that no one increases his share by depriving another of his resources.

If distributive justice did not matter to private law, we would have to ask why it should matter, in private law, if one person enriches himself by depriving another of his resources. Some theorists do not think it matters at all. Some believe that the point of law is to preserve public order. Others, whose views we will consider in detail, think that the desire to preserve one's own resources matters only because the law can handle the matter more efficiently than people can themselves. People will not buy guns if they are sure the law will protect them. Thus the law can prevent an inefficient over-production of guns. I'm not sure I understand that explanation. In the first place, some people buy guns not only to protect their own resources but take those of others. If law cured the problem, there would be no crime. Moreover, law and economics theories aside, most people think it is wrong for A to take B's resources, and not simply to avoid an economically inefficient overproduction of guns. But then we must consider why. At the moment, it is enough to say that there must be some reason B should have these resources instead of A which is not purely arbitary. That is simply another way of saying that there is a system for distributing resources in society which A should respect. It need not work perfectly. Perhaps B cannot put the resources to a better use than A, and in that sense, is less deserving of them. But if the system deviates from the ideal, there should be a pragmatic reason why it must. A must be asked to accept that it is better that B keep his resources than that every A, who thinks he can put them to better use, can redistribute wealth in his own favor at the point of a gun. Perhaps B acquired these resources by chance, or by placing his own greed ahead of the needs of his family. Still, without worse results, it is hard to see how to construct a system that rewards hard work and fortunate investments. If the system is so corrupt that it cannot give A any reason to respect what B considers to be his rights, I would not be unsympathetic to A. Robin Hood would not be a bad man if wealth were as arbitrarily distributed as those who praise him imagine. Absent that degree of corruption, however, it is hard to say how A could rip off B if he had to admit that the end result, if everyone followed his policy, would be that fewer people would have the resources they need, granted all the pragmatic compromises that must be made to secure them.

If I am right, Stephen Smith wrongly objects that by this view of distributive and commutative justice, a transaction could be fair 'only in societies—unlike any we know of—which are already distributively just'.[19] The question is one not only of fairness but of pragmatism.

In the chapters to come, we will argue that commutative justice is one of the key concepts needed to explain private law. While rooted in the Aristotelian tradition, the ideas just described again commend themselves to common sense. Most people think that external things can contribute to living a better life, and most, I believe, think it is

---

[19] Stephen A. Smith, 'In Defence of Substantive Fairness', *L. Quar. Rev.* 112 (1996), 138 at 147; Smith, *Contract Theory*, 355.

possible for people to have more or less than a fair share of them. Most think that it is impracticable to ensure everyone has a truly fair share since there must be incentives to conserve property and to labor, and society cannot reimburse everyone for any random loss. Nevertheless, while the distribution may fall short of the ideal, most people would agree that the law should protect a person's right to his own resources. If the distribution of resources can be improved, it should be done by a social decision, and not by individuals who go about redistributing wealth on their own. Thus the common sense views of most people may be better reflected in the Aristotelian tradition than in the more modern writers they are likely to encounter in school. Is that idea bizarre? And if not, how did we lose track of it?

II. The Break with the Aristotelian Tradition

A. The Jurists

As mentioned earlier, the late scholastics of the 16th and 17th centuries self-consciously reduced Roman law to a coherent system of doctrines and principles by drawing on the ethical theory of Aristotle and Thomas Aquinas. Many of their conclusions were accepted by the founders of the northern natural law school, Grotius and Pufendorf, although it is not clear how much of their original Aristotelian foundations these later writers understood. Many of the late scholastics' conclusions drifted through the late 17th and 18th centuries as their original philosophical foundations were forgotten. What did not happen, among the jurists, was the formation of some new synthesis explaining legal doctrine coherently in terms of one of the new philosophies of the 'Enlightenment'. Instead, jurists went on using concepts such as just price or equitable contract terms which had a meaning in the older philosophical synthesis but were now becoming incoherent.

The break came in the 19th century. Both civil and common lawyers tried to preserve a systematic legal doctrine while purging it of concepts of commutative and distributive justice which they had inherited from an earlier era and which no longer made sense to them. The key concept around which they tried to build private law was will. Will had figured in the earlier Aristotelian theories. According to Aristotle, in involuntary transactions, where one person took another's resources against his will, commutative justice required that he give them back or their monetary equivalent. In voluntary transactions—what we would call contracts of exchange—each party willed to give up some of his own resources in return for those of another. Commutative justice required that he do so at a price that enriched neither party at the other's expense. The innovation, for the 19th century will theorists, was that commutative and distributive justice no longer mattered. Contract simply meant that the law would enforce what the parties willed. Tort meant that one who invaded another's rights against his will had to pay. Property meant the right of the owner to do as he willed with his own.

Since the concept of will figured prominently in the philosophies present in their day—even though will was understood quite differently by utilitarians in England

and Kantians and Hegelians in Germany—it is tempting to imagine that the jurists, again, were borrowing from the philosophers. I think this is true only in a limited sense. The rise of modern philosophy had discredited almost any concept the jurists could build upon except that of will.[20] The jurists of the 19th century had little interest in trying to synthesize the philsophers' conceptions of law or will with their own work. That was not a task for which they were trained, and perhaps one in which they were not interested. They distanced themselves from the disputes of the philosophers and clung to the concept of will, chiefly, because, whatever it meant, it seemed to be the only concept that the 19th century philosophers regarded as sound. But that did not mean they took over the concept of will of the philosophers. The philosophers discussed the meaning of the will at length and in different ways. The jurists defined contract, tort and property in terms of will without explaining what the will is or why it matters.[21]

In England and the United States, it is hard to see the influence of any fashionable 19th century philosophical school of thought. Sir Frederick Pollock, who built the most elaborate will theory, explained that jurists should leave alone 'topics which ... may be philosophical, or ethical, or political, but are distinctly outside the province of jurisprudence'.[22] The 'business' of jurists is simply 'to learn and know ... what rules the State does undertake to enforce and administer, whatever the real or professed reasons for those rules may be'.[23]

Similarly, Ranouil observes in her study of the French will theorists that they seem hostile to philosophy, that they never cite Kant, and that, until the end of the 19th century, they never even speak of the autonomy of the will.[24] She concludes, nevertheless, that the will theorists must have been using the concept of autonomy of the will 'as Monsieur Jourdan used prose—without perceiving it'.[25] It would be more reasonable to conclude that the will theorists were not drawing on the ideas of Kant or any other philosophical, economic or political explanation of why the will was important.

In Germany, Savigny, who was one of the principal architects of the will theories, was also one of the most philosophical of German jurists. He gave an account of law that owed a good deal to Kant and Hegel. Law existed to protect freedom,[26] and its source was the *Volksgeist*—the unconscious mind or spirit of a particular people.[27] But neither he nor his followers rested their theories on a specifically Kantian or Hegelian conception of will. Indeed, Savigny sharply distinguished the legal concept of will from any philosophical conception: 'We in the area of law are not at all occupied with the speculative difficulties of the concept of freedom. For us, freedom is based

---

[20] Gordley, *Philosophical Origins*, 161–213.   [21] ibid. 214–29.

[22] Sir Frederick Pollock, 'The Nature of Jurisprudence Considered in Relation to some Recent Contributions to Legal Science', in Sir Frederick Pollock, *Essays in Jurisprudence and Ethics* (London, 1882), 19–20.

[23] Sir Frederick Pollock, *A First Book of Jurisprudence for Students of the Common Law* (London, 1896), 26–7.

[24] Valérie Ranouil, *L'Autonomie de la volonté: naissance et évolution d'un concept* (Paris, 1980), 9, 53–5, 79.

[25] ibid. 70.

[26] Friedrich Carl von Savigny, *System des heutigen Römischen Rechts* 1 (Berlin, 1840–8), 331–2.

[27] ibid. 1.19; Friedrich Carl von Savigny, *Vom Beruf unsrer Zeit für Gesetzgebung und Rechtswissenschaft* (Heidelberg, 1840), 8.

simply on the appearance, that is, on the capacity, of making a choice among several alternatives.'[28]

This approach set them up for the critiques of the 20th century. Contract cannot mean just what the parties will, for sometimes they are bound to terms they never considered, and at other times they are not bound to supposedly unfair terms to which they did agree. Tort cannot mean intentionally invading the rights of another, for there must be some other standard, other than the will of the parties or the 'will' of the law, that explains how those rights should be bounded. Property cannot mean that the owner has the right to do what he will with his own since his rights to do so are limited by the effect on his neighbor. And it is hard to explain the law of unjust enrichment in terms of anything the parties willed. Consequently, in the 20th century, among jurists, there has been a revolt against the systems built by the 19th century jurists. But it would be a mistake to think of it as a revolt against 19th century philosophy. The only point at which the 19th century jurists trusted the 19th century philosophers was they thought they could build on the concept of will, and they even thought they could do so without any philosophical commitment as to what the will might be.

B. The Philosophers

Today, however, contemporary jurists are taking on a task the 19th century jurists, perhaps wisely, avoided. They are trying to understand private law in philosophical terms. What is extraordinary is that the terms are those of the philosophers of 19th century. The law and economics movement descends lineally from utilitarianism. Jurists such as Weinrib and Benson are building on the rights-based theories of Kant and Hegel. Jurists such as Stephen Smith think our only alternatives are 'utilitarian' or 'rights based'.[29]

It would be out of place here to write a general critique of modern philosophy, but something should be said about the assumptions on which these attempts are based. Underlying them all are conceptions of will or choice and why it matters, although these conceptions are different from one other and from that of the Aristotelian tradition. According to one conception, which can be traced to the utilitarians, the task of the law is to see that people's preferences are satisfied to the greatest extent possible. Choices matter because they reveal the parties' preferences. According to the other conception, derived from Kant and Hegel, law is obligatory because it is rooted in human freedom or autonomy. Choices matter because they express freedom or autonomy. In both cases, will or choice is central. As we have seen, the conceptions of these contemporary jurists or the 19th century philosophers should not be confused with those of the 19th century will theorists. The will theorists had little to say about the philosophical meaning of will. They simply adopted a simplistic idea of what the will meant and impressed it into service.

These alternatives to the Aristotelian tradition arose from the crisis through which philosophy passed in the 17th and 18th centuries. Descartes founded modern critical philosophy on a new method in which the only permissible starting points were

---

[28] Savigny, *System*, 3: 102.   [29] Stephen A. Smith, *Contract Theory* (Oxford, 2004), 46–8.

matters that could not be doubted, and the only legitimate conclusions were those reached from them by deductive logic. Reason was equated with deductive logic. As we have seen, writers in the Aristotelian tradition thought that moral decisions were made, not by deductive logic, but by a human capacity for rational decision which they called prudence. If they had been asked why they believed there was such a capacity—why they believed some choices were right and others wrong, and that people had the capacity to discern the difference—they would have answered that if one denied these principles, human choice would no longer be meaningful. Therefore, these were first principles. They believed that one established a first principle dialectically: by showing that to deny it led to an absurdity. That was not the idea of the new critical philosophers. They were willing to entertain the possibility that human choice was not meaningful; indeed, that the entire world around them did not exist. The only indubitable starting points they would permit were propositions the denial of which would entail a logical contradiction, such as *cogito ergo sum*, or for the empiricists, immediate sense experience.

Applying the new method, philosophers soon discovered that there was no way to prove deductively that some choices were normatively better than others. John Locke and David Hume concluded that one could only say that the person choosing felt a desire or inclination for something, an inclination that could not be rooted in reason. According to Locke, 'the philosophers of old did in vain inquire whether the *summum bonum* consisted in riches, or bodily delights, or virtue or contemplation; they might have as reasonably disputed, whether the best relish were to be found in apples, plums or nuts'.[30] According to Hume, ' 'Tis not contrary to reason to prefer the destruction of the whole world to the scratching of my finger'.[31]

Hume concluded that normative statements are merely statements about one's inclinations. One cannot say that these inclinations are better or worse. The new method of doubting whatever cannot be shown by deduction had led exactly where an Aristotelian would have expected: there is no reason to believe that human choice has normative value. For an Aristotelian, the very fact that the method led to that conclusion would show that the method is wrong.

After Hume, it might have seemed that philosophers must either reject modern critical philosophy or stop theorizing about ethics. Instead, some of them tried to construct an ethical theory while agreeing with Hume that one cannot say that some choices are normatively better than others. There were two ways to try to do so. One was to claim that choosing in accord with one's inclinations or desires is normatively good whatever the objects of one's choice may be. The other was to claim that choosing according to inclination is not normatively good, and then to find some normative foundation for making a choice other than desire or inclination. Utilitarians such as Jeremy Bentham went the first way. They claimed that what matters normatively is to maximize satisfaction or pleasure, which can, in principle, be measured in units of pleasure and pain called utility. Kant and Hegel went the second way. They claimed that what matters normatively is that a choice be made freely or autonomously. They

---

[30] John Locke, *Essay on Human Understanding* II.xxi.55, in *The Works of John Locke*, 1 (1823), 273.
[31] David Hume, *A Treatise of Human Nature* (L. A. Selby-Bigge, ed., London, 1888), 416.

defined freedom as choice without regard to the choice-maker's inclinations or purposes.

Now, two centuries later, contemporary jurists are looking in the same two directions. What has changed, I believe, is that few of them are really willing to take seriously the intellectual premises that their philosophical predecessors recognized were crucial to the enterprise in which they were engaged. The founders of utilitarianism believed there were units of 'utility' or pleasure or satisfaction to be maximized. Kant and Hegel believed in freedom as a capacity to choose without regard to one's own inclination or purposes. For the most part, the modern jurists who are their heirs do not regard those concepts as central and perhaps not even as defensible. They fail to see that, without them, one cannot make sense of the traditions on which they attempt to build.

1. Utilitarianism and law and economics

a. Choice

According to Bentham, what matters is satisfaction or pleasure. It can, in principle, be measured in units of pleasure and pain called 'utility'.[32] More pleasure is better than less. Bentham claimed that, in general, 'utility is maximized by allowing people to choose for themselves' since 'no man can be so good a judge as the man himself, what gives him pleasure or displeasure'.[33] Hence the importance of will or choice.

One notorious problem with the theory is that to turn pleasure or satisfaction into a normative principle seems to violate our deepest feelings about morality. It is true that pleasure or satisfaction, for Bentham, is not the same as physical gratification. A dedicated scholar or a martyr for a noble cause supposedly finds study or martyrdom more satisfying than their other alternatives or they would do something else instead. Nevertheless, it is strange to think that what ultimately matters is satisfaction, whatever its source, whether it comes from study or serving a noble cause or idleness or drinking or drugs. No one would think the horror of a rape accompanied by torture is lessened to the extent the perpetrator enjoyed himself. Anyone would be appalled to find his child took pleasure in tearing the wings off flies.

John Stuart Mill tried to escape by claiming that pleasures differed not only in quantity but in quality. 'Human beings have faculties more elevated than the animal appetites.' One could 'assign to the pleasures of the intellect, of the feelings and imagination, and of the moral sentiments a much higher value as pleasures than to those of mere sensation'.[34] Critics have pointed out that this answer hardly solves the problem. If the activities of higher value are preferable simply because they are more pleasurable, then pleasure still determines the value of an activity. If they are preferable because they are higher, and higher because they engage our more elevated and distinctively human faculties, then we are back in an Aristotelian world in which some ways of living are more worthwhile than others whether or not they happen to be more pleasurable.

---

[32] Jeremy Bentham, *Principles of Morals and Legislation* (J. H. Burns and H. L. A. Hart, eds., London, 1970), I.i–iv. 11–12; IV.i–vi. 38–40.   [33] ibid. XIII.iv. 159.

[34] John Stuart Mill, *Utilitarianism* (O. Priest, ed., New York, 1957), 11.

Moreover, for Bentham's utilitarianism to work, 'pleasure' or 'satisfaction' must be something that accompanies all choices and for the sake of which all choices are made. But why should one think so? It is true that if one person drinks beer on a hot day, another studies, and a third suffers martyrdom because his convictions require it, all three did what they preferred to do under the circumstances. But why should one think that these choices are made to obtain some single thing called 'pleasure' or 'satisfaction' that accompanies every choice? It is like saying that because people regard what they choose as choice-worthy, their choices are accompanied by 'choice-worthiness', and they choose in order to get as much of it as they can.

Fifty years ago, Paul Samuelson noted that many economists 'have ceased to believe in the existence of any introspective magnitude or quantity of a cardinal, numerical kind'.[35] They had also discovered that they did not need traditional utilitarianism to build their descriptive models. To draw supply and demand curves, they merely needed to assume that people do prefer some courses of action to others. One could speak of preferences and preference satisfaction without imagining there is some quantity that people are maximizing when they choose what they prefer.

J. R. Hicks claimed that this approach had liberated economists from philosophical commitments. They no longer needed to be utilitarians.[36] That is true. Economists themselves sometimes fail to realize how completely the new approach has emancipated them. Some seem to think that when people make choices, they must be maximizing something, even if it is not utility.[37] Under the new approach, however, people need not be maximizing anything at all. Suppose that this morning, in order of preference, I would like to wear my blue, my brown and my green sports jackets. Suppose that this afternoon, I will go to a committee meeting, because it needs to be done; if there were no meeting, I would shop for groceries, because that needs to be done, too; and if neither needed to be done, I would read a book. The new approach, in effect, assigns numbers to each of these possible choices which indicate the order in which I prefer them. Assigning the numbers says nothing about how or why I make these choices. The new approach assumes no more than that people have preferences, which, by the new approach, is merely to assume that people make choices.

To make normative claims, however, one cannot get away with saying so little. Those who make such claims have attached normative value to 'efficiency' or 'wealth maximization', which they define in terms of preference satisfaction. For Pareto, 'efficiency' is improved if one can increase one person's ability to satisfy his preferences without decreasing that of others. To make normative claims for efficiency, one must assume that it is good for people to satisfy more of their preferences. Why should that be?

One possible answer is that satisfaction is good, whatever a person happens to find satisfying. But that answer is really a return to the utilitarian assumptions that economists have rejected. It treats 'satisfaction' as something that accompanies every choice and for the sake of which every choice is made.

[35] Paul Anthony Samuelson, *Foundations of Economic Analysis* (Cambridge, Mass. 1976), 91.

[36] J.R. Hicks, *Value and Capital* (Oxford, 1939).

[37] e.g., Michael Trebilcock, *The Limits of Freedom of Contract* (Cambridge, Mass., 1993), 2–3 ('[E]conomics assumes that individuals . . . attempt to maximize their desired ends (which may be of infinite variety')).

Another possible answer is that it is good for people to get what they prefer as long as what they prefer is good. To say so is to go in the same direction as John Stuart Mill. As before, we must then assume that some choices are better and worse, and that people have some capacity to choose for the better. We will have returned to something like the Aristotelian idea of a normatively good life and capacities or virtues that enable one to live it.

A third possible answer is to claim that it is good for people to satisfy more of their preferences without regard to whether they thereby live a normatively better life or a more pleasurable or satisfying one. Preference satisfaction means that one gets what one chooses, and a person who does so is *ipso facto* better off.

Sometimes economists seem to give that answer. They define a 'preference' as that which a person actually chooses. 'Thus,' Samuelson observed, 'the consumer's market behavior is explained in terms of preferences, which are in turn defined only by behavior. The result can very easily be circular...'.[38] Circular or not, this procedure is unacceptable for one who claims that preference satisfaction is normatively good. The idea that preference satisfaction is good in itself is hardly a self-evident premise.

Indeed, it contradicts common sense. An example I have used more than once is a hypothetical case I put to seven well-known economists and members of the law and economics movement, one of whom won the Nobel prize. A man whose yacht was sinking radioed his position to the coastguard and was told that, for whatever reason, it could not reach him for six days. He got into a lifeboat with a six-pack of beer, which is all that he had on the yacht to drink. He knew (never mind how) that if he drank one can each day, he would survive. Instead, he drank four cans the first day, two the second, and was found dead on the sixth. Is this efficient? Six economists said yes. The seventh (as it happens, the Nobel prize winner), said that it couldn't happen.

Economists who take this position are making a much more radical claim than Aristotle. He merely said that sometimes we choose rightly. They are saying that *ipso facto* all choices are right.

We should not conclude that economics is a false science or that its conclusions do not have normative value. We should conclude that efficiency or wealth maximization are of normative value precisely to the extent that people practice Aristotelian virtues of prudence, courage, and temperance that the economists never mention.

Amartya Sen is something of an exception. In his seminal work *On Ethics and Economics*, he claimed that 'the distancing of economics from ethics has impoverished welfare economics, and also weakened the basis of a good deal of descriptive and predictive economics'.[39] As part of his program for a rapprochement, Sen distinguishes a person's 'well-being' from what makes a person feel happy or what he desires or happens to value. 'Well-being' is truly valuable. We need not suppose that 'whatever

---

[38] Samuelson, *Foundations of Economic Analysis*, 91. Similarly, Leff objects that it is 'definitionally circular' to say 'what people do is good, and its goodness can be determined by what they do'. Arthur Allen Leff, 'Economic Analysis of Law: Some Realism about Nominalism', *Va. L. Rev.* 60 (1974), 451 at 458.   [39] Amartya Sen, *On Ethics and Economics* (Oxford, 1987), 78.

a person happens to value [is] valuable (i) unconditionally, and (ii) as intensely as it is valued by the person'.[40]

Well-being is ultimately a matter of valuation, and while happiness and the fulfilment of desire may well be valuable for the person's well-being, they cannot—on their own or even together—adequately reflect the value of well-being. 'Being happy' is not even a valuational activity, and 'desiring' is at best a consequence of valuation. The need for valuation in assessing well-being demands a more direct recognition.[41]

It would seem, then, that there is a life to be lived which is truly of value, and an ability to see what that life entails, although we can be mistaken. It is not an accident that Sen began his book by quoting Aristotle to the effect that there is an 'end of man' which politics must serve, and that it serves that end by making use of ' "the rest of the sciences," including economics'.[42] He is closer to the Aristotelian tradition than the small circle of modern ideas which he wishes to escape.

b. Distributive and commutative justice
For a utilitarian, the point of acquiring things is not to live a good life but to obtain pleasure or satisfaction. Consequently, the optimal distribution of resources is the one that will maximize pleasure. Some utilitarians said that ideally, this distribution would be equal since spending an extra dollar presumably gives less satisfaction to a rich man than a poor one. Others said that some pleasures, such as the appreciation of art or music, are of a higher nature and therefore more satisfying than others such as drinking beer. Those capable of the higher pleasures should have more resources.

As before, however, the test of a utilitarian theory is not that, when a sufficient number of background conditions are satisfied, it can produce results which non-utilitarians have regarded as fair for thousands of years. One who believed the theory only then, and would reject it otherwise, is really not committed to the theory. And, indeed, if we change the background conditions, the theory produces results that few would regard as normatively sound. Few would think a person who takes intense pleasure in watching movies about chainsaw massacres, or in defacing or destroying works of art, or in causing pain to others, is, for that very reason, entitled to more resources than another person who takes moderate pleasure in good music or art or in relieving pain.

In any event, few people who subscribe to theories based on preference satisfaction still believe that there is something called satisfaction that accompanies all objects of choice, and that choices are made to obtain as much of it as possible. They do not claim one can compare the importance of one individual's preferences with those of another. Consequently, most of them have stopped making normative claims as to how resources should be initially distributed. The claim instead is that, given any initial distribution, one can explain why, normatively, one person cannot take another's things, and that a person who is willing to pay the most for them should get them. Only then can we arrive at a state in which it is impossible to make anyone better off, in terms of his own preferences, without making someone else worse off. Such a state is said to be 'Pareto efficient'.

---

[40] ibid. 42.   [41] ibid. 46.   [42] ibid. 3.

To illustrate, suppose Ann has something she does not want for which Bob will pay $65 and Cara only $60. If Cara were to get it, it would still be possible to move to a state in which she and Bob will both be better off: she could resell to Bob. Only if Bob buys the object in question is a further improvement no longer possible.

This argument assumes that the mere fact that Bob has certain preferences doesn't make anyone else worse off. It may. As Michael Trebilcock and Richard Posner have noted, his preferences may drive up the price of something that others want.[43] In the example just given, if Ann sells directly to Bob, Cara will be worse off than if Bob hadn't wanted the object in question since she could then have bought it for $60. Moreover, the mere fact that a person gratifies his own preferences may distress others.[44] Even if Cara didn't want the object herself, she might not want Bob to have it because she hates or envies Bob or because the object is a rooster that Bob wants for cockfighting, which she thinks is immoral.

These problems arise because the objective is to maximize preference satisfaction. From an Aristotelian standpoint, the objective is different. It is to enable each person to have the resources he needs to live a good life. As already explained, ideally, each person should have a share of purchasing power that reflects what he needs for such a life. To the extent that this ideal is realized, and that each person chooses rightly how to spend his share, goods and services move to their normatively best uses. That is so even though the particular goods and services each person can buy are affected by the choices of others.[45]

Moreover, from an Aristotelian standpoint, not all preferences should be gratified. It is quite possible that if Cara hates or envies Bob, her preference that he suffer, or not prosper, is wrong. So may be Bob's preference for cockfighting. If so, his preference harms himself because he leads a less worthwhile life. Cara should be distressed if she cares about Bob. The difficulty is resolved to the extent that Bob and Cara prefer what they should. Because virtue is its own reward it is also what an economist might call a free lunch.

A further difficulty is that Bob may discover he really is worse off paying $65 for the object. Benson and Trebilcock have called this problem the 'Paretian dilemma': a contract only makes both parties better off *ex ante*, and nothing in the theory explains why that is better than to make them better off *ex post*.[46] From an Aristotelian standpoint, one could ask whether the risk Bob runs of being worse off *ex post* is one which, for the reasons described earlier, a person should be allowed to take, and whether Bob was prudent to do so. To ask those questions, one needs to talk about prudence and distributive justice. As Guido Calabresi has noted, as long as there are *ex post* losers, 'we

[43] Trebilcock, *Freedom of Contract*, 58; Richard Posner, 'Utilitarianism, Economics and Legal Theory', *J. Leg. Stud.* 9 (1979), 103 at 114. A similar point is made by Dworkin, Ronald Dworkin, 'What is Equality? Part 2: Equality of Resources', *Phil. & Pub. Affairs* 10 (1981), 283 at 307–8.

[44] Trebilcock, *Freedom of Contract*, 62–3, 243. See Guido Calabresi, 'The Pointlessness of Pareto: Carrying Coase Further', *Yale L.J.* 100 (1991), 1211, 1216–17.

[45] Consequently, a single rare stamp should command a high price if several people wanted it, although Trebilcock seems to think such a price would violate the theory of justice I am defending. Trebilcock, *Freedom of Contract*, 90.

[46] Peter Benson, 'The Idea of a Public Basis of Justification for Contract', *Osgoode Hall L.J.* 33 (1995), 273 at 284–87; Trebilcock, *Freedom of Contract*, 244.

will not be achieving an improvement according to the strict Pareto standard . . . [W]e could say that we do not *care* about these losers, . . . but that lack of care implies a distributional theory that has all too conveniently been kept out of sight.'[47]

A still more fundamental objection to attaching normative significance to Pareto efficiency is that the normative claim is circular. The claim is that it is normatively better that goods go to whomever will pay the most for them. Supposedly, the answer is that unless they are sold to that person, it will still be possible for a further transaction to make everyone better off and no one worse off. That transaction is possible, however, only if the rule of law is in force that a person can sell what he owns to whomever will pay most for it. To make a normative claim, one must not only assume this rule is in force but that it should be. But that is, in effect, to assume that goods should go to whomever will pay the most for them—which was the conclusion to be proven.

To illustrate, suppose we are in a society in which nearly everything is owned by a small group who live in decadence while the rest go hungry. Suppose Bob is one of the rich and will pay Ann $65 for a side of beef for which Cara, who is starving, cannot pay more than $1. Why would it be an 'improvement' for Bob to have it? Many people might think it a definite improvement if someone like Robin Hood stole the meat and gave it to Cara. If Bob then offered to buy it back from her for $65, many people might think it a still further improvement if someone stole the $65 from Bob as well. These 'improvements', of course, can only be made by violating the rule that Ann, who owns the beef, is free to sell it to Bob if he offers to pay more than anyone else. If we assume that rule will be followed, then, even if Cara owned the beef, both Cara and Bob will prefer for Bob to acquire it at a price that Cara will accept. But to conclude that it is normatively better for Bob to end up with the beef, we need to assume, not only that this rule will be followed but that, normatively, it should be. That is to assume the conclusion: people who are willing to pay the most for things ought to have them.

Moreover, the proposition assumed is far from obvious. As we have seen, in the Aristotelian tradition, that proposition about commutative justice rests on certain premises about distributive justice. The distribution of wealth may be imperfect, but it must still be worth protecting if one is to insist that people do not steal and pay for what they take. As will be described later, writers in the Aristotelian tradition claimed that in extreme circumstances, when a person was starving, the normal rules of commutative justice did not apply, and he had the right to take what he needed to live without the owner's permission. In time of war or famine most governments ration goods rather than leave their allocation to the market. Economists might object that necessity, war, famine and the extremely unfair distribution of wealth are aberrational circumstances to which their theory does not apply. But whether a situation counts as aberrational depends upon one's theory of distributive justice. An economist who claims to be agnostic about the justice of the initial distribution of resources cannot claim that a move to Pareto efficiency is an improvement.

---

[47] Guido Calabresi, 'The New Economic Analysis of Law: Scholarship, Sophistry or Self-Indulgence?' *Proceedings of the British Academy 1982* 68 (1983), 85 at 96.

Some writers make normative claims for what is called 'Kaldor–Hicks' efficiency or for 'wealth maximization', which Richard Posner admits is formally identical.[48] Goods are supposed to go to whomever would pay the most for them whether he actually has to pay or not. Since those who lose out are not compensated, the usual objection is that one cannot assume that the change is normatively for the better.[49] Suppose, Ronald Dworkin argues, that Derek's book is worth $2 to him and $3 to Amartya. Wealth would be maximized if somebody (an imaginary tyrant) forcibly transferred the book to Amartya, who then does not need to pay for it. But there is no reason to think the transfer is an improvement unless we assume, gratuitously, that the book will provide more satisfaction to Amartya than to Derek.[50]

Posner answered Dworkin by saying that the figures chosen are deceptive. The transfer 'probably will increase the amount of happiness', meaning satisfaction, if the book were 'worth $3000 to Amartya and $2 to Derek'.[51] He also said that wealth maximization is conducive, not only to satisfaction, but to freedom, self-expression and other uncontroversial goods.[52] That answer raises one of the graver problems with utilitarianism: we have to imagine that satisfaction or happiness is a quantity or 'amount'. In addition, it seems, we have to imagine that there are amounts of freedom and self-expression. Then we must assume that these amounts are maximized (at least probably) when goods and services go to a person who will pay much more for them than others. And that assumption supposedly does not depend on any assumptions about the nature of his preferences or about how purchasing power is distributed.

In one essay, however, Posner defended wealth maximization, not on these grounds, but by claiming the results will be consistent with our moral intuitions. When wealth is maximized, people must benefit others to secure benefits for themselves, they will have 'economic liberty', and they are likely to practice 'traditional ("Calvinist" or "Protestant") virtues'.[53] According to Posner, the principle of wealth maximization also suggests that resources should be initially distributed in a way that answers to our moral intuitions. People should have the right to their own labor or to determine their own sex partners. Wealth will be maximized if they do by avoiding the transactions costs people would incur buying these rights back if they initially belonged to others.[54] Posner acknowledges that very poor people will not be entitled to support, and that those whose 'net social product is negative' through no fault of their own may starve. That 'grates on modern sensibilities' yet he 'see[s] no escape from it' that is consistent with any major modern ethical theory.[55]

With that line of argument, we have come full circle. Centuries ago, philosophers decided that our moral intuitions should not be the test of what is normatively good.

[48] Richard A. Posner, 'The Value of Wealth: A Comment on Dworkin and Kronman', *J. Leg. Stud.* 9 (1980), 243 at 244.

[49] Calabresi, 'The New Economic Analysis', 89 ('who ever believed that wealth maximization without regard to its distribution could qualify as the goal of law in a just society?'); Hugh Collins, 'Distributive Justice through Contracts', *Current Legal Prob.* 45 (1992), 49 at 51 ('what is important is the ability of each individual to pursue a meaningful life, and the fulfilment of that aim involve some sacrifice of collective prosperity').   [50] Ronald M. Dworkin, 'Is Weath a Value?' *J. Leg. Stud.* 9 (1980), 191 at 197, 199.

[51] Posner, 'The Value of Wealth', 245.   [52] ibid. 344.

[53] Posner, 'Utilitarianism, Economics and Legal Theory', 122–4.   [54] ibid. 126.

[55] ibid. 128.

That presumption started them down the path to utilitarianism, and then to efficiency and wealth maximization. In his fidelity to that tradition, Posner does not build his theory on our intuition that some preferences are normatively better than others. Yet in the end he wants our moral intuitions to vindicate the enterprise. Moreover, it seems that the point of the enterprise is to find amoral reasons, such as minimizing transactions costs, for conclusions that correspond to certain moral intuitions, for example, that we should not rape or enslave others, and that we should live by some traditional but selectively chosen platitudes. Why, one wonders, do we need amoral reasons for trusting our moral intuitions if, in the end, we have to trust them anyway? And if we are supposed to trust them, why should we ignore them, for example, by letting a person starve, when we cannot find an amoral reason in support? If this is journey's end, we ought to reconsider why we embarked on the journey.

My conclusion, again, is not that economics is false science or that its conclusions have no normative significance. On the contrary, its conclusions are valid provided the members of society actually practice virtues of prudence, temperance, fortitude and justice that economists never discuss.

2. *The Kantian and Hegelian tradition*

a. Choice

The other approach, which traces back to Kant and Hegel, values choice because it values autonomy or freedom. In one respect, the starting point is like that of Bentham. Kant and Hegel described one's choices as based on desire or inclination. According to Kant, to pursue happiness (*Glückseligkeit*) or act on the principle of self-love (*Selbstliebe*) means to seek pleasure (*Lust*) and avoid displeasure (*Unlust*).[56] As with Bentham, the terms 'pleasure' and 'pain' are not used to describe physical sensations. Supposedly, a person can perform even the most altruistic acts out of desire or inclination. According to Kant, some people are so constituted that 'without any other motive of vanity or self-interest, they find a pleasure in spreading joy around them, and can take delight in the satisfaction of others . . .'.[57] They are nevertheless acting out of a desire to get what they happen to want.

In contrast to Bentham, however, Kant and Hegel denied that choices prompted by desire or inclinations are morally significant. A person who follows his desires or inclinations is not acting morally. Indeed, he is not acting freely because his choice depends on something he does not choose: namely, what his desires and inclinations happen to be.[58] They embarked on what an Aristotelian would regard as a doomed enterprise: to explain how a choice can be free and morally significant without regard to the value of what one seeks to have or to do by choosing.

This enterprise required them to define 'freedom' in an odd way. To be free, to most people, means to decide for oneself such matters as for whom to vote, whether to marry, whether to buy a new car, or whether to study law rather than medicine. For

---

[56] Immanuel Kant, *Kritik der praktischen Vernunft*, 129, in Immanuel Kant, *Werke in sechs Bänden* 4 (W. Weischedel, ed., Darmstadt, 1956), 107.

[57] Immanuel Kant, *Grundlegung zur Metaphysik der Sitten* 24, in 4 *Werke* 7.

[58] Kant, *Grundlegung der Metaphysik der Sitten*, 79–80.

Kant and Hegel, these choices are not free if they are made in order to have the president or spouse or car or career that one wants. Although people do make such choices to have what they want, freedom means that a person acts, not because he wants something, but because he is a free and rational being. To be free, an action must have its source in one's self rather than one's inclinations.[59]

The question thus becomes: what would a free and rational being choose, not because it is good for himself or others, but simply because he is free and rational? Kant said that a rational being would choose according to the ultimate principle of rationality: the law of non-contradiction. Such a choice is free because it has its source in one's rational nature and not in one's inclinations. Since the law of non-contradiction means that contradictory propositions cannot both be true, Kant concluded that a rational being would act according to a maxim that at the same time he could will to be universal law.[60] Otherwise, he would be willing a contradiction.

Few people today, even those committed to the Kantian tradition, really think it is possible to get from the law of non-contradiction to rules of conduct. Most would credit Kant with a basic moral insight: that one should not expect other people to abide by rules which one will not abide by oneself simply because they are not to one's own advantage. But that is a different proposition than claiming that one can base morality or law on deductions from the law of non-contradiction. It is a different proposition than claiming that an action is moral precisely because it does not reflect what one wishes to accomplish but rather one's allegiance to universal law.

Hegel realized that some other way had to be found to get from the concept of a free and rational being to institutions such as promise or contract. To do so, he invented a strange method which was neither deductive logic nor a functional analysis but seems to have the properties of both. According to Hegel, the free will, in order to be self-determining, must embody itself in something that is other than the will itself and nevertheless is not determined by inclination. Therefore, a person must have the capacity to own 'things', 'things' being whatever is not free.[61] But the will does not achieve its full determination merely by owning things since it is then related merely to that which is other than itself. It becomes fully actualized only through relation to another will, and does so through contract where the will of one party, with respect to something owned, becomes identical to the will of the other, so that ownership is transferred.[62]

My problem is that I don't see why this explanation counts as an explanation. Like deductive logic, this method tries to show there is a necessary relationship among concepts: the will is free, an external thing is not free and therefore other than the will. But it is not deductive logic of the sort a mathematician uses. Like a functional analysis, it concerns how a free being would solve some sort of a problem: such a being needs to be actualized or determined or embodied. But it is not a functional analysis. Nothing is said about why a free being encounters such a problem or the constraints under which he must solve it. If the explanation is neither logical nor functional, it is hard to see what it explains.

---

[59] Kant, *Grundlegung der Metaphysik der Sitten*, 79–80.   [60] ibid. 51.

[61] Georg Wilhelm Friedrich Hegel, *Grundlinien der Philosophie des Rechts* (G. Lasson, ed., Leipzig, 1911), §§ 41–6.   [62] ibid. §§ 71–5.

Few legal theorists today are Hegelians. Peter Benson and Alan Brudner are notable exceptions.[63] It is to their credit that they see clearly what Hegel saw: that if one wishes to get from the idea of a free and rational being to law, one cannot do so as Kant did, by way of the categorical imperative. One cannot do so at all unless Hegel's method is valid. If it is not, then the entire Kantian–Hegelian enterprise was impossible from the start.

Most contemporary theorists who write in the Kantian tradition are no longer engaged in this enterprise. They do not try to show that a free and rational being would regard certain rules as binding without regard to any purpose that such a being wants to pursue. They are Kantians only in the sense that they place freedom or reason at the apex of their theories. But then, how is one to get from such empty concepts to any definite conclusions about law? The difficulties are illustrated by the work of Charles Fried and Ernest Weinrib.

Fried places freedom at the apex. 'In order that I be as free as possible, that my will have the greatest possible range consistent with the similar will of others, it is necessary that there be a way in which I can commit myself.'[64] But as Benson notes, to think of freedom as a range of choice which should be the largest possible is to imagine that a quantity of freedom can be larger or smaller.[65] But what would make one range of choices larger or smaller than another?[66] It cannot be the number of alternatives among which a person might choose, whether he wants them or not.[67] It cannot be the extent to which a person can choose what he wants since, then, the scope of each person's freedom would depend on the extent of his desires.

In contrast, although Weinrib speaks of freedom, he places rationality or coherence at the apex of his theory. He tries to show that there is a rational structure immanent in law as we know it. This structure, he believes, is captured by the Aristotelian concept of commutative (or corrective) justice. For example, a contract of exchange is a single transaction in which each party transfers something equivalent in value to what he receives.[68] While his conclusion sounds Aristotelian, Weinrib claims that his approach is Kantian because it values rationality without regard to the purposes of the parties or society.[69] He links his position to Kant's by pointing out that for Kant, a free choice is one made with regard to its rational form but not with regard to any particular purpose.[70]

[63] Peter Benson, 'Abstract Right and the Possibility of a Nondistributive Conception of Contract: Hegel and Contemporary Contract Theory', *Cardozo L. Rev.* 10 (1989), 1077; Alan Brudner, 'Reconstructing Contracts', *Toronto L.J.* 43 (1993), 1.

[64] Charles Fried, *Contract as Promise* (Cambridge, Mass., 1981), 13. As Benson notes, in doing so, he breaks with Kant. Kant wanted to conceive of duty, not in terms of purpose, but 'in complete abstraction from our wants and needs'. Benson, 'Abstract Right', 1109.   [65] Benson, 'Abstract Right', 1109.

[66] As Johnson notes in his criticism of Fried, 'individual autonomy can be maximized and distributed in many different ways...'. Conrad D. Johnson, 'The Idea of Autonomy and the Foundations of Contractual Liberty', *Law and Philosophy* 2 (1983), 271 at 283.

[67] As noted by F. H. Buckley, 'Paradox Lost', *Minn. L. Rev.* 72 (1988), 775 at 816, 824; Trebilcock, *Freedom of Contract*, 165.

[68] Ernest J. Weinrib, *The Idea of Private Law* (Cambridge, Mass., 1995), 73, 83.

[69] ibid. 212–13.

[70] ibid. 83, 90, 97; Ernest J. Weinrib, 'Law as a Kantian Idea of Reason', *Colum. L. Rev.* 87 (1987), 472 at 483; Ernest J. Weinrib, 'The Jurisprudence of Legal Formalism', *Harv. J. of Law & Pub. Policy* 16 (1993), 583 at 590.

Nevertheless, his real reason for wanting to abstract from purpose seems to be that, otherwise, private law as we know it would not be coherent. That is what his arguments against a purposive account are designed to prove. Unlike Kant, he does not try to show that any free and rational being must respect the rules of commutative justice.[71]

Consequently, the question that Ken Kress and others have asked Weinrib is: why, then, does coherence matter?[72] His answer to Kress was that any justification of anything must be coherent.[73] That is true, but one cannot ask people to obey rules or a society to enforce them merely because they are coherent. It is perfectly coherent, from a certain point of view, to drive at 60 miles per hour on a freeway regardless of curves, the presence of other vehicles, or whether one will go off a cliff. To be sensible as a guide for action, coherence must enable one coherently to achieve what is worth achieving. Moreover, even if coherence were a value in itself, Weinrib doesn't claim the rules of law as we know them are the only coherent ones possible.

The problem here is like the one encountered by contemporary theories of preference satisfaction. Once one rejects the original utilitarian claim that choices are made for the sake of pleasure or satisfaction, 'preference satisfaction' means little more than 'choosing'. Similarly, once one rejects the Kantian and Hegelian claim that a free and rational being would be bound by certain rules without regard to his purposes, 'freedom' and 'rationality' mean little more than 'choosing' and 'thinking coherently'. While those ideas might figure in a theory of law, one cannot build a theory on them alone.

b. Distributive and commutative justice

As noted earlier, the starting point for Kant and Hegel was in one way like that of the utilitarians. They agreed that one cannot say that the purposes that people pursue are better or worse. All one can say is that people seek what they desire. Kant called the ability to satisfy one's desires without interference 'external freedom'. He contrasted it sharply with 'internal freedom', which meant choosing without regard to what one desired.[74]

For Kant, as for the utilitarians, the satisfaction of one person's desires often means that those of another person cannot be satisfied. Given his principles, he had to find a normative solution that did not depend on the importance of the desires themselves. The importance of desires could not depend on the normative value of what is desired without returning to the Aristotelian idea that some purposes are normatively of greater value than others. It could not depend on the pleasure or satisfaction of gratifying them because, as we have seen, Kant did not ascribe normative significance to the gratification of a desire.

---

[71] As noted by Stephen R. Perry, 'Professor Weinrib's Formalism: The Not-so-empty Sepulchre', *Harv. J. of Law & Pub. Policy* 16 (1993), 597 at 603.

[72] Ken Kress, 'Coherence and Formalism', *Harv. J. of L. & Pub. Policy* 16 (1993), 639 at 682; Luidger Röckrath, 'Umverteilung durch Privatrecht?' *Archiv für Rechts- und Sozialphilosophie* 83 (1997), 506 at 513.

[73] Ernest J. Weinrib, 'Formalism and Practical Reason, or How to Avoid Seeing Ghosts in the Empty Sepulchre', *Harv. J. of L. & Pub. Policy* 16 (1993), 683 at 695.   [74] Kant, *Metaphysik der Sitten*, 318.

The answer, Kant claimed, is that each person should act so that his freedom can coexist with every other person's freedom according to a universal law.[75] The freedom he is speaking about here is 'external freedom': gratifying one's desires without impediment. The 'universal law', by Kant's principles, cannot depend on the importance of the desires gratified. Therefore, such a law must assign resources to people without regard to the importance of their desires, and then allow each to gratify his own desires only from his own resources.

Kant tried to derive rules for assigning resources from the idea of the will itself. He thought he could show that one had a right to one's body, to one's labor and to appropriate anything that was not previously owned by someone else. People could alter these entitlements by consent, through exchange, gift or inheritance, but not without consent through force or fraud.

The attempt is not convincing. For example, according to Kant, the will would pointlessly lose some of its freedom if a person could not appropriate something that no one else owned or was using. Kant concluded that each person invariably has an unlimited right to do so. But the argument proves, at most, that the prior possessor should have some right to appropriate such a thing under some circumstances.[76] According to Kant, I have exclusive rights over my body, my labor and the exploitation of my own abilities because otherwise I would be treated as a thing rather than a person.[77] But unless a person is completely deprived of all external freedom, why is he a 'thing' rather than a person whose entitlements are minimal?

Hegel realized that more was necessary. As described earlier, he said that property exists because the free will, in order to be self-determining, must embody itself in something that is other than the will itself. Slavery rose and fell, he thought, because of some ultimately self-frustrating effort of the will to determine itself in relation to something that must be conceived as a thing and yet is not a thing.[78] As noted earlier, my problem is that while these arguments claim to be deductions, they are not deductive, and while they describe the will in terms of purposes, they are not functional in any ordinary sense.

With the exception of Peter Benson and Alan Brudner, few people who write in the Kantian and Hegelian tradition today try to get from the concept of will to rules for assigning resources. One reason is that they doubt it is possible to do so. But another is that, if the rules are derived in this way, people can have very different amounts of resources for reasons that seem arbitrary. People may have more than others if they are lucky enough to inherit more or to be the first to appropriate a gold mine, a valley or possibly a continent. John Rawls thinks it objectionable even to allow people to become wealthier because they have superior abilities since their superiority is a matter of chance.[79] Admittedly, any normative theory of the distribution of resources must recognize that, as a practical matter, chance is going to affect the distribution. In Kant's theory, however, the chance events are not random deviations from the ideal. They are the very operation of the rules that are said to assign resources justly.

[75] ibid. 337.   [76] ibid. 354.   [77] ibid. 345–6.

[78] Hegel, *Grundlinien der Philosophie des Rechts*, §§ 57, 356.

[79] John Rawls, *A Theory of Justice* (Cambridge, Mass., 1971), 101–2.

We cannot escape from these difficulties unless we recognize that the purposes people pursue are normatively important and that, in relation to these purposes, one person may have more and another less than he should. Ernest Weinrib, who writes in the Kantian tradition, agrees that a theory of distributive justice must take the well-being of people into account.[80] But it is hard to see how to take account of well-being without considering the importance of the purposes people pursue, and then we have left the Kantian and Hegelian tradition behind. The difficulties are illustrated by the theory of John Rawls which Weinrib believes to be compatible with his own ideas.[81]

According to Rawls, ideally, each person should have an equal share of resources. The reason is that people would agree on this principle if we imagine them deciding how to distribute resources without knowing the role they will occupy in society or the particular purposes they will choose to pursue. According to Rawls, if a person does not yet know whether he will be A pursuing A's purposes or B pursuing B's, he will want them each to have an equal share. He will not give B a greater share at A's expense lest he turn out to be A.[82]

The conclusion sounds like the principle of distributive justice that Aristotle said would be favored in a democracy. For Aristotle, however, the point of distributing resources is that people can use them rightly. The reason for distributing them equally is that in a democracy, as distinguished from an aristocracy, a greater capacity to make the right choices does not entitle a person to make more choices. When differences in capacity are set aside, each citizen counts merely as a person who needs resources to live well. He receives the same power to obtain them as anyone else.

In contrast, for Rawls, the distribution cannot proceed on the assumption that there are normatively better choices. The criterion is whether the distributor would equally prefer to be any of the persons to whom he has distributed resources, whatever the goals of each may be. That is really a criterion of preference satisfaction: what matters is what sort of life the distributor would prefer to have. But then, what is the criterion for preferring one life to another?

Suppose, first, that the distributor actually knew what goals A and B would pursue with their resources. He would have to distribute resources so that he would equally prefer to be A or to be B without passing a normative judgment on their goals. But then he would implicitly apply some standard of what makes a life preferable that does not call for a normative judgment. Rawls would not want that standard to be satisfaction, pleasure or something similar. If that were the standard, we would be back to a form of utilitarianism. Like Bentham, we would then have to imagine satisfaction or pleasure as a homogeneous something which people obtain in varying but comparable quantities whatever goals they pursue. Moreover, if we wanted A and B to be equally satisfied, we would violate both the spirit of Rawl's project and our common sense notions of justice. The spoiled and arrogant person who can scarcely be made happy with a kingdom should have more than a kingdom just because he is so hard to please.

Suppose, then, that the distributor is not allowed to know what A's and B's goals will actually be. He might then give them an equal share of purchasing power because

---

80 Weinrib, 'Formalism and Practical Reason', 684, 686.   81 ibid. 688–90.
82 Rawls, *Theory of Justice*, 12, 18–19, 136–7.

there is an equal chance that A's life will be as preferable as B's. That procedure merely dodges the question just raised. What does it mean for two lives to be equally preferable? It means nothing unless there is some standard by which two lives can be compared. This standard cannot depend on a normative judgment of what goals are worth pursuing. As before, all that seems to be left is some notion of satisfaction or pleasure. But then again we are back to a form of utilitarianism with all its problems. Again, in principle, A should have more resources than B if they would make his life equally satisfying. That seems unfair. Strangest of all, if our objective is make A's and B's life equally preferable, why is the distributor not allowed to know what their goals are?

IV. Conclusion

As noted earlier, William James, without meaning to be complimentary, once called scholasticism 'common sense made pedantic'. The basic principles on which the late scholastics explained private law sound like matters of common sense even centuries later. While there is no one right way to live one's life, there are better and worse ways to live it, and each person has some capacity to discern the better from the worse. External things can contribute to living a better life, and of these it is possible to have more or less than a fair share. While it is impracticable to secure an ideally fair share for each citizen, the distribution of resources should be improved, when feasible, by social decisions, and it should be protected against those who deprive others of the share they currently possess. I think anyone who had not been educated out of these positions by the work of modern philosophers would accept them as common sense. And once one does accept them, one is speaking of 'prudence', 'distributive justice', and 'commutative justice' whether one uses that terminology or not.

Much more, admittedly, needs to be explained. As said earlier, while Aristotelian philosophy was grounded in common sense, it was linked to a larger metaphysical view of the world. Though it may appeal to our common sense, we would like to know how that matches the common sense of other cultures. Still, if what are ultimately Aristotelian concepts explain our own law, which is rapidly becoming the law of the world, we should ask why these concepts work so well. If they do, anthropologists and metaphysicians should consider why.

2

Differences Among Legal Systems

I. Differences that can Arise from Common Principles

One way to proceed is to begin with the principles of prudence, distributive and commutative justice just described and to show how they resolve problems of property, tort, contract and unjustified enrichment. We will be doing so throughout this book. In doing so, as described earlier, we will not be attempting to deduce rules from principles by deductive logic as some of the rationalistically inclined jurists of the 17th and 18th centuries wished to do. As described earlier, our approach will be like that of writers in the Aristotelian tradition. The relationship between principle and rule, and between higher and lower level principles and rules, is not only conceptual but teleological. Rules are explained by the purposes they serve much as one would explain the biological function of an organ or of a part of a machine. At the summit of the explanation should be the principles that describe what the society and its members ultimately wish to achieve. As we have seen, for Aristotle and Aquinas, this purpose is not merely survival and reproduction but a truly human life in which, so far as possible, each person's distinctively human capacities are realized.

A second way to proceed, however, is to see how legal systems actually resolve problems and ask what principles can explain their solutions. People can often see that a result is right even if they cannot explain why in principle it should be. That must be so, if, as we have said, people have an ability to see what is right and wrong which is not reducible to deductive logic. Thus if a principle really does explain why the result is right, it should be reflected in what people do even if they have not been able to articulate it.

Hugo Grotius described the difference between these methods by saying that one can investigate fundamental legal principles—or, as he put it, the 'natural law'—in two ways. One could use 'the *a priori* method [and] show the necessary agreement or disagreement of a thing with [the] reasonable and social nature' of a human being. Or one might proceed '*a posteriori*' and 'infer that a thing is part of the law of nature which is accepted as such among all . . .'.[1] Throughout this book, we will using both of these methods.

A perennial objection to either of them is that the rules of various legal systems differ. How can that be if they are ultimately based on the same principles? To answer

---

[1] Hugo Grotius, *De iure belli ac pacis libri tres* (B. J. A. de Kanter-van Hetting Tromp, ed., Leiden, 1939), I.i.12.

that question, we will have to say more about how, according to the Aristotelian tradition, people could know what rule was most appropriate.

As we have already seen, for Aristotle and Aquinas, systematic reasoning from principles is not the only way that people can tell what rules are appropriate, even if they reason in terms of purpose rather than deductive logic. People choose the actions that contribute to a distinctively human life, by exercising an ability which Aristotle and Aquinas called prudence.[2] Prudence enables them to see that certain actions are right even though they cannot explain why it is so. Thus many people can see that murder is not right even though they could not give a good definition of murder or explain precisely why it is wrong.

In making rules and deciding cases, people exercise two aspects of prudence[3] which Aristotle called *synesis* and *gnome*. *Synesis* is good judgment in framing rules. *Gnome* is good judgment in deciding particular cases.[4] People with these abilities can frame a rule well, or decide a case well, even though they may not be able to explain systematically in terms of a higher purpose why the rule is well framed or the case rightly decided.[5] Aristotle seems simply to have been discussing a difference in people's virtues or abilities. He did not identify them clearly with the official roles of people in his own society. In contrast, Aquinas identified them with the roles of legislator and judge.

Ideally each of these capacities could play a role which complements that of the others. Ideally, *synesis* would always enable law makers to see what rule would give the right result in the largest number of cases. At least as Aquinas interpreted Aristotle, *gnome* would complement this ability. It would enable judges to see when the special circumstances of a particular case require a deviation from the rule. According to Aristotle and Aquinas, because rules serve purposes, circumstances can always arise in which following a rule would not serve its purpose and consequently a deviation is necessary.[6] Thus, even with the best framed rules, *gnome* is needed to see when to deviate.[7] Finally, by reasoning systematically, ideally, one could explain the appropriateness of each rule and of each deviation in terms of the higher principles which make them appropriate. And while that knowledge is not necessary in order for rules and cases to be well framed and decided, still, it should be of assistance. As Aristotle said, if we know what is good '[w]ill not the knowledge of it have a great influence on life? Shall we not, like archers who have a mark to aim at, more often hit upon what is right?'[8]

Each of these abilities is imperfect. That suggests one reason why legal systems may differ. Those who fashioned the rules of one system may simply be mistaken. Still, the jurist should not simply reject any conclusion that contradicts his systematic reasoning as a mistake in logic. He should investigate why, historically, the mistake came about,

---

[2] Aristotle, *Nicomachean Ethics* VI.v; Thomas Aquinas, *Summa theologiae* II–II, Q. 47, a. 2.

[3] In the technical vocabulary of Aquinas, they are quasi-potential parts. *Summa theologiae* II–II, Q. 51 pr.

[4] Thomas Aquinas, *Summa theologiae* I–II, Q. 95, a. 1; Q. 96, a. 6; II–II, Q. 51, aa. 3–4; *In decem libros Ethicorum expositio* VI, lectio ix; Aristotle, *Nicomachean Ethics* VI. xi. Throughout, I do not consider to what extent Aquinas' interpretations were faithful to Aristotle.

[5] Thomas Aquinas, *Summa theologiae* I–II, Q. 95, a. 2, ad 3; Aristotle, *Nicomachean Ethics* VI. xi.

[6] *Nicomachean Ethics* V.x; *Summa theologiae* II–II, q. 120, a. 1.

[7] *Summa theologiae* I–II, Q. 96, a. 6.   [8] *Nicomachean Ethics* V. i 1094ᵃ.

and how it happened to be made by people with the abilities just described. He may even wish to re-examine his own systematic reasoning to be sure it is they who are mistaken. We will try to give such an historical account on the occasions in this book when we claim a rule is simply mistaken.

On a deeper level, however, the fact that each of these capacities is imperfect suggests a reason, aside from mistake, that legal systems may differ. A legal system may be relying on one of these capacities for fear of making a mistake if it should rely on another. In our imperfect world, law makers may be uncertain what rule to frame; judges may be uncertain how to decide a case; and those who reason systematically about law may often find themselves stymied. Differences may emerge among legal systems even when they rest on the same principles because they are confronting the same uncertainty and responding to it in different ways, each of which has its own advantages and disadvantages. In that case, each system may make mistakes, but one cannot say that the approach of any system is wrong.

Suppose that after giving the matter his best thought, the law maker has trouble seeing what to do. He finds it hard to frame a law that accurately delimits the class of cases in which a given result is appropriate. One alternative is to frame the best rule he can, even though he knows it fits these cases only roughly. For example, in French law, a person is strictly liable in tort for harm caused by any object in his custody or *garde*.[9] I doubt if the French really think that they have drawn the line just where it should be. But it is not clear just where the line should be. Or, for example, in medieval law, relief was given when the contract price deviated by more than 50 percent from the fair price.[10] While the rule is clear, one cannot help feeling that more matters than simply the percentage deviation.

That is one alternative for the law maker: to frame a rule as well as he can and hope for the best. That is all he could do if the only ability that mattered were *synesis*. But an alternative is to dispense with a clear general rule and fall back on the ability to see what result is appropriate in particular cases. Aquinas discussed the possibility of running the entire system of justice that way. Every case would go to the judges with no laws to guide them. He said there were three disadvantages in doing so. First, it is easier to find a small number of able rule makers than a large number of able judges. Second, rule makers have more time to think and can consider a larger range of possible cases. Finally, the rule makers are legislating for the future and may be more impartial and dispassionate.[11] Nevertheless, if the law maker were really unsure what to do, he might find these risks preferable to that of laying down the wrong general rule. Differences between legal systems might then arise, not because of any difference in principle, but because different law makers deal with uncertainty in different ways.

The law maker who finds it difficult to frame a general rule and wishes to deal with an area of law case-by-case has two alternatives. He could make a list of cases himself in

---

[9] French Civil Code (*Code civil*), art. 1384, as it is presently interpreted. Here, and in discussion §§ 138(1) and 242 of the German Civil Code, I am not suggesting that the drafters of the codes had the present-day interpretations in mind. I am describing the advantages and disadvantages of keeping these provisions as they are now interpreted.

[10] See generally James Gordley, 'Just Price', *The New Palgrave Dictionary of Economics and the Law* 2 (ed. Peter Newman, London, 1998), 410.   [11] *Summa theologiae* I–II, Q. 95, a. 1, ad 2.

which he believes that a given result is proper. Or he could allow judges to decide what result is proper as cases arise. An example of the first approach is the German law governing strict liability. There is no general rule. There are special statutes imposing liability without fault, for example, for the operation of trains,[12] aircraft,[13] automobiles,[14] and electric and gas installations.[15] The judges do not add to the list even when the cases seem analogous.[16] Similarly, in France, there is no general rule against enforcing a hard bargain. The French Civil Code says that relief will be given only in cases provided for by statute. Special statutes protect, among others, those who sell land at less than five-twelfths the just price,[17] or who pay an excessive amount for fertilizer, seeds and fodder,[18] or for a rescue at sea[19] or after an aviation accident[20] or who receive too little for artistic or literary property.[21]

One advantage of making such a list in advance, rather than leaving the matter to judges, is that the law will be more certain. No one has to wonder what the judges will do. A disadvantage is that a law maker, who must consider these cases abstractly, may be less able to see the proper result than a judge, who considers them in a concrete factual setting. Another disadvantage is that when a law maker does not think of all the cases that may arise, there will be gaps. As Hein Kötz has said of the German rules on strict liability:

'It is far from obvious why a person should be strictly liable if he decides to move earth by means of a light railway while he is liable only for negligence if he uses heavy bulldozers. And why should an injured person's right to damages depend on whether the accident took place on board a steamer or a train? And if a motorized conveyance causes injury, why should liability depend on whether it is a chairlift, a motor car, a motorboat, a light railway, a hoist, a funicular, or an escalator?'[22]

Moreover, whatever the law maker may say, judges may try to fill these gaps. Then the advantage of certainty is lost. French courts have given relief for an unfair price outside the statutory list of cases by finding fraud, duress or mistake, even though the victim had neither been told a lie nor threatened, and his only mistake concerned the value of what he bought or sold.[23]

Consequently, a law maker might allow judges to decide particular cases as they arise. Here, again, he has two alternatives. He might list cases, as before, but allow the judges to add to the list. That is the approach, for example, of the European Council Directive on Unfair Terms in Consumer Contracts.[24] It lists a large number of

[12] Haftpflichtgesetz, § 1 I.   [13] Luftverkehrsgesetz, § 33.   [14] Strassenverkehrsgesetz, § 7.
[15] Haftpflichtgesetz, § 2 I.
[16] Konrad Zweigert and Hein Kötz, *Einführung in die Rechtsvergleichung* (3rd edn., Tübingen, 1996), 656.
[17] French Civil Code (*Code civil*), art. 1674.   [18] Law of July 8, 1907.
[19] Law of April 29, 1916, art. 7.   [20] Law of May 31, 1925, art. 57.
[21] Law of March 11, 1957.
[22] Konrad Zweigert and Hein Kötz, *An Introduction to Comparative Law* (T. Weir, trans., 2nd edn., 1987), 698–9. The text translated here was unchanged in the third German edition. Zweigert and Kötz, *Einführung*, 662–3. For a similar criticism, see Karl Larenz and C.-W. Canaris, *Lehrbuch des Schuldrechts* 2(2) (13th edn., Munich, 1994), no. 80 I 2 c.
[23] Cass. req., 27 Apr. 1887, D.P. 1988.I.263; Cass. req., 27 Jan. 1919, S. 1920.I.198; Cass. civ., 29 Nov. 1968, Gaz. Pal. 1969.J.63; Cour d'appel, Douai, 2 June 1930, Jurisp. de la Cour d'appel de Douai 1930.183; Cour d'appel, Paris, 22 Jan. 1953, Sem. jur. 1953.II.7435.
[24] European Community Council Directive 93/13/EEC of 5 Apr. 1993.

presumptively unfair terms, but contains a muddy general clause which allows a judge to find other terms invalid as well. That approach avoids gaps. It still has the disadvantage that the law maker, considering some of these cases in the abstract, may find it harder to see the right result than a judge who considers them in the concrete.

Instead, and to avoid that disadvantage, the law maker may not make a list but simply enact an unclear rule, thereby allowing judges to decide cases as they arise. The unclear rule may either be definite enough to give some guidance, or it may be completely vague. The American rule on strict liability gives some guidance: the defendant is liable if he conducts an 'abnormally dangerous activity'.[25] The rule is too imprecise to enable an American lawyer to tell what cases it covers. He would not guess from the rule that driving cars is not included while ground damage from aircraft may be, even though aircraft are safer than cars. When he wants to know what activities are included, he turns to a list which is so long that I consign it to a footnote, but which includes blasting, storing explosives or large quantities of water, crop dusting, and possible ground damage by aircraft and harm caused by nuclear power.[26] Nevertheless, the rule gives some guidance.

Alternatively, the law maker could promulgate a vague rule that allows judges to do what seems right in particular cases without much if any guidance. An example is relief from hard bargains under two of the general clauses of the German Civil Code: § 138(1) which says that a contract is void if it violates good morals (*gute Sitten*), and § 242 which says that a contract must be performed in good faith (*Treu und Glauben*). Nobody knows what they mean.

Again, there are pros and cons to each approach. Giving guidance is an advantage but only if the guidance is good. It may not be since, by hypothesis, the law maker is not sure how to describe the class of cases that call for a particular result. Maybe it is good for judges to consider whether an activity is 'abnormally dangerous'. If George Fletcher is right, however, what should matter is not whether it is dangerous but whether it creates a risk which is non-reciprocal: the defendant endangers others more than they endanger him.[27] If Fletcher is right—and we will argue later that he is[28]— perhaps the American rule points in the wrong direction.

In contrast, one advantage of a vague rule is that it allows time to gather experience before any guidance is given. The very vagueness of the German rule about good faith has enabled German jurists to see that the term 'good faith' covers different types of cases: for example, the implication of ancillary contractual terms, the abuse of contractual rights, and the effect of changed and unforeseen circumstances.[29] That brings jurists a

---

[25] *Restatement (Second) of Torts*, sec. 519.

[26] 'water collected in quantity in a dangerous place, or allowed to percolate; explosives or inflammable liquids stored in quantity in the midst of a city; blasting; pile driving; crop dusting; the fumigation of part of a building with cyanide gas; drilling oil wells or operating refineries in thickly settled communities; an excavation letting in the sea; factories emitting smoke, dust or noxious gases in the midst of a town; roofs so constructed as to shed snow into a highway; . . . a dangerous party wall', and possibly 'ground damage from aviation', and 'rockets and nuclear energy'. W. Page Keeton, Dan B. Dobbs, Robert E. Keeton and David G. Owen, *Prosser and Keeton on the Law of Torts* (5th edn., St Paul, Minn., 1984), 549–50, 556.

[27] George P. Fletcher, 'Fairness and Utility in Tort Theory', *Harv. L. Rev.* 85 (1972), 537.

[28] Chapter 7 III A.

[29] Günter Roth in H. Heinrichs, *Münchener Kommentar zum Bürgerlichen Gesetzbuch*, Band II (3rd edn., Munich, 1994), no. 93 to BGB § 242.

step closer to developing clearer rules for each type of case. Similarly, in the United States, courts initially gave relief for violations of 'privacy' without any clear idea what 'privacy' might mean. Drawing on their experience, William Prosser distinguished four types of cases in which relief was given: commercial appropriation of name or image, intrusion into seclusion, disclosure of embarrassing private facts, and putting the plaintiff in a false light.[30] It was then possible to frame more definite rules.

We have seen, then, that when the law maker is unsure of how to frame a rule, an alternative is to rely on the ability to decide particular cases appropriately even absent a rule. Indeed, some people think that a major difference between civil law and common law jurisdictions is that the former rely more on the rules contained in civil codes, and the latter on the ability of judges to decide particular cases. I think this contrast can easily be exaggerated. But to the extent it is true, it is a further instance of how the use of these abilities can be alternatives. If they are alternatives, each with its pros and cons, then, again, laws may differ not because of a difference in principle but because of the way of handling uncertainty.

The other ability described earlier is the capacity to explain rules systematically in terms of principles. Historically, some legal systems have been more interested in finding such explanations than others. Ancient Roman law, as has often been noted, was not very systematic. As mentioned earlier, it was first systematized in the 16th century when the late scholastics or Spanish natural law school tried to explain Roman rules by Aristotelian and Thomistic principles.[31] As we will see, before the 19th century, the common law was not organized systematically by doctrines but by writs or forms of action.[32]

As before, if the law maker is unsure of how to frame a rule, an alternative would be to rely on this ability to explain rules by principles.[33] Even if we cannot frame a rule, it may still be possible to see the principle at stake. Indeed, according to Aquinas, it is often easier for us to see the more general principles than their more specific consequences.[34] Over some domain of cases it must be true that *pacta sunt servanda*, that one who is at fault for injuring another must make compensation, that an owner can do with his property as he wishes, and that one who is enriched at another's expense

---

[30] William Prosser, 'Privacy', *Calif. L. Rev.* 48 (1960), 383.

[31] James Gordley, *The Philosophical Origins of Modern Contract Doctrine* (Oxford, 1991), 69–111.

[32] ibid. 134–60.

[33] The ability to explain rules can also be used to evaluate a rule even when we do not know the principles on which it is ultimately based. We might be able to see that a certain rule is inconsistent with any plausible explanation. For example, there is no generally accepted theory of why the law sometimes gives relief from an unfair bargain. Even without such a theory, however, one could still raise questions about the medieval rule mentioned earlier which gives relief whenever the contract price deviates from a fair price by more than 50 percent. This rule, unlike § 138(2) of the German Civil Code, ignores the question of whether the advantaged party obtained more favorable terms by exploiting the 'distressed situation, inexperience, lack of judgmental ability or grave weakness of the will' of the disadvantaged party. Without a theory of why relief is given, one cannot tell whether these factors should matter in principle. But one can say that even if they do not—even if all that matters in principle is the extent of the deviation from a fair price— these factors should still be relevant. It is hard to tell what price may have been fair when the contract is concluded. It is more likely to have been unfair when the disadvantaged party is less able to protect himself. His ability to do so should therefore matter even if the question in principle should be the extent to which the terms of the contract are unfair. [34] *Summa theologiae* I–II, Q. 94, a. 4.

must disgorge the enrichment. Otherwise there would be no law of contracts, torts, property and unjust enrichment. It is more difficult to get from these principles to clear rules. Thus, in the absence of a clear rule, the law maker might tell judges to be guided by the principle.

A difficulty, however, is that any single principle is unlikely to be all that matters. General principles of the kind just described nearly always need to be qualified by other principles. Consequently, if the law maker states only one principle, there is the danger that judges may think they should follow it invariably, as though it is all that matters. One reason that French jurists do not accept relief for *imprévision* or changed circumstances[35] may be that their Code does not mention that doctrine but it does contain the principle of *pacta sunt servanda*.[36] The reason, I believe, is the historical accident that the drafters worked from the treatises of Jean Domat and Robert Pothier who happened not to mention the doctrine of changed circumstances although it was widely accepted at the time. Similarly, the United States Supreme Court protects freedom of expression zealously. Perhaps it would do so less zealously if the American Constitution also mentioned human dignity,[37] honor,[38] and personality[39] as the German Constitution does.

Nevertheless, there are situations in which a rule maker may want judges to follow a principle invariably, as though it were all that matters, even if it is not. Where there is no clear rule, deviations from the principle create uncertainty, even though the deviations are necessary to reach the right result in particular cases. Certainty may be worth the price of sometimes reaching the wrong result. In English law, a contract is enforced without regard to whether there has been a violation of good faith.[40] In French law, as just noted, it is enforced without regard to whether circumstances have changed. The reason is probably not that the English and French think *pacta sunt servanda* is all that matters, like the 19th century will theorists. More likely, they fear that people will not be sure when their contracts are enforceable. Similarly, the United States Supreme Court has sometimes behaved as though all that matters is freedom of expression. According to the Court, the Constitution is violated if a newspaper is held liable for printing the name of a rape victim while her assailant is still at large.[41] Perhaps the Court mistakenly thinks that freedom of expression is all that matters. But it may fear that editors will be unsure of when they will be liable for publishing information.

Legal systems may differ, then, because the people's capacities are imperfect. When they cannot frame clear rules that accurately describe when a certain result is to be reached, they may handle the problem of uncertainty differently. This does not mean that the law of one system is wrong. It does not mean that it is based on different underlying principles. Indeed, recognizing the reason for the difference may be a guide to discovering a common underlying principle.

There is another reason, apart from human fallibility, why laws may differ even when the underlying principles are the same. As Aquinas himself noted, different laws

---

[35] François Terré, Philippe Simler, and Yves Lequette, *Droit civil: Les obligations* (7th edn., Paris, 1999), no. 441, pp. 428–9.   [36] French Civil Code (*Code civil*), art. 1134.
[37] German Constitution (*Grundgesetz*), art. 1.   [38] ibid. art. 5(2).   [39] ibid. art. 2(1).
[40] See Guenter H. Treitel, *The Law of Contract* (9th edn., London, 1995), 226.
[41] *Florida Star* v. *BLF*, 491 US 524 (1989).

may be consistent with the same principles.[42] Sometimes, when that is so, which law to enact is a matter of indifference. Theft should be punished but the exact length of the sentence is more or less arbitrary. We all must drive on the right side of the road or the left to avoid head-on collisions, but which side is a matter of indifference.

For present purposes, it is important to see that sometimes the choice of which law to enact is not a matter of indifference even though the underlying principle is the same. Indeed, even when it is, the choice of which law to enact may be one which people rightly regard as shaping their values and culture and hence making them the sort of people they are.

That may be so for two reasons. One is that circumstances differ, and the laws appropriate in one set of circumstances may not be appropriate in the other. The second is that, even when the circumstances are the same, laws can differ even when they are based on the same principles.

First, different laws may be appropriate because of different circumstances, and yet we may rightly perceive the difference as entailing a difference in values or culture. Let me give an example. In pre-commercial societies, when people make gifts, the recipient is often obligated to give back something equivalent but as yet unspecified. When people in these societies exchange, they often form stable trading relationships with particular partners. Each party to the relationship is obligated to exchange when the other asks, and to exchange at a price that remains stable despite changes in supply and demand.[43] It is not like our own society, where gifts are often made to enrich another party at the donor's expense, and where a person can exchange with whomever he wants and charge what the market will bear. Anthropological studies have suggested that the rules of pre-commercial societies make sense given their circumstances. There are few ways to store wealth. Therefore, it makes sense to give gifts in order to have a claim for help in the future. Markets are thin or non-existent, and so supply or demand can swing wildly from day to day. Therefore, it makes sense to trade with a regular partner who will not exploit a temporary advantage and who, in return, is not to be exploited.[44] That is not to imply that people in these societies saw their rules as appropriate only under certain circumstances. They might have trouble imagining it could ever be proper for a donee not to give in return, or for a person to raise the price he charges a regular customer. They have never had occasion to consider how circumstances might be different, and what it would be proper to do then.

People in these societies regard certain conduct as wrongful which we regard as appropriate, and in that sense their values differ from ours. Moreover, this difference is likely to be linked to many other differences in attitudes and behavior. They cannot behave to each other like modern creditors or merchants. Their relationships require trust, and for trust to flourish, relationships must be deeper, more personal, and not restricted to mere economic need. This difference will in turn affect people's character,

---

[42] *Summa theologiae* I–II, Q. 95, a. 2, ad 3; Q. 96, a. 1; Q. 97, a. 1.

[43] James Gordley, 'Contract in Pre-Commercial Societies and in Western History' in *Contracts in General*, vol. 7 of the *International Encyclopedia of Comparative Law* (Arthur von Mehren, ed., Tübingen, 1997), 2–9.

[44] See ibid. for an attempt to explain the contract law of pre-commercial societies by these considerations.

personalities, and their image of themselves and others. In that sense, one can speak of a difference in culture.

My point is a simple one. To speak of a difference in values or culture in this sense is not to speak of a difference in principles. If the principles were different, which set of rules is appropriate would not depend on the circumstances. One could not analyze the rules as a response to the difference in circumstances. And one would fail to see that if one of us were transported to such a society with our values and culture intact, our standard of conduct would then be inappropriate. It would be wrong to accept a gift and then fail to reciprocate. It would be wrong to trade with someone who demands less than he might and then to refuse to make a similar concession when the occasion arises.

Suppose now that the circumstances as well as the principles on which the laws are based are the same. In the Aristotelian tradition, it is still possible that the laws might differ. Moreover, the difference can matter very much. It need not be a matter of indifference like whether we drive on the left or the right side of the street.

That sounds odd. As I am using the term, principles are the ultimate standards by which we judge what is better or worse. If two rules are equally consistent with the same principles, neither of them could be better than the other. It would seem that the choice between them must be a matter of indifference.

To see why that is not so for Aristotle and Aquinas, we must come back to their idea of how people make choices. As noted earlier, when people choose, they exercise the virtue of 'prudence'. Prudence is an ability to recognize that certain choices contribute to the life that people should live, and are therefore good choices, whereas others detract from such a life, and are bad.[45] When an action contributes in one way and detracts in another way from such a life, prudence enables a person to weigh the good and bad consequences. Of course, he may be mistaken. He may see only the contribution that the action makes to his life and think it is all that matters, or he may exaggerate the extent to which it contributes. Yet it is also possible, for Aristotle and Aquinas, that after all the good and bad consequences are taken into account, neither choice is superior, and yet the choice is important. Suppose, for example, someone is asking himself whom to marry or whether to have a career in law or in medicine. Choices like these are not a matter of indifference. They shape people's lives. Yet there may be no right answer.[46] As mentioned earlier, according to Aquinas, there is no one right way for God to have made the world.[47] He could have made any world that is good, and the goodness of all possible worlds cannot be rank-ordered. As we have seen, according to Aquinas, that is also why people have free will, not simply to choose between good and evil, but to choose which of many possible good lives to live.[48]

[45] Aristotle, *Nicomachean Ethics* VI.v; Thomas Aquinas, *Summa theologiae* II–II, Q. 47, a. 2.

[46] Some modern philosophers also believe that there may be no right answer when a choice is based on more than one principle and that nevertheless the choice may be important. See e.g. Joseph Raz, *The Morality of Freedom* (Oxford, 1986), 332; Isaiah Berlin, 'Alleged Relativism in 18th Century Legal Thought', in Henry Hardy, ed., *The Crooked Timber of Humanity* (New York, 1991), 70 at 79–80; Christopher L. Kutz, 'Just Disagreement: Indeterminacy and Rationality in the Rule of Law', *Yale L. Jour.* 103 (1994), 1023–9. Here I cannot describe the ways in which their positions coincide with and diverge from that of Aquinas.   [47] Thomas Aquinas, *Summa theologiae* I, Q. 19, aa. 3, 10.

[48] ibid. I–II, Q. 10, a. 2; Q. 13, a. 6.

Making laws is similar. When the law maker exercises that aspect of prudence called *synesis*, he weighs the good and bad consequences of a law. Sometimes a single choice is right. Sometimes he is left with a range of alternatives. Therefore it is possible for different law makers to choose different laws even though they are acting under the same circumstances and even though they are judging what is good and what is bad according to the same principles.

An example may be the protection that modern legal systems give to freedom of expression, dignity and privacy. As we will see, civil law systems such as those of France and Germany give considerably more protection to privacy than American law, which in turn gives more protection to the freedom of the press.[49]

One might think that the Americans, Germans and French disagree over the importance of freedom of expression as opposed to dignity,[50] or, as I think, that Americans have a greater fear of muzzling the press.[51] Even then, one could not say that their principles are different. Americans believe in dignity, and French and Germans in freedom of expression. All of them believe in freedom of the press. The disagreement could be over which of two principles, in which they both believe, is most important. Nevertheless, it is important to see that their laws might differ even if there were no disagreement over which principle was of the greatest value. One has to choose whether to protect privacy and dignity even when, as a result, people must be more careful what they write and say and the press will be more restrained. This decision is not necessarily made by asking which principle is more important. There may be no right answer to that question, and it may be acknowledged that there is no right answer. Nevertheless, one still has to choose.

Choices like that shape societies, making one different in character from another. In that sense one can speak of a difference in values or culture. Yet that may be so absent any disagreement about principles or their relative importance. To be a lawyer rather than a physician, I need not believe that doing justice is more important than saving lives even though I will then be more occupied with the former than the latter. I can love my own wife or my own country the best without thinking there is something the matter with all the others.

This is one of the clearest instances I know of in modern private law in which the principles, or at least the importance accorded these principles, seems to differ. Yet even here we cannot be sure that it does. The example illustrates how easy it is to make the methodological error of assuming that people must believe in different things because they adopt different rules. If that is our method, we will find ourselves postulating a difference in principles or in the weight accorded them whenever rules differ. In fact, two people whose laws differ, each of whom prefers his own laws, might have to talk a long time to discover whether they disagree in principle or not.

We have seen, then, that underlying principles may be the same even when legal systems differ. We have seen that the differences themselves may be guides to the underlying principles.

---

[49] Chapter 11 II B.

[50] See James Q. Whitman, 'The Two Western Cultures of Privacy: Dignity versus Liberty', *Yale L. Jour.* 113 (2004), 1151.   [51]Chapter 11 II B 5–6.

It is worth noting in conclusion that this analysis delimits what jurists can and cannot hope to know about the basis of their own law or the reasons for differences in legal systems. If laws differ because people disagree about principles, scholars can describe the disagreement. Perhaps they can help to resolve it. If laws differ because circumstances are different, scholars can describe how the difference in circumstances makes each law appropriate. Perhaps their explanation can help in redesigning the law to make each even more appropriate to its own circumstances. But if laws differ even though the principles and circumstances are the same, then scholars have reached the limit of analysis. The only explanation can be historical: to describe the previous choices which are like this one and which made the societies what they are. The problem is like accounting for what people do. Sometimes their actions are due to their goals and principles, and to the circumstances in which they are acting, including the natural abilities which they possess. But sometimes one can only explain what they are doing by telling the story of how they came to be who they are. It would seem that law implies uniformity and individuality the opposite. Yet one needs the one to explain the other.

II. Differences Absent Common Principles: A Note on the Common Law

Thus far, we have seen why the laws of legal systems may differ even though they are based on common principles. Sometimes, legal systems may value the same ends but may pursue one at the expense of the other. They may do so, we have seen, even when they do not regard the end they prefer as of greater value. Sometimes, they may be pursuing the same ends but may be using different means because of differences in circumstances. Sometimes the differences may simply reflect differences in how to deal with uncertainty. Comparing differences such as these will help to identify common principles.

Sometimes, however, this sort of comparison is not possible because the rules of different legal systems were fashioned to perform different purposes. I am not speaking here about what one might call differences in culture. As we have just seen, cultures that share the same values may nevertheless give some values precedence over others, and that is so, paradoxically, even if they do not believe that one of these values is more important in principle than the others. As we have also seen, sometimes one can explain differences between vastly different societies—for example, between pre-commercial societies and our own—as different ways of achieving similar ends, even though the ways these ends are achieved will in turn affect what the members of these societies value.

Nevertheless, even in otherwise similar societies, rules can be compared only to the extent that they are means to a common end. We will have to be alert to the possibility that they are not when we compare the rules of civil law systems with each other. But we will have to be still more wary when we compare the rules of common law and civil law systems.

As has often been said, Roman jurists focused on substantive law, leaving problems of procedure to one side. Consequently, the medieval jurists who harmonized their texts were clarifying rules of substantive law which the late scholastics could then relate to principles and doctrines of commutative justice. The common law was the opposite. From its inception until after 1800, the common law was organized procedurally, in terms of writs or forms of action. In Sir Henry Maine's phrase[52], rules of substantive law were secreted in the interstices of rules of procedure. Hence the question was rarely which of the parties should prevail as a matter of substantive right. It was which party should prevail given the writ or form of action the plaintiff had brought.

A writ was needed for the plaintiff to bring a case before the royal courts. Eventually the number of writs was limited. These writs were not supposed to constitute an enumeration of the substantive rights that courts ought to protect. They were a procedural limitation on the types of cases the royal courts would hear. The limitation was based on tradition, not on any deliberation about the sorts of cases they ought to be hearing. After the number was fixed, the judges bent and stretched them to make them fit new cases. Their willingness to do so, however, was not always based on a desire to produce substantively fair results. It was often based on their sense of how far it was appropriate to bend and stretch. It was sometimes based on their respect for rules inherited from still earlier times. It was affected by their sense of what issues could be litigated under fact-finding procedures quite different than our own.

Sometimes, the peculiarities of the writ system had such an effect on the result of a case that the outcome did represent the court's judgment as to what, substantively, the parties' rights should be in a given factual situation. If so, one can compare their decision with those of courts or legislators facing the same question. The common law courts may have expressed themselves in a very different vocabulary than that of the civil law. But the difference does not show that its decision rests on different concepts or principles. It may rest on the same underlying principles. That may be so even if the outcome of the case is different in common law than it would be in civil law. We have seen many reasons why courts can reach different results even though the underlying principles are the same. Nevertheless, to the extent that the common law courts explain this result in terms which are foreign to the civil law, there is the danger of taking the difference in terminology too seriously and imagining that the common law and civil law rest on fundamentally different concepts. We will see instances in this book in which historians have done so.

Other times, however, the peculiarities of the writ system did effect the result which common law courts reached. The result represents the best a court could do given the traditional limitations on the writ the plaintiff had brought. It would be a mistake to think that a decision represents the court's judgment of what the substantive rights of the parties should be if the peculiarities of the writ system could have been set aside. The difference between the outcome in civil and common law cannot be explained simply as a different way of accomplishing a similar purpose. The result at common law was affected by an additional purpose foreign to the civil law: that of bringing the result within a recognized form of action.

[52] Sir Henry Maine, *Dissertations on Early Law and Custom* (London, 1891), 389.

The significance of these differences was often neglected during a great attempt to rationalize the common law that was made during the 19th and 20th centuries. In the 19th century, the forms of action were abolished. The plaintiff no longer needed to specify the writ he was bringing to seek relief. Supposedly, the law was not otherwise changed. The plaintiff could receive relief only in cases in which he would previously have been entitled to it. In fact, however, a great change had been taking place in the way in which Anglo-Americans thought about the common law. Before the 19th century, they had thought in terms of writs, each with its own rules. The 18th century jurist Blackstone had been almost the only one to try to organize the common law intellectually. He was the first to teach it in a university. His book, *Commentaries on the Laws of England*,[53] was almost the only legal literature on private law other than books about common law estates and the reports and abridgments of decided cases. The first treatise on the common law of contracts was written by Powell in 1794.[54] The first treatises on the common law of torts were written by Hilliard in 1861.[55] The first treatises on the law of unjust enrichment appeared in the 20th century.

The treatise writers of the 19th century described the common law in an ever more systematic fashion. They claimed merely to be explaining what the judges had been doing all along. But, as we will see, in the process, they changed the substantive law as well. They reorganized the common law by borrowing massively from civil law literature. Doctrines originally framed by the late scholastics and preserved by the northern natural lawyers were said, first, to be principles of universal jurisprudence, and then teachings of the common law. In the end, not only had the common law been reorganized along civil law lines in terms of property, tort, contract and, eventually, unjust enrichment. Not only had many of the traditional rules disappeared, but some of the traditional rules, whose significance could only be understood within the writ system, had been grafted onto civil law doctrines. They were explained as though they served the same purposes as civil law rules even though they would not have been formulated as they were absent the intricacies of the writ system.

Consequently, we will have to be especially wary about comparisons between common and civil law. We will have to be aware that sometimes what amount to differences in vocabulary have been interpreted as differences in underlying principle. We will have to recognize that sometimes rules which can only be understood within the framework of the writ system have been interpreted as though they were determinations of what the substantive rights of the parties should be. The problem is so pervasive that each part of this book will begin with an evaluation of the differences between common and civil law and how they came to be.

---

[53] William Blackstone, *Commentaries on the Laws of England* (London, 1765–9).
[54] John J. Powell, *Essay on the Law of Contracts and Agreements* (London, 1790).
[55] Francis Hilliard, *The Law of Torts or Private Wrongs* (Boston, 1861).

PART II
PROPERTY

Property

In civil law countries, the 19th century will theorists defined property in terms of the will of the owner to do as he willed with his own. They did not discuss why there should be property at all or what purposes the institution serves. Consequently, their approach created a number of intractable problems.

One, to be investigated in the next chapter, is why the law protects one who is not the owner but merely the possessor of property. As we will see, although this question was widely debated in the 19th century, and civil lawyers are still living parasitically off the debate, the question became unanswerable as soon as ownership had been defined as the will theorists had done. As we will see, the English joined the continental debate when Sir Frederick Pollock devised a clever theory in which he defined rights of ownership in terms of possession. Today, English jurists regard this theory, not as a response to a continental problem, but as ancient common law lore. We will see that instead it was a genuine step forward in response to the problem that continental jurists had raised and the key to resolving it.

A second question is how far the rights of a possessor or owner extend. To say that he can do as he will with his own does not answer that question. We will break it down into three questions to be discussed in three following chapters. One is the extent to which a person may use his property in a way that interferes with his neighbor's use. This is the question that common lawyers know as 'nuisance' and French and German lawyers as *troubles de voisinage* or *Immissionenrecht*. The next is to what extent neighbors can reset the limits the law prescribes by a voluntary agreement that binds their successors, an arrangement which common lawyers call a covenant or easement and civil lawyers call a servitude. Then we will discuss the extent to which property rights should include rights to the use of other resources that do not belong to any single proprietor. We will discuss only one such case, which will serve as a paradigm: the right to water.

A final question is how rights to property can be lost or gained other than by consent, be it through purchase, inheritance, or gift. Again, one cannot answer this question by simply defining property as the right to do as one wills with one's own. One has to ask why property should belong to one person rather than another. In one chapter, we will see how a proprietor can lose his rights because another is in a state of necessity or has been in possession for a long period of time. In the next, we will see when he can gain rights by find, capture or discovery.

Throughout this book, as mentioned earlier, we will be drawing on writers in the Aristotelian tradition. While they wrote a great deal about what we call contracts, torts and restitution, they wrote comparatively little about the questions of property law just described. Nevertheless, I will try to show that their insights into the purposes of property and the nature of commutative justice can best explain how these questions should be answered.

3

Possession and Ownership

I. A Preliminary Note on the Differences Between Common and Civil Law

A. Differences in the Structure of Property Law

As just mentioned, during the 19th and 20th centuries, there was an effort to rationalize the common law. Formerly, common lawyers had organized their thinking in terms of writs. Now they did so in terms of fields of law such as property, tort, contract and unjust enrichment which had been familiar to civil lawyers for centuries. In the process, a great deal was borrowed from the civilians. But there was also an effort to try to state what fundamental principles distinguished the one legal system from the other.

Some common law property rules were quite different than those of civil law but did not rise to the level of fundamental principles underlying the law of property. For example, traditionally, in common law, an owner had the right to control the future use of his property by creating any of a bewildering variety of 'future interests'. Leaseholds were treated as a type of property right which traditionally made it difficult to recognize ongoing contract-like duties between the lessor and the lessee. When land was sold to more than one person, the rights of the purchasers turned on who had a title that a court of equity would recognize. These differences will not be treated here. The law of future interests chiefly concerns family planning and inheritance, which is beyond the scope of this book. Also beyond its scope are how particular arrangements such as lease or sale or partnership should be governed. The rules of equitable title have lost much of their traditional significance with enactment of recording statutes. In any event, none of these rules concerns fundamental principles of the law of property.

Most jurists would say that the common law and civil law rules of property differ in two fundamental respects. One is that the civil law recognizes a limited number of types of interests in property—it has a *numerus clausus*—whereas the common law allows private parties considerably more freedom in the types of interests which they can create. The second is that the civil law recognizes 'ownership' or 'absolute owner-ship' whereas the common law does not clearly distinguish ownership and possession.

The first of these differences will be discussed in a later chapter concerning servitudes or property-like interests which one person can have in another's land. We will see that while the common law is more flexible in allowing such interests to be created, this flexibility is to be understood as a means to purposes which civil law systems are also trying to achieve, and that civil law systems themselves differ in the degree of flexibility that they permit to achieve these purposes. If, in so basic an area as servitudes, the flexibility of the common law can be understood as tool, analogous to the tools of the civil law and serving the same ends, then we can see that it is not a difference in the fundamental principles underlying property law, even though we will not be examining other contexts in which this difference can matter. It is a difference, and only a difference in degree, in techniques employed to accomplish common ends.

B. Possession and Ownership

This chapter will consider the second difference between the two systems: that supposedly, the civil law is based on a concept of 'ownership' that is foreign to the common law. Supposedly, the common law conceives of the protection of ownership much like the protection of possession. In the end, we will have a better understanding, not only of the difference between civil and common law, but why possession without ownership is protected in both systems.

The difference between the civil law concept of 'ownership' and common law conceptions is usually illustrated by mentioning either the common law estates or the identification of ownership and possession.

The common law estates, it is sometimes said, are not 'ownership' but interests which one can have in land. Even fee simple is not 'ownership' but simply the largest interest that the common law recognizes. We will not linger over this idea because it is difficult to see what it could mean. Civil law systems recognize interests in property such as usufruct that are not as extensive as full ownership. They recognize that more than one person can have real rights in the same land. The rights of a person with full ownership in civil law are much the same as those of one who holds a fee simple at common law. What can it mean to speak of a basic structural difference between the civil law and common law approach?

To be taken more seriously is the idea that civil law and common law take a radically different view of the relationship between ownership and possession. Supposedly, while the common law blurs these concepts, '[c]ontinental law makes a sharp distinction'.[1] The accounts that continental and Anglo-American jurists give of these institutions do seem to be polar opposites. Typically, continental jurists say that the owner has the right to possession while the mere possessor does not. Then they try to explain why the law protects someone who is acting without right. In contrast, Anglo-American jurists—and particularly the English—say that the common law 'never bothered much with the idea of ownership',[2] 'never applied the conception of ownership to land',[3] 'never really disentangled [the concept of ownership] from that of possession'.[4]

---

[1] Jacob Houdyn Beekhuis, 'Civil Law', in 'Chapter 2 Structural Variations in Property Law', 3 at 18 in *International Encyclopedia of Comparative Law* 6 *Property and Trust* (Frederich Henry Lawson, ed., Tübingen, 1973).   [2] Michael Harwood, *Modern English Land Law* (2nd edn., London, 1982), 503.
[3] Edward Hector Burn, *Cheshire and Burn's Modern Law of Real Property* (16th edn., London, 2000), 26.
[4] Robert Megarry and H. W. R. Wade, *The Law of Real Property* (5th edn., London, 1984), 104.

In the common law, supposedly, ownership or title to land is based on the fact of possession or the best right to possession.[5] Title is therefore relative. The person with possession has title against anyone who does not have a better right.[6] A 'better right' is a right based on still earlier possession.[7]

The reason, supposedly, is an ancient indigenous difference between common and civil law. Here we will examine and reject the evidence that the difference is ancient and indigenous. Then we will see that it arose as an English response to a paradox in civil law theory.

Supposedly, the common law never protected ownership as such. To support that proposition, English authors nearly always cite actions to recover land. Indeed, for much of English history, there was no action to recover chattels but only land. The medieval actions did not protect ownership or possession of land but rather 'seizin'. One who had been seized and was dispossessed would bring an action called 'novel disseizin' to get his land back. The heir of someone who had been seized would bring one called 'mort d'ancestor'. The closest thing to an action based on ownership was the 'writ of right', but even this was an action to protect seizin since the party who prevailed was the party who could trace his claim to the earliest person to have seizin.[8] In contrast, the civil law protects either ownership or possession. The plaintiff recovers if he can prove he is the owner (in an action known as *rivendicazione, revendication* or *Vindikation*) or if he can prove he was wrongfully dispossessed by the defendant (in an *azione di reintegrazione, action en réintégrande* or *Besitzentziehungsklage*).

For centuries, however, the common law has protected both ownership and possession, not by the medieval writs, but by an action known as 'ejectment'. Fifty years ago, two eminent English historians argued over whether the rise of the action of ejectment marked a change in 'theory' from the older notion of seizin to a civilian-like notion of ownership and possession. Sir William Holdsworth claimed that it did. A plaintiff in ejectment will prevail if, like a plaintiff in a continental real action, he can show he is the true owner or has been in possession for the period necessary to acquire title. He will not prevail if his period of possession was shorter or if the defendant can show title in a third party (the so-called defense of *ius tertii*). He will also prevail if, like a plaintiff in a continental possessory action, he can show the defendant ousted him from possession.[9] A. D. Hargreaves challenged him, arguing that the concept of seizin still mattered although the English courts were losing sight of it 'in a fit of absentminded-ness'.[10] A 'yearning for ownership' had 'infect[ed] the terminology of ejectment' ever since 'a spate of loose language set in ... with the sentimental liberalism of the [eighteen]-fifties'.[11] Nevertheless, the decisions of these courts could be explained without using the idea of ownership. According to Hargreaves, the reason a plaintiff in

[5] See Megarry and Wade, *Real Property*, 104; Burn, *Real Property*, 26; Harwood, *Land Law*, 503.

[6] Megarry and Wade, *Real Property*, 106; Burn, *Real Property*, 26–7; Harwood, *Land Law*, 503; Kevin Gray and Susan Francis Gray, *Elements of Land Law* (3rd edn., London, 2001), 96–7.

[7] See Megarry and Wade, *Real Property*, 107; Harwood, *Land Law*, 503.

[8] A. W. B. Simpson, *A History of the Land Law* (2nd edn., Oxford, 1986), 38.

[9] Sir William Searle Holdsworth, *History of English Law* 7 (Boston, 1926), 57–81.

[10] Anthony Dalzell Hargreaves, 'Terminology and Title in Ejectment', *L. Quar. Rev.* 56 (1940), 376 at 398.

[11] ibid. 387.

ejectment prevailed if he proved possession for the statutory period was not because he proved his title but because, under an old English rule, that period established a presumption of 'livery of seizin'.[12] The reason plaintiff prevailed if he proved he was wrongfully dispossessed was not that he had been wrongfully dispossessed but that he had been disseized.[13]

As I have shown in more detail elsewhere,[14] neither of these opinions is consistent with the English cases through the mid-19th century. From the 17th century onward, English judges had said that to recover in ejectment, the plaintiff must have title. Lord Holt said so in the 17th century,[15] and Lord Mansfield in the 18th.[16] But it does not follow that Holdsworth is right that the plaintiff had to prove title to recover. It was not clear, in the cases just mentioned, that either party did have title. Moreover, in a subsequent case, even though the plaintiff could not prove he had been in possession for the 20 year period necessary to obtain title, Lord Mansfield allowed the jury to infer possession for the requisite 20 years.[17] In the 19th century, courts continued to say that the plaintiff must recover on his title. Nevertheless, they allowed him to recover if he proved forcible dispossession[18] and sometimes if he merely proved possession[19] on the grounds that he had produced evidence from which title could be inferred. If the plaintiff had been forcibly dispossessed, they allowed him to recover, saying that forcible dispossession was evidence of title. If Hargreaves were right, these courts should not have mentioned title since what mattered was not title but seizin. If Holdsworth was right, they should have insisted that plaintiff actually prove that he did have title.

Instead, the courts had been reaching results pragmatically without any clear theory in mind. They might have done so indefinitely except that, in the mid-19th century, some cases finally came before them in which the plaintiff plainly did not have title. They could no longer say that his prior possession or forcible dispossession was evidence of title. They had to say either that he could not recover or that he need not have title to do so. Initially, in 1849, in *Doe dem. Carter* v. *Barnard*, they gave the first answer.[20] Then, in 1865, in *Asher* v. *Whitlock*,[21] they flip-flopped and gave the second. While *Asher* made it clear that a prior possessor without title could recover his land, that proposition is accepted by civil law systems as well. It hardly commits the common law to a distinct theory about the relationship of ownership and possession. And even if it had, this theory would have emerged only in 1865.

---

[12] ibid. 382–3.   [13] ibid. 379–80.

[14] James Gordley and Ugo Mattei, 'Protecting Possession', *Am. J. Comp. L.* 44 (1996), 293 at 319–29.

[15] *Stokes* v. *Berry*, 2 Salk 421, 91 Eng Rep 366 (KB 1699) (plaintiff recovers because 'the possession of twenty years shall be a good title').

[16] *Doe dem. Haldane & Urry* v. *Harvey*, 4 Burr 2484, 2487, 98 Eng Rep 302, 304 (KB 1769) ('plaintiff can not recover but on the strength of his own title').

[17] *Denn ex dem. Tarzwell* v. *Barnard*, Cowp 595, 98 Eng Rep 1259 (KB 1777).

[18] *Doe dem. Hughes* v. *Dyeball*, M & M 345, 173 Eng Rep 1184 (NP 1829); *Doe dem. Humphrey* v. *Martin*, Carr & M 32, 174 Eng Rep 395 (NP 1841); *Davison* v. *Gent*, 1 H & N 744, 156 Eng Rep 1400 (Ex 1857).

[19] Compare *Doe dem. Smith & Payne* v. *Webber*, 1 Ad & E 119, 10 Eng Rep 1152 (KB 1834) (plaintiff recovers) with *Doe dem. Wilkins* v. *Marquis of Cleveland*, 9 B & C 864, 109 Eng Rep 321 (1829) (plaintiff does not recover).   [20] 13 QB 945, 116 ER 1524 (1849).

[21] LR 1 QB 1 (1865).

II. The Theoretical Controversy

The distinction that in principle separates the common and civil law is therefore neither traditional nor indigenous. In fact, it was born of the conceptual debates of the 19th century. Continental conceptualists defined the owner as a person with the right to use the property in question as he willed. He therefore had the right to its possession. It then seemed that they must define the possessor who is not an owner as a person without this right. Having done so, they entered a theoretical box canyon from which they never emerged. Protection of mere possession became inexplicable. In response to this continental debate, Oliver Wendell Holmes suggested and Sir Frederick Pollock developed in detail the idea that possession gives a kind of title. Their idea became commonly accepted among common lawyers, and, as we shall see, there is much to be said for it as an explanation, not only of common law but of civil law. It was, indeed, a different explanation than that accepted by most civil law jurists but it was a response to their theories, not an ancient principle of common law.

A. The German Debate

Continental thought about possession was shaped by a great debate in Germany in the 19th century in which Savigny and Ihering were the foremost participants. Today, even outside Germany, jurists typically explain that there are two theories of why possession is protected. One, for which they often cite Savigny, is to preserve public order. The other, for which they often cite Ihering, is to provide a more complete protection for the true owner. These are almost the only explanations that French jurists give.[22]

The German debate is a case study in the consequences of the assumption that only the owner can have a genuine right to possess. That was Savigny's premise. Possession is a physical situation that corresponds to the legal situation called ownership. The owner has the legal power, and the possessor the physical power, to deal with an object as he wishes and to exclude all others from using it.[23] Therefore, according to Savigny, the question was 'how possession, without any regard to its own lawfulness, can be a basis for rights'.[24]

---

[22] Jean Carbonnier, *Droit civil tom 3 Les Biens* (19th edn., Paris, 2000), § 122, p. 208; Ambroise Colin, Henri Capitant, and Léon Juilliot de la Morandière, *Traité de droit civil tom 2 Obligations Théorie générale Droits réels principaux* (10th edn., Paris, 1959), § 446, p. 242; Gérard Cornu, *Droit civil tom 1 Introduction Les Personnes Les Biens* (4th edn., Paris, 1990), §§ 1155–6, p. 362; Christian Larroumet, *Droit civil tom 2 Les Biens Droits réels principaux* (1985), §§ 64–5, pp. 45–6; §§ 66–7, pp. 46–7; Gabriel Marty and Pierre Raynaud, *Droit civil: Les Biens* (2nd edn., 1980), § 14, pp. 14–15. Some jurists also mention that the owner who leaves his land idle is not making economic use of it, and that the law should protect third parties who innocently buy from the person in possession, believing him to be the owner. They seem to be using these considerations to explain why the possessor gains title with the passage of time. Alex Weill, François Terré, and Philippe Simler, *Droit civil: Les Biens* (3rd edn., Paris, 1985), § 54, pp. 63–4; § 55, pp. 64–5; Henri Mazeaud, Léon Mazeaud, Jean Mazeaud, and François Chabas, *Leçons de droit civil tom 2 Biens Droit de propriété et ses démembrements* (8th edn., Paris, 1994), §§ 1413–14, pp. 190–1.

[23] Friedrich Carl von Savigny, *Das Recht des Besitzes* 2–3 (6th edn., Giessen, 1837), 2–3.

[24] ibid. 9.

Answering Savigny's question was one of the major intellectual projects of the 19th century German jurists. Rarely if ever have more brilliant legal minds clashed. Yet they found no convincing answer. Whenever one German jurist suggested a solution, another was able to explain why it would not work.

Savigny claimed to have explained the protection Roman law gave a possessor. In Roman law, an owner could recover his property by bringing an action called *vindicatio*. A possessor, whether he was the owner or not, could bring actions known as possessory interdicts. In a *vindicatio*, Savigny pointed out, 'it is entirely irrelevant how the other party came into possession since the owner has the right to exclude him from possession'.[25] In contrast, 'all of the possessory interdicts ... presuppose an act that is unlawful by its form':[26] an interference with possession.[27] Savigny concluded that the interdicts were a kind of tort action given the victim of such an unlawful interference. He pointed out that the interdicts, like other Roman tort actions, lay only against the perpetrator or his estate, and could be brought only within a year.[28]

One difficulty with Savigny's theory was that in other ways the Roman interdicts were not like tort actions. As critics pointed out, the plaintiff's remedy was not damages but recovery of possession.[29] Moreover, the defendant could be liable without fault.[30] Indeed, the plaintiff had to prove the defendant violently dispossessed him only if he brought the interdict *unde vi*, an action to recover land. He did not need to prove violence or even bad faith if he brought the interdict *uti possedetis* to protect his possession of land when it was threatened or disturbed but not lost, or if he brought the interdict *utrubi* to recover or protect the possession of movable property.[31] Also, the interdicts only protected one who claimed the object in his own right. They did not protect lessees and others who based their right on the right of another. That was odd if they were supposed to provide tort-like protection against unlawful acts.[32] Finally, the possessory interdicts could be brought by a thief or a robber but Roman tort actions could not.[33]

More important for our purposes, however, is the way Savigny answered the theoretical question why the law should protect a possessor if possession was not in itself a right worthy of protection. According to Savigny, '[a]n independent right of the person ... is not violated but the situation of the person is altered to his disadvantage; the unlawfulness, which consists in the use of force against this person, can only be eliminated with all of its consequences by the restoration and protection of the factual situation to which the force extended'.[34]

---

[25] ibid. 9.   [26] ibid. 8.

[27] '[T]he right which mere possession gives consists only in the claim which the possessor has to interdicts when a certain form of interference occurs.' Therefore, the interdicts were a type of tort action. ibid. 31–3.   [28] ibid. 32–3.

[29] Anton Randa, *Der Besitz mit Einschluß der Besitzklagen nach österreichem Rechte* (3rd edn., Leipzig, 1879), § 8, p. 274; Carl Georg Bruns, *Die Besitzklagen des römischen und heutigen Rechts* (Wiemar, 1874), § 7, pp. 49–51.   [30] Bruns, *Besitzklagen* § 7, pp. 49–51.

[31] Rudolph von Ihering, *Über den Grund des Besitzesschutzes Eine Revision der Lehre vom Besitz* 17–19 (2d edn., Jena, 1869), 17–19; Heinrich Dernburg, *Pandekten* 1 (4th edn., Berlin, 1894), § 170, p. 402

[32] Randa, *Besitz*, § 8, p. 274; Ihering, *Lehre vom Besitz*, 9–12.

[33] Ihering, *Lehre vom Besitz*, 15–16 (noting that thief and robber do not have protection under *actio furti* and *lex Aquilia*, and citing 47.2.12.1; 47.2.76.1; arg. 9.2.17.6).   [34] Savigny, *Recht des Besitzes*, 41.

That answer is not perfectly clear. It suggests two rather different explanations for the protection of possession, each of which had its champions among the German jurists. According to the first, the law protects the peace and order of society against unlawfulness and force. According to the second, the law protects the victim himself. The victim has a legally protectable claim against unlawful interference even though he does not have a legally protectable claim to possession.

The first explanation was accepted by Rudorff in the 19th century[35] and by most German jurists today.[36] Supposedly, relief is given merely because public order has been disrupted and not because the plaintiff has a protectable interest. German critics have raised some powerful objections. If the plaintiff has no protectable interest in maintaining his possession, then the unlawfulness or disruption of public order cannot consist in the mere fact that the plaintiff was deprived of possession. It must be found in the unlawful or disruptive way in which the defendant deprived him of it. But relief is given when there has been dispossession without violence or a breach of the peace:[37] for example, when defendant took plaintiff's hat by mistake in place of his own.[38] Moreover, it is hard to see why public order should be protected by a civil action, rather than by administrative or police measures, if no one has suffered an injury to any protectable interest.[39] Nor can one see why the successful plaintiff should recover possession.[40] His incentive to defend public order by bringing the action will then depend on the value of what he has lost, a consideration which, by hypothesis, has nothing to do with the extent to which public order has been disrupted.[41]

In the 19th century, most German jurists turned to the second explanation instead. The possessor should be protected against interference even though his possession itself is not worthy of protection. According to Puchta, Windscheid, Bruns and Randa, the reason was that the possessor's will was actualized or expressed in his exercise of dominion over an object. The will was worthy of protection without regard

---

[35] Adolphus Rudorff, 'Über den Rechtsgrund der possessorischen Interdicte', *Zeitschrift für geschichtliche Rechtswissenschaft* 7 (1831), 90 at 110–14.

[36] G. Seuffert, in Julius von Staudinger, *Kommentar zum Bürgerlichen Gesetzbuch* (11th edn., Berlin, 1956), vor § 854 no. 3; Martin Wolff and Ludwig Raiser, *Sachenrecht Ein Lehrbuch* (10th edn., Tübingen, 1957), § 17, p. 52; R. Haase in *Munchener Kommentar zum Bürgerlichen Gesetzbuch* (Munich, 1981), vor § 854 no. 7; Julius von Gierke, *Das Sachenrecht des bürgerlichen Rechts* (4th edn., Berlin, 1959), § 9 I 2, p. 22; Friedrich Lent and Karl Heinz Schwab, *Sachenrecht Ein Studienbuch* (19th edn., Munich, 1983), § 3 IV, p. 13; O. Mühl, in Hans Theodor Soergel and Wolfgang Siebert, *Bürgerliches Gesetzbuch* (11th edn., Stuttgart, 1978), vor § 854 no. 13. It has been accepted as a partial explanation by E. Wieser, 'Der Schadensersatzanspruch des Besitzers aus § 823 BGB—*BGH JZ 1954, 613*', *Juristische Schulung* 10 (1970), 557 at 559–60; Harry Westermann, *Sachenrecht* (6th edn., Karlsruhe, 1990), § 8, 3 pp. 78–9.

[37] Ihering, *Lehre vom Besitz*, 8; Hans Joseph Wieling, *Sachenrecht* 1 (Berlin, 1990), 3 III b, p. 127.

[38] Phillip Heck, *Grundriß des Sachenrechts* (Tübingen, 1930), § 3, 6, p. 12; Hans Joseph Wieling, 'Grund und Umfang des Besitzschutzes', in *De iustitia et iure Festgabe für Ulrich von Lübtow zum 80. Geburtstag* (Manfried Harder and Georg Thielmann, eds., Berlin, 1980), 550 at 576.

[39] *Sachenrecht* III 3 b, p. 127; Wieling, 'Grund und Umfang', 576–7; Heck, *Grundriß*, § 3, pp. 12–13; Westermann, *Sachenrecht*, § 8, 3, pp. 78–9.   [40] Weiling, *Sachenrecht*, 3 III b, p. 127.

[41] In the 19th century, a further objection was that a concern for public order cannot explain why Roman law gives no remedy to a person such as the lessee who is not claiming in his own right. Randa, *Besitz*, § 8, p. 276; Georg Friedrich Puchta, *Vorlesungen über das heutige römischen Recht* 1 (Rudorff, ed., 2nd edn., Leipzig, 1849), § 122, p. 244; Georg Friedrich Puchta, 'Über die Existenz des Besitzrechts', in Georg Friedrich Puchta, *Kleine Zivilistische Schriften* (F. Rudorff, ed., Leipzig, 1851), 239 at 259, 262.

to whether this exertion of dominion was rightful or wrongful.[42] To interfere with another's exercise of will was to interfere with his freedom or personality,[43] or to violate the principle that each person is the equal of every other.[44] Today, Wieling takes the same approach.[45]

The advantage of this approach, as Puchta and Randa pointed out, is that the victim is protected simply because the act of dispossession interferes with his will, not because the act that interferes is unlawful in any other respect.[46] The difficulty is that the law does not protect people against any interference with their will. It protects them against dispossession. German critics have made this point in various ways. Ihering argued that the law does not protect the will regardless of what is willed but rather defines the circumstances in which the will is protected.[47] Heck noted that while one can always expand a word like 'personality' to cover any instance in which one gives relief, doing so does not explain why relief is given.[48] Julius von Gierke observed that any protection the law could afford is protection of the personality in some sense.[49] So what is special about possession?

Indeed, if the possessor who is not the owner is acting without right, the law is protecting the will to do something wrongful. Even if, in the abstract, the will should be protected, it is hard to see why the will to do wrong should be.[50] Moreover, the law is not simply protecting the will of the possessor but settling a conflict among different people's wills. By taking an object, a dispossessor allows his will to override that of the earlier possessor. By keeping it, the earlier possessor allows his own to override the will of all those who come later. Respect for the will does not explain why the earlier possessor should win.[51] Nor does it explain why physical possession matters. If the law were merely protecting a person's will to appropriate an object, it would protect that will however it were expressed, whether physical possession was taken or not.[52]

As Bruns noted, the theories just discussed did not protect possession as such.[53] Ihering recognized that to explain protection, one needed to identify some substantive right in need of protection. In his theory, however, this substantive right was not possession itself. It was ownership. By protecting possession, the law gave a more effective

---

[42] Georg Friedrich Puchta, *Cursus der Institutionen* 2 (3rd edn., Leipzig, 1851), § 224, p. 333; Puchta, *Vorlesungen*, § 122, p. 243; Georg Friedrich Puchta, 'Zu welcher Classe von Rechten gehört der Besitz?' in Puchta, *Kleine Schriften*, 255–6; Bernhard Windscheid, *Lehrbuch des Pandektenrechts* 1 (3rd edn., Düsseldorf, 1873), § 148, p. 401; Carl Georg Bruns, 'Das heutige römische Recht', in F. von Holtzendorff, *Encyclopädie der Rechtswissenschaft* (Leipzig, 1870), 247 at 293; Carl Georg Bruns, *Das Recht des Besitzes im Mittelalter und in der Gegenwart*, § 58, pp. 491–2 (Tübingen, 1848); Randa, *Besitz*, § 8, p. 284.

[43] Puchta, *Vorlesungen*, § 122, p. 243; Bruns, *Römische Recht*, 293; Randa, *Besitz*, § 8, p. 284.

[44] Windscheid, *Lehrbuch*, § 148, p. 401 n. 6.

[45] Wieling, *Sachenrecht*, 3 III b, p. 128; Wieling, 'Grund und Umfang', 577–8.

[46] Puchta, *Vorlesungen*, § 122, p. 244; Randa, *Besitz*, 290.

[47] Ihering, *Lehre vom Besitz*, 31–4.   [48] Heck, *Grundriß*, Excurs I, p. 488.

[49] Gierke, *Sachenrecht*, § 9 I 2, p. 23.

[50] Ihering, *Lehre vom Besitz*, 31–4; Gierke, *Sachenrecht*, § 9 I 2, p. 23; Wolff and Raiser, *Sachenrecht*, § 17, p. 52 n. 1.   [51] Dernburg, *Pandekten*, § 170, p. 403.

[52] Ihering, *Besitzschutzes*, 37–8. In the 19th century, another objection was that such an approach could not explain the failure to protect a person such as the lessee who did not claim the object in his own right. Ihering, ibid. 38–9.

[53] As noted by Bruns, *Besitzklagen*, § 26, pp. 265–66, speaking of the theory of Savigny, Rudorff, Puchta, Bruns, Windscheid and Randa.

protection to ownership.[54] The owner would not have to prove his title when dispossessed.[55] The protection given possessors who were not owners was an 'unavoidable consequence', a 'price' paid for protecting owners.[56] According to Ihering, this theory explained why the Roman possessory interdicts did not look like tort actions, and why they could not be brought by a person such as a lessee not claiming in his own right.[57]

Few German jurists have agreed with Ihering.[58] Critics pointed out that his theory does not explain why a possessor is protected when he clearly is not the owner;[59] indeed, why he is sometimes protected even against the owner.[60] Moreover, it rests on the assumption that the person dispossessed is most often the owner, an assumption Ihering himself had questioned.[61]

One begins to suspect that these theories do not work because of the feature they have in common: they give no reason to protect possession as such. The one German jurist who tried to give one was Dernburg. Possession should be protected because it is 'the factual order of society (*tatsächliche Gesellschaftsordnung*), the given division of physical goods. It grants the individual directly the instruments of his activity, the means for the satisfaction of his needs.'[62] If so, one might wonder, why is possession not a right belonging to the possessor? Dernburg denied that it is.[63] He explained that the owner, and not the possessor, has the right to possess. But if that is so, why should possession be protected?

Phillip Heck, developing Dernburg's insight, tried to answer that question while maintaining, with Dernburg, that the possessor did not have a genuine right to possession. Heck did so by claiming that the law does not protect possession as such but rather the continuity of possession. The law recognizes 'the need to protect the continuity of the relationships in life where possible', Heck said, citing Dernburg. 'Continuity is recognized as a good without regard to whether a definite right is present.'[64] 'Everyone knows from his own experience that adjustment to the loss of the use of a thing can lead to difficulties and damage.'[65] For Heck, the difficulties and damage against which the possessor is protected are not the loss of thing itself but the consequences of interrupting its use.

---

[54] Ihering, *Lehre vom Besitz*, 45–6.   [55] ibid. 47–54.   [56] ibid. 55.

[57] Consequently, some critics have pointed out that his theory does not explain why the German Civil Code does protect persons such as the lessee. Wieling, *Sachenrecht*, at 3 III b, p. 127; Wieling, 'Grund und Umfang', at 575; Gierke, *Sachenrecht*, § 9 I 2, p. 23.

[58] An exception is Wieser, *Sachenrecht*, 559–60. Unlike Ihering, he believes the goal of the law is to protect, not only owners, but all possessors worthy of protection, and that protection of the unworthy is the price one pays. He does not explain what other than ownership would distinguish the worthy from the unworthy possessor.

[59] Randa, *Besitz*, § 8, p. 276; Dernburg, *Pandekten*, § 170, p. 403; Heck, *Grundriß*, Excurs I, p. 488; Wieling, *Sachenrecht*, 575.   [60] Randa, *Besitz*, § 8, p. 276; Heck, *Grundriss*, Excurs I, p. 488.

[61] Ihering, *Lehre vom Besitz*, 25–7.   [62] Dernburg, *Pandekten*, § 170, p. 404.

[63] ibid. § 169, p. 398.

[64] Heck, *Grundriss*, § 3, p. 13. Similarly, '[t]he attack on continuity is always an injury to interest, a loss of something of value to life. Consequently, it must be remedied until a better right is established.' 'The protected legal good is the organizational value of possession' (ibid.). Protection is given because of 'the value . . . that continuity has for people in the relations of life' (ibid. Excurs I, p. 487).

[65] ibid. Excurs I, p. 487.

The trouble is that it is hard to see why continuity of possession merits legal protection if possession itself does not. Critics have made the same objection to protecting continuity that they would make to protecting possession as such: the theory cannot explain protection of a wrongdoer.[66] As one critic pointed out, the fact that everyone has an interest in keeping what he possesses does not explain why we protect it.[67]

Other German jurists have pointed out that the protection given possession is like that given property rights. But they have not developed a theory different than the ones already discussed. Bruns tired of his will theory and suggested that the reasons for protecting possession must be found in possession itself.[68] But he denied that possession could be a right,[69] and found no reason for protecting it other than the value placed on freedom.[70] Fritz and Jürgen Baur have said that 'in possession itself is a value that the law wishes to protect'.[71] But they accept Heck's theory. Gierke criticized Savigny, and Westermann criticized the will theorists, for failing to realize that the protection of possession is the protection of an economic asset (*Vermögen*).[72] Nevertheless, Gierke explained protection by the need to maintain public order, and Westermann tried to combine that theory with Heck's. Gierke, E. Wolf, M. Wolff, Raiser, Enneccerus and Nipperdey have concluded that possession must be some sort of right since it can be conveyed and inherited.[73] But none of them has turned this insight into a new theory.

B. The Anglo-American Sequel

As we have seen, the doctrine that English law does not distinguish clearly between ownership and possession, but is based on who can show the 'better right' by tracing his rights to the earlier possessor, is neither indigenous nor ancient. For centuries, English judges decided cases pragmatically without benefit of the doctrine of relative title or any other theory of what the relationship might be between ownership and possession. The doctrine first appeared clearly in the writings of Sir Frederick Pollock although he may have borrowed a suggestion of Oliver Wendell Holmes. Holmes and Pollock were familiar with the German debate and were trying to respond to it. While they both thought their theories would explain English law, their theories had little to do with any feature of the law that was distinctively English.

Holmes criticized the German debate in his book *The Common Law*. He complained that German scholars began with Kantian philosophical principles and then 'cunningly adjusted' them to explain the Roman law. He hoped to do better by improvising principles to explain the common law, 'a far more developed, more rational and mightier body of law than the Roman'.[74] At common law, possession and

---

[66] Wieling, *Sachenrecht*, n. 37, at § 3 III b, p. 127; Wieling, 'Grund und Umfang', 576–7; Gierke, *Sachenrecht*, n. 36, at § 9 I 2, p. 23; Westermann, *Sachenrecht*, n. 36, at § 8, 3 pp. 78–9.

[67] Wieling, *Sachenrecht*, n. 38, at 576–7.   [68] Bruns, *Besitzklagen*, § 26, p. 273.

[69] ibid. § 27, p. 292.   [70] ibid. § 27, p. 290.

[71] Fritz Baur and Jürgen Baur, *Lehrbuch des Sachenrechts* (15th edn., Munich, 1989), § 9 I 3, p. 71.

[72] Gierke, *Sachenrecht*, § 9 I 2, p. 23; Westermann, *Sachenrecht*, § 8, 3 p. 78.

[73] Gierke, *Sachenrecht*, § 5 I, p. 9; Ernest Wolf, *Lehrbuch des Sachenrechts*, § 2 A III b, p. 34 (Cologne, 1971); Wolff and Raiser, *Sachenrecht*, § 3 III, p. 19; L. Enneccerus and H.C. Nipperdey, *Allgemeiner Teil des Bürgerlichgen Rechts: Ein Lehrbuch* (15th edn., Tübingen 1959), § 80 I 1, p. 478.

[74] Oliver Wendell Holmes, Jr., *The Common Law* (Boston, 1881), 210.

ownership had been protected in a single action, the action of ejectment. It was originally a lessee's remedy, and had become available to owners and possessors who made a fictitious allegation that they had made a lease. Paradoxically, the features of ejectment that struck Holmes as more rational were due, historically, to the fact that it had originally protected a lessee.[75] At common law, in contrast to Roman law, a lessee could sue, and the defendant could plead his title in defense. Holmes developed a theory of possessory intent which he cunningly adjusted to explain these features.

He discussed the relationship between ownership and possession in his final paragraph. '[R]ights of ownership', he said, 'are substantially the same as those incident to possession ... The owner is allowed to exclude all, and is accountable to no one. The possessor is allowed to exclude all but one, and is accountable to no one but him.'[76] Whenever he could, Holmes had tried to present his ideas as descriptions of the action of ejectment at common law. This time, Holmes did not mention any feature peculiar to ejectment. He seemed to be discussing ownership and possession considered abstractly.

Possibly, this passage inspired the theory of relative title developed by Holmes' friend, Sir Frederick Pollock. Holmes wrote in 1881. Pollock described his theory in 1888, in his *Essay on Possession in the Common Law*, and in 1896, in his *First Book of Jurisprudence*.

Unlike Holmes, Pollock admired German scholarship and was willing to borrow from it. In his *Essay*, like the Germans, he initially described the owner as the person with the right to possess.[77] Consequently, he acknowledged that '[w]hy the law should ascribe possession to wrongdoers may be difficult to explain completely'.[78] In the *Essay* and in his *First Book*, he accepted explanations like those of the German jurists: protecting the wrongdoer is necessary to protect third parties, or the true owner, or the order of society, or the mere will of the possessor.[79]

His break with the German tradition was to formulate, and then exploit, an alternative distinction between an owner and a possessor. The owner had rights against everyone, and the possessor had rights against everyone except the owner. In his *Essay*, Pollock defined 'possession in fact' as the fact of control. In contrast, 'possession in law' is:

the fact of control coupled with a legal claim and the right to exercise it in one's own name against the world at large, not as against all men without exception. We say as against the world at large, not as against all men without exception. For a perfectly exclusive right to the control of anything can belong only to the owner ...[80]

Defined in this way, possession is a relative ownership, ownership as against everyone but the true owner. While Pollock may have borrowed this idea from Holmes, he thought it resolved a difficulty with the position of German authors such as Savigny: 'When possession as such is regarded as the proper subject of protection, that is to say, when dispossession without just cause (apart from any violence or physical damage

---

[75] ibid. 210–11.   [76] ibid. 246.

[77] Sir Fredrick Pollock and Robin Samuel Wright, *An Essay on Possession in the Common Law* (Oxford, 1888), 1–3. Pollock wrote parts I and II, which we will be quoting throughout, and Wright wrote part III.

[78] ibid. 3.

[79] ibid. 3–4; Sir Fredrick Pollock, *A First Book of Jurisprudence for Students of the Common Law* (London, 1896), 174–5.   [80] Pollock and Wright, *Essay*, 16.

incidental to the act) is treated as calling for a remedy, then the relation to ownership becomes apparent'.[81] Possession must be a right like ownership because it is protected for its own sake, not because of something else, such as the accompanying violence. As we have seen, the failure to recognize that possession was protected for its own sake was, indeed, a source of continual trouble for the 19th century Germans. Pollock was right to try to escape, and his attempt to do so shows he had learned a lesson from the difficulties the German scholars were encountering.

Certainly, Pollock was not developing a theory of the principles behind English law. Indeed, in his *First Book of Jurisprudence*, Pollock presented his theory as one that could explain both English and Roman law:

It may be worth remarking that in general terms that the relations of possession and ownership in Roman and English law, the difficulties arising out of them, and the devices resorted to for obviating or circumventing those difficulties, offer an amount of resemblance even in detail which is much more striking than the superficial and technical differences. We cannot doubt that these resemblances depend on the nature of the problems to be solved and not on any accidental connection. One system of law may have imitated another in particular doctrines and institutions, but imitation cannot find place in processes extending over two or three centuries, and whose fundamental analogies are externally disguised in almost every possible way.[82]

III. A Lesson to be Learned

While he did not explain how common and civil law differ, nevertheless, I believe that Pollock came close to resolving the problem that had so preoccupied the 19th century jurists: why is possession to be protected? He recognized that the problem was insoluble once one accepted the premise of most of the German jurists: that ownership was defined by the right to have one's possession protected. He concluded that possession must be a right something like ownership.

His mistake, in my view, was that he went too far. He did not merely conclude that possession must be a right worth protecting. He decided it was a right differing from ownership only because of the number of people against whom the right could be asserted. Consequently, possession 'is a kind of title'.[83] It 'may have all or most of the advantages of ownership against every one but the true owner, in other words, it may confer a relatively good title'.[84] '[W]e treat the actual possessor not only as legal possessor but as owner, as against every one who cannot show a better right . . .'.[85] It followed, he thought, that the prior right must be the better right. Possession conferred 'a right in the nature of property which is valid against every one who cannot show a prior and better right'.[86] '[E]very possession must create a title which, as against all subsequent intruders, has all the incidents and advantages of a true title.'[87]

Pollock's explanation escaped the problems the German jurists encountered although he did not consider all of its logical consequences. Does the possessor have a title which, like an owner's, would not be extinguished when he abandoned the

---

[81] Pollock, *First Book*, 169.   [82] ibid. 179.   [83] Pollock and Wright, *Essay*, 19.
[84] Pollock, *First Book*, 178.   [85] ibid. 172.   [86] Pollock and Wright, *Essay*, 93.
[87] ibid. 95.

property? May anyone who has been in possession even for a day claim the property until the statute of limitations runs from any current possessor who cannot trace title flawlessly from a prior possessor. If so, one should spend one's next vacation taking brief possession of as many English houses as possible in hopes of returning years later and finding them occupied by someone who cannot prove title. There is no reason to think English law would allow one to do so, and American law certainly would not.[88]

IV. Why Protect Possession?

As we have just seen, it would be more descriptive of continental and Anglo-American law to say that possessor has a right to possession but one that is not as extensive as the

---

[88] According to Lord Macnaghten, delivering the judgment of the Privy Council in *Agency Co.* v. *Short*, 13 AC 793, 799 (1888), 'the possession of the intruder, ineffectual for the purpose of transferring title, ceases upon its abandonment to be effectual for any purpose'. In that case, the court held that the statute of limitations did not run against the owner after the intruder left. In the Australian case of *Allen* v. *Roughly*, [1955] 94 CLR 98, Judge Williams applied Lord Macnaghten's statement to the relations between prior and subsequent possessors. The prior possessor, who left plaintiff the land in his will, died in 1895, and defendant did not take possession until 1898. Williams said he 'cannot accept' the rule that prior possessor is presumed to be seized in fee if it 'means that the presumption in his favour continues after he has abandoned the possession and would be available against any person who subsequently entered into possession so that any plaintiff who could prove prior possession at any time could recover the land against any subsequent possessor' (94 CLR at 114–15). He said that the rule proposed by Holdsworth that plaintiff must prove title 'refers and refers only, to cases where a person in possession abandons the land so that a succeeding intruder does not disturb an existing possession in any one. If an existing possession is disturbed, the person in possession can sue the disturber as a trespasser. Proof that he is in possession confers on him a good title against the whole world, except those who show a better title' (94 CLR at 115). Nevertheless, Williams held against the defendant on the ground that his possession was adverse.

In the United States, settlers often occupied land without formal title and later moved away. It was settled early on that unless a prior possessor intended to relinquish possession temporarily, he could not recover the land from a later possessor. Chief Judge Kent said in *Smith dem Teller* v. *Lorillard*, 'the prior possession of the plaintiff [must not have been] voluntarily relinquished without the animus revertendi, (as is frequently the case with possessions taken by squatters)' (10 Johns 338, 356, 4 NYCL 1057, 1064 (1813)) (but prior possessor recovers because he did not relinquish voluntarily but was expelled by British troops in 1776). When plaintiff had simply moved off, the lack of an animus revertendi would be presumed unless he could prove the contrary. Thus, in 1887, the United States Supreme Court held that when a prior possessor died intestate, his heir, who had moved away after one year, could not recover the property against a subsequent possessor who had moved on seven years later (*Sabariego* v. *Maverick*, 124 US 261 (1887)). The court said that 'in cases where the proof on the part of the plaintiff does not show a possession continuous until actual dispossession by the defendant, or those under whom he claims, the burden of proof is upon the plaintiff to show that his prior possession had not been abandoned' (124 US at 300). In other cases, plaintiffs surmounted this burden, for example, by showing they had spent large sums of money making improvements, the value of which had been appropriated by defendant (*National Milling & Mining Co.* v. *Piccolo*, 54 Wash 617, 104 P 128 (1909)), or by showing the premises had been left vacant because their tenant had moved off without their knowledge (*Jackson dem Murray* v. *Denn*, 5 Cowen 200, 8 NYCL 625 (1825)), quoted in *Sabariego* v. *Maverick*, 124 US 261, 300 (1887), or because they were driven off by foreign troops (*Smith dem Teller* v. *Lorillard*, 10 Johns 338, 4 NYCL 1057 (1813)). In the absence of such circumstances, some courts have simply said that 'possessory title continues only as long as possession is held, and after it has ended there can be no recovery from one who subsequently takes possession (or otherwise invades the premises)' (*Marinaro* v. *Deskins*, 344 SW 2d 817 (Ct App Ky, 1961)) (plaintiff, tracing title through the heirs of a prior possessor, cannot recover because the heirs failed to assert their claim for nearly 30 years while defendant was in possession after the prior possessor's death).

right of the owner. In particular, it is much more easily lost. We can conclude that a difference in the conceptions of ownership and possession is not a fundamental principle distinguishing the civil and the common law.

Nevertheless, the debate between the civil and common lawyers can teach us a good deal about why the right to possession should be protected. Pollock did not ask why. He simply wished to escape the conceptual paradox which arose for the Germans when they defined the owner as a person with the right to possession, which implied that the mere possessor had no such right. The writers in the Aristotelian tradition knew that possession was to be protected, but, disappointingly, they had little to say about why it should be. Yet a good explanation can be found by drawing on their ideas of possession and property. The insights relevant here were most clearly captured by Hugo Grotius.

The first is a parable—if you like—about how things become property in the first place. Once there was enough for everyone to take what he liked. As that situation gave way to one of scarcity, people acquired title to land which they occupied. In our terminology, there would originally have been possession without title. With the coming of scarcity, there could be title with or without possession.

Indeed, legal systems where there is no scarcity of land have recognized possession without title. Traditional land tenure in Africa is an example. Rattray described such a system in his classic work on the law of the Ashanti of West Africa. Among the Ashanti, land used for hunting and gathering was held in common. Private rights in this land would have been an inconvenience to everyone, as Rattray points out. Hunters want to follow an antelope wherever it goes.[89] In contrast, farmland belonged to a particular person or a family group. Nevertheless, according to Rattray, it was not owned in the Western sense. The person or group to whom it belonged had only the right to clear it and farm it.[90] The right was initially acquired by applying to a chief who would assign a plot that previously belonged to the hunting and gathering land.[91] Once the plot was assigned, no one else could use it. The chief himself could not take it back except for non-payment of an annual tax or rent equal to the value of it.[92] The person to whom the plot belonged could sell it, and his heirs could inherit it.[93] The right to use the plot lasted, however, only as long as it was farmed, or more technically, only as long as the claimant 'was able to point out some trees—kola, plantain, palm oil—which he had once cultivated, and still grew and bore fruit'.[94] When cultivation ceased, the land became, once again, land that anyone could use for hunting and gathering, and that the chief could reassign to someone else.

Similar systems of landholding were found throughout sub-Saharan Africa where land was abundant relative to the population.[95] The 'cardinal principle', according to Kwamena Bentsi-Entchill, 'is that land first reduced to cultivation from virgin forest

[89] Robert Sutherland Rattray, *Ashanti Law and Constitution* (Oxford, 1929), 345.

[90] ibid. 340–66.   [91] ibid. 350–1.   [92] ibid. 350–1, 353.   [93] ibid. 353–4, 356.

[94] ibid. 352. A right to use land held by someone not a subject to this chief may have reverted immediately when it was not cultivated (ibid. 353).

[95] Kwamena Bentsi-Enchill, 'The Traditional Legal Systems of Africa', in 'Chapter 2 Structural Variations in Property Law', 68 at 88–9. 3 in *International Encyclopedia of Comparative Law* 6 *Property and Trust*.

becomes the property of the person or persons who clear it'.[96] The cultivator's interest is freely alienable to other members of the same group.[97] It is lost when the cultivator abandons the land, but it is otherwise indefeasible.[98]

This system struck Rattray, and might strike most people, as quite fair. Land was abundant. Therefore, a person could appropriate it for farming without diminishing the resources available to others. To clear and farm the land required hard work. No one was allowed to appropriate the value of someone else's labor. No one was allowed to appropriate land and not use it.

This system might also strike a modern economist as efficient in a society in which land itself is not a scarce resource. A person will invest labor in clearing and cultivating the land up to the point where the marginal cost of so doing equals the marginal product he can obtain from it. He can sell his rights to someone else for whom the costs of cultivation are smaller or the returns greater. Indeed, the only feature of the system whose fairness or efficiency one might question is that the chief gets a sheep every year for allotting land. That task is unnecessary if land is not scarce since one could simply allow the first person to clear it to use it. The chief's sheep is like a tax, justified, if at all, by the public functions he performs.

Ownership is a solution to two problems that did not arise among the Ashanti where land was abundant, and private land had only one productive use. One is how to allocate scarce resources among people who want them. Under a system of ownership, one normally acquires resources by buying them. The other is the problem of deciding how resources will be used. Under a system of ownership, this decision is left to the owner. Even his decision to leave the land idle is normally respected.[99]

If we regard ownership functionally, as a means of solving these two problems, we will not conclude that only the owner can have a right to use property. We will merely conclude that the owner will prevail in a conflict with somebody else about how and for whose benefit the property may be used. There may be other conflicts to which the owner is not a party: between a possessor and a non-possessor, a former and a subsequent possessor, a party dispossessed and the party who dispossessed him. The owner may have an interest in how such conflicts are resolved. But none of them is a conflict between the owner and a non-owner about the use of the property. The principle that the owner would win if there were such a conflict does not tell us who should win when there is not.

There is nothing contradictory, then, about recognizing a right in the possessor, good against anyone else, to use the property until the owner appears and asserts his own rights. Indeed, if we imagine the non-owner can use the property without hurting the owner, it would be strange not to recognize such a right. At least the property will have been put to some use.

That brings us to a second conclusion of Hugo Grotius. Granted that, according to commutative justice, the benefit of resources belongs to the owner, nevertheless, the

---

[96] ibid. 81.

[97] ibid. 89; Taslim Olawale Elias, *The Nature of African Customary Law* (Manchester, 1956), 165.

[98] Bentsi-Entchill, *Traditional Legal Systems*, 89; Elias, *African Customary Law*, 163.

[99] While, according to Elias, under traditional African land law the possessor can decide to what use his land should be put, the only uses seem to be cultivation and building a dwelling. Elias, *African Customary Law*, 166.

ultimate purpose of resources is that they shall be used. Thus Grotius argued that non-owners should have a 'right of innocent use', a right to use another's property provided they could do so without injuring the owner.[100] This conclusion followed from the functional or teleological approach which writers in the Aristotelian tradition took to rights of ownership. Private property exists to avoid the disadvantages that would arise if everything were owned in common: people would not work and they would quarrel over how things were to be divided.[101] But rights of ownership should extend no further than necessary to serve this purpose.[102]

The question, then, is whether the non-owner's possession of the property may hurt the owner. It might do so in several ways. It might endanger or depreciate the property. It might also prevent the owner from putting the property to a use of his own.

Paradoxically, even in these cases, there is good reason for recognizing a right in the possessor good against other non-owners. If even the possessor's use is not 'innocent' in the sense that it does not hurt the owner, it is likely to be the most 'innocent' use to which anyone may put the property. The property is likely to be better cared for if it is in the hands of a single possessor while the owner is absent. Moreover, on his return, the owner will have a single defendant to sue for any damage he has suffered.[103]

One would want to recognize a right in the possessor, then, for two different reasons although the consequences will be similar in practice. One reason is that the possessor's use may be the best use of the property. In a system of ownership, the owner has the right to decide its best use. But sometimes, he is not actively exercising that right. It is better for this right to be exercised by someone else than by no one at all. The other reason is that even if the possessor's use may harm the owner, it may cause less harm if the possessor's right is protected against non-possessors than if it is not protected at all.

In both cases, the law is not simply protecting the possessor against dispossession. It is protecting him so that he can benefit from his possession. Nevertheless, there is a difference. In the first case, the possessor obtains the benefit without hurting the owner. His possession is protected because it is better that someone should benefit than that no one should. In the second case, the possessor is hurting the owner. He is protected only because otherwise the harm to the owner would be greater. His possession is protected to give him an incentive to protect the property from others and so minimize the harm the owner may suffer.

Although, in both cases, the law should recognize a right to possess, the right should not be as extensive as ownership. An owner has typically paid for his property. Therefore, there is a reason for respecting his decision to warehouse it by leaving it idle. If that is not the best economic use, the owner is the one who will suffer. The possessor, however, is protected only so that the property will be used and cared for by someone. The reason for protecting him ceases as soon as he ceases to use and care for

---

[100] Hugo Grotius, *De iure belli ac pacis libri tres* (de Kanter-van Hetting Tromp ed., Leiden, 1939), II.ii.11.   [101] ibid. II.ii.2.4.

[102] ibid. II.ii.6.1.

[103] Also, if this defendant ousted the owner, and the owner is not allowed to recover against one who later acquires possession in good faith, the owner will be able to recover his property more easily if he finds this defendant still in possession since he will not have to prove bad faith.

it. Moreover, because the owner typically has paid for the property, it will usually be more unfair to deprive him of it than to deprive the possessor. The possessor will suffer a loss only to the extent he has invested labor or expense in improving the land. If he has made no investment, to deprive him of the property might be unfair in the sense that he is being treated arbitrarily, but it will not be unfair in the sense that he has suffered a loss.

We can see, then, why in many of the systems we have examined, the prior possessor cannot assert his rights after he has voluntarily departed. When he has ceased to use or care for the property, there is no reason to protect his rights.

4

The Extent of the Right to Use Property: Nuisance, *Troubles de Voisinage* and *Immissionenrecht*

Some doctrines prescribe to what extent an owner may use his own property without interfering with the use of others. They will be examined in this chapter.

In discussing ownership and possession, we saw that common law conceptions emerged in response to a civil law debate. By examining this debate and the response, we could better understand why both systems protect the possessor who lacks title.

The doctrines that govern how an owner or possessor may use property emerged quite differently. So far as I can tell, the Germans, French and common lawyers arrived independently at solutions to the problems which they call *Immissionen, troubles de voisinage* and nuisance. Indeed, they represent a rediscovery of the solution of one of the greatest medieval jurists, Bartolus of Saxoferrato. Despite their independent origin, they are quite similar. The similarity suggests that there are common underlying principles which explain why different jurisdictions have found these solutions appropriate. Yet Western jurists have been unsuccessful in identifying these principles. We will examine the doctrines themselves, and ask what principles can explain them.

I. Common Solutions

In continental Europe before the enactment of modern civil codes, limits on a person's use of his property were described in two short Roman texts. One text reported that the jurist Aristo 'does not think that smoke can lawfully be discharged from a cheese shop onto the buildings above it'. The text added: 'He also holds that it is not permissible to discharge water or any other substance from the upper onto the lower property, as a man is only permitted to carry out operations on his own premises to this extent, that he discharge nothing onto those of another'.[1] The other text implied that one could nevertheless 'create a moderate amount of smoke on his own premises, for example, smoke from a hearth'.[2] So the question arose, what principled distinction might there be between the smoke of the cheese shop and that of the hearth?

---

[1] Dig. 8.5.8.5 (Ulpian).   [2] Dig. 8.5.8.6 (Ulpian).

Accursius, author of the influential *Ordinary Gloss* to the *Corpus iuris civilis*, despaired of finding an answer. Unlike water, he said, 'smoke naturally disperses'. He could not distinguish the smoke of the cheese shop from that of the hearth. He concluded that the text about the cheese shop could not mean what it said. Instead, 'the person with the upper premises is required to bear the smoke, and on that account not to have windows'.[3] His critic, the ultramontane jurist Iacobus de Ravanis, pointed out that the text in question 'says the complete opposite of what the *Gloss* says'.[4]

Distinguishing the cheese shop from the hearth proved to be difficult. According to Odofredus, the owner of the cheese shop was liable because one cannot use one's land in a way that annoys others: *unusquisque debet facere in suo quod non officiat alieno*.[5] Restated in a different form by Blackstone (*sic utere tuo ut neminem laedas*),[6] this maxim was repeated endlessly by common law judges. But the maxim does not explain why one is free to operate a hearth even if it does annoy others. Modern common lawyers have said the maxim is useless because it does not explain which annoyances are permissible.[7]

Iacobus de Ravanis proposed a different distinction: one cannot discharge anything onto another's property that disturbs the owner.[8] That solution was suggested by Aristo's remark that one must 'discharge nothing onto [the premises] of another'. This solution was repeated by the great medieval jurist Baldus degli Ubaldi,[9] and was popular among the Dutch and German jurists of the 17th and 18th centuries.[10] But, again, it does not explain the hearth, which discharged smoke onto another's property.

Bartolus of Saxoferrato, perhaps the greatest of the medieval jurists, found a way out of these difficulties:

I think the following is to be said: Sometimes the owner of the lower premises makes fire in the usual way for the ordering of his family, and then he may do it lawfully, and he is not liable if the smoke ascends unless he acts with an intention to injure. In the same way, if the owner of the upper premises lets water flow in some way that is normal, for his water clock, he is not liable if some descends unless he acts with an intention to injure. But if the owner of the lower premises wants to make a shop or inn where he is continually making a fire and a great deal of smoke, he is not allowed to do so, as in this text. In the same way, if the owner of the upper premises lets water flow beyond what is normal, he is not allowed to do so, as this text says.[11]

---

[3] Accursius, *Glossa ordinaria* (Venice, 1615), to Dig. 8.5.8.5 to *ad iure*.

[4] Albericus de Rosate Bergamensis, *In primam ff. veter. part. commentaria* (Venice, 1585) (photographic reproduction, *Opera iuridica rariora*, vol. 21, 1974), to Dig. 8.5.8.5, no. 5 (describing the opinion of Iacobus de Ravanis).

[5] Odofredus, *Lectura super digesto veteri* (Lyon, 1550) (photographic reproduction, *Opera iuridica rariora*, vol. 2), to Dig. 8.5.8.5.

[6] William Blackstone, *Commentaries on the Laws of England* 2 (Chicago, 1979), *306.

[7] W. V. H. Rogers, *Winfield and Jolowicz on Tort* (14th edn., London, 1994), 404.

[8] Albericus de Rosate, *Commentaria* to Dig. 8.5.8.5 no. 5 (giving the opinion of Iacobus de Ravanis).

[9] Baldus degli Ubaldi, *Commentaria Corpus iuris civilis* (Venice, 1577), to Dig. 8.5.8.5.

[10] e.g. Johann Brunnemann, *Commentarius in quinquaginta libros Pandectarum* (Genoa, 1762) ('in suo enim cuique facere licet, quatenus nihil in alienum immittit'); Dionysius Gothofredus, *Corpus iuris civilis… cum notis integris Dionysii Gothofredi, Antonii Anselmo, Simonis von Leuwen* (Antwerp, 1726) to Dig. 8.5.8.5 n. 37 ('immittere… vel… projicere non licet'); Johannes Voet, *Commentarius ad Pandectas* (The Hague, 1726), lib. VIII, tit. 5, § 5 ('cuius ire liceat in suo facere ea, quibus vicino nocet, si prosit sibi; observandum tamen, cuique in suo hactenus facere licere, quatenus nihil in alienum immittit').

[11] Bartolus de Saxoferrato, *Commentaria Corpus iuris civilis* (Venice, 1615), to Dig. 8.5.8.5.

For Bartolus, then, two things mattered: the extent of the interference, and whether the interfering use of the land was ordinary.

For a long time, most jurists ignored this solution although, intermittently, elements of it resurfaced. In 1658, Caspar Manzius said that what mattered was whether the smoke was 'great and abnormal'.[12] Jean Domat said that 'the character of the locality' mattered, meaning, presumably, what was normal in a locality.[13] Robert Pothier said that it mattered whether the smoke 'is too thick or too much of an interference'.[14]

Since the 19th century, however, most Western legal systems have adopted a solution like that of Bartolus. Assuming the defendant was not making a disturbance simply to irritate the plaintiff, and that the defendant could not avoid the interference by some reasonable measures, then whether the defendant is liable depends on the degree of interference and whether the interfering use of land is normal.

This solution was rediscovered, independently so far as I can tell, in Germany, France and common law jurisdictions. In Germany, it was rediscovered by Rudolf von Ihering. He pointed out that property rights would be worthless if a property owner either could disturb his neighbor at will or could not disturb him at all. An owner who could disturb his neighbors at will could make their land valueless by some pestilential use of his own. An owner who could not disturb them at all could not cook or use heat if they objected to the odors or smoke. Ihering concluded that an owner's rights must depend on the degree of interference and the normal use of land.[15] By and large, the 19th century Pankdektists agreed.[16] A solution that depended on these factors was adopted by the German Civil Code[17] and eventually borrowed by the Swiss[18] and the Italians.[19]

Even though similar factors had been mentioned by Domat and Pothier, the French Civil Code contained no general provision about disturbances among neighbors. French courts give relief, however, when a disturbance exceeds that which is 'normal' among neighboring properties. What is normal is judged by the character of the locality.[20]

---

[12] Casparus Manzius, *Tractatus de servitutibus personalibus* (Ingolstadt, 1658), tit. 2, quest. 56, no. 272 ('fumum tamen gravem et insolitum non nisi servitutis in superiora aedificis immittere licet').

[13] Jean Domat, *Les Loix civiles dans leur ordre naturel* (2nd edn., Paris, 1713), liv. 1, tit. 12, § 4, 9–10.

[14] Robert Pothier, *Traité du contrat de société*, App. 2, *Du voisinage*, § 241, in *Oeuvres de Pothier annotées et mises en correlation avec le Code civil et législation actuel* (Bugnet, ed., 2nd edn., Paris, 1861).

[15] Rudolph von Ihering, 'Zur Lehre von den Beschränkungen des Grundeigenthümers im Interesse der Nachbarn', *Jahrbücher für die Dogmatik des heutigen römischen und deutschen Privatrechts* 6 (1863), 81 at 94–6.

[16] e.g. Karl Vangerow, *Leitfaden für Pandekten-Vorlesungen* (Marburg, 1847), § 297, Anm. II; Bernhard Windscheid, *Lehrbuch des Pandektenrechts* 1 (7th edn., Frankfurt am Main, 1891), § 169.

[17] German Civil Code (*Bürgerlichesgesetzbuch*), § 906.

[18] Swiss Civil Code (*Zivilgesetzbuch*), § 684.   [19] Italian Civil Code (*Codice civile*), § 844.

[20] Gérard Cornu, *Droit civil Introduction Les Personnes Les Biens* (4th edn., Paris, 1990), § 1096; Murid Ferid and Hans Jürgen Sonnenberger, *Das Französische Zivilrecht* 2 (2nd edn., Heidelberg, 1986), § 3 C 191; Boris Starck, Henri Roland, and Laurent Boyer, *Droit civil Obligations Responsabilité délictuelle* (2nd edn., Paris, 1985), § 310; Alex Weill, François Terré, and Philippe Simler, *Droit civil Les Biens* (3rd edn., Paris, 1985), § 309.

In common law jurisdictions such as England and the United States, an interference with a neighbor is actionable when it is 'unreasonable'.[21] Everyone agrees, however, that an interference may be 'unreasonable' even if an owner was not careless, and so his conduct was not 'unreasonable' as the term is understood in the law of negligence.[22] Although English and American jurists list several considerations which determine the 'reasonableness' of an interference, the ones that matter in cases such as the cheese shop and the hearth are the extent of the interference and whether land is used in the way normal in a given locality.[23]

II. Difficulties Explaining the Solution

A. Difficulties in the 19th Century

Although Western legal systems have adopted much the same solution, there has never been a consensus as to why this solution is appropriate. Since it was widely adopted in the 19th century, one might expect that it fit well with 19th century ideas of tort and property. It did not. Nineteenth century jurists were comfortable with tort liability based on fault and much less so with liability absent fault.[24] Yet they acknowledged that a landowner could be liable absent fault for disturbing a neighbor. Moreover, their ideas about property seemed actually to contradict their solution to the problem of interferences among neighbors.

Typically, 19th century jurists subscribed to will theories of property. By definition, property meant that an object was completely subject to the will of its owner.

---

[21] e.g. England: Margaret Brazier, *The Law of Torts* (8th edn., London, 1988), 321; Simon Deakin, Angus Johnson, and Basil Markesinis, *Tort Law* (5th edn., Oxford, 2003), 455; United States: *Restatement (Second) of Torts*, §§ 822, 826 (1979); W. Page Keeton, Dan B. Dobbs, Robert E. Keeton, and David G. Owen, *Prosser and Keeton on the Law of Torts* (5th edn., St Paul, Minn., 1984), 629.

[22] England: Brazier, *Torts*, 321; Deakin *et al.*, *Tort*, 455; United States: *Restatement (Second) of Torts*, § 826(b); Keeton *et al.*, *Torts*, 629.

[23] England: Brazier, *Torts*, 322–7 (extent of the harm and suitability of the locality; she also says that the impracticability of preventing the interference and the social value of the plaintiff's activity bear on reasonableness, but she clearly does not mean that the plaintiff loses if his activity is of purely personal value and it is impracticable to prevent the interference); Deakin *et al.*, *Tort*, 455–71 (duration of interference and character of neighborhood; they also mention fault, but say that a nuisance is actionable without fault; they mention the abnormal sensitivity of plaintiff's activity as bearing on reasonableness, which is discussed later in this chapter); Rogers, *Tort*, 407–8 (extent of the harm and nature of the locality); United States: *Restatement (Second) of Torts*, §§ 829, 831; Keeton *et al.*, *Torts*, 629 (amount of harm and nature of the locality; they also mention use of land, presumably meaning whether the use is abnormally sensitive, a topic to be discussed later in this chapter; they mention the possibility of spreading losses by insurance or by shifting a loss to the general public but they do not cite any cases which turned on this consideration).

[24] Germany: Georg Friedrich Puchta, *Vorlesungen über das heutige römische Recht* 2 (2nd edn., Leipzig, 1849), § 261; Windscheid, *Lehrbuch* 1, § 101; see Reinhard Zimmermann, *The Law of Obligations: Roman Foundations of the Civilian Tradition* (Cape Town, 1990), 1034–5; France: Charles Aubry and Charles Rau, *Cours de droit civil français* 4 (4th edn., Paris, 1869–71), § 446; Alexandre Duranton, *Cours de droit français suivant le Code civil* 13 (3rd edn., Paris, 1834), 741; Léobon Larombière, *Théorique et pratique des obligations* 5 (Paris, 1857), 738, 767; François Laurent, *Principes de droit civil français* 20 (Paris, 1869–78), §§ 387, 550, 589, 639; Common law: Sir Frederick Pollock, *The Law of Torts* (13th edn., London, 1929), 506–7; Oliver Wendell Holmes, Jr., *The Common Law* (1881), Boston, 77–129.

'Property', said Puchta 'is the total legal subjection of a thing'.[25] 'According to its basic concept,' said Arndts, 'property is the right belonging to a person of complete domination over a physical object'.[26] Consequently, though the German jurists accepted Ihering's solution to the problem of interferences among neighbors, it was hard for them to relate this solution to their concept of property. Neighbors' rights were limited and yet property rights were by their very nature unlimited. Typically, the German jurists described the Roman text about the cheese shop as 'a limitation of ownership by positive law (*gesetzliche Beschränkung des Eigenthums*).'[27] According to Windscheid, the limitation was a good one because 'reckless realization of the consequences of the concept of ownership is not possible without serious disadvantages'.[28] But it was still a limitation by positive law of the owner's rights, as though the law first conferred these rights and then immediately found it necessary to take some back.

The 19th century French jurists encountered the same difficulty. According to Aubry and Rau, 'property . . . expresses the Idea [*sic*] of the most complete legal power of a person over an object and can be defined as the right by virtue of which a thing is submitted in an absolute and exclusive manner to the will and the conduct of a person'.[29] Laurent explained that a proprietor could use his thing however he wishes until prohibited by law or until he injured the rights of others.[30] According to Demolombe, 'an absolute right property confers upon the master a sovereign power, a complete despotism over the thing'.[31]

Having defined property as a seemingly limitless right, they found it difficult to explain how the limitless rights of two adjoining landowners could be limited vis-à-vis each other. According to Aubry and Rau, the 'respective rights of [the] proprietors' of adjacent land were in a 'conflict [that] cannot be resolved except by means of certain limits imposed on the natural exercise of the powers inherent in property'.[32] Demolombe observed that if all proprietors could 'invoke their absolute right, it is clear that none would have one in reality'. What would be the result? 'It would be war! It would be anarchy!' Similarly, Laurent thought that '[a]ccording to the rigor of the law, each proprietor would be able to object if one of his neighbors released on his property smoke or exhalations of any kind, because he has a right to the purity of air for his person and his goods'.[33] If that were so, he admitted, the existence of towns would be impossible.[34]

Thus the French jurists, like the Germans, found themselves saying that property rights were by their nature so unlimited that, if owners were allowed to exercise their rights, property would become worthless. Such a conclusion exemplifies Ihering's complaints about the *Begriffsjurisprudenz* of the times. A concept like property was

---

[25] Georg Friedrich Puchta and Adolf Rudorff, *Cursus der Institutionen* 2 (3rd edn., Leipzig, 1851), § 231.

[26] Ludwig Arndts von Arnesberg, *Lehrbuch der Pandekten* (14th edn., Stuttgart, 1889), § 130.

[27] Puchta, *Cursus* 2, § 231; Karl von Vangerow, *Leitfaden für Pandekten-Vorlesungen* (Marburg, 1847), § 297, Anm. II; Windscheid, *Lehrbuch* 1, § 169.   [28] Windscheid, *Lehrbuch* 1, § 169.

[29] Aubry and Rau, *Cours* 2, § 190.   [30] Laurent, *Principes* 6, § 101.

[31] Charles Demolombe, *Cours de Code Napoléon* 9 (Paris, 1854–82), § 543.

[32] Aubry and Rau, *Cours* 2, § 194.   [33] Laurent, *Principes* 6, § 144.

[34] ibid. In a later volume of his work, Laurent finally decided that '[t]he Code was wrong to say that the owner has the right to enjoy and to dispose of his thing in the *most absolute manner* . . .'. Laurent, *Principes* 20, § 417. Nevertheless, he did not suggest any other way that property could be defined.

not defined according to the purposes of recognizing property rights. It was defined in a way that thwarted these purposes. In any event, the 19th century jurists failed to develop a concept of property that could elucidate the solution they had adopted to the problem of interferences among landowners.

B. Difficulties since the 19th Century

In the 20th century, jurists became skeptical of *Begriffsjurisprudenz*. Although German jurists occasionally describe their law of *Immissionen* as a limitation on ownership, they seem to have in mind, not an abstractly defined concept of property, but the rights conferred on a proprietor by article 903 of the German Civil Code.[35] Since the early 20th century, jurists have preferred to discuss problems in terms of underlying interests or overarching policies. Unfortunately, these discussions have not shed much light on why an owner's right to interfere with his neighbors should depend on whether the interference is large and abnormal.

Some jurists have pointed out that if neighbors could use their property any way they wish, one use would interfere with the other, and both properties could become valueless.[36] That, of course, is the argument Ihering made in the 19th century. But it is a purely negative argument that shows why the rights of owners cannot be absolute. It does not explain why their rights should be limited in one way rather than another.

Some jurists have said that the appropriate solution is one that balances the interests of neighboring landowners.[37] That statement is true but unilluminating if it merely means that neither landowner can use his property however he wants. It is not true if it means that courts actually balance the importance of each owner's interest in using his land in a particular way and allow the most important interest to prevail. When an interference is great and abnormal, the aggrieved landowner generally has a remedy regardless of the importance of the interests at stake.

It is true that the remedy the aggrieved party receives may depend on the importance of his interest. In Germany, France and most American states, the defendant will not be forced to stop interfering if his activity is of considerably greater value than the harm done by the interference, and he has picked an appropriate place to carry it on.[38] Nevertheless, the plaintiff can recover damages. Italian commentators claim that their rule is similar[39] despite the language of the Italian Civil Code, which says that an

---

[35] e.g. Peter Bassenge in Otto Palandt, *Bürgerliches Gesetzbuch* (62nd edn., Munich, 2003), to § 906 no. 1.

[36] e.g. Germany: Herbert Roth in *J. von Staudingers Kommentar zum Bürgerlichen Gesetzbuch* (Neubearbeitung, Berlin, 2002), to § 906, no. 1; Italy: Andrea Tabet, Enzo Ottolenghi and Gabriella Scaliti, *La proprietà* (Turin, 1981), § 111.

[37] Germany: Roth, *Staudingers Kommentar*, to § 906, no. 1; Franz Jürgen Säcker in *Münchener Kommentar zum Bürgerlichen Gesetzbuch* (2nd edn., Munich, 1986), to 906, no. 1; Italy: Tabet *et al.*, *Proprietà*, § 132; England: K. Stanton, *The Modern Law of Tort* (London, 1994), 390; Australia: Rosalie P. Bolkin and J. L. R. Davis, *The Law of Torts* (Sydney, Aust., 1991), 187.

[38] Germany: German Civil Code (*Bürgerlichesgesetzbuch*) 906(2); France: Cornu, *Biens*; Starck *et al.*, *Obligations*, § 332; Geneviève Viney and Patrice Jourdain, *Traité de droit civil: Les obligations: Les effets de la responsabilité* (2nd edn., Paris, 2001), § 53; United States: *Boomer v. Atlantic Cement Co.*, 257 NE2d 870 (NY, 1970); Keeton *et al.*, *Torts*, 630–2, 637–41; also in Australia: Bolkin and Davis, *Torts*, 189.

[39] Antonio Gambaro, *La proprietà Beni, proprietà, comunione* (Milan, 1990), 385; Ugo Mattei, *La proprietà immobiliare* (Turin, 1993), 160–1; Tabet *et al.*, *Proprietà*, § 139.

emission exceeding normal levels of tolerability may still be justified by 'the needs of production'.[40] A stricter rule is followed in England where it has been claimed that merely to award damages would amount to private expropriation.[41] One suspects that the result, paradoxically, is that courts sometimes refuse to declare a valuable activity to be a nuisance to avoid shutting it down, thus leaving the plaintiff with no remedy. If so, however, the practice is a side effect of the belief that one who conducts a valuable activity should not escape by merely paying damages. No legal system, in principle, allows the defendant to escape liability because his activity is more valuable.

Some French jurists have said that to interfere with one's neighbors is an abuse of right (*abus de droit*).[42] In French law, however, abuse of right means that the abuser acted reprehensibly. He was negligent, or he acted solely to annoy his neighbor, or he used his right to property in a manner inconsistent with its social ends.[43] But as French jurists themselves have noted, the person who interferes with his neighbors often has done nothing reprehensible.[44] Indeed, French courts may award compensation but refuse to order him to stop.[45]

As one might expect, some American jurists have tried to base a solution on economic principles. Until 1960, it was widely believed that the reason a property owner must pay for interfering with his neighbor was that otherwise his own level of production would be inefficiently high. He would be using up the resources of his neighbors without paying for them. Therefore, he would overproduce just as a car company would if it did not have to pay the cost of the steel it used up.

It was never clear how to get from this general concern with overproduction to the specifics of the law of nuisance. But in any event, economic analysis of the problem changed drastically in 1960 when Ronald Coase published his famous article, 'The Problem of Social Cost'.[46] Coase argued that when there are conflicting activities, one cannot say which of them is imposing a cost on the other. A cement plant will impose a cost on nearby farmers if the farmers have no remedy, but if they can obtain compensation for the harm, they will be imposing a cost on the cement plant. Coase then showed that if the farmers and the cement company could costlessly negotiate, the use of resources will be efficient whether or not the law holds the company liable for harm to the farmers. Whether it is liable or not, the company will take any measure that prevents harm (such as installing anti-smoke devices, cutting production or even closing the plant) if and only if the cost of the measure is less than the harm that the measure would prevent. If the company is held liable for harm to the farmers, it will take only those measures that cost less than the harm for which it will otherwise have to pay. If the company is not liable, however, and the farmers can costlessly negotiate, they will pay the company to take any measures that cost less than the harm that they

[40] Italian Civil Code (*Codice civile*), § 844(2).

[41] *Elliott* v. *Islington London Borough* [1991] 10 EG 145; *Munro* v. *Southern Dairies* [1955] VLR 332; *Miller* v. *Jackson* [1977] QB 966; Deakin *et al.*, *Tort*, 486 (with some critical remarks).

[42] Their opinions are described by Starck *et al.*, *Obligations*, §§ 315–25; Weill, *Biens*, § 313.

[43] Starck *et al.*, *Obligations*, §§ 315–25.

[44] Philippe Malaurie and Laurent Aynès, *Cours de droit civil: Les Obligations* (9th edn., Paris, 1998), § 57; Starck *et al.*, *Obligations*, §§ 315–25; Weill, *Biens*, § 313.

[45] Cour d'appel, Toulouse, 17 Mar. 1970, JCP 1970.II.16534.

[46] *J. of L. and Econ.* 3 (1960), 1.

will otherwise suffer. Coase concluded that the same amount of cement and agricultural products would be produced and the same preventative measures taken regardless of whether the cement company is liable.

Of course, whether the law holds the company liable does change the financial well-being of the parties. If the farmers have no remedy, they will be poorer and the cement company will be richer than if the situation were reversed. For an economist, however, a difference in the way wealth is distributed is neither efficient nor inefficient. Efficiency means, to an economist, that resources are used as well as may be given a particular distribution of wealth.

Coase's conclusion was disconcerting to many Americans. Scholars such as Guido Calabresi have shown how one can still argue that it is efficient to hold the cement company liable.[47] They have pointed out that in the real world, neighboring landowners usually cannot negotiate costlessly. Often, there will be one cement company but many farmers. The farmers will find it hard to speak with one voice. Some will refuse to pay their share of any money to be paid to the cement company, hoping for a free ride, and that circumstance will reduce the amount that the farmers as a group are willing to pay. Moreover, the cement plant may know better which measures can prevent harm, how much harm they will prevent, and their cost. Therefore, to optimize production, the law should place liability on the cement company. It will then take all economically appropriate measures to reduce harm without the need for negotiations. Of course, sometimes it will have to pay for harm it could not have prevented but if so, as Coase has shown, the result will still be efficient.

This argument proves that sometimes, despite Coase, holding the cement company liable is efficient. But the argument is not a good explanation of existing law. It does not explain why, in the legal systems we have examined, a court will give a remedy even if it is convinced that no economically feasible measure can prevent the harm. If no measure is feasible, it does not matter that the farmers cannot negotiate costlessly. There is nothing for them to negotiate about. Nor is there any point in holding the company liable to give it an incentive to take measures to prevent harm since there are no measures to take.

As we have seen, in modern legal systems, whenever a court awards damages instead of ordering some preventive measure to be taken, it must first determine that no feasible measure would prevent the harm. In virtually every case, then, if the court's own determination is correct, awarding damages is economically pointless. An economist might say that a court might entertain doubts about the correctness of its own determination and award damages to give the defendant an incentive to take any feasible measures there may be. That seems thin. In any event, courts award damages even when they are convinced there are no economically feasible measures to be taken.

Moreover, the economic answer to Coase does not explain the intuitions most people have about why the cement company should pay, intuitions that are shared by law makers and judges, and consequently have shaped existing law. Most people are

---

[47] Calabresi's arguments were addressed to the analogous problem of strict liability for accidents. See G. Calabresi, *The Cost of Accidents* (1970), 135–403; Guido Calabresi, 'Transactions Costs, Resource Allocation and Liability Rules, A Comment', *J. of L. and Econ.* 11 (1968), 67 at 71–3.

not worried about optimizing investments in agriculture and cement production. They feel that if the cement company does not pay, an injustice will be done to the farmers. It is hard to think that scholars such as Calabresi would really want the cement plant to escape liability even if that result were efficient. Thus the question remains, why, as a matter of justice, the farmers should be compensated.

III. An Explanation Based on Commutative Justice

A. Commutative Justice

As described earlier, Aristotle distinguished distributive justice, which gives every citizen a fair share of resources, from commutative justice, which preserves the share that belongs to each. Commutative justice requires that neither party gain at the other's expense.[48]

So far as I know, the jurists who wrote in the Aristotelian tradition never applied this principle to the Roman text about the cheese shop. The reason may be that when they thought of commutative justice in involuntary transactions, they had in mind two types of cases: those in which one party gained by taking or using something that belonged to the other party, and those in which one party culpably harmed the other party or his property. Aristotle had mentioned both of these cases.[49] As we will see, writers in the Aristotelian tradition used them as the basis for their doctrines of unjust enrichment and tort.

The case of the cheese shop did not fit easily into this schema and that may be why the natural lawyers neglected it. The owner of the cheese shop had not used his neighbor's property but rather interfered with his neighbor's use of it. But he was not at fault. He had not built his fire in order to bother his neighbor, and he need not have built it negligently.

Still, in my view, the principle of commutative justice can explain why a landowner should be liable for interferences that are abnormal and grave. The principle is that no one should gain through another's loss. The application of the principle is easiest to see if we begin with the simpler cases and work our way to those that are more complex.

Imagine a community in which everyone is doing the same thing: for example, a rural community in which everyone raises animals. Imagine that each person raises the same number of animals. The smell of each person's animals bothers his neighbors, and in this sense, imposes a cost on them. Nevertheless, while each person is deriving a benefit for himself by imposing a cost on others, no person is a net gainer or a net loser. No one has gained overall at anyone's expense.

Suppose next that one of the farmers acquires a taste for American rock music and likes to play it loudly. His neighbors hate the music and protest. This farmer is now deriving what he regards as an advantage—an advantage his neighbors do not share—by interfering with them in a way that they do not interfere with him. In this sense, he

---

[48] Aristotle, *Nicomachean Ethics* V.ii.
[49] Aristotle, *Nichomachean Ethics* V.ii. 1130^b–1131^a; V.iv. 1131^b–1132^b.

has gained at their expense. As a matter of commutative justice, he should not be allowed to do so.

This example may seem artificially easy because the offending farmer's activity did not benefit any of his neighbors in any way. Moreover, it was an activity of dubious value. But even in the case of a valuable activity that benefits everyone, some people will gain at the expense of others provided that the benefit that each receives is not perfectly correlated with the harm that each suffers. Suppose a railroad spur is built into the rural locality with a station and large livestock pens, and the noise of the trains and livestock awaiting shipment bothers the farmers who live near the tracks. The railroad gains, as do all the farmers, but the gain is secured at a disproportionate expense to the farmers who are bothered. In this sense, some people gain at the expense of others. As a matter of commutative justice, the railroad should pay compensation. It will then adjust its fares to recover the amount it has paid. In the end, all the farmers will pay for the disturbance in proportion to the use they make of the railroad.

Suppose next that a merchant moves into the community and opens a store to sell goods to the farmers who previously had driven to a nearby town to shop. The merchant is bothered by the smell, and he does not own any animals himself. As in the previous cases, then, other people interfere with him in a way in which he does not interfere with others. Nevertheless, one cannot say that the farmers gain at his expense. He has come into the rural locality to gain an advantage he could not obtain in a locality with a different character. By locating near the farmers he can sell goods to them. He incurs the disadvantages of proximity in order to secure its advantages.

The principle that one should not gain at another's expense thus leads to the rule that modern legal systems typically apply: a person is liable for interferences with his neighbors that are grave and abnormal. Indeed, this explanation of the rule resembles one suggested by the French jurist Louis Josserand: that the person who profits from an activity should pay for the harm it does.[50] Modern French jurists have rejected his view on the ground that it does not explain why one pays only for abnormally large interferences.[51] But the answer to that objection, as we have seen, is that small normal interferences cancel each other out so that no one is a net gainer or loser.

The principle that no one should gain at another's expense also explains why, in exceptional cases, a person should not be held liable even though the disturbance is abnormal and grave. In one such instance, the aggrieved party is disturbed only because his own activity is abnormally sensitive. The disturbance is due as much to the

---

[50] Louis Josserand, *De l'esprit des droits et de leur relativité: Théorie dite de l'abus des droits* (Paris, 1927), 18–19. The explanation defended here also resembles what Professor Richard Epstein describes as a reason for relaxing the true principle, which, in his view, is that any physical invasion of another's land should be actionable. Where the interference is not abnormally grave, he says, the law tolerates it because all the parties mutually benefit from this rearrangement of their rights, the transactions costs of a voluntary rearrangement of rights by the parties themselves are high, and the 'presence of implicit in kind compensation from all to all . . . precludes any systematic redistribution of wealth'. Richard A. Epstein, 'Nuisance Law: Corrective Justice and its Utilitarian Constraints', *J. Leg. Stud.* 8 (1979), 49 at 78–9. Epstein does not explain very clearly why each person should have, in principle, a right against any physical invasion, a right which, as we have seen, would render everyone's land valueless. Epstein himself admits, moreover, that on his view, it is hard to explain why the extrasensitive plaintiff does not recover (ibid. 92).

[51] Starck *et al.*, *Obligations*, § 328; Weill, *Biens*, § 314.

fact that he, for his own advantage, has chosen to carry on such an activity as to the fact that the other party, for his advantage, carries on an activity that interferes with it. One can no longer say that one party is gaining at the other's expense. The aggrieved party should not recover.

In modern law, typically, he does not recover. In common law jurisdictions, it is a defense that the plaintiff was only disturbed because his own activity was abnormally sensitive.[52] For example, a plaintiff who was using special paper which required cool moist air did not recover against his downstairs neighbor, who, because of his own business requirements, had made the air warm and dry.[53] The owner of a drive-in theater did not recover when the lights of a toll road service center interfered with his films.[54] Under German law, an owner cannot recover damages under article 906(2) of the Civil Code unless his own activity is normal for the locality. Some French commentators favor a similar result, although the case law is not clear.[55]

In another exceptional type of case, the defendant's activity was not abnormally offensive in the locality at one time but it later became so. Suppose, for example, that people build houses in a rural locality until the normal use of land is residential, and the residents are bothered by the smell of the animals raised by the last remaining farmer. It is possible, of course, that the farmer will not suffer a loss even if he is forced to relocate at his own expense. It may be that he could sell his land profitably for housing sites and has not done so in the hope that the residents will pay him an additional amount simply to get rid of the smells. In that case, he would be trying to make a further profit at their expense. Nevertheless, it is also possible that the farmer will lose money if he has to sell and relocate. In that case, if he is not compensated, the transformation of the locality from rural to residential, which has benefitted the homeowners, will have taken place at his expense. It may be that the farmer should move elsewhere. But by the principle we have been defending, he should be compensated.

In cases of this type, however, modern legal systems typically do not compensate the defendant even though the plaintiff moved into the area knowing of his activity. In France, the defendant usually loses.[56] Some French jurists think he should win.[57]

---

[52] England: Deakin *et al.*, *Tort*, 466–7; Stanton, *Tort*, 391; Brazier, *Torts*, 318; United States: Keeton *et al.*, *Torts*, 628–9.

[53] *Robinson* v. *Kilvert* [1889] 41 Ch D 88. Courts have differed, however, on what is an ultrasensitive activity. Compare *Bridlington Relay Ltd.* v. *Yorkshire Electricity Board* [1965] Ch 436, [1965] 1 All ER 26 (plaintiff cannot recover when defendant's power line interferes with the television relay service it provides to its customers) with *Nor-Video Services Ltd.* v. *Ontario Hydro* (1978) 84 DLR (3rd) (Ont.) (plaintiff recovers interference with television transmission because watching television is ordinary use of premises) and *Page County Appliance Center* v. *Honeywell*, 347 NW2d 171 (Iowa 1984) (plaintiff recovers for interference with television sets on display in his store because television is ubiquitous).

[54] *Belmar Drive-In Theater* v. *Illinois State Toll Highway Comm.*, 216 NE2d 788 (Ill. 1966).

[55] Cornu, *Biens*, § 1109; Weill, *Biens*, § 317; compare Cour d'appel, Nancy, 12 Apr. 1923, Gaz. Pal. 1923.1.743 (owner of clinic can complain of factory) with Trib. gr. inst., Riom, 17 March 1965, D. 1965. 547 (activity must bother a normal person, not one who is sick and hypersensitive).

[56] Weill, *Biens*, § 317; Cornu, *Biens*, § 1108. Compare Cass., 1e ch. civ., 20 Feb. 1968, D. 1968.350 (priority does not matter when house built near factory); Cass., 2e ch. civ., 22 Oct. 1964, D. 1965.344 (same); Cass., 2e ch. civ., 29 June 1977, D. 1978. Inf. rap. 35 (priority does not matter when house build near sawmill) with Cass. 3e ch. civ., 14 Nov. 1985, J.C.P. 1986.IV.42 (hotel/bar cannot complain of noise and odors from nearby restaurant because it knew of them when it moved in).

[57] Alain Sériaux, *Droit des obligations* (Paris, 1992), § 122.

They point to a French statute which says that those who build in an area cannot complain about interferences that existed before the building permit was issued.[58] In Germany, the defendant loses.[59] He loses in England[60] even though Blackstone said he should win.[61] He usually loses in the United States[62] despite the complaints of some authors that the opposite result would promote efficient land use development.[63] He usually loses in Italy,[64] despite the language of the Italian Civil Code which says that the courts should take account of priority.[65]

The best explanation of why he loses is that, although in principle he should be compensated, in practice, there are two serious obstacles to doing so. First, there is the difficulty of determining whether the defendant will actually suffer a loss if he sells his land and moves. The fact that the other farmers have already moved out without the threat of legal action suggests that they did profit. Of course, the remaining farmer may have made investments in his land that the others did not. But a court might suspect that he has stayed on merely in hope of exacting money from his neighbors in addition to a profit he will make on a sale.

Second, if the defendant prevailed, it would not be easy to devise an appropriate remedy. If a court allows him to stay, he will be able to exact from the homeowners an amount that reflects, not the loss he suffers if he moves, but the aggravation he causes if he stays. He would then profit at their expense. But if the court orders the farmer to move and the homeowners to pay the expenses of relocating him, the question arises which of the neighbors are to pay. Moving the farmer benefits all of them but only some neighbors may be plaintiffs in the lawsuit. If the plaintiffs pay, then the other neighbors will be gaining at their expense. Moreover, if everyone knows in advance that only the plaintiffs will pay, few neighbors will choose to be plaintiffs, and the result will be still more unfair. Nevertheless, a court would find it difficult to make every neighbor pay his share. There is usually no procedural mechanism to force a neighbor who is not a party to the lawsuit to pay. Even if there were, it would be hard for a court to determine how much each should pay since it will never be clear how much the presence of the farmer bothered any particular neighbor.

In the unique circumstances of one famous American case, *Spur Industries, Inc. v. Del E. Webb Development Co.*,[66] neither of these obstacles was present, and the court awarded a farmer his costs of relocating. An American real estate developer had acquired a huge tract of previously rural land, and built a small city with thousands of houses as well as parks, golf courses, swimming pools and recreation centers. He sold the houses to older people who had retired from their jobs. The defendant, who raised animals, was sued by residents who were bothered by the smell. The court ordered

---

[58] French Code of Building and Dwellings (*Code de construction et habitation*) L. 122–16.

[59] Roth, *Staudingers Kommentar*, to § 906 no. 220.

[60] Deakin *et al.*, *Tort*, 482; Rogers, *Tort*, 429–30; Stanton, *Tort*, 405.

[61] Blackstone, *Commentaries*, *403.

[62] Keeton *et al.*, *Torts*, 635–6. Cases that seem to hold that coming to a nuisance is a defence often involve factual situations that are distinguishable: e.g. *Bove* v. *Donner-Hanna Coke Corp.*, 258 NYS 229 (NY 1932) (entire locality was industrialized when plaintiff moved in).

[63] William Baxter and Lillian Altree, 'Legal Aspects of Airport Noise', *J. of L. and Econ.* 15 (1972), 1.

[64] Mattei, *Proprietà*, 164; Tabet *et al.*, *Proprietà*, § 15.

[65] Italian Civil Code (*Codice civile*), § 844(2).   [66] 494 P2d 700 (Ariz. 1972).

the farmer to move but required the developer to pay his expenses. Under the circumstances, there was little reason to suspect that the farmer could profit by selling his land for housing. Housing in the area was attractive primarily because those who bought from the developer—and only those who bought from him—could use the golf courses, swimming pools, and recreation centers. Moreover, since the court could hold the developer liable, it could avoid the unfairness of requiring only those neighbors who were plaintiffs to pay. The case suggests that the reason the defendant usually is not compensated is because of the practical difficulties that are usually present.

There are other instances in which the principle we are defending, however correct, must give way because of practical difficulties. Many of them are cases in which the defendant's activity is normal in kind for an area but interferes with others to an abnormal degree.

In some cases of this type the defendant should not be held liable even though his activity interferes with others more than they interfere with him. Suppose that in the rural community we have imagined, everyone had raised the same number of animals. Then a newcomer bought the land of ten prior residents who moved away. He now raises ten times as many animals as everyone else, making ten times the gain that they do and causing ten times as much smell. It is still not the case that he is gaining overall at the expense of his neighbors. His presence in the community causes them no additional disturbance. He is richer than they are, but his activity is no more a source of harm to them than if they had ten poorer neighbors instead of a single rich one.

Sometimes, however, the defendant's activity will cause an additional disturbance. For example, while everyone raises animals, he might have a feedlot which concentrates more animals in a smaller area. In such a case, he is obtaining a gain for himself in which his neighbors do not share by causing the additional disturbance. In principle, he should compensate them. French and Italian authorities are correct, then, when they say that the plaintiff should recover when an interference is normal in kind but abnormal in degree.[67]

In practice, however, courts cannot be as sensitive to differences in the degree of the interference as they can to differences in kind. It will necessarily be harder to prove that an interference is abnormally grave.

This problem of proof explains why many courts are reluctant to give relief against so-called 'negative interferences' such as a building that blocks a neighbor's light, air, view, chimney, or television reception. In principle, it should not matter that the interference is 'negative'. A person who builds an apartment building in a neighborhood of single family homes obtains a benefit for himself by interfering with his neighbors more than they interfere with him. Typically, however, the interferences differ in degree but not in kind since every building blocks the neighbors' light, air or view to some extent. Consequently, it is difficult to determine what degree of interference calls for a remedy.

This difficulty explains why, although some legal systems allow a plaintiff to recover for 'negative interferences' in extreme cases, no system treats them the same way as

---

[67] France: Cass. 2e ch. civ., 3 Jan. 1969, J.C.P. 69.II.15920 (liability for 'usage, même normale' if the 'troubles dépassent les inconvenients normaux'); Cornu, *Biens*, § 1096; Starck *et al.*, *Obligations*, § 310; Italy: Tabet *et al.*, *Proprietà*, § 112.

physical interferences. Plaintiffs bothered by the height of buildings have occasionally recovered in France.[68] Swiss law has recently allowed plaintiffs to recover for 'negative interferences'.[69] Most German authorities say they cannot[70] but some say a plaintiff might win in an extreme case.[71] In common law jurisdictions, there is usually no action for obstructing light and view.[72] Yet one American court found for a plaintiff whose solar energy cells had been blocked.[73]

The same difficulty arises in the case of indecent or aesthetically objectionable activities. Such activities can be offensive to most people. Those who carry them on are therefore benefitting (in their own view) at their neighbors' expense. In principle, they should be liable. But indecency and ugliness are matters of degree. It is hard to say at what point an interference warrants a remedy. Moreover, with indecency and ugliness, it is hard to be sure the plaintiff is really objecting because the activity is carried on nearby rather than merely because it is carried on at all.

These difficulties explain why courts are reluctant to give a remedy against such activities. They do so sometimes in common law jurisdictions[74] and in Switzerland.[75] But the courts have been cautious. They have enjoined brothels,[76] sex shops,[77] and, occasionally, undertaking establishments[78] but not unsightly piles of junk.[79] In Italy and Germany, most commentators say that such activities cannot be stopped;[80] indeed, the courts have refused a remedy even against neighboring brothels.[81] Nevertheless, the Italian *Corte di cassazione* said that it would grant a remedy if the brothel was run indiscreetly so that the neighbors had to witness indecent activities.[82] The German *Bundesgerichtshof* noted that the activities of the brothel were not visible and had not reduced value of plaintiff's property.[83] Some commentators think the result would be different if they had.[84] Moreover, while the *Bundesgerichtshof* refused a

---

[68] Cass., 2e ch. civ., 3 Dec. 1964, D.S. 1965.J.321 (height of 11-story building makes the chimney of a three story building useless); Ferid and Sonnenberger, *Französische Zivilrecht*, § 3 C 192.

[69] Bernhard Peter Tuor, Jörg Schmidt, and Alexandra Rumo-Jungo, *Das Schweizerische Zivilgesetzbuch* (12th edn., Zürich, 2002), 888.

[70] BGH, 21 Oct. 1983, BGHZ 88, 344 (height of building interferes with television reception); Bassenge, *Palandt*, to § 906, no. 4; Säcker, *Münchener Kommentar*, § 906, no. 20; Roth, *Staudingers Kommentar*, to § 906, no. 122.   [71] Jan Wilhelm, *Sachenrecht* (Berlin, 1993), § 377.

[72] England: Deakin *et al.*, *Tort*, 463–4; Stanton, *Tort*, 391; United States: Richard A. Epstein, *Cases and Materials on Torts* (6th edn., Boston, 1995), 694.

[73] *Prah* v. *Maretti*, 321 NW2d 182 (Wis. 1982). In *Tenn* v. *889 Associates, Ltd.*, 500 A2d 366 (NH 1985), the court said that in principle, a nuisance action could be brought for blocking light and air, but held for the defendant, noting that he proposed to build a building no higher than that of the plaintiff.

[74] England: Brazier, *Torts*, 318; United States: Keeton *et al.*, *Torts*, 622.

[75] See BG, 25 June 1982, 108 1a BGE 140 at 144–5; Tuor *et al.*, *Schweizerische Zivilgesetzbuch*, 887–8.

[76] England: *Thompson-Schwab* v. *Costaki*, [1956] 1 All ER 652, CA; United States: *Tedeschi* v. *Berker* 43 So. 960 (Ala. 1907).   [77] *Lows* v. *Floringplace Ltd*, [1981] 1 All ER 659.

[78] *Howard* v. *Etchieson*, 310 SW2d 473 (Ark. 1958).

[79] *Mathewson* v. *Primeau*, 395 P2d 183 (Wash. 1964).

[80] Germany: Bassenge, *Palandt*, to § 906, no. 4; Säcker, *Münchener Kommentar*, to § 906, no. 20; Wilhelm, *Sachenrecht*, § 378; Italy: Tabet *et al.*, *Proprietà*, § 121.

[81] Italy: Cass., 26 Apr. 1951, Foro it. 1952.I.349; Germany: BGH, 12 July 1985, BGHZ 95, 307.

[82] Foro it. 1952.I.349–50. It also may have mattered that operation of the brothel was legal in Italy at the time.

[83] BGHZ 95 at 309–10.

[84] Roth, *Staudingers Kommentar*, to § 906, no. 131; Fritz Bauer, *Lehrbuch des Sachenrechts* (15th edn., Munich, 1989), § 25 IV 2 b cc.

remedy for such eyesores as a dump for building materials in a residential area[85] and an automobile scrapyard near a hotel,[86] it has hinted, at least, that it might give one in a more extreme case.[87] Thus the pattern is like the one we saw in the case of 'negative interferences': concern coupled with great caution.

With ugly and indecent activities, as with 'negative interferences', the theory we have defended explains both the concern and the caution. In principle, the plaintiff should win, but in practice it is hard to draw the line. With physical interferences such as noise, smoke, and odors, the theory explains why the plaintiff wins when the interference is abnormal and grave. If the theory is correct, then the ancient problem of the Roman cheese shop can be resolved by the still more ancient principle: no one should gain at another's expense.

[85] BGH, 7 Mar. 1969, BGHZ 51, 396.　　[86] BGH, 15 May 1970, BGHZ 54, 56.
[87] BGH, 15 Nov. 1974, NJW 1975, 170.

5

Private Modification of the Right to Use Property: Servitudes

The previous chapter dealt with a person's right to use his property in a way that interferes with others. This one will discuss how such rights can be changed by private arrangement. A landowner may agree to some change in his rights that binds, not only himself, but anyone who owns his land thereafter. The common law refers to such an arrangement as an easement or covenant, although here we will refer to it, continental fashion, as a servitude. The beneficiary of a servitude may be another landowner and his successors. In some legal systems, it may be instead a particular person independent of what land he owns.

In discussing ownership and possession, we saw that the differences between common and civil law arose in response to a debate as to why the possessor should be protected. In discussing rights to interfere with another's use of his property, we saw that different legal systems had arrived at similar solutions independently, and yet the similarity suggested there must be common underlying principles although there had been no common discussion of what they were. Servitudes are different. The law that governs them varies, not only between civil law and common law jurisdictions, but within them. The differences are not the result of any dialogue as to what the law should be. Nor can any legal system state with clarity what principles should govern the law of servitudes. One might wonder if there is any principled explanation.

Nevertheless, I and—independently—Ben Depoorter and Francesco Parisi[1] believe we have identified a principle that explains when the law should enforce a servitude. The variety and confusion arise because the principle is hard to translate into a clear legal rule. The principle itself, however, is fairly simple. A servitude is created by parties who believe that it will serve their mutual interest. They expect the cost or inconvenience to the owner of the burdened property to be less than the advantage that the servitude confers on whomever it benefits. Therefore, the beneficiary is willing to pay an amount that compensates the owner of the burdened property for the cost or inconvenience. I, Depoorter and Parisi agree that what matters in principle is whether this relationship is likely to persist: whether the advantage of the servitude to those who succeed to its benefits will continue to outweigh the cost or inconvenience

---

[1] Ben W. F. Depoorter and Francesco Parisi, 'Fragmentation of Property Rights: A Functional Interpretation of the Law of Servitudes', *Global Jurist Frontiers* 3 (2003), article 2. http://www.bepress.com/gj/frontiers/vol3/iss1/art2.

to those whom it burdens. If so, in principle, the law should recognize and enforce the servitude. Otherwise it should not.

Depoorter and Parisi have an economic explanation of why the persistence of this relationship of advantages and costs should matter. If the cost to the owner of the burdened land becomes greater than the advantage of the servitude to whomever it benefits, it will be in the interest of the parties to terminate the servitude. The owner of the benefitted land will agree to terminate it only if he is compensated. Bargaining over his compensation entails transactions costs. Moreover, the parties may fail to agree, particularly if there are several of them, and so fail to arrive at a mutually desirable result. In either case, the result is economically inefficient.

My explanation is in terms of commutative justice rather than economic efficiency. The point of commutative justice is, so far as feasible, to preserve each person's share of the wealth of the community. In the circumstances just described, the owner of the dominant estate may be able to demand more than the value of the benefit which the servitude confers on him. It is unfair of him to do so. Even if he does not, sale of the property could result in a chance gain for one party or a chance loss for the other. If there is no reason why one party should be permitted to make such a gain or to suffer such a loss, that would also be unfair.

The first part of this chapter will take a comparative look at the law of servitudes. It will be seen that even the variety and confusion is understandable if the underlying principle is what I, Depoorter and Parisi take it to be. The chapter will then explain why I find my explanation of this principle in terms of commutative justice more compelling that Depoorter and Parisi's economic explanation.

I. The Law of Servitudes

Both common and civil law systems typically distinguish between restraining the owner of the burdened property from exercising a right and requiring him to act affirmatively. He may be restrained from exercising a right in two ways. The benefit-ted party may be entitled to do something on his land to which he could otherwise object. Or he may no longer be entitled to do something on his own land which he otherwise could do. In either case, we will say that the burden on him is 'passive', meaning that he is not required to act. Common and civil law systems also typically distinguish between servitudes which benefit the owner of a particular piece of land and those which benefit a person regardless of what land he owns. Anglo-American lawyers say that a servitude of the first type is 'appurtenant' to the estate which it benefits; one of the second type is 'in gross'. In Germany and Switzerland, a servit-ude of the first type is called a *Grunddienstbarkeit*; one of the second type, if the burden is passive, is a *beschränkte persönliche Dienstbarkeit* (Germany) or a *Personaldienstbarkeit*. Both have a 'servient estate' or property on which the burden is imposed. A servitude of the first type has a dominant estate (*herrschende Grundstuck*) as well. In some countries a servitude of the second type is not recognized. We will first discuss the case in which the burden is passive and the servitude is appurtenant—that is, the beneficiary is whoever owns a particular piece of land.

Then we will move on to burdens which require action and beneficiaries who need not own any particular piece of land.

A. A Passive Burden Benefitting the Owner of Particular Land

In civil and common law systems, a servitude which imposes a passive burden for the benefit of whoever owns particular land is enforceable. The question is when. European civil codes say that it must be of 'advantage' or 'utility' to the property that is benefitted. For example, it must be of 'advantage to the use of' the benefitted property (German Civil Code),[2] 'to the advantage of' that property (Swiss Civil Code),[3] for its 'use or utility' (French Civil Code), for its 'utility' (Italian Civil Code).[4]

Anglo-American law is similar in result but requires a bit of explanation. It distinguishes 'easements', which are enforceable in courts of law, from 'equitable servitudes', which are enforceable in courts of equity. Easements are affirmative if the beneficiary has the right to do something on the burdened property to which its owner could otherwise object, and 'negative' if the owner is prevented from doing something he otherwise could do. It is commonly said that either type of easement must 'confer a benefit on the dominant tenant as such' rather than some 'personal advantage' on its owner.[5] It cannot 'benefit the landowner personally'.[6] That sounds like the requirement we have encountered in civil law systems.

Nevertheless, while it is true that any easement the common law recognizes will fit that description, traditionally the requirement has been narrower. Negative easements have been limited to a fixed number: a court will enforce them when the owner is not to block windows, not to interfere with the flow of air through a defined channel, not to remove support for a building, or not to interfere with the flow of water through an artificial stream.[7] English and American judges have been reluctant to hold that other limits on what an owner can do are enforceable as easements although American courts have occasionally done so.[8] Much of the reason, historically, was that easements could be acquired by prescription and could be enforced against an owner who bought without knowledge of them.[9] It would have been dangerous to say that an owner could not do something on his land merely because he hadn't done it during the period necessary for prescription to run. It would also have been unfair to subsequent purchasers ignorant of their existence especially because England did not have a system for keeping public records of land titles until 1925. Moreover, new affirmative easements were traditionally permitted only when they resembled those previously recognized. Kevin and Susan Gray believe this requirement is still part of

---

[2] German Civil Code (*Bürgerlichesgesetzbuch*), § 1019 (hereinafter cited as BGB).

[3] Swiss Civil Code (*Zivilgesetzbuch*), art. 730 (hereinafter cited as ZGB).

[4] Italian Civil Code (*Codice civile*), art. 1027.

[5] Sir Robert Megarry, Sir William Wade, and Charles Harpum, *The Law of Real Property* (6th edn., London, 2000), § 18–045.   [6] Peter Sparkes, *A New Land Law* (2nd edn., Oxford, 2003), 722–3.

[7] Jesse Dukeminier and James E. Krier, *Property* (5th edn., New York, 2002), 855.

[8] e.g. *Petersen* v. *Friedman*, 328 P2d 264 (Cal App 1958) recognized an easement protecting a party's view. English courts will not do so. *Campbell* v. *Paddington Corp.* [1911] 1 KB 869; Kevin Gray and Susan Francis Gray, *Elements of Land Law* (3rd edn., London, 2001), 470; Sparkes, *New Land Law*, 724.

[9] Dukeminier and Krier, *Property*, 856.

English law.[10] Peter Sparkes believes it is not. Lord Evershed 'broke the mold', he believes, in *Re Ellenborough Park*,[11] recognizing a new easement to build a private garden. According to Sparkes, that was a move in the right direction since the requirement that new easements resemble established ones was 'inherently conservative' and a 'hit or miss way of dealing with new technological developments'.[12] If he is right, then, in the case of negative easements, the common law requirement is like those of the civil law systems we have discussed. In any case, any easement that Anglo-American law will enforce, affirmative or negative, would fall within the civil law requirement.

Other arrangements restricting what an owner can do on his own property became enforceable in courts of equity—as distinguished from courts of common law—as 'equitable servitudes'. Enforcing them did not present the dangers just described. They could not arise by prescription, and they were enforceable only against one who purchased the land with actual or constructive notice of them. Traditionally, equitable servitudes are enforceable only if they 'touch and concern' the use of land, or, as it is sometimes phrased, only if they 'benefit or accommodate' the dominant estate.[13] In the United States, the drafters of the *Restatement (Third) of Property, Servitudes* have proposed to abolish this requirement.[14] Scholars are debating whether it is advisable to do so.[15] Richard Epstein believes that the 'touch and concern' requirement only made sense because the English did not have public records of land titles until recently.[16] But that cannot be the only reason. The requirement is much like the one we have seen in European civil codes. Whatever 'touches and concerns' land use or 'benefits' or 'accommodates' the benefitted land will presumably be to its 'advantage' or 'utility'.

Thus the rules of different legal systems are much the same. The difficult question is what they really mean. Jurists in different systems describe them in a similar but confusing way. Atias in France[17] and Cafaggi in Italy[18] explain that the servitude must benefit the property, not its owner personally. Terré, in France, says that it must benefit the property, and not the proprietor more than the property,[19] or at least it must benefit him *en sa qualité de propriétaire* and not in his 'personal interest'.[20] According to Ghedini in Italy[21] and Brehm and Berger in Germany,[22] the benefit

[10] Gray and Gray, *Land Law*, 472.   [11] [1956] Ch. 131.   [12] Sparkes, *New Land Law*, 725.
[13] Gray and Gray, *Land Law*, 625.   [14] § 3.2 (2000).
[15] Compare Richard A. Epstein, 'Notice and Freedom of Contract in the Law of Servitudes', *Calif. L. Rev.* 55 (1982), 1353 (in favor) with Gregory S. Alexander, 'Freedom, Coercion and the Law of Servitudes', *Cornell L. Rev.* 73 (1988), 883 (opposed).
[16] Richard A. Epstein, 'Covenants and Constitutions', *Cornell L. Rev.* 73 (1988), 906 at 909.
[17] Christian Atias, *Droit civil: Les Biens* (4th edn., Paris, 1999), no. 174.
[18] Fabrizio Cafaggi in Paulo Cendon, *Commentario al Codice civile* (Turin, 1991), no. 1.6 to art. 1027.
[19] François Terré & Philippe Simler, *Droit civil: Les Biens* (Paris, 1998), no. 797.
[20] Terré and Simler, *Les Biens*, no. 823.
[21] Luca Ghedini in Giorgio Cian and Alberto Trabucchi, *Commentario breve al Codice civile* (Padua, 1999), no. 1.2 to art. 1027.
[22] Wolfgang Brehm and Christian Berger, *Sachenrecht* (Tübingen, 2000), § 21, no. 20. According to Baur, the servitude must benefit the estate 'as it is configured' (*wie es gestaltet ist*). Fritz Baur, *Lehrbuch des Sachenrechts* (15th edn., Munich, 1989), 299. That captures the idea that something must set this particular property aside from property in general, but taken literally, it is too broad. It would cover my hypothetical case, described later, of the visibility of a statue.

must be 'objective' and 'connected to the property'. According to Kevin and Susan Gray in England, the right must confer 'a benefit on the dominant tenement as distinct from offering some purely personal advantage or facility to the dominant owner'.[23] One could quote any number of similar statements.

What do they mean? Susan French, who drafted the *Restatement* proposal to abolish the touch and concern rule, believes that this requirement means nothing definite. She regards it as a blanket delegation of discretion to a judge to terminate a servitude if he regards it as objectionable. One can understand her point of view. It is not clear what it means to say that a burden benefits a piece of land as distinguished from its owner. Land itself does not benefit. Owners of land do. Presumably, she would find the rules of civil law systems unclear for the same reason. She believes that any servitude should be enforced unless it offends the constitution, statute, or a public policy.[24]

It is true that sometimes the reason a servitude is not enforced is that it violates a public policy, whether or not the policy is expressed in a constitution or statute. For example, there is a controversy over whether a court should enforce a servitude prohibiting the owner of the burdened land from opening a competing business such as a hotel. Courts in Germany,[25] Switzerland,[26] in the United States,[27] and sometimes in France[28] have been willing to do so. Courts in England,[29] and, on other occasions, in France[30] have refused. It is not helpful to analyze these cases, as some courts and scholars have done, by asking whether the benefit in question is 'personal'.[31] The question is whether such arrangements should be considered illegitimate attempts to charge monopoly prices or, instead, as legitimate attempts to protect one's investment against the risk of losing business in the future. That is a hard question to answer but it is the one that matters, and it is one of public policy. Similarly, because of public policies against discrimination or in favor of free speech, American courts have refused to enforce servitudes which discriminate against minority groups[32] or handicapped people[33] or which abridge the freedom of speech.[34] Whether to uphold servitudes that

---

[23] Gray and Gray, *Land Law*, 462.

[24] Susan F. French, 'Servitudes, Reform and the New Restatement of Property: Creation, Doctrines, and Structural Simplification', *Cornell L. Rev.* 73 (1988), 928 at 940.

[25] Wolfgang Ring in Julius von Staudinger, *Kommentar zum Bürgerlichen Gesetzbuch* (Munich 1994), no. 13 to § 1090.   [26] BG, 9 June 1988, BGE 114 II 314.

[27] Richard R. Powell and Michael Allan Wolf, *Powell on Real Property* (New York, 2000), § 60.06[3][b]. One of the last hold-outs was Massachusetts, which finally decided to enforce such a restriction in *Witinsville Plaza, Inc.* v. *Kotseas*, 390 NE2d 243 (Mass. 1979).

[28] Cass. civ., 27 Nov. 1907, D. 1908.1.460 (hotel, cabaret or café although the court calls the arrangement a *créance*, not a servitude).   [29] *Hill* v. *Tupper*, (1863) 2 H & C 121, 159 Eng Rep 51.

[30] Cass. req., 8 July 1851, D. 1851.1.188 (agreement not to take cinders from burdened land which would compete with business on benefitted land); Cass. 3e ch. civ, 18 Mar. 1987, D.S. 1988. somm. 177 (agreement not to sell petroleum products); Cour d'appel, Paris, 7 July 1989, D.S. 1990. somm. 77 (agreement not to open medical office).

[31] e.g. Cass. req., 8 July 1851, D. 1851.1.188; Terré and Simler, *Les Biens*, no. 824; Gray and Gray, *Land Law*, 462.

[32] *Shelly* v. *Kraemer*, 334 US 1 (1948) (exclusion of black people held to violate the Constitution).

[33] *Deep East Texas Regional Mental Health & Mental Retardation Services* v. *Kinnear*, 877 SW2d 550 (Tex Civ App 1994) (exclusion of mentally retarded violates Fair Housing Act).

[34] *Gerber* v. *Longboat Harbour North Condominium*, 724 F Supp 884 (MD Fla 1989) (covenant that prohibits flying the American flag is unenforceable).

impose age limits in residential communities or prescribe what color one can paint one's house depends on what sort of freedom it should be our policy to encourage: freedom to live in a more uniform community if one chooses or freedom to be different wherever one lives. In all these cases, what is at stake is a distinct public policy which transcends the law of servitudes.

But these are not the kinds of cases that concerned the drafters of the European codes, or for that matter, the judges who created the 'touch and concern' requirement or the jurists who distinguish benefits to the property from benefits to the person. We can understand their concern by some common sense examples where the proper legal outcome seems clear. It seems plain that a neighbor should be able to acquire a right of way over my adjoining land or the right to prevent me from blocking his window. But he should not—and in the legal systems just described, he cannot—acquire a servitude that allows his child to come into my house to practice the piano or that prevents me from impairing the visibility from a nearby park of a statue of himself which he has erected on his property. He could acquire these rights by a contract with me but he cannot make them pass with the land to succeeding owners.

These seem to be the kinds of cases that jurists have in mind when they ask whether a benefit is enjoyed by property as distinguished from its owner personally. Professor French is right that this formulation cannot be correct if it is taken literally. She is also right that expressions like 'touch and concern'—or for that matter, 'advantage' or 'utility' to the benefitted estate—are not clear either. Still, all of these phrases seem to express imperfectly a shared insight and one which is not clarified by merely asking, as Professor French does, whether a public policy is offended.

Our examples help to clarify this insight. When the servitude was established, the right of way and the right to an unblocked window were sufficiently valuable to my neighbor that he was willing to compensate me for granting him these rights. Had the cost or inconvenience to me of granting these rights outweighed their benefit to my neighbor, I would not have been willing to grant them for any compensation he would have been willing to pay. There is no reason to think that these rights will be more burdensome to my successor in title or less valuable to my neighbor's successor. Thus, if the rights did not run with the land, his successor would have to re-acquire them from mine.

It is not so with his child's use of the piano or the statue's visibility from the park. There is no reason to think my successor will have my tolerance for the musical efforts of children or that my neighbor's successor will have a child who needs piano practice but lacks a piano. There is no reason to think that his successor will have any interest in whether the public can see the statue. It is more likely that the burden to my successor would exceed the value of these rights to that of my neighbor. Consequently, if they ran with the land, the arrangement would have to be undone. If my neighbor's successor insisted, my successor would have to pay him to terminate it.

These examples suggest, then, that the question should be: which is more likely, that an arrangement that is more valuable to my neighbor than burdensome to myself will also be more valuable to his successor than burdensome to mine? Or that it will be less valuable than burdensome? To put it another way, the question should be: which is more likely, that if the arrangement does not run with the land our successors will want to remake it? Or that if it does they will want to undo it?

If we ask this question, we can make sense of traditional formulas that speak of what 'touches and concerns' or 'benefits' or 'advantages' or is of 'utility' to land, or what benefits land as distinct from conferring a personal advantage on its owner. Of course, land does not benefit. Owners benefit. But these formulas draw our attention to whether future owners—of whom we know nothing except that they will own the same land—are likely to benefit in the same way as the present owner. If so, it is likely that they will benefit to the same extent. If they do, it is likely the value of the arrangement to them will still exceed its burden to the property subject to the servitude.

B. The Owner of the Burdened Estate Must Act Affirmatively

Legal systems are less uniform when the burden is not passive, when, instead, an owner is required to act affirmatively. With the possible exception of England, the legal systems we are describing will readily permit such a servitude when it is a means to securing the benefit of the passive burden and in this sense ancillary.[35] An example is a duty to open a sluice[36] or to maintain a right of way.[37] When the servitude is not ancillary, modern legal systems differ. They range from extreme suspicion to broad tolerance. Some legal systems do not enforce such a servitude. Some take account of how the affirmative burden relates to the use of land. Some limit the time period during which such a servitude will be enforced. Some, in effect, allow the burdened owner to buy his way out by awarding damages but refusing to compel performance. Finally, there are some in which, supposedly, any affirmative duty is enforceable as a servitude although one doubts if any sort of duty would actually be enforceable in practice. Varied as they are, each of these approaches can be understood as a way of dealing indirectly with the problem already discussed: to enforce the servitude if its relative costs and advantages are likely to be the same for the successors of those who created it, and who otherwise would have to remake the arrangement, but not if the cost is likely to exceed the advantage to the successors, who then would have to unmake it.

1. Jurisdictions in which affirmative duties are unenforceable

Traditionally, neither Roman law[38] nor common law enforced a servitude that required performance of an affirmative act, at least if the act was not ancillary to a passive

---

[35] France: Atias, *Les Biens*, no. 201; Terré and Simler, *Les Biens*, no. 806; Italy: Cafaggi in Cendon, *Commentario*, to art. 1030; Germany: Brehm and Berger, *Sachenrecht*, § 21 no. 20; Switzerland: ZBG, art. 730(II); Jörg Schmid, *Sachenrecht* (Zürich, 1997), no. 1264; BG, 12 June 1980, BGE 106 II 315, 317. In England, neither easements nor equitable servitudes can require a property owner to act affirmatively. Gray and Gray, *Land Law*, 475–6, 621–2. Courts have refused to recognize an easement to supply water, as distinguished from one to permit its passage. *Rance* v. *Elvin*, (1985) 50 P & CR 9 (CA). Yet they enforced an easement to repair a boundary fence. *Jones* v. *Price*, [1965] 2 QB 618. Courts of law, as distinguished from courts of equity, have traditionally enforced so called 'real covenants'. Like easements and equitable servitudes, these are burdens that run with the land. They, however, can be promises to do affirmative acts. In England, however, they are enforceable only when they are made between a landlord and his tenant. In most American states, they are enforceable at least as long as one party owns an interest in the other's land. Powell and Wolf, *Real Property*, § 60.04[3][b]. Since easements count as an interest in land, any promise to perform a duty ancillary to an easement is therefore enforceable against successors in title.

[36] Cass. civ., 22 Nov. 1892, D.P. 1894.1.45 (France).

[37] BGB, § 1021 (Germany); BG, 5 Dec. 1995, BGE 122 III 10, 12 (Switzerland).　　　[38] Dig. 8.1.15.1.

burden. Modern French,[39] Italian[40] and English law[41] still refuse to do so. So does the law of the German federal state Nordrhein-Westfalen unless the act is payment of money.[42]

If, in the interest of simplicity, the law ought to give a 'yes' or 'no' answer to the question of whether such servitudes are enforceable, then this traditional 'no' answer makes sense. Most often, the ease with which a landowner can perform an affirmative act, and the advantage he can confer on the owner who is benefitted, depend, not on what land he owns, but upon who he is, and sometimes on who the benefitted landowner is. If I agree to tend your garden, or to serenade you on the guitar once a week, there is no reason to think that the next person who owns my land will have my skill or enthusiasm for gardening or music, or that the next person who owns your land will share your appreciation of my skills, let alone those of my successor. Thus, while the cost of the arrangement may be less to me than the advantage it confers on you, there is no reason to expect the relative cost and advantage to be the same for those who succeed us.

While that is so as a general rule, nevertheless, it will not be so in every case. Just because a person owns the burdened property, he might be able to provide a benefit more cheaply or conveniently than other people. For example, he might be providing heat, and be able to provide it more cheaply because his property is located nearby since it is difficult to transport hot air or hot water much of a distance. Moreover, the benefit may be one, like heat, that the successor to the benefitted property is likely to want as much as the present owner. If these conditions are met, future owners are likely to find the arrangement as mutually advantageous as their predecessors. If it did not come to them along with the land, they would want to make the arrangement themselves.

In another type of case, one or more property owners are both burdened and benefitted. For example, each is burdened by an obligation to pay to maintain some facility such as a swimming pool, and each is benefitted by the right to use it. The benefit to each is greater than it otherwise would be because of the characteristics of the land that each owns: for example, it is located near the swimming pool. Successors may be as likely as present owners to want such a benefit and to consider it worth the price, either because most people want such a benefit, or because people who want such a benefit are particularly likely to buy property to which such a benefit is attached. If these conditions are met, then, again, the burden and benefit should run.

---

[39] Atias, *Les Biens*, no. 174; Terré and Simler, *Les Biens*, no. 746.

[40] Italian Civil Code (*Codice civile*), art. 1030; Ghedini in Cian and Trabucchi, *Commentario*, no. 1.1 to art. 1030.

[41] An easement cannot require an affirmative act. *Regis Property Co. Ltd.* v. *Redman* [1956] 2 QB 612 (obligation to secure a supply of hot water cannot be an easement). Neither can an equitable servitude. *Haywood* v. *Brunswick Permanent Benefit Building Society*, (1881) 8 QBD 403 (covenant to build and repair cannot be enforced in equity). See Gray and Gray, *Land Law*, 475–6 (easements), 621–2 (equitable servitudes); Sparkes, *New Land Law*, 724 (easements); 732 (equitable servitudes). A 'real covenant' is a promise that runs with the land and is enforceable at law rather than in equity. It can require an affirmative act. But in English law, as will be seen, a real covenant can only be made by those in a 'tenurial' relationship such as a landlord and tenant. It cannot be made between neighboring landowners.

[42] Preussisches Ausführungsgesetz zum BGB, art. 30, 20 Sept. 1899, GS 177.

Such cases illustrate when it would make sense for burdens and benefits to pass to successors in title. Seeing intuitively that it does make sense, some French courts have bent the law to enforce such arrangements as servitudes. The *Cour de Cassation* did so when a coal mine agreed to provide a neighboring glass works with the coal it would need even though the mine bore the cost of the activity necessary to provide the coal.[43] On another occasion it enforced an arrangement in which the seller of residential parcels retained title to the streets and agreed to maintain them. The owners of the parcels received the right to use the streets and were to pay a certain sum for their maintenance.[44]

Cases like these suggest that a flat refusal to enforce affirmative duties as servitudes goes too far.

2. Jurisdictions which consider the relationship of the burdened to the benefitted property

Consequently, it is understandable that some jurisdictions take direct account of the relationship between the burdened and the benefitted property. The problem which they then encounter is the one we encountered in discussing passive burdens: how to state with precision what this relationship must be.

As with passive burdens, typical formulations are so general as to seem meaningless or misleading. Perhaps the most general one is that of American courts. They say, as with passive burdens, that the affirmative action must 'touch and concern' the burdened property and, perhaps, the benefitted property as well.[45] The trouble is how to explain what 'touch and concern' might mean. We have already seen the difficulties that American jurists have encountered in giving that phrase a definite meaning.

The Swiss Civil Code contains a formula which is somewhat more definite but, for that reason, is also misleading: the performance must either be produced by the economic nature of the burdened property, or it must meet the economic needs of the benefitted property.[46] As we have seen, however, it should matter whether the person who owns the burdened property can provide the benefit in question more easily just because he owns it. It should also matter whether the affirmative action necessary to provide the benefit can be taken by him more easily than by others because he is the owner. Consequently, it isn't enough to ask, as the Swiss Code does, whether the benefit is produced by the economic nature of the burdened property. That requirement would be met whether the benefit is heat from a furnace or cars from a factory. Moreover, it goes too far to say, as the last part of this Code provision does, that the performance need only meet the economic needs of the benefitted property. Think of an arrangement to do the neighbor's gardening, or, if that seems insufficiently economic, of one to plant and harvest a neighbor's crops. Or imagine an arrangement to build and maintain a warehouse on another's land. Of course, these are not the sorts of cases Swiss jurists have in mind when they interpret the Code. A textbook example of a performance due to the economic nature of the property is supplying produce from the land. A textbook example of an activity that serves the economic needs of

---

[43] Cass. civ., 9 Jan. 1901, D. 1901.I.450.   [44] Cass. civ., 5 May 1919, D. 1923.I.230.
[45] Powell and Wolf, *Real Property*, § 60.06[2][c].   [46] ZGB, art. 782(3).

the benefitted property is the maintenance of a boundary wall.[47] These are the cases the jurists, and presumably the drafters, wish to cover, but the language of the Code goes beyond them.

One way to avoid such overly general formulations is to enumerate a few clear cases in which a servitude will be enforced without providing a general formula. For example, in Baden-Württemberg[48] and Rheinland-Pfalz,[49] the only servitudes that impose affirmative duties and can be established permanently are those to maintain installations for electricity, heat, warm water, or components of the soil, and, in Rheinland-Pfalz, to pay money. Those do seem to be cases in which, traditionally at least, the person owning nearby property could provide a benefit more cheaply than others. But they are not the only such cases. The disadvantage of dispensing with a general formula and enumerating clear cases is that it is hard to reach the same result in cases requiring like treatment.

3. Jurisdictions that impose time limits

Another type of limitation is a restriction on the length of time that servitudes establishing affirmative duties can be enforced. In Switzerland, the owner of the burdened property can terminate the servitude after 30 years, although he must pay compensation.[50] In Baden-Württemberg,[51] Bremen,[52] and Rheinland-Pfalz[53] such a servitude can last only for the burdened property owner's lifetime. In Rheinland-Pfalz, if the owner is a juridical person, it can last only 30 years.[54]

Imposing a time limit makes sense if, as I have suggested, what ultimately matters is whether the advantage of the servitude to the benefitted property continues to exceed its cost to the burdened property. One way to seek an answer, as we have just seen, is to ask whether the advantage and cost are likely to be the same for the successors of the parties who made the arrangement. But an indirect approach is simply to assume that the balance of advantage and cost will remain stable but only for a period of time.

4. Jurisdictions which limit the remedy to recovery of damages

As already mentioned, this chapter will suggest a reason why the law should not enforce servitudes when the cost or inconvenience for one party is greater than the benefit they bring to the other: in that event, the benefitted party can then charge more to terminate them than the amount by which he benefits. That, we will argue, is unfair. If so, then there is still another way to deal with the concerns raised by servitudes imposing affirmative duties. The law can allow the owner of the burdened

---

[47] Schmid, *Sachenrecht*, no. 1447.

[48] Ausführungsgesetz zum BGB, § 33, 26 Nov. 1974, Gesetz und Verordungsblatt 498.

[49] Ausführungsgesetz zum BGB, § 22, 18 Nov. 1976, Gesetz und Verordungsblatt 259.

[50] ZGB, arts. 787–8 (unless united with servitude which provides for a passive burden): art. 788(3); BG, 28 Apr. 1967, BGE 93 II 71, 76; Schmid, *Sachenrecht*, no. 455.

[51] Unless the burden is to maintain installation for electricity, heat, warm water, or components of the soil or to pay money. Ausführungsgesetz zum BGB, § 33, 26 Nov. 1974, Gesetz und Verordungsblatt 498.

[52] Ausführungsgesetz zum BGB, § 26, 18 July 1899, Sammlung des bremischen Rechts 400 a 1.

[53] Ausführungsgesetz zum BGB, § 22, 18 Nov. 1976, Gesetz und Verordungsblatt 259.

[54] Unless the burden is to maintain installation for electricity, heat, warm water, or components of the soil or to pay money (ibid.).

property to escape the servitude by paying the amount necessary to compensate the benefitted party for the loss of his benefit. The advantage of this approach is that it prevents the type of unfairness just described. The disadvantage is one that arises with any forced sale of a right. It is hard to be sure how much the benefit in question is really worth to the person entitled to it.

In some American states, this approach is a by-product of the way courts have dealt with what are called 'real covenants'. Traditionally, real covenants, like easements, were enforceable in courts of common law where the remedy was damages, unlike equitable servitudes, which were enforceable in courts of equity where the remedy was an injunction. The difference in remedies has been preserved even though courts of common law and equity have now been merged.[55] Moreover, traditionally, real covenants can impose affirmative burdens while easements and equitable servitudes cannot. For that reason, English courts severely limit their enforceability. The parties to a real covenant must be in a 'tenurial relationship', which nearly always means they must be landlord and tenant.[56] In some American states, however, real covenants can be made by neighboring landowners.[57] To the extent that these states have preserved the traditional rule that an affirmative duty can only be imposed by a real covenant, the result is that a landowner subject to such a duty can escape by paying damages. He will not be forced to perform.

In Switzerland, provided that 30 years have elapsed, a similar result is reached by allowing the owner of the burdened property to terminate the servitude if he pays compensation to the other party. He can only do so, however, after the end of 30 years.[58] Thus, again, the benefitted party cannot refuse to terminate the easement unless he is paid more than the amount by which he benefits.

As noted earlier, instead of following the traditional rule, some American jurisdictions will enforce an arrangement which calls for the performance of an affirmative duty as an equitable servitude. Supposedly, a court would then issue an injunction that the duty be performed. And yet, some courts have refused to do so. In *Oceanside Community Assn.* v. *Oceanside Land Co.*,[59] the court would not require the developer of a residential area to maintain a golf course even though it acknowledged that this obligation did run with the land. It said that an injunction, presumably the cost to the

---

[55] Dukeminier and Krier, *Property*, 868–9.

[56] Megarry, Wade and Harpum, *Real Property*, § 15–004.

[57] The English requirement that the parties who enter into a real covenant but are in a special relationship is called 'horizontal privity' as distinguished from the 'vertical privity' which exists between the parties who established the covenant and their successors. In some American states, the 'horizontal privity' requirement has been stretched so that in practice it allows any neighboring landowners to make a real covenant. That is not so in all states. In some, horizontal privity only exists if the parties are in a tenurial relationship or if they both own interests in the same land: for example, if one has an easement in the land of another. Consequently, promises of affirmative duties which are ancillary to easements are enforceable. But in many states, parties who derive their title from a common source are also deemed to be in horizontal privity. For example, if A conveys part of his land to B, or part to B and the rest to C, A can impose a real covenant on one parcel for the benefit of the other. Powell and Wolf, *Real Property*, § 60.04[3][c]. The result is that in practice any neighboring landowners can make a real covenant. If they are not already in horizontal privity, they convey their parcels to a 'straw'—for example, their lawyer's secretary—who then reconveys the parcels to them subject to the covenant. Since they now derive their title from a common source, the horizontal privity requirement is met. Since, with the help of a lawyer, the parties can always meet the horizontal privity requirement. The *Restatement (Third) of Property, Servitudes*, § 2.4 proposes to abolish it.

[58] ZGB, arts. 787–8.   [59] 147 Cal App 3d 166 (1983).

developer, would exceed the benefit to the homeowners. Instead, the court imposed an 'equitable lien' on the property for the amount of harm it estimated that the homeowners had suffered.

5. Jurisdictions which impose no limitations

In Germany, the drafters of the Civil Code rejected the Roman rule that a servitude could not require an affirmative action. They left the task of imposing limits to the German federal states. Some states have not imposed any limits. In others the only limitation is on the time period during which a servitude will be enforced. Supposedly, then, in these states a servitude could provide for any kind of affirmative duty. Seeing, however, is believing. I know of no case in which a German court has enforced affirmative duty to tend a neighbor's garden or serenade him on the guitar. If such a case arises, one hopes it will have the good sense not to do so.

C. Benefits that Do Not Depend on Ownership of Particular Land

Both common law and civil law systems also differ when the burden runs, not to the benefit of the owner of particular land, but to a person regardless of what land, if any, he owns. Some jurisdictions such as France,[60] Italy,[61] and England[62] refuse to recognize such a servitude. English courts follow a precedent laid down for easements in 1850,[63] and then extended by analogy to equitable servitudes.[64] Most American states preserved the English rule, not as to easements, but as to equitable servitudes,[65] although the *Third Restatement* wants them enforced as well.[66]

In contrast, some jurisdictions do enforce servitudes which benefit a person regardless of what land he owns. Most American states do so in the case of easements, and Germany and Switzerland do so in the case of all servitudes whether the duty in question is passive (a *beschränkte persönliche Dienstbarkeit* in Germany, a *Personaldienstbarkeit* in Switzerland) or the performance of an affirmative act (*persönliche Reallast* in Germany, *Personalgrundlast* in Switzerland) without limiting the permissible content of such servitudes.[67] Nevertheless, all of these jurisdictions impose limits on the power of the

---

[60] Terré and Simler, *Les Biens*, no. 796. French jurists rest this conclusion on art. 686 of the Civil Code which says that a servitude can only be imposed 'on an estate for an estate'.

[61] Cafaggi in Cendon, *Commentario*, no. 1.6 to art. 1027.

[62] Gray and Gray, *Land Law*, 459–60 (easements); 622–3 (equitable servitudes); Sparkes, *New Land Law*, 722 (easements); 734 (equitable servitudes).   [63] *Ackroyd* v. *Smith*, (1850) 10 CB 164, 138 Eng Rep 68.

[64] *London County Council* v. *Allen*, [1924] 2 Ch 379. As mentioned, common law recognizes a third kind of servitude, the real covenant, but in England it can only be established when the parties are landlord and tenant.

[65] Powell and Wolf, *Real Property*, § 60.04[3][b]; Uriel Reichman, 'Toward a Unified Concept of Servitudes', *S. Calif. L. Rev.* 55 (1982), 1179. That is curious, as James Krier has noted, since the rationale for the refusal to enforce such equitable servitudes in England was the analogy to easements. Dukeminier and Krier, *Property*, 891–2.   [66] § 2.6 Comment d.

[67] Except that the burdened owner cannot have given away the complete right to use his property since then the arrangement would be a usufruct. Ring in Staudinger, *Kommentar*, no. 3 to BGB § 1090 (Germany); Schmid, *Sachenrecht*, no. 1324. The Swiss Code mentions certain *Personaldienstbarkeiten* the law will recognize, but no limit is imposed because, according to the provision, the law will also enforce 'other' servitudes. ZGB, art. 781.

beneficiary to assign his rights to a third party. In the United States, he cannot do so in the case of some easements,[68] although the *Restatement Third of Servitudes* rejects this limitation.[69] In Germany, the beneficiary cannot assign his rights.[70] If the parties so specify, he may by contract allow a third party to use his rights.[71] In Switzerland, if the burden is passive, he cannot do so unless the parties so specify.[72] If the burden is an affirmative act, it is debated whether he may do so at all.[73]

Not only is there no uniform rule as to how such servitudes should be treated, there is no clear explanation of why they should be treated differently. Some Anglo-American scholars have said that the reason may be to avoid the difficulties of modifying or terminating them if the beneficiaries are unknown.[74] But that problem could be solved, as the *Third Restatement* and the German Civil Code provide, by allowing a court to terminate them if it is impossible or impracticable to locate beneficiaries.[75] According to others, the reason is to protect the owner of the burdened property against an increase in use and hence in the burden.[76] But that problem could be solved, as it has been by some American courts,[77] by refusing to allow the transferee to make a greater use of the servitude than the transferor.

Presumably, when the parties establish such an arrangement, the advantage to the benefitted party exceeds the cost or inconvenience to the party burdened. The question we have asked throughout this chapter is whether this relationship is likely to be the same for their successors. Which is more likely, that if the arrangement does not run with the land, their successors will want to remake it? Or that if it does, they will want to undo it? If that is the question that matters, then there are two reasons why the law should be suspicious of servitudes that benefit a person regardless of what land he owns.

First, it may be that this person can obtain the same benefit elsewhere with no more cost and inconvenience. Since he need not be located nearby, he may be able to derive the same benefit as easily from comparable property. Suppose, for example, the servitude is to boat or hunt, that the person benefitted must pay a certain amount each year for this privilege, and that there are many comparable locations for boating or hunting. If so, the person benefitted should not be obliged to obtain the benefit from the property subject to the servitude. He should be free to go wherever he can obtain it most cheaply. Otherwise, the owner of the burdened property will be able to make him pay to terminate their arrangement so that he can do so. Nor should the owner of the burdened property be obliged to provide the benefit if he can no longer do so as

---

[68] Powell and Wolf, *Real Property*, § 34.16; *Restatement (First) of Property*, § 489 (1944); Dukeminier and Krier, *Real Property*, 830; Alan David Hegi, 'The Easement in Gross Revisited: Tranferability and Divisability since 1945', *Vanderbilt L. Rev.* 39 (1986), 109, at 113–23.   [69] § 4.6.

[70] Ring in Staudinger, *Kommentar*, no. 3 vor 1090–3; Baur, *Lehrbuch*, 305.

[71] Baur, *Lehrbuch*, 305.   [72] Schmid, *Sachenrecht*, no. 1437.

[73] ibid. no. 1444. In any event, the benefitted party cannot compel performance but only sue for damages (ibid. no. 1445).

[74] Gray and Gray, *Land Law*, 461 (easements), 623 (equitable servitudes); Dukeminier and Krier, *Property*, 889–90 (equitable servitudes). This argument is criticized in Michael F. Sturley, 'Easements in Gross', *L. Quar. Rev.* 96 (1980), 557, at 562–7.

[75] *Restatement (Third) of Property Servitudes*, § 7.3; BGB, § 1112.

[76] Dukeminier and Krier, *Property*, 830; Hegi, 'Easement in Gross', 128–34.

[77] *Miller* v. *Lutheran Conference & Camp Ass'n*, 200 A 646 (Pa 1938).

cheaply and conveniently as others. If he is required to provide it, the benefitted party will be able to make him pay to terminate their arrangement even though doing so imposes no cost on the benefitted party. Of course, in such a case, parties with their eyes open would not want to establish a servitude running with the burdened property. Supposing, however, that at least one of them had his eyes closed, a court would have no reason to enforce such a servitude and a good reason not to do so: to prevent one party from holding up the other.

Second, it may be that the inconvenience to the owner of the burdened party depends on the identity of the person benefitted. The inconvenience I suffer if I have granted boating or hunting rights to someone whose habits I know will increase if he transfers them to someone who plays loud music when he boats or takes wild shots when he hunts. Thus even if such a servitude should be created, there may still be a reason why it should not be assignable.

In other situations, neither of these concerns would arise. Suppose, for example, the servitude is for the right to string power or telephone lines across the burdened property, or to erect poles to support them. It is not the case, at least after the lines are in place, that the power or telephone company can derive the benefit as easily from any other property. Nor does the inconvenience to the burdened property owner depend on which telephone or power company happens to own them. Indeed, if such a servitude could not be created, the company would have to repurchase its right to maintain its lines from every successive owner. If such a servitude could not be assigned, it could never transfer its lines to another telephone or power company without paying every property owner for the right to do so.

Most of the legal systems we have examined try to lay down clear 'yes' or 'no' rules. They say that servitudes are, or are not, enforceable when the benefit does not run to a particular piece of land; if enforceable, that they are or are not assignable. We can now see that there are difficulties with any such rule because some of these servitudes, but not others, should be enforceable, and some, but not others, should be assignable. It is understandable, then, that when legal systems lay down 'yes' or 'no' rules under such circumstances, the rules are not the same. Every 'yes' or 'no' rule works well in some cases and not in others.

One way to avoid that difficulty is not to lay down 'yes' or 'no' rules. For example, American courts have decided on a case-by-case basis whether easements in gross are assignable with no clear rule to guide them, let alone a yes-or-no rule. The clear cases are like those in our illustrations. As Powell noted, 'almost without exception' American courts have allowed the assignment of easements for 'for railroads, for telephone and telegraph and electric power lines, [and] for pipelines . . .'.[78] According to Krier, 'almost the only easements in gross that are not assignable under modern cases are recreational easements (easements for hunting, fishing, boating and camping)'.[79] Even then, courts have sometimes upheld the assignment of such a right when the recreational easement was granted for commercial purposes.[80] In such a case, it is

---

[78] Powell and Wolf, *Real Property*, § 34.16.   [79] Dukeminier and Krier, *Real Property*, 830.
[80] *Miller* v. *Lutheran Conference and Camp Ass'n*, 200 A 646 (Pa 1938) (noting that 'there is an obvious difference . . . between easements for personal enjoyment and those designed for commercial exploitation').

unlikely that the benefitted party could simply change his location without a loss of custom even if another were available. Moreover, the grantor would have been aware that the easement would be used by people he did not know. In general, then, the courts behave as though their concerns, albeit unarticulated, are those we just described. If they are the concerns that matter, it would be better for a court to take them directly into account. They are only approximated by the rule of the *First Restatement* that an easement is assignable if it has a commercial character.[81] They are disregarded by the rule of the *Third Restatement* which allows any easement to be enforceable and assignable. In effect, the *Third Restatement* replaces the traditional approach with a 'yes' rule which is clear but works well in some cases and not in others.

Nevertheless, if we take a closer look at systems that have adopted a 'yes' or 'no' rule we can see how they can accommodate situations in which it does not work well. In Germany and Switzerland, so far as I know, a court has not enforced a servitude when the beneficiary could as easily have derived the benefit elsewhere. Since it would not be in the interest of both parties to establish such a servitude, it is not surprising that such cases would rarely arise. Moreover, the rules about assignability do little harm in cases like the power or telephone lines. The Swiss rule merely creates a presumption. In such cases the parties will escape it by expressly providing that the servitude is assignable. In Germany, the beneficiary will almost always be an legal entity such as a corporation. In all likelihood, a court would apply by analogy § 1059a of the Civil Code which allows another unassignable interest—a usufruct—to be transferred from one such entity to another.[82]

France and England have the opposite problem. According to their 'no' rule, servitudes are enforceable unless they benefit whoever owns particular land. Thus their courts generally reach the right result in cases like those of boating and hunting rights.[83] The problem is what to do with case like those of the power lines.[84] It has been solved

[81] *Restatement (First) of Property*, § 491. The assignability of others is 'to be determined by the manner or the terms of their creation' (ibid. § 492).

[82] Brehm and Berger, *Sachenrecht*, § 22 no. 1. BGB, § 1098(3) allows § 1059 to be applied by analogy to another right which is normally unassignable, a *Vorkaufsrecht*, which is the right to buy property on the same terms as a third party to whom it is offered. Section 1059 has been applied by analogy in other situations not covered by the letter of the Code. BGH, 9 July 1968, 50 EBGHZ 307. In doing so, the court noted that the normal prohibition of assignability 'is to protect the burdened party against a disagreeable change in the person of the benefitted party' and, in the case of a *Vorkaufsrecht*, to set a time limit within which the right must be exercised. When the right is given to a legal entity, '[t]his need for protection is narrower . . . because the person concerned will have the anonymity of the benefitted party and the unlimited duration of the right in mind' (50 EBGHZ at 310–11).

[83] Generally but not always. French courts have held that one cannot have a servitude to hunt on another's property (Cass. crim., 9 Jan. 1891, D. 1891.1.89), or to take 'secondes herbes'(Cass. civ., 3e ch. civ., 25 Mar. 1992, D.S. 1993.J.65). But they have not asked whether the beneficiary of such a right could as easily obtain the benefit elsewhere. That might or might not be true when the right to hunt on certain land was given to all inhabitants of a town (Cass. req., 14 Nov. 1932, D.H. 1932.586) or when the owner of 500 hectares sold 23 reserving the right to hunt there to his or her direct heirs so long as they were owners (Cass. civ., 3e ch. civ., 22 June 1976, Bull. civ. 1976.III. no. 280, p. 215), but, without such an enquiry, these servitudes were held to be unenforceable.

[84] Another problem, although one that does not need discussion here, is what to do when the person for whose benefit the servitude is nominally imposed is, in fact, a proxy for someone else who does own land and for whose benefit the servitude is really intended. The problem arises, for example, when a developer imposes identical servitudes on each parcel of land as he subdivides. When he parts with the last parcel, he

by special statutes and ordinances which create what the English call 'statutory easements'[85] and the French call *servitudes de l'utilité publique*. Examples are servitudes for electricity, gas, and water lines.[86]

Although these enactments allow the beneficiaries to be private companies as well as government entities,[87] nevertheless, one problem with this approach is that it creates the illusion that such servitudes should not exist as a matter of ordinary private law, that they should only be allowed when the public has a special interest. Thus Gray and Gray say that with the creation of statutory easements, 'the requirement of a dominant estate is abrogated to further certain public or community-related purposes'.[88] According to Christian Atias, while 'the will of the proprietors . . . exercises a certain influence' on ordinary servitudes, *servitudes de l'utilité publique* are founded 'on the public interest' and therefore 'resist and restrain their will'.[89] If our approach is correct, that claim is misleading. The question to be asked is ultimately the same whether or not the servitude benefits the owner of particular land. The difference is that when it does not do so, the question will sometimes be answered differently. In any case, there is nothing more public about a gas line than a ski lift except that more people use the gas line, and would suffer greater hardship if they could not. Those differences do not justify refusing to enforce servitudes in favor of the operator of the ski lift.

In France, the idea that such servitudes are created for public purposes, unlike the servitudes of private law, has had the ill consequence that, in principle, the burdened property owner cannot demand compensation unless the statute or administrative act in question so provides. He does not need to do so when a *servitude de l'utilité publique* is established with his consent since he can refuse to assent unless he is compensated.[90] But in most cases, the servitude is imposed on his land whether he agrees or not.[91] Since 1857, French courts have held that he has no right to be compensated.[92] One source of confusion is that many different restrictions on the rights of a landowner count as *servitudes de l'utilité publique*. French courts and jurists do not distinguish among them when they ask whether the landowner should be compensated. Some of these restrictions are what an American jurist would call 'regulations' as distinguished from 'takings': for example, limits imposed for reasons of aesthetics or public health on what the landowner can build.[93] It would be odd if he could demand compensation for these. Other *servitudes de l'utilité publique* allow the kind of interferences with a landowner which, if done without statutory authority, common lawyers would call nuisances, and the French would call *troubles de voisinage*. In many legal systems,

---

owns no more land, and the restrictions he imposes would seem to be for the benefit of no land at all. Here the servitude is really established for the benefit of one who owns land. Quite sensibly, both the English and French have allowed substance to prevail over form so that the owners of parcels previously conveyed can enforce the restrictions against those who bought subsequently. Gray and Gray, *Land Law*, 624, 1172–8; Fréjaville, note to Cour d'appel, Amiens, 1 July 1952, D. 1953.J.153, at 154.

[85] In addition, 'numerous bodies have been given specific authority to enforce restrictive covenants in gross' (Gray and Gray, *Land Law*, 624).

[86] England: Gray and Gray, *Land Law*, 461; France: Terré and Simler, *Les Biens*, no. 332.

[87] England: Gray and Gray, *Land Law*, 461; France: Terré and Simler, *Les Biens*, no. 333.

[88] Gray and Gray, *Land Law*, 461.   [89] Atias, *Les Biens*, no. 170.

[90] Terré and Simler, *Les Biens*, no. 335.   [91] ibid. no. 334.

[92] Conseil d'Etat, 5 Feb. 1857, D. 1857.III.74.   [93] Terré and Simler, *Les Biens*, no. 329.

rightly or wrongly, whether a landowner should be compensated in such cases is thought to be problematic. Some French jurists have argued that owners should not be compensated for the burden of a *servitude de l'utilité publique* because they sometimes benefit without paying from the presence of public works in their neighborhood; therefore they should not be compensated when the public works interfere with them.[94] That argument, valid or not, addresses cases in which the interference is nuisance-like: for example, the servitude means that the landowner must put up with more noise or smoke. That situation seems different from one in which the servitude allows another person to build poles or installations to support power lines, ski lifts, or cable cars. French courts must have seen intuitively that there is a difference. They have made an exception to the general rule by requiring compensation when the servitude is for power lines.[95] If such an exception is warranted, however, they should rethink the question of when, in principle, an owner can demand compensation. It is a question that cannot be answered 'yes' or 'no' when heterogenous burdens are grouped together as *servitudes de l'utilité publique*. One reason the classification is heterogeneous, and analysis is obscured, is that some servitudes are so classified simply to escape the rule that a private law servitude must benefit a specific piece of property.

Another problem with this rule it that sometimes, even though a servitude should be enforced, there is no applicable statute or ordinance. When there is not, a court has two choices: to defer to the rule and refuse to enforce the servitude, or to wriggle around it. The highest French court acted in the first way when it held, first in 1936 and again in 1984, that the operator of a ski lift could not have enforceable servitudes in the properties it crossed.[96] A 1941 statute permitted servitudes for a cable car line[97] but a ski lift was not a cable car. In 1985, the legislature solved the problem by permitting servitudes for lifts in a provision of a statute concerning the protection and development of mountains.[98] As this example shows, a disadvantage of recognizing such servitudes only when provided by statute is that one must wait for the legislature to act. Another is that the legislature cannot envision every situation in which a servitude should be permitted. Suppose the lift is not on a mountain but across a park or zoo or valley?

The other alternative would be to twist the rule that the servitude must benefit some parcel of land. If any land is owned by the benefitted party, a court could claim that the servitude was established for the benefit of that land. One English court has said that the statutory easement of a utility company really does satisfy common law requirements because they are for the benefit of whatever land the utility company owns outright plus its 'incorporeal hereditaments', that is, its similar rights to run its lines over other lands.[99] If courts took that approach, they would not need a statute. But if courts believe such servitudes should be enforced, they should not need to twist the rules by making an argument that English scholars have rightly called disingenuous.[100] As Michael Sturley has said, a company that wants rights over a landing pad for its

---

[94] ibid. no. 335. [95] Cass. civ., 6 Jan. 1930, S. 1930.1.337; Cass. req., 3 June 1935, S. 1935.1.246.
[96] Cass. civ., 30 June 1936, D.P. 1938.1.65; Cass. civ., 3e ch. civ., 12 Dec. 1984, JCP. 1985.II.20411.
[97] Law of 8 July 1941. [98] Law of 9 Jan. 1985, art. L. 145-1–L. 145.3, Code de l'urbanisme.
[99] Re Salvin's Indenture [1938] 2 All Eng Rep 498, 506. [100] Gray and Gray, *Land Law*, 461 n. 15.

helicopter shuttle should not have to claim that these rights are for the benefit of its West End office.[101]

In any event, whether such servitudes are enforced by enacting statutes or by disingenuous argument, the fact that the French and English want to enforce them shows that it cannot be right in principle to do so only when they benefit particular land. The 'yes' or 'no' rule covers too much ground.

II. An Explanation Based on Commutative Justice

We have seen, then, that we can make sense even of the differences among legal systems by a fairly simple principle. The parties are willing to create a servitude when the advantage to the party who benefits exceeds the cost and inconvenience to the party who is burdened. What matters in principle is whether this relationship is likely to persist. If it is likely to do so, the law should recognize the arrangement as a servitude. Otherwise, the successors of the present owners will have to remake it. If the relationship is unlikely to persist, the law should not do so. If it did, the successors would have to unmake it.

We will now consider why this principle matters, why it is better to limit the occasions on which the successors of the present owners may remake or unmake the arrangement. Depoorter and Parisi have given an economic explanation.[102] If the arrangement must be remade, the party to be burdened can demand compensation. If it must be unmade, the party benefitted can do so. Bargaining over his compensation entails transactions costs. Moreover, the parties may fail to agree, particularly if there are several of them, and so fail to arrive at a mutually desirable result. In either case, the result is economically inefficient.

I find that explanation plausible only in the case of neighborhood restrictions covering many parcels of land such as those in housing developments. There, indeed, imposing or abrogating them requires the consent of so many people that the difficulties of bargaining with everyone and of going forward if anyone refuses to consent may be formidable. They are analogous to the difficulties presented by acquiring a large number of contiguous parcels to build a factory or office building. The result is often inefficient. Nevertheless, the law of servitudes is far more ancient than neighborhood restrictions and applies to many other arrangements as well. In the classic case in which there is one burdened parcel and one benefitted parcel or person, it is hard to see why the transactions costs or the chances of failing to reach agreement would be larger than for any other voluntary transaction. The parties are often bargaining under conditions of bilateral monopoly: each party can only deal with the other to get what he wants. Depoorter, Parisi, and other members of the law and economics movement[103] believe that under these conditions, bargaining will cost more and is more likely to fail. I don't see why, except that one party may waste time before giving in to try to convince the other of his determination to get a better bargain. It is hard to believe

[101] Sturley, 'Easements in Gross', 567–8.
[102] Depoorter and Parisi, 'Fragmentation of Property Rights'.
[103] e.g. Richard A. Posner, *Economic Analysis of Law* (6th edn., NY, 2003), 120.

that since the time of the ancient Romans the law of servitudes has been aimed at preventing the parties from wasting their time.

A better explanation is in terms of commutative justice. In a situation of bilateral monopoly, a party may demand more for assuming a burden or relinquishing a benefit than the amount by which he will be inconvenienced or benefitted. It is unfair of him to do so. Even if he does not, if such an arrangement has to be remade or unmade because one of the parcels has changed owners, the change in ownership will cause a chance gain for one party or a chance loss for the other. That is also unfair. As we have seen, according to Aristotle, distributive justice ensures that each citizen has a fair share of resources such as wealth or honor. Commutative justice preserves the share of each. Here I will claim that this concept can explain why hold-ups and chance gains and loss should be prevented where possible, and consequently why the law of servitudes should prevent them when it can.

A. Hold-ups

One way in which a rule could lead to a random change in the distribution of resources is by permitting a hold-up. A hold-up happens when one party exploits a bilateral monopoly to extract a higher price for resources than he otherwise could. As we have noted, writers in the Aristotelian tradition believed that even though changes in prices altered a person's share of wealth, these changes often had to be tolerated because prices must change to reflect need, scarcity, and cost.[104] They identified the fair price with the competitive market price which did reflect these factors.[105] Modern economics gives us a clearer picture of what would happen if prices were not allowed to change in response to supply and demand. There would be shortages of goods or queues of would-be buyers. The change in prices both provides an incentive to produce more goods and allocates goods among buyers according to their willingness to pay rather than their place in line. In a hold-up, however, a party is able to charge more simply because he is the only seller. An example would be a person who owns the only strip of land along a river through which a mine can sink a pipe to get the water it needs to operate. The high price the landowner demands neither encourages the production of more such strips of land nor allocates the right to lay a pipe among potential buyers. There is only one strip, and one mining company that wants this right. The gain the landowner is seeking need not be tolerated for the reasons that increases in market prices are tolerated. Absent any other justification, it should not be. And in fact, statutes in some American states allow mine owners, homeowners or farmers to condemn the right to lay pipes or utility lines across adjoining property.[106] Such statutes were upheld by the United States Supreme Court even in the era when it regarded private property rights as sacrosanct.[107]

---

[104] Chapter 1 I.   [105] Chapter 16 I A 1.

[106] John P. Dwyer and Peter S. Menell, *Property Law and Policy: A Comparative Institutional Perspective* (Westbury, NY, 1998), 739.

[107] *Clark* v. *Nash*, 198 US 361 (1905) (owner of farm can condemn right of way for irrigation ditch); *Strickley* v. *Highland Boy Gold Mining Co.*, 200 US 527 (1906) (mine owner can condemn right of way for aerial bucket line).

If the parties have to remake a servitude when land is resold, the party who is to re-assume a burden can hold the other up by demanding more than the amount necessary to compensate him for doing so. If the parties have to unmake it, the party who is to give up the benefit can hold the other up by demanding more than the amount necessary to compensate him for its loss. The rule that will prevent the largest number of hold-ups is one that will allow burdens and benefits to pass as servitudes only when it is more likely that otherwise, the new owners will find it advantageous to remake them.

Of course, a hold-up can also occur when a servitude is first created. Whenever the advantage to the party who will be benefitted exceeds the cost or inconvenience to the party to be burdened, the latter may demand a share of the benefit in excess of his cost or inconvenience in return for his assent. Most of the time, the law has to tolerate this behavior. The alternative would be to cause a forced sale. There would then be a risk of under-compensating a property owner for the burden he assumes. This danger does not arise in the case of servitudes intended to pass with the land. The party bearing a burden has already been compensated. Either he was compensated by the benefitting party when the servitude was first established, or he was compensated by receiving a lower price for the land if he was a later purchaser.

Nevertheless, in extreme cases when servitudes are first established different legal systems have been willing, in effect, to compel a forced sale and thus to prevent a hold-up. As mentioned, in dry parts of the United States, statutes were enacted, and upheld as constitutional, which allowed mine owners to lay pipes across adjoining property to obtain the water necessary to work them. In French, German, and Swiss law, a person whose property lacks access to public roads[108] can demand a right of way for them if he pays compensation. In England and the United States, when property is land-locked, a court will 'imply' an 'easement by necessity' across property from which the landlocked parcel was severed.[109] If a person accidentally builds so as to encroach on adjoining land, German and Swiss law allows him to stay provided he compensates the other party.[110] When the encroachment is small, American courts have reached similar results by awarding damages rather than issuing an injunction.[111] French courts have refused to help in such situations[112] but they have been criticized for failing to do so.[113]

---

[108] *Code civil*, art. 682; BGB, § 917; ZGB, art. 694. One French case allowed a right of way for aerial cable cars. Cass. civ., 24 Feb. 1930, DP 1932.1.9. Another French case did so for connections to public utilities, a case provided for expressly by the Swiss Civil Code (ZGB, art. 691.) Cass. civ., 22 Nov. 1937, DP 1938.1.62.

[109] Gray and Gray, *Land Law*, 496–8; Powell and Wolf, *Real Property*, § 34.07. In New Zealand, a right of way is provided for by statute if compensation is paid. Property Law Act 1952, s 129B. It is not clear in England whether a right of passage will be applied to connect with public utilities. Gray and Gray, *Land Law*, 499.

[110] BGB, § 912 (requiring that he must not have done so intentionally or by gross negligence); ZGB, art. 674(3) (requiring that he act in good faith and that the other party could have known he was building across the boundary). [111] *McKean* v. *Alliance Land Co.*, 253 P 134 (Cal 1927).

[112] Cass. civ., 3e ch. civ., 3 Mar. 1981, Gaz. Pal. 1981.Pan.270.

[113] Terré and Simler, *Les Biens*, no. 249.

B. Chance Gains and Losses

When a servitude must be remade, even absent a hold-up, the share of resources a person commands will have changed by chance. As we have noted, some chance gains and losses have to be tolerated.[114] It will often not be feasible to try to distinguish which of them result from chance and which result from investment. Indeed, a gain is often the result of both: an investment is made on the chance of a gain, in which case the gain is not a pure windfall. Absent a justification, however, if preserving the existing distribution where possible is a worthwhile goal, chance gains and losses should be prevented.

In speaking of chance gains and losses, I mean a loss or gain that was not certain to occur when the servitude was established or which was not certain to occur when it did. If it had been certain to occur when it did, each party would simply be receiving what he paid or was paid for. A party who suffers a predictable loss at a predictable moment of time will simply have paid less, like a person who leases property for one year, knowing with certainty that he will lose the right to possession at the end of that period. He did not suffer a chance loss. Nor did he make a chance gain when he was allowed to keep possession until the year ended.

If the loss or gain was unexpected, it may have been completely unforeseen, in which case it will not have been reflected in the compensation paid to assume the burden of the servitude. Or it may have been partially unforeseen, and then one party will have received less or more compensation reflecting the uncertainty.

If the law must permit a chance loss or gain, the worst rule is one in which the magnitude and likelihood of the loss is completely unforeseen and therefore will not be reflected in the compensation at all. A better rule permits a chance loss or gain when the parties can adjust the compensation to reflect the risk. The best rule would prevent the chance gain or loss entirely, or minimize the instances in which such gains or losses will occur.

Suppose that the law did not recognize a servitude when the successors of the present owners will regard the burden imposed on the one as less costly or inconvenient than the advantage that accrues to the other, and therefore are likely to remake the arrangement if the burdens and benefits do not pass with the land. One party will bring the arrangement to an end by selling his parcel. His successor will not experience a chance gain or loss. He will buy at a price that reflects the absence of a servitude. But the other party will have a chance gain if the burden or benefit to him lasted a longer or shorter time than was expected or a chance loss if they lasted a shorter or a longer time. I don't believe the converse is true: that there will be chance gains and losses if the agreement must be unmade because the burden to one party is greater than the benefit to the other. In that event, the successors of those who made the arrangement will buy in at a price that reflects the need to unmake it. But, as already described, one party will still be able to hold the other up.

---

[114] Chapter 1 I.

III. Conclusion

For all their variety, then, the rules governing servitudes in civil and common law systems can be explained by a fairly simple principle. Servitudes should be enforced when, if they were not, the successors of the current landowners would be likely to remake them. They should not be enforced when, if they were, the successors would be likely to unmake them. That way the law can prevent hold-ups and chance gains and losses. It is good to prevent them if, as Aristotle thought, as a matter of commutative justice, the current distribution of resources should be protected against random changes.

6

Rights Annexed to the Use of Property: The Case of Water Rights

Previous chapters discussed a person's rights to use his property and how these rights may be privately modified. Sometimes, however, a person makes a claim to use resources which he does not own and which the owner of these resources did not grant him, if, indeed, they have a private owner. The rules that govern such situations will be affected by the kind of resources in question. Nevertheless, we can see the underlying principles that should govern the rights to such resources by examining a paradigm case: that of water rights.

In discussing nuisance, *troubles de voisinage* and *Immissionenrecht*, we saw that different legal systems applied similar rules. We identified a principle that could explain them. In discussing servitudes, we saw that different systems applied different rules. Nevertheless, we could identify a principle that could explain the differences. In discussing water rights, we will have to proceed differently. In some legal systems, it is not clear how water rights are actually assigned because allocation is committed to an administrative authority. In other legal systems, however—notably, the common law, France and countries that have been influenced by French law such as Italy—we must admit that the rules that are supposed to govern water rights are at variance with the principles which, according to our approach, should govern. In fact, the one legal system with rules our principles can easily explain is not modern. It is the *ius commune*, the Roman law of medieval Europe.

We will begin by describing the rules of the *ius commune*. We will then see that even though writers in the Aristotelian tradition did not discuss this problem, the rules of the *ius commune* can be explained by the principles of commutative justice. We will then confront the question of why the rules of leading modern legal systems are different. We will argue that the difference was due to an error produced by an historical accident.

I. The *Ius Commune*

Roman law provided a rule governing the right to water for irrigation. It said nothing about the right to water for other uses such as to operate mills. As we will see in this section, the medieval jurists, notably the most famous of them, Bartolus of Saxoferrato, saw that the rules to govern water for mills should be different. In the next section, we will see why they were right.

A rescript of the Emperors Antonius Augustus and Verus Augustus provided 'that water from a public river for irrigating fields should be divided according to possession (*pro modo possessionis*)...',[1] meaning, one presumes, in proportion to acreage. That was the interpretation of Bartolus. He said that the text meant water 'is to be divided according to size (*secundum mensuram*)'.[2]

There were no Roman texts dealing with diversion of water for mills. An interdict lay against doing anything to a public river 'which makes the water to flow otherwise than it did in the previous summer' so as to injure neighboring owners.[3] But 'flow otherwise' was interpreted to 'refer, not to the quantity of water flowing but... to the manner and direction of its current'. One could not make the water 'deeper or narrower and hence swifter to the inconvenience of those nearby'.[4] Consequently, as Alan Watson noted, this interdict was not granted against one who diverted water but against one who changed the flow and so injured another's property.[5]

Consequently, Bartolus had to improvise when he considered whether 'if I have a mill below and others make a mill above so that they impede me, may they do this?' It was an old question, he said, which had been argued by 'Franciscus Accursius and other doctors of Bologna', then the center for legal studies. 'They all inclined to the view' that 'if, indeed, the river was public, as is every river that flows perpetually[6]... [and] the first person had his mill lawfully... the second person cannot act or take away from him the advantage that he lawfully began [to derive] from what is public'.[7]

Bartolus agreed and said that the result should be the same if the second person builds below the first mill and backs up the water so as to impede its operation.[8] He described the water as 'public' and quoted a text which said 'whenever anything is done in a public place, it should be permitted on condition that it causes no injury to anyone'.[9] He compared the situation to an encounter between carts on a public road: the first one to enter prevails. It was like two people who want to build on a strip of beach where anyone was entitled to build: the first to begin building prevails.[10]

Thus there was one rule for farmers irrigating their lands, and a different one for those who built mills. As we will see, on our principles, that was the right result.

II. How Water Rights Should be Assigned in Theory

As we have seen, according to Aristotle, distributive justice ensures that each citizen has a fair share of resources such as wealth or honor. Commutative justice preserves the share of each. Here, an appeal to principles of commutative justice might seem to lead in a circle. It would seem that to decide who is being deprived of resources, we must know to whom those resources belong. But here the very question is to whom

---

[1] Dig. 8.3.17.

[2] Bartolus de Saxoferrato, *Commentaria corpus iuris civilis* (Venice, 1615), to Dig. 8.3.17.

[3] Dig. 43.13.1.pr.   [4] Dig. 43.13.1.3.

[5] Alan Watson, 'The Transformation of American Property Law: A Comparative Law Approach', *Ga. L. Rev.* 24 (1990), 163 at 175.   [6] Citing Dig. 43.12.1.3.

[7] *Commentaria* to Dig. 43.12.2 [vulg. 11.2], no. 2.   [8] ibid. no. 8.

[9] Dig. 43.8.2.10.   [10] *Commentaria* to Dig. 43.12.2 [vulg. 11.2], no. 10.

the water belongs. Nevertheless, as we will see, from the standpoint of commutative justice, some rules for initially assigning such rights are better than others. Some rules make it less likely that the distribution of wealth will be changed by a chance event thereafter.

Depending on how water rights are assigned, the distribution of wealth may be changed by chance losses and gains and by hold-ups, all of which were mentioned in discussing servitudes.[11]

Chance losses and gains may be either forfeitures or windfalls. A forfeiture is the unexpected loss of a right, or of the enjoyment of a right, for which a person has paid. By unexpected, I mean that the loss was not certain to occur at the time he paid. If it was certain, then he simply received what he paid for. He merely paid less, like a person who leased property for one year, knowing with certainty that he would lose the right to possession at the end of that time. He did not suffer a random loss. If the loss was unexpected, it may have been completely unforeseen, in which case it will not have been reflected in the price he paid for the right in question. Or it may have been partially unforeseen, and then he will have paid a lower price which reflects the uncertainty.

If one must permit a forfeiture, the worst rule, from the standpoint of commutative justice, is one in which the magnitude and likelihood of the loss are completely unforeseen and therefore will not be reflected in the price that is paid for the right that may be lost. A better rule permits a forfeiture when the price discounts for the risk. But the best rule would be one that avoids or minimizes the random loss rather than one that merely allows it to be taken into account in advance.

A second way in which a rule could lead to a random change in the distribution of wealth is by permitting a windfall. A windfall is a gain that is the result of chance. As we have already noted, some chance gains have to be tolerated.[12] One purpose of establishing private property is to reward work and care or other investment. It will often not be feasible to try to distinguish gains which result from chance from those that result from investment. Indeed, a gain is often the result of both: an investment is made on the chance of a gain, in which case the gain is not a pure windfall. Moreover, another object of recognizing property rights is to prevent quarrels. One can imagine circumstances in which allowing a person to own an object he has come upon by chance would best prevent them. Absent a justification, however, a rule should not permit a windfall. It would be wrong to grant the right to all the water in a river to whoever was lucky enough to be the first to settle on its banks.

A third way in which a rule could lead to a random change in the distribution of wealth is by permitting a hold-up. As noted earlier, a hold-up occurs when one party exploits a bilateral monopoly to extract a higher price for resources than he otherwise could. As we have seen, writers in the Aristotelian tradition believed that even though changes in prices altered a person's share of wealth, these changes often had to be tolerated because prices must change to reflect need, scarcity and cost.[13] In a hold-up, however, a party is able to charge more simply because he is the only seller.

As between the two parties to the transaction, a hold-up may or may not be a windfall for the party who gains or a forfeiture for the party who loses. It is not a windfall if the

[11] Chapter 5 II. [12] Chapter 1 I. [13] ibid.

party who gains paid extra for resources in the expectation that he could hold someone up. It is not a forfeiture if the victim paid less.

These considerations suggest a first principle for allocating water rights: if the needs of those competing for water are known, rights to use water should be assigned to those most likely to place the highest value on these rights. That sounds like a rule based on economic efficiency, and it may well be efficient because it avoids the costs that would otherwise be incurred in reselling the rights in question to those who value them more. But, as we can now see, it is also a rule grounded in commutative justice because it best avoids windfalls and hold-ups. Suppose the law assigns water rights to a person who is likely to place a lower value on them than others. For the sake of concreteness, imagine that he has been assigned these rights because he owns land by a river, and that they extend beyond the amount of water he is likely to use himself. One possibility is that he did not pay an extra amount for the land that brings with it these rights. In that case he has received a windfall as in the example earlier in which the right to all the water in a river is assigned to the first person who happens to settle on its banks. The other possibility is that he has paid extra for the right to use water which he does not expect to use himself. The only reason he would do so is to resell his water rights at a profit to others. In that case, presumably, he hopes that he will be able to charge them more than he paid himself because he expects to have the advantages of a bilateral monopoly. They will have to deal with him because there are few other people from whom they can buy water. In that case, he is making his profit by a hold-up.

As an illustration, suppose that farmers own plots of land of different sizes but comparable fertility along a river. They all use the water for irrigation, and a given amount of water improves the yield per acre by the same amount on each farmer's land. This improvement follows the law of diminishing returns so that each extra gallon produces less of an improvement than the previous one. Still, there is not enough water for all the farmers to use as much as they would wish. In this situation, the rule that allots each farmer an amount of water proportional to his acreage will assign water rights to the person most likely to place the highest value on them. If any farmer receives more than that amount of water, the extra would be worth more to the other farmers who have less. The farmer with more water would profit by selling it to them. If he did not pay a higher price for his land originally on account of the extra water, he receives a windfall. If he did, very likely, he paid the higher price only because he could resell the water to others at a price that reflects difficulties they would have buying it elsewhere. He is profiting from a hold-up.

This argument, it should be noted, makes no assumptions about whether the amount of water in the river is the same every year or whether it fluctuates. Each year, allotting each farmer an amount proportional to his acreage will assign the water to the person who puts the highest value on it, which is desirable for the reasons just given.

We have been supposing that the relative needs of those competing for water are known initially. If they are not, we need a different rule. A rule that assigns water to the person who later proves to need it the most will lead to forfeitures. Suppose that, as in the case just described, farmers are using water for irrigation but later a mine unexpectedly opens nearby. Or suppose that one person builds a mill, and later someone else unexpectedly wants to build another mill which will hamper the operations of the first. The latecomers may place a higher value on the right to use the water than those who were there earlier. But the farmers or the first builder will suffer a forfeiture if the right to use the water is assigned to the latecomers. If the forfeiture was not entirely unexpected, the price they paid for their land will have been discounted to reflect the chance at the time they purchased that a forfeiture will occur. But as we have seen, it would be better if they were not exposed to a chance of loss at all. As before, it does not matter to the argument whether the amount of water is the same every year or fluctuates. As long as there is not enough water for all, fluctuation merely affects the amount of the forfeiture.

To prevent the forfeiture, the right to the water should be assigned to the prior user. The problem then is to prevent him from holding up the latecomer by charging a price that reflects, not his own loss, but the other's gain. The best solution would be to force him to sell the right to the latecomer at a price which does reflect his own loss. Equivalently, he could be allowed to recover damages but not to enjoin the latecomer.

We can see, then, that we need two different rules.[14] When the relative value that people will place on water in the future is known at the time they buy their land, then each should have the right to use an amount of water that is proportional to its value to them. They should share, whether the same amount of water is available each year or whether scarcity alternates with abundance. When it is uncertain who will value the water most, the right should be assigned to the first to use the water. If the latecomer values the water more, he should pay for it. That is so, at least, when it is feasible to require one to sell this right to latecomers for an amount that reflects one's loss.

Most real world situations in which farmers are competing for water for irrigation probably resemble our first example. Most situations in which a latecomer puts water to an industrial use probably resemble our examples of the mine and the mill. To the extent that is so, it would make sense to have a rule that apportions water in proportion to use for irrigation and a prior appropriation rule for industrial uses such as mills. As we have seen, those were the rules of the *ius commune*.

We can also see why, in a system of apportionment, it makes sense that those with land along a watercourse have the right to use the water as contrasted with a prior appropriation system, in which the first user is protected independently of what he owns. We saw in our example of the farmers that what should matter is whether the needs of those competing for water are known in advance when each person acquires his rights. Assigning water rights only to those with land along the watercourse may approximate this requirement. The needs of those along the watercourse will be most easily known. If someone at a distance were to purchase access rights and divert water, he would most likely be an unexpected latecomer whose needs were not foreseen. He would be like the mine owner or the second mill builder. Of course, if he had been diverting water from the beginning, his needs might have been as predictable as those of the other farmers. But that might be the exceptional case. If one wanted a simple rule to delineate those whose needs were most likely to be known in advance, it might be the rule that one must own land along the bank.

---

[14] In these two situations. Another situation, and one that needs a still different rule, is when an upstreamer is fouling the water. That situation is like the ones discussed in the Chapter 5.

It should be stressed, however, that these rules would only give the right results to the extent that diversions of water for irrigation or industrial uses such as mills resemble our examples. They might not. Many western American states rejected riparian rights doctrine and adopted a rule of prior appropriation. That rule was seen to be more suitable not only for mines but for irrigation. Under their circumstances, the situation of the irrigators may have been less like that of the farmers in our example and more like that of the mine or mills. In the west, the farmers and ranchers were often not living side by side along the banks of a river. The water had to be brought down from the mountains to a dry plain through artificially constructed channels built by water companies.[15] The members of agricultural communities on the plains shared the water among themselves like the farmers in our example. But, under the rule of prior appropriation, the water company which first built such a channel and diverted water had the right to divert the same amount every year. That is as it should be because of the uncertainty, when a first channel is built, whether a second will be built later on and what needs it will serve. A prior appropriation rule makes sense even though the water is used for irrigation.

Conversely, two mills might have stood near each other time out of mind, gradually but predictably expanding their size until their operations interfered with each other. It would then make sense to make them share the water according to their needs like the farmers in the first example.

III. Water Rights in Modern Legal Systems

As mentioned earlier, some modern legal systems have adopted permitting systems which make it difficult to tell to what extent the allocation of water rights corresponds to the principles just described. For example, in Germany water use is governed by a permit system established by statute. In Germany, the permit (*Bewilligung*)[16] entitles a person to use a certain amount of water for a certain purpose.[17] A permit is not necessary if the water can be used without an essential reduction of the flow.[18] If the grant of a permit will adversely affect the right of another, and there is no way to avoid the adverse effect, then the permit can still be granted 'on the grounds of the general welfare' but the person who loses his right to water must be compensated.[19] The federal statute does not say who is to make compensation, but the laws of many German federal states provide that it is the person benefitted.[20] The statutes of most

[15] Joseph L. Sax, Barton H. Thompson, Jr., John D. Leshy, and Robert H. Abrams, *Legal Control of Water Resources: Cases and Materials* (3rd edn., St Paul, Minn., 2000), 596–8. James B. Wadley, 'The Law of Water', in Richard R. Powell and Michael Allan Wolf, *Powell on Real Property* (New York, 2001), § 65.07[2] mentions that one reason western states adopted prior appropriation systems was that 'the actual place of use was generally remote from the source of supply'.

[16] Gesetz zur Ordnung des Wasserhaushalts in der Fassung der Bekanntmachung vom 12. November 1996 (BGBl. I S. 1696) (*Wasserhaushaltsgesetz* or WHG). § 2. Alternatively, he can obtain 'permission' to use the water (*Erlaubnis*) but then his use is less completely protected.   [17] ibid. § 8(1).

[18] ibid. § 24(1).   [19] ibid. § 8(3).

[20] Paul Gieseke, Werner Wiedemann, and Manfred Czychowski, *Wasserhaushaltsgesetz Kommentar* (6th edn., 1992), to § 20, no. 12.

German federal states also provide that once a permit has been granted, the right to use water is to be protected in the same way as a property right under the German Civil Code.[21] Consequently, a person who interferes with such a right will be ordered to desist and be held liable for damages in tort.[22] In the case of ground water, a permit is not necessary when it is used for domestic purposes, farming or livestock.[23] There is no comparable provision for water from lakes, rivers, or streams. So, although the statute reaches the right result in cases like our examples of the mine and the mill, it is hard to say how it would handle our example of the farmers.

There are other modern legal systems, however, in which the problem is not simply that we cannot tell to what extent the rules allocate water rights in accordance with the principles we have just described. They have adopted rules which do not give the right results if our analysis is correct. The most notable examples are the common law and French law since the 19th century and legal systems French law has influenced such as that of Italy. Consequently, we must ask why they adopted such rules and how the rules have been applied. We have stressed that it is usually easier for jurists or judges to see that a result is appropriate than to explain why.[24] The fact that these modern systems have adopted rules at variance with our approach is prima facie evidence that our approach is wrong.

We will see, however, that these rules were not adopted because the results they produced seemed right in practice. In common law jurisdictions, they were adopted by jurists who focused their attention, not on practical results, but on a theoretical dispute over what principles should matter. The debate was typical of the conceptual approach of the time, and begged the ultimate question to be answered. In France, similar rules were adopted but almost without deliberation. Without discussion of their merits, the drafters of the French Civil Code took these rules, out of context, from the works of treatise writers on whom they habitually relied. Moreover, in both common law jurisdictions and those influenced by French law, courts and legislatures have modified the results in practice so that they accord more closely with the principles we have described. Thus in neither case were the rules adopted by reaching results which seemed sensible in practice. They were adopted for other reasons, and in order to reach more sensible results, courts and legislatures have been moving away from them.

A. The Common Law

1. The traditional rules

Before the 19th century, English law did not have a clear rule governing a person's right to divert water. His prior use affected his rights but it is not clear how and to what extent. In *Luttrel's Case* in 1600, the plaintiff pleaded that he had a prescriptive right: his use of the water for his mills was so old that memory ran not to the contrary. The court rejected the defendant's argument that this right had been extinguished when the plaintiff replaced his fulling mills with mills to grind grain.[25] But it would be

---

[21] ibid. to § 8, no. 7.   [22] ibid. no. 8.   [23] WHG, § 33(1).   [24] Chapter 21.
[25] *Luttrel's Case*, 4 Coke 86a, 76 ER 1065 (KB 1600).

hasty to conclude that plaintiff would have lost absent a prescriptive right.[26] The court was not deciding such a case. The plaintiff in *Luttrel's Case* may not have known what the court would do, and therefore pled his prescriptive right in order to put his best foot forward. The court did not concern itself with what do on other facts.

Sometimes plaintiffs won without pleading a prescriptive right or that memory runs not to the contrary. They won by pleading that they had a mill *ab antiquo*,[27] or the water's former course was *antiquus*[28] or it then flowed 'customarily and as it ought' (*consuevisset et debuisset*).[29] Some judges said such words amount to a claim of use from 'time immemorial',[30] and some said that they did not.[31] In any event, the plaintiff won without pleading or proving that his mill had stood immemorially or any particular length of time. The jury was left to decide whether the mill was 'ancient' or the water had been flowing 'customarily and as it ought'. Carol Rose believes these expressions meant that the plaintiff's use must have 'been in place for a generation or so'.[32] She notes, however, that 'ancient' may have meant 'something akin to "former" or "earlier" '.[33] Indeed, 17th and 18th century authors used the word 'ancient' sometimes to refer to the distant past and sometimes to mean 'former'.[34] Since the final decision was up to the jury, all one can say is that the longer the mill had stood, the greater must have been the plaintiff's confidence that he would win.

Moreover, some plaintiffs won, or courts said that they might, even if their mills were newly erected. Sometimes they won alleging that the watercourse, though not the mill, was ancient, and so gained a considerable advantage, since most watercourses fit that description. But it was not clear that this allegation was necessary.[35] Indeed, in one 17th century case, the plaintiff won despite defendant's objection that he alleged neither the mill nor the watercourse to be ancient.[36] In another, he won without the defendant raising the point.[37] In yet another case, Matthew Hale said by way of dictum that one need not plead one's mill was ancient; one could win if it was newly erected.[38]

Had the law clearly been as Hale thought, then a plaintiff with an older mill would not have bothered to plead that it was 'ancient'. The plaintiffs who did so must have

---

[26] For Watson and Lauer, the case stands for that proposition. Watson, 'Transformation of American Property Law', 210; T. E. Lauer, 'The Common Law Background of the Riparian Doctrine', *Missouri L. Rev.* 28 (1963), 60 at 83–4.   [27] *Russell and Handfords Case*, 1 Leo. 273, 74 Eng Rep, 248 (KB 1583).

[28] *Richards* v. *Hill*, 5 Mod 206, 87 Eng Rep, 611 (KB 1695).

[29] Anonymous, Cro Car 449, 79 Eng Rep, 1031 (KB 1638).

[30] *Tenant* v. *Goldwin*, 2 Raym. Ld. 1089, 1094, 92 Eng Rep, 222, 225 (1705).

[31] *Palmer* v. *Keeblethwaite*, 1 Shower, KB 64, 64, 89 Eng Rep, 451, 451 (KB 1686).

[32] Carol M. Rose, *Property and Persuasion: Essays on the History, Theory, and Rhetoric of Ownership* (Boulder, Colo., 1994), 169.   [33] ibid. 169 n. 20.

[34] For examples, see *Oxford English Dictionary* (Oxford, 1971), v. 'ancient' A I 1, A I 2.

[35] Compare *Le Countee de Rutland* v. *Bowles*, Palm 290, 81 ER 1087 (KB 1622), where the court did not seem to attach importance to that allegation, with *Keeblethwait* v. *Palmes*, Comb 9, 90 Eng Rep, 311 (KB 1686), where the point was stressed by counsel, and it is not clear what the court thought.

[36] *Sands* v. *Trefuses*, Cro Car 575, 79 Eng Rep, 1094 (KB 1639).

[37] *Glyn* v. *Nichols*, Comb 44, 90 Eng Rep, 333 (KB 1687).

[38] *Cox* v. *Matthew*, 1 Vent 237 (KB 1673). Hale said the result would be different if the defendant 'used to turn the stream as he saw cause'. It is hard to read that passage as Maass and Zobel do, to mean that priority alone doesn't matter. Arthur Maass and Hiller B. Zobel, 'Anglo-American Water Law: Who Appropriated the Riparian Doctrine?' in C. J. Friedrich and S. E. Harris, *Public Policy: A Yearbook of the Graduate School of Public Administration, Harvard University* 10 (1960), 109 at 127.

thought the law was not so clear. Again, they were putting their best foot forward. Plaintiffs with younger mills must have been facing a risk. They could plead their mill was 'ancient' and hope the jury would agree, or not do so, and hope that the court would think it did not matter.[39]

In the 18th century, Blackstone said that the rule in England was simply one of priority: 'If a stream be unoccupied, I may erect a mill thereon, and detain the water; yet not so as to injure my neighbour's prior mill, or his meadow: for he hath by the first occupancy acquired a property in the current'.[40] He oversimplified. While that formulation was consistent with the language of some of the decided cases, it ignored the uncertainty of the case law.

2. Nineteenth century innovation

Blackstone innovated in another way as well. As Rose notes, it was an innovation in English law to explain why priority mattered in terms of 'occupancy', the idea that whoever first appropriated something had a right to it.[41] Indeed, it was an innovation in Anglo-American law to try to explain water rights by general principles.

Courts and scholars continued the search for principles in the 19th century. But Blackstone's rule of priority came into competition with another principle and lost. The other one was expressed by Ellenborough in 1805 in *Bealey* v. *Shaw*.[42] The plaintiff, who had built his mills in 1787, prevailed over the upstream proprietor who had enlarged his own in 1791. Lawrence, Le Blanc, and the judge below thought he should win because of priority: a person could appropriate water not previously appropriated, and any water left over could then be appropriated by someone else.[43] But Ellenborough thought that 'independent of any particular enjoyment used to be had by another, every man has a right to have the advantage of a flow of water on his own land without diminution or alteration'. The prior 'occupation of another' mattered only if it created a prescriptive right.[44] In 1818 in *Saunders* v. *Newman*,[45] he reiterated this view while Holroyd took the same position as Lawrence and Le Blanc.

For a while there was a duel. The view that the use of water belonged to whomever first appropriated it was taken by Holroyd and Bayley in 1824,[46] and Tindal in 1831.[47] Bayley and Tindal explained that until appropriated, it was *publici iuris*—it belonged to the public.[48] But Ellenborough's view prevailed. It was adopted by Leach

---

[39] Thus, unlike Lauer, I don't think one can describe the case law in terms of direction and development. Lauer, 'Common Law Background', 81–96.

[40] William Blackstone, *Commentaries on the Laws of England* 2 (London, 1766), 403.

[41] Rose, *Property and Persuasion*, 173.   [42] 6 East 207, 102 Eng Rep, 1266 (KB 1805).

[43] 6 East at 211, 102 Eng Rep, at 1268 (trial judge); 6 East. at 217–18, 102 Eng Rep, at 1270 (Lawrence); 6 East at 218, 102 Eng Rep, at 1270 (Le Blanc). Maass and Zobel, 'Anglo-American Water Law', 131, take them to mean that the defendant had a prescriptive right to any water he had been diverting for 20 years, but they are speaking of the water he was diverting before plaintiff built, some of which had been diverted for less than 20 years.

[44] 6 East at 214–15, 102 Eng Rep, at 1269 (as he put it, the use must have 'existed for so long time as may raise the presumption of a grant').   [45] 1 Barn & Ald 256, 260, 106 Eng Rep, 95, 96–7 (KB 1818).

[46] *Williams* v. *Morland*, 2 B & C 910, 915, 107 Eng Rep, 620, 622 (Holroyd); 2 Barn & Cress at 913, 107 Eng Rep, at 621 (Bayley) (KB 1824).

[47] *Liggins* v. *Inge*, 7 Bing 682, 693, 131 Eng Rep, 263, 269 (CP 1831).

[48] 2 B & C at 913, 107 Eng Rep, at 621 (Bayley); 7 Bing at 693, 131 Eng Rep, at 269 (Tindal).

in 1823 in *Wright* v. *Howard*,[49] and by Denham in 1833 in *Mason* v. *Hill*[50] which followed *Wright*. *Mason* was followed in 1849 in *Wood* v. *Waud*, the court noting that the defendant could not interfere with 'the natural state of the river',[51] and in 1851 in *Embrey* v. *Owen* where Parke explained that '[t]he right to have the stream flow in its natural state without diminution or alteration is an incident to the property in the land through which it passes'.[52] In these cases, again, the question was not who should win but why. In *Bealy, Saunders, Wright, Mason*, and *Wood* the plaintiffs who prevailed were prior users.[53] In *Embrey*, the plaintiff lost because the defendant had not perceptibly diminished the flow of water.

The American path was similar. Before Ellenborough's 1805 opinion in *Bealey* v. *Shaw*, American law was unsettled although a rule of priority had been adopted in an early New Jersey case.[54] In New York, such a rule was mentioned approvingly by Judge Spencer in 1805 in *Palmer* v. *Mulligan*.[55] Nevertheless, citing Ellenborough, Judge Thompson said that plaintiff had a right to the flow of water without 'diminution or alteration' unless defendant could establish a prescriptive right.[56] Speaking for the court, he took the same view in 1818 in *Platt* v. *Johnson and Root*[57] which was followed in later New York cases.[58] That rule was adopted in Connecticut in 1818,[59] in New Hampshire in 1824,[60] in Illinois in 1842,[61] and in Vermont in 1856.[62] It was also approved by three very influential American jurists: Joseph Angell in his treatise on *Watercourses* in 1824,[63] Joseph Story in his leading opinion in a federal case, *Tyler* v.

[49] 1 Sim & St 190, 57 Eng Rep, 76 (Ch 1823).   [50] 3 Barn & Adol 304, 110 Eng Rep, 114 (KB 1833).

[51] 3 Exch 748, 773–4, 154 Eng Rep, 1047, 1057–8 (Ex 1849).

[52] 6 Exch 353, 369, 155 Eng Rep, 579, 585 (Ex 1851).

[53] Although in *Saunders*, if Ellenborough had had his way, a new trial would have been needed to establish the size of plaintiff's former mill which had burned and been rebuilt during the period of prescription. 1 Barn & Ald at 260, 106 Eng Rep, at 96–7.

[54] *Merritt* v. *Parker*, 1 NLJ 526, 532 (NJ 1795) (Kinsey, J)('the defendant by the erection of the dam had appropriated [the water] to his own use, and had acquired a property in [it]').

[55] 3 Cai R 307, 312 (it is a 'familiar maxim' that 'as plaintiff's mills were first erected' defendant cannot interfere with them; holding, nevertheless, for the defendant on the grounds that the interference was insignificant).

[56] 3 Cai R at 316 (but the other judges held for the defendant because the interference with the plaintiff's operations was not significant).

[57] 15 Johns 213 (NY 1818) (but the result was not affected as the prior downstream mill owner recovered because of the extent of the harm done to him).

[58] e.g. *Merrit* v. *Brinkerhoff and van Wagenen*, 17 Johns 306 (1820) (but the result was not affected because defendant's use was found to be excessive); *Arnold* v. *Foot*, 12 Wend 331 (NY 1834) (but the result was unaffected because prior downstream user recovered against the upstreamer who diverted the water for irrigation); *Reid* v. *Gifford*, 1 Hopk 416 (1825).

[59] *Ingraham* v. *Hutchinson*, 2 Conn (2 Day) 584, 590–1 (1818) (the result was not affected since plaintiff had acquired a prescriptive right); followed in *Twiss* v. *Baldwin*, 9 Conn (9 Day) 291 (1832) (the result was not affected since plaintiff's use was prior, and the court held for him because defendant was acting in a way that hurt the plaintiff without benefitting himself); *Buddington* v. *Bradley*, 10 Conn (10 Day) 213, 218–20 (1834) (the result was not affected because the downstream plaintiff's use was prior).

[60] *Runnels* v. *Bullen*, 2 NH 532, 537 (1824) (dicta).

[61] *Evans* v. *Merriweather*, 4 Ill (3 Scam) 492 (1842) (but the result was not affected because the downstream plaintiff's use was prior).

[62] *Snow* v. *Parsons & Parsons*, 28 Vt (2 Will) 459 (1856) (the result was not affected because the plaintiff's use was prior, and defendant's liability turned on whether he had significantly interfered with plaintiff).

[63] Joseph K. Angell, *A Treatise on the Common Law, in Relation to Watercourses* (1st edn., Boston, 1824), 37–40.

Wilkinson, in 1827,[64] and Chancellor Kent in his *Commentaries* in the third volume, published in 1828.[65] Story and Kent were then quoted by Pollock in *Wood* v. *Waud*[66] and by Parke in *Embrey* v. *Owen*.[67] As in England, the question in nearly all the American cases just mentioned was not who should win but why: for example, the victorious plaintiff was also the prior user, or the victorious defendant had a prescriptive right or was also the prior appropriator or had not significantly interfered with the plaintiff.[68]

In Massachusetts, Chief Justices Parker and Shaw fought a rearguard action in a series of cases in which upstream plaintiffs sued downstreamers who had obstructed their operations by backing up the current. Parker did so despite initial hesitation,[69] deciding against a defendant in 1821 because there was 'obstruct[ion] of a mill already existing'.[70] He did so again in 1828, because '[t]he plaintiff had a right to calculate upon the state of things as they existed when he erected his mill'.[71] Shaw took a similar view in an 1830 case[72] and defended it at length in 1844 in his leading opinion in *Carey* v. *Daniels*,[73] which ranks with Story's decision in *Tyler* v. *Wilkinson* as one of the most thoughtful American decisions on water rights of the 19th century. Perhaps he wrote with such care because in 1833, the Court of King's Bench had taken the opposite view in *Mason* v. *Hill*. Nevertheless, Shaw surrendered after the decisions in *Wood* v. *Waud* and *Embrey* v. *Owen* in 1849 and 1851. He stopped mentioning priority. He said, as the court had said in *Embrey*, that each proprietor is bound 'so to use his common right, as not essentially to prevent or interfere with an equally beneficial enjoyment of the common right, by all proprietors'.[74] In 1854, when a trial judge had told the jury that 'priority of use... could never deprive the owner... of the right to enjoy a similar use of the water', Shaw said that the judge 'rightly stated' the law.[75]

3. Explanations

a. Economic explanations

According to some historians, the change just described represented an adjustment of the law to changed economic conditions. I don't believe so. At stake, for the judges themselves, was a theoretical question about the nature of water rights, and one which

---

[64] 24 Fed Cas 472 (1827) (Case no. 14312) (the result was not affected because the defendant, who won on the basis of a prescriptive right, was also the prior appropriator).

[65] James Kent, *Commentaries on American Law* 3 (1st edn., New York, 1828), 353.

[66] 3 Ex at 768–9, 154 Eng Rep, at 1055–6.   [67] 6 Ex at 368–9, 155 Eng Rep, at 585.

[68] *Platt* was an exception: the court found against a prior downstream mill owner who was harmed by defendant's mill. One might count *Reid* v. *Gifford* as another exception. While the plaintiff who successfully asserted a prescriptive right was also a prior possessor, apparently, his case had previously been dismissed because he had not alleged such a right. 1 Hopk at 418–19.

[69] See *Colburn* v. *Richards*, 13 Mass (13 Tyng) 420 (1816) (Parker, J)(distinguishing an earlier case (*Weston* v. *Alden*, 8 Mass (8 Tyng) 136 (1811)), on the grounds that there, the plaintiff had no prescriptive right).   [70] *Hatch* v. *Dwight & Brunell*, 16 Mass (16 Tyng) 289, 296 (1821).

[71] *Sumner* v. *Tileston*, 24 Mass (7 Pick) 198, 203 (1828).

[72] *Bigelow* v. *Newell*, 27 Mass (10 Pick) 349, 357 (1830).   [73] 49 Mass (8 Met) 466 (1844).

[74] *Elliot* v. *Fitchburg R.R. Co.*, 64 Mass (10 Cush) 191, 196 (1852).

[75] *Thurber* v. *Martin*, 68 Mass (2 Gray) 394, 395–6 (1854). Although previously he seems to have lapsed into his former opinion in *Hazen* v. *Essex Co.*, 66 Mass (12 Cush) 475, 476–7 (1853).

they resolved improperly because, in the conceptualist period in which they lived, they treated it as an either-or question about the nature of such rights.

According to Morton Horwitz, the change in water law in the 19th century was due to a desire to favor, and indeed to subsidize, economic growth. He regards the pre-19th century rules as 'anti-developmental'. They were based on two 'potentially contradictory' theories. One was priority. The other was the idea that a proprietor is entitled to the 'natural use' of his property or (equivalently, it seems for Horwitz) to the 'natural flow' of the river.[76] Protection of the natural use, according to Horwitz, was 'explicitly anti-developmental'. Protection of priority was functionally so 'because [w]here two neighboring parcels of land were underdeveloped, each owner could claim a right based on priority to prevent further development'.[77] The desire to promote economic growth, according to Horwitz, inspired opinions as different Story's and Shaw's. As we have seen, Story rejected the priority rule. In *Tyler* v. *Wilkinson*, he said that everyone had a right to water 'according to the natural current' but that if the use of this right was 'reasonable', only a person who suffered 'injury' from diversion of the water could object.[78] Although Horwitz regards the reference to natural flow as anachronistic, he claims that Story 'acknowledged that the utilitarian criterion of valuable use was the ultimate source of legal rules'.[79] In *Cary* v. *Daniels*, Shaw said that one had the right to use water in a way that 'is reasonable, conformable to the wants of the community, and having regard to the progress of improvement in hydraulic works'.[80] His premise, according to Horwitz, was 'the desirability of maximizing economic development even at the cost of equal distribution'.[81] His decision 'tended to erode a standard of proportionality' by denying 'that large cotton mills had to pay their own way to the extent that their operation exceeded the limits of proportional appropriation'.[82]

Alan Watson has pointed out in detail that Horwitz reads a good deal into his sources.[83] For example, Story and Shaw did not say that utilitarian criteria are the ultimate source of legal rules, or that economic development should be maximized at the cost of equal distribution. They said that they would not protect an unreasonable use of water while disagreeing about whether priority matters.

Also, Horwitz' dichotomy between older and newer rules is wrong. Even by his own account, the older rules were not based on proportionality, and so Shaw could not have eroded such a standard. Priority did matter. But the pre-19th century courts, like Shaw, were protecting prior mill owners, not the owners of undeveloped land. Moreover, courts did not mention 'natural use',[84] and they were not concerned about 'natural flow' until the 19th century. In 1625, one judge did say that water could not be diverted 'having taken a certain course naturally', but the point he wished to make was that water rights exist 'by natural right' (*ex iure naturae*) and therefore, unlike easements, are not extinguished by common ownership.[85] Natural flow became

[76] Compare Morton J. Horwitz, *The Transformation of American Law, 1780–1860* (Cambridge, Mass., 1977), 32 ('natural use' contrasted with priority) with ibid. 33 ('natural flow' contrasted with priority).

[77] ibid. 32.   [78] 24 Fed Cas at 474.   [79] Horwitz, *Transformation*, 39.

[80] 49 Mass (8 Met) at 475–6.   [81] Horwitz, *Transformation*, 41.   [82] ibid.

[83] Watson, 'Transformation,' 186–216.   [84] ibid. 192–3.

[85] *Shury* v. *Piggot*, 3 Bulstr 339, 81 Eng Rep, 280 (KB 1625), as noted by Maass and Zobel, 'Anglo-American Water Law', 125–6.

important to 19th century courts that rejected a rule of priority because, if everyone had the same right to appropriate water, one needed a base line for determining whether any had been appropriated. Some courts became concerned about natural flow for another reason as well. When a rule of priority was rejected, the prior appropriator was protected only if he had a prescriptive right. Thus the difficult question arose of whether he acquired one if he altered the natural flow of the current for the necessary period but without harming anyone. Story said that the plaintiff had no cause of action absent harm as long as defendant's use was reasonable. If so, to protect his rights, the plaintiff would have to build his own mill. English courts eventually held that the plaintiff could recover absent actual harm provided the alteration was perceptible. This solution became known as the 'natural flow' rule as distinguished from Story's 'reasonable use' rule. But it, too, answered a question that arose in the 19th century because a priority rule had been rejected.

Carol Rose has a different economic explanation. As mentioned earlier, in her view, the traditional rule protected a person who had diverted water for about a generation. It was replaced by the priority rule when, with technological change, people came to think that 'the first capital expenditure marked the most valuable use' rather than that 'the use in place for many years was superior'.[86] The priority rule was discarded in turn because it worked well in cases where the 'damage stemmed from backflow at an easily ascertainable dam downstream', and therefore conflicts were typically between two parties, one of whom could buy the other out. The transactions costs of buying out claimants became prohibitive when 'a new kind of case...began to appear' which 'concerned interruption of the flow and pollution from upstream sources'.[87] There were then more potential claimants.

We have seen, however, that the traditional rule was also one of priority. While that rule survived longer in Massachusetts, the Massachusetts courts did not distinguish between upstream and downstream interference. As mentioned earlier, the cases before them did concern backflow. But that would seem to be a coincidence. In England, the defendant had built upstream in three of the four cases in the early 19th century in which some judges endorsed the priority rule.[88] Other jurisdictions were rejecting the priority rule at the same time that the Massachusetts courts were preserving it. The upstream cases were not 'a new kind' preceded by the backflow cases. Indeed, as we have seen, both types of cases had been mentioned by the medieval jurist Bartolus. Again, while pollution by upstreamers might involve many potential plaintiffs, most of the cases concerned disputes among neighboring mill owners where the number of claimants would not have been large. Moreover, after rejecting the priority rule, the English adopted a 'natural flow rule'. That is odd if they were worried about the transaction costs of buying out downstreamers.

There are other obstacles to any economic explanation. As noted earlier, nearly always, when courts rejected the priority rule, the result would have been the same if they had not. Either the victorious plaintiff was also the prior user, or he lost for

---

[86] Rose, *Property and Persuasion*, 178.   [87] ibid. 179.

[88] *Bealey* v. *Shaw*, 6 East 207, 102 Eng Rep, 1266 (KB 1805); *Williams* v. *Morland*, 2 Barn & Cress 910, 107 Eng Rep, 620 (KB 1824); *Liggins* v. *Inge*, 7 Bing 682, 131 Eng Rep, 263 (CP 1831). The backflow case was *Saunders* v. *Newman*, 1 Barn & Ald 256, 106 Eng Rep, 95 (KB 1818).

reasons which were not inconsistent with the priority rule. Courts were not changing the rule to change the result in the cases before them.

Moreover, the economic problem of competition for mill sites was not new in the 19th century. It had existed in basically the same form at least since the Middle Ages. It does not seem to have arisen as a legal problem in Roman times. In the first century BC, Roman engineers added gears to a water mill and so increased its power sixfold from 0.5 to 3 horsepower.[89] Yet, as we have noted, we find no mention in Roman law of mutual interference among mills. Perhaps mills were far apart because estates were large. Perhaps it was cheaper to have slaves use their time grinding grain with hand mills when they were not sowing and reaping. In the Middle Ages, plots of land were smaller, and even serfs lived on grain they grew on their own plots. Moreover, there was a revolution in mill technology. Cams enabled the mill to change rotary motion to a continual pounding by raising and releasing trip hammers. Mills could then be used to make beer, paper, hemp, and leather and to process cloth. One industry after another was mechanized culminating in an explosion of fulling mills in the 13th century.[90] As early as the 11th century, the Domesday Book reported 5,624 water mills in England, and on some rivers, an average of three mills per mile.[91] It is hard to know whether disputes over mill sites were more or less frequent than during the industrial revolution of the 19th century. Nineteenth century mills were bigger. But in the Middle Ages, water was almost the only source of power except for animals and wind, and transportation costs were high, so that it would have been more important to locate a mill conveniently. Be that as it may, once the problem of mutual interference arose frequently enough to demand attention, its legal parameters were the same. Someone built a mill, and someone else diverted water upstream or caused backflow. It would not matter whether water was plentiful elsewhere where people were not quarreling over it.

b. The theoretical dispute

It would be better not to look for economic motives which the judges did not mention but to their own explanation of what they were doing. In water rights, as in many other fields of law, Anglo-American judges were trying to formulate and justify a general rule for the first time. The premise of those who rejected the priority rule was that each proprietor has an 'equal right' or 'common right' to use the water.[92] Therefore, prior appropriation cannot matter. If it did, the prior appropriator would have deprived his neighbors of their equal right. As Leach said in *Wright* v. *Howard*: 'Every proprietor has an equal right to use the water which flows in the stream, and consequently no proprietor can have the right to use the water to the prejudice of any other proprietor'.[93] Story developed this point in his opinion in

[89] Jean Gimpel, *The Medieval Machine: The Industrial Revolution of the Middle Ages* (New York, 1977), 7–8.
[90] ibid. 13–15. [91] ibid. 12.
[92] *Platt* v. *Johnson and Root*, 15 Johns 213, 218 (NY 1818)('equal right'); *Merrit* v. *Brinkerhoff and van Wagenen*, 17 Johns 306, 321 (1820) ('equal right'); *Embrey* v. *Owen*, 6 Exch 353, 372 155 Eng Rep, 579, 587 (1851) ('equal right'); *Twiss* v. *Baldwin*, 9 Conn (9 Day) 291, 306 (1832) ('common right'); *Runnels* v. *Bullen*, 2 NH 532, 537 (1824) ('equal right'); *Evans* v. *Merriweather*, 4 Ill (3 Scam) 492, 496 (1842) (right to participate in a 'common benefit').
[93] *Wright* v. *Howard*, 1 Sim & St at 203, 57 Eng Rep, at 82, quoted in *Mason* v. *Hill*, 3 Barn & Adol 304, 312, 110 Eng Rep, 114, 117 (KB 1833).

Tyler v. *Wilkinson* which, he later said, 'fully recognized and acted upon' Leach's opinion in *Wright*.[94]

[T]he river being common to all proprietors on the river, no one has a right to diminish the quantity which will, according to the natural current, flow to a proprietor below or to throw it back on a proprietor above. This is the necessary result of the perfect equality of right among all the proprietors of that which is common to all.[95]

Blackstone had said that the prior appropriator acquired his right by first 'occupancy' like the right to a wild animal acquired by capturing it. But occupancy, Story objected, 'supposes no ownership already existing, and no right to the use already acquired. But our law annexes to the riparian proprietors the right to the use in common as an incident to the land.'[96]

The argument is not unanswerable. It assumes that each proprietor has a right to use the water, whether he is currently using it or not, rather than the right to use it only if he does so first. In *Carey* v. *Daniels*, Shaw conceived of the right in the latter way. It is like a right to use the highway: 'whilst one is reasonably exercising his own right, by a temporary occupation of the street with his carriage or team, another cannot occupy the same place at the same time'.[97] The same view was implicit in the earlier statements of Bayley and Tindal that water, until appropriated, was *publici iuris*—something that belonged to the public. To conclude that the prior appropriator deprives others of their equal right to use the water, we must conceive of their rights as Leach and Story did. If we follow Shaw, the prior appropriator does not deprive them of any rights although he does deprive them of the benefit of being able to appropriate the water later on. We can understand, then, why the protagonists in this debate reached different conclusions. Their starting points were different conceptions of the right at stake.

If we then ask why each believed his own starting point to be correct, we are asking a question which, very likely, the protagonists could not have answered themselves. If they had an answer which seemed satisfactory, very likely, they would have presented it. It might seem even more conjectural to ask why Shaw's position lost out to that of Leach and Story.

Nevertheless, it may be helpful to compare this debate to the one we have already described which occurred in the Middle Ages in which a position like Shaw's did win out. We can consider what differences in circumstances made Shaw's position seem less persuasive in the 19th century.

Bartolus gave an explanation like that of Shaw. The key to the problem is that the river is 'public'. Bartolus relied on a text that said, 'whenever anything is done in a public place, it should be permitted on condition that it causes no injury to anyone'.[98] The texts that Accursius had cited for the contrary position were not in point because they did not deal with 'public' waters.[99] For Bartolus, the situation was like an

[94] *Webb* v *Portland Mfg. Co.*, 29 Fed Cas 506 (1838) (case no. 17,322). Scholars have said he restated Leach's ideas. Samuel C. Weil, *Water Rights in Western States* 1 (3rd edn., San Francisco, 1911), 764; Maas and Zobel, 'Anglo-American Water Law', 133.   [95] 24 Fed Cas at 474.
[96] 24 Fed Cas at 474.   [97] *Carey* v. *Daniels*, 49 Mass (8 Met) 466, 478 (1839).
[98] Dig. 43.8.2.10.   [99] *Commentaria* to Dig. 43.12.2 [vulg. 11.2], no. 2.

encounter between carts on a public road: the first one to enter prevails. It was like two people who want to build on a strip of beach where anyone was entitled to build: the first to begin building prevails.[100] Similarly, the first to draw water from a public river may do so if it is 'without injury to those nearby'. He then answered the objection of a hypothetical interrogator: 'You say, is it not always an injury to those nearby since then one cannot make his own building? I answer that he does not suffer injury or harm but he does not acquire an advantage, and these are not equivalent or the same in meaning (*ratio*).'[101] For him as for Shaw, water is public before appropriation, and therefore the first appropriator does not violate anyone's rights—or, as Bartolus puts it, he does not legally harm or injure anyone—though he does deprive him of the benefit of being able to appropriate the water later on.

Bartolus' position seems to have prevailed among the jurists of his time but, in the 19th century, Shaw's did not. Two circumstances may have made it more difficult for Shaw. First, medieval Roman lawyers were more comfortable with the legal concept of rights acquired by first appropriation. They had seen it in more contexts. To a common lawyer, what first comes to mind is acquiring a wild animal by catching it. As Story pointed out, however, that case seems inapposite since no one has any rights in the animal. Shaw's illustration seems more in point: the first person to occupy a given spot on the highway has the exclusive right to be there even though everyone has the right to use the highway. But a common lawyer might find that illustration recherché. A person would rarely want to appropriate another's spot. Moreover, it is not a clear example of a right that a common law court would protect as such. Supposing someone pushed another out of his spot on the highway, the occupant would recover for battery simply because he was pushed, not because of some quasi-proprietary interest in the spot. The right to be there would become an issue only if the defendant had owned the spot and pled as a defense that he was removing a trespasser. Bartolus' illustration was blocking another's movement along a public road. Such a case was not decided by a common law court until *Bird* v. *Jones*[102] in 1845, and then it was held that the plaintiff could not recover for false imprisonment. Indeed, it is hard to think of a common law action to vindicate a right to use a public place except possibly an action of public nuisance where the plaintiff has been specially affected. In contrast, in Roman law, an action for *iniuria* could be brought by a person who was obstructed from going to the public baths or the theater.[103] An interdict 'to prevent anything from being done in public places or ways' could be brought against one who did something there that harmed another.[104] An example was Bartolus' illustration of a house built on a beach. In Roman law, the shores were not private property.[105] Anyone could build there, but this interdict could be brought if he impeded the use of others.[106] His illustration of two carts meeting was not made up for the occasion but had already been put by Accursius who had used it to show how the right to use public space depended on priority.[107] Shaw's task may have been harder because common law protection of rights to use public places was much less developed.

---

[100] ibid. no. 10.   [101] ibid. no. 5.   [102] 7 Ad & E (NS) 742, 115 Eng Rep, 688 (1845).
[103] Dig. 43.8.2.9.   [104] Dig. 43.8.2.pr.   [105] Dig. 43.8.3; I. 2.1.1.   [106] Dig. 43.8.4.
[107] *Glossa ordinaria* to Dig. 43.8.2.2 to *ad optinendum*.

Second, in the 19th century, common law judges were trying to formulate a general rule to govern water rights. They had not previously formulated one. Perhaps because of the conceptualism of their time, they thought the subject should be governed by one general rule. In contrast, when Bartolus discussed the problem of mills, he was adding interstitially to Roman rules that governed other problems of water rights. He was not claiming that all such problems should be settled by a rule of priority. As we have already seen, he accepted the Roman rule that 'water from a public river for irrigating fields should be divided according to possession (*pro modo possessionis*)...',[108] meaning, according to Bartolus, that it was to be divided according to size or acreage (*secundum mensuram*)'.[109] He did not see a contradiction between having a rule of proportionality govern this situation and a rule of priority govern the diversions of water that can be made without injury to anyone. Indeed, after discussing this text, he immediately mentions such diversions and cites to his discussion of mills.[110]

Thus Bartolus and his contemporaries could espouse a rule of priority in certain situations while allowing others to be governed by a balancing rule or a rule of proportionality. The 19th century judges talked as though some general principle must govern water rights in every situation. A more flexible and less conceptualist approach might have recognized that different rules can be appropriate to different situations.

4. The law in practice

a. The United States
In the United States, as noted earlier, riparian rights systems which apportion water to each proprietor along a water course have been rejected in whole or in part in western states. The eight most arid states (Arizona, Colorado, Idaho, Montana, Nevada, New Mexico, Utah, and Wyoming) repudiated them very early and entirely.[111] They adopted a prior appropriation system in which the right to use water belongs to the first to put the water to a beneficial use. In most of these states, water rights can then be transferred to another person.[112] If our theory is correct, this system gives the right result in cases like our examples of the mine and the mill. In cases like our example of the farmers, the result would be the wrong one. Nevertheless, even though these states have a single rule, that rule may often give the right result even when water is used for irrigation. As described earlier, in these states, diversion of water for irrigation in these states often bears more resemblance to our examples of the mine and mill than to that of the farmers.

Nine other less arid states have adopted a hybrid system which combines riparian rights and prior appropriation.[113] A riparian rights system governs those who own land along a watercourse. Their conflicts are governed by riparian principles: they must share with each other. A prior appropriation system governs anyone else who uses water. Conflicts among them are resolved in favor of the first to appropriate.[114] These states approximate our theoretical ideal of one rule for cases like our example of the farmers and another for those like our examples of the mine and mill.

---

[108] Dig. 8.3.17.   [109] *Commentaria* to Dig. 8.3.17.   [110] ibid.
[111] David H. Getches, *Water Law* (St Paul, Minn., 1984), 85;
[112] *Powell on Real Property*, § 65.07[7].   [113] *Powell on Real Property*, § 65.10[1].
[114] Getches, *Water Law*, 204.

In these states, when those along the watercourse begin using water which they have not used before, and divert it from those whose rights rest on prior use, a conflict arises between the principles that ordinarily govern systems of riparian rights and systems of prior appropriation. A system of riparian rights would allow them to do so even at the expense of prior users. Nearly all states with a hybrid system have enacted statutes resolving this conflict in favor of the prior appropriator. Unused or 'non-vested' riparian rights are extinguished.[115] That is as it should be if our theory is correct. As we have seen, in theory, the reason it would matter whether people own land along the watercourse is that their needs are most likely to be known initially. If they put water to a new use, it makes sense to protect prior appropriators against them.

Most states in the east have retained a system of riparian rights. But 16 of them have enacted permit systems.[116] Typically, a permit must be granted for all pre-existing uses. A pre-existing use is a vested right, and it cannot be taken without compensation.[117] In some states, permits are granted in perpetuity; in others, for terms deemed to be sufficiently long to allow the holder to recoup his investment.[118]

In four of these states, irrigation is exempted from the permit system.[119] Those states, like the hybrid states, thus have two rules which may approximate our theoretical ideal: those who wish to irrigate are subject to a riparian system, and others are protected if they are the first to receive a permit. In the remaining states, it is hard to tell to what extent the system requires people to share water, as a riparian system would, or simply to have a prior permit. At least the prior user has more protection than riparian rights doctrine would allow.

Thus far, we have seen how prior users have been protected by departures from a system of riparian rights. We will now consider how cases have been decided under riparian rights doctrine. We will see that the prior user has fared better than one might expect.

When riparian rights systems were first adopted in the 19th century in England and the United States, nearly all of the cases concerned mills and other industrial uses. That seems strange, if our theory is correct, since these are the very cases in which the court should have protected the prior users. But as it happened, in nearly all of these cases, the recognition of riparian rights did not affect the outcome. In England, a rule of priority was rejected by one or more judges in decisions stretching form 1805 to 1851: *Bealey* v. *Shaw*,[120] *Saunders* v. *Newman*,[121] *Wright* v. *Howard*,[122] *Mason* v. *Hill*, *Wood* v. *Waud*, and *Embrey* v. *Owen*.[123] In *Bealy*, *Saunders*, *Wright*, *Mason*, and *Wood* the plaintiffs who prevailed were prior users.[124] In *Embrey*, the plaintiff lost because the defendant had not perceptibly diminished the flow of water. During roughly the same period, American judges rejected a rule of priority

---

[115] Getches, *Water Law*, 200–1; *Powell on Real Property*, § 65.10[1].

[116] *Powell on Real Property*, § 65.09[3][c].

[117] William Goldfarb, *Water Law* (2nd edn., Chelsea, Mich., 1988), 26, 27–8.   [118] ibid. 28–9.

[119] ibid. 27.   [120] 6 East 207, 102 Eng Rep, 1266 (KB 1805).

[121] 1 Barn & Ald 256, 106 Eng Rep, 95 (KB 1818).

[122] 1 Sim & St 190, 57 Eng Rep, 76 (Ch 1823).   [123] 6 Exch 353, 155 Eng Rep, 579 (Ex 1851).

[124] Although in *Saunders*, if Ellenborough had had his way, a new trial would have been needed to establish the size of plaintiff's former mill, which had burned and been rebuilt during the period of prescription. 1 Barn & Ald at 260, 106 Eng Rep, at 96–7.

in New York,[125] Connecticut,[126] New Hampshire,[127] Illinois,[128] Vermont[129] and, in federal court, in 1827 in Story's celebrated opinion in *Tyler* v. *Wilkinson*.[130] As in England, the question nearly always was not who should win but why. For example, the victorious plaintiff was also the prior user, or the victorious defendant had a prescriptive right and was also the prior appropriator or had not significantly interfered with the plaintiff.[131] Courts established the riparian rights doctrine in cases in which prior users were not facing chance losses.

Having done so, however, the courts had endorsed a doctrine which, if our theory is correct, was inadequate in two ways. It did not protect prior users in cases like our examples of the mine and the mill. Moreover, as originally conceived, it did not protect proprietors along the river adequately in cases like our example of the farmers needing water for irrigation. As we have seen, the judges who recognized riparian rights said that each person with land along a river had an equal right to use the water. If our theory is correct they should be required to share the water according to their need. Today, they are made to share. It is textbook law today that quarrels are supposed to be umpired by the principle of 'reasonable use'.[132] Courts are supposed to decide which uses are the most reasonable. But that was not the original understanding of riparian rights.

The principle of reasonable use was supposedly formulated by Story in his opinion in *Tyler* v. *Wilkinson*. His reference to 'reasonable use' must be read in context. As noted earlier, Story said that 'no one has a right to diminish the quantity which will, according to the natural current, flow to a proprietor below...'.[133] Indeed, every owner 'has a right to the use of the water flow... in its natural current without diminution or obstruction'.[134] He used the phrase 'reasonable use' to make the point that, nevertheless, a proprietor cannot complain about any diminution or obstruction.

---

[125] *Platt* v. *Johnson & Root*, 15 Johns 213 (NY 1818) (but the result was not affected as the prior downstream mill owner recovered because of the extent of the harm done to him); *Merrit* v. *Brinkerhoff and van Wagenen*, 17 Johns. 306 (1820) (but the result was not affected because defendant's use was found to be excessive); *Arnold* v. *Foot*, 12 Wend 331 (NY 1834) (but the result was unaffected because prior downstream user recovered against the upstreamer who diverted the water for irrigation); *Reid* v. *Gifford*, 1 Hopk 416 (1825).

[126] *Ingraham* v. *Hutchinson*, 2 Conn (2 Day) 584, 590–1 (1818) (the result was not affected since plaintiff had acquired a prescriptive right); followed in *Twiss* v. *Baldwin*, 9 Conn (9 Day) 291 (1832) (the result was not affected since plaintiff's use was prior, and the court held for him because defendant was acting in a way that hurt the plaintiff without benefitting himself); *Buddington* v. *Bradley*, 10 Conn (10 Day) 213, 218–20 (1834) (the result was not affected because the downstream plaintiff's use was prior).

[127] *Runnels* v. *Bullen*, 2 NH 532, 537 (1824) (dicta).

[128] *Evans* v. *Merriweather*, 4 Ill (3 Scam) 492 (1842) (but the result was not affected because the downstream plaintiff's use was prior).

[129] *Snow* v. *Parsons & Parsons*, 28 Vt (2 Will) 459 (1856) (the result was not affected because the plaintiff's use was prior, and defendant's liability turned on whether he had significantly interfered with plaintiff).

[130] 24 Fed Cas 472 (1827) (case no. 14312) (the result was not affected because the defendant, who won on the basis of a prescriptive right, was also the prior appropriator).

[131] See n. 124–30, *supra*. *Platt* was an exception: the court found against a prior downstream mill owner who was harmed by defendant's mill. One might count *Reid* v. *Gifford* as another exception. While the plaintiff who successfully asserted a prescriptive right was also a prior possessor, apparently, his case had previously been dismissed because he had not alleged such a right. 1 Hopk at 418–19.

[132] *Powell on Real Property*, § 65.06[4][b]; Goldfarb, *Water Law*, 22–3; Getches, *Water Law*, 50–1.

[133] 24 Fed Cas at 474.   [134] ibid.

'There may be, and there must be allowed of that which is for the benefit of all, a reasonable use. The true test of the principle and the extent of the use is, whether it is of injury to the other proprietors or not.'[135] Thus Story meant that if one proprietor diverted the current, another proprietor could only complain if he was harmed. Yet the 'reasonable use' doctrine came to mean that one proprietor could harm another provided a court decided his use of the water was 'reasonable'. If our theory is right, that result is correct to the extent that means that farmers like those in our example must share water in proportion to their needs. And yet it was a departure from Story's original conception of what it meant for each proprietor to have an 'equal right'.

According to the *Restatement (Second) of Torts*, reasonableness depends on 'consideration of the interests of the riparian proprietor making the use, of any riparian proprietor harmed by it and of society as a whole'. Factors affecting reasonableness include:

(a) [t]he purpose of the use, (b) the suitability of the use to the watershed or lake, (c) the economic value of the use, (d) the social value of the use, (e) the extent and amount of harm it causes, (f) the practicality of avoiding the harm by adjusting the use or the method or use of one proprietor or the other, (g) the practicality of adjusting the quantity of water used by each proprietor, (h) the protection of existing values of water uses, land, investments and enterprises, and (i) the justice of requiring the user causing harm to bear the loss.[136]

The last two of these factors suggest that the prior user may be entitled to some protection. All the rest suggests that the court is supposed to decide who needs the water most. What have courts actually been doing?

Frequently, at least, they have been acting as they should if the theory we have put forward is correct. Most disputes over water for irrigation probably resemble our case of the farmers in which, we saw, the water should be shared. In such disputes, courts have required the farmers to share.[137]

In other cases, one person built a mill and later another person wanted to build a mill that would hamper its operations. In such cases, it must be admitted, some courts have refused to protect the prior user on the ground that, in a riparian rights system, the result does not depend on priority but on the reasonableness of each party's use.[138] That is an accurate statement of the rules supposedly in force, and it is not surprising that courts have sometimes applied them. Even with such rules in place, however, some courts have protected the mill which was disturbed by the latecomer. The latecomer has been told that party who first built a mill was entitled to have the water flow in its

---

[135] 24 Fed Cas at 474.

[136] *Restatement (Second) of Torts*, § 850A (1979). Similarly, *Powell on Real Property*, § 65.06[4][b]; Goldfarb, *Water Law*, 23; Getches, *Water Law*, 53–4.

[137] *Hough* v. *Porter*, 95 P 732; (Ore 1908); *Clark* v. *Allaman*, 80 P 571 (Kan 1905); *Meng* v. *Coffee*, 93 NW 713 (Neb 1903) *McCook, Irrigation & Water Power Company* v. *Crews*, 96 NW 996 (Neb 1903); *Barrett* v. *Metcalfe*, 12 Tex Civ App 247; 33 SW 758 (1896); *Mud Creek Irrigation, Agricultural, and Manufacturing Company* v. *Vivian*, 11 SW 1078 (Tex 1889); *Wadsworth* v. *Tillotson*, 15 Conn 366 (1843); *Weston* v. *Alden*, 8 Mass (7 Tyng) 136 (1811); *Gillett* v. *Johnson*, 30 Conn 180 (1861) (but prior user prevails because diversion is not reasonable in quantity).

[138] e.g. *Bullard* v. *The Saratoga Victory Manufacturing Company*, 77 NY 525 (1879); *Dumont* v. *Kellogg*, 29 Mich 420 (1874).

accustomed manner.[139] Or he has been told that he diverted too much because the water was needed by the old mill.[140] In one case, he was told he could not divert water from a mill for steam locomotives, because different rules applied when he was not merely diverting water but taking it away.[141] When a salt company diverted water from a mill, the court said that its use was not 'reasonable'. What struck the court as unreasonable was that to allow the diversion when a party came 'long afterward and with knowledge of the facts established its plant...would amount to a virtual confiscation of the property of small owners in the interest of a strong combination of capital'.[142] In all of these cases, though the court claimed to be applying riparian rights doctrine, it protected the prior user.

Moreover, sometimes, when the priority of a mill was ignored, the situation may have been less like the mill in our example and more like that of farmers competing for water to irrigate. Mills had operated near each other for many years, each gradually expanding, and knowing the other was doing the same, until, foreseeably, their needs conflicted.[143] In other cases, the prior user diverted water to a mill and the latecomer wanted to use it for irrigation.[144] Perhaps his needs should have been anticipated.

In another sort of case, farmers were using water for irrigation and a mine unexpectedly opened near them. In such cases, courts have protected the prior users rather consistently. Farmers prevailed against an aircraft company that opened a plant that required diversion of 150 million gallons per year. The court said the diversion was so vast that the stream ceased to flow and therefore was unreasonable.[145] A rancher prevailed against a mining company diverting the water for its mine. The court upheld the view of the court below that its 'business might reasonably require more than he could take consistently with the rights of the plaintiff'. It only had the right to use the water 'without materially diminishing it in quantity'.[146] Municipalities and water companies that buy river or lake front property to divert water for the domestic use of towns have consistently lost even in cases in which the issue never arose of whether this use was riparian.[147] So have those who divert so much water that they lower the level

[139] *Mason* v. *Whitney*, 78 NE 881 (Mass 1906) (dicta); *Cox* v. *Howell*, 65 SW 868 (Tenn 1901); *Woodin* v. *Wentworth*, 23 NW 813 (Mich 1885); *Thunder Bay River Booming Company* v. *Speechly*, 31 Mich 336 (1875); *Harding* v. *The Stamford Water Company*, 41 Conn 87 (1874); *Burden* v. *Stein*, 27 Ala 104 (1855); *Parker* v. *Griswold*, 17 Conn 288, 300 (1845); *King* v. *Tiffany*, 9 Conn 162 (1832); *M'Calmont* v. *Whitaker*, 3 Rawle 84 (Pa 1831).   [140] *Timm* v. *Bear*, 29 Wis 254, 268 (1871).

[141] *Garwood* v. *N.Y. Central & Hudson R. R.R. Co.*, 83 NY 400 (1881).

[142] *Strobel* v. *The Kerr Salt Company*, 58 NE 142 (NY 1900).

[143] See *Keeney & Wood Mfg. Co.* v. *Union Mfg. Co.*, 39 Conn 576 (1873); *Davis* v. *Getchell*, 50 Me 602 (1862); *Hoy* v. *Sterrett*, 2 Watts 327 (Pa 1834). The last case was then treated as dispositive, without any discussion of the facts, in *Whaler* v. *Ahl*, 29 Pa 98 (1857); *Hartzall* v. *Sill*, 12 Pa 248 (1849); *Hetrich* v. *Deachler*, 6 Pa 32 (1847).   [144] *Pyle* v. *Gilbert*, 265 SE2d 584 (Ga 1980); *Tolle* v. *Correth*, 31 Tex 362 (1868).

[145] *Weaver* v. *Beech Aircraft Corp*, 303 P2d 159 (Kan 1956).

[146] *Wheatley* v. *Chrisman*, 24 Pa 298 (1855).

[147] *City of Battle Creek* v. *Goguac Resort Association, Ltd*, 148 NW 441 (Mich 1914); *Kennedy* v. *Niles Water Supply Co.*, 139 NW 241 (Mich 1913); *Pine* v. *Mayor of New York*, 103 F 337 (SDNY 1900); *Smith* v. *The City of Brooklyn*, 54 NE 787 (NY 1899); *Valparaiso City Water Company* v. *Dickover*, 46 NE 591 (Ind App 1897); *East Jersey Water Co.* v. *Bigelow*, 38 A 631 (NJ 1897); *Rigney* v *The Tacoma Light & Water Company*, 38 P 147 (Wash 1894); *The Borough of Ashland* v. *Haupt*, 17 A 436 (Pa 1889); *Ulbricht* v. *Eufaula Water Company*, 6 So 78 (Ala 1888) (water company enjoined from causing plaintiff any sensible injury or damage but entitled to take water as long as it does not harm him); *The Acquackanonk*

of a lake.[148] In one such case the court said that the plaintiffs, who owned hotels, clubs and fishing docks, were entitled to the 'natural' level of the lake.[149] In another, in which the defendant began diverting large quantities of water to create a rice paddy, the court insisted that the question was not whether the lake was drained below its customary level but whether the diversion of water was reasonable. It then held that it would be unreasonable for the defendant to drain the lake below its customary level since to do so would interfere with the plaintiff's boating and fishing.[150]

My colleague Joseph Sax has described what courts do in a manner very different than the *Restatement*:

When the competing activities are scalable (i.e. when they can be reduced proportionately without becoming infeasible), a 'share the shortage' philosophy can lead to pro rata reductions in water use. When that option is not available, courts may characterize one as the 'cause' of the interference to the other and require that use to make more substantial adjustments.[151]

I also have the sense that courts flip back and forth between requiring the parties to share and holding one party liable. In my view, the reason is not that the option of making them share is unavailable. It is that the paradigm 'scalable' case is agricultural use, where, as we have seen, the parties generally ought to share according to need. But in other cases, the courts have not made them share even when one party's need was great. Without admitting it, they protect priority. They do not do so invariably. But they do so often enough to show their discomfort with a system of riparian rights.

b. England

It is often said that a prior appropriation rule is appropriate for western American states because they are dry. If our view is correct, their dryness only accentuates the unfairness that would be found in wetter regions with a riparian rights regime. England is wet. And yet its riparian rights law has largely been replaced by a statutory scheme initially enacted by the Water Resources Law of 1991. Under the Act, a person who abstracts water or obstructs its flow must have a license[152] unless he owns contiguous land and takes less than 20 cubic meters a day for domestic or agricultural purposes other than spray irrigation.[153] The license specifies the quantity of water[154] and purposes for which it may be used.[155] Anyone with land next to a watercourse, or a right of access to the water, can apply for a license.[156] The National Rivers Authority can then grant it on such terms as it deems appropriate.[157] Nevertheless, it may not grant a license which derogates from a 'protected right'.[158] 'Protected rights' are those to take up to 20 cubic meters a day for domestic or agricultural purposes[159] and those

---

Water Company v. *Watson*, 29 NJ Eq 366 (1878) (relief denied on other grounds). See also *Helfrich* v. *Catonsville Water Company*, 22 A 72 (Md 1891) (landowner entitled to water his livestock even though it fouls the municipality's source of drinking water); *People* v. *Hulbert*, 91 NW 211 (Mich 1902) (same, although the landowner swam in the water to create a test case). Contra *City of Springfield* v. *Samuel Harris*, 86 Mass 494 (1862) (municipality prevails because quantity diverted found to be reasonable).

148 *Taylor* v. *Tampa Coal Co.*, 46 So2d 392 (Fla 1950).
149 *Webster* v. *Harris*, 69 SW 782 (Tenn 1902).   150 *Harris* v. *Brooks*, 283 SW2d 129 (Ark 1955).
151 Sax *et al.*, *Legal Control of Water Resources*, 26.   152 Water Resources Act, 1991 c. 57, §§ 24–5.
153 ibid. § 27(3)–(4).   154 ibid. § 46(2).   155 ibid. § 46(4).   156 ibid. § 35(2).
157 ibid. § 38.   158 ibid. § 39(1).   159 ibid. §§ 39(3), 27(6).

of people already holding licenses.[160] If the Authority derogates from a 'protected right', it is liable in damages for breach of statutory duty.[161] The Authority can modify or revoke a license.[162] If it does so, however, the Authority must pay compensation if the license holder '(a) has incurred expenditure in carrying out work which is rendered abortive by the revocation or variation; or (b) has otherwise sustained loss or damage which is directly attributable to the revocation or variation . . .'.[163] The result is that the prior user is protected in cases like the ones in our examples of the mill and mine. It is not clear what happens to cases like that of the farmers. To some extent, they may be sharing water in rough proportion to their need because they can take up to 20 cubic meters a day. In times of water shortage, the Act allows the Secretary of State to apportion water in virtually any way he sees fit.[164] We can conclude, at any rate, that the English have been unwilling to live with the consequences of the riparian rights system they adopted in the 19th century.

B. Water Rights in France and Italy

1. Origins

While the English and Americans adopted a riparian rights system without an argument that went to the merits of the issue, the French apparently did so with no argument at all. From thence it spread to countries influenced by the French Civil Code such as Italy.

French customary law, like the *ius commune*, protected the first to build a mill against anyone who diverted water.[165] There is no evidence that the drafters of the French Civil Code considered adopting this rule. They provided instead in what are now articles 644–5 that one who owned land on a 'running watercourse' could divert water for irrigation. If a dispute should arise among 'proprietors to whom these waters may be of use, the courts, in giving judgment, should reconcile the interest of agriculture with the consideration due to property rights . . .'. A rule of priority was replaced by one that allowed the needs of the parties to be balanced or weighed in some fashion.[166]

The multi-volume drafting history of the Code contains no discussion of the change. In all likelihood, the drafters had simply paraphrased the 17th century jurist,

---

[160] ibid. §§ 39(3), 48(1).   [161] ibid. § 60(2).   [162] ibid. §§ 52–54.

[163] ibid. § 61(1).   [164] ibid. §§ 73–6.

[165] Antoine D'Espeisses, *Traicté de l'ordre iudiciare observé ez causes civiles* (Lyon, 1677), tit. V, art. 3, sec. ix, no. 6, in *Les Oeuvres de M. Antoine D'Espeisses* 3.

[166] The similarity is sufficiently close that Samuel Weil argued these articles caused the change in Anglo-American water law. Supposedly, they inspired Kent and Story, who were familiar with French law. Their views were then adopted in England in *Wood* and *Embrey*. But the chronology is wrong. The priority rule was rejected by Ellenborough in 1805. He was unlikely to have been influenced by a provision in a Code passed a year before that does not even mention mills. It mentions irrigation and only later was held by French courts to apply to mills and other industrial uses. As we have seen, some American courts adopted Ellenborough's position before Story and Kent. Moreover Kent followed Story, and Story followed Leach. Leach's argument from equal right has a parallel in Domat but not in the Code. And the common law judges do not speak, like the Code, about a need to reconcile the interests of agriculture with property rights. They don't envision a conflict.

Jean Domat. Bonaparte had given them only three months to write a Code, and in their haste, they borrowed a great deal from Domat and from the 18th century jurist Robert Pothier. Neither had treated the diversion of water in their works on private law. But Domat had done so in his treatise on public law. Articles 644–5 of the Civil Code seem to be adaptations of the following passage:

[A]lthough one can divert water from a stream or river to water one's meadows or other land, or for mills or other uses, he must use that freedom in such a way that he does no harm either to the navigation in the river whose water he diverts, or in another that is made navigable by the water of the first, or to some other public use, or to neighbors who have a similar need and a like right. And if there is not enough water for all, or if the use that some make of it is injurious to others, all will be provided for, according to need, by the officers who have that responsibility.[167]

This passage described the power of the state to regulate navigable rivers, which were considered part of the public domain. To adapt it to private water rights, the drafters transferred to judges the power enjoyed by Domat's 'officers', thereby conferring on them a discretionary power which, as French scholars have noted,[168] is unparalleled elsewhere in the Code. They also changed the standard of 'similar need and like right' to a vaguer one: 'reconcile the interest of agriculture with the consideration due to property rights'. Thus the French system seems to be the result of the accident that the only passage in the works of Pothier and Domat dealing with water rights happened to be in Domat's treatise on public law.

2. The law in practice

a. France

While France adopted a system of riparian rights, courts have behaved like those in the United States, not invariably, but frequently enough to show discontent with the rules supposedly in force. They have required those who want water for irrigation and other agricultural purposes to share it.[169] But as in the United States, French courts have refused to allow latecomers to build dams which impaired the flow of water to a prior user's mill. They have said that the prior user has the right to have the water flow according to its 'natural course and level' (*son cours et son niveau naturel*)[170] or 'ordinary course' (*cours ordinaire*).[171]

Moreover, the latecomer has lost cases which resemble our example of the mine diverting water from prior users. A concessionaire for the distribution of electricity was held liable for diverting water from prior users and thereby 'disrupting the regime'

---

[167] Jean Domat, *Loix civiles dans leur ordre naturel: Le Droit public* (nouv. edn., Paris 1713), liv. i, tit. viii, sec. ii, § 11.

[168] Alex Weill, François Terré, and Philippe Simler, *Droit civil: Les Biens* (3rd edn., Paris, 1985), no. 224.

[169] Cour d'appel, Montpellier, 29 Oct. 1934, D.H. 1935.12; Cour d'appel, Montpellier, 12 Jan. 1870, D 1871.2.70; Cour d'appel, Bourges, 29 Jan. 1872, D. 1872.2.61. They have not done so in a situation which does not resemble our example: when there is such scarcity that irrigation by some farmers would use up all the water, they have allowed whoever happened to be upstream to take it all. Trib. civ., Baugé, 26 Apr. 1950, D. 1950.J.515; Cass., req., 21 Jan. 1901, D. 1901.1.336; Cour d'appel, Agen, 9 Feb. 1863, D. 1863.1.96. Also, a latecomer lost in Cass. req., 1 Apr. 1901, D. 1906.1.133 on the curious ground that the water never had and never could serve his land.   [170] Cass., ch. civ., 15 Feb. 1860, D. 1860.1.347.

[171] Cass., 3e ch. civ., 12 Oct. 1978, D.S. 1979.I.R.58.

of the stream.[172] So was a laundry.[173] According to an unsigned note to the case, 'one is permitted to suppose' that the court acknowledged 'a situation of fact' which apparently endured for 30 years. Those dwelling on the river 'perhaps seemed more worthy of interest than a commercial enterprise destroying, for the purpose of profit, an equilibrium long established'. Another plaintiff won who alleged that upstream users had disturbed the 'integrality' of the stream.[174] In finding for another plaintiff, the court said that he had a 'quasi-possession' in the flow of the water which defendant had disturbed by inserting a pipe.[175]

When the latecomer prevailed it was often in situations that do not resemble our examples of the mine and the mill. In one case, the reason the latecomer won, according to the court, was so that a prior state of affairs could be preserved. The commune of d'Epinoy had a stone pipe. An upstream mill owner enlarged his mill so that more water was sent downstream. The mill lost motive force because, as a result, more water had to go through the pipe. The mill owner sued successfully to have the size of the pipe altered so it would take only the same amount of water as before. The court said this result was necessary 'to maintain the parties in their respective rights, in assuring for each of them, without harm to the other, the same quantity of water originally attributed to them'.[176]

In another case, the defendant was allowed to divert water for his factory. But the situation may have resembled more closely our example in which farmers compete for water for irrigation. The defendant's predecessors had diverted water for a mill. The mill was so ancient that the defendant claimed he could divert water by seigneurial right. The court held that this right only extended to the operation of a mill. Nevertheless, the old valves were still in place 1 m. 10 cm. above the river bed, and the court approved using them as the measure of the parties' rights. It also said that the defendant could not take more water than he would have used for irrigation. This case, like some of the American cases we discussed, may have seemed like competition among age-old claims for water and not like disruption by an intruder.[177]

In other cases in which the latecomer won, the plaintiff could not establish that he had been hurt.[178] In others, he could not establish that he had been hurt by the defendant.[179]

Diversion of water for power is now governed by a statute enacted in 1919. The diverter is required to obtain a permit (*concession*) if he has a large operation or permission (*autorisation*) if he has a smaller one.[180] In either case,[181] he can divert

---

[172] Cons. d'Etat, 12 Feb. 1960, D. 1960.Somm.81.

[173] Cass., 3e ch. civ., 14 Oct. 1980, D.S. 1981.IR.511.

[174] Cass., 1e civ. ch., 12 Mar. 1968, D.S. 1968.Somm.86.

[175] Cours d'appel, Rennes, 15 Feb. 1980, D.S. 1983.I.R.13.

[176] Cass., ch. civ., 15 Jan. 1850, D. 1850.1.172.   [177] Cass. req., 4 May 1887, D. 1887.1.199.

[178] Cass., 3rd ch. civ., 4 Feb. 1975, D.S. 1975.I.R.100; Cass., req., 10 Mar. 1879, D. 1880.1.31; Cass. civ., 23 Jan. 1923, D. 1925.1.190.   [179] Cour d'appel, Dijon, 8 May 1895, D. 1895.2.309.

[180] Law of 16 Oct. 1919, art. 1 (as amended by law 80–531 of 15 July 1980, art. 24), art. 2 (as amended by law 84–512 of 29 June 1984, art. 8).

[181] After art. 16 bis was added to the law of 16 Oct. 1919 by the law 85–30 of 9 Jan. 1985, art. 90, which extended to authorizations the rules that previously applied to permits.

water to the prejudice of prior users[182] but he must pay them compensation.[183] Since the diverter is like the mine owner or the second mill builder in our examples, that would be the right result.

b. Italy

Under the influence of the French Civil Code, Italy adopted similar rules. According to article 910 of the Italian Civil Code, which governs 'private waters': 'The proprietor of land crossed by non-public water which flows naturally and to which others do not have a right may, as it passes, to use it for the irrigation of his land and for the use of his industries but must return the run-off and residue to its ordinary course'. But in 1994, all of the watercourses in Italy were declared to be 'public' by the 'legge Galli'.[184] They are therefore governed by the *Regio Decreto* of 1933.[185] Article 2 of this decree provides that to be entitled to use water, a person must receive a permit (*concessione*) through a procedure which is designed to weigh the public interest with the private interest of the applicant. Article 45 provides that the permit can be taken away, and the right to use the water given to another applicant, but in that event, an indemnity must be paid.[186]

Unless the permit is taken away, the permit holder is protected even if a new permit is granted to someone else which conflicts with his own. Article 19 provides that the new permit 'is intended to be made within the limits in which water is available'. The person who obtains it 'is exclusively responsible for any injury which may be done as a result of it to the rights of a third party'.

The right to water of the permit holder is protected by Italian tort law against anyone who does not have a permit.[187] If the offender is a public entity, it cannot be enjoined from diverting water. But the *Corte di cassazione*, the highest court for civil matters, has held that the entity must pay damages in tort.[188] The result is, in effect, a forced sale.

Indeed, a public entity which does have a permit has been held liable in tort to a prior user who does not. The *Ente Nazionale per L'Energia Elettrica* (ENEL), which had a permit, diverted so much water in a time of scarcity as to interfere with irrigation in the valley below its installation. It was sued by the *Consorzio per l'Incremento delle Irrigazioni* which represented the farmers. The farmers based their claim, not on a permit but on 'ancient use' (*per antico uso*). The *Corte di cassazione* awarded damages

---

[182] Law of 16 Oct. 1919, art. 4 (as modified by Decree 67–885 of 6 Oct. 1967, art. 4).

[183] Law of 16 Oct. 1919, art. 6.

[184] 1. 36/94, art 2: 'All surface and subterranean waters though not extracted from the subsoil are public and constitute a resource which is safeguarded and utilized according to the criterion of solidarity'. This principle was affirmed by art. 1, c. 1 of Dcr 238/1999 (Regolamento recante norme per l'attuazione di talune disposizioni della legge 5 Jan. 1994, n. 36, in materia di risorse idriche): 'All surface and subterranean waters, including those gathered in reservoirs and cisterns, belong to the state and are part of the public domain'.   [185] 11 Dec. 1933 n. 1775.

[186] Art. 45(3): 'when, in the unreviewable judgment of the Minister of Public Works, having heard the Consiglio superiore, the provision of water [to the former right holder] . . . is excessively onerous in relation to the value of the preexisting use, the party with the right to that use is to be indemnified by the party newly receiving a permit according to the terms of the law on expropriation'.

[187] Cass. 6 Dec. 1974 n. 4051 (defendants forbidden from diverting waters which belonged to the plaintiff by prior permit and ancient use).   [188] Cass. 16 Jan. 1985 n. 95; Cass. 18 Mar. 1992 n. 335.

in tort, citing article 19, and concluding that the permit doesn't entitle ENEL to take water from anyone with a 'prior title' (*titolo anteriore*).[189]

IV. Conclusion

Some rights, like the right to use water, are annexed to the rights of an owner to use his own property. We have seen that the way in which these rights are initially allocated will affect the chances that the value of a proprietor's resources will be changed by the events we have referred to as forfeitures, windfalls, and hold-ups. The proprietor will lose a right he paid for, or gain a right for which he did not, or be able to take advantage of a bilateral monopoly to take advantage of another's need for resources. Forfeitures, windfalls and hold-ups all infringe on the principle of commutative justice that each person's share of resources should be preserved so far as feasible.

As we have seen, when the needs of proprietors are known in advance, the ideal rule would be to allocate resources such as water in proportion to their needs. When they are not known in advance, the best rule would allocate the first user the resources he needs, and compel later users to pay him for any resources they wish to divert. To prevent a hold-up, the ideal rule would allow the latecomer to pay a price that reflects the loss the diversion causes the first user, not the value of the resources to the latecomer.

As we have seen, this solution was approximated by the medieval *ius commune* which required proprietors along a watercourse who were using the water for irrigation to share in rough proportion to their needs, but protected the first person who built a mill against diversion of water by later builders. Such a rule has been rejected by leading modern legal systems—notably by common law jurisdictions and those influenced by French law. Yet, as we have seen, these systems adopted their rules, not because they worked well in practice, but for reasons which do not compel respect. Since then, they have been moving away from them in the direction our principles call for.

---

[189] Cass. 18 Mar. 1992 n. 3353.

7

Loss of Resources Without the Owner's Consent: Necessity and Adverse Possession

I. Necessity

A. Origins

The doctrine of necessity was foreign to Roman law although later jurists used it to explain Roman legal texts. The doctrine was first formulated by the medieval canon lawyers. Aquinas and the late scholastics then explained it by drawing on Aristotelian ideas about the purpose of property. It was then rejected by the will theorists of the 19th century but managed to survive in the United States and resurface in Germany because it commended itself to common sense.

The Roman legal texts on which later jurists drew allowed one person to enter another's land without permission: for example, to look for a fugitive.[1] They allowed a person to preserve his own life or property by destroying that of another: for example, if he pulled down his neighbor's house to save his own from a fire. Thus, what we would call necessity was sometimes a defense against an action under the Roman *lex Aquilia* for damage done unlawfully.[2] Finally, there were rules allowing the captain of a ship to jettison cargo to save the ship. The passengers whose goods had been saved had to compensate those whose goods were thrown overboard. These rules were similar to modern admiralty law, and indeed, were the historical ancestors of that law.[3]

The medieval canon lawyers generalized to formulate a doctrine of necessity. Unlike the Roman lawyers, they were not dealing with the problem of who should pay if cargo was jettisoned or a house destroyed or a fugitive chased onto someone else's land. They were trying to determine when one was guilty of the sin of greed. In one of the texts that Gratian incorporated into his *Decretum*, Saint Ambrose denounced a person who 'sees always gold, always silver' and 'asks gold even in his prayer and supplication to God'. He goes on:

But, you say, what is the injustice if I diligently care for my own without seizing what is another's? Oh, imprudent saying! Your own you say? What things? From what horde did you

---

[1] Here is how these situations were described by a medieval lawyer (as it happens, a canonist): 'There are cases in which one is allowed to pass through another's field: if there is a servitude, C. 3.34.11, or if one wants to dig up one's own treasure, Dig. 10.4.19 (at the end), if my fruit fell into your field, D. 43.27.1, when I am looking for a fugitive, Dig. 11.4.4 . . . and when a public road is destroyed, Dig. 8.6.14.1'. *Glossa ordinaria to Gratian, Decretum ad* D. 1, c. 2. [2] Dig. 9.2.49.1.

[3] Dig. 9.2.2 pr.

bring them into this world? When you came into the light, when you left your mother's womb, stuffed with what possessions and goods, I ask, did you come? . . . Let no one call his own what is common.[4]

Maybe Ambrose merely meant that people shouldn't be piggy. Nevertheless, the literally minded canon lawyers tried to figure out when and in what sense private property could be 'common'? They said that property was not meant merely for the benefit of the owner, so that if a person had more than enough for himself, he should give the rest away. They also said that in a state of necessity, property became literally common. In addition to canon law texts, they cited the Roman rules on jettisoning cargo at sea.[5]

While the canonists had formulated a general doctrine of necessity, they explained it only in the way just described: by citing texts. Eventually, Aquinas found a philosophical explanation by drawing on Aristotle. As we have seen, Aristotle thought that human beings needed external things to lead a distinctively human life. Nevertheless, he rejected the view of his teacher Plato that all property should be in common. If it were, Aristotle said, '[t]hose who labor much and get little will necessarily complain of those who labor little and receive or consume much'.[6] Aquinas gave a similar explanation.[7] Going beyond Aristotle, he claimed that this account or private property could explain the canonists' doctrine of necessity. In considering 'whether it is lawful to steal through stress of need' Aquinas said:

[T]he division and appropriation of things which are based on human law do not preclude the fact that man's needs have to be remedied by means of these very things . . . If the need be so manifest and urgent, that it is evident that the present need must be remedied by whatever means be at hand (for instance, when a person is in some imminent danger, and there is no other possible remedy) then it is lawful for a man to succor his own need by means of another's property, by taking it either openly or secretly: nor is this properly speaking theft or robbery.[8]

This explanation was adopted, first by the so-called late scholastics of the 16th century, and then by the northern natural law school of the 17th and 18th centuries.[9] They all say that the rights of a private owner are therefore qualified, and must yield in

---

[4] *Decretum* D. 47, c. 8.

[5] *Glossa Ordinaria* to *Decretum* to D. 47, c.8 to *Commune*. That interpretation seemed to collide with another text that was eventually included in a collection of papal decisions called the *Decretals of Gregory IX*. The text, taken from an early manual for priests prescribing penance to those who confessed their sins, said that 'if a person stole food, clothing or money because of necessity, being hungry or naked, he should do three weeks penance, and if he returned what he stole, he should not be compelled to fast'. *Decretals* 5.18.3. The difficulty for the canonists was why a person who stole in time of necessity should have to do penance at all, even a light penance, since by their doctrine all things were in common, and therefore he should not have committed a sin. The standard gloss to the *Decretals* resolved the problem by assuming the text was speaking of moderate necessity: 'From the facts that penance is imposed, it may be gathered that the necessity was moderate. Penance would not have been imposed if it had been great . . . for in necessity all things are common.' *Glossa ordinaria* ad *Decretals* 5.18.3. to *poenitentia*. [6] *Politics* II.v.

[7] *Summa theologiae* II-II, Q. 66, a. 2.   [8] *Summa theologiae* II-II, Q. 66, a. 7.

[9] Leonardus Lessius, *De iustitia et iure, ceterisque virtutibus cardinalis libri quatuor* (Paris, 1628), lib. 2, cap. 12, dub. 12; Ludovicus de Molina, *De iustitia et iure tractatus* (Venice, 1614), disp. 20; Domenicus Soto, *De iustitia et iure libri decem* (Salamanca, 1553), lib. 5, q. 3., a. 4; Hugo Grotius, *De iure belli ac pacis libri tres* (B. J. A. de Kanter-van Hetting Tromp, ed., Leiden, 1939), II.ii.6–7; Samuel Pufendorf, *De iure naturae et gentium libri octo* (Amsterdam, 1688), II.vi.5.

certain cases to the needs of another. The standard example is the taking of property
by a person in urgent need.[10] Here is the way it was presented by Leonard Lessius:

I say...one may take another's thing when one is in extreme necessity because, in extreme
necessity, one needs what is necessary to preserve one's life. This is the common opinion of the
doctors. The proof is that in extreme necessity all things are common—which is a received
axiom—not that ownership is transferred.... All things are common insofar as the right to use
them is concerned, and so a person who is pressed by these difficulties can lawfully take them.
He has the right to any thing to the extent it is necessary, and he may help himself or another
person by its use. The reason for this is that the end of inferior things is to serve men through
necessity, so that through them men may preserve and maintain their lives. Therefore this right
belongs to all by nature. Nor can the division of things introduced by the law of nations take
away this right, for the law of nations presupposes the law of nature and does not destroy it particularly as to what is necessary to preserve life. The division of things must therefore be deemed
to have been made with a reservation to each person of this natural right to whatever is necessary
to maintain his life. Otherwise the division would not have been done in a rational way.[11]

Grotius added that if 'it is possible, restitution [must] be made' for the goods that were
taken.[12]

Explanations of this sort were common on into the eighteenth century. By the nineteenth century, in continental Europe, they had almost vanished. In the nineteenth
century, jurists tried to explain property, not by asking about the purposes that
property should serve, but by the concept of will. Property, by definition, meant that
the will of the owner determined the use to which the property could be put.

Nineteenth century French jurists said that this idea was enshrined in the French
Civil Code. Article 544 provided: 'Property is the right to enjoy and dispose of things
in the most absolute manner provided that one does not make a use of them that is
prohibited by statute or regulation'. This sentence had been taken almost verbatim
from the eighteenth century jurist Robert Pothier whose conceptions of law were
nearly always an unoriginal restatement of the teachings of the natural law school. It is
unlikely that when Pothier wrote these words he had in mind any different theory
of property than Grotius. It is even more unlikely that the drafting committee of
the French Civil Code, in the few months available to it, devised a new theory of
property and had it in mind when they borrowed the words of Pothier. Nevertheless,
the nineteenth century French jurists claimed that this provision required them to
define property solely in terms of the will of the owner.[13]

The 19th century German jurists defined property in the same way. According to
Bernard Windscheid, one of the greatest jurists of the century:

To say that a thing belongs to a person is to say that his will is decisive for it in its totality of its
relationships. The significance is two-fold: (1) the owner may provide as he will concerning the

---

[10] Lessius, *De iustitia et iure*, lib. 2, cap. 12, dub. 12; Molina, *De iustitia et iure*, disp. 20; Soto, *De iustitia
et iure*, lib. 5, q. 3, a. 4; Grotius, *De iure belli ac pacis*, II.ii.6–7; Pufendorf, *De iure naturae*, II.vi.5.

[11] *De iustitia et iure*, lib. 2, cap. 12, dub. 12.   [12] *De iure belli ac pacis*, II.ii.2, 6–9.

[13] Charles Aubry and Charles Rau, *Cours de droit civil français d'après la méthode de Zachariae*, 2 (4th
edn., Paris, 1869), § 190; François Laurent, *Principes de droit civil français*, 6 (3rd edn., Paris, 1875), § 101;
Charles Demolombe, *Cours de Code Napoléon*, 9 (3rd edn., Paris, 1882), § 543.

thing; (2) another person may not provide for the thing in a manner contrary to his will (these are the positive and negative sides of ownership).[14]

They concluded that there should not be a doctrine of necessity. The first draft of the German Civil Code provided in what is today § 903: 'The owner of a thing may treat it as he pleases and exclude others from any dealing with it insofar as statutes and the rights of a third party are not to the contrary'. Necessity was not supposed to be an exception.

Nevertheless, in the United States and Germany, the doctrine survived, less because it was supported by a widely accepted theory, than as a matter of common sense. In 1908, in *Ploof* v. *Putnam*, a pier owner was held liable when his employee cut loose the plaintiff's ship which the plaintiff had tied to the pier to save it in a storm.[15] In 1910, in *Vincent* v. *Lake Erie Transportation Co.*, it was held that a ship owner might lawfully remain moored to plaintiff's pier during a storm but that he must pay for the harm done to the pier.[16]

Moreover, in Germany, the second drafting commission adopted the doctrine for reasons that were more pragmatic than conceptual. They adopted § 904 of the German Civil Code:

The owner of a thing is not entitled to prohibit another from dealing with the thing when such conduct is necessary to avoid a present danger, and the damage threatened by it is unreasonably large compared to the damage arising to the owner from dealing with his thing. The owner can require compensation for the damage that occurs to him.

The drafting commission explained:

The unacceptability of the legal situation [under the first draft] is apparent without further argument when one considers some practical examples of its application. According to the draft, it is against the law for a drowning man to climb on another's boat to rescue himself. The owner of the boat who is himself not in danger is entitled . . . to push him back in the water. The draft forbids one to tear down another's fence during a conflagration to permit entry of fire fighting equipment or to break into a neighboring house which is the only possible point from which the work of extinguishing the fire can be directed. In all such cases, the draft will recognize a person's defense as lawful self defense. These results are insupportable and irreconcilable with other principles recognized by law. The draft acknowledges the right [of the owner of property with no access to the public street] to obtain a right of way by necessity . . . , and it permits a person to enter another's property to find and carry off any of his own property that has come there by chance . . . . The most striking example, however, of giving way to lower rights before a higher interest counter to them is the right of expropriation. The fundamental idea of this manifestation of right is that action taken through necessity will be declared to be in accordance with law insofar as it manifests the importance of higher interests over lower ones, that is, to the extent that it is a function performed as a duty to the community. There should be no contradiction between rights and laws of morality. Every private right carries the inherent limitation that it must give way to the general interest, and when such a higher interest is present is decided by the judgment of the community.[17]

---

[14] Bernhard Windscheid, *Lehrbuch des Pandektenrechts* 1 (7th edn., Düsseldorf, 1891), § 167.

[15] *Ploof* v. *Putnam*, 71 A 188 (Vt 1908).   [16] 124 NW 221 (1910).

[17] *Protokolle der Kommission für die zweite Lesung des Bürgerliches Gesetzbuches* 4 (Berlin, 1899), § 419, p. 214.

Today, the doctrine is generally accepted in the United States and Germany. Certain French jurists are trying to read it into French law[18] although their illustrations are not in point: for example, a party was held not to be liable—not because necessity justified the use of another's property—but because he took a risk of injuring someone which was justified under the circumstances, or, to put it another way, because he was not negligent.[19]

B. The Justification for the Doctrine

In 1926, in his classical article, Francis H. Bohlen defended the result in *Vincent* v. *Lake Erie*. He argued: 'As between the individuals concerned, it is obviously just that he whose interests are advanced by the act should bear the cost of doing it rather than that he should be permitted to impose it upon one who derives no benefit from the act'.[20]

Consequently, the ship owner in *Vincent* was privileged to tie up to the pier. As to when person had such a privilege, Bohlen said:

'Upon one thing there is substantial agreement. An act intended to invade another's legally protected interests is privileged only if done to protect or advance some public interest or an interest of the actor. If the act is done only for the protection of one of the actor's interests, it must be an interest of a value greater than, or at least equal to, that of the interest invaded . . .'[21]

Bohlen's view passed into the *Restatements* of restitution and torts. According to the *Restatement of Restitution*: 'A person who is privileged to harm the land or chattels of another while acting to preserve himself or a third person or to preserve his things or those of a third person is under a duty to make restitution for the harm done . . .'.[22] According to the *Restatement (Second) of Torts*, which does not differ materially from the first, 'One is privileged to enter or remain on land in the possession of another if it is or reasonably appears to be necessary to prevent serious harm' to the actor, his land or chattels or, absent the third party's objection, to those of a third party. If he does so, however, 'he is subject to liability for any harm done . . .'.[23]

---

[18] Boris Starck, Henri Roland, and Laurent Boyer, *Obligations 1: Responsabilité délictuelle* (4th edn., Paris 1991), §§ 300–1; François Terré, Philippe Simler, and Yves Lequette, *Droit civil: Les Obligations* (7th edn., Paris, 1999), § 704. The popularity of the doctrine is recent. In 1976, Charbonnier was one of the few to discuss it. He concluded that 'the maxim that necessity has no law is traditional and has the value of customary law'. Jean Charbonnier, *Droit civil* (Paris, 1976), § 45. He admitted that his position had little support in the case law. He mentioned an old criminal case in which a Cour d'appel stretched the text of the Criminal Code to acquit a girl, poor and hungry but not actually starving, who stole bread. The court found that the girl did not have a wrongful intention even though, according to art. 379 of the Criminal Code, all that is necessary is simply the intention to appropriate an object. Cour d'appel, Amiens, 22 Apr. 1898, S. 1899.II.1.

[19] E.g. Cass. 2e ch. civ., 8 Apr. 1970, JCP. 1970.J.136 (defendant not liable for breaking down a bathroom door to rescue a trapped child even though he inadvertently caused the child's eye to be injured by a piece of glass); Trib. d'instance, Charolles, 13 Mar. 1970, JCP 1970.J.16354 (defendant not at fault when he had to brake suddenly to avoid injuring a pedestrian).

[20] Francis H. Bohlen, 'Incomplete Privilege to Inflict Intentional Invasions of Interests of Property and Personality', *Harv. L. Rev.* 20 (1926), 307 at 316.   [21] ibid. 314.

[22] *Restatement of Restitution* § 122 (1937).   [23] *Restatement (Second) of Torts* § 195 (1965).

As my colleague Stephen Sugarman has noted, Bohlen and the *Restatements* seem to rely implicitly on a notion of unjust enrichment.[24] But by their formulation, a person would seem to be unjustly enriched whenever he threatens another's property to save his own. But if that is so, the law of necessity collides with the law of negligence. As Robert Keeton noted in 1959 in a well-known article: '[T]here is a kind of enrichment of oneself to the detriment of others when one operates an automobile non-negligently; it is not, however, unjust enrichment. It does not give rise to liability.'[25]

Indeed, as we will see later on, the question of whether a person was negligent turns on a balancing of the possibility of harm to someone else's life or property against that to his own. American jurists refer to this balancing as the 'Learned Hand formula' because it was proposed by Judge Learned Hand in *United States* v. *Carroll Towing Co.*[26] As we will see, while some modern scholars have interpreted the Hand formula as a sort of economic calculus of risks and benefits, the idea that one is behaving without negligence when one chooses the lesser evil, taking into account its probability, commends itself as a matter of common sense, and has been endorsed by continental jurists with little sympathy for law and economics. Indeed, as we will see, writers in the Aristotelian tradition regarded this balancing of evils as an exercise of the virtue of prudence.[27] If that is so, however, it cannot be that one must pay compensation when one imperils another's property to avoid a greater peril to one's own. If that were so, there would be no law of negligence.

Some jurists have tried to avoid the difficulty by saying that the doctrine of necessity privileges a person intentionally to endanger another's property. Therefore, the doctrine of necessity applies to risks created intentionally but not to those negligently created. While one finds hints of such an approach in American writers, it has been adopted by the German courts. To do so, they have made use of a concept of 'conditional intent' even though this concept was not developed to distinguish cases of necessity from cases of negligence but to explain how a person can be held to be intentionally responsible for consequences he did not intend. According to Hein Kötz:

A person acts intentionally when he knows that his conduct will lead to an unlawful violation of another's body, property or 'similar right' (*sonstiges Recht*) and who attains this result wilfully and consciously. The party need not have done so with a 'direct intention'; he need not have the purpose of interfering with these rights of legal interests. Rather, it is enough if he recognized the possibility of such an interference, and proceeded to act despite this knowledge, taking into account that action may occur, although he may even hope that it does not (conditional intent). Thus, one who flees from an accident and runs over a policeman standing in his way has intentionally injured him even if he hopes the policeman can reach safety by a sudden leap. It is enough if the person fleeing took account of the injury to the policeman in the event that it should occur as a consequence of his act which is certainly regrettable but which is subordinated to his purpose of fleeing.[28]

---

[24] Stephen Sugarman, 'The "Necessity" Defense and the Failure of Tort Theory: The Case Against Strict Liability for Damages Caused While Exercising Self-Help in an Emergency', issues in Legal Scholarship, (2005), http://www.bepres.com/ils/iss7/art1, 11, 15.

[25] Robert Keeton, 'Conditional Fault in the Law of Torts', *Harv. L. Rev.* 72 (1959), 401 at 414.

[26] 159 F2d 169 (2nd Cir 1947).   [27] Chapter 10 II C.

[28] Hein Kötz, *Deliksrecht* (3rd edn., Frankfurt-am-Main, 1983), 61.

As we will see later, this concept has been applied, unsuccessfully, to explain why one should be responsible for the unintended consequences of unlawful acts.[29] As applied to the problem of necessity, it leads to odd results. In one case, a German naval vessel ran aground. A second naval vessel attempted to pull her free. To do so the captain dropped anchor even though he knew that somewhere below him was an electric cable. Although the captain was not negligent in dropping anchor, the court held the German navy liable under the doctrine of necessity.

[T]he captain of the torpedo boat threw the anchor over and let it take hold although he knew that the anchor would penetrate the ground and took into account the possibility that the cable would be broken or injured. He tried to avoid or minimize such an injury to the cable. Nevertheless, in the event that these efforts were unsuccessful, he willed the action upon the cable as a consequence of the naval maneuver which he considered to be necessary and had carried out.[30]

In another case, the defendant motorist, to escape collision with a negligently driven vehicle whose driver was never identified, drove into the wrong lane and struck the plaintiff's car. The defendant was not negligent because risking collision with the plaintiff was a more reasonable course of action than driving head on into the third party. But the plaintiff claimed compensation under § 904 of the Civil Code. The plaintiff had harmed her car (or risked doing so) to prevent greater damage to his own. The court rejected this argument, refusing to hold the defendant liable:

a claim for compensation for harm by an owner under § 904, sentence 2, of the Civil Code is only possible when the defendant knows and wills to deal with the owner's thing under the circumstances of necessity of § 904, sentence 1. For that to be so, the party taking the action must at least conceive of the damage to the object as a possible consequence of his interference with the sphere of legal rights of another, and he must take account of it and consent.[31]

As a German jurist noted, speaking of the case of the motorist, the distinction does not make much sense. 'Taking into account a higher danger to other people's legally protected interests is part of daily life in modern traffic . . .'. Nevertheless, he thought that in case of the motorist, 'a claim under § 904 of the Civil Code was rightly rejected' even though 'the decision cannot be justified by dogmatically watertight arguments'.[32]

That is to put it mildly. As we will see, even German jurists who are suspicious of economic formulations of the law of negligence agree that one is not negligent, and therefore not liable, when one has endangered another's property to avoid a greater peril to someone else's. Now we are asked to believe that the difference between the captain dropping anchor when he knew it might cut a cable and the motorist pulling into the opposite lane is that in the one case, the captain 'willed the action on the cable' although he hoped to avoid it while the motorist did not 'conceive of the damage' of a collision as the possible consequence of pulling into a lane reserved for on-coming traffic. According to this formulation, the more carefully one understands the risks of one's action the more likely one is to be liable. That can't be.

---

[29] Chapter 10 I B.   [30] RG 29 Apr. 1926, RGZ 113, 301.
[31] BGH, 30 Oct. 1984, Vers R 1985, 66.
[32] R. Walter Dunz, Note to BGH, Decision of 10 Oct. 1984, Vers R 1985, 335.

As we will see, American jurists have stretched the concept of intentional wrong in a different way to explain why sometimes a wrongdoer is liable for consequences he did not intend. They have said that the consequences are intended if the actor knows they will come about with 'substantial certainty'. At a later point, we will see the difficulties of that approach.[33] Here it is enough to note that as applied to the doctrine of necessity, it leads to paradoxes as difficult as the German doctrine. It cannot be that liability turns on the probability that harm will come to the plaintiff. The defendant has acted reasonably whether he takes a chance of damaging the plaintiff's property to avoid a chance of harming something of greater value or whether the risk is 50 percent, 80 percent or 100 percent. There is no reason why, at some point, his action should count as intentional and he should be liable for behaving reasonably.

In the United States, though jurists are stymied, proponents of the law and economics movement have stepped into the breach. According to them, the doctrine of necessity produces efficient outcomes. They define efficiency in terms of the increased 'preference satisfaction', the amount of the increase depending on the amount a person is willing to pay to have his preference satisfied. To explain *Ploof* v. *Putnam*, Richard Posner noted that the pier owner wasn't present, and was held liable when his employee cut loose the ship that moored to his pier. In the absence of the pier owner, 'negotiations were, in the circumstances, infeasible'.[34] The negotiations would have led to an efficient result. In discussing *Vincent* v. *Lake Erie*, he argued that by imposing tort liability, the court is reflecting the contract the parties 'would have made had they had the opportunity to negotiate. . . '.[35] But in *Ploof*, the court rested its decision, not on the defendant's absence, but on the plaintiff's 'necessity'.[36] If it meant what it said, then, as in Germany and other civil law countries, it would have held the pier owner liable if he cut the ship loose. Suppose that he did so out of sheer cussedness after the plaintiff offered him a fortune to refrain. Would that result be efficient? I think an economist would have to say so. He defines efficiency in terms of preference satisfaction, and cussedness is as much a preference as any other. Suppose, after negotiating, the owner accepted plaintiff's promise of a fortune for permission to tie up. Would that also be efficient? Certainly, but would any court enforce it?[37]

More fundamentally, however, the economic analysis begs the very question we have been considering. Does the pier owner have the right to receive compensation if the ship owner ties up to his dock, as the necessity doctrine maintains? Or does the ship owner owe nothing because, by the law of negligence, he has behaved reasonably? Only after resolving that question can we imagine hypothetical contracts between the two parties. Instead of resolving it, the economic analysis assumes it has been answered in the dock owner's favor.

Stephen Sugarman, who is critical of the doctrine of necessity, has noted that, very often, its proponents merely appeal to common sense. According to Bohlen, 'it is

---

[33] Chapter 10 I B.   [34] Richard Posner, *Economic Analysis of Law* (5th edn., Boston, 1998), 190.

[35] William M. Landes and Richard A. Posner, 'Salvors, Finders, Good Samaritans, and Other Rescuers: An Economic Study of Law and Altruism', *J. Leg. Stud.* 7 (1978), 83 at 113 n. 74.

[36] 71 A at 189 ('necessity . . . will justify entries upon land and interferences with personal property that would otherwise be trespasses').   [37] See Sugarman, 'The "Necessity" Defense', 81.

obviously just that he whose interests are advanced by the act should bear the cost of doing it . . .'.[38] The philosopher Joel Feinberg put this case:

Suppose that you are on a backpacking trip in the high mountain country when an unanticipated blizzard strikes the area with such ferocity that your life is imperiled. Fortunately, you stumble onto an unoccupied cabin, locked and boarded up for the winter, clearly somebody else's private property. You smash in a window, enter, and huddle in a corner for three days until the storm abates. During this period you help yourself to your unknown benefactor's food supply and burn his wooden furniture in the fireplace to keep warm.[39]

According to Feinberg, 'everyone' would agree that although you acted justifiably you ought to pay. Sugarman is sceptical about arguments based on what everyone might think.[40] Sugarman is not so sure everyone would think that way. But the appeal to common sense is, in my view, a powerful argument. The Romans had no general doctrine of necessity but gave relief in cases where we would apply that doctrine. The 19th century jurists defined property as an unrestricted right to use one's own and yet in both the United States and Germany, necessity was recognized as an exception, again on the basis of common sense. While Sugarman's views may differ, those he criticizes would not have appealed to common sense had they not believed that most people would regard that appeal as persuasive. According to the German jurist Dunz, it makes sense that the motorist who pulls into another's lane should not be liable if he did it to escape a greater danger even though he believes this view cannot be defended by 'watertight logic'. If the distinction between necessity and negligence is perceived so widely, it seems hard to believe it has no rational basis.

Here, I think it is helpful to see how the distinction was formalized by the writers in the Aristotelian tradition. Thomas Aquinas had said that a person might violate commutative justice either by interfering with another's property in a wrongful manner (*acceptio rei*) or simply by having what belonged to another (*ipsa res accepta*).[41] The late scholastics examined this last possibility more closely. Suppose he no longer had another's property. He was liable, they said, if he had benefitted by its use. They thus recognized unjust enrichment as a distinct ground for relief from negligence or intentional harm, and the northern natural lawyers followed them.[42] As we have seen, they thought of the doctrine of necessity as a qualification on the rights of the owner of property. Given the purposes of creating private rights in external things, these rights had to give way before the greater need of another. But the person in greater need had still used another's property and therefore must still pay compensation even though he did not act wrongfully. The compensation was due, not for wrongful use, but simply for the use of what belonged to another.

Every now and then a modern jurist has raised such a consideration but often with reservations. Keeton admitted that it could be used to distinguish *Vincent* v. *Lake Erie* from cases of negligence: 'The distinction between using another's person or property

---

[38] Bohlen, 'Incomplete Privilege', 316.

[39] Joel Feinberg, 'Voluntary Euthanasia and the Inalienable Right to Life', *Philos. and Pub. Affairs* 7 (1978), 93 at 102.   [40] Sugarman, 'The Failure of Tort Theory', 17, 98.

[41] *Summa theologiae* II-II, Q. 62, a. 6.

[42] Molina, *De iustitia et iure*, disp. 718, no. 2; Lessius, *De iustitia et iure*, lib. 2, cap. 14, dub. 1, no. 3; Grotius, *De iure bellis ac pacis*, II.x.5; Pufendorf, *De iure naturae et gentium*, IV.xiii.9.

and increasing risks to his person or property may be useful in expressing a limit in the scope of the concept of unjust enrichment as customarily understood . . .'. But, he added, 'it is far from clear that this limit is sound'.[43] Jules Coleman claimed that the ship owner in *Vincent* and the hiker in Feinberg's hypothetical should be liable because they gained by 'taking of what another has a well-established right to'.[44] But he acknowledged that to 'have suggested that the basic concept may be that of a "taking" . . . only shifts the burden to an analysis of which are takings in the sense that requires compensation. I do not have a fully worked out analysis of a "taking" but I did not want the reader to think I had not realized the importance of developing one.'[45] In contrast, without reservations, Daniel Friedman has maintained that 'a person who obtains—though not necessarily tortiously—a benefit at the expense of another through appropriation of a property or quasi-property interest held by the other is unjustly enriched and should be liable to the other for any benefit attributable to the appropriation'.[46] My colleague Stephen Sugarman has criticized him for not explaining why 'appropriation' should matter.[47]

I don't think the matter is that mysterious. When a person owes compensation under the doctrine of necessity, the reason is precisely that he has used another person's property. We can see why that should be if we consider the reason that writers in the Aristotelian tradition gave for the existence of private property. They said that private property was instituted only to overcome the disadvantages of a state in which all property was held in common. In a state without private property, resources would go as of right to the person who had the best use for them. One might describe such a world by saying that all rights and duties were governed by what American jurists call the Learned Hand formula. Everything would depend on a balancing of the potential gains and losses to one party or the other and the risks associated with them.

According to writers in the Aristotelian tradition, the function of rights to private property is to avoid the disadvantages of such a state: to avoid quarrels over who has the best use for resources and to provide and incentive to produce resources and care for them. It does not follow, as we saw in considering nuisance, that the owner has a right to use his resources in any way he sees fit.[48] It does not follow, as we will see in considering negligence and strict liability, that he is to be indemnified whenever his resources are damaged or his activities damage another.[49] But it does follow that the owner's right to the exclusive use of his property is not absolute. Because of the purposes for which property rights are instituted, we must sometimes return to a state in which they do not apply and the right to use property depends solely on who has the greatest need.

---

[43] Keeton, 'Conditional Fault', 417–18.

[44] Jules Coleman, 'Corrective Justice and Wrongful Gain', *J. Legal. Stud.* 11 (1982), 421 at 423.

[45] ibid. 423 n. 2.

[46] Daniel Friedmann, 'Restitution of Benefits Obtained through the Appropriation of Property of the Commission of a Wrong', *Colum. L. Rev.* 80 (1980), 504 at 509.

[47] 'For this to be a normative rather than a descriptive theory, however, Friedmann must explain what is an appropriation of a property interest in way that convinces us that, in such a case, the defendant's enrichment is indeed unjust. More precisely, he must tell us, in terms relevant to Vincent, which he supports, why the use of the loaded word "appropriation" is seemly. I am not persuaded that he has done so.' Sugarman, 'The "Necessity" of Defense', 35. [48] Chapter 4 III.

[49] Chapter 10 II and III.

II. Adverse Possession and Prescription

A traditional rule, known as adverse possession in common law[50] and prescription in civil law, deprives an owner of his property if another has been in possession of it long enough. As Henry Ballantine put it, that 'sounds at first blush like title by theft or by robbery, a primitive method of acquiring land without paying for it'.[51]

Not only is the institution ancient, however, but so are the justifications given for it.[52] For Ballantine, there was one justification only: 'the great purpose is to automatically quiet all titles which are openly and consistently asserted, to provide proof of meritorious titles, and correct errors in conveyancing'.[53] A similar justification had been given centuries earlier by Soto, Lessius, and other late scholastics. The purpose, Soto said, was 'the public good, that is, that ownership shall be certain, and errors shall be undone through the passage of time, and the possession of things shall be secure'.[54] As authority, they quoted a Roman text that made much the same point.[55]

Ballantine noted that were this the only reason, '[i]f we had a scientific system for the registration of titles, adverse possession would be of far less importance'.[56] As the British jurists, Kevin and Susan Gray observed, '... that the 1998 Law Commission, in announcing its vision of a future founded on a "culture of registration," simultaneously recommended changes in the law of adverse possession that would significantly diminish the right of the squatter to derogate from the right of the registered proprietor of the land'.[57] Indeed, prescription is of much less importance in German land law, which does have a scientific system of recording titles in a land register or *Grundbuch*. Entries in the *Grundbuch* can be changed due to the passage of time only under the most restricted circumstances. Section 927 of the German Civil Code provides that the right of an owner can be changed after the passage of 30 years only if the person registered as owner is dead or missing and no entries have been made affecting the property during that period. Indeed, the drafters of the German Civil Code claimed that to permit prescription would be incompatible with the purpose of the land registration system. 'Prescription would be incompatible with the purpose of

---

[50] In common law, the word 'prescription' is used for obtaining rights such as easements in another's property by long use.

[51] Henry Ballantine, 'Title by Adverse Possession', *Harv. L. Rev.* 32 (1918), 135 at 135.

[52] Not counting a modern one invented by Oliver Wendell Holmes. He said that 'It is in the nature of man's mind. A thing which you have enjoyed and used as your own for a long time ... takes root in your being and cannot be torn away without your resenting the act and trying to defend yourself. ... The law can ask no better justification than the deepest instincts of man.' Oliver Wendell Holmes, Jr., 'The Path of the Law', *Harv. L. Rev.* 10 (1897), 457 at 476–7. I cannot imagine the state of law if, generally speaking, the deepest instincts of man to resent and strike back were regarded as legal justifications.

[53] Ballantine, 'Adverse Possession', 135.

[54] Soto, De *iustitia et iure*, lib. IV, q. 5. Similarly, Lessius, *De iustitia et iure*, lib. 2, cap. 6, dub.17, no. 50.

[55] The text speaks of *usucaptio*, one way in which ownership could be acquired by continued possession. It said: '*Usucaptio* was introduced for the public good, that is, so that the ownership of things should not be uncertain for a long period, possibly forever, granted that the period of time prescribed should be sufficient for owners to inquire after their property'. Dig. 41.3.1.   [56] Ballantine, 'Adverse Posessession', 143.

[57] Kevin Gray and Susan Francis Gray, *Elements of Land Law* (3rd edn., London, 2001), 240–1, quoting Law Commission and HM Land Registry, *Land Registration for the Twenty-First Century*, Law Comm. no. 254 (Sept. 1998), ¶¶ 11.10, 11.56.

the land register because the purpose of the register is to make ownership knowable, and to permit prescription would in large measure contradict this measure . . .'.[58]

Nevertheless, perennially, jurists have given another justification for adverse possession or prescription: land should belong to the person who is putting it to use, not to an owner who has not behaved like an owner and has not even checked to see how his land is being used. Soto objected that 'many think' the owner loses his property because of 'negligence inquiring after his thing'; for 'the foundation of this judgment is that the laws of prescription appear to be made only or principally as a penalty for the negligence of the owner'.[59] Ballantine criticized those who thought the policy of adverse possession was 'to reward those using land in a way beneficial to the community' and 'to penalize the negligent or dormant owner for sleeping on his rights'.[60] Yet many Anglo-American[61] and French[62] jurists have been comfortable with both theories, or, at least, they have placed them side by side as the two policies informing adverse possession and prescription. The law and economics scholars Robert Cooter and Thomas Ulen have presented both as economic justifications of adverse possession.[63]

Anglo-American and French jurists have not thought it necessary to explain which of these justifications is correct because, as long as one does not sufficiently trust the system of land registration, either can explain the rules they have inherited. Most of the rules are similar under the law of England, the United States, France and, for that matter, under the *ius commune* of the Middle Ages. To eventually obtain title, the intruder must actually take possession of the land;[64] his behavior must be public and open.[65] He must remain in possession continuously,[66] although possession counts as continuous if he voluntarily transfers his interest in the property to another person who can then count the prior period of possession as his own.[67] Common lawyers call this 'tacking' the previous period of adverse possession to the new one. The owner is protected, to some extent, if he is under certain disabilities in asserting his rights, in

---

[58] *Protokolle der Kommission zur Ausarbeitung einer bürgerlichen Gesetbuches* (Berlin, 1881–9), 3950–1, in Horst Heinrich Jakobs and Werner Schubert, eds., *Die Beratung des bürgerlichen Gesetbuches in systematischer Zusammenstellung der unveröffentlichten Quellen Sachenrecht* 1 (Berlin, 1985), 560.

[59] Lessius, *De iustitia et iure*, lib. 2, cap. 6, dub.17, no. 50.

[60] Ballantine, 'Adverse Possession', 135.

[61] Gray and Gray, *Land Law*, 242–4; Abraham Bell and Gideon Parchomovsky, 'Pliability Rules', *Mich. L. Rev.* 101 (2000), 1 at 56–7; see Carol Rose, *Univ. of Chi. L. Rev.* 52 (1985), 73 at 79 (she has a more sophisticated analysis, however, of the role of possession in preserving clarity as to title).

[62] François Terré and Philippe Simler, *Droit civil: Les biens* (5th edn., Paris, 1998), nos. 443–4; Gabriel Marty and Pierre Raynaud, *Les Biens* (2nd edn., Paris, 1980), no. 284; Christian Atias, *Droit civil: Les biens* 1 (Paris, 1980), no. 147.

[63] Robert Cooter and Thomas Ulen, *Law and Economics* (4th edn., Boston, 2003), 154–6.

[64] On the *ius commune*, see Lessius, *De iustitia et iure*, lib. 2, cap. 6, dub. 1.

[65] French Civil Code (*Code civil*) art. 2229 ('public, unequivocal and à titre de propriétarie'; Gray and Gray, *Land Law*, 263–4 ('open') (English law); Richard Powell and Michael Allan Wolf, *Powell on Real Property* 16 (New York, 2000), ¶ 91.04 ('open & notorious') (US law).

[66] French Civil Code (*Code civil*), art. 2243; Gray and Gray, *Land Law*, 263 (English law); Powell and Wolf, *Real Property*, 91.07 (US law); Lessius, *De iustitia et iure*, lib. 2, cap. 6, dub. 16 (*ius commune*).

[67] French Civil Code (*Code civil*), art. 2235; Gray and Gray, *Land Law*, 247, 279–80 (English law); Powell and Wolf, *Real Property*, ¶ 91.10 (US law); Lessius, *De iustitia et iure*, lib. 2, cap. 6, dub. 14, no. 48 (*ius commune*).

particular, if he is a minor or a lunatic.[68] There is less consensus on whether the intruder must have acted in the good faith belief that he was entitled to possess the land. The medieval canon law insisted that he must act in good faith, and claimed that this rule bound secular as well as church courts.[69] Under French law, bad faith lengthens the term required for prescription.[70] In America, bad faith may or may not be an obstacle to prescription, and jurists disagree as to the number of states in which it is.[71] In England, the good or bad faith of the intruder does not matter.[72]

These rules were consistent with either of the two traditional explanations: that of clearing title, and that of transferring ownership from one who did not use his property to one who did. The question of whether or not to allow a bad faith possessor to profit had little to do with either rule. Some French jurists have claimed that the rules protecting owners under a disability are hard to explain if the sole purpose of the rule is to clear title.[73] But the law could have the policy of making title certain and still wish to give those who have title a chance to protect it. Indeed, the same Roman text that said that the rights of long continued possession are 'introduced for the public good ... so that the ownership of things should not be uncertain for a long period' added 'that the period of time prescribed should be sufficient for owners to inquire after their property'.[74]

Perhaps the most serious debate over which of these two purposes underlies the rules just described took place among the late scholastics. The reason for their interest is not one that would trouble modern jurists. They were writing about both law and morals. Granted that a possessor became entitled to property by operation of law, was he morally entitled to it? If not, he would seem to have a moral obligation to return the property or its value. Thomas Aquinas thought that he did, invoking Aristotle's idea that commutative justice maintains equality in the share of resources of the parties. Aquinas put the case of 'one who consumes the thing of another ... it being understood that he has such a right by prescription'. He answered that 'if equality is not restored, it cannot be just, that granted he does not have an action in civil law against the one who consumed, he does according to divine law'.[75] He seems to have in mind, not the use of land, but something like wine which cannot be used without consuming it.[76] His question, however, was straightforward. Granted that there might be legal reasons for taking away one person's property and giving it to another, on what moral ground could the new owner justly retain the property?

---

[68] French Civil Code (*Code civil*), art. 2252; E. H. Burn, *Cheshire & Burn's Modern Law of Real Property* (16th edn., London, 2000), 984–5; (English law); Powell and Wolf, *Real Property*, ¶ 91.10 (US law); Lessius, *De iustitia et iure*, lib. 2, cap. 6, dub. 3, no. 14 (*ius commune*).

[69] *Decretales Gregorii ix, Corpus iuris canonici* 2 (E. Freidberg, ed.), 2.26.20. For a discussion of the varying interpretations and exceptions that jurists placed on this prohibition, see Lessius, *De iustitia et iure*, lib. 2, cap. 6, dub. 6.   [70] French Civil Code (*Code civil*), 2262, 2265.

[71] Compare Richard H. Helmholz, 'Adverse Possession and Subjective Intent', *Wash. U. L. Quar.* 61 (1983), 331 with Roger A. Cunningham, 'Adverse Possession and Subjective Intent: A Reply to Professor Helmholz', *Wash. U. L. Quar.* 64 (1986), 1.   [72] Gray and Gray, *Land Law*, 277.

[73] Alex Weill, François Terré, and Philippe Simler, *Droit civil: Les biens* (3rd edn., Paris, 1985), no. 460.
[74] Dig. 41.3.1.

[75] Thomas Aquinas, *Quaestiones quodlibitales*, in Thomas Aquinas, *Opera omnia* 9 (Parma 1852–73), Quodlibet 12, art. 25, p. 459 at 628.

[76] He draws this distinction elsewhere. *Summa theologiae* II-II, Q. 78, a. 1.

In the 17th century, Iohannes Medina thought that the previous owner had been justly deprived of his property because prescription was 'a penalty for negligence' which also served 'to avoid negligence in the future'.[77] It would seem to follow the new owner was bound to return the property only if the old one had been negligent in his care of it. According to Lessius, this was the view of many jurists.[78] Some said, according to Soto, that even the negligent former owner still had a moral right to his property unless the negligence constituted serious wrongdoing that would justify depriving him of his property.[79] But how often, Soto asked, would that happen? Like prodigality, negligence in the use of one's property would rise to the level of a serious wrong only if it violated some important moral obligation: for example, to provide for one's family. But the person in straightened circumstances who was having trouble providing for his family would rarely neglect to look after his property.[80] The true answer, according to Lessius and Soto, was that the purpose of prescription was the public good in quieting title. Their opponents answered that even if some were 'lord of the world, he would not be the owner of the things [in it], so that he could take away things as he pleased'.[81] Lessius and Soto answered that, nevertheless, he could transfer ownership when the public good so required.[82] This is one of the rare instances in which they seem to have disagreed with their intellectual hero, Thomas Aquinas.

This debate is illuminating because both sides seem to have lost, and seeing why they lost may clarify the rationale for adverse possession. The adversaries of Soto and Lessius lost because they could only think of one reason an owner could lose title: confiscating it was a penalty for some wrong he had done. By this rationale, title was not owed as a matter of justice to the adverse possessor. The owner lost it because he was a wrongdoer. Prescription therefore was something like a criminal penalty. But what could he have done that was so wrong as to warrant forfeiting his property? The only answer seemed to be that he was negligent in looking after it, and, as Soto pointed out, that would only be seriously wrong if, for example, his family were in need. So for this rationale to explain adverse possession we must imagine, as Soto said, that prescription aims at taking property away from needy people who despite their need don't bother to use or sell it. That can't be right.

But neither, it would seem, is the explanation of Lessius and Soto. If someone is not using their property, it may be in the public good for the government to give it to someone who will then have a clear title or who may put it to a productive use. But one cannot say that the government can take property without compensation simply to achieve some public benefit. Stated as an abstract proposition, even Soto and Lessius would have had to agree.

This debate illuminates, then, what seems to be the inherent difficulties of either of the traditional explanations of adverse possession. Since the state ordinarily doesn't confiscate property without compensation for any reason other than severe wrongdoing, why does it do so in this one case: when the owner neglects to use his property for a sufficiently long time? Since the state cannot ordinarily take property without

---

[77] Iohannes Medina, *De rerum dominio, earum restitutione et reliquis contractibus* (Cologne, 1607), Q. 16, p. 133.   [78] Lessius, *De iustitia et iure*, lib. 2, cap. 6, dub. 17, no. 50.

[79] Soto, *De iustitia et iure*, lib. IV, q. 5.   [80] ibid.   [81] ibid.

[82] ibid.; Lessius, *De iustitia et iure*, lib. 2, cap. 6, dub. 17, no. 50.

compensation even for sound public reasons, how can it do so here whether the benefit sought is that titles may be clarified or property used productively?

In my view, the only way out of this dilemma is to recognize that when an owner does not intend to put property to productive use, he does not have ownership in its true sense. One cannot explain his rights in terms of the reasons for having the institution of ownership.

We discussed these reasons when we dealt with the difference between possession and ownership.[83] As we saw, many societies in which land is not scarce do not distinguish between ownership and possession, at least in the same way modern legal systems do. The land belongs to the person who clears and plants it. He can lease it to another and while remaining the owner—in that sense, ownership and possession can be separated. But when the land is no longer used, it is no longer owned. When no one is in possession, the land goes back into a common stock and may be assigned to someone else who will put it to use. As we saw, such a system would be fair if we consider the reasons why, according to writers in the Aristotelian tradition, private property rights should be instituted at all. They avoid quarrels while encouraging people to produce and care for resources.

Ownership is a solution to two problems that did not arise in societies like these where land was abundant, and private land had only one productive use. One problem is how to allocate scarce resources among people who want them. Under a system of ownership, one normally acquires resources by buying them. The other is the problem of deciding how resources will be used. Under a system of ownership, this decision is left to the owner. Even his decision to leave the land idle is normally respected. Under normal circumstances, this modern model also serves the purposes which the Aristotelian writers identified for private property. It prevents quarrels and encourages people to produce and care for resources. Ownership serves these purposes because once a resource such as land is scarce it commands a price. People normally will not buy it unless they have a productive use for it. If they do not, normally they will sell it.

It is possible, however, to have an aberration: a person who pays so little attention to what he owns that he neither sells it nor intends to put it to a productive use. His failure to use it is not even due to a desire to conserve a natural habitat or to warehouse it for use in the future. He has made no such decision at all. It follows that the reasons for recognizing ownership over land that is not in productive use do not apply to such a person. He is not an owner for any of the reasons for which the law recognizes owners. Consequently, there is no reason why the law should extend to him the protection it normally does to owners.

If that is so, we can see why, in this case uniquely, the law will not protect him, so that the land will be put to productive use by someone else, or so as to avoid quarrels by clarifying doubts about title. The reason is not that the law has a general policy of reallocating land to what it deems to be more productive uses or of abrogating titles to avoid confusion. It is because, given the reasons for the institution of ownership, certain so-called owners should not be protected because they have not taken it upon themselves to allocate land to its most productive use, and their conduct has only muddled titles.

---

[83] Chapter 3 III.

The proper conclusion, then, is not that of Professor Ballantine, the drafters of the German Civil Code, and the British Law Commission: that a clear system of land registration will solve all the problems to which the traditional doctrines of adverse possession and prescription are addressed. It is that the traditional doctrines themselves do quite a good job of handling a distinct problem: how to avoid protecting the rights of those who claim ownership but who, given the purposes of that institution, should not be recognized as owners.

8

Acquisition of Resources Without a Prior Owner's Consent: Minerals, Capture, Found Property

I. Possession as the Origin of Property

One person may voluntarily transfer property to another. As we will see, writers in the Aristotelian tradition described these transfers as acts of commutative justice, if they were intended to obtain an equivalent for what was given, or as acts of liberality, if they were intended to enrich the other party at the giver's expense. Alternatively, a person may acquire property that did not previously belong to anyone else. Under Roman law, he might catch an animal or find an object which no one else owned or whose owner could not be identified. Often, he obtained title to such an object by *occupatio* or taking possession of it.

Some modern philosophers have seen in *occupatio* or first possession or in some kindred concept the origin of all property. For John Locke, since each person owned his own labor, one who mixed his labor with an object thereby became its owner.[1] He left it unclear what one had to do to mix one's labor with an object beyond taking possession of it. According to Immanuel Kant, one could appropriate anything that was not previously owned or used by someone else. He rested this idea on the will. The will would pointlessly lose some of its freedom if a person could not appropriate something that no one else owned or was using.[2] For both philosophers, after resources had originally been acquired in these ways, they could then be legitimately transferred from one person to another by agreement in the absence of force or fraud.

For Locke and Kant it was important to explain how ownership was originally acquired for reasons that were foreign to the Aristotelian tradition. For the Aristotelian writers, property existed so that, to the extent possible, people could live a truly human life. Ideally, resources would be held in common and would be distributed according to what each person deserved. Admittedly, different regimes would have different ideas of desert. However that might be, private property was instituted to overcome the disadvantages of holding property in common: there would be

[1] John Locke, *Second Treatise of Government*, in *Two Treatises of Government* (P. Laslett, ed., Cambridge, 1963), § 25.
[2] Immanuel Kant, *Grundlegung zur Metaphysik der Sitten* 354, in Immanuel Kant, *Werke in sechs Bänden* 4 (W. Weischedel, ed., Weisbaden, 1956–64), 107.

endless disputes, people would take less care to manage property well, and some would work hard and get less while others worked less and received more. As a result, the ideal had to be compromised. To avoid these disadvantages, one could not distribute all the property of the rich, or the unvirtuous rich, among those deemed more deserving.

Consequently, while writers in the Aristotelian tradition sometimes describe possession or *occupatio* as the origin of property, they do so for a different purpose and with different consequences. They imagine the world as originally sparsely populated. Its resources belonged to everyone. If the population could have remained small and people could have stayed on good terms, there would have been no need for private property. As Lessius and Grotius point out, resources could have been shared as they are among members of religious orders. But given the need to introduce private rights, people adopted one of two rules: to divide up what they held as a common stock or to grant the right to resources to the first person to take possession of them. The reason for the latter rule was not that a person had an inherent right to anything with which he mixed his labor or exerted his will. It was simply a convenient rule when the world was a largely empty place with plenty for everyone to appropriate. As Lessius put it, 'For the posterity of Adam were coming as it were into a house filled with things so that whoever occupied a thing first became its owner'.[3] Indeed, one could hardly imagine, when the population of the earth was small, that its original inhabitants would make some express decision about to whom all its resources should belong. At any rate, it was not a rule of inherent right. The state could—and Roman law did[4]—make a rule that the finder of treasure must give half of it to the owner of the land on which it was found.[5] The state could make a rule that newly discovered minerals belonged to the state and not to the finder.[6] Moreover, writers in the Aristotelian tradition regarded distributive justice as an ongoing duty of the state. They were not claiming that the current distribution of resources must be just because the initial distribution was just since it was based on a just principle of private appropriation, and subsequent transfers of resources were just because, absent force or fraud, they were based on agreement. Had they thought so, it would have been meaningless for the Aristotelian writers to claim that distributive justice was based on merit, that in a democracy merit meant equality, and that in an aristocracy, it meant virtue. Aquinas describes distributive and commutative justice in organic terms as ongoing requirements for the health of the civic body: distributive justice governs the order of the whole state to the individuals which are its parts, and commutative justice governs the order of one part to another.[7]

This approach avoided the difficulties of Locke's and Kant's position. Locke never gave a good account of what it means to mix one labor with a thing or why one should thereby own it. As Carol Rose says, quoting Robert Nozick: 'Suppose I pour a can of tomato juice into the ocean: do I now own the seas?'[8] Moreover, while Kant is right

[3] Leonardus Lessius, *De iustitia et iure, ceterisque virtutibus cardinalis libri quatuor* (Paris, 1628), lib. 2, cap. 5, dub. 1.   [4] I. 2.1.39.

[5] Aquinas, *Summa theologiae* II-II, Q. 66, a. 5, ad. 2; Lessius, *De iustitia et iure*, lib. 2, cap. 5, dub. 15, no. 59.

[6] Lessius, *De iustitia et iure*, lib. 2, cap. 5, dub. 12, no. 51.

[7] Aquinas, *Summa theologiae* II-II, Q. 61, a. 1.

[8] Carol Rose, 'Possession as the Origin of Property', *U. Chi. L. Rev.* 53 (1985), 73, 74, quoting Robert Nozick, *Anarchy, State and Utopia* (New York, 1974), 175.

that the will would be constrained for no reason if no one could use what another person was not using, that argument proves at most that the prior possessor should sometimes have the right to appropriate an object. It does not prove he should have the exclusive right to whatever he first appropriates, be it a gold mine, a valley, or for that matter a continent.[9]

Nevertheless, the discussions of the rights of first possession by late scholastics and northern natural lawyers seem lame. Usually, they assert that the first possessor has a right without explaining why. Part of the reason may be that the problem cannot be framed in terms of commutative justice, the concept on which they most frequently rely. By hypothesis, the resources in question did not previously belong to anyone. Therefore one who appropriates them can hardly have violated commutative justice by taking what belongs to another. Part of the difficulty, however, was that these writers did not effectively deploy the other concepts which the Aristotelian tradition did provide: the concept of distributive justice and the justifications for instituting rights to private property. As we will now see, these concepts bring one closer to an explanation of how legal systems treat the rights of a first possessor although they cannot provide all the answers.

II. Acquisition of Resources without a Prior Owner's Consent

A. Distributive Justice

In the Aristotelian tradition, resources in principle belong to everyone. Ideally, distributive justice would be done by allocating them according to merit, although, as we have seen, different regimes will differ over what constitutes merit. If that is the case, it is hard to see why very precious resources such as minerals should belong to the finder. The only reason would seem to be to provide an incentive to search for them. As the Aristotelian tradition recognized, one reason for recognizing private rights is to provide an incentive for them to be produced. But that does not explain why the finder should have the right to whatever he finds, however great its value may be. Nor does it explain why he should have the right to resources he finds by chance. For that matter, it is hard to see why, on Aristotelian grounds, minerals should belong to the person on whose land they happen to be found unless he paid a higher price for the land because he knew or suspected the resources were there. The only reason would seem to be that, as explained earlier, the owner of property has the right, not simply to its market value, but to the personal value he places on it, like someone whose house is worth more to him than the amount he could sell it for. He bought the right to this personal value when he bought the house. It may be that there is no way to exploit the resources found under his land without dispossessing him or destroying this personal value. It may be that this personal value is hard to estimate. But if the value of the minerals is so great that it is clear he would exploit them himself if he could, even though he would forfeit this personal value, then the only reason he should have the right to

---

[9] Chapter 1 II B 2 b.

the minerals is the difficulty of estimating the personal value he would lose if they were exploited and he were not allowed to keep the proceeds. But that is merely a problem of uncertainty. It would seem that when the value of the minerals is great enough, it should be resolved by compensating the owner by a generous amount that in all probability will make him happy they were found though he cannot keep their value for himself.

Lessius said that as a general rule gold or metals belonged to the finder at least if they were found on the shore or in rivers or other property which was not privately owned. But he said that the state might own these minerals if it granted concessions to those who search for them and if it compensated the landowner if they were found on private land.[10] It is hard to see why, on Aristotelian principles, this rule, which Lessius says the state may adopt, should not be the general rule. It provides both an incentive to find minerals and compensation to owners who lose the use of the land on which they are found. It recognizes that in principle, resources are held in common until the state makes some distribution of them in accordance with distributive justice.

Consequently, it is reasonable that many modern legal systems have enacted a rule like the one that Lessius describes.

In German law, one needs a permit from the state to prospect (*Erlaubnis*) or to exploit a mineral discovery (*Bewilligung*). He can obtain one even if he is not the owner of the land on which the minerals are located.[11] The owner of that land can grant him a right of exploitation, but if he refuses, the person with the permit to exploit them can compel such a right to be granted although the owner is then entitled to damages.[12] Jürgen Baur calls this law a form of expropriation that can be required when it serves the public interest.[13] If our approach is correct, it would be more accurate to say that the former proprietor owns the land without which the minerals cannot be exploited and the state owns the minerals. Thus it is less an expropriation than a means of settling conflicting land rights in favor of the person whose interest is of greater value. It is like accession in which one who paints on another's canvas can keep the painting but must pay compensation for the canvas.

French law is similar. Minerals such as coal, iron, salt, gold, silver, petroleum and natural gas belong to the state, not to the surface owner. The state grants a concession for their exploitation.[14] The holder of the concession must pay the surface owner an annual sum which reflects his interference with the surface owner's use of his land.[15] The courts have held that he is also liable for any damage he causes to the surface owner's property whether he is at fault or not.[16]

English law is much the same. Traditionally, the crown had the right to deposits of gold and silver.[17] Now, coal,[18] oil, and natural gas[19] also belong to the state.[20] The state

---

[10] Lessius, *De iustitia et iure*, lib. 2, cap. 5, dub. 12, no. 51.   [11] Bundesberggesetz, §§ 11–13.
[12] ibid. §§ 77 ff.   [13] Jürgen Baur, *Sachenrechts* (17th edn., Munich, 1999), § 30 II.
[14] Decree no. 80–204 of 11 Mar. 1980.
[15] *Code minier*, 16 Aug. 1956, as modified by Law of 16 June 1977, art. 37.
[16] Gérard Cornu, *Droit civil: Introduction: Les personnes: Les Biens* (4th edn., Paris, 1990), no. 1520.
[17] Case of Mines (1568), 1 Plowd 310, 336, 75 ER 472, 510.
[18] Coal Industry Act 1994, ss 1(1), 7(3).   [19] Petroleum Act 1998, ss 1(a), 2(1).
[20] See generally Kevin Gray and Susan Francis Gray, *Elements of Land Law* (3rd edn., London, 2001), 21–2.

grants licenses to search for and extract such minerals for whatever consideration it sees fit. The landowner is entitled to compensation for whatever ancillary rights are necessary for their exploitation.[21]

The exception is the United States in which, in principle, minerals belong to the owner of the land. Perhaps the explanation lies in the peculiarities of the settlement of the American continent in which it was thought desirable to encourage a small population to exploit an abundance of resources as quickly as possible. Perhaps it lies in a traditional American prejudice against an active role for the state, of which more will be said later.

B. Incentives for the Exploitation of Resources and the Prevention of Quarrels

Aristotle and Aquinas gave three reasons why rights to private property should be instituted. Two of them have to do with incentives: if property is common, people will not be careful to preserve and manage it; moreover, people will be reluctant to work. The third reason is to prevent quarrels. If resources are allocated according to who deserves them, whatever the standard of desert may be, there will be more quarrels than if resources have clearly designated owners. A rule awarding property to the first to take possession may be a means both of providing incentives and of preventing quarrels. To the extent work and care are necessary to take possession, bestowing a right on the first possessor may provide an incentive for this work and care. Moreover, if a clear rule is needed to decide to whom property should belong, first possession may provide the clearest rule possible.

This observation is not original. It was made by Carol Rose in her 1985 article 'Possession as the Origin of Property'. She begins by considering the classic early case of *Pierson* v. *Post*,[22] in which the court awarded a dead fox, not to the hunter who had pursued it diligently, but to an interloper who appeared and killed it. As she notes, '*Pierson* . . . presents two great principles, seemingly at odds, for defining possession: (1) notice to the world through a clear act, and (2) reward to useful labor'.[23] Thus, as she points out, the majority believed that by awarding the fox to the possessor it established a clear rule valuable 'for the sake of certainty, and preserving peace and order in society' and for avoiding 'a fertile source of quarrels and litigation'.[24] The dissent, noting that the fox is a 'noxious beast' whose destruction is 'a public benefit' thought 'our decision should have in view the greatest possible encouragement to the destruction' of such an animal. Therefore, the pursuing hunter should prevail for 'who would keep a pack of hounds; or what gentleman would mount his steed, and for hours together . . . pursue the windings of this wily quadruped if . . . a saucy intruder, who had not shared in the honors or labors of the chase' could take the animal for himself.[25] Here, the two principles seemed to work against each other. The first possession rule would be more clear but would award the fox to the 'saucy intruder'. A different rule would be less clear but would reward the labor of the hunter.

---

[21] Mines (Working and Facilities and Support) Act 1966, s. 8.
[22] 3 Cai R 175 (NY Sup Ct 1805).   [23] Rose, 'Possession', 181.   [24] 3 Cai R at 179.
[25] 3 Cai R at 180.

In a more typical case, however, the first possession rule would serve both purposes at once: absent the intruder, it would both be clear and reward the hunter's efforts. Similarly, a rule that lost property belongs to the finder if he takes appropriate steps to locate the true owner provides both an incentive to locate the true owner and a clear rule as to who should have the object if these efforts fail. Both purposes are worthwhile if, as Aristotle and Aquinas thought, property rights are established both to prevent quarrels and to provide incentives for useful work. It is not surprising, then, that, subject to exceptions we will describe, the rule that wild animals belong to the first to take possession was adopted, not only by Anglo-American law, but, for example, by Roman,[26] French,[27] Italian,[28] and German[29] law as well. Anglo-American,[30] French,[31] Italian,[32] German,[33] and other modern[34] legal systems also adopted the rule that lost objects belong to the finder at least if he takes appropriate steps to locate the true owner, which may include leaving the property at a specially authorized bureau.

Nevertheless, in light of these considerations, we can see why the first possession rule is a notorious source of difficulty whether it is applied to previously unowned objects such as wild animals or to objects that have been lost, mislaid or concealed by an unknown owner. To begin with, the first possession rule will not always provide the best incentive for useful labor. That was the point the dissent made in *Pierson* v. *Post*. In cases where it clearly provides the wrong incentives, American courts, at least, have been willing to discard or redefine the rule. For example, in *Ghen* v. *Rich*,[35] complainant had been hunting fin-back whales by shooting them with bomb-lances fired from guns. When killed, this species of whale immediately sinks to the bottom but resurfaces within a matter of days. The respondent (as the defendant is called in an admiralty case) bought a whale which had drifted into shore from a person who had taken first possession of it. The court ruled in favor of the libellant (as the plaintiff is called) who had killed the whale. The court noted that there was a custom among whalers that the animal belonged to whoever had killed it. But the court said that even absent the custom, the common law might reach the same result.[36] Otherwise 'this

---

[26] Dig. 41.1.1.1.

[27] Alex Weil, François Terré, and Philippe Simler, *Droit civil: Les Biens* (Paris, 1985), no. 402.

[28] Italian Civil Code (*Codice civile*), art. 923, although Law no. 968 of 27 Dec. 1977 declares wild animals to be part of the patrimony of the state and provides that they do not belong to the captor unless he obeys the rules laid down by the law.

[29] German Civil Code (*Bürgerlichesgesetzbuch*) [hereinafter BGB], §§ 958, 960.

[30] The classic case holding that the finder has a right against anyone but the true owner is *Armory* v. *Delmirie* (1722) 1 Strange 505 (KB). Many American states have enacted legislation requiring finders to deposit the property in a designated place or to give notice that it has been found. Jesse Dukeminier and James E. Krier, *Property* (4th edn., New York, 1998), 124–5.

[31] French Civil Code (*Code civil*), art. 717(2); Weil *et al.*, *Droit civil: Les Biens*, no. 411. In France, by municipal ordinance, the finder is usually required to leave the object with a lost and found bureau (ibid.).

[32] Italian Civil Code (*Codice civile*), arts. 927–9. The finder must first leave the object with an official (*sindico*) (art. 927), who must give notice that the object was found (art. 928).

[33] German Civil Code (*Bürgerlichesgesetzbuch*) [hereinafter BGB], §§ 965–83; *Codice civile*, arts. 927–9. In Germany, he must first take the object to an authorized bureau. BGB § 965.

[34] Roman law, apparently, did not recognize such a rule except in the case of treasure, where it is assumed the owner cannot be found, as will be described later on. See Dig. 6.1.67; Max Kaser, *Das Römische Privatrecht* 1 (Munich, 1955), 359. [35] 8 F 159 (D Mass 1881).

[36] 8 F at 162.

branch of industry must necessarily cease, for no person would engage in it if the fruits of his labor could be appropriated by any chance finder'.[37]

In other cases, it will be harder to tell which rule will provide the right incentives. For example, the court in *Ghen* v. *Rich* says that whalers follow two different customs in hunting other species of whales. According to one, whoever first harpooned the whale is entitled to capture it even if the whale breaks free from the boat. According to the other, he is entitled to capture the whale only as long as it remains attached to boat by a line.[38] The court implied it was willing to follow whatever custom whalers had adopted. In the absence of a custom, however, it would be difficult to tell which rule provides the best incentives.[39] One would have to know a good deal about the industry in question. One could not tell by a legal analysis, and certainly not by an analysis of what constitutes 'possession'.

A similar problem arises when a hunter captures an animal on another person's land. Should the animal belong to the hunter so as to give him an incentive to hunt or to the landowner to give him an incentive to acquire and preserve property where valuable animals may be found? It is not surprising that legal systems differ. Under French law, hunting rights belong to the owner of the land.[40] According to some distinguished French jurists, however, game caught on his land in violation of his rights belongs to the hunter.[41] Originally, under the German Civil Code, the animal belonged to the hunter, wherever it was caught,[42] but a later statute provided that it belongs to whoever has the right to hunt on the land in question.[43] That right belongs to a person who owns more than 75 hectares of land; if he owns less, he shares the right with other smaller landowners.[44] In Anglo-American law, animals caught on another's land belong in principle to the landowner.[45] Nevertheless, some American courts have been willing to imply that the hunter had an implied license to hunt on wild and unenclosed lands.[46] Presumably, the owner acquiring such land did not do so to have a stock of valuable animals which was diminished by the hunter's capture. Otherwise a license would not have been implied. One could give the hunter an incentive to hunt without diminishing the owner's incentive to acquire and preserve land for the sake of hunting.

One problem, then, is to determine when a first possession rule provides the right incentives. Another problem is to determine what rule to apply when there are two possible clear rules, either of which could be used to avoid quarrels. For example, if one person finds an object on another's land, does the object belong to the finder who first took possession or to the owner of the land on which the object was found? If the only point of the rule is simply to provide clarity, it does not matter whether the law adopted either rule or whether, as in later Roman law[47] and modern French[48] and German law,[49] it awarded half the value of the object to the finder and half to the

---

[37] 8 F at 162.   [38] 8 F at 160.

[39] See Robert C. Ellickson, 'A Hypothesis of Wealth-Maximizing Norms: Evidence from the Whaling Industry', *J. Law Econ. & Org.* 5 (1989), 83.   [40] *Code rural*, art. 853.

[41] Weil *et al.*, *Droit civil: Les Biens*, no. 402.   [42] BGB §§ 958, 960.

[43] Bundesjagdgesetz, § 7.   [44] ibid. §§ 7–9.

[45] *Blades* v. *Higgs*, (1895), 11 HL Cas 622; *State* v. *Repp*, 73 NW 829 (Iowa 1898); *Rexroth* v. *Coon*, 223 A 37 (RI 1885).   [46] *McKee* v. *Gratz*, 260 US 127 (1922).

[47] As prescribed by Hadrian. I. 2.1.39.   [48] *Code civil*, art. 716(1).   [49] BGB § 984.

owner. It should be noted, however, that even these rules are less clear than they appear. In one case, a customer found cash in a supermarket. A German court awarded it to the supermarket owner to whom it was delivered on the grounds that he was the finder.[50]

Anglo-American law has done a still worse job of providing a clear rule. It sometimes applies the one rule and sometimes the other. As a result, the case law is contradictory. In an English case, a commercial traveler, not the shopkeeper, was allowed to keep the notes someone accidentally dropped on the floor of a shop.[51] In an American case, the barber, and not the one who found it in his shop, was allowed to keep a pocket book.[52] In another, one who found a pocket book on the customer's table in a bank was held not to have the rights of a finder.[53] There is no way for legal analysis to determine which of these cases were decided correctly. Legal analysis can only determine the proper scope of a rule by asking what function it serves. When the function is to provide clarity, and there is more than one possible clear rule, there is no way to decide which rule is better. The difficulties of the Anglo-American approach are only aggravated by trying to reconcile the cases by drawing distinctions that are still less clear. Examples are distinctions between property which has been lost by the owner and property which was mislaid in the sense that it was voluntarily left by an owner who forgot to pick it up,[54] or between property found in a part of the owner's land that was public or private.[55] It is often impossible to tell whether an object was lost or mislaid, or to say if a part of the property to which the finder was lawfully admitted is public or private.

I do not mean to suggest that continental systems have entirely escaped these difficulties by their rule that an object should belong half to the owner and half to the finder. There is another rule that the owner of land owns even those parts of it of whose existence he is unaware (with the exception, in some systems, of mineral rights). This rule, again, is laid down for the sake of clarity. While it may sometimes furnish owners with an incentive to buy land in order to explore it, it also applies when the owner had no idea what the land might contain and paid no extra price for it. How, then, is one to decide whether something of value on the land is to be regarded as part of it, which therefore belongs to the owner, or as a found object, which belongs to both him and the finder? French courts have held that a Roman mosaic[56] and an ancient artifact found at some depth beneath the surface[57] belong to the owner of the land exclusively. Some German jurists claim that fossils and historical objects buried in the land are to be treated like treasure: they belong equally to the finder and the landowner.[58] Nevertheless, some German Länder have adopted different rules.[59] The

---

[50] BGH 101, 193.   [51] *Bridges* v. *Hawkworth* (1851), 21 LJ 75 (QB).

[52] *McAvoy* v. *Medina*, 11 Allen 548 (Mass 1866).   [53] *Kincaid* v. *Eaton*, 98 Mass 139 (1867).

[54] e.g. *McAvoy* v. *Medina*, 11 Allen 548 (Mass 1866); *Toledo Trust Co.* v. *Simmons*, 3 NE 2d 661 (Ohio App 1935).

[55] E. L. G. Tyles, N. E. Palmer and Crossley Vaines, *Personal Property* (5th edn., London, 1973), 426. See *Pyle* v. *Springfield Marine Bank*, 70 NE2d 257 (Ill App 1956); *Toledo Trust Co.* v. *Simmons*, 3 NE2d 661 (Ohio App 1935).   [56] Cass. req., 13 Dec. 1881, D.P. 1882.1.55.

[57] Trib. civ. Aix., 17 Jan. 1898, D.P. 1898.2.507.

[58] Henrik Hefermehl in Walter Erman, *Handkommentar zum Bürgerlichen Gesetzbuch* (8th edn., Münster, 1989), to § 984, no. 1; Baur, *Sachenrechts*, § 53gVI.   [59] Baur, *Sachenrechts*, § 53gVI.

same thought—that some found objects constitute part of the land—may explain why English courts held in favor of the owner when gold rings were found embedded in the mud at the bottom of the owner's pool[60] or a prehistoric boat underneath his land was found by an excavator.[61]

My conclusion is that all these rules can be explained by the considerations that Aristotle and Aquinas gave for instituting private property: to provide incentives for useful work and to prevent quarrels. Often, a rule conferring ownership on the first possessor serves both of these purposes. But to tell what rule provides the best incentive will often require an inquiry which is industry specific, to which traditional legal analysis will not give answers. Moreover, there will often be no way to analyze which of several clear rules to apply in the interest of avoiding quarrels, or, once more than one rule must be adopted, to decide how to draw the line between them. Certainly, one cannot resolve these problems by analyzing the concept of possession.

---

[60] *South Staffordshire Water Co.* v. *Sherman*, [1896] 2 QB 44.

[61] *Elwes* v. *Brigg Gas Co.*, LR 33 Ch D 562 (1886). According to Tyles *et al.*, *Personal Property*, 422, what mattered in these cases was that the object in question was 'under the land or attached thereto'.

PART III
TORTS

Torts

The modern civil law and common law of torts have a different structure. Civil law systems generally have a unified action in tort based on fault, though they recognize special cases of strict liability. At common law, to prevail, the plaintiff must bring the facts of his case within a list of recognized torts. In both systems, however, jurists analyze the plaintiff's conduct by asking whether he was at fault for acting intentionally or negligently or liable because his action was one that gives rise to strict liability. In both systems, jurists ask whether the harm the defendant suffered is of a kind for which the law will give a remedy. We will see in the next chapter that this form of analysis came from the civil law. In the 19th century, it was grafted on the common law, which produced a series of anomalies that it is difficult to explain. In the chapter following, we will discuss the concepts of intent, negligence and strict liability. Two further chapters will deal with two situations in which it is disputed whether the plaintiff should have a remedy for the kind of harm he has suffered. One is when the harm is done to intangible interests variously described as dignity, reputation, privacy or *Persönlichkeit*. The second is when the plaintiff has suffered a pure economic loss not due to harm caused to his person or property.

9

The Structure of the Modern Civil and Common Law of Torts

Neither the ancient Roman law nor the traditional common law had much to say about torts in general. They recognized what we would call particular torts, each with its own rules. The civil law eventually arrived at a unified concept of tort. Roman distinctions were regarded as peculiarities of Roman positive law and many eventually disappeared. As we will see, this change was again the work of the late scholastics of the 16th and early 17th centuries for whom the Roman actions were all directed at doing what Aristotle described as commutative justice in involuntary transactions. By this view, the defendant was liable if he was at fault for injuring the rights of the plaintiff. Liability without fault, which existed in Roman law, remained, but it was never satisfactorily explained. Again, many of their conclusions remained to shape modern civil law after the Aristotelian ideas on which they were originally based had been forgotten. Articles 1382–3 of the French Civil Code and § 823(1) of the German Civil Code contain general provisions imposing liability on one who intentionally or negligently injures another's rights, although the German Code enumerates these rights and the French Code merely speaks of 'harm' to the plaintiff (*dommage*). Neither code deals with strict liability, and the deficiency has been supplied, in France, by creative judicial interpretation, and in Germany, by special legislation.

Common law tort law developed differently. In 1800, it was still a law of particular torts, each with its own rules. In the 19th century and early 20th century, in an effort to rationalize the common law, Anglo-American jurists borrowed the ideas of continental writers and used them to reorganize pre-existing law. They classified the traditional tort actions according to whether liability turned on intention, negligence or strict liability. They tried to identify the rights that each traditional action was designed to protect. They could go only so far in that direction, however, and still present their work as an explanation of the law they had inherited. The result is a tort law in which traditional actions are still recognized and have been reinterpreted according to continental ideas, leaving inherited anomalies. We will describe the anomalies before moving on, in later chapters, to problems which common and civil law lawyers face in common.

I. The Emergence of the Modern Civil Law

Gaius was the first Roman jurist to distinguish two general classes of obligations, *delictus* and *contractus*, tort and contract.[1] Since this distinction resembles the one Aristotle

---

[1] G. Inst. 3.88.

drew between involuntary and voluntary commutative justice, modern scholars believe Gaius may have taken it from Aristotle.[2] But Gaius did not follow out the implications of these definitions or look for general principles of tort or contract law. Like the other Roman lawyers, he discussed particular torts.

Two of these torts became the basis for later continental law. One was an action under the *lex Aquilia*. It is the ancestor of provisions such as articles 1382–3 of the French Civil Code and § 823(1) of the German Civil Code. Today, French and German lawyers will sometimes say that these provisions create an 'Aquilian' liability. There were two basic requirements for an action under the *lex Aquilia*. One was that the defendant had to be at fault to be liable. That requirement will be described later on. In general, however, fault meant causing harm either intentionally or negligently, as it does in the modern legal systems. There were certain cases left over—we would call them cases of strict liability—in which the plaintiff was allowed to recover but not under the *lex Aquilia* because the defendant was not at fault.[3] Eventually, the Romans lumped them together as 'quasi torts' (*quasi ex delicto*).[4]

Under Roman law, the plaintiff could recover under the *lex Aquilia* only if he suffered certain types of harm. One Roman text said that the plaintiff had an action even if 'the harm was not done physically nor an object physically injured'.[5] But in almost all the Roman examples, the plaintiff has lost the use of a physical object even if it was not physically injured: for example, he could recover for the loss of a cup whether it was smashed or thrown into a river where he could not get it back. The plaintiff could not recover if he himself was physically injured.

The closest the Romans came to allowing such an action was to let him recover if his son was injured while still under his authority. Here are two (almost the only two) texts that indicate that he can. Both are from the jurist Ulpian.

'Julian also puts his case: A shoemaker, he says, struck with a last at the neck of a boy who was freeborn and whom he was teaching because he had done badly what he had been shown and so knocked out his eye. On these facts, Julian, says that the action for *iniuria* does not lie because he struck him not with the intent to insult but in order to correct and teach him. He wonders whether there is an action for breach of the contract for his services as a teacher, since a teacher is only permitted to punish lightly, but I have no doubt that an action can be brought against him under the *lex Aquilia*.[6]

'If a man kills another in wrestling or boxing, provided he kills him in a public match, the *lex Aquilia* does not apply because the harm appears to have been done in the cause of glory and virtue and not for the sake of injury.... This applies when a son under authority has been hurt.'[7]

Beginning in the Middle Ages, the Roman texts were interpreted to allow recovery for many other types of harm although the jurists never arrived at a clear rule. The Glossators (the jurists who wrote from about 1100 under the mid-13th century) said

---

[2] Reinhard Zimmermann, *The Law of Obligations: Roman Foundations of the Civil Law Tradition* (Juta, 1990), 10–11; Max Kaser, *Römische Privatrecht* (Munich, 1959), 522; A. M. Honoré, *Gaius* (Oxford, 1962), 100; Helmut Coing, 'Zum Einfluß der Philosophie des Aristoteles aud die Entwicklung des römischen Rechts', *Zeitschrift der Savigny-Stiftung für Rechtsgeschichte, Rom. Abt.* 69 (1952), 24–59.

[3] See ibid. 953–87, 998–1017.   [4] Inst. 4.5.   [5] Inst. 4.3.16.   [6] Dig. 9.2.5.3.

[7] Dig. 9.2.7.4.

that the plaintiff could recover if he was physically injured, citing the first of the two texts just quoted. Citing the second text, the jurist Azo (who died about 1210) said that there could be recovery if a person was killed, whether or not he was a son in authority. The plaintiffs in such an action would be his heirs and relatives. By the 17th century it was widely accepted that his wife and children could recover for loss of support. By that time, it has also become accepted that the plaintiff could recover for pain and suffering.[8] Whether he could recover for economic harm that was not accompanied by physical loss was less clear, but, as we will see later on, jurists sometimes gave examples in which he did so.[9] Thus, a remedy came to be given under the *lex Aquilia* for more kinds of harm than in Roman times.

Another Roman action was given for *iniuria*. It could be brought for many different kinds of offensive behavior: a blow, an imminent attempt at a blow,[10] entering a house without permission,[11] composing a derogatory song,[12] beating someone's slave,[13] 'accosting' a woman[14] or following her 'assiduously,'[15] or using 'base language'.[16]

As in other areas of law, the late scholastics tried to explain Roman law with the philosophical principles of Aristotle and Thomas Aquinas. As noted earlier, Aristotle distinguished distributive justice, which secures each citizen a fair share of whatever resources were to be distributed, from commutative justice, which preserves the share of each citizen. When citizens exchange resources voluntarily, commutative justice requires that they do so at a just price, a price that preserves their share. If one citizen is involuntarily deprived of resources by another, commutative justice requires the person who did so to restore his victim's share of resources.[17] The late scholastics identified these two kinds of commutative justice with *contractus* and *delictus*—with contract and tort.

Having taken that step, the late scholastics concluded that the distinctions between the *lex Aquilia iniuria* and the other particular Romans torts were merely matters of Roman positive law. In principle (or as they put it, as a matter of natural law), the defendant should be liable whenever, through his own fault, he deprived the plaintiff of anything that belonged to him as a matter of justice.[18] They were not very specific about what belonged to a person as a matter of justice. Nevertheless, Aristotle had mentioned 'honor' as well as 'money' as one of the objects of distributive justice,[19] and 'abuse' and 'insult' as examples of involuntary transactions that violate commutative justice.[20] The late scholastics concluded that violations of commutative justice were rectified not only by recovery under the *lex Aquilia* but in the action for *iniuria* as well. In the action for *iniuria*, the plaintiff recovered for insult, which deprived him of his reputation or his dignity.

---

[8] Zimmermann, *Law of Obligations*, 1024–6.   [9] Chapter 10 I.   [10] Dig. 47.10.15.1.
[11] Dig. 47.2.21.7.   [12] Dig. 47.10.15.27.   [13] Dig. 47.10.15.34.
[14] Dig. 47.10.15.20.   [15] Dig. 47.10.15.22.   [16] Dig. 47.10.15.21.
[17] *Nicomachean Ethics* V.ii 1130ᵇ–1131ᵃ.
[18] For examples, Lessius said that by a 'thing' (*res*) taken from the owner he understands not only an object such as a horse, clothes or money but 'what is owed as a matter of justice . . . such as a legacy left another or something which has been sold but which I still have'. Leonardus Lessius, *De iustitia et iure, ceterisque virtutibus cardinalis libri quatuor* (Paris, 1628), lib. 2, cap. 7, dub. 5, no. 19.
[19] *Nicomachean Ethics* V.ii 1130ᵇ.   [20] *Nicomachean Ethics* V.ii 1131ᵃ.

At the same time, for reasons we will examine later, the late scholastics were wedded to an Aristotelian conception of voluntary action that meant that the defendant should be liable only for fault. That was no obstacle to explaining the *lex Aquilia* and the action for *iniuria*. It was an obstacle to explaining the instances in which the Romans imposed strict liability. The late scholastics concluded that these, too, were instances of Roman positive law which had no principled explanation.

Grotius borrowed many of his conclusions from the late scholastics, and this was an instance. Like the late scholastics, he found no principled explanation for strict liability.[21] In discussing tort law, he stated the same general principle:

'By a wrong, we mean every fault, whether of commission or of omission, which is in conflict with what men ought to do, either generally or because of some special characteristic. From such a fault, if damage is caused, an obligation arises by the law of nature, namely, that the damage should be made good.

Damage, *damnum* (perhaps from *demo*) is when a man has less than what is his, whether it be his by mere nature or by some human act in addition such as ownership, agreement or statute. Things which a man may regard as his by nature are life, not indeed to throw away but to keep, his body, limbs, fame, honor, and his own acts. The previous part of our treatise has shown how each man has what is his own by property law and by agreements and not only with respect to property but also with respect to the actions of others . . .'[22]

This text had an enormous influence on the history of tort law. It was followed by many jurists including the 18th century French jurist Robert Pothier who influenced the drafters of the French Civil Code, although unlike Grotius, he did not try to enumerate the different types of harm for which one could recover.[23]

When the French drafters wrote articles 1382–3, they paraphrased Pothier. Article 1382 of the French Civil Code provides: 'Any act of a person which causes harm to another obligates the person through whose fault the harm (*dommage*) occurred to make compensation for it'. Article 1383 provides: 'A person is liable for the harm that he causes not only by his acts but by his negligence or imprudence'. French commentators explain (correctly) that article 1382 was meant to govern harm caused intentionally. Taken together, then, these provisions mean that the defendant is liable if he intentionally or negligently causes 'harm' to the plaintiff. Nothing in the French Civil Code explains what is supposed to count as 'harm'. French courts have had to work that out for themselves.

The analogous provisions of the German Civil Code are a bit different. According to section 823(1): 'A person who intentionally or negligently unlawfully (*widerrechtlich*) injures the life, body, health, freedom, property or similar right (*sonstiges Recht*) of another is bound to compensate him for any damages that thereby occur'. The addition of the word 'unlawfully' makes explicit what is implicit in the French Code: that in certain cases, such as self-defense, one is not liable for intentionally harming another. Also the German provision enumerates various types of harm for which the plaintiff can

---

[21] Hugo Grotius, *De iure belli ac pacis libri tres* (B. J. A. de Kanter-van Hetting Tromp, ed., Leiden, 1939), II.xvii.21.   [22] Ibid. II.xvii.1–2.
[23] Robert Pothier, *Traité des obligations* (Paris, 1761), nos. 116, 118.

recover. Since the drafters found it impossible to enumerate all of them, they added that he could recover for violation of any 'similar right'.

Whatever might count as a 'similar right', it is clear that the drafters believed that there were certain harms for which the defendant should not be liable. In particular, the drafters believed that for pragmatic reasons, the defendant should not recover for harm to privacy or dignity. As we will see in a later chapter, German courts now permit recovery anyway, despite the text of the Code.

Moreover, they believed that he should not be liable if he negligently inflicted what we now call a 'pure economic loss'. Section 826 allowed the plaintiff to recover for such a loss only if the defendant caused it intentionally. As we will see in a further chapter, this limitation has largely remained although the drafters based it on a conceptual argument that was far more persuasive in their time than ours.

Neither the German nor the French Code contained a general principle concerning strict liability. Like the late scholastics and the northern natural lawyers, the German and French drafters could not see a general principle that could explain liability without fault. As we will see, however, strict liability did not disappear in French and German law. The French eventually read strict liability into one of the less clear provisions of their Code. Even before the German Code was drafted, the legislation had provided for special cases in which the defendant was liable without fault.

To summarize, the civil lawyers began with a set of torts they inherited from Roman law. The medieval jurists extended the harms for which one could recover under one of these torts, the *lex Aquilia*. The late scholastics identified tort as a branch of law concerned with doing commutative justice in involuntary transactions. They formulated the general principle, which the northern natural lawyers accepted, that one who causes another harm through fault is obligated to make compensation. This general principle passed into modern French and German law, although the German drafters made certain exceptions to the types of harm for which one could recover. Neither the late scholastics, nor the northern natural lawyers, nor the French or German drafters found or enacted a general principle governing strict liability although rules of strict liability lingered on. The end result, in civil law, was a structure in which the key categories were liability for harm, or at least certain harms, caused by fault, and a miscellany of cases of strict liability.

II. The Emergence of the Modern Common Law

A. The Traditional Forms of Action

In a famous speech, Maitland claimed that while 'the history of English law is not yet written', someday, that history will show the origin, in the forms of action, of 'the great elementary conceptions, ownership, possession, contract, tort, and the like'.[24] But as

---

[24] Frederick William Maitland, 'Why the History of English Law is Not Written', in *The Collected Papers of Frederic William Maitland* 1 (H. A. L. Fisher, ed., Cambridge, 1911), 480 at 484.

Charles Donahue has observed, 'we know a considerable amount more today than we did when Maitland wrote.... Relatively little of the history of the forms of action seems to deal with "the great elementary conceptions" like ownership, possession, tort, and contract.'[25] As we will see, however, the common lawyers had been borrowing from the civil lawyers. We have already seen that supposedly distinct common law concepts about the relationship between ownership and possession were developed in reaction to a 19th century debate among civil lawyers.[26] We will now see that many supposedly common law ideas about tort were borrowed from still earlier civil law jurists. As Simpson has shown, a series of translations in the early 19th century enabled common lawyers to read the work of continental jurists such as Grotius, Pufendorf, Pothier, and Domat in English even if they were unable to do so in the original.[27] Some of the most important concepts they introduced into the common law were to be found in these authors.

The common lawyers had not thought in terms of tort. They thought in terms of actions for trespass in assault and battery, trespass *quare clausum fregit* (later called trespass to land), trespass *de bonis asportatis* (later called trespass to chattels), trespass on the case and so forth. Blackstone said that 'personal actions' at common law were either 'founded on contracts' or 'upon torts or wrongs'.[28] He was borrowing a distinction which, as we have seen, went back to the Roman jurist Gaius and which civil lawyers had regarded as basic for centuries.

Beginning with Blackstone, treatise writers began to remodel what they now called the common law of tort along civilian lines. As we have seen, by early modern times, continental writers had organized their law of torts around two basic ideas which the common lawyers then borrowed. One was the idea that the plaintiff could recover if the defendant harmed him by violating one of his rights or legally protected interests. As we have seen, modern civil codes take such an approach. Some jurists and some codes attempted to list these rights.

That was not the traditional approach of the common law. Traditionally, whether the plaintiff could recover depended on whether he could bring his case within one of the traditional forms of action. The forms of action were not a list of protection-worthy interests. They were the end result of centuries of bending and stretching a fixed number of writs. The number of writs reflected 12th century ideas about what cases the king's courts should hear.

Nevertheless, beginning with Blackstone, common law treatise writers identified the forms of action with different rights or interests which the law was attempting to protect. Blackstone distinguished actions that protected personal property (trespass *de bonis asportatis* and trover), those that protected real property, (trespass *quare clausum fregit*), and those that protected the 'personal security of individuals' against injuries to 'their lives, their limbs, their bodies, their health or their reputations'.[29] Injuries to personal security were redressed by actions for menace and assault in the case of threats, and, in the case of actual injury, by actions of battery for harm life and limb,

---

[25] Charles Donahue, *Why the History of Canon Law is Not Written* (London, 1986), 6.
[26] Chapter 3.
[27] A. W. B. Simpson, 'Innovation in Nineteenth Century Contract Law,' *L.Quar. Rev.* 91 (1975), 247 at 247.　　　　　[28] 3 William Blackstone, *Commentaries on the Laws of England* 3 (1766), 117.
[29] ibid. 3. 119.

actions of malpractice and nuisance for harm to health, and actions of libel and slander for harm to reputation. As we will see, while the treatise writers of the 19th and early 20th centuries proposed different classifications, like Blackstone, they looked for a correspondence between forms of action and interests to be protected.[30]

A second fundamental idea was that there were three distinct grounds for holding a person liable in tort. In principle, he might have harmed someone intentionally, or negligently. He might also be liable for engaging in an activity for which he is strictly liable although this was a category, for many centuries, no one could explain by any general principle. Again, in civil law this distinction was ancient.

Again, however, this was not the approach of the traditional common law. Traditionally, a plaintiff could sue in trespass or in trespass on the case. There is a long-standing debate over whether the plaintiff was liable in either action absent fault. As Milsom and Fifoot have pointed out, the question is misleading because, traditionally, the common lawyers did not clearly distinguish fault-based and strict liability.[31]

If the plaintiff sued in trespass, he did not need to allege fault. He might simply allege, for example, that the defendant shot him or struck him. The defendant might then 'plead the general issue' by answering with the set phrase 'not guilty'. Or he might make a special plea, in effect, admitting the trespass and offering some justification. There was no clear answer to the question whether either course of action would allow a defendant to escape liability if he was not at fault in the sense in which civil lawyers or modern common lawyers understand fault. If he answered, 'Not guilty', the jury was supposed to decide whether the plaintiff's allegations were true or false. It is hard to know what juries did.[32] Presumably, the defendant escaped liability if the jury felt that the shooting or striking of the defendant was really not something he did, that he was the passive instrument of forces of nature, a third party, or the animal he was riding. Possibly, they decided in the defendant's favor if they concluded he had not committed a trespass or wrong, whatever that might have meant to them. In trespass, the common law did not have a rule when the defendant pleaded the general issue but a procedure: let the jury decide.

Alternatively, the defendant might plead, in justification, that he was not at fault. It was not clear what would happen then. Defendants did so in only a few cases, and the remarks of the judges are confusing and seem contradictory. Some judges said that the defendant was not liable if he had done his best,[33] some said that he was,[34] and

---

[30] ibid. 3. 19–27.

[31] S. F. C. Milsom, *Historical Foundations of the Common Law* (2nd edn., London, 1981), 392–8; C. H. S. Fifoot, *History and Sources of the Common Law: Tort and Contract* (London, 1949), 189, 191.

[32] Milsom, *Historical Foundations*, 393.

[33] e.g. *The Thorns Case*, YB Mich 6 Ed 4, f 7, pl 18 (1466) (Choke, CJ: 'As to what has been said that they [thorns] fell *ipso invito* [on another's land], this is not a good plea; but he should have said that he could not do it in any other manner or that he did all that was in his power to keep them out'); *Millen* v. *Fandrye* Popham 161 (1626) (defendant excused because he has 'done his best endeavor'); *Wakeman* v. *Robinson*, 1 Bing 213 (1823) (Dallas, CJ: 'If the accident happened entirely without default on the part of the defendant or blame imputable to him, the action does not lie').

[34] *The Thorns Case*, YB. Mich 6 Ed 4, f. 7, pl 18 (1466) (Littleton, J: 'If a man suffers damage, it is right that he be recompensed'); *Bessey* v. *Olliot*, Sir T. Raym. 421, 467 (1682) (Sir Thomas Raymond: 'in all civil acts the law doth not so much regard the intent of the actor as the loss and damage of the party suffering'); *Leame* v. *Bray*, 3 East 593 (1803) (Grose, J: 'if the injury be done by the act of the party himself at the time or he be the immediate cause of it, though it happen accidentally or by misfortune, yet he is answerable in trespass').

some said he could escape liability if his conduct were the product of 'unavoidable necessity'.[35] It is very difficult to know what these statements meant to those who made them. The judges themselves may not have been thinking in terms of a clear distinction between fault-based and strict liability. For example, in *Weaver* v. *Ward*, the court said the defendant would be excused if he were 'utterly without fault', if the accident were 'inevitable', and if he 'had committed no negligence to give occasion to the hurt'.[36] As Fifoot said of this case, ' "[f]ault," "inevitable accident," "negligence" are words used indiscriminately without reflection and almost without meaning'.[37]

The plaintiff who wished to avoid these uncertainties might sue, not in trespass, but in trespass on the case. The difference was not so much in the substantive law, but that he was then able to allege, not simply that the defendant shot or struck him, but particular circumstances that showed the defendant had acted wrongfully. Sometimes, in describing the situation, the plaintiff did allege that the defendant acted negligently.[38] Even then, it isn't clear what the allegation meant.[39] It might or might not mean negligence in the modern (or ancient Roman) sense. Certainly, judges did not instruct the jury to ask themselves whether the defendant had behaved like a reasonable person. In any event, the defendant might also bring an action of trespass on the case without alleging negligence.[40]

Blackstone did not even attempt to read the civil law distinctions among intent, negligence and strict liability into the common law. As we will see, the treatise writers of the 19th and early 20th centuries regarded them as fundamental.[41] They tried to understand some of the forms of action as intentional torts, and others as based on negligence or strict liability.

These civil law ideas were introduced as part of the process described earlier in which legal doctrines are formulated in an effort to make sense of the case law. A point was reached, however, in which that process could not be carried to completion without eventually snapping the historical links that still bind the common law to the old forms of action. The process stopped well before completion. There was only so far the common law jurists could go and still present their doctrines as an interpretation of the law they had inherited.

B. Legally Protected Interests

Hilliard and Addison, in two of the first treatises on tort law, explained that for the plaintiff to recover, he must have suffered some 'injury'[42] or 'damage'.[43] Pollock and Salmond, in their more systematic works, said that he must have suffered some

---

[35] *Dickenson* v. *Watson*, Sir T. Jones 205 (1682) (defendant who had shot the plaintiff and pleaded accident not excused 'for in trespass the defendant shall not be excused without unavoidable necessity').

[36] *Weaver* v. *Ward*, Hobart 134 (1616).   [37] Fifoot, *History*, 191.

[38] Milsom, *Historical Foundations*, 394.

[39] ibid. 399; A. I. Ogus, 'Vagaries in Liability for the Escape of Fire', *Cam. L. J.* 27 (1969), 104, at 105–6.   [40] ibid. 394.

[41] See John Wigmore, 'Responsibility for Tortious Acts: Its History', *Harv. L. Rev.* 7 (1894), 315.

[42] Francis Hilliard, *The Law of Torts or Private Wrongs* 1 (Boston, 1859), 83–4.

[43] C. G. Addison, *Wrongs and their Remedies: A Treatise on the Law of Torts* 1 (F. J. P. Wolferston, ed., 4th edn., Albany, NY, 1876), 2.

'harm'.[44] Later writers such as Harper and Prosser spoke of the violation of 'interests demanding protection'[45] or 'legally recognized interests'.[46] All of them, like Blackstone, tried to identify the traditional forms of action with the protection of distinct types of interests or the prevention of distinct types of harm, damage or injury. At the same time, they tried to formulate a definition or list of the elements that the plaintiff must establish to recover under each of the forms of action. Judges traditionally had not decided cases by asking what type of harm the plaintiff had suffered or by formulating such lists. They decided them by looking for resemblances to clear cases in which an action would surely lie.

One problem for the treatise writers was to find a formula that could fit decisions that had not been made by a formula but by looking for such resemblances. It was like that of a British colonial administrator demarcating a boundary line between a tribe that claimed the hills and one that claimed the lowlands. A further problem was that the cases did not always correspond closely to a distinct interest worthy of protection. When they did, it was easy for the treatise writers to define a particular tort in terms of that interest. For example, false imprisonment could be defined in terms of confinement which deprived the plaintiff of his freedom of movement. Otherwise, unless the treatise writers were to challenge the cases, their choices were limited. They could devise a formula that fit the cases and then invent some reason why it corresponded only roughly to an interest worth protecting. They could redescribe the interest in question to make it fit their formula more closely. Or they could ignore the problem.

For example, the earliest treatise writers said that battery protected a person against bodily harm. Yet bodily harm was not all that mattered, as one can see from their definitions of battery, which still looked more like graphic images than boundary lines. Battery is 'violence' inflicted on a person[47] or as 'an angry, rude, insolent or revengeful touching'.[48] Later definitions are less graphic. For example, according to Bigelow and Salmond, battery is an 'application of force' to 'the person of another' that is 'unpermitted'[49] or 'without lawful justification'.[50] But force did not mean harm. Even a person who had not been harmed could recover.[51] Some writers did not try to explain why. Some found a reason why legal protection extended beyond the

---

[44] Sir Frederick Pollock, *The Law of Torts: A Treatise on the Principles of Obligations Arising from Civil Wrongs in the Common Law* (8th edn., London, 1908), 6; Sir John W. Salmond, *The Law of Torts: A Treatise on the English Law of Liability for Civil Injuries* (4th edn., London, 1916), 8.

[45] Fowler Vincent Harper, *A Treatise on the Law of Torts: A Preliminary Treatise on Civil Liability for Harms to Legally Protected Interests* (Indianapolis, 1933), 5.

[46] William L. Prosser, *Handbook of the Law of Torts* 8–9 (Indianapolis, 1941). Similarly, *Restatement of Torts*, § 1 cmt. d (1934) ('legally protected interests'); *Restatement (Second) of Torts*, § 1 cmt. d (1965) (same).

[47] Hilliard, *Torts*, 1, 201; Francis M. Burdick, *The Law of Torts: A Concise Treatise on the Civil Liability at Common Law and under Modern Statutes for Actionable Wrongs to Person and Property* (2nd edn., Albany, NY, 1908), 268.

[48] Hilliard, *Torts*, 1, 201. See Addison, *Wrongs*, 2, 692 ('the person of a man is actually struck or touched in a violent, rude or insolent manner'); Burdick, *Torts*, 268 ('touching of another in anger'); Thomas M. Cooley, *A Treatise on the Law of Torts or the Wrongs which Arise Independent of Contract* (Chicago, 1880), 162 ('injury . . . done . . . in an angry or revengeful or rude or insolent matter').

[49] Melville M. Bigelow, *Elements of the Law of Torts for the Use of Students* (3rd edn., Boston, 1886), 101.

[50] Salmond, *Torts*, 382

[51] e.g., Bigelow, *Torts*, 101 ('any forcible contact may be sufficient'); Salmond, *Torts*, 382 (force may be 'trivial').

interest supposedly in question. The reason, according to Clark, was 'the very great importance attached by the law to the interest in physical security'.[52] According to Seavy, a 'very slight interference is sufficient' because the interest 'in bodily integrity' is one of the 'most highly protected'.[53] Salmond redescribed the interest in question: it is 'not merely that of freedom from bodily harm, but also that of freedom from such forms of insult as may be due to interference with his person'.[54] Harper, Prosser, and the *Restatements* agreed,[55] and so were able to redefine battery in a way that fit the cases and also corresponded to the interests that Salmond had identified: plaintiff can recover for 'unpermitted unprivileged contacts with [his] person'[56] and for 'harmful or offensive touching'.[57] English writers do so today.[58]

Similarly, according to the earlier treatise writers, an action of assault was supposed to protect a 'right not to be put in fear of personal harm'.[59] Yet, as one can see even from the graphic, image-like descriptions of the earliest treatise writers, this action did not protect against all reasonable fear of harm, or only against fear of harm. They described assault as ' "an unlawful setting upon one's person"; or a threat of violence exhibiting the intention to assault, and a present ability to carry the same into execution';[60]; an 'attempt . . . to offer with force and violence to do hurt to another'.[61] Later writers, somewhat more tamely, defined assault as 'an attempt, real or apparent, to do hurt to another's person, within reaching distance';[62] 'an attempt with unlawful force to inflict bodily injury upon another, accompanied with the apparent present ability to give effect to the attempt if not prevented'.[63] None of them claimed, however, that the plaintiff could recover always or only when he had been put in fear. As before, some like Seavy said that the reason was the importance of personal security as though that explained the matter.[64] Harper, Prosser, and the *Restatements*, however, redefined the interest at stake as 'the interest in freedom from apprehension of a harmful or offensive contact'.[65] That interest corresponded to their more precise definition of assault: it required the 'apprehension of a harmful or offensive contact' where apprehension simply means the awareness that such a contact may imminently occur.[66] They did not explain why the law should protect such a rarefied interest.

Similarly, the plaintiff's property was supposedly protected by an action by trespass to land, and his reputation by actions for libel and slander. Yet the plaintiff could recover for trespass if the defendant entered his land even if he did no physical

[52] George L. Clark, *The Law of Torts* (Columbia, Mo., 1922), 10.

[53] Warren Seavey, 'Principles of Torts', *Harv. L. Rev.* 56 (1942), 72.   [54] Salmond, *Torts*, 383.

[55] Prosser, *Torts*, 44–5; Harper, *Torts*, 38; *Restatement of Torts*, ch. 2, titles of topics 1 & 2 (1934); *Restatement (Second) of Torts*, ch. 2, titles, topics 1 & 2 (1965).   [56] Prosser, *Torts*, 43.

[57] Harper, *Torts*, 39. See *Restatement of Torts*, §§ 13, 15, 18–19 (1934); *Restatement (Second) of Torts*, §§ 13, 15, 18–19 (1965).

[58] R. F. V. Heuston and R.A. Buckley, *Salmond and Heuston on the Law of Torts* (21st edn., London, 1996), 120.

[59] Cooley, *Torts*, 161. See Burdick, *Torts*, 266 ('the right to live in society without being put in reasonable fear of unjustifiable personal harm').   [60] Hilliard, *Torts*, 1, 197.

[61] Addison, *Torts*, 2, 690.   [62] Bigelow, *Torts*, 98.   [63] Cooley, *Torts*, 160.

[64] Warren Seavey, 'Principles of Torts', *Harv. L. Rev.* 56 (1942), 72.

[65] Prosser, *Torts*, 48; Harper, *Torts*, 43 (same, but speaking of a 'harmful or offensive touching'); *Restatement of Torts*, ch. 2, title of topic 3 (1934); *Restatement (Second) of Torts*, ch. 2, title of topic 3 (1965).

[66] Prosser, *Torts*, 48; Harper, *Torts*, 43; *Restatement of Torts*, § 21 (1934); *Restatement (Second) of Torts*, § 21 (1965).

damage. He could recover for libel and certain types of slander if the defendant 'published' a defamatory statement, whether or not the plaintiff's reputation suffered, or suffered with anyone whose opinion mattered to him. This time, none of the treatise writers managed to redescribe the interest at stake to make it conform to the circumstances under which the plaintiff could recover. Some of them found reasons why the law would impose liability when no harm was done. Some said that the law 'presumes'[67] or 'implies'[68] damage. According to Cooley, it does so in the case of defamation because it would be 'unjust' to deprive a plaintiff of recovery who could not prove he had been harmed.[69] According to Salmond, '[t]he explanation [is] that certain acts are so likely to result in harm that the law prohibits them absolutely and irrespective of the actual issue'.[70] According to Seavy, the reason was that like the interest in bodily integrity, the interests in 'reputation, together with those in the possession and ownership of land, are the most highly protected'.[71] Some merely let the matter pass.

The objective of the treatise writers was to make the common law more rational by explaining it in terms of underlying interests. Paradoxically, their efforts in this direction became an obstacle to further efforts. Their explanations made it sound as though somebody—'the law'—had already decided what interests were worth protecting and how to protect them. Supposedly, for example, the law had decided to protect one's interest in not being offended but only against offence by physical contact; it had decided to protect one's freedom from the apprehension of imminent harmful or offensive physical contact whether one was put in fear or not; it had decided not only to protect one's interest in land or reputation but to allow recovery even when neither had suffered harm. The treatise writers suggested that the law had made all these decisions without saying that they themselves agreed on the merits.

In fact, such decisions had never been made. Trespass in assault and battery dates from a time when breaches of the peace often led to private vengeance, when the distinction between civil and criminal liability was not yet clear in everyone's mind, and when the very concept of tort as a distinct body of law was centuries off. The rules governing trespass in land were laid down before there were declaratory judgments. As Prosser himself observed, an action in trespass was used, not merely to redress an injury, but to vindicate 'a legal right without which the defendant's conduct, if repeated, might in time ripen into prescription'.[72] The rules for defamation were developed at a time when fact-finding was more difficult and the value placed on freedom of speech was quite different. Historically, it would be hard to reconstruct what the common law judges had in mind when they delimited the traditional forms of action. Surely, however, they were not considering what interests each form of action should protect and the best way to protect them.

One unfortunate consequence is that common lawyers are still taking many propositions as settled which, in fact, have never been considered on their merits. It is far from obvious that even the least unwelcome physical contact should trigger the plaintiff's right to recover for having been offended; or that absent fear, freedom from the apprehension of imminent unwelcome contact is worth protecting; or that

---

[67] Hilliard, *Torts*, 1, 87.   [68] Burdick, *Torts*, 338.   [69] Cooley, *Torts*, 30–1.
[70] Salmond, *Torts*, 12.   [71] Seavey, 'Principles of Torts'.   [72] Prosser, *Torts*, 81.

blanket rules should exempt the plaintiff from having to prove that his land or reputation were really harmed.

A second unfortunate consequence is that protection in tort law has been possible only by confusing the boundaries of old torts or inventing new ones. The result has been doctrinal categories that are neither rational nor traditional. The work of the treatise writers made it painfully clear that tort law protected some interests while neglecting others that are often as important. One way to fill the gaps would have been to change the formulas the treatise writers had devised to make them correspond to interests that should be protected. Instead, gaps were filled by creating new torts alongside the old, judicially or by legislation, and, when that process did not occur fast enough, fudging by the use of one of the traditional torts. As a result, some interests are now protected by a number of different torts. Some torts protect a number of different interests. Some of the new torts destroy the limitations imposed by old formulas, and yet the old formulas remain. Thus, the work of the treatise writers became an obstacle to the very goal they were pursuing: an orderly and systematic description of the common law of tort in terms of the interests that should be protected.

For example, one interest protected by the tort of battery is freedom from bodily harm. But the treatise writers did not define the tort in terms of bodily harm, but in terms of 'violence' or 'force' or, later, in terms of 'touching' or 'contact'. But it would be bizarre to deny people protection against bodily harm inflicted without physical contact. In part, the gap has been filled by construing the requirement of contact broadly. Salmond, for example, thought that the defendant would not be liable if bodily harm 'is inflicted otherwise than by the application of physical force, for example, by administering a deleterious drug'.[73] Later treatise writers such as Prosser and Harper would say that the drug touched or made contact with the plaintiff.[74] The gap has also been filled by recognizing liability for bodily injury caused without physical contact In the famous English case of *Wilkinson* v. *Downton*, a woman suffered physical injury out of anxiety for her husband when the defendants had told her, falsely, that he had been injured.[75] As John Fleming has noted, liability in such a case means that the traditional requirement of physical contract is no longer a barrier to recovery. *Wilkinson* 'finally committed our law to the proposition that, in the absence of a privilege, all intentional infliction of *bodily* harm is actionable regardless of the means employed to procure it, be it by direct physical aggression, injurious words or by setting in motion a force which directly or indirectly accomplishes the desired result'.[76] In the first *Restatement*, this result was accommodated by providing that '[t]he rules which determine an actor's liability for the infliction of bodily harm otherwise than by harmful bodily contact' are the same as those that determine 'liability for the infliction of a harmful bodily contact'.[77] In the second *Restatement*, the result was reclassified as an instance of the new tort of intentional infliction of emotional distress.[78] Whatever the label, it is hard to see what useful purpose is served by defining battery in terms of contact and then explaining that contact is unnecessary to be held liable. Indeed, as

---

[73] Salmond, *Torts*, 384.   [74] Prosser, *Torts*, 44; Harper, *Torts*, 41.

[75] *Wilkinson* v. *Downton*, 2 QB 57 (1897).

[76] John G. Fleming, *The Law of Torts* (8th edn., Sydney, 1992), 34.

[77] *Restatement of Torts*, § 17 (1934).   [78] *Restatement (Second) of Torts*, §§ 17, 46 (1965).

Fleming points out, with physical injuries, it is hard to see 'any point in distinguishing intentional from negligent torts, seeing that...liability could have been based on fault, embracing both negligent and intentional conduct'.[79]

According to Harper, Prosser and the *Restatements*, another interest protected by the tort of battery is freedom from offensive contact. Protection of that interest is said to explain why the plaintiff could traditionally recover if his body was not harmed but the defendant had struck his hat, his walking stick or the horse he was riding.[80] Protection of personal dignity against insult, however, is not limited to instances of physical contact. A plaintiff might be able to recover in defamation. While the treatise writers generally said that this tort protects one's interest in a good reputation, they acknowledged that the plaintiff could sometimes recover absent any allegation of misconduct if he had been insulted or made to look ridiculous.[81] For example, in one famous case, a man who had consented to have his picture used in an advertisement recovered for libel because the picture had made him look ludicrously deformed.[82] A plaintiff whose dignity was offended might also recover for trespass to land, even if the defendant had not harmed his property, provided the defendant had entered it. For example, a gas company was held liable when its meter reader screamed insults at a woman because he made the mistake of putting his hand in her doorway, thereby committing trespass.[83] In the United States, a plaintiff may also recover under the new tort of intentional infliction of emotional distress. American courts have sometimes held defendants liable for cruel practical jokes[84] and for insulting words.[85] In England, a plaintiff can recover[86] under the Protection from Harassment Act of 1997 for 'a course of conduct...which amounts to harassment of another...'.[87] English commentators have said that 'harassment...is capable of embracing, for example, persistent following, questioning or "door stepping" by journalists, methods of debt collection which are humiliating or distressing, or conduct in the course of a neighborhood dispute which is designed to annoy...'.[88]

According to the earlier treatise writers, the tort of assault protects against fear of bodily harm; according to the later ones, against the more rarified mental state of apprehension of imminent harmful or offensive contact with the person. It did not protect one against threats of immediate bodily harm, however credible they might be, provided these threats were made without any menacing gestures.[89] It did not protect one against threats to one's property. Nor did it protect one against threats of harm in the future. According to Blackstone, the victim of such a threat could bring

---

[79] ibid. 34.   [80] Prosser, *Torts*, 45; Harper, *Torts*, 40–1.

[81] Hilliard, *Torts*, 1, 267; Burdick, *Torts*, 302; Salmond, *Torts*, 451; Harper, *Torts*, 499; Prosser, *Torts*, 783.

[82] *Burton* v. *Crowell Publishing Co.*, 82 F2d 154 (2d Cir 1936) (L. Hand, J). The case the earlier treatise writers cite is *Cook* v. *Ward*, 6 Bing 409 (1830) (liability in defamation for a humorous story).

[83] *Bouillon* v. *Laclede Gaslight Co.*, 129 SW 401 (Mo App 1910).

[84] e.g., *Nickerson* v. *Hodges*, 84 So 37 (La 1920).

[85] e.g., *Wiggs* v. *Courshon*, 355 F Supp 206 (SD Fla 1973).

[86] A civil remedy is permitted by s. 3 of the Protection from Harassment Act 1997, c. 40.

[87] ibid. s. 1.

[88] W. V. H. Rogers, *Winfield & Jolowicz on Tort* (15th edn., London, 1998), 88–9.

[89] Hilliard, *Torts*, 1, 198; Salmond, *Torts*, 383; Clark, *Torts*, 15; Cooley, *Torts*, 29; Harper, *Torts*, 44; Prosser, *Torts*, 50.

an action for 'menace'.[90] This possibility was ignored by the treatise writers after Pollock observed that in most of the cases, the plaintiff had recovered for a threat to his servants rather than himself.[91] Sometimes, however, the plaintiff who was in fear of harm to his property could bring an action in nuisance to have the cause of the fear removed. In the United States, the victim of a threat of future harm to person or property can now recover under the new tort of intentional infliction of emotional distress. In a famous case, the defendants were held liable for threatening to beat up the plaintiff and wreck his truck.[92] In England, the plaintiff can recover under the Protection from Harassment Act for 'course of conduct causes another to fear, on at least two occasions, that violence will be used against him . . .'.[93] Apparently, the gang lord who can induce compliance with a single threat comes off much better than the thug of lesser credibility who has to repeat himself. In either case, whether with the addition of the judicially created American tort or the statutorily created English one, it is again difficult to see why it is sensible to have three torts protecting one interest.

The tort of trespass to land was generally said to protect one's property. As we have seen, however, if the defendant entered plaintiff's land, the plaintiff could recover even if his property had not been harmed. As a result, plaintiff could recover in trespass if the defendant entered plaintiff's premises and violated his privacy, for example, by reading his papers, planting a microphone, eavesdropping, or taking photographs. In the United States, if the defendant violates the plaintiff's privacy without entering his property, for example, by taking his picture with a telephoto lens or eavesdropping with a parabolic microphone, plaintiff can now recover for the new tort of 'intrusion into seclusion'.[94] Two torts protect one interest.

The torts of libel and slander were generally said to protect the plaintiff's reputation. Except in the cases of ridicule which were just mentioned, the plaintiff was protected only if the defendant's statements were defamatory: the statement had to lower him in the esteem of the community. He could not recover if the statements gave him a reputation he did not want or deserve if they did not lower him in anyone's esteem. This limitation was overcome in two ways. First, defendants were held liable for alleging, for example, that the plaintiff was insane or had been raped, even though, as Prosser noted, such statements 'would be likely to arouse only pity or sympathy in the minds of all decent people'.[95] Second, in the United States, the plaintiff has been allowed to recover under the new tort of 'false light'.[96] For example, members of a family held hostage by criminals could recover for a false but not defamatory account of their actions.[97] A further limitation on libel and slander was that the plaintiff could not recover if the defendant's statement was defamatory but true. In the United States, it has been overcome by allowing the plaintiff to recover for the new tort of 'disclosure of embarrassing private facts'.[98] Yet another limitation was that in certain cases, the

---

[90] Blackstone, *Commentaries*, 3. 120 (requiring, however, that there be some actual injury such as 'through fear . . . a man's business is interrupted').   [91] Pollock, *Torts*, 220.

[92] *State Rubbish Collectors Ass'n* v. *Siliznoff*, 240 P2d 282 (Cal 1952).

[93] Protection from Harassment Act 1997 c. 40, s. 4(1).

[94] See *Restatement (Second) of Torts*, § 652B (1965).   [95] Prosser, *Torts*, 780.

[96] See *Restatement (Second) of Torts*, § 652E.

[97] *Time, Inc.* v. *Hill*, 385 US 374 (1967).   [98] See *Restatement (Second) of Torts*, § 652D.

plaintiff could not recover in slander without proving special damages even for words that did obvious harm to reputation: for example, when school officials accused a high school girl of sexual misconduct. To be actionable, such statements had to constitute 'slander per se': that is, they had to concern whether one was unfit for a trade or profession, whether one had a loathsome disease, or whether one had committed a serious crime. Sexual misconduct was actionable without proof of special damages only in states that had imitated England's Slander of Women Act, and only then, if the plaintiff was a woman.[99] In the United States, this limitation was overcome in cases like those just described by allowing the plaintiff to recover anyway, and impounding the cases under the new tort of 'intentional infliction of emotional distress'. Thus four torts protect the interest in reputation. In England, most of these gaps have simply been left unplugged. Thus an interest in reputation is partially protected, but along lines drawn long ago under very different historical circumstances.

In the United States, where new torts have been created to plug these gaps, nevertheless, sometimes the doctrinal category will affect whether the plaintiff recovers when his interests are violated. If the plaintiff is insulted, he may find it easier to recover if the defendant nudged him, or committed technical trespass, or ridiculed him in print in a way judged to be defamatory. He may find it more difficult to recover if he must sue for intentional infliction of emotional distress for then, to go to the jury, he must convince the judge that defendant's conduct was highly offensive to a reasonable person. For similar reasons, he might find it easier to recover for an invasion of privacy accompanied by a technical trespass. If his reputation has been hurt, recovery in defamation will be harder in some ways and easier in others than recovery for disclosure of embarrassing private facts or being placed in a false light. It will be easier because he need not establish the defendant publicized a statement but merely that he 'published' it—that is, that he communicated it to any third party. His recovery will be more difficult because he will be subject to special rules that govern such matters as slander per se and privilege. All of these differences exist simply because we have preserved the definitions of particular torts bequeathed us by the treatise writers. They do not exist because anyone has decided that they should.

But even if there were no practical consequences, this list of particular torts forfeits the advantage that a rational doctrinal system should bring: namely, to help focus on what ultimately matters. A limitation on recovery does not matter if it is established for one tort only to be undermined by another. What does matter, as the treatise writers recognized, is the interests we wish to protect. They recognized that to give a rational account of tort law, we should explain our rules in terms of these interests. That goal is not furthered by a list of torts whose boundaries pay so little regard to which interests are being protected.

C. Intent, Negligence and Strict Liability

The second fundamental idea on which the Anglo-American treatise writers rebuilt tort law is that there are three distinct grounds for holding a person liable: he might

---

[99] Slander of Women Act 1891, 54 & 55 Vict ch 51. See Prosser, *Torts*, 804.

have harmed someone intentionally, or negligently, or by engaging in an activity for which he is strictly liable. Here, a critical change that made their work possible was the recognition by judges of a separate tort of 'negligence'. This change took place during the period they were writing, the late 19th and early 20th centuries. Most of them approved, although it is hard to say whether the judges who made the change did so because of their approval. A first step was to hold that the plaintiff could not recover for bodily injuries which the defendant caused accidentally and without negligence. In the United States, this step was taken in Massachusetts in 1851 by Chief Justice Shaw who cited as authority Greenleaf, a law professor at Harvard and author of a treatise on evidence.[100] In England, it was not taken until 1891.[101] It was then illogical not to do the same with damage to property. As Prosser noted, it was 'no great triumph of reason' to hold that if a streetcar jumped its track, its operator was liable for injuring a pedestrian only if he was negligent but for injuring the plate glass window behind the pedestrian whether he was or not.[102] The courts changed the rule for damage to chattels and eventually for damage to real property, but it took time. In his first edition, written in 1941, Prosser could only say that 'indications are' that the old rule for trespass to land 'is undergoing modification'. The indications he cited were the first *Restatement of Torts* and four cases, three of them decided in the 1870s.[103]

Meanwhile, the treatise writers were discussing the common law in terms of intent, negligence and strict liability. In his early treatise, Addison claimed that negligence did not matter.[104] Hilliard claimed that it did.[105] More significantly, however, in the truly systematic treatises of Salmond and Pollock, the discussion was organized around these grounds for liability. According to Salmond, '[i]n general, though subject to important exceptions, a tort consists in some act done by the defendant whereby he has wilfully or negligently caused some form of harm to the plaintiff'. There must be (a) damage and (b) 'wrongful intent or culpable negligence'.[106] Pollock claimed that in the case of 'personal wrongs' such as battery, assault, false imprisonment, slander and libel, liability is imposed where, 'generally speaking, the wrong is wilful or wanton. Either the act is intended to do harm, or, being an act evidently likely to cause harm, it is done with reckless indifference to what may befall by reason of it.'[107] In contrast, in the torts of nuisance and negligence, according to Pollock, the defendant was generally held liable for 'negligence', that is 'for a failure to observe due care and caution'.[108] Insofar as liability for intent and negligence was concerned, he concluded that 'the Roman conception of delict agrees very well with the conception that appears really to underlie the English law of tort'.[109] To complete the resemblance, English law imposed strict liability for 'the ownership and custody of dangerous things', as in *Rylands* v. *Fletcher*, where the owner of a resevoir was held liable without fault when the water escaped.[110] Such liability 'has its parallel in Roman law' in liability

---

[100] 60 Mass 292 (1850). He also cited *Wakeman* v. *Robinson*, 1 Bing 213 (1823), cited earlier to show that judges had made confusing and seemingly contradictory statements.

[101] *Stanley* v. *Powell*, 1 QB 86 (1891).   [102] Prosser, *Torts*, 77–8.

[103] ibid. 78, citing *Nitro-Glycerine Case, Parrott* v. *Wells Fargo & Co.*, 15 Wall 524 (US Sup Ct 1872), 21 L Ed 206; *Brown* v. *Collins*, 53 NH 442 (1873); *Losee* v. *Buchanon*, 51 NY 476 (1873); and cf. *Dobrowolski* v. *Penn. R. Co.*, 178 A 488 (Pa 1935).   [104] Addison, *Torts*, 2, 691.

[105] Hilliard, *Torts*, 1, 83–4, 104–5, 109.   [106] Salmond, *Torts*, 8.   [107] Pollock, *Torts*, 9.

[108] ibid. 11, 18.   [109] ibid. 17.   [110] ibid. 8.

'quasi ex delicto'.[111] In the United States, *Rylands* was followed in a line of cases eventually establishing a rule of strict liability for dangerous activities. In 1994, this interpretation of *Rylands* was repudiated by Lord Goff in *Cambridge Water Co Ltd* v. *Eastern Counties Leather plc*.[112] He regarded *Rylands* as having established a remedy akin to nuisance for the activities of landowners that harm their neighbors although, unlike the typical nuisance case, *Rylands* imposed liability for damage resulting from an 'isolated escape...'. As we have seen, the typical English nuisance case concerns whether one party has made a use of his land that interferes excessively with his neighbors. It is hard to see how clarity is promoted by impounding under the tort of nuisance both activities excessively interfering with land use and those leading to strict liability for a so-called isolated escape from land. Be that as it may, as we have seen, Anglo-American jurists, like their continental brethren, tried to distinguish particular torts as to whether the defendant is liable for acting intentionally, for acting negligently, or (with some qualifications added in England in 1994) whether he was engaged in an activity for which he is strictly liable.

Once 'negligence' had been recognized as a separate tort, it seemed to follow that the defendant must have acted intentionally to be liable for a tort such as battery. He could not be strictly liable, or there would be no point to the new tort of negligence: if he were negligent, then the proper action was 'negligence' rather than battery. But what, precisely, must the defendant intend? As we have just seen, Pollock said the 'wrong' must be 'wilful'. The defendant is liable if 'the act is intended to do harm'. That was the accepted view in the civil law tradition on which Pollock was drawing in which liability for acting intentionally or negligently is liability based on fault or misconduct. The common law forms of action, however, had not generally required that the defendant intend to do harm or wrong, and they could not be made to do so without considerable retailoring.

Pollock addressed the problem when he discussed trespass to land and to chattels. He acknowledged that the defendant might be liable absent such an intent to do harm. There was an 'absolute duty not to meddle...with land or goods that belong to another'.[113] For a moment, he contemplated discarding this rule as an archaism. 'We are now independent of the forms of action... [A] rational exposition of tort law is free to get rid of extraneous matter brought in, as we have shown, by the practical exigency of conditions that no longer exist'.[114] Nevertheless, he thought that the traditional rule was innocuous enough to retain because it usually gave the right result. 'A man can but seldom go by pure unwitting misadventure beyond the limits of his own dominion.'[115] 'If not wilfully or wantonly injurious, it is done with some want of due circumspection, or else it involves the conscious acceptance of a risk.' Thus in all but 'exceptional cases', strict liability would not result in 'real hardship'.[116] For Pollock, then, in principle, intent-based liability required an intention to do harm wrongfully. Liability for trespass to land and chattels was not based on intent.

The problem, however, extended beyond trespass to land and chattels. Traditionally, liability for battery, assault, false imprisonment and defamation had not turned on

---

[111] ibid. 18.   [112] [1994] 2 AC 264 (HL).   [113] ibid. 10.   [114] ibid. 15.
[115] ibid. 16.   [116] ibid. 11.

whether the defendant had acted intentionally anymore than on whether he had acted negligently. Consequently, the defendant could not escape by proving that he had been mistaken as to the identity of the victim, or the existence of a privilege, or whether a statement was defamatory, anymore than he could escape liability for trespass to land by proving he was mistaken as to privilege or ownership. One approach would have been to say, as Pollock did, that since we are now independent of the forms of action, and since negligence has emerged as an independent tort, we should re-examine whether such a defendant should be liable. Nevertheless, that was not the approach that was taken by the treatise writers who were his near contemporaries. They took it for granted, as he did, that if liability were to be based on intent, the intent that mattered was an intent to do harm or wrong. But they invented reasons why the law imposed liability anyway. According to Vold, the defendant was liable for mistakes in identity because 'the risk . . . should be placed on the intentional wrongdoer rather than his innocent victim'.[117] He did not explain why an actor who made a reasonable mistake should count as a wrongdoer. According to Smith, 'an *intentional* entry standing alone and unexplained involves fault'.[118] He did not ask why the law will not let such a person make an explanation. Salmond thought that the reason was 'the evidential difficulties in which the law would find itself involved if it consented to make any inquiry into the honesty and reasonableness of a mistaken belief which a defendant set up as an excuse for his wrongful act'.[119] He did not say why the defendant was held liable even if there were no evidential difficulties. These writers thus suggested that the law had already considered and answered a question which, in fact, no one had faced: whether, if liability were to depend on intent, the defendant should be held liable absent an intent to do wrong or harm.

This approach paved the way for the quite different one taken by Seavy, Harper, Prosser and the *Restatements*.[120] They took it for granted that the defendant could be liable absent such an intent. By their approach, however, the reason was that the intention that mattered was not an intention to do harm or wrong. According to Seavy, it was the intention 'to deal with the things or with the interests of others'. He claimed that '[t]he liability of one whose words unexpectedly prove to be defamatory can be based, in most instances, on his intent to deal with another's reputation'. '[M]ost nuisance cases', he said, 'involve a realization by the defendant that he is interfering with the factual interests of others'.[121] Similarly, Harper claimed that the intention that matters is 'to violate a legally protected interest of the plaintiff'.[122] In the case of trespass to land or chattels the defendant need merely intend 'the immediate effect of his act which constituted the interference with plaintiff's possession'.

---

[117] Lawrence Vold, *Neb. L. Rev.* 17 (1938), 149.

[118] Jeremiah Smith, 'Tort and Absolute Liability—Suggested Changes in Classification—II', *Harv. L. Rev.* 30 (1917), 319.   [119] Salmond, *Torts*, 116.

[120] Beale had yet another explanation. He said that someone who enters land mistakenly thinking it is his own 'acts on a mistake as to his own authority'. The mistake cannot 'give him an authority which in law or in fact he lacks'. Joseph H. Beale, 'Justification for Injury', *Harv. L. Rev.* 41 (1928), 553. He did not explain why one who enters land without authority and without believing that he has authority is liable only if the entry is negligent but one who makes such a mistake is liable without negligence.

[121] Seavey, 'Principles of Torts'.   [122] Harper, *Torts*, 41.

Therefore a mistake as to ownership or privilege was no defense.[123] To be liable for defamation 'the defendant must have intended to publish the defamatory matter, i.e., he must have voluntarily published the statement which harms the plaintiff's reputation and thus invades his legally protected interests'. But he need not have intended that anyone's reputation be harmed.[124] Similarly, Prosser said that the intention that matters is not a desire to do harm but 'an intent to bring about a result which will invade the interests of another in a way the law will not sanction'.[125] He drew the same conclusions as Harper. So did the *Restatements*.[126]

Harper claimed that his position rested on a 'fundamental principle of policy' which was based on 'such deep-rooted notions of fairness and justice that [it] will be found applicable to all legal phenomena in the law of tort'. The principle was that '[c]onduct threatens the interests of others in such a manner that it becomes the basis of tort liability only when the actor intends to invade such interests, is negligent toward such interests, or when the conduct is ultra-hazardous with respect to such interests'.[127] But by Harper's definition of intention, one can intend to invade another's interests without intending harm or wrong or even knowing that one is invading the interests of another. Surely there is nothing deep-rooted about the idea that such a person should be held liable.

Prosser's explanation was that the law is concerned about 'the social consequences that will follow'.[128] He claimed that if the law allowed mistake in ownership as a defense, 'the property rights of every owner would be threatened'.[129] It is the same with 'innocent publisher' of words 'as against the helpless victim whose reputation is blasted his act has been regarded, whether rightly or not, as a social menace, and so unreasonable in itself'.[130] This explanation is thin. The recognition of negligence as a separate tort means that, in principle, it is not enough that one person has caused harm to another. To be liable for negligence, he must have acted unreasonably. It is hard to see why a person who intends no harm and acts reasonably should be regarded as a threat to property rights or a social menace because he has some innocent intention. Prosser may not have believed his own explanation.[131]

Indeed, after the recognition of a tort of negligence, it is anomalous to hold such a person liable. Suppose a boy taps or kicks another playfully and thereby causes him some serious but unforeseeable injury. Liability for battery depends on whether the incident occurred on the playground, where there might be an 'implied license' to do so, or in the classroom, where there is not.[132] Suppose the defendant sets up a charcoal

---

[123] ibid. 55. [124] ibid. 504. [125] Prosser, *Torts*, 40–1.

[126] *Restatement of Torts*, § 13, § 13 cmt. d, § 158, § 158 cmt. e, § 577, § 580 (1934); *Restatement (Second) of Torts*, § 13, § 13 cmt. c, § 158, § 158 cmt. f (1965). In response to the constitutional challenges to no-fault liability, the second Restatement changed its rules to include a requirement of fault for liability in defamation. *Restatement (Second) of Torts*, §§ 580, 581.

[127] Harper, *Torts*, 6. 'Liability is not imposed unless the actor has conducted his activities in such a manner as to come within one of the foregoing classes' (ibid. 12).

[128] Prosser, *Torts*, 9. 'So far as they can be rationalized, it must be on the ground that it is acts which are unreasonable or socially harmful, from the point of view of the community as a whole, rather than the sole matter of individually questionable conduct, with which the law of torts is concerned' (ibid. 9–10).

[129] ibid. 9. [130] ibid. 9.

[131] It explained the rules in question only '[s]o far as they can be rationalized' (ibid. 9–10). He admitted that the rules are historical survivals (ibid. 9). [132] See *Vosburg v. Putney*, 50 NW 403 (Wis 1891).

burner near the border of his own land, builds a fire, and a freak wind carries a spark that sets fire to his neighbor's crops or house. Liability for trespass to land depends on whether he was correct in thinking that he had placed the burner on his own side of the property line. Suppose a person smashes another's car. If he did so while driving his own, liability turns on whether he was driving negligently. But if he bought that car from someone who did not have title, then, even though he has every reason to think he owns it, according to common law doctrine, he should be liable no matter how carefully he was driving. Suppose someone writes about how outrageously a fictitious person with an unlikely name is behaving abroad, and by pure chance, someone actually has that name, and some reader might think the article was about him. Again, the defendant is supposed to be liable.[133]

The anomaly is all the greater when we recognize that sometimes a defendant is not liable if he reasonably believed that he was not acting wrongfully. A defendant can escape liability for battery if he had a reasonable belief that he was acting in self-defense even though he was wrong.[134] And yet a reasonable mistake as to identity or privilege does not excuse him. The defendant is excused if he made a reasonable mistake as to whether his conduct would result in an entry on land or harm to another's chattels. He is excused if he made a reasonable mistake as to whether he must tie up at defendant's pier to save his life or property in a storm.[135] He is not excused if he is reasonably mistaken as to privilege or ownership. If a third party reads a defamatory statement which the defendant sent the plaintiff, the defendant is not liable if he had no reason to know the letter would be opened by another.[136] He is liable if he sent the letter to a third party but had no reason to know the statement was false, or would hurt anyone's reputation.

Recognizing a reasonable belief as a defense in the cases just mentioned leads to a further anomaly: a defendant can be held to have committed an intentional tort when he merely behaved unreasonably. The defendant who unreasonably believes he is under attack is liable for battery. The defendant who unreasonably believes his life or property is in danger in a storm and ties up at plaintiff's pier is liable for trespass. The defendant who unreasonably believes that a third party will not open his letter to the plaintiff is liable for defamation. And the fact that he is liable for an intentional tort may change the extent to which he is liable. As Prosser noted, in the case of intentional torts, '[m]ore liberal rules are applied to the consequences for which he will be held liable, the certainty of proof required, and the type of damage for which recovery is to be permitted, as well as the measure of compensation'.[137]

Nor do the difficulties end there. Suppose the harm the defendant intended was not precisely the one he caused. Explaining whether the defendant is liable[138] is complicated in common law because, according to Harper, Prosser, and the *Restatements*, the intention that mattered was not an intention to do harm or wrong. Therefore it was not enough to say that the defendant was liable if he wrongfully intended one

---

133 *E. Hulton & Co.* v. *Jones*, [1910] AC 20.
134 *Restatement of Torts*, § 63(1)(a) (1934); *Restatement (Second) of Torts*, § 63(1) (1965).
135 *Vincent* v. *Lake Erie Transportation Co.*, 124 NW 221 (Minn 1910).
136 *Restatement of Torts*, § 577 (1934); *Restatement (Second) of Torts*, § 577(1) (1965).
137 Prosser, *Torts*, 39–40.   138 Discussed in Chapter 10 I B.

harm and did another, or if he wrongfully intended to harm one person and harmed another. According to them, the intention that gives rise to liability is specific to each tort: to make unauthorized contact, to create the apprehension of unauthorized contact, to enter land, to meddle with chattels, to make a statement. Yet they acknowledged that a person was sometimes held liable for committing one tort when he intended to commit a different one, or to a different person, or sometimes even when he acted intentionally but his intention did not correspond to any specific tort.

They handled this problem by adding three new epicycles to what was already an overly complicated doctrinal system. First, the intention that gave rise to liability for one tort was sometimes defined to include the intention to commit another. For example, the intention requisite for battery was defined to include the one requisite for assault: 'the intention of inflicting a harmful or offensive contact . . . or putting the other . . . in apprehension thereof'.[139] Conversely, the intention necessary to commit an assault was to include the intention necessary to commit a battery.[140] Indeed, according to Prosser it would be sufficient to have the intention necessary to commit false imprisonment.[141] The trouble with this solution is that it explained nothing. It simply smuggled a conclusion into a definition.

Second, the intent to commit one tort or to commit it upon one person was said to 'transfer' to consequences which, if intended, would constitute a different tort or which had been suffered by a different person.[142] That was supposed to explain cases of the kind just mentioned in which A shoots at B and hits C. As Prosser himself noted, however, to speak of 'transferred intent' was 'obviously only a fiction'.[143] His explanation of the doctrine was that '[h]aving departed from the social standard of conduct [the defendant] is liable for the harm which follows from his act although he does not intend it'. The doctrine is 'illustrative of the general attitude of the courts as to the imposition of responsibility on an intentional wrongdoer'.[144] That explanation does not work when the defendant was not an 'intentional wrongdoer' and did not intentionally depart from 'the social standard of conduct' even though he had the intention supposedly necessary to trigger liability.

Third, the victim was said to have 'intended' consequences which he did not desire as long as he was 'substantially certain that they would occur'.[145] The cases Prosser cited for it in his first edition are not at all in point.[146] But in any case, as we will see, why this principle should apply in tort law is far from clear. In any event, this principle does make it possible to hold a person liable when the result he intended would not

---

[139] *Restatment of Torts*, § 18(1) (1934); *Restatement (Second) of Torts*, § 18(1) (1965).

[140] Prosser, *Torts*, 52; *Restatement of Torts*, § 21(1) (1934); *Restatement (Second) of Torts*, § 21(1) (1965).

[141] Prosser, *Torts*, 52.

[142] ibid. 47; William L. Prosser, 'Transferred Intent', *Tex. L. Rev.* 45 (1967), 650.

[143] Prosser, *Torts*, 47.　　[144] ibid. 48.

[145] *Restatement of Torts*, § 13 cmt. d; § 21 cmt. d; § 35 cmt. d (1934); *Restatement (Second) of Torts*, § 8A cmt. b (1965).

[146] Prosser, *Torts*, 41: 'The driver who whips up his horses with a loud yell while passing his neighbor's team will not be credited when he denies that he intended to cause a runaway'; citing *Lambet* v. *Sehreyer*, 152 NW 645 (Minn 1915) 'and the defendant on a bicycle who rides down a man in full view on a sidewalk where there is ample room to pass may find the court unwilling to accept his statement that he did not mean to do it', citing *Mercer* v. *Corbin*, 20 NE 132 (Ind 1889).

constitute a tort provided the consequences, if intended, would do so and they were 'substantially certain' to follow.

In the next chapter, we will see that we do not have to smuggle conclusions into definitions, or to speak of transferred intent or substantial certainty to explain the results just described.[147] But in any event, as applied to the common law torts, this approach multiplies the instances in which a person who intended no harm or wrong was held liable even though he did not act negligently. Suppose a manufacturer's representative tests fly spray in the plaintiff's husband's store, hoping to persuade him to stock it, and she becomes sick because of a previously unsuspected allergy. Liability depends on whether there was an implied revocation of the representative's license to make the experiment.[148] Suppose the defendant dumps waste water which, unforeseeably, contains contaminants which make his next door neighbor sick. Liability depends on whether he wanted the water to enter his neighbor's land, or was substantially certain it would do so. Suppose, without negligence, the defendant accidentally shoots his hunting partner. If we apply the doctrine of transferred intent, he is liable if they happen to have wandered onto the land of a third party even though they believe they are in a national park, unless we say the injured party is *in pari delicto* because he, too, is a trespasser, in which case the defendant's liability would turn on whether the victim happened to have some implied license to be there which the defendant himself did not.

III. Conclusion

By early modern times, continental writers had organized their law of torts around two basic ideas which the common lawyers then borrowed. One was the idea that the plaintiff could recover if the defendant harmed him by violating one of his rights or legally protected interests. The second was that there were three distinct grounds for holding a person liable in tort. In principle, he might have harmed someone intentionally, or negligently. He might also be liable for engaging in an activity for which he is strictly liable although this was a category, for many centuries, no one could explain by any general principle, and which recent English law has called into question.

In contrast, until the 19th century, English law was organized by writs. The writs were not a list of interests deemed worthy of legal protection. Nor, in what we now call tort law, were the categories of intent, negligence and strict liability distinguished with any clarity. Beginning with Blackstone, the Anglo-American treatise writers, with the help of their courts, tried to reorganize their law around the principles which, for centuries, had been fundamental to civil law. The result was only partially successful. There was only so far the treatise writers could go and still present their doctrines as a rationalization of English case law. It is unfortunate that they could not go further. By and large, the elements that they did not assimilate clash with the continental system they borrowed. The result is often neither rational nor traditional.

---

[147] Chapter 10 I B.   [148] *Brabazon* v. *Joannes Bros. Co.*, 286 NW 21 (Wis 1939).

Salmond and Prosser made the first systematic attempts to liberate the common law from the forms of action. Salmond said:

'In earlier days, [the forms of action] filled the law with formalism and fiction, confusion and complexity, and though most of the mischief that they did has been buried with them, some portion of it remains inherent in the law of the present day. Thus if we open a book on the law of torts, however modern and rationalized, we still hear echoes of . . . old controversies . . . , and we are still called upon to observe old distinctions and subtleties that have no substance or justification in them but are nothing more than an evil inheritance from the days when forms of action and of pleading held the legal system in their clutches'.[149]

That is true. But, if our argument has been correct, his approach and that of the other treatise writers made escape impossible. He asked: 'Does the law of torts consist of a fundamental general principle that it is wrongful to cause harm to other persons in the absence of some specific ground of justification or excuse, or does it consist of a number of specific rules prohibiting certain kinds of harmful activity, and leaving all the residue outside the sphere of legal responsibility?'[150] He thought that the second alternative was correct. It is not surprising that he concluded that 'even at the present day, all satisfactory definition and classification of the different species of injuries must be based on the old procedural distinctions between forms of action'.[151] Once that decision had been made, there was no way to escape the 'mischief' he himself had criticized. It would be better to say with Pollock that '[w]e are now independent of the forms of action'. Therefore 'a rational exposition of tort law is free to get rid of extraneous matter brought in, as we have shown, by the practical exigency of conditions that no longer exist'.[152]

---

[149] John W. Salmond, 'Observations on Trover and Conversion', *L.Q. Rev.* 21 (1905), 43.
[150] Salmond, *Torts*, 9.   [151] ibid. 182.   [152] Pollock, *Torts*, 15.

10

The Defendant's Conduct: Intent, Negligence, Strict Liability

As we have seen, civil law systems have generally recognized three bases for liability in tort: intent, negligence and strict liability, although civil law jurists have often been at a loss to explain the last of these, and it was omitted by the drafters of the French and German Civil Codes. We have also seen how the common lawyers borrowed this structure from the civil law although they failed to purge it of remnants of their traditional system of writs. We will now consider why liability should be imposed on these three grounds.

Again, we will be drawing on Aristotelian ideas of commutative justice. We will also be drawing on other Aristiotelian ideas about the nature of voluntary action.

I. Intent

A. Liability for the Intended Consequences of Intentional Conduct

According to Aristotle, one type of commutative justice is observed in transactions that are involuntary, and another in transactions that are voluntary. Involuntary transactions include those which are 'clandestine, such as theft, adultery, poisoning, procuring, enticement of slaves, assassination, false witness' and others which are 'violent, such as assault, imprisonment, murder, robbery with violence, mutilation, abuse, insult'.[1]

Commutative justice meant that when one person deprived another of resources, the balance had to be restored by taking resources from the person who had gained to compensate the one who had lost. Thus, in involuntary transactions, Aristotle maintained, 'the judge tries to equalize things by means of the penalty', taking away the 'gain' of one party and restoring the 'loss' of the other.[2] He admitted that it seems odd to speak of a 'gain' when one person has wounded another. Nevertheless, Aristotle maintained that 'when the suffering has been estimated, the one is called loss and the other gain'.[3]

Some modern scholars have found it difficult to see how holding the defendant liable to the plaintiff is supposed to restore equality by eliminating these gains and losses. Suppose, as Aristotle mentions, someone does commit murder but out of

---

[1] Aristotle, *Nicomachean Ethics* V.iv 1131ᵃ.   [2] ibid. V.iv 1132ᵃ.   [3] ibid.

hatred rather than for financial gain. George Fletcher has observed that the person who pays compensation for harming another will be poorer than he was initially unless he happens to have profited by an equivalent amount.[4] Conversely, suppose one party gains from a wrong done to another but without causing his victim a loss. Jules Coleman has noted that equality will not be restored if the defendant keeps the gain.[5]

In the Aristotelian tradition, a first step toward an explanation was taken by the teacher of Thomas Aquinas, Albert the Great. He said that 'the one who acts has more of what he wants, and the one who suffers has less . . . and this is appropriately designated by the name gain and loss'.[6] Aquinas clarified: a 'person striking or killing has more of what is evaluated as good, insofar, that is, as he fulfills his will, and so is seen to receive a sort of gain'.[7] 'To gain', then, means to fulfill one's will. One who took or used or harmed another's resources for his own ends had 'gained', and therefore must pay compensation, whether or not his ends were achieved, and whether or not he had made a financial gain by pursuing them.

On this view, a defendant was liable because he 'fulfils his will'. Consequently, it explained why a person would be liable for harm he inflicted intentionally. For Aristotle and Aquinas, an act was voluntary when a person exercises the abilities that make him human: his reason and will. Through reason, he understands the ends he might seek and the courses of action by which he might pursue them. Through will, he chooses among them. One who voluntarily kills another out of hatred had therefore 'gained' in the sense that he had chosen to harm another in order to accomplish an end of his own. My late colleague, David Daube, has shown rather clearly that Aristotle had only intentionally inflicted harm in mind.[8] How the scholastics eventually extended this theory to explain liability for negligence will be discussed at a later point. We can see, then, why, despite Fletcher's objection, commutative justice restores a pre-existing equality even when the defendant has not profited financially from the plaintiff's loss. By voluntarily harming the plaintiff, he has chosen to use the plaintiff's resources for his own ends. The pre-existing equality that commutative justice seeks to restore is a state in which each party can pursue his own goals only out of his own resources.

We can also see, despite Coleman's argument, why commutative justice does not require taking away the defendant's gain if the plaintiff has not suffered a loss. In that case, the defendant has not achieved his own ends at the plaintiff's expense. As Aquinas noted, when commutative justice required restitution, '[t]he chief end . . . is not that he who has more than his due may cease to have it, but that he who has less

---

[4] George P. Fletcher, 'Corrective Justice for Moderns', *Harv. L. Rev.* 106 (1993), 1658 at 1668 (reviewing Jules L. Coleman, *Risks and Wrongs* (Cambridge, 1992)). See Stephen Perry, 'The Moral Foundations of Tort Law', *Iowa L. Rev.* 77 (1992), 449 at 454.

[5] Jules L. Coleman, 'Property, Wrongfulness and the Duty to Compensate', *Chi-Kent L. Rev.* 63 (1987), 451 at 461–2.

[6] Albertus Magnus, *Ethicorum libri decem*, lib. V, tract. ii, cap. 6, no. 25 in *Opera omnia* 7 (A. Bourgnet, ed., Paris, 1891).

[7] Thomas Aquinas, *In decem libros Ethicorum Aristoteles expositio* (A. Pirotta, ed., Maritti, 1934), lib. V, lectio vi, no. 952.

[8] David Daube, *Roman Law: Linguistic, Social and Philosophical Aspects* (Edinburgh, 1969), 131–56.

than his due may be compensated'.[9] Aquinas concluded that though it might be appropriate to take away the defendant's gain by criminal sanctions,[10] the defendant did not have to pay if the plaintiff was not harmed: for example, if plaintiff's use of his resources was unimpaired as when the defendant took a light from the plaintiff's candle;[11] if the plaintiff was never harmed because the defendant's plan miscarried,[12] or if the plaintiff had already been compensated by another tortfeasor.[13]

There is a feature of this Aristotelian account which I find, not only attractive, but necessary to any sound theory of tort law. It explains why the plaintiff should recover, and recover from the defendant. The defendant has profited—in the sense of getting what he wants, or seeking to do so—at the plaintiff's expense. As Jules Coleman once noted, the proposition 'the plaintiff has lost' is 'analytically' different than the proposition that 'the defendant should be liable'.[14] A good theory of tort needs to explain why these two consequences should go together. Otherwise, it must explain tort law in terms of two distinct and only casually related policies: a concern about the defendant's conduct and a concern about the plaintiff's loss.

If one is simply concerned about the former, one will conceive of tort law as an indirect way of accomplishing ends that are directly addressed by criminal law: deterring the defendant from harming others or punishing him. At best, one could then explain why under some circumstances these goals are better effectuated by allowing private recovery in tort. One could never explain as a general principle why the plaintiff should compensate the defendant for the harm he has suffered. The harm the plaintiff has suffered will bear no necessary relationship to the need for deterrence or the punishment the plaintiff deserves. Some intentional wrongs are more or less difficult for the law to deter. Some are more or less vicious and deserving of punishment. Regardless, the plaintiff will recover only the amount by which he was harmed. If he was killed, he will not even recover that. Conversely, if one were solely concerned about compensating the plaintiff for the harm he has suffered, it would not seem to matter whether the defendant hurt him intentionally. It would not be clear why his recovery should be limited to the assets of the defendant. It would make more sense to have some system of social insurance. In contrast, if one believes in commutative justice, there is a reason that the plaintiff should be compensated by one who has profited, or attempted to profit, by seeking to accomplish his own goals at the plaintiff's expense.

B. Liability for the Unintended Consequences of Intentional Conduct

Suppose, however, one party was not seeking to accomplish his goals by harming the other in the way he did. The harm he happened to inflict was unintended and perhaps even unforeseen. A person strikes another to render him unconscious so as to steal his wallet and inadvertently maims him. Jurists take it for granted that he is liable for the injury he actually caused. A person shoots to harm one person and by accident harms another whom he had no reason to suspect is in the vicinity. As we will see, modern

---

[9] Aquinas, *Summa theologiae* II-II, Q. 62, a. 6, ad 1.   [10] ibid. Q. 62, a. 3.   [11] ibid.
[12] ibid. Q. 62, a.7, ad 2.   [13] ibid.   [14] Coleman, 'Property', 461.

common law or civil law jurists have not found a good solution to these problems, and neither, for that matter, did the late scholastics or the northern natural lawyers. That is paradoxical because, as we will see, Thomas Aquinas had a good solution which he borrowed from the medieval canon lawyers. Had the late scholastics accepted it, as they did so many of Aquinas' conclusions, the northern natural lawyers might have done so as well, and it might have passed into the mainstream of the civil law. Strangely enough, it was discredited by, of all people, the late scholastics.

1. Modern solutions

A party who did not desire the harm is sometimes held liable, supposedly, because he knew or thought it would occur. In the United States, it is commonly said that a person is liable if knew with 'substantial certainty' that the harm would occur. The famous case is *Garratt* v. *Dailey* where a child removed the chair in which an older woman had begun seating herself.[15] She was hurt when she struck the ground. The court held that the child need not have desired that the woman strike the ground in order for his action to count as intentional. It was enough that he was substantially certain she would.

One of the difficulties with this solution is that conceptually, it is hard to see why an action should be viewed as intentional simply because it is more likely to occur by some unspecified degree. Another difficulty is to see why liability should be limited to cases of substantial certainty. If it is reasonable to hold the child liable if he knows the woman has a 100 percent chance of striking the ground, why isn't it reasonable to do so if he knew the chances were 80 or 60 or even 10 percent?

As mentioned earlier, German jurists avoid such problems by speaking of 'conditional intent'.[16] Even if a person does not desire the consequence of his action, but envisions it, and mentally accepts it, he is deemed to have intended it. The difficulty here is to explain what it means to envision an action and mentally accept it. Presumably, it does not mean that the person in question is liable for any harm his action may foreseeably bring about. If so, a person would be liable for intentionally inflicting, not only for all harm that he negligently inflicts, but for all the harm that he foresees may result even from a non-negligent action.

When one person harms another while intending to harm someone else whom he does not know or envision he might harm, jurists are divided on whether he should be held liable. In Anglo-American criminal law, he is held responsible by invoking a doctrine known as 'transferred intent' or 'transferred malice'. If A inadvertently harms B while intending to harm C, his intention to harm C is said to 'transfer' to the harm done B.[17] In Italy, article 82 of the Criminal Code provides that one who mistakenly harms a different person than he intended will be held responsible as though his intention had not miscarried.[18] The Italians do not have a similar doctrine in tort.[19] It is not

---

[15] *Garatt* v. *Dailey*, 279 P.2d 1091 (Wash 1955).   [16] Chapter 7 I B.

[17] As the Model Penal Code puts it, the requirement that the defendant have acted 'purposefully' is satisfied even if the actual result is different only in that a different person or property is affected. Model Penal Code, § 2.03(2)(a).   [18] Italian Criminal Code (*Codice penale*), art. 82.

[19] Nevertheless, the defendant might be civilly liable under art. 185, par. 2 of the Italian Criminal Code (*Codice penale*) which says that 'every crime that has caused a harm . . . obligates the guilty party to make compensation . . .'.

clear whether the English have a similar doctrine in tort[20] although in two old English cases[21] and one recent one in Northern Ireland[22] liability was imposed. American lawyers say that the intent to commit a tort can be transferred from one victim to another and from one tort to another so that if A shoots at C or at C's dog he will be liable if he hits B.[23]

Italian critics have claimed that their rule violates the principle, enshrined in their constitution,[24] that a person is criminally responsible only for his 'personal' fault.[25] English and Americans have called this doctrine 'a curious survival of the antique law',[26] an 'archaic survival',[27] 'an historical aberration',[28] 'an arbitrary exception to normal principles'.[29] No one believes that A's intention to harm C really transmutes to an intention to harm B.[30] To say so merely expresses the conclusion that A should

---

[20] Some say that liability even for an intentional wrong is limited to the foreseeable consequences. E.g., R. F. V. Heuston and R. A. Buckley, *Salmond and Heuston on the Law of Torts* (21st edn., London, 1996), 511 Others think an English court might follow the Canadian case of *Allan* v. *New Mt. Sinai Hospital*, [1980] 125 DLR 3d 276, in which the court said that there would be liability for the unforeseeable consequences as well. See John Fleming, *The Law of Torts* (8th edn., North Ryde, Aust., 1992), 25 (approving the rule); K. M. Stanton, *The Modern Law of Tort* (London, 1994), 101 (asking if it is part of English law). But *Allan* was not like the American transferred intent cases. Defendant, who had committed a battery by giving the plaintiff an injection over his protest, was held liable for consequences to which he was abnormally and unforeseeably susceptible.

[21] *Scott* v. *Shepard*, [1773] 2 Wm Bl 892, 96 Eng Rep 525 (defendant liable when he had thrown a fire cracker toward one person who threw it toward another who threw it toward the plaintiff); *James* v. *Campbell*, [1832] 5 Car & P 372, 172 Eng Rep 1015 (defendant liable when he tried to hit one person in a fistfight at a parish dinner and accidentally struck the plaintiff).

[22] *Livingstone* v. *Ministry of Defence*, [1984] NI 356 (CA) (plaintiff struck by bullet aimed at someone else).

[23] e.g., *Alteiri* v. *Colasso*, 362 A2d 798 (Conn 1975) (defendant liable when he hit the plaintiff with a rock thrown in order to frighten someone else); *Singer* v. *Marx*, 301 P2d 440 (Cal App 1956) (same, except the rock was thrown to hit someone else). In other cases sometimes cited as authority for the doctrine of transferred intent courts have reached similar results but have spoken of the 'unlawfulness' of the defendant's action. E.g., *Talmage* v. *Smith*, 59 NW 656 (Mich 1894) (a man threw a stick at two boys who were trespassing on his property but struck a third boy who, he claimed, was out of sight); *Lopez* v. *Surchia*, 246 P2d 111 (Cal App 1952) (defendant shot when he had not been attacked with deadly force, and therefore he is liable when a bystander is accidentally hit); *Morrow* v. *Flores*, 225 SW2d 621 (Tex App 1949) (same); *Carnes* v. *Thompson*, 48 SW2d 903 (Mo 1932) (if defendant struck at plaintiff's husband, he is liable if he accidentally hit the plaintiff).

In Anglo-American criminal law, the doctrine of transferred intent permits the 'intention' to be transferred from one person to another or one physical object to another but not from one crime to another. According to the Italian Criminal Code (*Codice penale*), art. 83, except as provided by art. 82 (described in the text), a person who causes an 'event' other than the one he intended is liable for the event he caused 'for negligence' (*a titolo di culpa*). Commentators disagree whether this provision means he is punished as though he caused this event negligently or whether he is liable only if he caused it by his negligence. See Giovanni Fiandaca and Enzo Musco, *Diritto penale: Parte generale* (3rd edn., Bologna, 1995), 581 (taking the former position); Ferrando Mantovani, *Diritto penale: Parte generale* (3rd edn., Padua, 1992), 386 (supporting the later position on the grounds that in cases of doubt one must follow the principle that punishment is due only in cases of personal fault); Francesco Antolisei and Luigi Conti, *Manuale di diritto penale: Parte generale* (13th edn., Milan, 1994), 392–3 (same).

[24] Italian Constitution, art. 27, par. 1.   [25] Fiandaca and Musco, *Diritto penale*, 576–81.

[26] William L. Prosser, 'Transferred Intent', *Texas L. Rev.* 45 (1967), 650.

[27] Cardozo in *Sinram* v. *Penn. R.R. Co*, 61 F2d 767, 770 (2nd Cir 1932).

[28] Don Stuart, *Canadian Criminal Law* (Toronto, 1982), 196–7.

[29] Glanville Williams, *Criminal Law: The General Part* (2nd edn., London, 1961), 134. Similarly, Martin R. Gardner, 'The Mens Rea Enigma: Observations on the Role of Motive in the Criminal Law Past and Present', *Utah Law Rev.* (1993), 635, at 734 ('an unnecessary exception').

[30] Douglas Husak, 'Transferred Intent', *Notre Dame J. of L. & Pub. Policy* 10 (1966), 65 at 83.

be held responsible.[31] According to Ernest Weinrib, the doctrine is anomalous because '[t]he duty breached by the defendant must be with respect to the embodiment of the right whose infringement is the ground of the plaintiff's cause of action'.[32] Some Americans believe that the doctrine should be abolished. If A was not negligent, he should not be liable in tort except possibly for assault.[33]

The trouble is, illogical as the doctrine appears to be, it enables courts to reach results that seem to be more in accord with an ordinary sense of justice than those they would reach otherwise.[34] If A aims at C and shoots B, few people would want to treat him the same way as if he missed.[35] Those who disagree, Husak suggests, should ask themselves how they would react if A shot first at B and then at C, meaning to kill them both, and due to some freak event (chance ricochets or gusts of wind) the bullet meant for B hit C and vice versa.[36] Is it really possible that A is not liable?

Prosser said that while 'it would be easy to dismiss all this as one more illustration of the survival of absolute rules.... nevertheless... as between the innocent plaintiff struck by the bullet and the guilty defendant who fired it with intent to kill another man, it put the loss on the one upon whom it ought in obvious justice to fall'.[37] And so we have a curious state of affairs. A thoroughly illogical doctrine is needed to reach an 'obviously' just result.

The difficulty of achieving logical consistency even without the doctrine of transferred intent is illustrated by the experience of legal systems that have no such doctrine. Germany is a good illustration. In German criminal law, if A shoots at C and kills B, he is guilty of attempting to murder C and, at most, of negligently killing B.[38] The result is said to be the same in tort.[39]

In tort, however, German courts have held the defendant liable when he inflicted a different kind of harm than he intended on the same person. That result seems intuitively correct but is reached at the cost of logical consistency. In such cases, German courts have applied a general rule that once the defendant has violated a right of the plaintiff enumerated in Section 823 of the Civil Code, he is liable even for unforeseen

---

[31] Husak, 'Transferred Intent', 67; Paul H. Robinson, 'Imputed Criminal Liability', *Yale L. Jour.* 93 (1984), 609 at 619.   [32] Ernest Weinrib, *Duke L.J.* 44 (1994), 277, at 295, 295 n. 42.

[33] That seems to be Prosser's view of what we would conclude if we applied tort principles logically. Prosser, 'Transferred Intent,' 660, 652.

[34] Husak, 'Transferred Intent', 70. See Robinson, 'Imputed Criminal Liability', 619 (speaking of a 'community consensus').

[35] As in other respects, the sense of justice in Dodge City on the American frontier may have been different. In 1878, Jim Kennedy shot at Mayor Dog Kelley and killed Dora Hand by mistake. He was tracked down and arrested by a blue ribbon posse composed of Wyatt Earp, Bat Masterson, Charlie Bassett and Bill Tilghman, only to be acquitted. The reason, according to John Myers' interpretation, was that 'Kelley had not even been hit so there was no reason for him to squawk, and Miss Hand had not been shot on purpose, so it was ridiculous to talk about assaulting with intent to kill'. John Myers, *Doc Holliday* (London, 1973), 91.

[36] Husak, 'Transferred Intent', 70.   [37] Prosser, 'Transferred Intent', 662.

[38] Adolf Schönke and H. Schröder, *Strafgesetzbuch Kommentar* (24th edn., Munich, 1991), no. 57 to § 15; BGH, 10 Apr. 1986, EBGHSt 34, 53 (defendant who tried to run down one person in his car and accidentally struck another is liable for attempted murder as to the first and for the negligent infliction of bodily harm as to the second).

[39] In OLG, Schleswig, 10 Aug. 1976, NJW 1977, 718, the court held that if the defendant hit the plaintiff with an object thrown at another, he would be liable to the plaintiff for negligence, not for an intentional wrong. The court, however, was not deciding a case in which defendant argued he was not negligent as to the plaintiff. Plaintiff's injury was covered by an insurance policy if harm was inflicted negligently but not intentionally.

consequences.[40] Section 823 says that the defendant is liable for intentional or negligent injury to plaintiff's life, body, health, freedom of movement or 'similar' right. Economic harm does not count as the invasion of a 'similar' right. The defendant is liable for causing economic harm only if he does so intentionally, and then only if the harm he inflicts is the harm he intended. But if he negligently or intentionally injures plaintiff's life, body, health or freedom, he is liable for unforeseen consequences.[41]

One result is that in Germany, as in the United States, the defendant must 'take the plaintiff as he finds him'. If he causes him a physical injury, he will be liable if the injury is more severe because the plaintiff had some unforeseeable physical condition.[42] But another result is that the defendant who violated one of the plaintiff's protected rights is liable for the unforeseen consequences to some quite different interest. For example, in one case, plaintiff's property was destroyed in an allied bombing raid in the Second World War. He claimed he could have saved his property had he not been arrested by German authorities on information given them by the defendant. He was allowed to recover if he could prove the giving of the information was unlawful.[43]

Such a result raises the same problems as the doctrine of transferred intent. The defendant is held liable for harm he neither intended nor negligently caused. Why should it matter that this harm was the accidental consequence of a harm that he did intend? If he should be liable for this sort of accident, why shouldn't he be if, by accident, the victim was a third party?

In German law, it is easier to see these anomalies because the German jurists are precise about the grounds for giving relief. Nevertheless, the same difficulty is implicit in the tort law of other continental legal systems. Typically, their codes contain a general provision that the defendant is liable for harm he causes negligently or intentionally.[44]

---

[40] German writers distinguish two causal relations: that between the defendant's act and a violation of one of the rights enumerated in section 823 (*haftungsbegründende Kausalität*) and that between the violation and any further harm of whatever type that the plaintiff suffers (*haftungsausfüllende Kausalität*). Karl Larenz and Claus-Wilhelm Canaris, *Lehrbuch des Schuldrechts* 2(2) (13th edn., Munich, 1994), § 27 III b 1. The first of these causal relations also embraces unforeseen consequences. Nevertheless, a limit is imposed by the requirement that the plaintiff must cause these consequences negligently or intentionally. Wolfgang Grunsky in Kurt Rebmann and Franz Juergen Säcker, *Münchener Kommentar zum Bürgerlichen Gesetzbuch* (Munich, 1985), vor § 249 no. 38. There is no analogous requirement that the plaintiff must intentionally or negligently bring about the consequences of the initial violation of a right.

[41] According to some German jurists, defendant is liable provided that his violation of plaintiff's rights was the 'adequate cause' of the harm done, meaning that the harm 'would not appear wholly improbable from the standpoint of an experienced observer'. Larenz and Canaris, *Lehrbuch*, § 27 III b 1. Others say that the defendant is liable only if the harm suffered falls within the 'protective purpose of the norm' that was violated. Larenz and Canaris, *Lehrbuch*, § 27 III 3; Grunsky in *Münchener Kommentar*, vor § 249, no. 43. All agree, however, that the defendant may be liable even for harm that he could not foresee.

[42] e.g., BGH, 17 Oct. 1955, BGHZ 18, 286, 289 (defendant liable for plaintiff's adverse reaction to an injection even if it was due to abnormal susceptibility); RG, 26 Apr. 1937, RGZ 155, 38, 41 (defendant liable for consequences of accident that were due to plaintiff's nervous condition).

[43] BGH, 8 Mar. 1951, NJW 1951, 596 (holding the loss of freedom was the 'adequate cause' of the loss of property).

[44] e.g., French Civil Code (*Code civil*), arts. 1382–3; Italian Civil Code (*Codice civile*), art. 2043. The New Dutch Civil Code (*Burgerlijk Wetboek*), art. 6.162 is an exception. It provides that a person is responsible if his action was 'due to fault or another ground which, according to statute or the opinion of society, should make him accountable'. But the provision is not meant to impose liability for the unforeseen consequences of unlawful acts. It was meant to deal with cases in which a person is held liable even though he is not personally to blame for the way he acted. It was thought, for example, that a novice driver or newly trained

Logically, these provisions seem to leave only two alternatives: to deny relief for harm that was neither foreseeable nor intended, or to give relief and claim that somehow the harm was caused negligently or intentionally.

In France, a hunter came on the plaintiff's land in violation of a French statute and in defiance of posted no trespassing signs. The plaintiff angrily grabbed away his firearm, knocked it against a cement block, and was injured when it fired. The highest court, the *Cour de Cassation*, allowed him to recover.[45] It did not say whether it regarded the consequences of the defendant's intentional wrong as, in some mysterious way, intended as well, or whether it thought that a prudent hunter would remove his cartridges when entering another's land for fear that the owner would grab away his gun and injure himself by knocking it against a cement block.

American law might not be more consistent even if, like continental legal systems, it rejected the doctrine of transferred intent. Yet the doctrine of transferred intent seems to be illogical. What is to be done?

2. An older solution

Before the 19th century, English jurists did not speak of transferred intent. They said that if A unintentionally harmed B, he was responsible if he was engaged in an unlawful activity. He would be liable if he shot B when aiming at C or trespassing on B's land because these were unlawful activities. One can find that doctrine in Blackstone[46] and Hale[47] who took it from Coke[48] who took it from Bracton.[49] As Shulz has shown,[50] Bracton took it from the famous 13th century canon lawyer Raymond of Penafort.[51] Raymond had simply been stating the opinion generally accepted among the canon lawyers of day. Italian scholars say that this medieval doctrine also inspired article 82 of their Criminal Code.[52]

Although, in the 19th century, English jurists thought it more sensible to speak of transferred intent, we will argue that this older solution, which can still be glimpsed in the language of some judicial opinions,[53] was actually the best one. If we examine the origins of the doctrine, we will see it was accepted because of the range of cases in which it produced sensible results. It is, of course, a viable doctrine only if one can explain (1) what should count as an unlawful activity, (2) what the causal relation

---

physician should be liable if he fails to act like a more experienced person although he is not at fault. It was thought more honest to acknowledge that liability is imposed without fault than to say, as other legal systems do, that the defendant was 'negligent' as judged by an 'objective standard'. See *The Netherlands Civil Code Book 6: The Law of Obligations: Draft Text and Commentary* (The Netherlands Ministry of Justice, Leyden, 1977), 384–5.

[45] Cass., 2e ch. civ., 14 Dec. 1987, arrêt no. 1.307 (unpublished).

[46] William Blackstone, *Commentaries on the Laws of England* 4 (London, 1776), *182–3.

[47] Matthew Hale, *Historia Placitorum Coronae* 1 (S. Emlyn and G. Wilson, eds., London, 1800), *471–7. See also ibid. *429–30, *431, *466.

[48] Edward Coke, *The Third Part of the Institutes of the Laws of England* (London, 1817), *56–57.

[49] Bracton, *De legibus et consuetudinibus Angliae* 2 (G. E. Woodbine and S. E. Thorne, eds., Cambridge, Mass., 1968), *f. 120b–121, p. 341.

[50] F. Schulz, 'Bracton and Raymond de Penafort', *L. Quar. Rev.* 61 (1945), 286 at 289–90.

[51] Raimundus de Penafort, *Summa de poenitentia* (Xaverio Ochoa and Aloisio Diez, eds., Rome, 1976), II. i. 3.   [52] Fiandaca and Musco, *Diritto penale*, 574; Antolisei and, *Manuale Conti*, 361.

[53] e.g, *Wyant* v. *Crouse*, 86 NW 527 (Mich 1901).

must be between that activity and the harm it unforeseeably causes, and (3) why one who engages in such an activity should be responsible for that harm. These are difficult questions. As we will see, even though Aquinas accepted the doctrine, many of the late scholastics rejected it because they thought that they could not answer them consistently with the principles of Aquinas and Aristotle. As mentioned, if they had accepted this solution, Grotius and Pufendorf might have done so as well, and the doctrine might have passed into modern law. Instead, it died out in continental Europe in the 16th and 17th centuries.

We will examine, first, why the doctrine initially seemed attractive, second, why it was rejected and third, why rejecting it was a mistake.

a. Its initial acceptance

The earlier canonists rested the doctrine that one was liable for the unintended consequences of unlawful acts on three texts in the *Decretum*, a collection of authorities made by Gratian about 1140. One was a vague statement by St Augustine that no one can be blamed for doing what is 'good and lawful'.[54] Another was a ruling by the Council of Worms in 868 that a person who cuts down a tree which crushes a passer-by 'while carrying out some necessary work' need only do penance if he acted 'by will or by negligence'.[55] The third was a decision by Pope Urban I that a priest who killed a boy by throwing a stone should do penance as a homicide but would not be suspended from his functions as those guilty of homicide usually were. The text said nothing about why the priest threw the stone.[56]

Just because their authorities said so little, the canonists found themselves improvising. The earliest canon lawyers to consider the problem said that the priest would not be guilty if he threw the stone for a 'reason' (*causa*)[57] or 'good reason' (*iusta causa*)[58] and did so with 'diligence' in a place where people were not walking. Later canonists explained that the priest had a 'reason' to throw the stone if he was engaged in a 'lawful' activity rather than an 'unlawful' one.[59] The priest would not have been guilty if he threw the stone to chase a wild boar or a pig out of a field of grain unless he had been careless.[60] He would be guilty if he engaged in an unlawful activity or failed to use the diligence he should.[61]

After the doctrine became generally accepted, popes referred to it in their own decisions which were in turn regarded as authoritative. Raymond of Penafort included two such decisions in an authoritative collection he assembled known as the *Decretals*

---

[54] C. 23, q. 5, c. 8.   [55] Dig. 50, c. 50.   [56] Dig. 50, c. 37.

[57] Paucapalea, *Summa über das Decretum Gratiani* (J. F. Schulte, ed., 1891; repr. Aalen, 1965), to D. 50, c. 37.

[58] Stephanus Tornacensis, *Die Summa über das Decretum Gratiani* (J. F. Shulte, ed., repr. Aalen, 1965), to D. 50, c. 37.   [59] Huguccio, *Summa*, Admont, Stiftsbibliothek, MS 7, to D. 50, c. 37, f. 71ra.

[60] *Glossa Palatina*, Vatican City, Biblioteca Apostolica Vaticana, Cod. palatini latini MS. 658, to D. 50, c. 37, f. 13va; Huguccio, *Summa* to D. 50, c. 37, f. 71ra; Iohannes Teutonicus, *Glossa ordinaria*, Vatican City, Biblioteca Apostolica Vaticana, Cod. palatini latini MS 624, to D. 50, c. 37 to *Clerico*, f. 40rb.

[61] e.g. *Glossa Palatina* to D. 50, c. 37, f. 13rb; Huguccio, *Summa* to D. 50, c. 37, f. 71ra; to D. 50, c. 44, f. 72va; to D. 50, c. 50, f. 73ra; Iohannes Teutonicus, *Glossa ordinaria* to D. 50, c. 37 to *Clerico*, f. 40rb; Guido de Baisio (Archidiaconus), *Archidiaconus super Decretum* (Lyon, 1549), to D. 50, c. 37; to D. 50, c. 44 to *casu*. For other references, see Stephan Kuttner, *Kanonistische Schuldlehre von Gratian bis auf die Dekretalen Gregors IX* (Vatican City, 1935), 201 n. 1, 202 n. 1.

of Pope Gregory IX. In one, the pope exonerated a chaplain who had gone riding to restore his appetite after an illness and killed someone when the reins broke.[62] In the other, he exonerated a priest who was building a church and killed a co-worker by dropping a load of wood on him. In both decisions, the pope noted that the activity was a lawful one.[63] As a 16th century critic pointed out, these texts supported the doctrine only by negative inference: because a priest engaged in a lawful activity was exonerated, one was asked to infer that the priest engaged in an unlawful one would be held responsible.[64] Nevertheless, the canon lawyers read these texts as authority for their doctrine, and, indeed, they read the doctrine into other papal decisions that had never mentioned it.[65]

The canon lawyers, then, did not accept this doctrine on authority. Neither did they do so for any theoretical reason. Instead, they seem to have liked it because it produced results that seemed intuitively correct. They gave some instances in their commentaries. One was the hypothetical case just mentioned of a priest who kills a boy when he throws a stone to chase a boar or pig from a grainfield. He was not to be held responsible, but, presumably, he would be if he had thrown at another boy. Raymond of Penafort said that a person would not be responsible for homicide if he threw a stone at his own animal and killed someone. He would be responsible if he threw the stone at another person's horse or cow in order to steal it.[66] A person who cut down his own tree with due care would not be responsible if it fell on someone. He would be responsible if he had been unlawfully cutting down another person's tree.[67] Sinibaldus Fliscus, later Pope Innocent IV, put the case of man who advised someone else, not to kill anyone, but to perform an act which might cause someone to die: for example, to fire a ballista or to capture a castle or to attack a person who might defend himself. He rejected the opinion of some jurists that the man would be innocent of homicide only if 'if it were plausible that the act could be done without a person's death'. The better opinion, he said, was that he would be innocent only if the action that he had advised were lawful: for example, to attack a malefactor lawfully in order to apprehend him.[68]

In one respect, the canonists were in the same position as some modern jurists. Results such as these intuitively appealed to them but they could not explain why.

---

[62] *Decretales Gregorii* ix 5.12.13.   [63] ibid. 5.12.25.

[64] Domenicus Soto, *De iustitia et iure libri decem* (Salamanca, 1553), lib. 5, q. 1, a. 9.

[65] e.g. *Glossa ordinaria* to *Decretales Gregorii* ix 5.12.14 (Venice, 1595); Raimundus de Penafort, *Summa de poenitentia* II.i.3; Hostiensis, *Summa aurea* (Venice, 1574), rubr. *Qua poena feriatur* sub *De homicidio volunatrai, vel casuali*, f. 359; Bernardus de Montemirato (Abbas Antiquus), *Commentaria ad libros Decretalium* (Venice, 1588), to *Decretales Gregorii* ix 5.12.13.

[66] Raimundus de Penafort, *Summa* II.i.3.   [67] ibid.

[68] Sinibaldus Fliscus (Innocent IV), *Commentaria in apparatus in v libros Decretalium* (Frankfurt, 1570), to X 5.12.12. Another and less fortunate example was based on a remark by Gratian that a blind man would be guilty if he injured someone while hunting with a javelin. Huguccio, *Summa* to C. 15, q. 1, dicta Gratiani post c. 2, f. 264rb; Iohannes Teutonicus, *Glossa ordinaria* to C. 15 q. 1 dicta Gratiai post c. 2 to *penitus*, f. 162 rb. The example was not a good one because the blind man should not go hunting precisely because it was too risky. As a critic pointed out, one did not need their doctrine to explain why someone was responsible in such cases. Leonardus Lessius, *De iustitia et iure, ceterisque virtutibus cardinalis libri quatuor* (Paris, 1628), lib. 5, cap. 9, dub. 15, no. 106.

b. Its rejection

This doctrine was endorsed in the 13th century by Thomas Aquinas. This is one of the rare instances in which the late scholastics rejected one of his conclusions.

The late scholastics rejected the doctrine because of the difficulties mentioned earlier. Some thought that it could not satisfactorily explain which unlawful acts gave rise to liability nor the causal relationship necessary between such an act and the harm that ensued. Others rejected it because they could not see why the perpetrator of an unlawful act should be held responsible for its chance consequences. To do so seemed to them to violate some basic principles of Aristotelian and Thomistic moral philosophy even though Aquinas himself had said that a person is responsible for the unintended consequences of an unlawful act.

Cajetan and Soto supported the doctrine but recognized that it would be absurd to hold a person liable for the consequences of any unlawful act. A priest should not be liable if he killed a co-worker while repairing a church on a religious holiday when he was forbidden to work.[69] If he was forbidden for religious reasons to ride a horse[70] or to hunt[71] he should not be responsible if he killed someone when his horse bolted or his arrow missed its mark. Soto argued that even though adultery is unlawful, if an adulterer was attacked by the husband and killed him in self-defense, the adulterer should not be held responsible for his death.[72]

Cajetan and Soto recognized, then, that a person was responsible for the consequences of some unlawful acts but not others. But they never satisfactorily explained the difference. In trying to do so, they became entangled in the second difficulty mentioned earlier: explaining the causal relationship necessary between that act and the unforeseen result. Suppose one person struck and killed a person whom he wished to strike but not to kill. Cajetan thought he would be responsible for homicide because 'the blow is a path (*via*) to death'. In contrast, riding a horse or hunting is not 'generically (*de genere suo*) a path to death'.[73] Soto agreed. As he put it, the unlawful activity must be a cause of death 'generically' (*de genere suo*), 'by its nature' (*ex natura sua*) or '*per se*'.[74] But it is not at all clear, even in the scholastic terminology of the time, what it meant to say an act was 'generically' or 'by its nature' or '*per se*' a cause of death.

Molina and Lessius concluded that, absent negligence, no one is responsible for the unintended consequences of an unlawful act. They may have been influenced by the difficulties that Cajetan and Soto encountered. Their chief difficulty, however, was that they could not see why someone should be liable for chance consequences.

---

[69] Soto, *De iustitia et iure* V.i.9.

[70] Cajetan (Tomasso di Vio), *Commentaria* to Thomas Aquinas, *Summa theologica* (Padua, 1698), to II-II, Q. 64, a. 8; Soto, *De iustitia et iure* V.i.9.   [71] Cajetan, *Commentaria* to II-II, Q. 64, a. 8.

[72] ibid.

[73] Cajetan, *Commentaria* to II-II, Q. 64, a. 8. Lessius, who thought one was only responsible for harm caused intentionally and negligently, sometimes spoke of harm that arises 'from the nature of an action' (*ex natura actionis*). He seems to have meant harm that arises 'frequently' (*ut plurimum*) rather than 'rarely' (*raro*) and so that undertaking the action would be negligent. Lessius, *De iustitia et iure*, lib. 2, cap. 9, dub. 16, no. 111. He seems to have thought that Cajetan was referring to harm that naturally arose from an action in this sense. ibid. lib. 2, cap. 2, dub. 15, no. 106. But in that event, Cajetan would have agreed with Lessius that there were only two bases for liability. Instead, Cajetan and Soto were to preserve something of the old rule even at the cost of muddy expressions and apparent inconsistency.

[74] Soto, *De iustitia et iure* V.i.9.

As Lessius put it, these consequences 'were willed neither themselves nor as to their cause'.[75] They were simply a matter of 'chance'.[76] The old doctrine was wrong.

For them, to hold someone responsible for 'chance' consequences that he did not 'will' would violate basic principles of Aristotelian and Thomistic moral philosophy. As mentioned, for Aristotle and Aquinas, man is a rational animal who acts by reason and will. When he fails to do so, for example, because he is ignorant of what he is doing or because his body is moved by force, he acts involuntarily.[77] Because such actions do not proceed from his reason and will, they are not caused by him.

While we have taken pains to see this difficulty in its historical context, one can make similar objections today. The harm that occurred had only a chance relationship to the unlawful act. Why then should the perpetrator be responsible? Stephan Kuttner and Martin Gardner have criticized the earlier doctrine for purporting to rest on fault but actually establishing a form of strict liability.[78] Giovanni Fiandaca, Enzo Musco and others have made the same criticism of article 82 of the Italian Criminal Code.[79]

As soon as the medieval doctrine was subject to careful scrutiny, then, it collapsed. The difficulties we have described seemed insurmountable.

c. A reappraisal

But two features of this story should make us wonder if the older doctrine was rightly rejected. First, Molina and Lessius themselves seem to have had qualms about their own conclusions. There are indications that they, like ourselves, found it hard to reach intuitively correct results if a person is only held responsible for harm intended or caused negligently.

Molina was willing to deny that a person who, without negligence, cut down another person's tree should be held responsible if it fell on a servant or a cow,[80] and that a thief should be responsible if, without negligence, he set fire to the house from which he was stealing.[81] Suppose, however, the thief had entered the house at night and stepped on something valuable and broke it. Or suppose a person who struck another harmed him in a different way than he intended. At this point even Molina refused to exonerate him. In these cases, he said, the unlawful act was the sort that might lead to the harm that actually occurred (*res illicita ... est apta, ut damnum sequatur*). Consequently, 'it is easy for fault to be present' and 'much easier' for it 'to be presumed' to be present by the court.[82] He seems to be reassuring us that the court will always presume the thief or the assailant was negligent and so hold him responsible.

Lessius left himself no such line of retreat. Nevertheless, he did not discuss Molina's cases of theft and physical attack or the cases put by the medieval canon lawyers. He illustrated his thesis with Cajetan's examples of the priest who is forbidden to

---

[75] ibid. lib. 2, cap. 8, dub. 18, no. 103.   [76] ibid. no. 102.

[77] *Nicomachean Ethics* III.i; *Summa theologiae* I-II, Q. 6, aa. 1, 5, 8.

[78] Kuttner, *Kanonistische Schuldlehre*, 207; Gardner, 'Mens Rea', 734.

[79] Fiandaca and Musco, *Diritto penale*, 576–81.

[80] Ludovicus Molina, *De iustitia et iure tractatus* (Venice, 1614), disp. 728, no. 2 (reading *bovem* for *ovem*).

[81] ibid.   [82] ibid. no. 3.

hunt and the adulterer who defends himself without excessive force.[83] He added several examples of his own. Suppose someone kills Peter, and malicious accusers and witnesses later see to it that Paul is punished for the crime.[84] Suppose someone robs Peter's treasure and Peter subsequently dies of grief.[85] Suppose someone sells arms to a knight knowing that the knight might put them to a bad use.[86] According to Lessius, in none of these cases should a person be held responsible for the death he did not intend.

The examples make one suspicious. They seem carefully chosen to make the conclusion sound plausible. In some of them, the act in question was wrongful but it was not unjust. The perpetrator was not trying to achieve his ends by harming anyone: for example, he hunted or worked on Sunday or in violation of the rules of his religious order. In the others, someone other than the perpetrator behaved in a strange or unlawful way: the homicidal husband, the malicious witness, the inconsolable robbery victim, the knight who misuses weapons that he is entitled to carry. Arguably, in these cases, the causal chain is broken. Just because it might be broken, it seems less unjust to exonerate the perpetrator than in the cases put by Lessius' predecessors.

There is a second reason for suspicion. The late scholastics thought that Thomas Aquinas had violated his own principles by accepting the doctrine. If so, one wonders why Aquinas didn't see the difficulty himself.

The easiest answer is that Aquinas did not think there was a difficulty. He may well have thought that the perpetrator of an unlawful act did act voluntarily in the sense required by his principles. As we have seen, Aquinas thought a person must act voluntarily if the action is to be attributed to him *qua* human being rather than attributed to chance. He thought that to violate commutative justice, a person must voluntarily be seeking a gain for himself at the expense of another.

Certainly, the unlawful act itself was voluntary and can be attributed to the perpetrator. It was voluntary even though he did not foresee the harm it would cause. Moreover, if the perpetrator acted unjustly, he voluntarily sought his own ends by harming or depriving another person of the resources that belonged to him. He did seek to 'gain' through another's loss. Perhaps Aquinas thought it did not matter that he inflicted a different loss than the one through which he hoped to gain.

Earlier we saw that the late scholastic criticism can be restated in modern terms without losing its force. Whether or not Aquinas would have given the answer just described, it, too, can be restated rather simply. The defendant by mere chance did inflict a different loss than the one he intended. But it does not follow, as Molina, Lessius, Kuttner, Gardner, Fiandaca, and Musco thought, that holding him responsible is strict rather than fault-based responsibility, responsibility for chance rather than for choice. There are two senses in which one can say that the defendant inflicted the harm by chance: he could not foresee the harm, and he did not wish it to occur. But why should either of these make a difference?

---

[83] Lessius, *De iustitia et iure*, lib. 2, cap. 9, dub. 15, nos. 104–5. He added a similar case in which the priest who is an expert surgeon but prohibited by his religious station from practicing his art operates on someone skillfully but happens to kill him (ibid. no. 104).

[84] ibid. lib. 2, cap. 9, dub. 16, nos. 109–11.   [85] ibid. no. 113.   [86] ibid.

Whether the defendant could have foreseen the harm matters in a negligence case precisely because the defendant is held liable for imposing an undue risk on someone else. When, however, the defendant is held liable for harm inflicted intentionally, it does not matter whether his action created a large or a small risk of harm. It does not matter whether he himself thought it probable that he would succeed in inflicting it. At the end of the Faulkner's *Snopes Trilogy*, a man seeking revenge shoots Flem Snopes with a pistol so old and rusty that it was extremely unlikely to fire. Yet there is no doubt he was responsible when it did. That would still be so even if the pistol were so defective that he would not have been negligent if he fired it at someone as a joke. A person who succeeds in blowing up a building with a crudely made bomb or in shooting down a helicopter with a small caliber handgun will be held responsible however unlikely the outcome. Of course, the defendant's actions must have created some risk that harm would occur or else he could not be said to have caused the harm. But he is not held responsible because he created a risk. He is held responsible simply because he wanted the harm that he caused to occur.

Should it matter, then, that he caused, not the harm that he chose, but a different harm? Certainly, it matters from his own perspective. His intention to bring about the very harm he wished was thwarted. His own ends, which would have been advanced, in his view, by causing this very harm, were not realized. But a defendant's failure to achieve his ends hardly exonerates him in criminal or tort law. The greedy nephew who shoots his uncle is not exonerated if the uncle turns out to have been poor rather than rich or to have left all his money to the University of California. Though the characteristic about which the nephew was mistaken—rich or poor, testator or not—mattered very much to him, it only matters from his own perspective. Similarly, if he missed the uncle and killed a bystander, it also matters from his perspective that the man he killed is not one from whose death he expected to profit. But it is hard to see why it should matter to anyone else that the harm he inflicted was not the one he wished.

Moreover, the approach just described holds him responsible for a reason that answers to our sense of justice. Imagine a person's reaction if someone he loved were killed by a bullet aimed at another. If he were asked to regard the killing as merely an unfortunate accident, he might feel a sense of outrage. To explain that feeling, he might well say that the perpetrator should not have been trying to kill anyone at all. If he hadn't, the victim would still be alive.

If this approach is correct, then the other difficulties with the older doctrine can be resolved rather straightforwardly. As we have seen, Cajetan and Soto put cases in which it seems absurd to hold the defendant liable for the consequences of his unlawful act. But in those cases, the act in question was not unjust. The perpetrator hunted or worked on Sunday or in violation of the rules of his religious order. A person should not be liable for the unforeseen consequences of all unlawful acts. He should be responsible for the unforeseen consequences of acts that are unlawful because they are unjust to others because they harm or appropriate what belongs to them.

II. Negligence

A. Negligence in the Aristotelian Tradition

Some classical scholars have thought that Aristotle believed that a person owed compensation for harm caused negligently as well as intentionally. As mentioned earlier, my former colleague, David Daube, showed rather clearly that Aristotle had only intentionally inflicted harm in mind.[87] Daube claimed that anyone reading the *Nicomachean Ethics* without prior indoctrination by the classicists would arrive at his conclusion. He would be gratified to know that not only Thomas Aquinas but most modern tort theorists have done so.[88]

Whatever Aristotle may have meant, however, Roman law imposed liability for harm caused negligently as well as intentionally.[89] By the time that Aquinas was writing, the canon lawyers, following Roman law, had decided that a person who injured another through negligence or a lack of due diligence was not only morally guilty[90] but under a moral obligation to compensate the victim.[91] Consequently, though Aquinas understood Aristotle in the *Ethics* to be speaking of intentionally caused harm, he tried to explain liability for negligence on Aristotelian principles.

For Aristotle, as we have seen, a person, *qua* human being, acts through reason and will, and therefore is not liable for chance events but only for those that proceed from his reason and will. Aristotle concluded that he could not be praised or blamed for such actions.[92] Aquinas concluded that he could not be liable for them.

According to Aquinas, a person was responsible for negligence because it was a voluntary act depriving another person of what belonged to him, and therefore a violation of commutative justice. It was a voluntary act because it was a failure to exercise prudence.[93] Prudence, for Aristotle and Aquinas, was a cardinal virtue. Virtues were faculties, perfected through training, which helped a person to attain his end. Through prudence a person decides how to obtain those things that are good

---

[87] David Daube, *Roman Law* (Edinburgh, 1969), 131–56.

[88] Aquinas, *In decem libros aristoteles Expositio*, lib. V, lectio xiii, no. 1043; Jules Coleman, *Markets, Morals and the Law* (Cambridge, 1988), 197; Richard Posner, 'The Concept of Corrective Justice in Recent Theories of Tort Law', *J. Legal Stud.* 10 (1981), 187 at 190; Perry, 'Moral Foundations', 453. Wright's view, which seems impossible to square with the text, is that Aristotle distinguishes intent, negligence and strict liability as grounds for the duty to pay compensation: Richard Wright, 'Substantive Corrective Justice', *Iowa L. Rev.*77 (1992), 625 at 697–8.

[89] See generally Reinhard Zimmermann, *The Law of Obligations: Roman Foundations of the Civilian Tradition* (Juta, 1990) 953–1049.

[90] D. 50, cc. 49–50; X 5.10.7–13, Bernardus Papiensis, *Summa Decretalium* (E. Laspeyres, ed., Graz, 1956), lib. 5, tit. 10, §§ 5–6; Raimondus de Pennafort, *Summa*, lib. 2, tit. 1, § 3. See Kuttner, *Kanonistische Schuldlehre*, 213–27.

[91] *Glossa ordinaria* to X 5.36.5 *Casus*; to *non custovit*; to *reddet*; X 5.36.6 to *voluntarie*; X 5.36.9.

[92] Aristotle, *Nicomachean Ethics* III.i.

[93] More technically, negligence (*negligentia*) was a lack of solicitude (*sollicitudo*) or diligence (*diligentia*). Solicitude or diligence was the virtue that enables the alert, adroit performance of the 'chief act' of prudence, *praecipere*, which could be translated as 'to command' or 'to execute'. Prudence required three 'acts': to take counsel or to consider what should be done (*consiliari*); to judge or decide what should be done (*iudicare*); and to execute this decision (*praecipere*). See Aquinas, *Summa Theologiae* II-II, Q. 47, aa. 8–9; Q. 54, aa. 1–2; Q. 64, a. 8.

because they contribute to his end and to avoid those that are evil because they obstruct it.[94] He weighs the magnitude of the good result he seeks against that of the evil one he avoids. Thus any prudent person 'will accept a small evil in order not to obstruct a great good'.[95] Since prudence is concerned with the 'contingencies of action', the prudent person must also concern himself with probabilities, with 'what happens in the greater number of cases'.[96] A person who acted imprudently had chosen the lesser good ahead of the greater, or the good that was more remotely likely ahead of that which was more certain.

In my view, this approach to negligence has two advantages which more modern views do not. First, it links causation or agency to choice. Second, it gives a more coherent account of negligence than modern writers have done.

B. Negligence and Choice

In the case of intentionally inflicted harm, a person chooses to act so that harm will occur. In the case of negligently inflicted harm, he chooses an action that is inappropriate because harm may occur. In either case, the causing of harm is linked to choice. A human being acts by making choices. A person who did not choose in any sense for the harm to occur did not cause the harm *qua* human being.

In contrast, according to some modern tort theories, a person may be liable for harm that was not the result of any choice he should or could have made differently. Supposedly, he should be liable if he caused this harm. In these theories, then, causation must mean something different from choice. Indeed, Nils Jansen has criticized the theory I have just described precisely because it cannot account for what he takes to be a fundamental problem of tort law: why liability is imposed, whether or not one party gained but simply because another party lost.[97] But whether that is so is precisely the question in dispute.

Just what it means to say liability for negligence rests on causation independent of choice is hard to see. No one seems to think the defendant should be liable simply because an act he voluntarily performed happened to create a risk to the plaintiff. One cannot act without creating risks, and the plaintiff's own act created a risk to himself.[98] Nor does anyone claim that the defendant should be liable simply because his body played a causal role in the accident: for example, he landed on the plaintiff after he was thrown from an upstairs window. And certainly no one believes the defendant should be liable because absent his action, the accident would not have occurred. An accident has an infinity of but-for causes.[99]

Instead, the builders of such theories explain causation in such a way that it looks much like fault except for the absence of personal culpability or a personal choice that the harm should occur. These theorists hold the defendant liable for performing the

---

[94] ibid. II–II, Q. 47, a. 4, obj. 1; Q. 49, a. 8; Q. 51, a. 8, ad. 1.

[95] Thomas Aquinas, *De veritate*, Q. 5, a. 4, ad 4, in *Opera omnia* 9 (P. Fiaccadori, ed., 1859), 5.

[96] Aquinas, *Summa theologiae* II–II, Q. 49, a. 1; a. 8, ad 3.

[97] Nils Jansen, *Die Struktur des Haftungsrechts Geschichte, Theorie und Dogmatik ausservertragliche Ansprüche auf Schadensersatz* (Tübingen, 2003), 90–1.

[98] Perry, 'Moral Foundations', 463–5; Stephen R. Perry, 'The Impossibility of General Strict Liability', *Can. J.l. & Jur.* 1 (1988), 147 at 169.   [99] See Perry, 'Impossibility' 169.

sort of action that people ordinarily would be at fault for performing. Then they claim the defendant should pay because he caused any harm that occurred even if he were not at fault. They never adequately explain why, if liability does not rest on fault, fault should matter at all. In particular, they do not explain why the question of whether the defendant caused the harm should depend on whether some other person would have been at fault for acting as the defendant did.

In his early writings, Richard Epstein built a theory in which fault is supposed to be irrelevant. The defendant is liable if his action falls within one of four 'causal paradigms'. The paradigms, however, describe actions that people typically do not perform unless they are at fault:[100] the defendant applied force to the plaintiff's person or thing; he frightened the plaintiff; he compelled the plaintiff to act; or he created a dangerous condition that injured the plaintiff.[101] Epstein then describes defenses by which the defendant can escape liability. They look like typical cases in which a person ordinarily would not be at fault. For example, he is not liable if the plaintiff blocked his right of way, and whether the plaintiff did so depends on applicable state traffic laws.[102]

Epstein has argued that 'the proper conception of ownership compels the adoption of a strict liability principle' because ownership is typically defined in terms of inviolability, which suggests protection against all invasions.[103] But Epstein's theory does not protect the owner from all invasions. It only protects the owner against invasions that typically would be culpable if committed by someone other than the defendant. Epstein does not explain why the concept of property only requires protection against these invasions.

Other tort theorists have adopted a so-called 'objective' theory of negligence. According to Oliver Wendell Holmes, Stephen Perry, and Jules Coleman, the defendant is liable without personal fault if he deviated from the standard of conduct that a reasonable person would normally observe.

Holmes argued that if 'a man is born hasty and awkward... his slips are no less troublesome to his neighbors than if they sprang from guilty neglect'.[104] Sometimes, Perry argues in a similar way that negligence law is 'interest-sensitive', and 'determines liability by reference to a certain level of permissible risk'.[105] On this rationale, however, all that should matter is whether a person has created an above average level of risk. If so, he is more troublesome to his neighbors and should be held liable independently of whether he deviated from a standard of conduct that would guide a normal person, and independently of whether he chose to create this level of risk. But then there is no place to stop. The person who infects the plaintiff with a contagious disease, crashes into the plaintiff when his brakes fail through an undetectable defect, or lands on the

---

[100] On the normative character of Epstein's paradigms, see Ernest J. Weinrib, 'Causation and Wrongdoing', *Chi.-Kent L. Rev.* 63 (1987), 407 at 417; Posner, 'Concept of Corrective Justice', 195–6; Gary T. Schwartz, 'The Vitality of Negligence and the Ethic of Strict Liability', *Ga. L. Rev.* 15 (1981), 963 at 988–9.

[101] Richard A. Epstein, 'A Theory of Strict Liability', *J. Legal Stud.* 2 (1973), 151 at 166–9.

[102] Richard A. Epstein, 'Defenses and Subsequent Pleas in a System of Strict Liability', *J. Legal Stud.* (1974), 165 at 176.

[103] Richard A. Epstein, 'Causation and Corrective Justice: A Reply to Two Critics', *J. Legal Stud.* 8 (1979), 477 at 500.   [104] Oliver Wendell Holmes, Jr., *The Common Law* (Boston, 1881), 108.

[105] Stephen Perry, 'Loss, Agency and Responsibility for Outcomes: Three Concenptions of Corrective Justice', in Ken Cooper-Stephenson and Elaine Gibson, eds., *Tort Theory* (North York, Ont., 1993), 24 at 46.

plaintiff after being thrown out the window creates an above average risk at the moment before impact. His presence is no less troublesome for the fact that he could not help being there.

Perry has also defended such a theory by claiming people may be 'outcome responsible' even when they are not at fault. A person is 'outcome responsible' for events he could not help if he has voluntarily performed an act that 'contributed causally' to an injury in a way that is 'close and normatively significant' and would typically arouse in him a feeling of 'agent regret'.[106] Why such a person should be liable is left mysterious. If the defendant was not at fault, one wonders what could make his connection to the accident 'normatively significant', and how anything so illusive could be the basis of tort law.

Jules Coleman defends an objective theory on the grounds that '[t]he central concern of corrective justice is the *consequences* of various sorts of doings, not the character or culpability of the actor'.[107] Why someone should be responsible for consequences he could not prevent is again unclear. Coleman defines the defendant's conduct as 'wrongful' or 'injurious' by reference to a 'community standard' that supposedly he was unable to meet, and then asserts it is better a loss should fall on someone who has acted 'injuriously' than on someone who has not done so.[108]

Unlike Holmes, however, Coleman claims that the reason the defendant should be liable for deviating from that standard is not simply that his conduct is dangerous but that his actions are 'the consequences of agency, of the agent's causal powers'.[109] On this rationale, however, it is again difficult to see the relevance of an *objective* standard of conduct. It is odd to think that the extent of Al's causal powers depends on what Betty (and others, whose collective conduct forms the standard) can do. Moreover, according to Coleman, 'agency requires the ability to form intentions and to act accordingly'.[110] For that reason, he would not hold liable a person with bi-polar disease or catatonic schizophrenia since, according to Coleman, the former may be unable to form intentions and the latter 'to translate intentions into actions'.[111] If the reach of one's causal powers depends on one's intentions, however, it is hard to see why anyone should be liable who intended no harm to the plaintiff and tried to take every appropriate precaution to avoid harming him.

Holmes and Coleman claim that their 'objective' theory best explains modern law.[112] Actually, it does not. In American law, as in that of other major legal systems,

---

[106] Perry, 'Moral Foundations', 498–9, 503; Perry, 'Loss', 40–4; Stephen Perry, 'Comment on Coleman: Corrective Justice', *Ind. L.J.* 67 (1992), 381 at 399.

[107] Jules Coleman, 'Tort Law and the Demands of Corrective Justice', *Ind. L.J.* 67 (1992), 349 at 370. See Coleman, *Risks and Wrongs*, 333–5; Coleman, *Markets*, 174; Jules Coleman, 'The Mixed Conception of Commutative Justice', *Iowa L. Rev.* 77 (1992), 427 at 442; Jules Coleman, 'Mental Abnormality, Personal Responsibility and Tort Liability', in Baruch Brody and H. Tristram Engelhardt, Jr., eds., *Mental Illness: Law And Public Policy* (Dordrecht, Neth., 1980), 107; Jules Coleman, 'Moral Theories of Torts: Their Scope and Limits: Part I', *Law & Phil.* 1 (1982), 371, 376–8.   [108] Coleman, *Risks*, 224–5, 334.

[109] Coleman, 'Mixed Conception', 442; Coleman, *Risks*, 334–5; Coleman, 'Tort Law', 371; Coleman, 'Mental Abnormality', 126–31. For a negative reaction, see Ernest J. Weinrib, 'Non-Relational Relationships: A Note on Coleman's New Theory', *Iowa L. Rev.* 77 (1992), 445 at 445; for a positive reaction, see Stephen Perry, 'Comment on Coleman: Corrective Justice', *Ind. L. Rev.* 67 (1992), 381 at 399.

[110] Coleman, 'Mental Abnormality', 130.   [111] ibid. 30–1.

[112] Holmes, *The Common Law*, 107–9; Coleman, 'Moral Theories I', 377–8; Coleman, *Risks*, 218–19, 333–4; Coleman, *Markets*, 174; Coleman, 'Tort Law', 370; Coleman, 'Mental Abnormality', 111–12.

the defendant usually is held liable if he fails to use the care a reasonable person would use.[113] Usually, however, that is the best, and, indeed, the only evidence of the care of which he was capable or would have been capable had he spent his life overcoming whatever hasty and awkward proclivities we suppose him to have inherited. In American, German, Italian and French law, the defendant with a physical handicap will be held only to the standard of a person with such a handicap.[114] Thus the defendant will escape liability if he can point to a physical condition for which he clearly was not responsible. That is as one would expect if, in principle, personal culpability matters.

Admittedly, mental handicaps are treated differently. In German, Italian and French law, insane persons and children may be required to compensate those they have injured.[115] In American law, the insane are also liable,[116] though children are not if they were engaged in appropriate activities and used the care to be expected of a child of similar age.[117] Except possibly in France, however, the reason does not seem to be allegiance to an objective standard of fault. In American law, an insane plaintiff is not held to an objective standard in proving contributory or comparative negligence.[118] The German and Italian Codes exonerate the insane or under-age defendant who cannot meet an objective standard from liability based on fault.[119] A duty of compensation is imposed by special provisions that allow the court to award an indemnity that is 'equitable' considering the financial resources of both parties if the plaintiff cannot recover from those in charge of caring for the insane person or the child.[120] Thus in American, German and Italian law, while the liability of the insane and of children may be a kind of strict liability, it is not simply an application of the ordinary standard of liability for fault.

[113] See, e.g., W. Page Keeton, Dan B. Dobbs, Robert E. Keeton, and David G. Owen, *Prosser and Keeton on the Law of Torts* (5th edn., St Paul, Minn., 1984), 173–5 (American law); Peter Hanau in *Münchener Kommentar zum Bürgerlichen Gesetzbuch*, (Kurt Rebmann and Franz-Jürgen Säcker, eds., 2nd edn., Munich, 1985), to § 276, no. 78 (German law); Luigi Gaudino in Paolo Cendon, ed., *Commentario al Codice Civile* (Turin, 1991), to § 2043, no. 8 (Italian Law); Gabriel Marty and Pierre Raynaud, *Droit Civil: Les Obligations* (2nd edn., Paris, 1988), no. 457, at 512–14 (French law); See generally, Francesco Parisi, *Liability for Negligence and Judicial Discretion* (2nd edn., Berkeley, 1992), 341–72; Mario Bussnani, *La Colpa Soggettiva* (Padua, 1991).

[114] See *Restatement (Second) of Torts*, § 283C (1965); Prosser and Keeton, *Law of Torts*, 175–6 (American law); Hanau, *Kommentar*, to § 276, no. 85 (German law); Bussani, *Colpa*, 7 (French law); Lina Bigliazzi Geri, Umberto Breccia, Francesco Busnelli and Ugo Natoli, *Diritto Civile* 3 (Turin, 1989), 702 (Italian law).

[115] For German and Italian law, German Civil Code (*Bürgerlichesgesetzbuch*) [hereinafter BGB], § 829; Italian Civil Code (*Codice civile*) § 2047. In France, an insane person was not liable until a 1968 statute changed the law: Law of 3 Jan. 1968, now French Civil Code (*Code civil*), § 489–2. See Marty and Renaud, *Obligations*, nos. 460, 463; Petrelli, 'La responsabilità civile dell'infermo di mente nell'ordinamento francese', *Riv. Dir. Civ.* 37 (1991), 77–86. Children were held to the standard of a child of their own age until the decision of 9 May 1984 by the highest French judicial authority, the *Cour de Cassation* meeting in *assemblée plénière*, D.S 1984.J.525. See Henri Mazeaud, 'La "faute objective" et la responsabilité sans faute', D.S. 1985.Chr.13 at 86–95 (1991); Petrelli, 'Responsabilità', at 77–86.

[116] *Restatement (Second) of Torts*, § 283B (1963); Prosser and Keeton, *Law of Torts*, 176–8; Stephanie I. Splane, 'Tort Liability of the Mentally Ill in Negligence Actions', *Yale L. J.* 153, 93 (1983), 153 at 155–6.

[117] *Restatement (Second) of Torts*, § 283A (1963); Prosser and Keeton, *Law of Torts*, 179–82.

[118] Prosser and Keeton, *Law of Torts*, 178; Splane, 'Tort Liability' 155–7.

[119] German Civil Code (BGB), §§ 827–8; Karl Schäfer in Julius von Staudinger, *Kommentar zum Bürgerlichen Gesetzbuch*, to § 828, no. 26 (12th edn., Berlin, 1986) (German law); Italian Civil Code (*Codice civile*), to §§ 2046; Venchiarutti, *Commentario*, at § 2046, no. 2.1 (Italian law).

[120] BGB § 829; Italian Civil Code (*Codice civile*), § 2047.

C. The Meaning of Negligence

As we have seen, in the Aristotelian tradition prudence was a virtue through which a person decides how to obtain those things that are good because they contribute to his end and to avoid those that are evil because they obstruct it. He weighs the magnitude of the good result he seeks against that of the evil one he avoids. He concerns himself with probabilities, with 'what happens in the greater number of cases'.[121]

Cajetan gave an example of how such factors might be taken into account in his commentary on Aquinas' *Summa theologica*. A canon law text in Gratian's *Decretum* said that parents are negligent if they fall asleep with children in their bed, and the children die because they are suffocated or crushed.[122] According to Cajetan, whether a nurse would be responsible in such a case depended on the circumstances:

[If] the bed is large and there is nothing else near it, the nurse is always accustomed to find herself in the same place and position in which she put herself to begin sleeping, and the implacability of the infant required it, she seems to be excused, because it is not rational when these things concur to fear the risk.[123]

According to Aquinas and Cajetan, then, a prudent person will weigh the good and evil consequences to be expected from each course of action. The fact that the baby will not otherwise stop crying can justify letting it sleep with the nurse. Indeed, the factors Cajetan expected a prudent nurse to take into account resemble those mentioned by Judge Learned Hand in *United States* v. *Carroll Towing Co.*[124] Hand said that a precaution should be taken if the burden it entails (B) is less than the loss that may occur (L) multiplied by the probability the precaution will prevent the loss (P).

Ernest Weinrib argued at one point that on Aristotelian principles the defendant should not be permitted to weigh these consequences. He should be liable as long as the risk he imposed on the plaintiff went beyond a certain level, taking account of both likelihood of an injury and its seriousness.[125] If that were so, negligence would no longer approximate an Aristotelian conception of imprudent action or a common sense notion of fault. We do not blame a person who fails take every possible precaution, however costly, to prevent risk from reaching a certain level, or exonerate him if he fails to take a simple precaution when the risk falls below it. Anyone would feel justified in driving faster to reach a hospital in an emergency.[126]

---

[121] Aquinas, *Summa theologiae* II-II, Q. 49, a. 1; a. 8 ad 3.   [122] C. 2, q. 5, c. 2.

[123] Cajetan, *Commentaria post*, Q. 64, a. 8.   [124] 159 F2d 169 (2nd Cir 1947).

[125] Ernest J. Weinrib, 'Understanding Tort Law', *Val. U.L. Rev.* 23 (1989), 485 at 518–19; Ernest J. Weinrib, 'Right and Advantage in Private Law', *Cardozo L. Rev.* 10 (1989), 1283 at 1304–5; Ernest J. Weinrib, 'Liberty, Community and Corrective Justice', *Can. J.L. & Jur.* 1 (1988), 3 at 4; Ernest J. Weinrib, 'The Special Morality of Tort Law', *McGill L.J.* 34 (1989), 403 at 410 He elsewhere seems to have been attracted by a test that would balance the cost of taking a precaution against the level of risk. Weinrib, 'Causation', 428. See Perry, 'Impossibility' 170 (apparently favoring a level of risk test).

[126] The common law authority usually cited for the level of risk test is Lord Reid's opinion in *Bolton* v. *Stone* [1951] AC. 850, cited by Weinrib, 'Understanding Tort Law', 518–19 and Perry, 'Impossibility', 170. The plaintiff, while standing near her house outside the cricket grounds, was hit on the head by a cricket ball. She claimed the grounds had been negligently constructed. Lord Reid did say that a person may not 'create a risk which is substantial', and that he would take no account of 'the difficulty of remedial measures'. [1951] AC at 867. But the reason he would not take such measures into account, he said, was: 'If cricket cannot be played on a ground without creating a substantial risk, then it should not be played there at all'. Possibly, all Lord Reid meant was that since one could avoid the danger in a seemingly costless way by

Nevertheless, while they thought that a prudent person would weigh factors like those of the Hand formula, Aquinas and Cajetan had a different idea than modern economists of what it meant to do so. Economists explain negligence law in terms of efficiency, and identify the B and L of the formula with the magnitude of social costs. Thomas Aquinas and Cajetan were discussing virtue. For them, an outcome is good or evil, and a prudent person will seek or avoid it, to the extent it furthers or detracts from the distinctively human life that is one's ultimate end. Moreover, they did not think that a prudent person could make his decision by any sort of calculus or deductive argument. He moves from the premise that 'the greater evil is to be avoided' to the conclusion 'this is the proper course of action' by means of a minor premise, 'this course of action avoids the greater evil' which is not itself demonstrable but is apprehended by a type of prudence (*intellectus* for Aquinas, *nous* for Aristotle) which has been translated as 'understanding' or 'intuition'.[127]

To economists, it seems unscientific to claim that decisions to risk life or property can be right or wrong according to such a higher normative standard, or that people possess a moral capacity to apply this standard. For the economists, the magnitude of a cost or benefit is determined by individual preferences or by individual preferences backed by cash. To the extent that the economists reach normative conclusions about what the law should be, however, it is not clear why this approach is supposed to be more scientific. Indeed, it is not clear that this approach is morally or logically defensible.

Once, economists spoke like utilitarians about individual preferences although not always consistently.[128] Preferences were psychological experiences of satisfaction or dissatisfaction. Modern economists now regard this approach as unscientific,[129] and, in any case, it would lead to some strange conclusions. In Dickens' *Tale of Two Cities*, a rich man races a coach through a crowded street and runs down the child of a poor family. It would be odd to think that he may not have been negligent if he really enjoys racing coaches, or if he is sadistic and enjoys running down children, and the child is unlikely to be happy growing up in squalor.

The contemporary approach is to deny that one can compare the strength of individual preferences and to speak only about how an individual allocates whatever resources he has in accordance with his own preferences.[130] Thus Richard Posner asks what course of action would maximize 'wealth' which 'is the value in dollars or dollar equivalents . . . of everything in society. It is measured by what people are willing to pay

playing cricket somewhere else, it was irrelevant that some other remedial measure, such as building a higher fence, was too expensive. That interpretation is consistent with his statement elsewhere in the opinion: 'In my judgment the test to be applied here is whether the risk of damage to a person on the road was so small that a reasonable man in the position of the appellants . . . would have thought it right to refrain from taking steps to prevent the danger'. (ibid.). In any case, Lord Reid's speculations on when liability might be imposed if a risk were substantial had no bearing on the outcome of the case. The defendant was held not to be liable, according to Lord Reid, because the risk was not substantial.

[127] See Aristotle, *Nicomachean Ethics* IV.xi; Aquinas, *Summa theologiae* II-II, Q. 49, c. 2.

[128] See Robert Cooter and Peter Rappaport, 'Were the Ordinalists Wrong about Welfare Economics?' *J. Econ. Lit.* 22 (1984), 507.   [129] Chapter 1 II B 1.

[130] For a challenge to this approach based on Aristotelian principles, see Robert Cooter and James Gordley, 'The Cultural Justification of Unearned Income: An Economic Model of Merit Goods Based on Aristotelian Ideas of Akrasia and Distributive Justice', in Robin Cowan and Mario Rizzo, eds., *Profits and Morality* (Chicago, 1995), 150.

for something or, if they already own it, what they demand in money to give it up.'[131] According to Posner, if one person walks fast and smashes another's oranges, the court would have to make a judgment as to how much the oranges were worth to the plaintiff and how much walking fast was worth to the defendant.[132] Presumably, in the case we were just considering, the court would have to compare the value the child puts on life (or the risk of it) with the value the rich man put on racing the coach. But what does this mean?

To begin with, we are dealing with a child. In an Aristotelian world, in which prudence is a virtue that develops with time and experience, we can say that the child is too young to place a proper value on his life. On Posner's principles, however, it is hard to see why we should not treat the child like any other individual with his own individual preferences and a rather limited income. If the child would risk his life for a gumdrop, so be it.

Next, even if we were dealing with a poor person of mature years rather than a child, we still need to know whether his life is to be valued in cash by the amount he would accept if the rich man had to pay him for endangering it, or by the amount he would offer the rich man for not doing so. Even in the first case, the result is unappealing. Whether the rich man is liable depends on whether his victim was so desperately poor as to have accepted little, and whether he is so rich, so enamored of racing, so indifferent to human life, or so genuinely sadistic, as to have paid much. Moreover, since the rich man is not liable unless he is negligent, he owes the poor person nothing as long as he would have paid an amount acceptable to the poor person even though the poor person was never offered and will never receive such an amount. Most of us deplore the terrible risks that many industrial workers once ran in return for a slight increase of their wages because of their extreme poverty. On Posner's principles, any sufficiently poor person could be exposed to the risks created by any sufficiently rich and indifferent or sadistic person for no compensation at all.

Matters are even less appealing if the life of the poor person is supposed to be valued by the amount that he would pay the rich man for not endangering him. All his wealth might be insufficient to buy protection from a risk so great that, despite his poverty, he would not choose to run it for a huge sum.

On Posner's principles, then, we do not know if the rich man is negligent until we know whether, so to speak, we should regard the racing of horses as belonging to the rich man unless the poor person can purchase it, or the freedom from risk as belonging to the poor person unless the rich man can purchase it. Posner does have a theory of how rights should initially be allocated but not one that provides a happy solution. He says that his wealth maximization principle 'ordains the creation of a system of exclusive rights' that ideally includes 'the human body and even ideas'. If transactions costs are zero, the economist is indifferent to where these rights are vested.[133] The right to the poor man's body might equally be assigned to the poor man as to the rich man. If transaction costs are positive, however, rights should be vested initially 'in those who are likely to value them most'. This, according to Posner, is the reason

---

[131]   Richard A. Posner, 'Utiliarianism, Economics, and Legal Theory', *J. Legal Stud.* 8 (1979), 103 at 119.
[132]   ibid. 120.   [133]   ibid. 125.

for giving 'a man the right to sell his labor and a woman the right to determine her sexual partners'. Were these rights initially given to others, they would be likely to repurchase them, and that would be a transactions cost.[134]

Even this honest but shocking fidelity to a bizarre principle does not lead to a coherent result. Whether the poor person should have the right to bodily protection against coaches depends upon which is more likely, that he would buy this right from the rich man to whom it was initially allocated, or that the rich man would buy it from the poor man were it allocated to him. But in the situation we have just described, the poor person so values that right that if he were allocated it initially, he wouldn't sell it at a price the rich man is willing to pay, but were it allocated initially to the rich man, the poor person has so little money, that he would be unable to buy it back.

Indeed, Posner's principles not only fail to explain the law of negligence but the law of intentional torts. Imagine a world in which the rights of the vast majority to sell their labor, to determine their sexual partners, and to be free from intentionally inflicted harm to their persons, have been allocated together with all the property to a small minority. There are no transaction costs, because the majority has nothing it can offer to repurchase all these rights. Thus on Posner's principles, even the recognition of intentional torts is not necessary to maximize wealth. It is the result of a supposedly arbitrary decision as to how rights are initially distributed.

These difficulties have been raised by putting hypothetical cases in which there is an aberrational distribution of wealth or an aberrational decision maker such a child or a sadistic or indifferent rich person. The economists' principles do not lead to such absurd results as long as one can assume that the preferences of individuals are formed with prudence and the cash that backs them is justly distributed. But that, of course, proves just the point that an Aristotelian would want to make. Their principles reach acceptable results only insofar as a society actually practices the virtues the economists reject in theory.

There is another difference between the Aristotelian account of negligence and that of modern economists. For the economists, the point of negligence law is not to compensate a person for a wrong done him in the past, but to provide the proper incentives for people to take the efficient level of precautions in the future. Tort damages functions like prices in a market.

In practice, however, negligence law does not work like a market. People often act negligently even when they know that they will have to pay fully for any harm they cause. The explanation for an Aristotelian is that prudence is a virtue we do not all perfectly possess. For an economist, however, the efficient action is supposed to follow once the incentives are right.

III. Strict Liability

A. A Theory Based on Commutative Justice

Although writers in the Aristotelian tradition assimilated the Roman law of negligence, they never adequately explained strict liability. As we have seen, their principles were incompatible with a theory of strict liability based on mere causation. Nevertheless,

---

[134] Richard A. Posner, 'Utiliarianism, Economics, and Legal Theory', *J. Legal Stud.* 8 (1979), 103 at 125.

one can see hints in contemporary and in earlier literature about how an Aristotelian explanation might be developed.

One of the concerns that led Epstein to his theory of strict liability sounds remarkably Aristotelian. He has argued the defendant should not be able to justify the loss imposed on the plaintiff by gains to himself.[135] Indeed, Kathryn Heidt has noted that, logically, Aristotle's theory ought to support liability for activities like disposing of toxic waste because they harm some people and produce a gain for others.[136] Frederick Sharp, in a student note, tried to develop a theory using Aristotle's definition of corrective justice. He seems to have rested it, in part, on notions of fault: the defendant is liable because he 'departed from the restricted standard of conduct owing to one's neighbors' and so created a hazard 'disproportionate to the expectations of citizens'.[137] Nevertheless, on Aristotelian principles, it does seem that a person might be liable simply because he has sought a gain for himself by imposing a risk of loss on another.

Occasionally, some of the earlier writers groped in this direction. One of the obstacles was the rather patchy pre-modern set of strict liability rules that they were trying to explain. The cases the Roman jurists classified as quasi-tort (*quasi delictus*) or tort without fault were, for the most part, of the kind American law treats with the doctrine of *res ipsa loquitur*. The defendant is likely to have been at fault though there is no direct evidence. For example, the plaintiff is struck by an object thrown from the defendant's window or hung by the defendant over the street, or he is robbed while staying in the defendant's inn.[138] In American law, the defendant would be presumed to be negligent but would be allowed to prove that he was not. In Roman law, he was simply held liable.

There were also cases in Roman law in which the defendant would be liable if he failed to exercise an extreme diligence that went beyond what an ordinary person would observe.[139] The defendant might also be liable without fault for damage done by his animal or through the fault of his slave, although he had the option of surrendering the animal or slave to the plaintiff rather than paying damages.[140] This was not the most promising set of rules to explain by a general theory of strict liability. But there were attempts.

In the 16th century, Molina struggled with the rule that sometimes one could be liable for failing to exercise the most extreme diligence. Nearly all of his contemporaries said that the rule could not be explained in principle or by natural law. Molina said that one was liable in principle if the activity was so dangerous that one should not undertake it except with the intention of paying for any harm that occurred.[141]

In the next century, Pufendorf found a reason why as a matter of natural law one might be liable for the acts of an animal: 'the owner gets the profit from his animal

---

[135] Richard A. Epstein, 'Intentional Harms', *J. Legal Stud.* 4 (1975), 391 at 398; Richard A. Epstein, *Takings: Private Property and the Power of Eminent Domain* (Cambridge, Mass., 1985), 40.

[136] Kathryn R. Heidt, 'Corrective Justice from Aristotle to Second Order Liability: Who Should Pay When the Culpable Cannot?' *Wash. & Lee L. Rev.* 47 (1990), 347 at 360–3.

[137] Frederick L. Sharp, Note, 'Aristotle, Justice and Enterprise Liability in the Law of Torts', *U. Toronto Fac. L. Rev.* 34 (1976), 84 at 90.　　　　　　　　　　　　　　　　　　　　[138] G. Inst. 4.5.

[139] The phrase *culpa levissima* in Dig. 9.2.44 was interpreted to require the extreme diligence of Dig. 13.6.18pr. and Dig. 44.7.1.4. See Zimmermann, *Law of Obligations*, 192–3, 1027–9.

[140] Dig. 9.1; 9.4.　　　　[141] Molina, *De iustitia et iure*, disp. 698, no. 3.

while [the victim] suffered loss from it'.[142] The French jurist Domat repeated this explanation, though he seemed to rest liability on fault in letting the animal escape.[143] These explanations are not well thought out, but they emphasize that the defendant creates a risk through an activity from which he profits.

I believe they point in the right direction. They point toward a theory of strict liability founded on the principle that the defendant should be liable if, in order to obtain a gain for himself, he exposed the plaintiff to an especially high risk of loss. We can see the justification for such a theory if we return to the reason given earlier why a society interested in preserving a given distribution of resources would not compensate everyone for accidental losses. If it did so, people who invested in particularly vulnerable forms of property or exposed themselves or their property to especially high risks would be using up more than their share of resources. By similar reasoning, those who profit by exposing others to especially high risks will be using up more than their own share if they are not held liable.

Thus, in a sense, Epstein was right when he objected to negligence law because the defendant should not be able to justify the loss the plaintiff suffers by the gain he himself hopes to receive. As Perry has pointed out, the difficulty with Epstein's argument is that whenever an accident occurs, both parties were pursuing an activity from which they expected to benefit, and the risk of an accident was due to both of these activities.[144] One might equally well say that the plaintiff, for his own benefit, created the risk. This difficulty vanishes, however, when the defendant exposes the plaintiff to an abnormally high risk of loss. If he can justify this extra risk by pointing to his own gain, he will have achieved this gain at the plaintiff's expense. On Aristotelian principles, he should not be allowed to do so.

This explanation parallels the one given earlier in discussing interferences among landowners.[145] If they all interfere with each other to the same degree to gain the same advantage, the losses cancel out. If one interferes with another in a manner that is abnormal and grave, he is imposing a cost which they are not imposing on him to gain an advantage in which they do not share, or at least, in which they do not share in proportion to the cost they bear. In the case of strict liability, again, the risk he imposes on others is abnormal and grave, and the benefit is one which they do not share at all, or at least in proportion to the risk they bear. In both cases, commutative justice requires compensation.

As with interferences among landowners, the case is clearest when the defendant's activity in no way benefits the plaintiff. For example, the defendant flies a glider for fun, knowing that when the wind fails he will have to land on a farmer's field, destroying his crops. Suppose, however, the plaintiff does benefit from the defendant's activity. He should still recover provided that the expected value of the harm he suffers is not correlated with the degree to which he benefits. Suppose a train occasionally throws sparks that consume the crops of nearby farmers who all use the railroad. If the railroad does not pay, the railroad will gain, and the injured farmers will lose. Even if

---

[142] Pufendorf, *De iure naturae et gentium* III.i.6.
[143] Jean Domat, *Les Loix Civiles Dans Leur Ordre Naturel* (Paris, 1713), liv. 2, tit. 8.
[144] Perry, 'Moral Foundations', 463–5; Perry, 'Impossibility', 169.   [145] See Chapter 4 III A.

we imagine that the railroad will pass on some of this gain to the farmers through decreased fares, the farmers who ship more crops or are less exposed to sparks will still gain at the expense of those who ship less or are more exposed. The losses due to the extra risks created by the railroad will not be borne by those who benefit from its presence in proportion to their benefit but by those who happen to be in the way of the sparks. Again, the reason for compensation is the same as in the analogous case among interfering landowners.[146]

The train and the sparks, like interferences among landowners, are often used to illustrate the thesis Ronald Coase advanced in a article, 'The Problem of Social Cost'.[147] He argued that one cannot say the farmer's loss was caused by the presence of the train anymore than the presence of the crops. He then showed that from the standpoint of efficiency, if transactions costs are zero, it does not matter whether liability is placed on the railroad or the farmers. In the former case, the railroad would be willing to take any precaution that cost less than the expected value of the harm it would prevent; and in the latter case, the farmers would be willing to pay the railroad to do so.

As in the case of interferences among landowners, scholars such as Guido Calabresi have reassured us about the implications of Coase's argument by pointing out that transactions costs usually are not zero and that the railroad may be best able to determine if a given precaution is efficient or not.[148] But most people do not feel the railroad should pay because they are worried about optimizing investments in farming and transportation. They feel that otherwise an injustice will be done to the farmer. It is hard to believe Calabresi would want the railroad to escape tort liability even if it were not the best cost avoider. The Aristotelian theory identifies a reason why it is not merely efficient but just that the railroad should pay: it gained through the farmer's loss.

A theory of strict liability based on these considerations would look much like George Fletcher's theory of liability for non-reciprocal risk. According to Fletcher, 'a victim has a right to recover for injuries caused by a risk greater in degree and different in order from those created by the victim'.[149]

Unlike Fletcher's theory, the Aristotelian account would only explain strict liability in terms of non-reciprocal risk. Fletcher tries to explain intentional and negligent torts as well. The difficulty is that the defendant is liable for acting intentionally or negligently even if the risk of his act is not 'greater in degree' than the risk created by acts that are not actionable. The defendant is liable if he shoots intending to kill even if he fired at such a distance that there was little chance of success. He is liable for negligence if he creates even a slight risk provided that the offsetting benefit of his action is still less.

Moreover, the theoretical basis for strict liability would be more clear and more solid in an Aristotelian account. This account, like Fletcher's theory, would hold the defendant liable if he chose to engage in an activity knowing it creates an abnormally

---

[146] ibid.

[147] R. H. Coase, 'The Problem of Social Cost', *J.L. & Econ.* 3 (1960), 1. See Chapter 4 II B.

[148] Guido Calabresi, *The Cost of Accidents* (New Haven, 1970), 135–403; Guido Calabresi, 'Transactions Costs, Resource Allocation and Liability Rules, A Comment', *J.l. & Econ.* 11 (1968), 67 at 71–3. See Chapter 4 II B.

[149] George P. Fletcher, 'Fairness and Utility in Tort Theory', *Harv. L. Rev.*85 (1972), 537 at 542.

high risk of harming the plaintiff. The Aristotelian account, however, can explain why the defendant is not liable unless he knew of the risk and chose to go ahead. It can explain why one who could not have known he is carrying a contagious disease is not liable. On Aristotelian principles one cannot attribute an action to a person unless he acted voluntarily. Fletcher claims that in his own theory the 'Aristotelian . . . categories' of compulsion and unavoidable ignorance should count as excuses.[150] But he does not explain why.

Again, the Aristotelian account can explain why the defendant is liable when the risk is abnormally high. He has gained at the plaintiff's expense. Fletcher does not base his theory on corrective justice. He rests it on the principle that 'all individuals in society have the right to roughly the same degree of security from risk'.[151] As Coleman correctly observes, on that principle everyone should have the right to compensation if he is harmed, not simply if he is hurt by a non-reciprocal risk.[152]

Another difference concerns what is meant by a risk that is 'different in order'. In the Aristotelian account, in principle, liability should be imposed on a defendant who, in pursuit of his own ends, subjected the plaintiff to an especially high risk—in Fletcher's terminology, a risk that is 'greater in degree'. To say the risk must be 'different in order', however, is simply to identify one way that courts may apply the principle pragmatically and heuristically. Human activities are so different and the risks they create so various that there is no bright line between ordinary and extra-ordinary risks. The law will have to make do with rough categories that work best in the generality of cases. For example, the law can impose liability on those who engage in an activity that is both less common and more risky than other activities. Roughly speaking, that is the sort of activity that is captured by Fletcher's phrase 'different in order'. In the Aristotelian account, it represents one possible and pragmatic way to apply the principle that defendant should be liable for creating an abnormally high risk.

B. Law the Theory Can and Cannot Explain

Despite the differences, the Aristotelian account, like Fletcher's, imposes liability for non-reciprocal risk. Therefore, like Fletcher's, it can explain why some modern legal systems commonly impose liability for carrying on an activity that is less typical and more dangerous than most. American courts have imposed liability for conducting an 'abnormally dangerous activity'.[153] Examples include blasting, storing explosives or large quantities of water, crop dusting, and possibly ground damage by aircraft and harm caused by nuclear power.[154]

---

[150] ibid. 552.

[151] ibid. 550.

[152] Coleman, *Risks* 266; Coleman, 'Moral Theories I', 389; Coleman, *Markets*, 194.

[153] *Restatement (Second) of Torts*, § 519 (1976); Prosser and Keeton, *Law of Torts*, 545–59.

[154] '. . . water collected in quantity in a dangerous place, or allowed to percolate; explosives or inflammable liquids stored in quantity in the midst of a city; blasting; pile driving; crop dusting; the fumigation of part of a building with cyanide gas; drilling oil wells or operating refineries in thickly settled communities; an excavation letting in the sea; factories emitting smoke, dust or noxious gases in the midst of a town; roofs so constructed as to shed snow into a highway; . . . a dangerous party wall', and possibly 'ground damage from aviation', and 'rockets and nuclear energy'. Prosser and Keeton, *Law of Torts*, 549–50, 556.

German courts have not recognized a general principle and will hold the defendant strictly liable only in cases recognized by specially enacted statutes. Most of these statutes, however, concern activities that are abnormally dangerous. The defendant is liable, for example, for the operation of trains,[155] aircraft,[156] automobiles,[157] and electric and gas installations.[158] The advantage of the German approach is that the law is made more certain since no one has to guess whether a court will consider an activity to be abnormally dangerous. The disadvantage is that to the extent a law maker does not think of all the cases that may arise, there will be gaps. It is worth requoting Hein Kötz:

It is far from obvious why a person should be strictly liable if he decides to move earth by means of a light railway while he is liable only for negligence if he uses heavy bulldozers. And why should an injured person's right to damages depend on whether the accident took place on board a steamer or a train? And if a motorized conveyance causes injury, why should liability depend on whether it is a chairlift, a motor car, a motorboat, a light railway, a hoist, a unicular, or an escalator?[159]

In Italian law, the burden of proof of negligence is reversed when the defendant has engaged in an abnormally dangerous activity.[160] One reason could be the difficulty of proving negligence. Nevertheless, the courts have made it so difficult for the defendant to exonerate himself, that in practice it amounts to a kind of strict liability for dangerous activities.[161]

An Aristotelian account of strict liability explains not only why strict liability should be imposed when activities are less common and more dangerous, but also two exceptions recognized by American and German law. First, the defendant is not liable if the plaintiff's activity is abnormally sensitive.[162] In the United States, a defendant was not held liable for blasting when the noise alarmed plaintiff's mink, and the mink then killed each other.[163] In Germany, an airline was not held liable when it alarmed silver foxes on plaintiff's farm who bit their cubs to death. The court stressed that the airplane was not dangerous to 'normally constituted animals'.[164] From an Aristotelian perspective, this exception makes perfect sense. The damage was as much due to the plaintiff's decision to pursue an activity that was abnormally dangerous.

Second, often strict liability has not been imposed when the plaintiff himself was a participant in the activity. For example, in American law traditionally,[165] and in German law,[166] although an airline is liable for ground damage when planes crash, it is not liable for damage to the passengers when they collide in the air. Although the owners of wild animals are usually held strictly liable, in the United States, a zoo was held

---

[155] Haftpflichtgesetz, § 1(1).   [156] Luftverkehrgesetz, § 33.   [157] Strassenverkehrgesetz, § 7.
[158] Haftpflichtgesetz, § 2(1).
[159] Zweigert and Kötz, *An Introduction to Comparative Law*, 698–9, quoted earlier Chapter 2 I. The text translated here was unchanged in the third German edition. Zweigert and Kötz, *Einführung in die Rechtsvergleichung* (3rd edn., Tübingen, 1996), 662–3. For a similar criticism, see Larenz and Canaris, *Lehrbuch*, 2(2): no. 80 I 2 c.   [160] Italian Civil Code (*Codice civile*), § 2050.
[161] Patricia Ziviz in Cendon (ed.), *Commentario*, 4 to § 2050, no. 1; Geri *et al.*, *Diritto Civile* 3: 757–59.
[162] *Restatement (Second) of Torts*, § 524A (1976).
[163] *Madsen v. East Jordan Irrigation Co.*, 125 P2d 794 (Utah 1942).
[164] RG, 4 July 1938, RGZ 158, 34.   [165] *Restatement (Second) of Torts*, § 520A (1976).
[166] Luftverkehrgesetz 1922, §§ 33 ff.

liable only on proof of negligence when a visitor was bit by a zebra,[167] and national parks have not been held liable when visitors were attacked by bears.[168] Again, the exception makes sense. In these cases one can no longer say that the defendant in order to obtain a benefit of his own has imposed a risk on the plaintiff. The plaintiff and the defendant to procure a joint benefit are engaged in the activity that creates the risk. Moreover, it is an activity from which the plaintiff benefits in rough proportion to the degree of exposure to the risk. If one person flies or visits a zoo or national park five times as much as another, he is roughly five times as likely to crash, to be bitten by a zebra or to be attacked by a bear.

Admittedly, there are other jurisdictions whose law cannot be explained in this way. We will consider two exemplary cases: England and France. In each case, the result has been a law which is difficult to defend in its own terms.

In England, in *Cambridge Water Co.* v. *Eastern Counties Leather*,[169] the House of Lords repudiated an interpretation which had widely been placed on *Rylands* v. *Fletcher*, a case which had been thought to establish a general principle of strict liability and therefore, the court noted, 'is generally regarded as an important landmark—indeed, a turning point—in the law of torts'. In *Rylands*, the defendant was held liable without fault when the water he collected in a reservoir flooded his neighbor's land. The land had once been mined and the water escaped through shafts which the defendant did not know existed. Lord Cairns had said he was liable because he made a 'non-natural' use of his land and therefore when 'the water came to escape' it was at his peril. Blackburn, who had held the defendant liable before the case reached the House of Lords, said that one 'who for his own purposes brings on his lands and collects and keeps there anything likely to do mischief if it escapes, must keep it at his peril'. Sir Frederick Pollock had regarded the case as one in which liability turned on 'the magnitude of the danger, coupled with the difficulty of proving negligence'. If that is so, then there is, in principle, no reason why liability should not depend on whether an object or activity is 'non-natural' as long as it is dangerous nor on whether the person brings the object or conducts the activity on his own land. In 1880, Bramwell recognized as much in his decision in *Powell* v. *Hall* in which he applied the principle of *Rylands* v. *Fletcher* when a traction engine on a public highway threw sparks which caused a fire on nearby land. He noted:

It is just and reasonable that if a person uses a dangerous machine, he should pay for the damage which it occasions; if the reward which he gains for the use of the machine will not pay for the damage, it is mischievous to the public and ought to be suppressed, for the loss ought not to be borne by the community or the injured person. If the use of the machine is profitable, the owner ought to pay compensation for the damage'.[170]

---

[167] *City & County of Denver* v. *Kennedy*, 476 P.2d 762 (Colo Ct App 1970) (though the court explained the result by the desirability of having zoos).

[168] *Rubenstein* v. *United States*, 338 F Supp. 654 (ND Cal. 1972), *aff'd*, 488 F2d 1071 (9th Cir 1973) (though the court explained the result by assumption of the risk).   [169] [1994] 2 AC 264 (HL).

[170] [1880] 5 QB 597. Similarly, in *Rigby* v. *Chief Constable of Northhamptonshire* [1985] 1 QLR 1242, the court said, per curiam and by way of dicta, '[t]he rule relating to the escape of dangerous things applies to the escape of dangerous things from the highway as well as escape from private land'. The plaintiff's shop was set on fire when police fired a canister of CS gas into the building in an effort to flush out a dangerous psychopath who had broken into it. The defendant was held negligent for not having fire-fighting equipment on hand.

As we have seen, this approach was accepted in the United States where liability is imposed for the conduct of an 'abnormally dangerous activity' whether or not conducted on the plaintiff's land.

The court could have decided *Cambridge Water Co.* without ruling on the correctness of this position. In that case, over a period of years, chemical solvent from defendant's tannery had seeped 173 miles underground to contaminate plaintiff's well. The lower court held that plaintiff could not recover 'unless the defendant could have foreseen that its activity might cause the harm the plaintiff suffered'. If the danger was unforeseeable, then a court should not find the defendant liable for conducting an abnormally dangerous activity.

Nevertheless, relying on an article by Newark,[171] the court interpreted *Rylands* as a case in which Blackburn was not laying down a new principle but following one which had been settled by the law of nuisance. The court noted, '[i]t is true that Blackburn ... never once used the word "nuisance," but three times he cited the case of fumes escaping from an alkali works—a clear case of nuisance'. Supposedly, Blackburn was simply applying the principles of nuisance to 'an isolated escape'. Echoing the Report of the Law Commission on Civil Liability for Dangerous Things and Activities,[172] the court expressed its concern over the 'uncertainties and practical difficulties of determining which things and activities are abnormally dangerous'.

Actually, Blackburn analogized the case, not only to alkali fumes, but to the acts of 'beasts' as when a person's 'grass or corn is eaten down by the escaping cattle of his neighbor . . .'. But even if he had based his opinion on cases of nuisance, it should be read to mean that in *Rylands* as in cases of nuisance the defendant should be liable without fault. Whether *Rylands* should be limited in the same way as the law of nuisance was a question not before him and which he did not address.

Indeed, there are only two ways that such a question can be answered. One is to see, by analogy to other cases, whether such a limitation makes sense. The other is to ask if it can be justified in theory. If we look at other English cases, we can see how little sense it makes to limit *Rylands* to defendant's activities on his own land, and how, in any case, a court must consider the degree to which an activity is dangerous.

If *Powell* v. *Hall* is no longer good law, it is hard to see why, if sparks from defendant's traction engine ignite the plaintiff's property, it should matter whether the defendant kept the engine on his own land or took it on the street. Moreover, defendant has been held liable when electricity[173] or gas[174] escapes from a cable or pipe which he has a statutory right or franchise to put in place. It is hard to see why he should be liable if he moves a dangerous substance through a channel which, by statutory right or franchise, he alone can use, rather than by a public highway which others can use as well. In *Crown River Cruises* v. *Kimbolton Fireworks*,[175] which was decided after *Cambridge Water Co.*, fireworks shot from a pontoon towed by a boat on the Thames set fire to a nearby boat engaged in the display. Because the fire was not completely extinguished, it later spread to the defendant's boat after both boats had been moored to the shore.

---

[171] 'The Boundaries of Nuisance', *L.Quar. Rev.* 65 (1949), 80.   [172] Law. Comm. 32 (1970).
[173] *Charing Cross Electricity Supply Co.* v. *Hydraulic Power Co.* [1914] KB. 772.
[174] *Northwestern Utilities Ltd.* v. *London Guarantee Ltd.* [1936] AC 108.
[175] *Crown River Cruises* v. *Kimbolton Fireworks* [1996] 2 Lloyd's Rep 533 (QB).

The court held that because the boats had been moored, they were to be treated in the same way as land, and so the defendant was liable for nuisance. It refused to apply *Rylands* v. *Fletcher* to the escape of fireworks from the pontoon because it was not moored. The court itself expressed doubt as to whether this distinction made sense.

In any event, a court will have to consider whether the defendant's activity was abnormally dangerous. In *Crown River Cruises*, in holding the defendant liable for nuisance for what *Cambridge Water Co.* would have called an 'occasional' escape, the court observed that 'the occasional holding of displays upon the Thames . . . can hardly be said to be an ordinary and reasonable incident of river life; rather are they an unusual and potentially dangerous state of affairs in relation to flammable property lawfully located within the fall-out zone'. Similarly, as Rogers and Winfield have observed of cases applying *Rylands*:

> Notwithstanding the refusal to develop *Rylands* v. *Fletcher* into a general principle of strict liability for ultra-hazardous activities, the *effect* of the case law seems to go some way along this road by excluding from the scope of the rule minor or common or domestic uses of things which have some potential for danger. So the following have been regarded as natural uses of land: water installations in a house or office;[176] a fire in a domestic grate;[177] electric wiring;[178] gas pipes in a house or shop;[179] erecting or pulling down houses or walls;[180] burning stubble in the normal course of agriculture;[181] the ordinary working of mines or minerals;[182] the possession of trees whether planted or self-sown;[183] or generating steam on a ship.[184] There has, however, been a greater willingness to apply the rule to the bulk storage or transmission of water[185] or gas or electricity,[186] or to the bulk storage of chemicals,[187] though the defence of statutory authority has in many cases prevented a decision in the plaintiff's favour.[188]

Indeed, it is hard to see how one would impose liability for harm done on a particular occasion by a 'non-natural' use of land without attending to whether the use was abnormal and dangerous. It may be true, as the court said in *Cambridge Water Co.*, that the law will be uncertain if it is left to judges to decide whether an activity is

176 *Rickards* v. *Lothian* [1913] AC. 263; cf. *Wei's Western Wear Ltd* v. *Yui Holdings Ltd* (1984) 5 DLR (4th).

177 *Sochacki* v. *Sas* [1947] 1 All ER 344.

178 *Collingwood* v. *Home and Colonial Stores Ltd* [1936] 3 All ER 200.

179 *Miller* v. *Addie & Sons* (Collieries) Ltd, 1934 SC 150.

180 *Thomas and Evans Ltd* v. *Mid-Rhondda Co-operative Society* [1941] 1 KB 381; cf. *Gertsen* v. *Municipality of Metropolitan Toronto* (1973) 41 D LR (3d) 646 (landfill project using household waste which generated methane gas, not a natural user).

181 *Perkins* v. *Glyn* [1976] RTR ix (note); cf. in the somewhat different climatic conditions of New Zealand, *New Zealand Forest Products Ltd* v. *O'Sullivan* [1974] 2 NZLR 80, where, however, negligence was clearly established. In *Metson* v. *De Wolfe* (1980) 117 DLR (3d) 278 at 283, it was said that there was no case in Nova Scotia: 'Where the application of the rule in *Rylands* v. *Fletcher* has been in any way modified or eroded for considerations of normal agricultural husbandry'.

182 *Rouse* v. *Gravelworks Ltd* [1940] 1 KB 489.

183 *Noble* v. *Harrison* [1926] 2 KB 332; cf. *Crowhurst* v. *Amersham Burial Board* (1878) 4 ExD 5 (poisonous yew tree).

184 *Howard* v. *Furness etc. Ltd* [1936] 2 All ER 781; *Eastern Asia Navigation Co. Ltd* v. *Freemantle* (1951) 83 CLR 353 (fuel oil store a natural user); *Miller Steamship Co. Pty. Ltd* v. *Overseas Tankship (U.K.) Ltd* [1963] 1 Lloyd's Rep 402 at 426.   185 *Rylands* v. *Fletcher* itself.

186 *Charing Cross Electricity Supply Co.* v. *Hydraulic Power Co.* [1914] 3 KB 772; *Northwestern Utilities* v. *London Guarantee and Accident Co.* [1936] AC 108.

187 *Cambridge Water Co.* v. *Eastern Counties Leather plc* [1994] 2 AC 264.

188 W. V. H. Rogers, *Winfield & Jolowicz on Tort* (15th edn., London, 1998), 548–9.

sufficiently abnormal and dangerous to warrant imposing liability. If so, then the solution ought to be a series of special statutes, as in Germany, despite the gaps in the law that would leave. But if courts have to make such judgments anyway to determine whether a use is 'non-natural', then the problem is not solved by the limit *Cambridge Water* supposedly placed on *Rylands* v. *Fletcher*.

The other question to ask is whether the limitation the court imposed in *Cambridge Water Co.* can be justified in theory. It cannot be if the theory of the law of nuisance presented earlier in this book is correct. There it was argued that a person should be liable as a matter of commutative justice if, to gain a benefit others do not enjoy, he imposes a burden on them which they do not impose on him. The argument we have made here for strict liability is exactly parallel. It is unfair for a person, to gain a benefit which others do not enjoy, to impose a risk on them which they do not impose on him. The court in *Cambridge Water Co.* rejected a rule 'which would lead to the practical result that the cost of damages resulting from [ultra-hazardous] operations would have to be absorbed as part of the overheads of the relevant business rather than be borne (where there is no negligence) by the injured person or his insurers, or even by the community at large'. But if our analysis was correct, that is precisely what the law of negligence seeks to do with operations that are abnormally disturbing to another's use of his property. It does not make sense to reject such a result on the grounds that the principles underlying *Rylands* v. *Fletcher* are merely those underlying nuisance.

Another notable instance in which the law of strict liability cannot be explained on the principles we have suggested is France. Articles 1382–3 of the French Civil Code impose liability for harm inflicted intentionally or negligently. Article 1384 provides: 'A person is liable not only for the damage he causes by his own act, but also for that caused by the acts of persons for whom he is responsible or of things that he has in his custody (*garde*)'. It is hard to know what the drafters meant by this provision. Much of their work was based on that of Domat and Pothier, who themselves were not clear about the status of strict liability. As described earlier, the Roman *edictum de feris* imposed strict liability for the keeping of animals. Domat explained the *edictum* by suggesting that a person who had custody or guard (*garde*) of a fierce animal was liable because he was at fault. But he also made an argument like the one which, as we have seen, Pufendorf made to defend strict liability: 'As he profits from the use he can make from this animal, being its owner, and as he can obtain possession of it again, having acquired it for money or by his own efforts, and having expended time and trouble to acquire some profit, he should answer'.[189] Although Pothier did not make this argument, he may not have regarded fault as the only basis for liability.[190]

---

[189] Domat, *Les Loix civiles*, liv. 2, tit. 8.

[190] Other paragraphs of art. 1384 modeled on Pothier impose liability on parents, teachers and guardians for harm done by those under their care and by masters for harm done by their servants. Pothier said that parents, guardians and teachers were not liable for torts they could not prevent committed by those under their authority. In contrast, masters were liable vicariously for torts of their servants even when they could not prevent them. They, apparently, were liable without fault, although Pothier threw this conclusion in doubt by adding: 'This has been established to render masters careful to employ only good servants'. Pothier, *Traité des Obligations*, § 121.

The ambiguities in Domat and Pothier passed into the Code. They can be seen in the legislative history of these provisions. Bertrand-de-Greuille explained the liability of the owner of animals by stating the 'general thesis' that 'nothing that belongs to a person can injure another with impunity'.[191] In contrast, Tarrible explained it by the principle that 'damage, to be subject to reparation, must be the effect of a fault or imprudence on the part of someone' since otherwise 'it is only the work of chance'.[192]

In any event, 19th century courts and commentators interpreted art. 1384 as an instance of the liability imposed by arts. 1382–3. The defendant was liable only if he was at fault.

In the late 19th century, however, the *Cour de Cassation* applied art. 1384 to the increasingly important problem of industrial accidents. In 1897, it allowed the widow of a worker fatally injured in the explosion of a steam tug to recover on the grounds that the explosion was the result of a defect in the tug for which the owner was responsible because the tug was under his *garde*.[193] Shortly thereafter the compensation of workers for job-related accidents was provided by the Law concerning Liability of 9 April 1898 for accidents. In 1919, however, the court applied art. 1384 to the dangers which had arisen from mechanized transport. The plaintiff recovered for damage caused to his property when a locomotive exploded.[194] Unlike Germany, France did not have a special statute governing railway accidents under which the plaintiff could otherwise recover. In 1930, the *Chambres réunies*—an assembly of all the judges of the *Cour de Cassation*—considered a case in which defendant's truck had knocked down and injured a child.[195] The *Cour d'appel* had denied recovery on the grounds that 'an accident caused by an automobile in movement, under the impulsion and direction of an individual, does not constitute the act of an object that one has under one's guard ... as long as it has not been shown that the accident was due to a defect in the automobile'.[196] The *Chambres réunies* rejected this distinction. Liability for automobile accidents was eventually dealt with by a special statute.[197] But the principle the court established lived on and remains the law of France: the defendant is liable without fault if an accident is due to an object under his *garde*. He can exonerate himself only by proving *cas fortuit* or *force majeure*.

The origins of this rule do not inspire confidence. The drafting history, while ambiguous, certainly does not suggest a clearly thought-out response to the question of when a person should be strictly liable. The rule was forged in situations such as

---

[191] Rapport fait par Bertrand-de-Greuille, Communication officielle au Tribunat, 10 pluviose, an XII (31 Jan. 1804), in P. A. Fenet, *Recueil complet des travaux préparatoires du Code civil* 13 (1827, repr. Paris, 1968), 477.

[192] According to Tarrible, vicarious liability and liability for animals are based on the principle that 'damage, to be subject to reparation, must be the effect of a fault or imprudence on the part of someone' since otherwise 'it is only the work of chance'. Discours prononcé par le Tribun Tarrible, Discussion devant le Corps Législatif, 18 pluviose, an XII (8 Feb. 1804), in Fenet, *Travaux préparatoires*, 13, 488.

[193] Cass., ch. civ., 16 June 1896, D. 1897.1.433.

[194] Cass., ch. civ., 21 Jan. 1919, D. 1922.1.25. The next year the court applied 1384 to a fire fed by casks of resin stored on the premises of a railroad company. Cass., ch. civ., 16 Nov. 1920, D. 1920.1.169. Its attempt to help victims of this type of accident was defeated by the enactment of the law of 7 Nov. 1922, which provides that when a person's property catches fire, he shall be liable only for fault.

[195] Cass, ch. réun., 13 Feb. 1930.1.57.

[196] That was how its decision was characterized by the *Chambre réunies* (ibid.).

[197] Law of 31 Nov. 1931 (no. 51–1508).

industrial and mechanized transportation accidents which later were, or could have been, dealt with by special legislation.

Moreover, if we examine how the rule has been applied, we can see that though the French courts have struggled toward a defensible system of liability, the rule itself has prevented them from ever attaining one. In the first place, they have had to decide what constitutes the 'act of an object'. They have not done so by asking whether the object was dangerous or not. According to some commentators, they will presume the accident was caused by an object if the object was in motion and if it made contact with the plaintiff.[198] Sometimes this distinction seems to explain the case law. The defendant has not been held liable when the plaintiff slipped on a floor[199] or walked into a glass door.[200] He was not held liable for swerving and crashing his car because another car was passing him.[201] Nevertheless, in the case of the floor, the court noted that the plaintiff had failed to show the 'covering' of the floor caused the accident. In the case of the glass window, it noted that the door was marked by two metal edges and a handle of gilded metal. In contrast, plaintiff recovered when he crashed into a car that was parked in such a way that it was difficult to see.[202] Similarly, in the case of the car that swerved, the court noted that the defendant had passed the plaintiff in a regular fashion. In contrast, the defendant was held liable when he made the plaintiff fall by skiing too close to him.[203] The true explanation of these cases seems to be that an accident is imputed to an object when the action or condition of the object was dangerous in a way that it is normally the duty of the defendant to prevent, despite the fact that in these cases the defendant could not have prevented the danger.

The same can be said of the defenses of *cas fortuit* and *force majeure*. The court exonerated a defendant who fired a bullet that ricocheted and hit the plaintiff when he was unable 'to foresee that the bullet would ricochet in the direction of his hunting partner'.[204] In contrast, the court said that the ricochet cannot be considered a case of *cas fortuit* when the defendant 'committed an imprudence in firing close to a road, where the ground was hard, and where there were a pole and apple trees that could have caused the ricochet'.[205] A driver who lost control of his car when it skidded on a patch of ice was exonerated because 'the formation of a patch of ice on the highway when the temperature is just below freezing is normally unforeseeable'.[206] In a similar case, he was not exonerated 'when there was no question of an icy condition that developed suddenly and could not have been foreseen.... Hence a prudent driver could have foreseen the icy condition.'[207] While *cas fortuit* and *force majeure* do not simply mean the absence of fault, they do seem to mean that the defendant's action was one for which he could not possibly be at fault.

---

[198] François Terré, Philippe Simler, and Yves Lequette, *Droit civil: Les obligations* (7th edn., Paris, 1999), no. 745.   [199] Cass., 2e ch. civ., 19 Nov. 1964, J.C.P.1965.2.14022.

[200] Cass., 2e ch. civ., 20 Mar. 1968, Bull. Civ. 1968.II no. 89.

[201] Cass., 2e ch. civ., 13 Mar. 1967, Bull. Civ. 1967. II no. 120.

[202] Cass., ch. civ., 5 Mar. 1947, D. 1947.J.296. The case turned on the court's conclusion (in 1947) that 'a vehicle parked at night on a public road, even though it is placed at the curb, cannot be considered as in a normal situation unless it is provided with the required lighting capable of revealing to others the obstacle that its presence represents'.   [203] Trib. gr. inst., Lyon, 24 Feb. 1971, J.C.P. 1971.II.16822.

[204] Cass., ch. civ., 9 Dec. 1940, D.A. 1941.J.33.

[205] Trib. civ., Chartres, 18 June 1941, D.A. 1942.J.13.

[206] Cass., 2e ch. civ., 29 June 1966, D. & S. 1966.J.645.

[207] Cour d'appel, Paris, 28 Oct. 1943, Gaz. Pal. 1943.II.269.

If this is how courts construe the requirement of an 'act of an object' and the defenses of *cas fortuit* and *force majeure*, then, it would seem, there could be only one way to justify the French law of strict liability. That would be to say that it imposes liability in situations in which the defendant is likely to be at fault. In that respect, it is like the Roman actions mentioned earlier in which the plaintiff could recover when he was struck by an object hung over the street by the defendant or thrown from the defendant's window. It is like the common law doctrine of *res ipsa loquitur* which creates a presumption of fault in situations in which the defendant is likely to have been negligent except that the common law doctrine allows the defendant to exonerate himself by proving the absence of fault.

There are two problems with this justification of the French version of strict liability. First, there are certain aspects of French law which it cannot explain. Suppose that possession of an object passes from one person to another. When bottles being transported by railroad exploded, a French court held the railroad was not liable.[208] That is as it should be if the point of the doctrine is to place liability on the party most likely to have been at fault—in this case, whoever was most likely to be at fault for whatever defect caused the explosion of the bottles. But in other cases when possession of an object has passed temporarily, French courts, despite the criticism of some commentators,[209] have refused to distinguish 'guard' of the object's structure from 'guard' of its conduct. If one party rents to another, 'guard' passes so that the party who rents becomes liable for defects in the object's structure as well as in its comportment.[210] That is not as it should be if liability is to be placed on the party most likely to be at fault.

Even if French law consistently did so, however, the question arises, if liability is placed on a party because he is likely to have been at fault, why he is not allowed to exonerate himself by proving he was not, as is the case with the common law doctrine of *res ipsa loquitur*. One reason may be that proof of whether there was fault is difficult and unlikely to be convincing. That may explain the Roman rules just mentioned. As we will see, it may explain the liability of the manufacturer of a defective product. But it can hardly explain liability for harm caused by 'objects' as a class with no attempt to discriminate between cases in which it is hard or easy for the defendant to prove convincingly that he was not at fault. If that is so, the only way to explain the extent of strict liability in France is by historical accident. Article 1384, which was drafted without any consideration of when the defendant should be strictly liable, simply spoke of the act of an 'object', and French courts were unwilling to retailor the text to apply only to cases in which strict liability can be rationally defended.

It is some confirmation of our theory, then, that it can provide a rational justification of the case law of some countries, and when it cannot, the law of those countries seems to lack a rational justification.

---

[208] Cass., ch. comm., 30 June 1953, J.C.P. 1953.II.7811.
[209] B. Goldman, *De la détermination du gardien responsable du fait des choses inanimées* (Paris, 1947), 208.
[210] Cass., ch. civ., 11 June 1953, J.C.P.II.7825.

11

Liability in Tort for Harm to Reputation, Dignity, Privacy, and 'Personality'

There have been major controversies over two questions concerning the scope of the rights which tort law should protect. One—the subject of this chapter—is whether and to what extent the law should protect rights to reputation, dignity, privacy and 'personality'. The other, which is the subject of the next, is the extent to which the law should exclude protection for pure economic loss.

It will be helpful to begin by considering the protection extended to reputation and dignity, both traditionally and by modern law. We will then turn to a miscellany of other rights often described along with reputation and dignity as rights to 'privacy' or 'personality'.

I. The Protection of Reputation and Dignity

A. Rights and Remedies

1. Civil law

a. Iniuria *in Roman law*
There is a story that a man named Lucius Veratius once walked about Rome, slapping whomever he met, followed by a slave who paid each person he struck the sum of 25 asses. The Twelve Tables provided this penalty for anyone who struck another. By the time of Lucius Veratius—the late third century BC—the amount had become trivial. According to the story, in response to his escapade, the praetors instituted an action by which an equitable amount was to be awarded to any victim of *iniuria*.[1] Eventually, the Romans allowed the action for many different offenses. The plaintiff could recover if the defendant beat his slave[2] or entered his house without permission.[3] He could recover if someone attacked him by composing or reciting a song,[4] or by assembling people at his house to raise a loud and offensive clamor.[5] The defendant was liable for *iniuria* if he 'accosted' a woman, which meant, according to the jurist Ulpian, that he used 'smooth words to make an attempt upon [her] virtue'.[6] He was also liable for using base language[7] or for following a woman 'assiduously'.[8] As we have

---

[1] Aulus Gellius, *Noctes atticae* (A. Lion, ed., 1825), lib. 20, cap. 1.   [2] Dig. 47.10.15.34.
[3] Dig. 47.2.21.7.   [4] Dig. 47.10.15.27.   [5] Dig. 47.10.15.2.   [6] Dig. 47.10.15.20.
[7] Dig. 47.10.15.21.   [8] Dig. 47.10.15.22.

seen, the action was also used to protect against what common lawyers would call nuisance: the upstairs neighbors could sue for *iniuria* when bothered by the smoke from a downstairs cheese shop.[9] It is hard to say what all these cases had in common except that someone's instrusive or offensive behavior bothered someone else without inflicting any physical damage.

The plaintiff could also be liable in *iniuria* for maligning the defendant: for example, by presenting a petition about him to the emperor.[10] Whether the Roman jurists thought truth was a defense is not so clear. According to one Roman text: 'It would not be fair (*bonum aequum*) for one who defames a pernicious person to be condemned, for the wrongs of such a person ought to be observed and made known'.[11] The 13th century jurist Accursius read the text broadly. It did not matter whether the wrong was revealed in judicial proceedings or 'extra-judicially' because, he said, the rationale of this provision was a general one: wrongs should be made known. Had his view had prevailed, the action of *iniuria* would have resembled the traditional Anglo-American law of defamation, at least when the defendant was accused of misconduct. But other jurists thought Accursius had gone too far. Cinus de Pistoia explained that it was wrong and inhumane (*iniuriosus et inhumanus*) to disclose another person's defects,[12] citing a Roman text which, in a different context, had called it 'inhumane' to disclose the extent of another's wealth.[13] As we will see, that became the accepted opinion except in cases in which the public interest was concerned and, perhaps, in cases in which the defendant acted in order to injure the plaintiff.

The Roman lawyers did not try to elaborate a general concept of tort or delict and explain how the actions recognized by Roman law were related. Neither did the medieval jurists. They were chiefly concerned with interpreting each Roman text. Their discussion of the relationship between *iniuria* and the other Roman actions[14] never went beyond some occasional musings on how, if the action was delictual, it could also be *ex bono et aequo*[15] as one text said that it was.[16] A systematic theory was first developed by the late scholastics and then borrowed, in part, by the northern natural lawyers.

b. The reconceptualization of the late scholastics and natural lawyers

The work of the late scholastics and natural lawyers is worth examining for its own sake. It was one of the most systematic efforts to understand the rights that should be protected and the proper remedies. It is worth examination for another reason as well. Their debate raised four questions which have figured in modern law. One is whether, as the medieval jurists thought, the revelation of true but embarrassing facts about another person should be actionable. It is in civil law systems and has become so in England and the United States where originally it was not. Second, should an

---

[9] Chapter 4 I.   [10] Dig. 47.10.15.29.   [11] Dig. 47.10.18.pr.

[12] Cinus de Pistoia, *In codicem commentaria* (Frankfurt-am-Main, 1578; repr. Turin, 1964), to C. 9.35.5, no. 10.   [13] C. 10.35.2 [vulg. 34.2].

[14] Manfred Herrmann, *Der Schutz der Persönlichkeit in der Rechtslehre des 16.–18. Jahrhunderts Dargestellt an Hand der Quellen des Humanismus, des aufgeklärten Naturrechts und des Usus modernus* (Stuttgart, 1968), 17.

[15] Bartolus de Saxoferrato, *Commentaria Corpus iuris civilis* (Venice, 1615), to D. 47.10.11.1, no. 1.

[16] Dig. 47.10.11.1.

action lie only for offences to dignity or reputation? The late scholastics and natural lawyers thought so, but modern legal systems have expanded relief in ways we will describe, even though doing so has raised distinctive problems. Third, should the defendant who has attacked another's reputation be compelled to retreat or apologize? For a long time, civil law required him to do so but that position is now universally rejected. Fourth, should he pay damages? Modern legal systems compel him to do so although the German Civil Code said he should not.

i. The nature of the right. The starting point for the late scholastics was the ethics of Aristotle, and the moral philosophy which Thomas Aquinas had developed on the basis of Aristotelian principles. According to Aristotle and Aquinas, the allocation of honor among citizens belongs to distributive justice which 'is manifested in distributions of honor or money or the other things that fall to be divided among those who have a share in the constitution . . .'.[17] The honor that belongs to each citizen is to be protected as a matter of commutative justice. According to Aquinas, a person's 'personal dignity' (*dignitas personae*) might be lost either 'secretly by false witness, detractions (*detractiones*), and so forth, or openly, when he is deprived of his reputation (*fama*) by being accused in court of law, or by public insult'.[18] If so, he was entitled to compensation, just as if his property were taken.

Consequently, the distinction among Roman actions was treated as a matter of Roman positive law. They were merged into a general law of tort, which has one purpose: to ensure compensation, as commutative justice requires, when one person has deprived another of something of value which belongs to him. Like property, 'personal dignity' belongs to a person and compensation must be paid for its loss. Indeed, his claim to reparation is stronger than for property because, Aquinas said, his reputation is worth more than his wealth.[19] The late scholastics agreed.[20]

Aquinas and the late scholastics then distinguished two ways in which in which 'personal dignity' or 'honor' could be impaired: detraction (*detractio*) and insult (*contumelia*). Detraction was 'impairing another's reputation (*fama*) . . . in secret'.[21] Insult was openly 'dishonoring someone' by doing 'that which is contrary to his honor in the presence of himself and others'.[22] Thus, Aquinas said, 'detraction differs in two ways from insult: . . . the insulting person speaks openly against someone, the detractor secretly . . . [and] the insulting person impairs honor, the detractor reputation'.[23] Aquinas apparently thought that the two criteria went together: honor is impaired openly because the offender wishes to show another person that he does not respect him, while reputation is impaired by talking about him to others because the offender wishes to change their opinion of him. Nevertheless, some of the late scholastics were troubled by having two different criteria. Some gave somewhat labored explanations of why the two criteria should go together. Cajetan said that while an absent person could be insulted, he would only be absent *per accidens* since person insulting him

---

[17] Aristotle, *Nicomachean Ethics* V.ii 1130[b].   [18] *Summa theologiae* II-II, Q. 61, a. 3.

[19] ibid. Q. 73, a. 3.

[20] Domenicus Soto, *De iustitia et iure libri decem* (Salamanca, 1553), lib. 4, Q. 6, a. 3; Ludovicus Molina, *De iustitia et iure tractatus* (Venice, 1614), IV, disp. 3, no. 2; Martinus Azpilcueta, *Commentaria . . . de detractione, fama et eius restitutione* (Venice, 1594), f. 1v, no. 399.

[21] *Summa theologiae* II-II, Q. 73, a. 1.   [22] ibid. Q. 72, a. 1.   [23] ibid. Q. 73, a. 1.

would intend him to learn of the insult.[24] Soto said that the difference in 'material object' (reputation versus honor) is less significant than the distinction in the way the impairment was involuntary (secret versus open).[25] Lessius said that honor (and so dishonor) is most directly (*potissimum*) exhibited face to face—implying that Aquinas had defined insult by putting the clearest or purest case.[26] De Lugo gave up trying to use both criteria. He said that the difference was simply that between impairment of honor and of reputation.[27]

Having defined insult and detraction, the late scholastics then read their definitions into the Roman action of *iniuria*. They cited Roman texts alongside Aristotle and Aquinas. Molina explained that the Roman texts that spoke of *contumelia* were using the term broadly to cover any harm to reputation or honor.[28]

Their analysis was part of a larger Aristotelian theory of why dignity and honor should matter. Aquinas and the late scholastics defined honor and reputation in terms of deference and esteem for the qualities and actions that contribute to a certain kind of life, the distinctively human life which they regarded as the ultimate end of a human being. Actions are good to the extent that they contribute to such a life either as an integral part or as instrumental to it. Virtues are acquired capacities to perform such actions. Deference and esteem are due to whatever contributes to such a life. Moreover, receiving deference and respect contributes to such a life by enabling a person to perform good actions.

Thus they defined honor as deference, acknowledgment, testimony or recognition of the excellence of another person.[29] It is due 'most properly' to virtue.[30] Nevertheless, it is due to any sort of excellence: to 'every perfection of rational nature'.[31] Nobility should be honored because it arises from excellent deeds; wealth, because it enables the possessor to perform them; both nobility and wealth because they are instruments of virtue.[32] Indeed, honor itself is worth having because it also is an instrument of virtue. A Christian, it might seem, should bear insults patiently, and so he should, said Aquinas, unless vindicating his honor was good either for the perpetrator or for oneself.[33] We should vindicate our honor, according to Molina,[34] if by doing so we can do good to others; according to Lessius, if by doing so we can better perform our office.[35]

Reputation is the esteem of others for one's excellent qualities.[36] It 'most properly' concerns esteem for another person's 'virtue and wisdom' since they are the qualities most proper to a human being, but in a secondary sense, reputation concerns the

---

[24] Cajetan (Tomasso di Vio), *Commentaria* to Thomas Aquinas, *Summa theologica* (Padua, 1698), II-II, Q. 72, a. 1.   [25] Soto, *De iustitia et iure*, lib. 5, Q. 10, a. 1.

[26] Lessius, *De iustitia et iure, ceterisque virtutibus cardinalis libri quatuor* (Paris, 1628), lib. 2, cap. 11, dub. 2, nos. 6–7.

[27] Iohannes de Lugo, *Disputationum de iustitia et iure* (Lyon, 1670), disp. 14, § 1, no. 4.

[28] Molina, *De iustitia et iure* IV, disp. 12.

[29] Soto, *De iustitia et iure*, lib. 5, Q. 9, a. 1 (*reverentia*); Lessius, *De iustitia et iure*, lib. 2, cap. 11, dub. 1, no. 2 (*testificatio*); de Lugo, *Disputationum*, disp. 14, § 1, no. 3 (*testificatio*); Molina, *De iustitia et iure* IV, disp. 1, no. 1 (*testimonio ac recognitio*).   [30] Soto, *De iustitia et iure*, lib. 5, Q. 9, a. 1.

[31] Lessius, *De iustitia et iure*, lib. 2, cap. 11, dub. 1, no. 2.   [32] ibid. no. 4.

[33] *Summa theologiae* II-II, Q. 72, a. 3.   [34] Molina, *De iustitia et iure* IV, disp. 20, no. 1.

[35] Lessius, *De iustitia et iure*, lib. 2, cap. 11, dub. 14, nos. 124, 126.

[36] ibid. lib. 2, cap. 11, dub. 1, no. 1.

opinion people hold of one's 'eloquence, nobility, strength, beauty, power, and the like'.[37] Like honor, reputation is worth having because it pertains to human perfection and enables one to do good.[38]

Writers in the Aristotelian tradition could then explain why—although they excepted certain cases in which the disclosure was in the public interest—it was not a defense to an action of *iniuria* that the plaintiff did not deserve honor or a good reputation, and the defendant had only told the truth about him or treated him as he deserved. Having an undeserved reputation, like having an undeserved fortune, is still of value because of the good it enables a person to do. Aquinas concluded that it would be a violation of commutative justice to deprive a person of an undeserved reputation.[39] Lessius and de Lugo explained that such a person was like one with goods in his possession that he did not own. Until deprived of them by legal proceedings brought for the purpose, he was entitled to keep them, and therefore entitled to redress against anyone who took or injured them.[40] Lessius, despite some doubts, thought it would be wrong to deprive someone even of a reputation he had preserved by fraud and lies. Such a person did not have the right to have his lies believed, but he did have the right to keep his wrongdoing a secret.[41] To illustrate their argument, suppose that a person has reformed, concealed his disreputable past, and now has a reputation which enables him to do good for others. Why should his past be revealed unless there is a danger that he may use his undeserved reputation to do further wrong? As we will see, however, where a person's past indicated that he might still be a threat to others, the late scholastics believed it should be a defense that the defendant told the truth.

In rough outline, this approach was preserved by the founders of the northern natural law school although the underlying Aristotelian analysis was not. Grotius explained that, in principle, compensation must be made whenever one person negligently or intentionally harms whatever belongs to another, including his reputation and honor.[42] 'From such a fault, if damage has been caused, by the law of nature an obligation arises, namely, that the damage should be made good.'[43] Damage, he explained, meant harm to whatever is one's own: life, body, limbs, reputation (*fama*) and honor (*honor*).[44] Pufendorf said the same, although he mentioned reputation and *pudicia*—chastity or virtue—rather than honor.[45] The late scholastic analysis of why dignity and reputation should be protected was largely ignored, not only by Grotius, Pufendorf and the other northern natural lawyers, but by the 17th and 18th century commentators on Roman law. Only occasionally one hears an echo, as when Lauterbach explained that one who debauches another's wife or daughter for physical gratification

---

[37] ibid. lib. 2, cap. 11, dub. 1, no. 1; de Lugo, disp. 14, § 1, no. 2.

[38] de Lugo, *Disputationum*, disp. 14, § 1, no. 2.

[39] *Summa theologiae* II-II, Q. 62, a. 2 ad 2; Q. 73, a. 1 ad 3.

[40] Lessius, *De iustitia et iure*, lib. 2, cap. 11, dub. 10, no. 67; de Lugo, *Disputationum*, disp. 14, § 2, no. 35.

[41] Lessius, *De iustitia et iure*, lib. 2, cap. 11, dub. 10, nos. 65–7.

[42] See Hermann, *Schutz der Persönlichkeit*, 33–7, who notes the change from the Roman and medieval jurists but not the debt to the late scholastics.

[43] Hugo Grotius, *De iure belli ac pacis libri tres* (B.J.A. de Kanter-van Hetting Tromp, ed., Leiden, 1939), II.xvii.1.   [44] ibid. II.xvii.2.

[45] Samuel Pufendorf, *De iure naturae ac gentium libri octo* (Amsterdam, 1688), III.i.1; III.i.3.

is liable for insult because he 'indirectly' intended an insult,[46] and therefore redress must be given as a matter of 'commutative justice'.[47]

ii. Remedies. Aristotle had said that, as a matter of commutative justice, one who deprived another of something that belonged to him was obligated to restore an equivalent. Thomas Aquinas and the late scholastics called this obligation one to make 'restitution'. That was the term that the canon lawyers had used when they explained the duty of a person who wishes to be forgiven to give back whatever he had unjustly taken.[48] As Soto said, that duty extended to 'everything whatsoever of which a person can be unjustly deprived'.[49] Thus restitution had to be made to one who had been deprived of dignity or reputation. The question was how.

The Roman law of *iniuria* required payment of damages. By the 13th century, the theologian Peter the Chanter (d. 1197)[50] and the canon lawyers, Hostiensis (d. 1271)[51] and Raymond of Penafort (d. 1275)[52] had said that to make restitution, a person who had harmed another's reputation should publicly announce that he had been in error or at least apologize. This was an idea with a future before it. Canon law courts began to require an offender to do so.

In the 13th century, such a requirement was not yet an established principle of canon law.[53] Nevertheless, it was the view of Raymond of Penafort, who, like Aquinas, was a member of the Dominican order and whose *Summa de poenitentia* was one of Aquinas' sources. His opinion surely carried weight with Aquinas. Again, Aquinas found an Aristotelian explanation of the remedy which was followed in turn by the late scholastics. The aim of commutative justice is to restore a party to where he had been before he was deprived of something that belonged to him. One who had taken away another's good name must restore it, or, if that cannot be done 'he must compensate him otherwise'.[54] 'Sometimes', Aquinas explained, 'it is impossible to restore what has been taken, as when a man has taken life or limb'.[55] In such a case, 'when that

---

[46] Wolfgang Lauterbach, *Collegii theoretico-practici* (Tübingen, 1793), to D. 47.10, § 1, X.

[47] ibid. XXIV.

[48] The locus classicus was a passage from a letter of St Augustine which Gratian had included in the *Decretum* which said that a person who has acquired another's property through sin is not doing penance if he refuses to return it but is pretending to do penance. *Decretum*, C. 14., q. 6, c. 1.

[49] Soto, *De iustitia et iure*, lib. 4, Q. 6, a. 3.

[50] Petrus Cantor, *Summa de sacramentis et animae consiliis* pars 3 *Liber casum conscientiae* (J.-A. Dugauquier, ed., Louvain, 1963), cap. 2, § 202. See Karl Weinzierl, *Die Restitutionslehre der Frühscholastik* (Munich, 1936), 132–46.

[51] Hostiensis (Enrico di Segusio), *Summa aurea* (Venice, 1574), V, § Quibus et qualiter, § Quid de accusatoribus, f. 425vb.

[52] Raimundus de Penafort, *Summa de poenitentia* (X. Ochoa and A. Diez, eds., Rome, 1976), lib. 2, tit. 5, no. 42.

[53] Peter the Chanter cited no authority but argues by analogy to robbery. Raymond cited *Decretum*, C. 14, c. 6, c. 1, described in the text, which says one must give back another's thing which is acquired by sin, C. 5, q. 1, c. 2, which says that one who has posted an accusation at night in a public place will not be suspended from communion or anathematized if he confesses, and Matthew 5:23 which says that you should go and be reconciled with your brother before presenting your offering at the altar. Hostiensis cited Raymond and *Decretales Gregorii ix* 5.34.10 (vers. *precipias*), which says that a person implicated in heresy should denounce the heresy in question at various public places. All of these sources are suggestive, but they do not show the existence of an established rule.					[54] ibid. ad 2.

[55] *Summa theologiae* II-II, Q. 62, art. 2, obj. 1.

which has been taken cannot be restored in equivalent, compensation should be made as far as possible: for instance if one man has deprived another of a limb, he must make compensation either in money or in honor . . .'.[56]

The late scholastics described how harm to honor and reputation might be repaired. In the case of honor, one might salute the offended party in a respectful and friendly way, invite him to dinner, and give him a place of honor.[57] In some cases, one might have to go further and ask the offended party's pardon.[58] Given that the late scholastics lived in a society that was unapologetically hierarchical, it is not surprising that many concluded that the need to apologize depended on one's status. De Lugo thought that superiors should rarely be obliged to ask pardon from subordinates, or masters, parents or teachers to do so from servants, children, or students. Often the offended honor of these people could be restored with a single word, and in all but rare cases, by a showing of kindness and benevolence.[59] Lessius described how the measures required would normally vary with the status of the parties. A friendly and respectful salutation would normally be enough from a superior to an subordinate or from a noble to a plebeian. With a person of equal condition, it would normally be enough to ask the offended party to dinner. But if the insult was serious, and committed by an inferior to his superior or often even by an equal to an equal, then the offender must ask pardon.[60] In an extreme case, for example, when a very serious insult had been offered to a nobleman, merely asking pardon would not be enough. One would have to ask it on bended knee with a rope around one's neck. Nevertheless, Lessius thought that, as a matter of justice, one need not ask pardon in this graphically humble way unless ordered to do so by a court.[61] De Lugo disagreed. Surely, he said, one who struck a nobleman publicly should do more than merely ask his pardon even if he was not ordered to do more.[62]

In the case of reputation, a person who had lied about another could make restitution by admitting that he had lied. A more difficult problem was how he could restore the other person's reputation when he had been telling the truth. To lie about his truthfulness would be morally impermissible. Aquinas suggested that he say that he had spoken wrongly and unjustly.[63] That would not be a lie even though it gave a false impression because it was wrong and unjust of him to have spoken, even though what he said was true. The trouble was, as several of the late scholastics observed, that though this tactic would work with simple people it probably would not with clever ones.[64] Molina proposed more subtle variations: 'When I said such-and-such of so-and-so, I thought that it was true, but having later taken more care, I have determined that I spoke wrongly'.[65] Or again: 'What I said of so-and-so I surely said out of malice, and, if necessary, I would swear under oath that I spoke out of malice, and so you are

---

[56] ibid. ad. 1.

[57] Lessius, *De iustitia et iure*, lib. 2, cap. 11, dub. 26, no. 144; de Lugo, dub. 15, § 4, no. 57.

[58] Cajetan to *Summa theologiae* II-II, Q. 62, a. 3.

[59] de Lugo, *Disputationum*, disp. 15, § 4, no. 57.

[60] Lessius, *De iustitia et iure*, lib. 2, cap. 11, dub. 26, no. 144.   [61] ibid. no. 145.

[62] de Lugo, *Disputationum*, dub. 25, § 4, no. 57.   [63] *Summa theologiae* II-II, Q. 62, a. 2, ad 2.

[64] Molina, *De iustitia et iure* IV, disp. 44, no. 1; Lessius, *De iustitia et iure*, lib. 2, cap. 11, dub. 20, no. 110.

[65] Molina, *De iustitia et iure* IV, disp. 44, no. 1; also recommended by Azpilcueta, *Commentaria*, f. 59r, no. 856.

not to believe any of it, but to strike it out of your mind'.[66] Unfortunately, an alert listener might notice that the speaker here never denied that he had spoken the truth. So could one go further and say that had spoken 'falsely' or 'in error'? The apparent meaning of those expressions is that he had said something false or erroneous. Yet they could have another meaning. 'False' can mean 'wrongful' or 'not in conformity with law', as when we say, in modern English, that a spouse or a coin is false. Saying that one spoke 'in error' might mean it had been an error to speak at all. De Lugo thought it was not a lie in these cases to use words that were ambiguous, even though one knew that listeners would take them in a false sense.[67] Molina and Lessius were of the same view, though they had doubts, and Lessius believed that one was not obligated to restore another's reputation by speaking in this way.[68] Soto thought that such statements were lies.[69]

If one could not completely restore another's honor or reputation by any of these means, then, as we have said, according to Aquinas, one must pay compensation.[70] On this question, the late scholastics disagreed. Lessius and de Lugo argued that since the harm done could not be undone with money, to pay money was not to restore an equivalent.[71] Soto and Molina disagreed,[72] although Molina added that as a practical matter, many people considered it shameful to accept money,[73] and that if the offended party wanted an apology, the offender could not pay money instead.[74] Their argument was that, as Aristotle had said, money was a universal measure of value. Lessius answered that it was only the measure of the value of things that people buy and sell.[75]

Grotius concluded that in the case of reputation or honor, 'reparation is made by confession of the fault, by manifestation of honor, by witness of innocence, and through other means which are similar to these. Nevertheless, such damage may be made good with money, if the injured party so desires, because money is the common measure of useful things.'[76] Curiously, he supported his argument by citing both Soto and Lessius.

The 17th and 18th century civil lawyers took a similar approach, albeit without the Aristotelian analysis. Whatever the Roman texts might say, they accepted a version of the practice of canon law courts which, by their time, was adopted by civil law. They allowed the plaintiff an action for what was known as an *amende honorable* or *recantatio, revocatio,* or *palinodia.* If he succeeded, the court forced the defendant to apologize or to admit that he had spoken an untruth.[77] That remedy was distinguished

---

[66] Molina, *De iustitia et iure*, IV, disp. 44, no. 2.

[67] de Lugo, *Disputationum*, disp. 14, § 2, no. 30.

[68] Molina, *De iustitia et iure*, IV, disp. 44, no. 2; Lessius, *De iustitia et iure*, lib. 2, cap. 11, dub. 20, no. 110.

[69] Soto, *De iustitia et iure*, lib. 4, Q. 6, a. 3.

[70] *Summa theologiae* II-II, Q. 62, a. 2, ad 1; ad 2 (at the end, presumably referring to ad1) (speaking of honor).

[71] Lessius, *De iustitia et iure*, lib. 2, cap. 11, dub. 16, no. 92; de Lugo, *Disputationum*, disp. 15, § 3, nos. 44–5.

[72] Soto, *De iustitia et iure*, lib. 4, Q. 6, a. 3; Molina, *De iustitia et iure* IV, disp. 44 no. 3.

[73] Molina, *De iustitia et iure* IV, disp. 46, no. 1.   [74] ibid. no. 2.

[75] Lessius, *De iustitia et iure*, lib. 2, cap. 11, dub. 16, no. 95.

[76] Grotius, *De iure belli ac pacis*, II.xvii.22.

[77] Udo Wolter, *Das Prinzip der Naturalrestitution in § 249 BGB Herkunft, historische Entwicklung und Bedeutung* (Berlin, 1985), 72. See generally Reinhard Zimmermann, *The Law of Obligations: Roman Foundations of the Civil Law Tradition* (Cape Town, 1990), 1072; C. von. Wallenrodt, 'Die Injurienklagen auf Abbitte, Widerruf und Ehrenerklärung in ihrer Entstehung, Fortbildung und ihrem Verfall', *Zeitschrift für Rechtsgeschichte* 3 (1864), 238.

from the *amende profitable* or *actio iniuriarum aestimatoria* by which the defendant was forced to pay a sum in compensation.

c. France

The drafters of the French Civil Code did not prescribe how dignity or reputation were to be protected. The cumulative effect of articles 1382 and 1383 was to impose liability on anyone who intentionally or negligently caused another person harm (*dommage*). The drafters were paraphrasing the 18th century jurist Robert Pothier from whom they borrowed many of their provisions. Pothier had said:

A delict is an act by which a person through intent or malice causes a damage or injury to another.

A quasi-delict is an act by which a person without malice but by inexcusable imprudence causes an injury to another.'[78]

Although Pothier had been much influenced by the leading natural lawyers, unlike Grotius, he did not try to specify the different types of harm for which one could recover. Nor did he mention, as Grotius did, that 'reparation is made by confession of the fault, by manifestation of honor, by witness of innocence' as well as by monetary compensation. Thus, as with the late scholastics and the natural lawyers, the distinction between the older Roman actions dropped from sight. But so did the idea that the protection of dignity and reputation required special remedies. That change occurred without debate. The drafters simply followed Pothier rather than Grotius. If Pothier had devoted a few more lines to his paraphrase of Grotius, the provisions of the Code might have been quite different.

In any event, Toullier[79] and Duranton,[80] the first commentators on the Code, do not mention the protection of dignity or honor. They simply say that anyone who is at fault for actions which are injurious or harmful to another must pay damages. In their leading treatise, Aubry and Rau explained that 'any right can be the matter of a delict—it matters little that this right concerns an external object, or one which is bound up with (*se confonde*) with the existence of the person to whom it belongs'.[81] In a footnote, they added: 'Consequently, for example, the honor and reputation of a person can be the matter of a delict'.[82] Without much argument, their position became standard among French commentators and courts.

Baudry-Lacantinerie and Barde dissented later in the century but by then they had to acknowledge that the weight of authority was against them. They directed their attack, not against compensation for loss of dignity or reputation in particular, but against any compensation for *dommage simplement morale* or harm that was merely non-pecuniary and non-physical. The role of pecuniary damages, they claimed, can only be to 'reestablish the wealth (*patrimoine*) of the person who obtains them by the

[78] Robert Pothier, *Traité des obligations* (Paris, 1761), nos. 116, 118.

[79] Charles Toullier, *Le droit civil français suivant l'ordre du Code* 11 (4th edn., Paris, 1824–37), no. 117.

[80] Alexandre Duranton, *Cours de droit français suivant le Code civil* 13 (3rd edn., Paris, 1834–7), nos. 704, 708.

[81] Charles Aubry and Charles Rau, *Cours de droit civil français* 4 (4th edn., Paris, 1869), no. 444.

[82] ibid. n. 4.

amount by which this wealth was unjustly diminished'. Moroever, '[i]t is scandalous that one can regard, as a matter of justice, the most sacred affections [and] the sufferings most worthy of respect'. Third, the amount of damages would necessarily be arbitrary.[83]

The third of these arguments, taken to its logical conclusion, would preclude compensation for suffering that was not *simplement morale* but was accompanied by physical harm—a position Baudry-Lacantinerie and Barde did not endorse. The first two are reminiscent of arguments made by some of the late scholastics although one can see a different conception of the right being discussed. As we have seen, Lessius and de Lugo argued that since the harm done could not be undone with money, to pay money was not to restore an equivalent.[84] Molina had noted that many people considered it shameful to accept money as compensation for a loss of dignity or reputation.[85] Nevertheless, Lessius, de Lugo and Molina, like others in the Aristotelian tradition, had regarded dignity and reputation as specific rights, like property, to be allocated according to distributive justice and protected according to commutative justice. Baudry-Lacantinerie and Barde regarded them as instance of *dommage morale*, of pain and suffering. They questioned whether mere pain and suffering calls for redress as a matter of justice. As Marcel Planiol and Georges Ripert characterized their position, 'the award . . . of an indemnity constitutes a pure gain and, for the [defendant], a private fine'.

'But', Planiol argued, 'why refuse this sum if, by the satisfaction the victim can procure with it, it at least attentuates his sufferings?'[86] Therefore, an attaint to reputation and honor called for compensation not only if there is 'monetary loss' but when the harm is purely '*morale*'.[87] Thus Planiol and Ripert also classed injuries to reputation and honor together with other sorts of *dommage morale* or pain and suffering. They thought compensation was in order because money could 'attenuate' these 'sufferings'. While the late scholastics who supported compensation regarded it as an equivalent, due as a matter of commutative justice, for a right lost, Planiol and Ripert regarded it as compensation for suffering. To support their view that the defendant must pay damages, they cited an uninterrupted case law stretching back to 1842.[88]

Today French jurists would still avoid damages for injury to dignity or reputation as compensation for *dommage morale*, or pain and suffering, since *dommage morale* encompasses whatever harm is not physical or pecuniary. They would also say that such an injury violates an amendment to the Civil Code passed in 1970: 'Each person has the right to respect for his private life'.[89] Yet despite the amendment, protection of this right remains much as Planiol and Ripert described it.

d. Germany

In Germany, except where superseded by the statutes of particular states, the older civil law remained in force before German unification. Commentators describe the

---

[83] Gabriel Baudry-Lacantinerie and Louis Barde, *Traité théorique et pratique de droit civil: Les obligations* 4 (3rd edn., Paris, 1908), no. 2871.

[84] Lessius, *De iustitia et iure*, lib. 2, cap. 11, dub. 16, no. 92; de Lugo, *Disputationum*, disp. 15, § 3, nos. 44–5.   [85] Molina, *De iustitia et iure* IV, disp. 46, no. 1.

[86] Marcel Planiol and Georges Ripert, *Traité pratique de droit civil français* 6 (Paul Esmein, ed., Paris, 2nd edn., 1952), no. 548.   [87] ibid.

[88] ibid. n. 5.   [89] Law no. 70-643 of 17 July 1970, art. 22, now *Code civil*, art. 9.

traditionally recognized remedies. One could bring an action for an apology or retraction. If one's dignity or reputation could not be restored in that way, one could seek monetary damages.[90]

The German jurists, like the French, found themselves redefining the right that these remedies were supposed to protect, but their problem was somewhat different. In France, where Roman law had been swept away by the Civil Code, the question became whether *dommage simplement morale* was *dommage* that was recoverable under articles 1382–3. In Germany, in those areas where Roman law remained in force, and in the universities, where it remained at the core of the curriculum, the question was the boundaries of the Roman action for *iniuria*. As the influence of the natural law schools waned, and as attention focused on the Roman texts themselves, it became less than clear that the action was meant simply to protect reputation and honor. For example, neither might be affected by coming on someone's land. A woman's reputation or honor would not necessarily be harmed if she were followed 'assiduously'. As we have seen, the Roman action protected a person against other interferences as well: for example, against unauthorized entry on his property or smoke from a downstairs cheese shop. Jurists made their peace with the texts as best they could. While Keller insisted the action was meant to protect honor, he conceded that the Romans had used the term *iniuria* in a broader sense, so that any injury that was not to one's physical or pecuniary assets counted as an injury to one's honor.[91] Thus the term 'honor' was stretched to cover any wrongful non-physical injury. According to Puchta: '*Iniuria* is an intentional wrong which is exclusively directed against the person of the victim without the intention of inflicting damage even if it should occur as a result of the act'.[92] It is clear in context that by 'damage' he meant the physical damage protected by an action under the *lex Aquilia* or the pecuniary damage protected by an *actio doli*. Thus the scope of the action of *iniuria* was defined negatively as including any harm that was not physical or pecuniary. Windscheid said that '[i]niuria is any unlawful act which entails a disregard for another's personality (*Persönlichkeit*)'.[93] He did not explain *Persönlichkeit*. In my view, we should resist the temptation to read too much into that word. As James Whitman rightly points out, it is 'a characteristically dense German concept with roots in the philosophy of Kant, Humboldt, and Hegel' according to which, as Edward Erble explains, people 'develop freely and self-responsibly their personalities'.[94] Doubtless, 19th century German jurists thought of law as a means of allowing people a free space for self-development, an idea they drew from philosophers such as Kant and Hegel. As Savigny said:

For free beings to exist together in contact, helping each other and unobstructed in their development, is possible only by recognition of an invisible boundary within which secure free

---

[90] e.g., Friedrich von Keller, *Pandekten Vorlesungen* (E. Friedberg, ed., Leipzig, 1861), § 376.

[91] ibid.   [92] Georg Friedrich Puchta, *Pandekten* (7th edn., Leipzig, 1853), § 387.

[93] Bernhard Windscheid, *Lehrbuch des Pandektenrechts* 2 (7th edn. Frankfurt-am-Main, 1891), § 472.

[94] James Q. Whitman, 'The Two Western Cultures of Privacy: Dignity Versus Liberty', *Yale L. J.* 113 (2004), 1151 at 1180, quoting Edward J. Erble, *Dignity and Liberty: Constitutional Visions in Germany and the United States* (Westport, Conn., 2002), 85.

room is won for individual existence and effectiveness. The rule which defines these boundaries and this free room is law.[95]

But Savigny denied that one could begin with the concept of free room for individual effectiveness and arrive by logic or reasoned agreement at the boundaries to be set by law. The law had a quite different source: the spirit or conviction of a people, its *Volksgeist*, which, curiously enough, for Savigny as for Windscheid, was expressed in the legal texts the German people had accepted as law, that is, in the Roman legal texts. Thus, as I have described elsewhere, jurists such as Savigny and Windscheid paid homage to Kantian and Hegelian ideas such as freedom and still managed to wall them off from the work of a jurist to make sense of the Roman texts.[96] I think Windscheid was doing the same thing here. For Windscheid, 'personality' was a term sufficiently large and vague to embrace the varied interests protected by the Roman texts dealing with *iniuria*. But his analysis of *iniuria* has no more to do with the philosophical meaning of that term than the ways in which his contemporaries dealt with the same textual problem.

One difficulty that confronted the German jurists, then, was the fact that the Roman texts concerning the action of *iniuria* protected more than dignity and reputation, and so the question arose of how to describe the interests the texts did protect. A second question was how dignity and reputation were to be protected. As mentioned, before German unification, absent a statute, German jurists followed the traditional modified version of the civil law in which a defendant could make a retraction or apology but would otherwise be condemned to pay damages. In 1872, however, the Criminal Code of the newly unified German state provided instead a criminal sanction for attacks on honor and reputation. As part of the criminal action, compensation could be awarded to the victim if he had suffered pecuniary damage.[97]

One purpose of the new provisions of the Criminal Code was to abolish the old remedies in which a court would demand that the defendant make a retraction or apologize. It was pointed out that it might be difficult to compel the defendant to do so, and compelling him might do little to ameliorate the situation of the plaintiff.[98] As we have seen, this problem had lurked in the background as soon as civil courts had tried to forge a legal remedy to compel conduct which canon lawyers and moral philosophers thought to be morally obligatory.

That left open the question whether, once the Criminal Code was in place, a plaintiff could only recover if he had suffered pecuniary damages as specified in the Code, or whether he could still bring a civil action for *iniuria* for monetary compensation for a loss of dignity or reputation. German jurists split on that question.[99] The split presumably was influenced by arguments at the time as to whether or not there should be an action for monetary damages for violations of reputation and dignity. The arguments of the German jurists against allowing the action were the same as those which

---

[95] Friedrich Carl von Savigny, *System des heutigen Römischen Rechts* 1 (Berlin, 1840–8), § 8.

[96] James Gordley, *The Philosophical Origins of Modern Contract Doctrine* (Oxford, 1991), 225–7.

[97] Strafgesetzbuch, § 188.   [98] Zimmermann, *Obligations*, 1090.

[99] For example, there was no civil action according to Aloys Brinz and Philipp Lotmar, *Lehrbuch des Pandekten* 2 (2nd edn., Goldberg, 1879), § 338. There was according to Heinrich Dernburg, *Pandekten* 2 (4th edn., Berlin, 1894), § 137.

Bauderie de Lacantinerie and Barde made in France. A loss of honor and good reputation could not be made good by the payment of money.[100] Moreover, it was squalid to seek money for their loss or for any other type of suffering. Hartman claimed that in this respect, the French law was 'absolutely foreign' to the 'feelings of the German people'. 'It contradicts the deepest German sensibilities to measure the most sacred feelings in base mammon and to compensate every violation of those feelings with a monetary payment.'[101] The drafters of the initial version of the German Civil Code, like the majority of French jurists, disagreed. The initial draft provided, in a provision which was the ancestor of what is now § 823, that a plaintiff could recover damages for injury to his 'honor' (*Ehre*) just as he could for injury to other enumerated rights such as life, health, freedom (meaning freedom of movement) and property. Here, honor was treated as a distinct right worthy of protection, not, as by Bauderie de Lacantinerie and Barde, merely as an instance of mental suffering. Proponents of this position argued that it was necessary to fill the gaps left by the provisions of the German Criminal Code. But the majority of the drafting committee rejected their argument. According to the official report of the debates:

> The majority, on the contrary, was of the view that the practical result would be that through this proposal all the inconveniences would be reintroduced against which the statute on the abolition of the *actio iniuriarum* had been aimed. If the main purpose is not the procurement of a payment of damages but the restoration of honor, one would be drawn to the conclusion that a declaration concerning one's honor, a retraction, or an apology would have to be made.[102]

The argument, then, was if one wished to protect honor, one would have to do so by means that had already been legislatively rejected: a court-compelled retraction or apology. A payment of money would not accomplish that objective. The reason, presumably, was either that money could not restore honor, or that it was squalid to ask for money when one's honor was offended.

At any rate, the final version of the German Civil Code made it as clear as possible that one could not recover damages for a loss of dignity or reputation except in certain special cases as when one's credit was hurt. Section 823(1) says that the plaintiff can only recover for injury to the 'life, body, health, freedom, ownership or similar right (*sonstiges Recht*) of another'. Injury to 'honor' (*Ehre*) had been deleted from the original version of this provision and was not supposed to be included as a *sonstiges Recht*. Section 823(2) said that the obligation to make compensation also rests 'on a person who infringes a statute intended for the protection of others'. As we have just seen, people are protected against defamation and insult by the German Criminal Code (*Strafgesetzbuch*). But to prevent them from recovering damages in tort, the drafters added in § 253: 'In the case of harm that is not economic, compensation in money can be demanded only in the cases specified by statute'. The Criminal Code provided for recovery only for pecuniary loss, and the Civil Code provided for 'fair compensation

---

[100] Zimmermann, *Obligations*, 1090–2.

[101] G. Hartmann, 'Der Civilgesetzenentwurf, das Aequitätaprincip und die Richterstellung', *Arch. civ. praxis* 73 (1888), 309 at 364.

[102] *Protokolle der Kommission für die zweite Lesung des Entwurfs des Bürgerlichen Gesetzbuchs* (Berlin, 1898), 641.

in money for non-economic harm' only 'in the case of injury to body or health or in the case of deprivation of liberty'.[103]

So it remained until the highest German Court for civil cases, the *Bundesgerichtshof*, chose to overturn the provisions of the Civil Code by invoking the post-war German Constitution (*Grundgesetz*). The Constitution provided in article 1(1): 'The worth of a human being is unassailable. It is the duty of all state power to attend to it and protect it.' It provided in article 2(1): 'Each person has the right to the free development of his personality (*Persönlichkeit*) insofar as he does not injure the rights of others and does not violate the constitutional order or moral law'. The *Bundesgerichtshof* held that these constitutional rights would lack adequate protection if a plaintiff could recover damages only if he had suffered pecuniary loss. In 1954, it declared that *Persönlichkeit*—'personality'—was a 'similar right' within the meaning of § 823(1) of the German Civil Code. It held that a newspaper had violated this right by publishing a letter written by a lawyer on his client's behalf as though it was written by him spontaneously and expressed his own views.[104]

German law therefore has become much like the law of France. There is a uniform action for damages in tort which embraces, not only injuries to property and person, but to a vague conglomeration of interests which the French describe as *dommage morale* or a private life and the Germans as rights to *Persönlichkeit*. Whatever else these rights include, they do encompass protection of one's dignity and reputation, most often, even if the defendant has lost his reputation because the plaintiff told the truth.

e. Overview

One can see a remarkable degree of continuity in the civil law. Rights to dignity and reputation have always been protected. The late scholastics developed a theory of what these rights were and why they should be protected, but their protection predated and outlasted their theory. The canonists and late scholastics endorsed remedies—apology and retraction—which were accepted by the civil law but have since passed away, yet the reason for the passing seems to have been a change of concern: from what a moral person should do to make up for his offense to what remedy would be legally effective. Their passing meant a return to the Roman remedy of monetary damages. The German Civil Code abolished the right to monetary damages because a majority of the drafters accepted the position—voiced by minorities long before and in other countries—that damages were not an acceptable compensation for the loss of dignity or reputation. But German courts reinstituted the remedy.

There is one difference from the past, however, other than the abolition of the remedies of apology and retraction. While dignity and reputation are protected, injury to these rights is now described in larger and vaguer terms. Their infringement is considered an instance, of *dommage morale* or an intrusion into 'private life' in France. It is considered a violation of personality or *Persönlichkeit* in Germany. It is not at all clear what the use of those terms has contributed to the development of the law protecting dignity and reputation. Those terms have been held to encompass other rights as well which we will consider later in this chapter.

---

[103] German Civil Code (*Bürgerlichesgesetzbuch*) [hereinafter BGB], § 847(1).
[104] BGHZ 13, 334.

Admittedly, however, one should not confuse this continuity in the law with continuity in how people have actually been protected. As mentioned earlier, in the hierarchical societies that preceded the rise of modern democracy, people were deemed to be have different degrees of honor and dignity, and the law protected their rights accordingly. Supposedly, however, everyone did have a right which the law would protect. Although one Roman text said that no *iniuria* could be suffered by a slave,[105] another said that '*iniuria* to the slave should not be left unavenged by the praetor, especially if it occurred by beating or torture, for it is obvious that the slave himself feels these things'.[106] Medieval jurists agreed that the slave could be the victim of *iniuria* although they differed as to the protection the law afforded him.[107] From the Middle Ages to the 18th century, jurists put cases in which the victims lack social status. According to Accursius, not only is it *iniuria* to try to make a chaste woman unchaste, as a Roman text said,[108] but to try to make an unchaste woman still less so.[109] To judge from the texts he cited, he also had in mind the unchaste of the lower classes.[110] Bartolus put the case of a landowner who caught a rustic fellow in his vineyard and beat him. Bartolus took it for granted that the rustic could normally recover for *iniuria*, and asked whether he could still recover if he had previously agreed that a vineyard owner could beat him if he were found there. He could recover, according to Bartolus, because the agreement 'contains something immoral (*turpe*), namely, that the owner could commit a wrongful act'.[111] As we have seen, 16th century examples of *iniuria* included maligning the skill of carpenters[112] or the private lives of seemingly

---

[105] I. 4.4.3

[106] Dig. 47.10.15.35. Another text may not do *iniuria* to another person's slave. C. 9.35.1. The point of this last text, according to Cinus, was that 'because a slave is considered as nothing (Quia servi nihil esse putanter) there was doubt as to whether he could suffer or commit *iniuria*, which is removed by this law'. Cinus de Pistoia, *Commentarius*, to C. 9.35.1.

[107] Azo noted that while, according to this text, the slave could be the victim of *iniuria*, it was not clear that he had an action in his own name. Azo Portius, *Ad singulas leges xii librorum Codicis Iustinianei commentarius* (Paris, 1577), to C. 9.35.1. Odofredus concluded that even for *iniuria* to the slave himself, the action must be brought by his master. Odofredus, *Lectura super Codice, Opera Rariora Iuridica* 2 (Bologna, 1969), to C. 9.35.1. Accursius reconciled these texts in a formalistic manner. While the slave had no action as a matter of *ius civile* or civil law, he did as a matter of *ius naturale* or natural law. *Glossa ordinaria* (Venice, 1581), to I. 1.4.3 to *nulla iniuria*. He had in mind a text which said that while a slave counts for nothing as a matter of civil law, the natural law is different because as a matter of natural law all men are equal. Dig. 50.17.33. His response might suggest that while some sort of natural right of the slave has been violated, he has no legal redress, but that does not seem to be what Accursius meant. The texts he cites are instances in which, expressly or by implication, the slave does have some form of legal redress. One of these texts says that if one slave does *iniuria* to another, one should proceed as though the master were the victim. Dig. 47.10.18.1. Accursius notes, 'sed non in tantum', meaning that the slave should recover, but not as much as if the victim had been his master (*Glossa ordinaria* to Dig. 47.10.18.1, citing Dig. 47.10.12 sec. pen., which observes that the severity of an *iniuria* depends on the status of the person offended). The other two texts allow a slave legal redress even against his own master. Dig. 1.6.2.; I. 1.8.2. Thus Accursius seems to have meant that the source of the slave's right is *ius naturale* rather than *ius civile*. In contrast, 17th and 18th century jurists generally held that while a slave is protected by praetor, he cannot suffer *iniuria qua* slave. Iohannes Voet, *Commentarius ad Pandectas* (5th edn., The Hague, 1726), to Dig. 47.10, § 4, p. 989; Arnold Vinnius, *In quatuor libros Institutionum imperialium commentarius academicus et forensis* (Venice, 1747), to I. 4.4.3.

[108] Dig. 47.10.10.   [109] *Glossa ordinaria* to Dig. 47.10.10 to *impudicus*.

[110] Dig. 11.3.1 last sec., which says that to corrupt a slave is to make a good slave bad or a bad one worse.

[111] Bartolus de Saxoferrato, *Commentaria* to Dig. 47.10.1.5 no. 3.

[112] Azpeilcueta, *Commentaria*, f. 8r nos. 458–9.

pious humble women (*mulierculae*) who live on alms.[113] A prostitute could not complain if someone said she admitted a man at night, but that was because she habitually did so, and so had no reputation to lose.[114] Analogously, a man who had committed 100 homicides could not complain if he was accused of 101st,[115] but he could if he was notorious for one type of wrongdoing but was accused of another.[116] Children and madmen could be insulted, and the jurists do not suggest that they must be upper class children or madmen.[117] I have read no source which claims that only the upper class had a legal right to vindicate their honor or reputation. While James Whitman notes that little protection was accorded the honor or dignity of the lower classes, his citations show, not that they were not legally entitled to redress, but that their chances of obtaining it were slight.[118] That is undoubtedly true. It is hard to imagine Leporello suing Don Giovanni for calling him a *birbone*. Reading the law in force to understand how rights were actually protected would be an historical mistake, like reading the Fourteenth Amendment to the American Constitution to learn how the rights of newly freed slaves were protected after the Civil War.

On the other hand, one can make the reverse mistake and conclude that the law has changed because of a change in how dignity and reputation are regarded in society. Many rules protecting property and contract have remained the same whether the they govern cows or computer chips, and whether the ownership of property is regarded as a source of social prestige or merely as a commodity. As we have seen, despite the continuity just described, there was both a conceptual change and a practical change in the rules protecting dignity and reputation. In my view, neither of them have much to do with changes in how dignity and reputation are regarded in society.

The conceptual change wrought by the late scholastics was to subsume the Roman actions for redress of injury within a common concept, the violation of commutative justice, and to limit relief to violations of dignity and reputation. Today, the rights are still protected although others are protected as well. These conceptual changes seems to have nothing to do with a change in the social significance of honor or dignity.

The practical change was first, to supplement the damage remedy of action of *iniuria* by claims for retraction or apology, and later, to abolish such claims. These claims had been recognized by the canon lawyers, theoretically explained by the late scholastics, adopted by the civil courts and persisted into the 18th century. In France, they were abolished almost by accident, since they had not been mentioned by Pothier and were not discussed by the drafters of the Code. They were abolished in Germany because the jurists of the time thought them insufficient to re-establish a person's good name. The alternatives, therefore, were to give a damage remedy or to deny any civil remedy at all. Some French and German jurists made the same arguments against a civil remedy: one could not restore honor by money, and that it was squalid for the plaintiff to try to do so. In France, these arguments did not prevail. In Germany, among a majority of the drafters, they did. In 1954, when German

---

[113] Soto, *De iustitia et iure*, lib. 5, Q. 10, a. 2.   [114] ibid. lib. 4, Q. 6, a. 3.

[115] Azpilcueta, *Commentaria*, f. 60r, no. 865.   [116] ibid. 59v, no. 858.

[117] Azpilcueta, *Commentaria*, f. 9r, no. 466; Lauterbach, *Collegii theoretico-practici* to D. 47.10, § 1, VIII; Iohannes Brunnemann, *Commentaria in quinquaginta libros pandectarum* (Genoa, 1762), to Dig. 47.10.3.

[118] Whitman, 'The Two Western Cultures of Privacy', 1165–6.

courts reinstituted the remedy for civil damages, they said that otherwise human dignity could not receive the protection mandated by the constitution. Doubtless, dignity and reputation were conceived more democratically by the post-war German judges than in the time of the drafters. But one cannot conclude that the drafters thought that their protection was less important than the post-war judges. One can say that the judges, unlike the drafters, thought that these rights could be adequately and honorably protected by remedy for damages. Had the drafters thought so, they would not have amended the original draft to abolish the right to money damages.

2. Common Law

a. Reputation

Traditionally, the only common law action that protected reputation was defamation. False statements of fact that injured the defendant's reputation were actionable but true statements were not. Unlike civil law, truth was an absolute defense whether the making of the statement was in the public interest or not.

In both the United States and England, some true statements that harm another's reputation have become actionable, not by changing the law of defamation, but by developing new causes of action. In the United States, courts have recognized a 'right to privacy' which, among other things, protects a plaintiff against the 'disclosure of embarrassing private facts'. From the beginning, however, this right was conceived to go beyond protection of dignity and reputation. The suggestion that courts recognize such a right was initially proposed in a famous article in 1890 by Samuel Warren and and his law partner, Louis Brandeis.[119] Warren was a person of high social stature who was offended when a description of one his society dinners appeared in a newspaper. A description of a high society dinner, in itself, would not lower the reputation of the hosts. The existence of a right to privacy was then claimed, and rejected, in 1902, in a widely discussed New York case, *Roberson* v. *Rochester Folding Box Co.*, in which much of the opinion was devoted to refuting Warren and Brandeis. In that case, the defendants had, without consent, used the picture of an attractive young woman with the caption 'Flour of the Family' on advertisements for Franklin Mills flour. Reaction to the decision was swift. New York passed a statute against using 'the name, portrait or picture of any living person' for 'advertising purposes or the purposes of trade'.[120] Some American courts then recognized the right not to have one's picture or name used in advertising as a matter of common law.[121] William Prosser, who tried to classify the cases which held a right to privacy was infringed, eventually called the right violated here the commercial appropriation of the name or likeness of another.[122] Violation of that type of right will be discussed later.

In other cases, however, true statements that clearly did affect one's reputation were held to be violations of the right to privacy. In 1927, the Kentucky Supreme Court held the defendant liable for putting up a large sign notifying passers-by that the plaintiff had persistently refused to pay a debt. The plaintiff said that his reputation

---

[119] 'The Right to Privacy', *Harv. L. Rev.* 4 (1890), 193.
[120] New York Civil Rights Law, § 50 (McKinney, 1976).
[121] *Pavesich* v. *New England Life Ins. Co.*, 50 SE 68 (Ga 1905); *Hinish* v. *Meier & Frank Co*, 113 P2d 438 (Or 1941).   [122] William Prosser, 'Privacy', *Calif. L. Rev.* 48 (1960), 383 at 389.

had been impugned: others 'had formed an evil opinion of him'. The court said his 'right to privacy' had been violated.[123]

At first, the cases protecting a 'right to privacy' seemed to lack any common thread. In the 1960 article just mentioned, Prosser classified these cases into four categories: '(1) Intrusion upon plaintiff's seclusion and solitude, including his private affairs[;] (2) Public disclosure of embarrassing private facts about the plaintiff[;] (3) Publicity which places the plaintiff in a false light in the public eye; and (4) Appropriation, for the defendant's advantage, of the plaintiff's name or likeness'. Prosser did not explore the underlying reasons for protecting the plaintiff in these four instances. He did not explain why a disclosure of embarrassing facts had to be 'public', why putting the plaintiff in a 'false light' should be actionable if doing so was not defamatory or the requirement that doing so must be by giving 'publicity' which placed plaintiff in a false light in 'the public eye'. He was unclear about the nature of the 'privacy' that these actions were supposed to protect. Nevertheless, through the influence of the *Restatement (Second) of Torts*, of which he served as Reporter, they became accepted as the basis the American law of 'privacy'.

Even though the defamation cases continued to speak of reputation, courts protecting the right of privacy most commonly characterized plaintiff's complaint as one for the mental suffering caused by plaintiff's action. Since different things will make different people suffer the *Second Restatement* tried to use more objective language: 'one who gives publicity to a matter concerning the private life of another' which is not a matter of legitimate concern is liable if 'the matter publicized would be highly offensive to a reasonable person . . . .'.[124] Thus the test is supposed to be not whether a person was insulted or his reputation impaired but whether a 'reasonable person' would be offended because of some revelation about his private life. And, as with Prosser, the disclosure must be made, not to a few individuals, but by giving the matter 'publicity'.

Whatever else this tort protects—and that will be considered later—it does protect a person against truthful statements which diminish his reputation unless—as often happens in the United States—the making of these statements is deemed in the public interest or protected by the constitutional right of freedom of speech. In *Melvin* v. *Reid*, the defendant was held liable for revealing (albeit using plaintiff's maiden name), that she had once been a prostitute who had been accused though acquitted of murder. She had since reformed, married into respectable society and made friends who did not know her past.[125] In *Briscoe* v. *Reader's Digest*,[126] the defendant was held liable for mentioning that the plaintiff had once stolen a 'valuable looking truck' and, after a gun battle with police, had discovered he had hijacked four bowling pin spotters. In the 11 years since that time, plaintiff had been 'entirely rehabilitated and has thereafter at all times lived an exemplary, virtuous and honorable life [and] assumed a place in respectable society'. In *Diaz* v. *Oakland Tribune*,[127] the plaintiff, a transsexual who had taken pains to keep that fact secret, recovered against a newspaper which revealed it. As will be described later, the scope of these decisions has been

---

[123] *Brents* v. *Morgan*, 299 SW 967, 968–70 (Ky 1927).

[124] *Restatement (Second) of Torts*, § 652D (1976).   [125] 297 P 91 (Cal App 1931).

[126] 483 P2d 34 (Cal 1971). For later applications of the same doctrine, see *Forscher* v. *Bugliosi*, 608 P2d 716 (Cal 1980); *Conklin* v. *Sloss*, 86 Cal App 3d 241 (1978).   [127] 139 Cal App 3d 118 (1983).

radically circumscribed by others which speak of legitimate public interest or freedom of speech. It is clear, however, that whatever other rights are protected by the tort of 'disclosure of embarrassing private facts', one has the right to have one's reputation protected against truthful disclosures.

One may well wonder, then, why the tort supposedly only protects against giving 'publicity' to the facts disclosed rather than against merely making the disclosure. The tort of defamation protects reputation but there is no analogous requirement: 'publication' is required but that means disclosure to any third party. As the courts mention, the reformed hijacker and prostitute and the transsexual suffered from the revelation of their past, but most acutely, one presumes, because of its influence on the opinion of those they knew, not those who did not know them, read their stories in a newspaper and forgot their names by the end of the day.

In contrast, English courts have said that they will not recognize a right to privacy.[128] Still, they have managed to protect truthful disclosures that harm another's reputation by developing a tort of breach of confidence. Initially, the action was one for disclosing information one had received in confidence. In *Stephens* v. *Avery*, it was held that plaintiff could recover from a defendant to whom she had revealed in confidence her lesbian relationship with a woman who, in a crime which made a sensation in the tabloids, had been killed by her husband.[129] American courts have not taken this path. When Ralph Nader recovered against General Motors for invading his privacy, one of the company's acts for which the court did not impose liability was the company's attempt to ferret out discreditable information Nader had imparted to his acquaintances.[130] Nevertheless, English courts have now transformed the action by dropping the requirement that confidence be reposed by the plaintiff in the defendant. That requirement was rejected in two decisions in which a well-known actor had granted exclusive rights to pictures about his wedding to one newspaper and they had been appropriated by another.[131] In *Campbell* v. *MGN Ltd.*[132] the House of Lords held that a newspaper had violated a fashion model's rights by publishing photographs of her arrival at a meeting of Narcotics Anonymous. She was a prominent person who had publicly denied taking drugs. All of the judges believed that because she had lied, the newspaper had the right to set the record straight. Whether they were right will be discussed later on. The issue then became whether the newspaper could also publish a picture of her emerging from a treatment center. That was a matter on which the judges disagreed. Nevertheless, all of them did agree that had she not been a public figure who had not lied, she would have an action for breach of confidence even though the newspaper told the truth and she had never reposed confidence in the newspaper. Lord Nicholls reaffirmed that English law recognized no general right of privacy. Yet he said the case turned on respect 'for one aspect of an individual's privacy' which 'lies at the heart of liberty in a modern state because [a] proper degree of privacy is essential for the well-being and development of an individual'. He did not confine the decision to disclosures about another's reputation. 'An individual's privacy can be invaded in ways

---

[128] *Wainright* v. *Home Office*, [2003] UKHL 53.   [129] [1988] 1 Ch 457.
[130] *Nader* v. *General Motors*, 255 NE2d 765 (NY 1970).
[131] *Douglas* v. *Hello! Ltd*, [2001] 2 WLR 992 (CA); [2003] EWHC 786 (Ch).
[132] [2004] UKHL.

not involving publication of information. Strip-searches are an example.' But he, like the other judges, refused to pass on how far such rights extend. As Basil Markesinis has noted, since the court did not recognize a 'right to privacy' and continued to speak of breach of 'confidence', it is not at all clear how far its decision extends.[133] One would think it extends very far. An action that began as one for breach of confidence now extends to the disclosure of 'private facts' absent anything one would normally call a confidential relationship. The court acknowledged that one must balance the harm done against the public interest in disclosure. Absent such an interest, however, it seems clear that despite the traditional limitations on the law of defamation, the disclosure of true facts that lower a person's reputation is actionable.

If that is so—except in cases in which the public has an interest in the disclosure—then all the legal systems we have examined have rejected the idea that a person has no right to a reputation that can be destroyed by revealing the true facts about him. It may seem that the law is then protecting a right he does not deserve. But a good reason for doing so was advanced by the late scholastics.[134] If a person is using an undeserved reputation to do harm, there is a public interest in exposing him. If he is not, as in the case of the reformed criminal who is now living a life of benefit to society, disclosure can only cause harm to him and others.

If that is so, then we should question the premise that all the judges accepted in *Campbell* v. *MGN Ltd.* They thought that once the plaintiff had publicly denied taking drugs, unlike other fashion models, the newspapers had the right to set the record straight on that issue, whether or not they could print pictures of her leaving a meeting of Narcotics Anonymous. But if a reputation is worth preserving, provided its preservation does good and not harm, why should that be true? She lied. One should not lie. But even Lessius, who had qualms about a moral reputation preserved by lies, did not think the truth could be revealed unless some public interest was at stake.[135] In this case, why is there any public interest in setting the record straight? It is not the case of a politician taking graft. It is the case of a role model—in sports, theater, or here in fashion—claiming virtues she does not possess. It has been said that hypocrisy is the tribute that vice pays to virtue. It is hard to see the public interest in rejecting that tribute.

b. Insult
The extent to which a person is now protected against insult or indignity is another question, and one which is again veiled by the description of the claim as one for invasion of privacy or disclosure of 'private facts'.

Traditionally, while the plaintiff could recover for false statements of fact, supposedly, he could not recover for insult. As mentioned earlier,[136] however, courts found various ways to award damages for insulting portrayals of the plaintiff by wedging them within one of the common law forms of action. Sometimes, what might pass as vituperation was read to imply a false statement of fact and hence as defamation.

---

[133] Basil Markesinis, Colm O'Cinneide, Jörg Fedtke, and Myriam Hunter-Henin, 'Concerns and Ideas about the Developing English Law of Privacy (and How Knowledge of Foreign Law Might be of Help)', *Am. J. Comp. L.* 52 (2004), 133.   [134] Chapter 11 I A 1 b i.

[135] Lessius, *De iustitia et iure*, lib. 2, cap. 11, dub. 10, nos. 65–7.   [136] Chapter 9 II B.

In 19th century New York, Horace Greeley not only said that James Fenimore Cooper was 'proud, captious, censorious, arbitrary, dogmatical, malicious, illiberal, vengeful and litigious'. That much would sound only insulting. But Greeley's newspaper said that Cooper was therefore in bad repute in Oswego where he lived. That was held to be actionable as a statement of fact.[137] Sometimes, as the treatise writers themselves acknowledged, plaintiffs recovered for defamation because they had been made to look ridiculous although no false statements were made.[138] In one American case, a man who had consented to have his picture used in an advertisement recovered because the picture had made him look ludicrously deformed.[139] Sometimes, a plaintiff recovered in defamation because a statement was made about him which was degrading but did not impute any dishonorable conduct. In an English case, a Russian princess recovered because she was depicted in a film as having been raped by Rasputin.[140] Rape is an extreme injury to human dignity, and hence to say that someone has been raped is to say her dignity was injured. But the film did not imply she was a woman of bad reputation. Sometimes, portraying the defendant in undignified circumstances was held to be defamation because of the possibility that people would assume he had consented to the portrayal. To imply that he consented was said to constitute a falsehood. That was the rationale of the English case of *Kaye v. Robinson*, in which newspaper photographers printed photographs they had published of a well-known actor who was hospitalized, seriously injured and, the court said, in no state to give his consent.[141]

At other times, courts have piggy-backed damages for loss of dignity onto some other tort. As mentioned, the traditional common law rule that any unauthorized contact with another's person constituted a battery—for example by striking his hat or walking stick—was acknowledged by the treatise writers as protection against contact which was not harmful but offensive.[142] According to Harper, Prosser and the *Restatements*, the interest protected in such cases was the freedom from offensive contact. Thus an unwanted kiss, however well intended, might be a battery.[143] In an American case, it was held to be a battery to blow cigar smoke into the face of one who was publicly warning about the dangers of secondary smoke. The court held that 'tobacco smoke, as "particulate matter," has the physical properties capable of making contact'[144] and therefore of constituting a battery.

---

[137] *Cooper v. Greeley*, 1 Denio 347 (NY 1845).

[138] Francis Hilliard, *The Law of Torts and Private Wrongs* 1 (Boston, 1859), 267; Francis M. Burdick, *The Law of Torts: A Concise Treatise on the Civil Liability at Common Law and Under Modern Statutes for Actionable Wrongs to Person and Property* (2nd edn., Albany, NY, 1908), 302; John W. Salmond, *The Law of Torts: A Treatise on the English Law of Liability for Civil Injuries* (4th edn., London, 1916), 451; Fowler Vincent Harper, *A Treatise on the Law of Torts: A Preliminary Treatise on Civil Liability for Harms to Legally Protected Interests* (Indianapolis, 1933), 499; William L. Prosser, *Handbook of the Law of Torts* (St Paul, Minn., 1941), 783.

[139] *Burton v. Crowell Publishing Co.*, 82 F2d 154 (2d Cir 1936) (L Hand, J). The case the earlier treatise writers cite is *Cook v. Ward*, 6 Bing 409 (1830) (liability in defamation for a humorous story).

[140] *Youssoupoff v. Metro-Goldwyn-Mayer Pictures*, 50 TLR 581 (CA 1934).

[141] *Kaye v. Robertson*, [1991] FSR 62 (CA).   [142] Prosser, *Torts*, 45; Harper, *Torts*, 40–1.

[143] R. F. V. Heuston and R. A. Buckley, *Salmond and Heuston on the Law of Torts* (21st edn., London, 1996), 120.

[144] *Leichtman v. WLW Jacor Communications, Inc.*, 634 NE 2d 697 (Ohio App 1994).

A plaintiff whose dignity was offended might also recover for trespass to land, even if the defendant had not harmed his property, provided the defendant had entered it. For example, a gas company was held liable when its meter reader screamed insults at a woman because he made the mistake of putting his hand in her doorway, thereby committing trespass.[145]

In the United States, rights against insult, and others as well, were protected by inventing a new tort: an action for intentional infliction of emotional distress. The starting point was an English case which need not be taken to stand for any such broad principle. In *Wilkinson* v. *Downton*,[146] the defendant, as a practical joke, told the plaintiff her husband had broken both legs in an accident and needed her help to get home. This was held actionable on the curious ground that the plaintiff had suffered, not merely emotional distress, but physical harm which the defendant was deemed to have intended, although the possibility of physical harm may not crossed his mind. In any event, American courts developed an action which is defined in the *Second Restatement of Torts* as 'intentionally or recklessly' causing 'severe emotional distress' to another by 'extreme or outrageous conduct'.[147]

Whatever else that broad language includes, it does include cases of insulting the plaintiff or, what is the same, portraying him in a degrading position, at least when the distress is regarded as 'severe' and the conduct 'extreme and outrageous'. For example, in *Halio* v. *Lurie*,[148] the plaintiff and defendant had been 'keeping company' for two years with the expectation of marriage, the defendant had then married another woman without telling the plaintiff, and then written her letters mocking her feelings toward him, and explaining she was a subject of amusement to his new wife and himself. In *Flamm* v. *Van Nierop*,[149] defendant was held liable for 'dashing at plaintiff with threatening gestures and malign looks accompanied by derisive laughter, walking closely behind or beside or in front of plaintiff on the public streets, telephoning plaintiff at his home and place of business and then either hanging up or remaining on the line in silence, and driving his automobile behind that of plaintiff at a dangerously close distance . . .'. Courts have been particularly sensitive to insults directed at racial minorities.[150] That is to be expected in a democracy, just as in the unapologetically hierarchical societies of the past, the law was especially sensitive to the dignity of the highly placed.

In England, where recovery is supposed to rest on breach of 'confidence', an action would seem to be limited the disclosure of 'private information'. But suppose the 'private information' is not objectionable because of what it reveals, but because it portrays the plaintiff in a position some might regard as degrading. In *Campbell*, the plaintiff recovered, not because the newspaper said she was a drug addict, but for publishing a picture of her taken outside a treatment center. The judges argued over whether this picture was in any way demeaning.

---

[145] *Bouillon* v. *Laclede Gaslight Co.*, 129 SW 401 (Mo App 1910).   [146] [1987] 2 QB 57.
[147] *Restatement (Second) of Torts*, § 46 (1966).   [148] 222 NYS 2d 759 (NY AD 1961).
[149] 291 NYS 2d 189 (NY AD 1968).
[150] E.g., *Alcorn* v. *Anbro Engineering, Inc.*, 468 P2d 216 (Cal 1970) (plaintiff called a 'god damn nigger' by his white foreman); *Gomez* v. *Hug*, 645 P2d 916 (Kan App 1982) (plaintiff, a county employee, called a 'fucking spic', a 'fucking Mexican greaser' and 'nothing but a pile of shit' by the county commissioner); *Wiggs* v. *Courshon*, 355 FSupp. 206 (SD Fla 1973) (plaintiff called a 'black son of a bitch' by the waitress who brought him his food).

It is worth noting, however, that the House of Lords wrote its decision after the enactment of the United Kingdom Human Rights Act 1998, incorporating in the domestic law of England the European Convention on Human Rights and in particular the guarantee of the right to privacy in Article 8 of the Convention. As we have seen, English courts claim they do not need to recognize a general right of privacy to afford this guarantee. It is enough to expand the actions they have. It is too soon to tell how far they will go in doing so.

3. Differences

In all the legal systems we have examined, one whose reputation is injured even by disclosure of the truth can sometimes recover damages. One whose dignity is injured by insult can sometimes do so except that in England he must bring his case within one of the recognized causes of action. Courts and commentators, however, are less likely to speak specifically of an offense to reputation or dignity but generally of *dommage morale, la vie privée, Persönlichkeit*, privacy, the disclosure of embarrassing private facts, the intentional infliction of mental distress, or breach of confidence.

Nevertheless, civil law systems are more inclined to allow one to recover for any infringement of dignity and reputation. Lawsuits rarely concern relatively trivial violations of others' rights. Still, in France and Germany, unlike the United States, conduct need not be outrageous or distress severe for the plaintiff to have an action. The reason, I believe, is a difference in the way these rights are regarded.

In the United States and England, the plaintiff was traditionally allowed to recover in defamation for any untruth that adversely reflected on his reputation, often without needing to prove mental distress or any other specific harm. In England, it is too soon to see what limits judges will impose on an action for breach of confidence. In the United States, however, in contrast to defamation, the *Restatement (Second) of Torts* allows recovery for the disclosure of embarrassing private facts only if 'the matter publicized would be highly offensive to a reasonable person . . .'.[151] It allows recovery for 'intentional infliction of emotional distress' only when the distress is 'severe' and caused by 'extreme or outrageous conduct'.[152] According to Official Comment d, 'The liability does not extend to mere insults, indignities, threats, annoyances, petty oppressions, and other trivialities. . . . [P]laintiffs must expect to be hardened to a certain amount of rough language.' By comparison, not only defamation, but other traditional torts such as trespass and battery are actionable whether or not the conduct was outrageous and regardless of how severely the defendant suffered.

In civil law systems it has always been otherwise. As we have seen, in Roman law, a defendant could be held liable for ridiculing the plaintiff in a song,[153] or 'accosting' a woman by using 'smooth words' to make an indecent proposal,[154] or for using base language.[155] Reinhard Zimmermann gives some examples from 18th century Germany. It was *iniuria* to taunt a person with his natural impediment by calling him a cripple or a hunchback, to use obscene language, particularly in the presence of a

---

[151] *Restatement (Second) of Torts*, § 652D (1965).   [152] ibid. § 46.
[153] Dig. 47.10.15.27.   [154] Dig. 47.10.15.20.   [155] Dig. 47.10.15.21.

virgin, to use the familiar form of address (*du*) when talking to someone of honorable status who should be addressed more formally (as *sie*) and to make faces or to stick one's tongue out at someone else.[156] Dignity was a right, and to violate it was therefore actionable.

Similarly, Jean Larguier and Anne-Marie Larguier[157] list expressions for which French courts have held the defendant responsible: 'bandit, riffraff (*canaille*), traitor, pirate, little demagogue, filth, mountain of dung, dirty sewer stream, tart kosher pork butcher, *buse* (which means 'buzzard' but can be used figuratively to mean blockhead), [and] paranoid'. In Germany, courts have acknowledged that one can be responsible for addressing a person by the familiar pronoun when it is intended as an insult[158] or for calling prison guards 'shit bulls' (*Scheissbüllen*).[159] While some of these French and German cases were criminal prosecutions, the same rules are supposed to apply as in civil cases.

If insult as such is actionable, it is not a defense that no serious harm was done. Defendants have to claim that the language they used was not insulting at all. In France, when a Jewish television journalist was called a 'tart kosher pork butcher *(charcutière)*' defendant had to claim that 'tart' plausibly could be understood as a compliment, 'butcher' was 'a profession perfectly worthy of esteem, evoking as well good health, a certain assurance of one's self' and, although a *charcutière* was the type of butcher who normally dressed pork, it could refer to a butcher who handled kosher meats. He lost as the court found he clearly had intended an anti-semitic insult.[160] In another French case, the defendant accused the plaintiff of 'hysteria'. The defense was that 'hysteria' refers 'to a sickness or, at the most, a disorder of the nervous system'. The court held the defendant responsible since, in context, the remark had nothing to do with plaintiff's medical condition but was meant as a reflection on her character.[161]

In a German case, a woman accused a man of insulting her by using the familiar pronoun even though, before they quarreled, they had lived in the same house and used the familiar term of address. The trial court held the man responsible for insulting her because she had told him she no longer wished to be addressed in the familiar way. The appellate court reversed, not on the ground that such an insult was insignificant, but that there was no clear proof that the expression was intended as an insult.[162] The woman who called the prison guards 'shit bulls' fared less well. The trial court held that in context the remark could be taken as 'a simple expression of displeasure over, "a most unlovable place and a protest against the treatment directed against the speaker and not as the abuse of an individual standing near her"'. The *Bundesgerichtshof* rejected that view. The words had been directed at the guards and accompanied by a threat to kick them in a delicate part of their anatomy.[163] In all these cases, the defense, then, was not that 'the plaintiff must be expected and required to be hardened

156 *Obligations*, 1065–6.
157 Jean Larguier and Anne-Marie Larguier, *Droit pénale special* (8th edn., Paris, 1994).
158 OLG, Düsseldorf, 10 Aug. 1989, JR 1990, 345.
159 OLG, Oldenburg, 31 July 1989, JR 1990, 1217.
160 Cour d'appel, Paris, 15 Feb. 1988, JCP 1988.II.21115.
161 Cass., Ch. crim., 3 Dec. 1970, pourvoi no. 69-92.381(unpublished).
162 OLG, Düsseldorf, 10 Aug. 1989, JR 1990, 345.
163 OLG, Oldenburg, 31 July 1989, JR 1990, 1217.

to a certain amount of rough language', as the *Second Restatement* put it, but that he had not been insulted. If he was, the defendant was held responsible.

These cases may make the civil law look overly sensitive and protective. In many of them, an American might regard the harm done as trivial and believe the defendant should simply have a thicker skin. One might imagine that those who live in civil law jurisdictions regard it as worse to insult someone and more egregious when one is insulted.

I, personally, have not noticed such a difference while living in European countries. But in any event, one cannot conclude that a right is taken more seriously simply because any violation is actionable. In common law, traditionally, one could recover for false statement that diminishes reputation whether or not it was outrageous or the damages severe. Unlike Europe, the common law plaintiff had an action whenever anyone set foot on his land. He could recover in battery for the most trivial of insults provided that it was accompanied by physical harm—being shoved, hit by a spitball, shot with a water pistol or, as we have seen, having smoke blown in his face. One cannot conclude that Americans do not care about true statements that injure reputation but are extremely sensitive to false ones, or that they object more than Europeans when someone cuts across their property, or that they regard a trivial insult accompanied by physical contract as inherently more serious than a grave one which is not.

I think a better explanation is that medieval English courts, for reasons that have nothing to do with modern American culture, happened to limit the traditional forms of action as they did. Why they did so is obscure, but it was not due to reflection on what wrongs the law in principle should address. As we have seen, except for Blackstone, it was only in the 19th century that jurists tried explicitly to identify rights that the traditional forms of action were supposed to protect. The result of that effort was to leave unexplained gaps in the rights protected. In the United States, in the 20th century, the torts of disclosure of embarrassing private facts and intentional infliction of emotional distress were invented to fill some of those gaps.

Just because these torts were novelties, it is understandable that jurists such as Prosser tried to promote them by limiting them to extreme cases. That sidestepped the charge that the courts would be flooded with trivialities. That fear had not inspired a demand to reform the traditional English forms of action where the courts are not jammed with such cases even though, as we have seen, the plaintiff can often sue over a triviality. Nor has such a fear induced Europeans to limit relief. People rarely sue over a triviality, and although one can find cases in which they have, European courts have not been swamped. As we have seen, when the Germans abolished a civil action for such harms from 1900 to 1954, the reason was not the frequency of lawsuits but doubts as to whether money damages were an appropriate remedy.

Moreover, the idea has been ingrained in civil law jurisdictions since the time of the late scholastics that rights to dignity and reputation are rights to be protected much in the same sense that property is a right. This idea endured long after Aristotelian theories concerned with why such rights should be protected were forgotten. In both Europe and America, this idea is obscured by speaking vaguely about *dommage morale*, privacy and *Persönlichkeit*. Surely, a person cannot be legally secured against every act that would diminish his privacy or hamper the free development of his personality.

In the United States, however, discussion began with the general idea 'privacy', and then conceived of privacy in terms of protection against 'embarrassment' or 'emotional distress', that is, in terms of mental suffering experienced by the plaintiff. The law cannot protect a person against any sort of embarrassment, emotional distress or mental suffering. Consequently, according to the *Restatement*, the facts disclosed must be 'be highly offensive to a reasonable person . . .'.[164] The 'emotional distress' must be 'severe'.[165] The rights protected by these new torts were therefore described differently than conventional rights. When the law protects property, for example, an American, like a European, would identify the right protected as property, not a right against the mental suffering caused by its loss. The taking of another's property, however trivial, is actionable, not because it causes mental distress, but because the owner has a right to his property. Civil lawyers treat dignity and reputation as distinct rights, like property, when they allow an action for their violation independent of whatever embarrassment or distress the plaintiff has suffered. They do so even though, like Americans, they now speak in terms of *dommage morale* or suffering, *Persönlichkeit*, or personality, or in terms of privacy.

Despite this general language, I believe that the civil lawyers have held on to a truth which Americans are only beginning to grasp. Dignity and reputation belong to a person in much the way property belongs to him. For practical reasons, such as to avoid a flood of litigation, one might allow these rights to be infringed, even though, as we have seen, that is not much of a danger. As we will see, these rights must also be limited by the public interest in the exchange of information. But otherwise, if they are rights which in principle should not be infringed, then what matters is their infringement, not whatever mental suffering it may or may not cause.

Robert Post has criticized the view that protection of the right to privacy in America is essentially a protection of 'injury to the inner person' to a 'plaintiff's emotions and his mental suffering'.[166] He points out that one simply cannot understand even America law in these terms. Redress is not given simply for causing mental suffering. One cannot explain the limits on relief by asking what is 'outrageous' or what emotional distress is 'severe'. Courts do not allow the answer to depend on the feelings of the individual plaintiff. Nor can it depend on an appeal to the feelings of a 'reasonable person' or 'community standards' since these are abstractions, and do not explain why some of these feelings or standards are legally relevant and others are not. Ultimately, Post argues, the rules at stake are normative standards of 'civility' which govern the 'deference and demeanor' which one individual has a right to expect from others in society. Post suggests that such rules constitute the society in which an individual lives, and therefore the status of an individual as a member of that society, which Post calls his 'social personality'. The law is concerned 'not [with] actual injury to the personality of specific individuals but rather on the protection of the personality which would be constituted by full observance of the rules of deference and demeanor, those whose violation would appropriately cause outrage and affront'. Post calls them 'civility rules'.[167] According to Post, these considerations explain why the victim need not

---

[164] *Restatement (Second) of Torts*, § 652D (1965).   [165] ibid. § 46.

[166] Robert C. Post, *Constitutional Domains* (Cambridge, Mass., 1995), 51.   [167] ibid. 56.

prove he has actually suffered. 'An intrusion on privacy is *intrinsically* harmful because it is defined as that which injures social personality'.[168] 'Dignitary harm depends not on the psychological condition of an individual plaintiff but rather on the forms of respect that a plaintiff is entitled to receive from others.'[169] The *Restatements* may speak of mental suffering, but, as Post points out, the *First Restatement* provided that damages could be awarded 'in the same way in which general damages are awarded for defamation'.[170] The *Second Restatement* provides that the plaintiff can recover damages for 'the harm to his interest in privacy' as well as for 'his mental distress'.[171] That makes sense only if we regard the harm to the plaintiff not merely as mental distress but in the violation of the civility with which he is entitled to be treated.

Post explains the American limitation to conduct that is 'highly offensive' by the danger that the legal system would 'otherwise be inundated by trivial lawsuits',[172] a concern which we have suggested may be exaggerated. But he regards 'dignitary harm' as a violation of a right which belongs to the plaintiff according to the 'civility rules' of a society rather than a protection against mental distress. I agree. Nevertheless, I think it would be clearer if, instead of speaking of 'civility rules' and 'social personality', we spoke in traditional terms of dignity (or honor) and of reputation. Dignity or honor refers to how a person should be treated in accord with what Post calls 'civility rules'. Reputation refers to the qualities which are esteemed in the society of which a person is a member and therefore belong to his 'social personality'.

In any case, even though our vocabulary may be different, if Post is right, to explain our protection of privacy, we must return to something like the late scholastics' explanation of *iniuria*. They described it as redress for violation of the rights to dignity and reputation which are accorded each person as a matter of distributive justice and to be protected as a matter of commutative justice. In the Aristotelian tradition, the rules of distributive justice constitute the structure of society. They concern not only property but, according to the late scholastics, honor and reputation. If honor and reputation are rights accorded to an individual, then they should be protected just as the law protects his property. That seems to me close to what Post says we must accept, not only to explain civil law, which in principle redresses any violation of these rights, but the American common law as well.

II. The Defense of Public Interest

A. Traditional Limits

1. The civil law

Although some medieval jurists said that the defendant should be liable if he spoke the truth in order to injure the plaintiff, *animo conviciandi*,[173] Iacobus de Ravanis claimed that the question should be whether the plaintiff had been accused of conduct for

---

[168] ibid.   [169] ibid. 58.

[170] ibid. 57, quoting *Restatement of Torts*, § 867 Comment d (1939).

[171] Post, *Constitutional Domains*, 57 quoting *Restatement (Second) of Torts*, § 652 H (1965).

[172] Post, *Constitutional Domains*, 65.

[173] Described by Iacobus de Ravanis, *Lectura* to C. 35.10.5.

which he is legally answerable. If so, the defendant should not be liable since there was a public interest in the revelation.[174] Petrus de Bellapertica took the same position in his *Lectura Institutionum*.[175] So did Dinus de Mugello.[176] But Petrus refined it in a *repetitio* on C. 9.35.5. The important question, indeed, is whether the disclosure is of aid or interest to the republic. But therefore, the defendant could even reveal matters for which the plaintiff was not legally answerable: for example, that the plaintiff had leprosy and might infect the city.[177] This solution became standard. It was adopted by Cinus de Pistoia[178] and by two of the greatest medieval jurists, Bartolus de Saxoferrato[179] and Baldus de Ubaldis, who added illustrations of what might interest the republic: for example, that someone is illegitimate and therefore incapable of holding some honor.[180]

In the 16th and 17th centuries, the late scholastics echoed the words of the medieval jurists: one could reveal matters that were of interest to the republic.[181] One could reveal the commission of a wrongful act so that it could be punished[182] but not if it had already been punished or was not legally punishable.[183] Molina said that one could reveal that a man was a leper[184] (echoing Petrus) or that he was illegitimate[185] (echoing Baldus). The jurists of the period added illustrations in which the revelation was justified, not by the interests of the republic as such, but by those of its citizens. One could inform a superior of the misconduct of a brother in a religious order.[186] One could expose those whose simulation of some virtue or skill threatened others: the unqualified doctor,[187] druggist,[188] artisan,[189] lawyer,[190] surgeon, knight, merchant, carpenter,[191] or, for that matter, the unqualified theologian.[192] In contrast, one could not expose the wrongs done by humble women (*mulierculae*) who, seeming to live pious lives, received alms.[193]

---

[174] Iacobus de Ravanis, *Lectura*, to C. 35.10.5.

[175] Petrus de Bellapertica, *Lectura Institutionum* (Lyons, 1536), repr. *Opera Iuridica Rariora* 11 (Bologna, 1970), to I. 4 *de iniuriis*.   [176] According to Cinus de Pistoia, *Commentaria*, to C. 9.35.5, no. 12.

[177] Petrus de Bellapertica, *Repetitio* in C. 9.35.5, no.16, in *Repetitiones in aliquot divi Iustiniani imp. Cod. leges* (Frankfurt-am-Main, 1571), repr. in Petrus de Bellapertica, *Commentaria in Digestum Novum repetitiones variae, Opera Iuridica Rariora*, 10 (Bologna, 1968) to C. 9.35.5, no. 16.

[178] Cinus de Pistoia, *Commentaria*, to C. 9.35.5, no. 12.

[179] Bartolus de Saxoferrato, *Commentaria*, to Dig. 47.10.18, no. 1.

[180] Ibid. to Dig. 47.10.18, no. 1.

[181] Soto, *De iustitia et iure*, lib. 5, Q. 10, a. 2; Molina, *De iustitia et iure*, IV, disp. 24, no. 2; disp. 38, no. 3.

[182] *Summa theologiae* II-II, Q. 62, a. 2 ad 2; Soto, *De iustitia et iure*, lib. 4, Q. 6, a. 3; Molina, *De iustitia et iure*, IV, disp. 38, no. 3.   [183] Molina, *De iustitia et iure*, IV, disp. 38, no. 3.

[184] ibid; see de Lugo, *Disputationum*, disp. 14, § 2, no. 110 (fending off plague).

[185] Molina, *De iustitia et iure* IV, disp. 38, no. 3.

[186] Lessius, *De iustitia et iure*, lib. 2, cap. 11, dub. 3, no. 11; Molina, *De iustitia et iure*, IV, disp. 24, no. 1; disp. 38, no. 3; de Lugo, *Disputationum*, disp. 14, § 2, no. 111.

[187] Soto, *De iustitia et iure*, lib. 5, Q. 10, a. 2; Molina, *De iustitia et iure*, IV, disp. 24, no. 2; Lessius, *De iustitia et iure*, lib. 2, cap. 11, dub. 10, no. 63; de Lugo, *Disputationum*, disp. 14, § 2, no. 109; Azpeilcueta, *Commentaria*, f. 8r, nos. 458–9.   [188] Lessius, *De iustitia et iure*, lib. 2, cap. 11, dub. 10, no. 63.

[189] De Lugo, *Disputationum*, disp. 14, § 2, no. 109.

[190] Lessius, *De iustitia et iure*, lib. 2, cap. 11, dub. 10, no. 63; Azpeilcueta, *Commentaria*, f. 8r, nos. 458–9.

[191] Azpeilcueta, *Commentaria*, f. 8r, nos. 458–9.   [192] Soto, *De iustitia et iure*, lib. 5, Q. 10, a. 2.

[193] ibid.

After the late scholastics, discussions of the problem typically became sketchy. Some jurists barely dealt with it. Some took the position taken by a few medieval jurists: what mattered was the defendant's intention. Had a clergyman denounced the plaintiff out of 'pious zeal'?[194] Was a criminal exposed in order to see justice done rather than to injure him? An affirmative answer was to be presumed if the crime was reported in a procedurally proper way.[195] Often, this criterion rode tandem with the question whether information is of public utility or interest. If so, supposedly, the defendant is not liable as long as he spoke without an intention to injure, for example, seeking justice rather than revenge.[196] The leading jurist Voet added that if the disclosure were for the good of the republic, the defendant's good intentions should be presumed.[197] As far as the defense of truth was concerned, not much had changed from the 13th century to the 18th.

2. The common law

Reputation was protected by the common law actions for defamation, libel and slander. Truth was a complete defense. Moreover, it was held in a series of cases that one who had spoken falsely was liable even if he reasonably believed his statement was true.[198] While the civil law defendant was liable for false statements made negligently or intentionally, defamation in England became what we would now call a 'strict liability' tort.

The public interest in disclosure was protected by recognizing qualified privileges. The privilege was 'qualified' in the sense that it could be overcome by a showing of 'actual malice'. 'Actual malice' or 'malice in fact' meant that the defendant knew the statement to be false or 'acted out of ill will or some other wrong motive' or that he made the statement 'recklessly' without regard to its truth or falsity.[199] At least that was the rule in England. Some American cases held that, to defeat the privilege, it is enough that the defendant acted 'negligently'[200] and others that it is enough that he acted in good faith.[201]

The existence of a qualified privilege was said to depend on whether the speaker, the audience or both have an interest in the making of the communication.[202] That covered cases of references for employment, and most often credit references. There was also a recognized privilege of 'fair comment' which protected opinions, as distinguished from facts, expressed on artistic and literary productions and other matters deemed to be in the public interest such as the conduct of public officials. Thus the traditional common law, like the civil law, was concerned both with the public interest and with why a false statement was made. Unlike the civil law, it regarded

---

[194] Lauterbach, *Collegii theoretico-practici* to Dig. 47.10, § 1, VI; Georg Adam Struve, *Syntagmatis iuris civilis pars altera* (Jena, 1663), Exerc. 48, to Dig. 47.10, § 56.

[195] Struve, *Syntagmatis*, Exerc. 48, to D. 47.10, § 55.

[196] Lauterbach, *Collegii theoretico-practici* to D. 47.10, § 1, XXII; Brunnemann, *Commentaria* to Dig. 47.10.18, no. 4.   [197] Voet, *Commentarius* to Dig.. 47.10, § 9, p. 993.

[198] *Bromage* v. *Prosser*, 4 B & C 247, 107 Eng Rep 1051 (1825); *Hulton & Co.* v. *Jones*, [1910] AC 20. See also *Cassidy* v. *Daily Mirror Newspapers, Ltd.*, [1929] 2 KB 331.

[199] *Clark* v. *Molyneux*, [1877] 3 QB 237.   [200] *Toothaker* v. *Conant*, 40 A 331 (Me 1898).

[201] *Barry* v. *McCollum*, 70 A 1035 (Copnn 1908).

[202] *Toogood* v. *Spyring*, 1 CM & R 181 (1834); See *Restatement of Torts*, §§ 594–6.

truth as an absolute defense even if a statement was not in the public interest. Liability for false statements depended on whether one could bring oneself within a recognized privilege, designed to protect communications in the public interest. If one could, usually, one was liable not for negligence but for 'malice', which blended considerations about defendant's ill-will with whether he knew the statement was false or was reckless with regard to its truth.

B. Democracy and the Mass Media

Traditionally, then, protection of the public interest had been primarily concerned with protecting the public against such matters as a particular person's crime, disease, or incompetence. With the rise of democracy and the increasing role of the mass media in forming opinion, it was recognized that the public had yet another interest: an interest in being educated and informed. This interest is recognized in England although it is too soon to see where its recognition will lead. It is recognized in the United States and in civil law jurisdictions also, often in very different ways.

1. The disclosure of true information which bears directly on public decision making

In a sense, when members of the public decide any issue, all of their opinions about their society and its past come into play. But it will be easiest to begin with the clear case in which the facts in question bear directly on some decision which, in a democracy, is entrusted to them: for example, the qualifications of public officials, their performance, and the prudence of the decisions they make. These decisions are in need of protection in a democracy which they would not receive in a society in which decisions are not entrusted to the electorate. Here, in common and civil law jurisdictions alike, the disclosure of such information, when true, is protected.

2. The disclosure of false information

False information benefits no one even if it does bear on public decision making. The question, however, is the standard of liability for false disclosures. The answer should depend on the value of communicating the information in question in light of the possibility that it might be true.

One approach, which was traditionally taken by the civil law, is to hold a person liable for a false statement made intentionally or negligently. That remains the rule in France and Germany where liability is subject to the ordinary rules of tort law provided by art. 1382–3 of the French Civil Code and § 823 of the German.

English law is similar. The House of Lords, in effect, adopted a negligence standard—or, as they might prefer to say, a standard of responsible journalism in 1999, in *Reynolds* v. *Times Newspapers*.[203] In that case, the House of Lords expanded the common-law qualified privilege of fair comment to provide special protection to the British media for reporting on matters of public interest. Such matters neither embraced anything of political relevance nor were restricted to politics in the narrow

[203] 3 WLR 1010, 1024 (HL 1999).

sense. In the leading opinion, Lord Nicholls listed ten factors relevant to whether a disclosure was privileged:

(1) The seriousness of the allegation. The more serious the charge, the more the public is misinformed and the individual harmed . . . (2) The nature of the information, and the extent to which the subject matter is a matter of public concern. (3) The source of the information. Some informants have no direct knowledge of the events. Some have their own axes to grind, or are being paid . . . (4) The steps taken to verify the information. (5) The status of the information. The allegation may have already been the subject of an investigation which commands respect. (6) The urgency of the matter. News is often a perishable commodity. (7) Whether comment was sought from the plaintiff . . . An approach to the plaintiff will not always be necessary. (8) Whether the article contained the gist of the plaintiff's side of the story. (9) The tone of the article. A newspaper can raise queries or call for an investigation. It need not adopt allegations as statements of fact. (10) The circumstances of the publication, including the timing.[204]

One of these standards concerns the degree to which the public is legitimately concerned with the information in question. Another concerns the degree to which the defendant may be hurt. The rest concern the care the publisher has taken to ascertain the truth. Thus the standard for liability seems indistinguishable from a standard of negligence.[205] In a later case, *Bonnick* v. *Morris*,[206] the Privy Council said that 'a journalist should not be penalized for making a wrong decision on a question of meaning on which people might reasonably take different views'.[207] In *Al-Fagih* v. *H H Saudi Research & Marketing*,[208] the Court of Appeal exonerated a newspaper which published allegations without trying to verify them because 'both sides to [the] political dispute [were] being fully, fairly and disinterestedly reported in their respective allegations and responses . . .'.[209] The standard seems to be one of responsible reporting—or, to put it another way, non-negligent reporting—even though that does not always imply a duty to verify what one prints.

American law is different. The seminal decision in *New York Times Co.* v. *Sullivan*.[210] There the *New York Times* had printed an advertisement condemning the treatment of civil rights advocates in the south during the de-segregation movement, and containing several misstatements of fact about a public official which the *Times* could have caught had it checked its own files. The standard adopted was not negligence but 'malice'. The Supreme Court, in this and subsequent decisions, made it clear that malice meant knowledge of or reckless disregard for the falsehood of the disclosure. It did not mean ill will, and was not enough that the *Times* had failed to check sources which it had readily available. Unlike *Reynolds*, this decision was not presented as an extension of the common law privilege of fair comment. According to the Supreme Court, it rested on the constitutional right to freedom of expression protected by the First Amendment to the United States Constitution.

We find, then, two standards: one of which asks if the publisher behaved negligently, and the other whether he intentionally or recklessly misstated the truth. We can understand their respective merits if we reflect back on our discussion of negligence.

---

[204] [2001] 2 AC 127 (HL).   [205] See the standard of negligence described in Chapter 10 II.
[206] [2002] UKPC 31.   [207] ibid. 24.   [208] [2002] EMLR 13 (Eng CA).
[209] [2002] EMLR 13, 52 (Simon Brown LJ) (CA).   [210] 376 US 254 (1964).

Negligence is a matter of balancing. A modern law and economics scholar thinks one must balance the cost and effectiveness of a precaution against the likelihood and extent of the damage that lack of such a precaution might cause. As we saw, writers in the Aristotelian tradition also thought one must balance prospective evils and their likelihood. In contrast to the modern economists, however, they thought the balancing was one of moral evils and was done by an ability they called prudence rather than by a calculus of economic costs.[211]

In either case, we can see whether, when it is not known whether information of importance to public decision making is false, the publisher's decision is different than, for example, the decision how fast to drive or what safety precautions to take in a factory. The driver or factory owner saves his own time or his own money if he does not take the precaution; he must weigh the value of this saving against the danger to others. The publisher must weigh the value of disseminating information of which he is not completely sure against the harm that will be done if it is false. Nevertheless, if he publishes, he does not get to keep the full value of releasing the information if it is true. In that respect, he is not like the driver who saves his own time or the factory owner who saves his own money. The publisher will profit to the extent he sells more newspapers, but he will not be reimbursed in proportion to the value of the information to the public. Moreover, if the information released is false, others will have a chance to correct the injury he has done, which is hardly possible in a traffic or industrial accident.

Thus, if one were to ask whether a publisher behaved negligently or irresponsibly in disclosing information, ideally, the answer should depend on a balancing of all the good and evil that the disclosure may do: the benefit, not simply to the publisher, but to the public if the information is true, and the harm, not simply to the plaintiff, but to the public if the information is false. Thus it was correct for the *Reynolds* court to consider, not only how careful the publisher was to check his information, but the value of it to the public and the possible harm to the defendant.

This is a difficult balance to strike. It is not clear, particularly on sensitive political issues, that one wants it to be struck by judges or juries. If there is a margin of error, as inevitably there will be, the publisher may keep silent since he may be liable for heavy damages and will profit only to the extent he can sell extra newspapers. That was surely one of the fears that lead to the rejection of a negligence standard in *New York Times Co.* v. *Sullivan*. In a time of unrest over the civil rights issue, it is far from clear that a southern judge and jury would attach the proper degree of importance to news about abuse of civil rights workers.

That publishers subject to a negligence standard do refrain from printing information they believe is true, or sufficiently likely to be true to warrant discussion, is shown in a thorough study of the English press by Russell L. Weaver, Andrew T. Kenyon, David F. Partlett, and Clive C. P. Walker.[212] It is impossible here to present their findings in full. They conclude, however, that even after *Reynolds*, English journalists routinely have their publications screened in advance by an attorney for potential

---

[211] Chapter 10 II.

[212] 'Defamation Law and Free Speech: Reynolds v. Times Newspapers and the British Media', *Vand. J. Transnat'l Law* 37 (2004), 1255.

liability, and that the fear of damages makes them reluctant to take risks unless they are quite sure they can prove they have a *Reynolds* defense. The authors note, for example, that 'BBC lawyers try to create a 20% margin for safety. In creating this margin, BBC lawyers recognize that witnesses sometimes change their minds, and at other times are forced to change their minds by opposing counsel.'

3. Affront to dignity that bears directly on public decision making

In France and Germany, insult may be actionable if it is directed against persons directly involved in political decision making such as politicians and political commentators. One cannot say so categorically. It is hard to draw the line between criticism and insult, and without criticism there would be no political discussion. But in France, as already mentioned, a newspaper reporter was held liable for calling a television journalist a 'tart kosher pork butcher'. As we have seen, it was not a defense that he intended an anti-semitic insult against a political journalist.[213] In a post-war German decision, a reporter was held liable for 'insult' though not 'defamation' for calling the German army a 'gigantic murder machine'. The court held that a reporter can use 'sharp and polemical expressions and overstated poster-like value judgments. [citation omitted] But nevertheless that does not legally justify vituperation, abuse and defaming as is the case here.'[214]

By comparison, in *Hustler Magazine* v. *Falwell*,[215] the United States Supreme Court held it was not actionable for a magazine to say that the Reverend Jerry Fallwell had his first sexual experience with his mother in an outhouse. The magazine was not liable for defamation because no one would have believed such a statement and because the page on which it appeared disclaimed its truth. It was not liable for insult, or, in American common law, for 'intentional infliction of emotional distress' because Falwell was politically active. The court said that '[i]f it were possible by laying down a principled standard to separate' this insult from the insulting but politically valuable cartoons by which Thomas Nast exposed the corruption of the New York 'Tweed Ring', 'public discourse would probably suffer little or no harm'. But the court could not see a principled distinction between the one and the other.

No one has commended the conduct of *Hustler Magazine*. Robert Post has defended the court's decision on other grounds: the rules of civility are as society makes them, and anyone has the right to challenge these rules. I don't see that argument. *Hustler* was not challenging prevailing rules of civility as one might do, for example, by declining a duel in a society in which it was expected one would accept after offending another. *Hustler* knew perfectly well that by prevailing rules of civility it was insulting Falwell. That was the point of its article.

Nevertheless, although I hate to say so, I believe the Supreme Court's decision was right. In political debate, no one can draw a line between permissible and impermissible civility. The United States once had a Sedition Law which nearly everyone today

---

[213] Cour d'appel, Paris, 15 Feb. 1988, JCP 1988.II.21115.
[214] BGH, 19 Jan. 1989, JZ 1989, 644. A seemingly opposite result was reached by the German Constitutional Court in BVerfG, 28 Aug. 1994, NJW 1994, 2943, which held a prominent anti-war activist could not be prosecuted for displaying a bumper-sticker 'soldiers are murderers'. But the Court did so by noting that in context, 'murder' did not have its normal meaning.   [215] 485 US 46 (1988).

would regard as unconstitutional. It was supposed to prohibit all criticisms that were designed to bring it into contempt—what we would call insults. Editors went to jail for making statements such as 'Downfall to the Tyrants of America', for calling the American military a 'standing army', for claiming that the government allowed the wealthy to benefit at the expense of the commoners and for criticizing the President, John Adams, for an 'unbounded thirst for ridiculous pomp, foolish adulation, and selfish avarice'.[216] No doubt, many felt that these epithets were unjustifiably offensive. But, in political controversies, it is dangerous for anyone, including the courts, to decide what is unjustifiably offensive and what is not.

4. *The disclosure of information that affects dignity or reputation is relevant to the public's understanding of society and themselves, but does not bear directly on public decision making*

We will see that civil law and American courts take drastically different approaches to what information they consider to be of legitimate public concern or, at least, to be protected as a matter of freedom of discussion. Civil law courts are inclined to find there is no legitimate public interest in information which does not serve to educate the public. Indeed, they often hold that such information cannot be published even it would have little or no effect on a person's reputation or dignity. American courts are likely to find there is a legitimate public interest in knowing things which one cannot imagine would put the public in a better position to understand themselves, their society or the political choices they must make. They will protect disclosures even at the expense of a person's dignity and reputation. With England, it is too soon to tell.

Before looking at these differences, however, we should note a similarity: the tendency of a publication to educate the public tends to influence decisions. That is so in the past as well as in both civil and common law jurisdictions, even though it often requires judges to bend the rules which differentiate these systems.

As we have seen, the late scholastics believed it was wrong, in principle, to reveal an unpleasant truth about a person's reputation absent a public interest. Education was valued in their day for a humanistic elite though not for all citizens, and history was a part of education. Consequently, they were stymied as to revelations about historical figures. Could Tacitus not reveal what Tiberius was up to on Capri? They therefore made an exception for historians who disclosed the faults of persons even when no one was any longer in danger.[217] They claimed that such writings were justified by the 'public good'.[218] That is the closest they came to the modern idea that the public good includes general education. And yet, they said, though historians should tell of 'wars, homicides and other matters which are not indecorous in illustrious men',[219] they should not report deeds which were merely shameful,[220] at least if they had hitherto been completely secret.[221]

Similar considerations seem to have affected both the civil law and common law. Whatever the formal rules may be, it has mattered whether the purpose of a broadcast

---

216 Ron Chernow, *Alexander Hamilton* (New York, 2004), 575.
217 Soto, *De iustitia et iure*, lib. 5, Q. 10, a. 2; Molina, *De iustitia et iure*, IV, disp 24, no. 9.
218 Molina, *De iustitia et iure*, IV, disp. 24, no. 9.   219 Soto, *De iustitia et iure*, lib. 5, Q. 10, a. 2.
220 ibid. lib. 5, Q. 10, a. 2.
221 ibid. lib. 5, Q. 10, a. 2; Molina, *De iustitia et iure*, IV, disp. 28, no. 2.

or a published work has been to enlighten the public (whether a particular court finds the article enlightening or not) or whether it has been a sensational piece in the tabloids. In France, as we will see, the general rule is that one cannot disclose information about a film celebrity without his implied consent. An article in *Lui* published 'numerous details relative to the private life of Chaplin and his family'. Rather than simply invoking the general rule, the court of appeal said that 'even if disclosure of these details would not have violated Chaplin's right to privacy if published in an historical study, it does here because *Lui* is not an historical journal'. The highest French court, the *Cour de Cassation*, upheld that decision adding that 'Presse Office has never claimed for the magazine *Lui* the character of a scientific and critical publication and did not present the article attacked as an historical study'.[222] Similarly, in France and Germany, the general rule is that one cannot publish criminal or shameful events in a person's past even where they had been reported at the time. Yet, in another French case, defendants were the writer and publisher of a book, '*A Toboggan in the Torment of the Franche-Comté 1940–45*,' a study of the Nazi occupation of the Franche-Comté, which, the author said, would describe 'historical truth down to its smallest details'. He mentioned a man who was tried and condemned as a traitor in 1946 'along with his mistress Mananges'. The French court refused to allow Mananges to recover. The *Cour de Cassation* explained that the reason was that the event had been reported in newspapers at the time. But that would not have bothered them in an ordinary criminal case. Perhaps they were more influenced by the observation of the Court of Appeal that 'he had the right as an historian to present the evidence of facts, without the consent of the interested parties, even if they touch on one's private life'. Similarly, a German court upheld the right of a newspaper to expose a former German *Sturmbahnführer* whom it accused of the deaths of 20 children. 'In informing, instructing and supporting the shaping of public opinion,' the court said, 'the press has a legitimate interest in reporting concretely the facts that are essential for evaluating a former period of time, in preserving the memory of the era of national socialist rule, in contributing to an impartial view by its readers of these horrible acts of power, and even to help toward a clarification of particular criminal acts through the publication of further details'.[223]

Although it is too early to tell what will happen in England,

tabloids like *The Sun* have found that they have a more difficult time taking advantage of the *Reynolds* defense. A solicitor for *The Sun* stated that, although he regards *Reynolds* as 'good pro-freedom of speech development,' he saw it as 'being of much less use to my newspapers (*The Sun* and *News of the World*) than to broadsheets like *The Times*'. He explained that papers that engage in 'red top tabloid sensationalism' find it difficult to take advantage of *Reynolds*. A solicitor for *The Times* stated, *The Sun* never does anything by halves. By contrast, since the BBC strives for objective reporting, it feels that it is more able to take advantage of the *Reynolds* defense.[224]

In the United States, as we have seen, a broad view has been taken of freedom of the press and of what is of legitimate public interest. Yet even there, the result the courts

[222] Cass., 2e ch. civ., 14 Nov. 1975, arrêt no. 729. pourvoi no. 74-11.278 (unpublished).
[223] OLG, Frankfurt, 6 Sept. 1979, NJW 1980, 597.
[224] Weaver *et al.*, 'Defamation and Free Speech'.

reach sometimes does seem to turn on whether the purpose of a story is public enlightenment or sensationalism. In *Buendorf* v. *National Pub. Radio, Inc.*,[225] an assassination attempt on President Gerald Ford was prevented by a man who struck the gun from the perpetrator's hand. A newspaper revealed that the man was a homosexual, a fact widely known, but not to members of his family. In denying recovery, the court noted that one purpose of the article was to educate the public by attacking the stereotype of homosexuals as lacking in virtues such as courage. In *Haynes* v. *Alfred A. Knopf, Inc.*,[226] plaintiff was denied recovery when a book about the history of black families moving to the north used the plaintiff as an example and contained information obtained from his ex-wife on the breakdown of their marriage and his own alcoholism and adultery. At the time the book was published, the plaintiff had remarried, he had a home, a steady job and was a deacon of his local church. The court held that '[a]n individual, and more pertinently perhaps the community, is most offended by the publication of intimate personal facts when the community has no interest in them beyond the voyeuristic thrill of penetrating the wall of privacy that surrounds a stranger'. In contrast, one of the author's major themes was the 'transposition virtually intact of a sharecropper morality characterized by a family structure "matriarchal and elastic" and by an "extremely unstable" marriage bond to the slums of the northern cities, and the interaction, largely random and sometimes perverse, of that morality with governmental programs to alleviate poverty'. It was a 'a story not only of legitimate but of transcendent public interest . . .'.

In contrast, in *Diaz* v. *Oakland Tribune*,[227] a newspaper was held liable for disclosing that the plaintiff, who had become a distinguished athlete, a high school president and a public opponent of the policies of school authorities, was in fact a transsexual, a fact that Diaz had made every effort to conceal. The article made a snide remark as to whether female classmates might prefer to take separate showers. One wonders if the result would have been the same if the article had not been not a slur but a serious study of transsexuality.

5. *Information that affects dignity or reputation but has little or no relevance to public education or decision making*

In civil law countries such as France and Germany, when information does affect dignity or reputation, courts are far more willing than in the United States to make judgments as to what the public should know. If they do not see any legitimate reason why the public should be concerned, they are willing to assume a matter is not of legitimate public interest. That is so even if the information concerns political figures. One can publish information as to the health of the head of state, François Mitterand.[228] One cannot disclose that a trial court judge had taken a vacation on account of 'nervous depression'.[229] One cannot describe 'an altercation' between Mrs. Dewi Sukarno, widow of the president of Indonesia, and Beatrice Chatelier, the former wife of Eddie Barclay 'for the handsome eyes of a Parisian playboy'.[230]

---

[225] 822 F Supp 6 (DC 1993).   [226] 8 F3d 1222 (7th Cir 1993) (Posner, J).
[227] 139 Cal App 3d 118 (1983).   [228] See Cours d'appel, Paris, 5 Dec. 1997, D.1998. I.R.32.
[229] Cass., 2e ch. civ., 27 Apr. 1988, pourvoi no. 86-13.303 (unpublished).
[230] Cass., 2e ch. civ., 5 Dec. 1979, arrêt no. 1.032, pourvoi no. 78-13.614 (unpublished).

Similarly, in post-war Germany, one cannot disclose that the wife of Prince Friedrich William of Prussia intended to divorce her husband. The Hohenzollerns were not a proper object of public attention '[s]ince, with an interruption, Germany has been a republic for fifty years, the House of Hohenzollern has had only historical significance since the abdication of Kaiser Wilhelm II'.[231] As will be described below, rarely will a French or German court allow a prior criminal's conviction to be reported long after the event. While the public has an interest in crime, there is no public interest in knowing who committed what crime long ago.

The European Court of Justice has taken a similar approach. In *Peck* v. *UK*[232] the Court found that the United Kingdom was in violation of Articles 8 and 13 of the Convention by failing to provide a legal remedy to prevent the publication of the CCTV footage of Mr Peck's suicide attempt, which occurred in a public place. The public, however, had no legitimate interest in watching a man kill himself.

Some American Courts once took a similar view as to past criminal records. In *Melvin* v. *Reid*, the Supreme Court of California held the defendant liable for making a movie about the plaintiff's past, using her maiden name, but revealing the fact that she had been a prostitute who had been tried and aquitted of murder.[233] In *Briscoe* v. *Reader's Digest*[234] the same court held that a newspaper could not publish the fact that the plaintiff, 11 years before, had stolen a valuable looking truck only to find it contained bowling-pin spotters.

Eventually, as we will see, the United States Supreme Court intervened and held that even to report details of a criminal's past life could be constitutionally protected if the information was a matter of public record. Even before that time, however, one can see an American unwillingness to pronounce on what the public legitimately needed to know. The *Restatement (Second) of Torts* had recognized as a defense the revelation of information that 'is . . . of legitimate concern to the public'.[235] By then, however, American courts had already construed the legitimate interest to the public to go beyond what an educated electorate needed to know in order to vote or to form an intelligent appreciation of the society in which they lived. In 1940, in the landmark case of *Sidis* v. *F-R Publishing Co.*,[236] the court held that the rights of a child prodigy, William Sidis, were not violated by an article exposing the fact that for many years he had retired from the world and sought a life of anonymity. The court did not explain how this disclosure had any educational value for the public.

In *Cape Publications, Inc.* v. *Bridges*,[237] an estranged husband had kidnapped his ex-wife at gunpoint, taken her to their former apartment and forced her to disrobe to prevent her escape. She escaped nevertheless clad only in a dishtowel. A newspaper

---

[231] OLG, Hamburg, 26 Mar. 1970, NJW 1970, 1325.

[232] (2003) EHRR 287 (App No 00044647/98). Similarly, in (2004) EHRR (App No 59320-00), the court held that one could not publish pictures of Princess Caroline of Monaco riding horses or pursuing other ordinary activities in public places because the public had no legitimate interest.

[233] 297 P91 (Cal 1931).   [234] 483 P2d 24 (Cal 1971).

[235] *Restatement (Second) of Torts*, § 652D (1976).   [236] 113 F2d 806 (2nd Cir 1940).

[237] 423 So 2d 426 (Fla App 1982), review denied 431 So 2d 988 (Fla 1983).

was allowed to print the picture it had taken of her in this position because it was newsworthy and therefore within the common law privilege.

The First Amendment of the United States Consitution has been construed to loosen the common law restraints on the disclosure of events that are supposedly of public interest. In *Cox Broadcasting* v. *Cohn*,[238] the Supreme Court held that the constitution required that journalists be able to disclose matters that were of public record, even though individual members of the public were unlikely to be familiar with such matters. Indeed, it could disclose any information that it had obtained lawfully. One wonders if anything is left of *Melvin* v. *Reid*, since, except in the case of juveniles, plaintiff's criminal background is normally a matter of public record. In *Oklahoma Publishing Co.* v. *District Court*,[239] the Supreme Court went further and held that journalists were constitutionally permitted to publish the name and picture of an 11 year old boy charged with delinquency for second degree murder. The proceedings were not a matter of public record but the court held it was enough that the press was present in the courtroom and the picture was taken as the boy left the courtroom. In *Florida Star* v. *B.J.F.*,[240] the Supreme Court held that a newspaper could not be held liable for publishing the name or a rape victim even when her assailant was still at large because the newspaper had obtained the information 'lawfully' from a police report even though the report was not a matter of public record. Apparently, a publisher is entitled to release any information that is true and lawfully obtained regardless of the consequences for the victim. A lower federal court held that *Sports Illustrated* could print a picture of a Pittsburgh Steeler fan with the zipper of his trousers open under the title 'A Strange Kind of Love'. The court noted that the picture had been taken in a public place.[241]

In *Howell* v. *New York Post, Inc.*,[242] the New York Supreme Court disregarded not only limitations as to where information was obtained such as from a public place or public record but also as to how it was obtained, lawfully or unlawfully. A *New York Post* photographer trespassed on the secluded grounds of a private psychiatric facility and took pictures of a group that included Hedda Nussbaum and Pamela Howell, the plaintiff. Nussbaum had attracted considerable public interest in a child abuse case a few months earlier. Howell had not been in the public eye at all. Her complaint and affidavit (accepted as true on appeal) alleged that it was imperative to her recovery that the hospitalization remain a secret from all but her immediate family, and had concealed her residence at the facility from her friends and family. That night, the hospital's medical director telephoned a *Post* editor requesting that the paper not publish any photographs of patients. The *Post* printed the photograph the next day. The court held it was entitled to do so. The *Post* did not even need to crop Howell's picture from the photograph on the grounds that '[t]he visual impact would not have been the same . . .'.

All of these cases involved media defendants, and all of them were decided on the right of the public to be informed on the events in question despite the hardship to the plaintiff. But when the question arises whether the information serves any purpose in educating the public, or bears on any decision they are called upon to make, one can

---

[238] 420 US 469 (1975).   [239] 430 US 308 (1977).   [240] 491 US 524 (1989).
[241] *Neff* v. *Time*, 406 F Supp 858 (WD Pa 1976).   [242] 612 NE 2d 699 (NY 1993).

imagine two sensible rules, each with its own advantages and disadvantages. One could allow a court to ask to balance the value of the disclosure in informing or educating the public against the harm done to the plaintiff. That has the danger of placing a power of censorship in the courts that could easily be abused. It was abused, in my judgment, in a case in which a post-war German court chose to interpret the words of an article literally which accused the army of being a 'murder machine' and held the publishers liable.[243] Alternatively, one could allow a court to permit publishers to make any disclosure which, at least arguably, educates the public, helps them to understand the society in which they live and better fits them to make public decisions. Then the courts will not be in the position of deciding what the public ought to know as long as there is any discernible reason why it is in their interest to know it.

Even by that more lenient standard, however, the American decisions are indefensible. Certainly, the public is better educated by knowing of the work of scholars, but their understanding is not helped by revelations about the seclusion sought by an eccentric genius. Certainly, the public should know about the problems of crime, but its understanding is not improved by a photograph of a woman escaping in a dishtowel, the remembrance of criminal convictions long forgotten, publicizing the trials of juveniles which are deliberately not made matters of public record or the disclosure of the names of rape victims. It is hard to see what of use the public learns from pictures of football fans with their zippers open or convalescents once involved in sensational events, let alone of their companions. One could only justify such disclosures if one believed there was no way of discerning what might or might not inform or educate the public. If that were so, it would be hard to see why the freedom of the press is regarded as a vital instrument for informing and educating them.

6. Information that neither affects reputation nor dignity nor is relevant to public education or public decision making

The public is interested in all manner of things that neither help them to form a deeper understanding of the world around them nor, on the other hand, do particular harm to the dignity or reputation of the person they learn about. Here again, there is a gulf between the approach of civil law jurisdictions such as France and Germany and the United States.

I think the difference is easiest to see with the publication of pictures, although the same point could be made about the details of people's lives. In France, what matters is consent, or presumed consent, but the rules on presumed consent are strict. In one French case, the newspaper *Paris-Match* was held liable for publishing a picture of one of the plaintiffs, a famous singer, in a public place in Paris with a young woman (also a plaintiff) on his arm. The newspaper did not say or suggest anything about their relationship. The highest French court, the *Cour de Cassation*, said:

if the publication of photographs of a public figure (*personne publique*) even without his express authorization does not constitute, in principle, an injury to his right to his image, that is only upon condition that the photographs in question concern exclusively his profession and not his

---

[243] BGH, 19 Jan. 1989, JZ 1989, 644.

private life... and, finally, if the reproduction of the image of a public figure in the conduct of his professional life is not, in principle, subject to obtaining his express permission nevertheless it is necessary that the interested party be considered as having tacitly authorized the reproduction of his image.

Here, the court noted, by his past conduct Jacques Brel 'manifested an evident desire to be extremely discrete'.[244]

In Germany, by statute, photographs of an individual can be published only in four cases:

1. Images in the area of contemporary history;
2. Images in which the people appear only as an incident in a landscape or similar locale;
3. Images of gatherings, processions, and similar events in which the person in question was a participant;
4. Images that are not made upon order insofar as their dissemination or display serves an important artistic interest.[245]

Of course, most of the cases are not only concerned with the use of the defendant's picture without his consent, but occur in some unflattering context. In France, a newspaper was held liable for printing the picture of a well-known actress, her eyes protected by glasses, and her face showing signs of suffering and of the effects of a recent illness.[246] In Germany, the plaintiff 'was pointed out as the example and prototype of the "satisfied German" by the caption'. Second, there was a danger that the public would confuse him with an SS general described on the same page. The court held that either ground was sufficient to support an action.[247]

American law is different. As we have seen, one cannot use the plaintiff's image commercially. But otherwise one can use it without consent. That is true in an embarrassing context such as one we have described: the Pittsburg Steelers fan with the zipper of his trousers open. But it is also true when the picture is used in an innocuous context: for example, the picture of a couple in an affectionate but not amorous pose in a public place to illustrate a human interest story.[248] I can understand perfectly well why plaintiffs would object when the picture places them in an unfavorable context. Indeed, in such a context they could well complain that their dignity suffers. I have more trouble understanding why some American plaintiffs complain and many European countries object to gathering or dissemination of information about people which in no way hurts them. Recently, this question has embroiled the United States with Europe in questions involving the gathering of information over the Internet. Article 2(a) of the Directive provides that ' "personal data" shall mean any information relating to an identified or identifiable natural person ("data subject"); an identifiable person is one who can be identified, directly or indirectly, in particular by reference to an

---

[244] Cass., 2e ch. civ., 8 July 1981, arrêt no. 1.013; pourvoi nos. 80-12.286, 80-13.079 (unpublished).

[245] Law Concerning the Right of Authors to Works of Pictoral Art and Photography (*Kunst Urheber Gesetz*), § 23. Although the European Court of Human Rights has held that even in the case of an historical figure—Princess Caroline of Monaco—the German Constitutional Court erred in allowing pictures of her riding horses and performing other ordinary activities. See n. 232 above.

[246] Cass., 1e ch. civ., 10 June 1987, pourvoi no. 86-16.185 (unpublished).

[247] BGH, 15 Jan. 1965, 1965 NJW 1374.

[248] *Gill* v. *Hearst Publications Co., Inc.*, 253 P2d 441 (Cal 1953).

identification number or to one or more factors specific to his physical, physiological, mental, economic, cultural or social identity'. Article 7(a) provides that 'personal data may be processed only if the data subject has unambiguously given his consent...'. Every subject has to be informed under Article 12(a) 'whether or not data relating to him are being processed and information at least as to the purposes of the processing, the categories of data concerned, and the recipients or categories of recipients to whom the data are disclosed'. According to Article 15(1) governing 'automated individual decisions',

Member States shall grant the right to every person not to be subject to a decision which produces legal effects concerning him or significantly affects him and which is based solely on automated processing of data intended to evaluate certain personal aspects relating to him, such as his performance at work, creditworthiness, reliability, conduct, etc.

There is obviously a difference here. Article 15 does not refer to specific information that would impugn a person's 'performance at work, creditworthiness, reliability, conduct, etc.'. It doesn't have anything to do with an individual's personal reputation or dignity but with the judgments that a computer can make by placing him in categories of people whose credit has been found more or less reliable. Similarly, the use of a person's picture is proscribed, not only in the cases we have mentioned in which he is reflected in an unfavorable light, but whenever he is singled out, without his consent for publicity.

As I noted earlier, I believe American courts are mistaken to permit disclosures which harm a person's reputation or dignity and are of little or no value to the public. Here, however, I must say that I believe civil law jurisdictions are mistaken to forbid disclosures which may be of little value to the public but do not affect a person's reputation or dignity. James Whitman has suggested that the French and Germans believe they have a right to present themselves to others in the way they wish—a sort of right to control their public image.[249] I have trouble imagining what such a right would entail. No one controls the impressions they make on other people. People who live in small towns, extended families, or move in small circles such as the academic community both benefit and suffer from what others think of them far more than they could from a remark about them in the press which affects neither their dignity or reputation. I cannot see why they should be protected against the latter when it is absurd even to imagine protecting them against the former.

6. Civil v. common law

There is considerable truth, then, in the common belief that when there is perceived to be a conflict, civil law jurisdictions will protect the individual while common jurisdictions will protect the media. I think it is a mistake, though, for James Whitman to describe the difference by saying Americans attach greater importance to freedom and the French and Germans to dignity. Whitman's image of American attachment to freedom is a man sitting on his property with a shotgun ready to defend himself against all intruders. His image of continental attachment to dignity is an

---

[249] Whitman, 'Two Western Cultures', 1165–6.

almost aristocratic sense of honor which is now believed to be the right of all citizens of a democratic society.[250] But the American decisions rarely deal with the freedom of the individual. They deal with the freedom of newspapers, broadcasters, data gatherers, and other media defendants. Conversely, as we have seen, French courts will protect individuals in cases that have little or nothing to do with honor or dignity. I find it easier to understand the difference in terms of a different attitude toward the media and toward trust in government action to control the media. American courts are reluctant to interfere when the media reports what some people clearly want to know, for whatever reason. French and German courts are inclined to think that the job of the press is to report what the public ought to know, at least without special permission from those affected, and less inclined to doubt their ability to discern what the public ought to know. To my mind, many of the differences would disappear if American courts would agree that there are clear cases in which a disclosure which hurts someone is of little or no value to the public, and if civil law courts would agree that the press should be able to print matters which harm no one, even if they contribute little or nothing to public education.

II. Other Rights to 'Privacy' and *'Persönlichkeit'*

A. Intrusion into Seclusion

In Roman law, the plaintiff could recover against someone who entered his house without permission.[251] It is not clear why. Was the unauthorized entry considered an insult? The late scholastic Molina discussed the case in which information about another is obtained wrongfully. It is wrongful to read another's letters without 'reasonable cause' (*rationabilis causa*), and especially to do so by entering a place that is shut (*locus clausus*).[252] Reasonable cause is present, for example, if the letter is opened by religious superiors who have suspicions of a subordinate, or, in wartime, by duly authorized government officials near the area of the hostilities.[253] According to Molina, the person whose letters are opened is entitled to redress if, as a result, he loses honor or reputation.[254] But that observation sidesteps the question of whether he can recover if he loses neither. It seems odd to say he has no redress since he has suffered a wrong. But if his honor and reputation are unaffected, it is hard to say the redress is for insult or detraction. Modern civil law systems, as we will see, ask whether the plaintiff's image or information about him has been used without his consent. Intrusion into a private place, even without physical entry, has been deemed evidence that the plaintiff would not have consented. Both German and French courts have held that, even absent physical entry the use of a telephoto lens is evidence that the plaintiff would not have consented to the photograph.[255]

---

[250] ibid.   [251] Dig. 47.2.21.7.
[252] Molina, *De iustitia et iure* IV, disp. 36, no. 2.   [253] ibid. no. 5.   [254] ibid. no. 3.
[255] See Trib. de grande inst., Paris, 29 May 1996, *Legipresse*, 1996, n°135-I, p. 122; BVerfGE 101, 361, NJW 2000, 1021.

In Anglo-American law, one who entered anyone else's land would have an action for trespass to land, even if no harm was done. The mere entry was considered a violation of rights in the land. Traditionally, the common law claimed that absent a physical trespass on another's land there was no action. Now, American courts have recognized, as a violation of the right to privacy, 'intrusion into seclusion',[256] which encompasses intrusion into any private space, whether or not by physical entry, and whether or not the space is owned by the victim. In *Nader* v. *General Motors*, the court held that while following Ralph Nader into a bank was permissible, standing where one could observe the denominations of the bills he was withdrawing was not. In England, after the furor over the death of Princess Diana, the Press Complaints Commission amended its Code of Practice to provide: 'The use of long lens photography to take pictures of people in *private places* without their consent is unacceptable'.[257] Basil Markesinis believes that 'the development of the law of confidence now appears to ensure that such use of tele and short lenses to photograph individuals in either private or public places may be relevant in determining whether a legitimate expectation of privacy was being infringed'.[258] He quotes Lord Woolf, who in *A* v. *B plc* suggested that breach of confidence could extend to cover 'an intrusion in a situation where a person can reasonably expect his privacy to be respected'.[259]

What, then, if the plaintiff attempts such an entry in order to obtain information to which he is not legally entitled and fails? Such cases hardly ever come to court. The plaintiff who brings them can almost always show some other injury. I don't know of any civil law cases in which the plaintiff was unable to do so, and Post has found few in the United States.[260]

While Post and I believe the plaintiff should recover in such cases, Post interprets them as an instance of what I would call insult. He believes eavesdropping and the like are a violation of 'civility rules'.[261]

I believe we have to distinguish three kinds of cases in which the plaintiff can show no injury except the intrusion itself. In all three cases, the intrusion is wrongful, and if we want to use words loosely, it is for that very reason an insult to the plaintiff. But if we use words more carefully, in some cases the intrusion is an insult in the same sense as striking another person or blowing smoke in his face. The point of it is to bring home to him that he is not being treated with dignity. A person might barge into his office without knocking, or enter his house when forbidden not to do so. That is not the case Molina envisioned in which a person reads another person's letters without his knowledge. There the idea is simply to gather information about him but not to embarrass him by the mere fact that his letters are opened. The offender might want to keep it secret that his letters were being opened.

In a second kind of case, a person's dignity is demeaned, not because his misbehavior is exposed, but because activities which are appropriate in private, and only in private,

[256] *Restatement (Second) of Torts*, § 652B (1965).
[257] Code of Practice, art. 3(ii).   [258] Markesinis *et al.*, 'Developing English Law of Privacy'.
[259] See A v. B plc [2003] QB 195 par 11.   [260] Post, *Constitutional Domains*, 57.   [261] ibid.

are witnessed by others. In an extreme case, a person might plant an eavesdropping device in a couple's room and listen to their most intimate conversations, or pretend to be a doctor to witness what it would be quite inappropriate otherwise to witness. In less extreme cases, one could simply imagine that a family's activities were observed through a long range telescope or recorded surreptitiously. The offense is not that the observer witnessed any activity that was inappropriate. It is that he witnessed activities that are spoiled as soon as they are no longer the private activities of a person, a couple, a family, or a group of friends, but open to public inspection. The offense is not an insult in the sense of a denigration of a person's dignity nor an attack on his reputation. It is an attack on those activities which have value at least in part because they are private and not shared with others.

In a third kind of case, the rule that holds a defendant liable for violation of privacy is purely prophylactic. The offender has not witnessed anything that impugns the dignity or character of the plaintiff. But he has taken measures which are wrongful precisely because they might have had that result. He has opened the plaintiff's letter and found nothing that was compromising or, for that matter, even intimate. He has planted an eavesdropping device in a couple's bedroom and heard nothing. After long hours of telescopic observation, he has seen nothing of interest.

In very few of such cases has the plaintiff bothered to bring suit. Post cites the case of *Hamberger* v. *Eastman*,[262] in which the plaintiffs' landlord installed an eavesdropping device in their marital bedroom. They recovered even though, as it happened, nothing was overheard. The plaintiffs did recover damages for harm they claimed to have suffered: impotence and frigidity after the discovery and removal of the device. It is quite unlikely that people who knew that nothing of interest had been overheard would have suffered in this way. The explanation of why they recovered, I believe, is one I gave earlier: that he who commits a wrong intentionally is liable even for the unforeseeable consequences of that wrong.[263] But he did commit a wrong. It was a wrong because it was designed to have the result of exposing intimate behavior that the defendant was not entitled to witness.

Post claims the landlord violated 'civility rules'. I think it would be more accurate to say that he attempted to violate the plaintiff's right to dignity and reputation, as we have defined it, but also their right to privacy, and should be held liable accordingly.

One consequence of this analysis is that the plaintiff should recover in situations in which no actual harm was done, and yet the act in question was wrongful. Suppose as soon as the device was discovered, the plaintiffs saw that it wouldn't work and suffered neither embarrassment nor any other harm. As will be described in a later chapter, it is perfectly appropriate for the law to give damages which cannot properly be described in the conventional categories of 'compensatory', 'restitutionary', or 'punitive'. They are not compensatory or restitutionary because the plaintiff was not harmed nor the defendant benefitted. They are not punitive because they are not intended to penalize

---

[262] 206 A2d 239 (NH 1964), cited ibid. 52.   [263] Chapter 10 I B.

the defendant. Their amount should not depend on his wealth or on the need to deter similar violations in the future.

This problem arises frequently in law. Suppose a doctor operates on a patient without his consent, or without informing the patient of the risks as he should to obtain informed consent. He has doubtless violated the patient's right to consent, even if the operation was successful and beneficial to the plaintiff, who, in all probability, would have consented had he been told the truth. There are two alternatives: to deny an action because the plaintiff was not harmed, or to grant one because one of his rights was wrongfully denied him—the right to informed consent.

One might describe a plaintiff's right to seclusion or to give his consent to such an operation as 'prophylactic': it exists only to protect the plaintiff against the possibility of harm. Nevertheless, it seems that a remedy should be given when such a 'prophylactic' right is violated simply because a right is violated and independent of any considerations of punishment or deterrence. If that is so, then an action for intrusion into seclusion is the vindication of a prophylactic right. If that is not so, then one must accept Post's thesis that rules of 'civility' encompass more than deliberate humiliation or attacks on one's reputation. I admit that I am troubled by the notion of awarding damages where there has been a violation of right but no harm, but I am more troubled by Post's thesis that one can award damages for a breach of the rules of 'civility' accepted in society. If that is so, I don't see how one can stop short of awarding damages whenever any convention of a particular society is violated.

B. Protection of Name or Image against Commercial Exploitation

As mentioned earlier, this right figured in one of the earliest right to privacy cases, *Roberson* v. *Rochester Folding Box Co.*, in which the defendants had, without consent, used the picture of an attractive young woman with the caption 'Flour of the Family' on advertisements for Franklin Mills flour. Reaction to the decision was swift. New York passed a statute against using 'the name, portrait or picture of any living person' for 'advertising purposes or the purposes of trade'.[264] Some American courts then recognized the right not to have one's picture or name used in advertising as a matter of common law.[265] In civil law systems, as we have seen, that right merges into a larger one: not to have one's picture used for any purpose at all absent a legitimate public purpose. Here we can only note that the extent to which a person has the exclusive right to commercial exploitation of his image or personality belongs to another topic too large to be considered here: the limits the law sets to what the plaintiff can commercially exploit. Rights to physical property, as we have seen, can be explained as a means of providing people with what they need to live a good life while giving incentives to work, to care for property and to take the risks bound up with doing so. Rights to benefit from patents and copyrights are often explained as a means of encouraging and rewarding inventors and authors. In cases in which one has worked

---

[264] New York Civil Rights Law, § 50 (McKinney 1976).
[265] *Pavesich* v. *New England Life Ins. Co.*, 50 SE 68 (Ga 1905); *Hinish* v. *Meier & Frank Co*, 113 P2d 438 (Or 1941).

10

to acquire a public image or persona in order to exploit it, one might explain his right to do so in the same way. Rights to trademarks are often explained as a means of avoiding confusion in the minds of the public. I believe the decision in *Roberson* was wrong. But I do not have a theory of why one has the right to the commercial exploitation of rights that neither belong to one as a matter of distributive justice nor provide an incentive for useful activity.

12

Liability in Tort for Pure Economic Loss

In some legal systems, the victim of a tort cannot recover for 'pure economic loss'. If the defendant had harmed his person or property or some other legally protected right, he can recover for the economic loss consequent on the injury. Otherwise, in principle, he cannot.

This rule has been adopted in some jurisdictions such as Germany, England and the United States and not in others such as France, Italy, and the Netherlands. Nevertheless, exceptions in special cases have been made by courts both in the jurisdictions that have adopted and in those which have rejected the rule.

The first part of this chapter will examine why the rule was adopted in jurisdictions such as Germany, England and the United States. As we will see, it was a creation of the 19th and early 20th centuries. Before that time, recovery for what we call economic loss was permitted, and the late scholastics of the 16th and early 17th centuries developed sophisticated reasons why it should be. The rule excluding recovery for economic loss was adopted for reasons which commended themselves to the 19th century conceptualists. Now that conceptualism has been discredited, these reasons have little appeal. The rule against the exclusion of economic loss survives largely because during the conceptualist era it became entrenched in the German Civil Code and the Anglo-American case law.

It doesn't follow that a rule excluding recovery for pure economic loss serves no useful purpose. Jurisdictions that purport to apply it sometimes make exceptions. Presumably, they find the application of the rule more acceptable in some cases than in others. Conversely, in those jurisdictions that reject the rule and still make exceptions, courts presumably encounter cases of economic loss in which they are not willing to allow the plaintiff to recover. The second part of this chapter will suggest why recovery of such losses is sometimes appropriate and why sometimes it is not.

I. Origins

A. Before the 19th Century

As we have seen, in England and the United States, an action for negligence was recognized only in the 19th century.[1] Before that time, the problem of how to limit liability in negligence could not exist. In continental law, however, an action for negligence or *culpa*

---

[1] Chapter 9 II A, C.

had been recognized since the time of the ancient Romans. Nevertheless, before the late 19th and early 20th centuries, the problem of limiting recovery for negligence either was not faced squarely by continental jurists or was resolved in other ways. It was not resolved by distinguishing between physical harm and economic loss. We will examine only the history of continental law because this problem did not exist in England until the late 19th century when an action for negligence was recognized for the first time.

1. The Roman tradition

In Roman law, the *lex Aquilia* allowed the plaintiff to recover for harm which the defendant had caused negligently or intentionally. There were originally two limits on recovery but both had disappeared by the Middle Ages.

One limit was that the defendant was liable under the *lex Aquilia* only if the damage was done in a physically direct way. Roman jurists effectively abolished this limit by granting the plaintiff an *actio in factum* or an *actio utilis* when he could not sue under the *lex* itself.[2] Eventually, Justinian's compilers rationalized this distinction by saying that an action under the *lex* could be brought where the defendant injured the plaintiff *a corpore in corpus*, 'by the body to the body', meaning that the harm had to be physical and to be physically inflicted by the defendant. The defendant would be liable, for example, if he struck and broke something that belonged to the plaintiff. The plaintiff was allowed to bring an *actio in factum* for harm that was *a corpore* but not *in corpus*, as for example, if the defendant tossed the plaintiff's ring in the river: the harm was done physically but the ring itself was not damaged but rather put beyond reach. The plaintiff was allowed to bring an *actio utilis* for harm that was neither *a corpore* nor *in corpus*, as, for example, if the defendant untied the plaintiff's slave so he could run away: like the ring, the slave was now beyond reach but this time the defendant himself had not physically moved him.[3]

Medieval jurists were not sensitive to the historical meaning of their texts. They tried to reconcile the texts logically, but since there were different ways that they could be reconciled, the medieval jurists were able to reach results that would have surprised the Romans. Had they wished to limit liability under the *lex Aquilia*, they could have held, for example, that an *actio in factum* or an *actio utilis* did not invariably lie, that the court had some power of discretion in allowing these actions that it did not have if the action were brought directly under the *lex Aquilia*. But they did not do so. The 13th century jurist Accursius, who wrote the Ordinary Gloss on the *Corpus iuris civilis*, did say that an *actio in factum* is given 'if equity persuades that an action be given'.[4] But it is clear from the authority he cites that he meant that, as a matter of equity, the plaintiff should have an action even if the damage is not *a corpore* and *in corpus*. He did not mean that such an action is subject to a special requirement that the plaintiff show it is equitable that he recover.[5] And indeed, a medieval plaintiff bringing

---

[2] Reinhard Zimmermann, *The Law of Obligations: Roman Foundations of the Civilian Tradition* (Cape Town, 1990), 993–6.   [3] I. 4.3.16. See *Zimmermann, Law of Obligations*, 996–7.

[4] Accursius, *Glossa ordinaria* (Venice, 1581), to Dig. 9.2.33.1 to *lege Aquilia* ('et hoc [giving an *actio in factum*] si aequitas suaderet actionem dari').

[5] In modern printed editions, the passage just cited ends 'alioquin contra ut s[upra] eo[dem titolo lex] quaemadmodum § sed et si tanto'. This means that an action is given only when equity so 'persuades'

an *actio utilis* would frame his complaint in the same terms as one bringing an action that lay squarely within the *lex Aquilia*. He would not add an allegation that his case is especially deserving and therefore he should have relief as a matter of equity.[6] As Brunnemann noted in the 18th century, it did not matter which action the plaintiff brought.[7]

A second limitation can be inferred from the texts in which the Roman jurists said that the plaintiff can recover. Nearly always, his tangible property has been damaged physically or else put beyond his reach as when his ring is thrown into the river or his slave is allowed to escape.[8] Two texts go further and let a father recover for the death of a son who is still *in manus*.[9] Perhaps it seemed odd that the father could recover for the death of a slave but not a son.[10] Or perhaps the loss of the son was seen as an economic loss because legally, as long as the son was *in manus*, the father had a right to any assets that the son possessed.

In any event, as mentioned earlier, this limitation disappeared in the Middle Ages. The two texts just mentioned were generalized to allow recovery when any person died. A surviving widow was thus able to recover for economic losses suffered when her husband died.[11]

With this limitation gone, medieval[12] and early modern jurists[13] simply said that the plaintiff could recover if he suffered damage, and that damage meant a diminution

because otherwise there would be a contradiction with the section that begins 'sed et si tanto' of the law that begins 'quaemadmodum' which is to be found in the same title (Dig. 9.2) as the law which Accursius is explaining. That must be a miscitation since there is no passage that exactly fits this description. But there is one that comes close: the passage beginning 'sed si tanto' in Dig. 9.2.29, which does begin 'quaemadmodum'. And that, indeed, is the citation given in several medieval manuscripts. Vat. Lat. 2511 f. 78va; Vat. Lat. 1410 f. 158va; Pal. Lat. 733 f. 180va. This passage says that there is no liability under the *lex Aquilia* if a ship hits another because of the overpowering force of the elements. The context of the passage, and Accursius' gloss to *dominium* make it clear that there would be an action had the navigators been at fault for managing the ship. Accursius says: 'Et sic collige hic a contrario in damnum dari quando non fiat fortuitus casus'. Thus, when he says that an action outside the terms of the *lex Aquilia* is to be given only if equity so 'persuades', all he seems to mean is that one is not to give such an action invariably since then one would do so even if the defendant were not at fault.

[6] For model complaints, see Odofredus, *Summa de formandis libellis* in *Refugium advocatorum* (Vale Argentorael, 1510). The volume is neither foliated nor paginated but the form for an *actio in factum* under the *lex Aquilia* is on what would be f. 11v and the one for an *actio directa* is on what would be f. 40v. The complaints are the same except that the factual situation differs as one might expect from the Roman sources.

[7] Johannes Brunnemann, *Commentarius in quinquaginta libros pandectarum* (ed. novissima, Coloniae Allogrum, 1762), to Dig. 2.9.7 no. 11.

[8] See Zimmermann, *Law of Obligations*, 1023–4. One Roman text did allow the the plaintiff to recover the value of property he never obtained because the defendant destroyed a will or some other document legally necessary to obtain it. Dig. 9.2.41. In that case, however, the will or the document had been destroyed, which may not have seemed much different than physically destroying any other physical asset. At least, that is how medieval jurists regarded the destruction of such documents in other contexts. E.g. *Glossa ordinaria* to *Decretales Gregorii ix* to 5.36.7.

[9] Dig. 9.2.5.3; Dig. 9.2.7.4. A person could also recover when, not knowing that he was a free man, he served in good faith as someone's slave. Dig. 9.2.13.pr. See Zimmermann, *Law of Obligations*, 1016–17.

[10] Zimmermann, *Law of Obligations*, 1015.   [11] ibid. 1024–5.

[12] Azo, *Summa Codicis* (Lyons, 1557), to Dig. 9.2 ('Et dicit damnum a demo vel a diminuatione patrimonium'); Hostienisis, *Summa aurea* (Lyon, 1556), lib. 5, rubr. 'de damno dato', no.1 ('Quid sit damnum. Diminutio vel redemptio patrimonii').

[13] Georgius Adamus Struvius, *Syntagma iurisprudentiae secundum ordinem pandectarum* (Jena, 1692), Exerc. XIV, lib. 9, tit. 2, no. xx ('Fundamentum et causa huius actionis est damnum iniuria datum, quod est

in his *patrimonium*. They did not distinguish between loss of a physical asset and other kinds of loss. Indeed, they occasionally put cases in which, they said, the plaintiff would recover although he suffered what we today would call pure economic loss. The medieval jurist Durandus said that the plaintiff could recover if the defendant put dung in the street in front of his house, and he therefore had to pay a fine imposed by statute.[14] One of the greatest medieval jurists, Baldus de Ubaldi, said that the plaintiff could recover against his secretary who revealed his secrets.[15] In the 16th century, Zasius gave the same opinion in the case of the secretary, citing Baldus.[16] In the 18th century, Lauterbach and Brunnemann said that a client could recover from an advocate who harmed him through lack of skill.[17] Horst Kaufmann has found many other examples from the practice of early modern times.[18]

Before the 19th century, then, jurists would not deny relief under the *lex Aquilia* on the grounds that the plaintiff had suffered a purely economic loss. It does not follow that the plaintiff could recover in all the cases jurists put today when they discuss the problem of economic loss.[19] The category of economic loss is ours, not theirs. We cannot assume that these jurists would have seen all cases of economic loss as similar to those in which they said the plaintiff should recover. They did say that the plaintiff could recover for damage, and that damage meant any diminution in his *patrimonium*. But jurists make general statements like this one to address questions that they have consciously in mind. The question before them was one the Romans had already asked and answered: whether he could recover for damages inflicted *non in corpus* and even *non a corpore*. We should be careful about reading their statements as answers to questions they were not asking.

2. The natural law schools

As mentioned earlier, neither the Romans nor the medieval jurists had been concerned with the theory or general principles of tort. The Romans had discussed concrete instances of recovery, and the medieval jurists had tried to reconcile Roman texts. In contrast, beginning in the 16th century, the late scholastics, and later, the northern natural law schools were looking for principles. They were the first to ask whether a

delictum privatum, quo patrimonium sive re aliena dolo aut culpa deminuitur'); Wolfgang Lauterbach, *Collegium theorico-practici* (Tübingen, 1707), to D. 9.2 no. vii ('ut itaque hoc delictum dicatur commissum, requiritur ut damnum sit datum pecuniarium, scilicet, quo alterius diminuitur patrimonium'); Arnold Vinnius, *In quatuor libros Institutionem Imperialium commentarius* (4th edn., Amsterdam, 1665), to I. 4.3 pr. ('Nam damnum ad ademptione, et quasi deminutione patrimonii dictum est'); Iohannes Gottlieb Heineccius, *Elementa iuris civilis secundum ordinem pandectarum* (5th edn., Traiecti ad Rhenum, 1772), to Dig. 9.2, § clxxxvi ('quia haec actio ad patrimonii deminutionem pertinet').

[14] Guilelmus Durandus, *Speculum iuris* (Basil, 1574), lib. iv, par. iv, De iniuriis et damno dato, § 2 (sequitur), no. 15.

[15] Baldus de Ubaldi, *Commentaria Corpus iuris civilis* (Venice, 1577), to Dig. 9.2.41 (vulg. 9.2.42) pr. in fine.

[16] Ulricus Zasius, *Commentaria seu Lecturas eiusdem in titulos primae Pandectarum* ad Dig. 9.2 no. l 39, in *Opera omnia*, 1 (Lyon, 1550) (repr. Scientia Verlag, Aalen, Darmstadt, 1966).

[17] Lauterbach, *Collegium theorico-practici* to Dig. 9.2, no. xv; Brunnemann, *Commentarius* to Dig. 9.2.8, no. 5.

[18] Horst Kaufmann, *Rezeption und Usus Modernus der Actio Legis Aquiliae* (Cologue, 1958), 46–56.

[19] As noted ibid. 58.

person should recover, not only when something that already belonged to him was harmed, but when he was prevented from obtaining something of value.

The late scholastics debated this question drawing on Aristotelian ideas of commutative justice. In involuntary transactions, commutative justice is violated when one person harms another without giving back what he took or making compensation.[20]

Thomas Aquinas had described what belongs to a person and the types of harm that one could suffer. The harm might be to a 'thing' that belongs to him. It might be to his 'person', and then, either to his person itself or to his dignity. It might be to his relationship with another person such as his wife or his slave.[21] As we have seen, the late scholastics concluded that the Roman distinctions between different actions were mere matters of Roman positive law. In principle and as a matter of commutative justice, a person should recover whenever he suffered harm.[22] Sometimes they merely stated this principle,[23] and sometimes they classified types of harm in much the same way as Aquinas.[24] Grotius was merely summarizing their conclusions when he gave his famous description of the basic principles of tort law quoted earlier: 'From ... fault, if damage is caused, an obligation arises, namely, that the damage should be made good'. 'Damage', he explained, 'is when a man has less than what is his ...'.[25]

Anyone who culpably deprived another of any of these 'things' therefore owed compensation. But suppose he prevented the other from obtaining something that might have been his. Did he owe compensation then? Aquinas had said yes, adding that the amount to be paid in compensation is not the same:

'[A] man is bound to make compensation (*restitutio*) for whatever of another's he harmed. But one is harmed in two ways. One way is that he is harmed because that which he actually has is taken, and compensation must always be made for such a harm by payment of an equivalent. For example, when one person harms another by destroying his house, he is bound to pay the amount that the house is worth. The other way is that someone harms another by preventing him from acquiring what he was on the way (*in via*) to having. And compensation of an equal amount need not be made for such harm, for it is less to have such a thing virtually than to have it actually. One who is on the way to acquiring a thing has it only virtually or potentially. Consequently, if he is paid as though he had the thing actually, he would not receive the value of what was taken as compensation but more, which is not required in making compensation, as noted in article 3. He is bound, however, to make compensation according to the condition of persons and affairs.'[26]

In article 3, which he cites, Aquinas had put the case of someone who unjustly prevents another from obtaining a benefice. He said that compensation must be paid,

[20] *Nicomachean Ethics* V.ii 1130^b–1131^a.

[21] Thomas Aquinas, *Summa theologiae* II-II, Q. 61, a. 3.   [22] Chapter 12 I.

[23] e.g. Domenicus Soto, *De iustitia et iure libri decem* (Salamanca, 1553), lib. 4, q. 6, a. 5; Ludovicus Molina, *De iustitia et iure tractatus* (Venice, 1614), disps. 315, 724; Leonardus Lessius, *De iustitia et iure ceterisque virtutibus cardinalibus libri quatuor* (Paris, 1628), lib. 2, cap. 12, dubs. 16, 18; cap. 20, dubs. 10–11.

[24] e.g. Lessius, *De iustitia et iure*, lib. 2, caps. 3, 9–12.

[25] Hugo Grotius, *De iure belli ac pacis libri tres* (B. J. A. de Kanter-van Hettinga Tromp, eds., 1939), II.xvii.1–2. For similar conclusions by other natural lawyers, see Samuel Pufendorf, *De iure naturae et gentium libri octo* (Amsterdam, 1688), III.i.2, III.i.3; III.i.6; Jean Barbeyrac, *Le Droit de la nature et des gens... par le baron de Pufendorf* (5th edn., Amsterdam, 1734), n. 1 to III.i.2; n. 1 to III.i.3; n. 4 to III.i.6. See generally Zimmermann, *Law of Obligations*, 1032–4.   [26] *Summa theologiae* II-II, Q. 62, a. 4.

but not for its entire value 'because the man had not yet obtained the benefice and might have been prevented from doing so in many ways'.[27] Similarly, if one person destroys seeds which belong to another and which have not yet grown, he need not make compensation for the value that the crop would have had at harvest.[28]

Disagreeing with Aquinas, Cajetan tried to distinguish the case of the seeds from that of the benefice. The person claiming compensation for the seeds had a right to them, and it was on this right that his hope to profit at harvest time was based. In the case of the benefice, the claimant never had either the right to it or to anything else. Therefore, Cajetan said, he was not entitled to compensation:

'[N]o reason can be seen why I am bound to make compensation in whole or in part for impeding someone from seeking a benefit to which he never had any right. It follows from this—that he never had any right in anything—that nothing was his, and consequently it follows that no compensation is due him. And if it be said that he has a right hoped for (*ius in spe*), that is not a valid consideration because a right in hope is not a right, just as wealth hoped for is not wealth. Moreover, compensation for a thing hoped for is given when a person is deprived of a right on which that hope is founded, as is shown when seeds are destroyed or the tools of a craft are taken away through the use of which a person's family is supported, and in similar cases.'[29]

As we will see, Cajetan's argument was to resurface in England and Germany in the late 19th and early 20th centuries and to inspire the prohibition against liability for pure economic loss. The late scholastics rejected it, however, with arguments that would have been as sound then as in their own time. They failed to see how it could matter from the standpoint of commutative justice whether or not a person's expectations of a benefit were 'founded' on something he presently owned. If he was unjustly deprived of that benefit, as a matter of commutative justice, he was entitled to compensation. Moreover, Cajetan assumed that a person who does not yet have the right to the benefit he is seeking has, at present, no rights at all. Therefore, he cannot have been deprived of a right. In that respect, his argument is conceptualistic: the conclusion follows only if 'having a right' is implicitly defined to exclude a person from having a right to seek a benefit to which he, as yet, does not have the right. Lessius answered that a person could have a right to something he had not yet acquired, for example, to a gift that had not yet been made to him. Such a right was not 'absolute' but 'conditional'. The recipient's right to a gift, for example, was 'conditional' on the decision of the potential donor to give it to him.[30] Molina distinguished two meanings of the phrase 'having a right':

'[A] person is said to have a right (*ius*) to something in two different ways. First, because it is in some way his or owed to him. When right is used in this sense, we distinguish right in a thing (*ius in re*) and right to a thing (*ius ad rem*). In another sense, a person is said to have a right to something, not because it is owed to him, but because he has the capacity (*facultas*) for it, so that one who contravenes that right does him an injury. In this sense, everyone can be said to have the right to use his own things, for example, to eat his own food, so that injury and injustice is

[27] *Summa theologiae* II-II, Q. 62, a. 3, ad 4.   [28] ibid. a. 4, ad 1 and 2.
[29] Cajetan, *Commentaria* to Thomas Aquinas, *Summa theologica* (Padua, 1698), to II-II, Q. 62, a. 2 ad 4.
[30] Lessius, *De iustitia et iure*, lib. 2, cap. 12, dub. 18.

done to him if he is impeded. Indeed, we say that the poor have the right to beg for alms, that one who works for pay has the right to hire out his services, and that everyone has the right to hunt and fish in places where it is not prohibited. Consequently, if anyone impedes them in these matters, he does an injury and injustice and has the duty to make compensation. . . .'[31]

Thus a person could have the right to seek what he had not yet acquired, and the violation of this right entitled him to compensation.

While the late scholastics generally agreed that Cajetan was wrong, there was less agreement about how much compensation should be paid in such cases. As we have seen, Aquinas said that one must pay, not the value of the benefice that was never obtained or of the crop never harvested, but a lesser amount, according to the state of 'persons and affairs', since the party entitled to compensation could have been prevented from obtaining these benefits in many ways. Soto disagreed. He claimed that a person who harmed another's crop intentionally should have to pay its full value at the time of harvest though one who did so negligently should pay only the amount Aquinas had described.[32]

That conclusion was rejected by Lessius, de Lugo, and Molina. Lessius and de Lugo explained that whether the wrong had been done negligently or intentionally, commutative justice entitles the victim only to an amount equivalent to the harm actually done.[33] That harm, according to Lessius, is the value of the crop at the time it was destroyed 'taking in account the circumstances prevailing then'.[34] Molina argued that if the owner were paid the value of the crop at harvest time, he would be over-compensated since the further off the harvest, the greater are the perils and labor necessary to produce the crop, and so the less it is worth.[35] Molina consequently came close to the concept that modern economists call the 'expected value' of an asset, although he did not express it mathematically as they do.

De Lugo came closer still. He agreed with Aquinas, Lessius, and Molina that compensation should be made 'according to the present value (*secundum valorem praesentem*) of the object in the state in which it was when destroyed'.[36] But he took them to mean that this amount was the price for which the object could then have been sold. That is so usually, de Lugo argued, but not always. It all depends on whether the owner of the object could have bought another like it. If a person's foal is killed, usually, he can buy another. If he does, he will not lose the profit he intended to make by later selling a fully grown horse. If he does not, then the reason he will not make this profit is his own decision not to replace the foal rather than the foal's death. In either case, he should only receive the price of the foal in compensation. Suppose, however, that he could not replace it because he lacked the money to do so. In that case, the foal's death did deprive him of the profit he would have made on the horse, and so he should recover that profit. Indeed, it may be impossible to buy something equivalent to the object that was destroyed. Buying another foal is easy but if crops are

---

[31] Molina, *De iustitia et iure*, II, disp. 727 no. 1.   [32] Soto, *De iustitia et iure*, lib. 4, q. 6, a. 5.

[33] Lessius, *De iustitia et iure*, lib. 2, cap. 12, dub. 19, no. 137; Iohannes de Lugo, *Disputationum de iustitia et iure* (Lyon, 1670), disp. 18, § 4, no. 79.

[34] Lessius, *De iustitia et iure*, lib. 2, cap. 12, dub. 19, no. 137.

[35] Molina, *De iustitia et iure*, III, disp. 726, no. 4.

[36] de Lugo, *Disputationum*, disp. 18, § 4, no. 81.

destroyed, it may be impossible to replace them by replanting the field that year. In that event, the owner should receive the profit he lost because he could not raise that crop, not merely the value of the crop when still immature. That conclusion, de Lugo said, was consonant with the principles of Aquinas, Lessius, and Molina although it seemed to contradict their views. De Lugo added that the owner's compensation, if he could not replace the crop, should not be the full value of a mature crop. A deduction should be made for the risks the owner would have faced and the expenses he would have incurred.[37]

Indeed, because value in the present depends upon what happens in the future, a person should be compensated for the loss of things that he hopes to obtain but does not yet have. 'You say', de Lugo challenged a hypothetical interlocutor, 'that the hope of this profit from a future object (*spes illa lucri ex rei futuri*) does not increase the value of this object itself'. But if that were so, one who ousted the owner of a field and occupied it without raising crops would merely need to give back the field without paying for crops that the owner could have raised had he not been ousted. As this example shows,

'this hope [of profit] is not based on the field alone, at least when effort and cultivation are wanted in order to profit, but, indeed, on the will of the owner who wants to till the field or to pasture animals and to expend the effort and care by which he adds something to the value of the field alone: the amount, that is, that the hope is worth then of profiting from the effort and care that the owner wants to expend.'[38]

In short, the opportunity to profit in the future has a value in the present, and the value of a field in the present depends upon such an opportunity.

Many rules of modern civil law can be traced back to Grotius and Pufendorf, who, in turn, had taken them from the late scholastics. If the late scholastics had agreed with Cajetan, perhaps something like the modern German and English rule against the recovery of pure economic loss would have become part of the civil law. Cajetan's position resembled the modern German and English rule although it did not go as far. He wanted to deny compensation to a person who lost his chance to get a benefit to which he 'never had any right'. The modern rule excludes recovery when the person had a right to the benefit under a contract with a third party.

In any event, the late scholastics rejected Cajetan's view, and Grotius and Pufendorf did not mention it. The debate was forgotten as soon as jurists no longer read the works of the late scholastics. As we have seen, however, it was rejected for reasons that can be readily understood today. Indeed, the late scholastics came close to the concept of expected value as a modern economist or jurist understands it.

B. The Rise of the Rule against Recovery of Pure Economic Loss

In the late 19th and early 20th centuries, a rule emerged, first in Germany, and then in England and the United States, that the defendant was not liable for 'pure economic harm' caused to the plaintiff. 'Pure economic harm' is harm unaccompanied by

---

[37] de Lugo, *Disputationum*, disp. 18, § 4, no. 81.   [38] ibid. no. 82.

physical damage to the plaintiff's person or property. The jurists who developed this rule defended it with an argument as conceptualistic as Cajetan's. It would have been as vulnerable as Cajetan's to criticisms like those of the late scholastics. Yet in a period of conceptualism, this argument prevailed.

1. Germany

In Germany, the idea that the plaintiff should not be able to recover for any sort of harm was suggested by the Roman texts which remained in force in much of Germany until 1900. As we have seen, in almost all the Roman examples, the plaintiff has lost the use of a physical object even if it was not physically injured: for example, he could recover for the loss of a cup whether it was smashed or thrown into a river where he could not get it back. In the universities, most jurists concluded that the defendant should be liable only for harm to defendant's person and property.[39] Some merely pointed to the texts. Others, such as Rudolf von Ihering, argued that liability would be too extensive unless limited in some way:

'Where would it lead if everyone could be sued, not only for intentional wrongdoing (*dolus*) but for gross negligence (*culpa lata*) absent a contractual relationship! An ill-advised statement, a rumor passed on, a false report, bad advice, a poor decision, a recommendation for an unfit serving maid by her former employer, information given at the request of a traveler about the way, the time, and so forth—in short, anything and everything would make one liable to compensate for the damage that ensued if there were gross negligence despite one's good faith ...'.[40]

Nevertheless, by the end of the century, it seemed as though this approach would be abandoned for a broader one. It had been challenged by jurists such as Otto von Gierke and Josef Kohler who argued that the defendant should be liable for violation of a panoply of rights that concerned plaintiff's freedom of action and personality.[41] In 1888, the highest German court for civil matters, then the *Reichsgericht*, allowed a plaintiff to recover whose person and property had not been injured. He had been temporarily unable to sell a product because the defendant had been 'negligent at least' in raising a claim of patent infringement.[42] Indeed, in their first draft, the First Commission charged with drafting the German Civil Code proposed the following provision: 'One who has caused another harm (*Schaden*) by intention or by negligence by an unlawful [*widerrechtlich*] act or omission is obligated to make him compensation'.[43] As in the

---

[39] e.g. Bernhard Windscheid, *Lehrbuch des Pandektenrechts* 2 (7th edn., Frankfurt-am-Main, 1891), §§ 451, 455; Karl von Vangerow, *Lehrbuch der Pandekten* 3 (6th edn., Marburg, 1863), § 681 n. 1.I (3); Karl Arndts von Arnesberg, *Lehrbuch der Pandekten* (14th edn., Stuttgart, 1889), § 324. See Zimmermann, *Law of Obligations*, 1036–8.

[40] Rudolph von Ihering, 'Culpa in contrahendo oder Schadensersatz bei nichtigen oder nicht zur Perfektion gelangten Verträgen', *Jherings Jahrbücher* 4 (1861), 12–13.

[41] Otto von Gierke, *Der Entwurf eines bürgerliches Gesetzbuch und das deutche Recht* (Leipzig, 1889), 264; Otto von Gierke, *Deutsches Privatrecht* 3 (Leipzig, 1917), 885–7; Joseph Kohler, 'Recht und Prozess', *Zeitschrift für das privat-öffentliche Recht der Gegenwart* 14 (1887), 1 at 4–5; Joseph Kohler, *Lehrbuch des bürgerlichen Rechts* 1 (Berlin, 1904), § 132; 2 (Berlin, 1906), § 190. See Karl Heinz Fezer, *Teilhabe und Verantwortung* (Munich, 1986), 456–65.   [42] RG, 3 Dec. 1888, ERGZ 22, 208 at 209.

[43] *Teilentwurf des Vorentwurfs zu einem BGB, Recht der Schuldverhältnisse*, no. 15, § 1.

French Civil Code, this provision puts no express limitation on the 'harm' for which one can recover. The Commission explained:

'Any act is not permitted in the sense of the civil law by which anyone impinges and violates the sphere of rights of another unlawfully in an unauthorized manner. For the sphere of rights of each person must be respected and left untouched by all other persons; whoever acts contrary to this general command of the law without there being any special grounds for justification has by that alone committed a tortious act.'[44]

Why, then, did the German Civil Code allow the plaintiff to recover only for the types of harm enumerated in what is now § 823? At one of its early meetings, the First Commission discussed 'what is to be understood as the "violation of a right" '. It might be 'only the violation of a legal order by an act prohibited by law as contrary to the legal order for the sake of himself'.[45] The Commission eventually chose the first of these alternatives. For the Commission, it seemed to follow that the violation of rights such as person and property is tortious because such rights are 'absolute' in the sense that they could be asserted against anyone. In contrast, a 'right of obligation' (*obligatorisches Recht*) such as a contract right was a right only against the other party to the contract. The Commission noted that a tort was not committed by the violation of such a right because it 'cannot be violated by anyone except the debtor [i.e., the party who is bound]'.[46] Consequently, the Commission added a final sentence to clarify the type of right that must be violated. It went without saying that the paradigm case of a violation of a right was an interference with property. The Commission added, 'The violation of life, body, health, freedom and honor are also to be regarded as the violation of a right in the sense of the previous provision'. This language had mixed fortunes before it passed into what is now § 823(1). At one point it was deleted as unnecessary. Later it was put back, with an explicit mention of the right of property and the subtraction of 'honor'. The phrase 'or similar right' (*sonstiges Recht*) was added because it had proven impossible to enumerate all of the ownership-like 'absolute rights' that a defendant could violate.

The drafters had not been discussing 'pure economic harm'. They were distinguishing between 'absolute rights', good against all the world, and 'relative rights', good against a particular party. But if one could not recover against a third party for interference with these relative rights (let alone mere economic opportunities), then it followed that one could not recover for what we now call pure economic harm. The German courts reached that conclusion soon after the Civil Code came into force. In 1901, it held that a defendant who interfered with the plaintiff's economic freedom of action had not violated his 'freedom' within the meaning of § 823(1).[47] In 1904, it held that economic harm (*Vermögensschädigung*) was not in itself harm to a right protected by § 823(1).[48]

---

[44] Werner Schubert, ed., *Die Vorlagen der Redaktoren für die erste Kommission zur Ausarbeitung des Entwurfs eines Bürgerlichen Gesetzbuches, Recht der Schuldverhältnisse, Teil 1, Allgemeiner Teil* 1 (Berlin, 1980), 657.   [45] *Protokolle* 1, 971–2.

[46] ibid. 1, 984, 986–7.   [47] RG, 11 Apr. 1901, ERGZ 48, 114.

[48] RG, 27 Feb. 1904, ERGZ 58, 24.

In Germany, then, the rule against recovery for pure economic harm originally rested on what today would seem a conceptualistic argument: if A interferes with B's performance of a duty that B owes to C, then C cannot recover against A because C was owed the duty by B, not by A. This argument is typical of the conceptualism of the 19th century—of what the Germans call *Begriffsjurisprudenz*. It does not consider what principle or purpose might be served by limiting the plaintiff's recovery. It tries to extract limits from the definitions of concepts, in this instance, from the concepts of absolute and relative rights. Today, it is generally recognized that one cannot proceed in that way. The definitions of absolute and relative right were not framed with the problem of limiting tort recovery in mind, and therefore one cannot expect these definitions to contain an answer to that problem. It is an historical accident that the Code was enacted just before conceptualism fell into disrepute.

Then there is one accident more. If the defendant should be liable for negligence only if he violates plaintiff's absolute rights, how can he be liable for causing the plaintiff an economic loss, as he is in Germany under § 826 of the Civil Code, if he acts intentionally in a way that violates 'good morals'? If the drafters had seen a contradiction here, they might have rethought limiting recovery in negligence to the violation of absolute rights. They did not see a contradiction because of the way in which they had classified 'unlawfulness'. When the defendant who intentionally caused economic harm was held liable, it was not because he had unlawfully violated plaintiff's rights but because he had violated 'good morals' within the meaning of § 826. And that settled that. No one asked why, if the defendant had not violated any of the plaintiff's rights, causing him an economic loss intentionally should ever be considered a violation of good morals.

2. The common law

In England, and consequently in the United States, it also came to be accepted that one could not normally recover in negligence for pure economic loss.[49] The English case commonly cited today to illustrate this rule is *Spartan Steel & Alloys Ltd* v. *Martin & Co. (Contractors) Ltd.* [50] The defendants cut the power line to plaintiff's factory causing material to solidify in its furnace. The plaintiff recovered for the loss it suffered because the material solidified but not for the profit it lost because it could not melt other material while the power was off. This rule predated *Spartan Steel*. It was judge-made, not statutory, and it was established by a series of cases rather than a single decision. Unlike Germany, one cannot find a single moment in which the rule became accepted. Nevertheless, one can see a turning point: a point at which the courts began to say that relief would not be given because of the kind of harm that the plaintiff had suffered. At this turning point, a critical role was played by the same conceptualistic argument that influenced the German drafters.

As we have seen, an action for negligence was recognized in England only in the 19th century, and then at a comparatively late date. The question of whether one

---

[49] W. V. H Rogers, *Winfield and Jolowicz on Tort* (15th edn., London, 1998), 134; K. M. Stanton, *The Modern Law of Tort* (London, 1994), 332, 353–54. See generally Michael Furmston, ed., *The Law of Tort: Policies and Trends in Liability for Damage to Property and Economic Loss* (London, 1986).

[50] [1973] 1 QB 27.

could recover in negligence for what we now call pure economic loss was faced only at the turn of the century. By that time, a few cases had been decided which courts and commentators thought in point. As we will see, however, though these courses denied recovery, they did not do so on the grounds that the loss was purely economic.

In 1875 in *Cattle* v. *The Stockton Waterworks Co.*,[51] defendant's negligence caused the flooding of a third party's land on which the plaintiff was building a tunnel. The court refused to allow him to recover for his extra expenses. In 1877, in *Simpson & Co.* v. *Thomson*,[52] an insurance company was denied recovery for the insurance money it had to pay for insured cargo that was lost when one of defendant's ships negligently struck one of his own ships containing the cargo. In 1908, in *Anglo-Algerian Steamship Co. Ltd.* v. *The Houlder Line, Ltd.*,[53] defendant had negligently damaged a third party's dock. Plaintiff was not allowed to recover for the loss he suffered when his ship was unable to use it.

Nevertheless, as Robby Bernstein has noted, the rationale of *Cattle* and *Simpson* 'had nothing to do with the fact that the plaintiff's loss was economic',[54] and the same can be said of *Anglo-Algerian Steamship*. One consideration, mentioned in *Cattle* and *Anglo-Algerian Steamship*, was that the damage was too 'remote'.[55] Another, mentioned in *Cattle*, *Simpson*, and *Anglo-Algerian Steamship* was that recovery would unduly multiply the number of possible plaintiffs: if a mine were flooded, those who worked there could recover their lost wages;[56] a doctor who had contracted to treat a man for a fixed fee for a year could recover from the negligent driver of a carriage who had injured his patient;[57] a traveler forced to find other accommodation could recover against a person who negligently damaged the inn where he planned to stay.[58] The first of these considerations has to do with causation; the second with a pragmatic desire to avoid an indefinite number of plaintiffs. Neither suggests that the plaintiff cannot recover what we now call economic loss. Indeed, in *Anglo-Algerian Steamship*, Walton indicated that under some circumstances, he could.[59]

Nevertheless, at the turn of the 20th century, a number of leading treatise writers placed a different interpretation on such cases. According to J. F. Clerk and W. H. B. Lindsell, *Cattle* stood for the principle that 'interference with rights of service or with rights of contract generally is not actionable'.[60] In that respect, such rights different from rights such as property which were 'unqualified'.[61]

A similar interpretation was adopted in the eighth edition of C. G. Addison's treatise on torts which, after his death, was published in 1906 by William Gordon and Walter Griffith. Although they styled themselves 'editors', they had found it necessary to rewrite the treatise extensively because it was unsystematic, they said, compared

---

[51] (1875) LR 10 QB 453.   [52] [1877] 3 AC 279 (HL).   [53] [1908] 1 KB 659.
[54] Robby Bernstein, *Economic Loss* (2nd edn., London, 1998), 11.
[55] LR 10 QB at 457; [1908] 1 KB at 665.   [56] LR 10 QB at 457.   [57] [1877] 3 AC at 289.
[58] [1908] 1 KB at 668.
[59] [1908] 1 KB at 664–5. He was speaking of what are now called cases of public nuisance in which the plaintiff is specially affected. As will be noted later on, today the rule is said to be different in nuisance than in negligence, but Walton was writing before that difference came to be accepted.
[60] John Frederick Clerk and WHB Lindsell, *The Law of Torts* (Wyatt Paine, edn., 3rd edn., London, 1904), 11. At another point they do suggest that the case turned on the remoteness of the damage (ibid. 133).   [61] ibid.

with the treatises of Sir Frederick Pollock and Clerk and Lindsell.[62] Since it contained 'little or nothing about the law of Negligence', they had written the chapter on that subject from scratch.[63] In it they explained that negligence was the breach of a duty, and that therefore the plaintiff is liable only 'where there is an obligation toward the plaintiff'.[64] 'It follows', they said, 'that if there is no duty to be careful there is no action for negligence', citing *Cattle* as an illustration.

Sir John Salmond adopted a similar interpretation of *Cattle* and of *Anglo-Algerian Steamship* in the second edition of his treatise on torts published in 1910. In *Cattle*, the principle was that 'nuisance is actionable only at the suit of the occupier or owner of the land affected by it; not at the suit of strangers whatever pecuniary interest they may have in the non-existence of the nuisance'.[65] In *Anglo-Algerian Steamship*, the principle was that '[n]egligent injury to property gives an action to the owner of that property, or to other persons having some proprietary interest therein, but not to mere strangers who are thereby subjected to pecuniary loss'.[66] Both cases were instances of *damnum sine iniuria*.[67] In later editions, he generalized the principle: 'He who does a wrongful act is liable only to the person whose rights are violated'.[68] As illustrations, he cited *Cattle* and *Anglo-Algerian Steamship Co.*[69]

Such an interpretation was adopted by Justice Hamilton in 1911 in deciding the case of *La Société Anonyme de Remorquage à Hélice* v. *Bennets*.[70] The defendant had negligently rammed and sunk a ship owned by a third party which the plaintiff had been towing under contract. The plaintiff was not allowed to recover the money he would have made under the contract. The plaintiff's attorney had argued that he should recover because the damage was not 'too remote'.[71] Instead of arguing whether it was or not, the defendant's attorney said, in the words of Salmond, that '[a]lthough there was a breach of duty followed by damage to the owner of the tow, there was only iniuria sine damno so far as the tug was concerned'.[72] Justice Hamilton agreed. Although the headnote to the case said that the plaintiff's harm was not the 'direct consequence of the negligence', Hamilton said that the plaintiffs must 'shew not only an iniuria, namely, the breach of the defendant's obligation, but also damnum to themselves in the sense of damage recognized by law'.[73] Like the treatise writers, he cited *Cattle* as authority.

After *Remorquage* came a long series of cases in which courts said that what mattered was not remoteness but the type of harm the plaintiff had suffered. In 1922, in *Elliott Steam Tug Co. Ltd.* v. *Shipping Controller*, the plaintiff did not recover under the common law for the profits he lost when the Admiralty requisitioned his tug. The reason, according to Scrutton, is 'not because the loss of profits during repairs is not the direct consequence of the wrong, but because the common law rightly or wrongly

---

[62] Charles Greenstreet Addison, *A Treatise on the Law of Torts or Wrongs and their Remedies* (8th edn., William E. Gordon and Walter Hussey Griffith, eds., London, 1906), viii.   [63] ibid. p. vii.

[64] ibid. 701.

[65] John W. Salmond, *The Law of Torts: A Treatise on the English Law of Liability for Civil Injuries* (2nd edn., London, 1910), 10.   [66] ibid. 10.

[67] ibid. 8, 11.

[68] John W. Salmond, *The Law of Torts* (8th edn., W. T. S. Stallybrass, ed., London, 1934), 133.

[69] ibid. 134, 135.   [70] [1911] 1 KB 243.   [71] [1911] 1 KB at 245.

[72] [1911] 1 KB at 246.   [73] [1911] 1 KB at 248.

does not recognise him as able to sue for such an injury to his merely contractual rights'.[74] A few years later, Oliver Wendell Holmes adopted this rationale in *Robbins Dry Dock Repair* v. *Flint*,[75] citing this language with approval. Later American cases cited *Robbins*.

In 1947, by way of dictum, Lord Roche said of *Remorquage* that '[i]f it was correctly decided, on which I express no opinion, I think it must depend on a view that one vessel (A) does not owe to the tug which is towing vessel (B) any duty not negligently to collide with (B)'.[76] Lord Simons said of the plaintiff in *Simpson* that '[t]he reason why he cannot recover is not because it could not be reasonably foreseen that he, or at least some insurer, would suffer, but because his loss is of a kind that the law does not regard as recoverable'.[77] He cited with approval *Remorquage* and its statement about *damnum* without *iniuria*.[78] In 1952, in *Best* v. *Samuel Fox & Co. Ltd.*, a wife was denied recovery for loss of consortium when her husband had been injured. Lord Goddard said that '[n]egligence, if it is to give rise to legal liability, must result from a breach of duty owed to a person who thereby suffers damage. But what duty was owed here by the employers of the husband to the wife?'[79] In 1955, in *Attorney-General for New South Wales* v. *Perpetual Trustee Co. (Ltd.)*, the government was not allowed to recover for loss of the services of a policeman whom the defendant had tortiously killed. Citing *Remorquage*, Viscount Simonds said: 'It is fundamental . . . that the mere fact that an injury to A. prevents a third party from getting from A. a benefit which he would otherwise have obtained, does not invest the third party with a right of action against the wrongdoer . . .'.[80] In 1966, in *Weller & Co.* v. *Foot and Mouth Disease Research Institute*, plaintiff could not recover for harm suffered to his business of auctioning cattle when the market for cattle was closed due to the escape of a virus from defendant Institute. Justice Widgery said that 'a duty of care which arises from a risk of direct injury to person or property is owed only to those whose person or property may foreseeably be injured by a failure to take care'.[81] In *Electrochrome Ltd.* v. *Welsh Plastics Ltd.*, plaintiff could not recover when defendant negligently cut off the supply of water from his factory. Justice Geoffrey Lane said that he 'adopt[ed] as correct' Salmond's statement that '[a] person who suffers damnum cannot recover compensation on the basis of iniuria suffered by another'.[82] In 1969, in *Margarine Union GmbH* v. *Cambray Prince Steamship Co. Ltd.*, plaintiff failed to recover the loss he suffered when goods were damaged that he did not own at the time that they were harmed. Justice Roskill said that he agreed with 'every word' of Widgery's judgment in *Weller*.[83]

As P. S. Atiyah observed,[84] and as we have just seen, in these cases the courts did not formulate a rule that expressly said that a plaintiff could not recover for pure economic loss. Nevertheless, this was an implication of what they had said. If the plaintiff could not recover when the defendant interfered with a contractual right, then surely he

---

[74] [1922] 1 KB 127, 140.   [75] 275 US 303 (1927).
[76] *Morrison Steamship Co. Ltd.* v. *Greystoke Castle*, [1947] AC 265, 280 (HL).
[77] [1947] AC at 305.   [78] [1947] AC at 306.   [79] [1952] AC 716, 730–1.
[80] [1955] AC 457, 484.   [81] [1966] QB 569, 587.   [82] [1968] 2 All ER 205, 206.
[83] [1969] 1 QB 219, 251.
[84] P. S. Atiyah, 'Negligence and Economic Loss', *L. Quar. Rev.* 83 (1967), 248 at 248.

could not be liable when he interfered with a mere expectation of receiving some benefit.

What is striking is the consistency not only in result but in rationale during this period of over 50 years. Supposedly, the fact that the plaintiff had a contract with a third party could not change the rights and duties of the plaintiff and defendant to each other. To be liable, the defendant must violate a right such as property which the plaintiff has against all the world, not merely against a third party. This is the same argument that we have seen in Germany.[85] It exemplifies a logical or conceptualist style of reasoning that seemed persuasive at the beginning of the century but has since been generally discredited. Even at the beginning of the century, the argument was not decisive. Then as now, the plaintiff could recover for economic loss in a variety of cases in which the defendant had caused the loss intentionally: for example, by threatening potential customers.[86] He could recover if the defendant created a public nuisance, for example, by blocking the street, and the plaintiff suffered some special economic harm that was not suffered by users of the street generally such as a loss of customers.[87] Treatise writers today simply say that the plaintiff can recover for such harm in nuisance but not in negligence without explaining why there should be such a difference.[88] Such cases can be distinguished in various ways from the ones we have just described. But if, as a matter of logic, the defendant should not be liable unless he violates a right that the plaintiff has against all the world, it is hard to see why he should ever be liable for preventing the plaintiff from entering into contracts or for interfering with their performance.

Twice during this long period, it seemed that a crack might be opening in the wall but both times it was plastered over. In 1932, in *Donoghue* v. *Stevenson*, it was held that one who negligently manufactured a product was liable to the ultimate consumer. Lord Atkin said: 'You must take reasonable care to avoid acts or omissions which you can reasonably foresee would be likely to injure your neighbor'. Neighbors, he explained, are 'persons who are so closely and directly affected by my act that I ought

---

[85] Whether the English treatise writers who first put forward this argument knew that German jurists had already done so is another question. That is certainly a possibility for Salmond. He was surely familiar with the German Civil Code and may have known of the work of the First Commission as well. His select bibliography in his book *Jurisprudence* shows a thorough knowledge of German writing on private law and a special admiration for Bernard Windscheid, one of the most distinguished members of the First Commission. He described Windscheid as 'one of the most distinguished German exponents of modern Roman law' and his book, *Lehrbuch des Pandektenrechts*, as 'an admirable example of the scientific study of a legal system'. John W. Salmond, *Jurisprudence or the Theory of the Law* (London, 1902), 654. Some have suggested that he used ideas taken from Windscheid in that book. Julius Stone, *Legal System and Lawyers' Reasonings* (Stanford, Cal., 1968), 141. See Alex Frame, *Salmond Southern Jurist* (Wellington, NZ, 1995), 63.

[86] Rogers, *Winfield and Jolowicz on Tort*, 133. The classic early case is *Tarleton* v. *M'Gawler*, 170 Eng. Rep. 153 (KB). Nevertheless, there is no general principle that anyone who intentionally causes another economic loss is liable. The plaintiff must sue for deceit, unfair competion or some other particular tort. See Margaret Brazier, *The Law of Torts* (8th edn., London, 1988), 103–50.

[87] *Fritz* v. *Hobson*, (1879) 14 Ch D 542 (obstruction in the highway costs plaintiff customers); *Rose* v. *Miles*, [1815] 1 KB 405 (obstruction of navigable creek forces plaintiff to move his goods by land).

[88] Rogers, *Winfield and Jolowicz on Tort*, 493; Stanton, *Modern Law of Tort*, 402. Thesiger, J did the same in *SCM*. Thesiger says economic loss rule applies in negligence but not in nuisance. *SCM (United Kingdom) Ltd.* v. *W.J. Whittall & Son Ltd.* [1970] 2 All ER 417, 430.

reasonably to have them in contemplation as being so affected...'.[89] In 1964, in *Headly Byrne & Co. Ltd* v. *Heller & Partners Ltd.*, defendants were held liable for pure economic loss. They were bankers who had negligently given incorrect information about a company's creditworthiness. Lord Devlin claimed that there was 'neither logic nor common sense' in distinguishing between a financial loss that was caused by physical injury and one that was caused directly.[90] But later courts held that these statements only applied to cases of negligently manufactured products and negligently provided information. They did not change the rule in cases like *Remorquage*.

Bernstein used the phrase 'historical accident' to describe the shift in rationale from *Cattle* to *Remorquage*.[91] As we can now see, it was the same sort of historical accident that occurred in Germany. The shift occurred because of the accident that a decision was made at a time when this conceptualistic rationale could find favor. In England, judges repeated it for over half a century, either because they still found it persuasive, or out of respect for precedent and the opinion of prior judges.

One might have expected that when this rationale no longer seemed persuasive, judges would react as Lord Devlin did in *Headley Byrne* and throw out the rule. Instead, Lord Denning kept the rule and threw out the rationale in his decisions in *SCM (United Kingdom) Ltd.* v. *W.J. Whittall & Son Ltd.*[92] in 1971 and *Spartan Steel* in 1973.

In both cases, the plaintiffs tried to recover the profits they lost when defendants negligently severed a cable, cutting off the power to their factory. *SCM* reached Lord Denning on appeal from a decision by Justice Thesiger which seems to have influenced his own thinking. Thesiger allowed the plaintiffs to recover. In doing so, he gave a new explanation of the prior decisions. As we have seen, they rested on a rationale that was logical and conceptualist. According to Thesiger, however, these decisions could not be explained logically. '[I]t is not always possible for the law to be logical.'[93] Indeed, he said, these decisions had not been the product of a logic but of common sense groping for reasonable results. '[T]he common law has always developed by experience rather than logic and by dealing with situations as they arise in what seems a reasonable way.'[94] One indication that judges had been 'dealing with situations as they arise' was the fact that they had stated the principle at stake in two different ways. Sometimes they had said that there was no duty, but sometimes that the harm was too remote.[95] The question should be whether it was reasonable for the plaintiffs to recover in this particular situation. Thesiger thought it was because the plaintiffs were 'so closely and directly affected' by the act of the defendant.

This decision was overturned on appeal. Nevertheless, in this case and again in *Spartan Steel*, Lord Denning also gave a new explanation of the prior decisions. The core of his analysis was much like that of Thesiger. Like Thesiger, he claimed that the rule followed in these decisions was not logical nor based on logic but on common sense. Thus Lord Devlin was only partially right when he said it could be defended by 'neither logic nor common sense'. 'There may be no difference in logic, but I think

---

[89] *Donoghue* v. *Stevenson*, [1932] AC 562, 580.   [90] [1964] AC 465, 517.
[91] Bernstein, *Economic Loss*, 11.   [92] [1971] 1 QB 337.   [93] [1970] 2 All ER 417, 431.
[94] [1970] 2 All ER 417, 431.   [95] [1970] 2 All ER 417, 431.

there is a great deal of difference in common sense. The law is the embodiment of common sense: or, at any rate, it should be.'[96] If we ask why the law has refused to allow the plaintiff to recover for pure economic loss, '[t]he reason is public policy'.[97] In deciding *SCM*, he observed that courts had sometimes said there was no duty and sometimes that the harm was too remote. He claimed 'it was plain' that the defendants owed a duty to the plaintiffs,[98] and seemed at one point to think that the policy concerns that are relevant might be captured by the phrase 'too remote'.[99] In *Spartan Steel*, however, he said, like Thesiger, that both expressions masked the considerations that had been truly important in the prior cases:

Sometimes I say: 'There was no duty.' In others I say, 'The damage was too remote.' So much so that I think the time has come to discard those tests which have proved so elusive. It seems to me better to consider the particular relationship in hand, and see whether or not, as a matter of policy, economic loss should be recoverable, or not.[100]

He was less clear about the policy at stake. In *SCM*, he said '[i]t is not sensible to saddle losses on this scale onto one sole contractor'. 'The risk should be borne by the whole community who suffer the losses, rather than rest on one pair of shoulders.... There is not much logic in this, but still it is the law.'[101] In *Spartan Steel* he mentioned this concern, and also the risk of too many claims, the belief of 'most people' that power shortages are 'a thing they must put up with', and the way such risks are allocated by legislation governing the industry.[102]

   The account that Justice Thesiger and Lord Denning gave of the history of the rule is history as a common law judge would like it to have occurred. Focusing on the situation before them, judges decide a case as common sense suggests, unsure as yet of the rule or principle to be followed, grasping it dimly but formulating it as best they can. Finally, after many cases are decided, experience makes it possible to see what is at stake more clearly than if one had tried to work out a rule or principle abstractly. Indeed, one may ultimately discover that the problem cannot be solved by a rule or principle that is logically satisfying but must be resolved, case by case, through the exercise of common sense.

   I do not deny that sometimes the common law does work that way. I have argued elsewhere that an advantage of the common law method is that it sometimes does.[103] But this time it did not. The courts had not been deciding cases on common sense grounds. They had been deciding them according to a rationale that had appealed on logical grounds to Clerk, Lindsell, Salmond, and the editors of Addison and before them to the German First Commission. Doubtless, the courts were relieved that this rationale imposed some limit on liability, a concern they sometimes mentioned. Their decisions may have been a product of that concern as well as the logical appeal of the rationale they adopted. But it does not follow that they placed the limit on recovery where they did by consulting common sense or experience.

---

[96] [1971] 1 QB at 344.   [97] [1971] 1 QB at 344.   [98] [1971] 1 QB at 343.
[99] [1971] 1 QB at 344–5.   [100] [1973] 1 QB at 37.   [101] [1971] 1 QB at 344.
[102] [1973] 1 QB at 38–9.
[103] James Gordley, 'European Codes and American Restatements: Some Difficulties', *Colum. L. Rev.* 81 (1981), 140.

Having adopted that rationale in 1911, the courts adhered to it thereafter. To show that they had shifted back and forth between this rationale and a concern for remoteness, Justice Thesinger and Lord Denning only cited pre-*Remorquage* cases such as *Cattle*, *Remorquage* itself, which only mentioned remoteness in the headnote, and cases which do not deal with pure economic loss but with physical harm occurring in some improbable way[104] or nervous shock on witnessing an injury to one's child.[105]

It is an historical accident that the rule was adopted at a time when the conceptualistic rationale for it seemed persuasive. To scrap the rationale and keep the rule as though it were the product of experience and common sense is to perpetuate the accident. I agree that there should be a limit on recovery in tort. The fact that this rule was adopted by accident does not prove that it sets the wrong limit. By coincidence, it might be the best rule from the standpoint of policy, common sense, experience. But that would be a remarkable coincidence.

II. A Rationale for Limiting Liability in Tort

It might seem there should be no limit on recovery in tort. A person who suffers economic harm is hurt just as badly as when a comparable amount of physical property is destroyed. Indeed, the value of physical property depends upon the economic benefit it can produce in the future. This point was made centuries ago by the late scholastics. As we have just seen, the rule excluding recovery for economic harm originated in the late 19th and early 20th centuries for reasons that appealed to the conceptualism of that time but do not seem persuasive now.

A law and economics scholar might find a reason for sometimes limiting recovery for pure economic loss but not one that would explain the law. His question would be who could prevent the loss at lowest cost. Suppose an electric cable is cut by an excavator, and a factory therefore loses profits. A law and economics scholar might ask which would cost less: for the factory to have a back up generator or the excavation company to incur extra expense to avoid cutting cables. But that inquiry would depend on the circumstances of each case, just like an inquiry into which party was negligent. Moreover, it cannot explain why the law should treat a pure economic loss differently than a physical loss.

We can find a better explanation if we first observe that even jurisdictions that prohibit recovery for pure economic loss will sometimes make exceptions. Presumably, at least on an intuitive level, they find the prohibition more sensible in some cases than in others. Conversely, jurisdictions that permit recovery for pure economic harm will also make exceptions. Presumably, on an intuitive level, they sometimes feel that to allow recovery is objectionable even though the rules of their jurisdiction permit it. That is not the behavior one would expect if the rule against

---

[104] *Woods* v. *Duncan*, [1946] AC 410, 421 (submarine sunk due to an 'extraordinary combination of circumstances'), cited by Thesiger, J in *SCM*, [1970] 2 All ER 431.

[105] *King* v. *Phillips* [1953] 1 QB 429, cited by Lord Denning in *Spartan Steel*, [1973] 1 QB at 36.

recovery for pure economic loss were always right or always wrong. It would then apply in the one case in the same way as in the other.

The differences make sense in terms of a principle we have already discussed. In considering distributive and commutative justice, we saw that while the society should try to promote and preserve a fair distribution of resources, it doesn't follow that those whose resources are destroyed by natural accidents should ipso facto be entitled to compensation. To do so would be to redistribute resources to those holding forms of property and engaged in activities that are more likely to result in accidents.[106] Commutative justice is not violated if they bear their own loss. In discussing nuisance, we saw that sometimes, an aggrieved party is only hurt because, for his own advantage, he has chosen to carry on an activity that is abnormally vulnerable to interference. Commutative justice is not violated if he is not compensated.[107] Similarly, in discussing strict liability, we saw that commutative justice is not violated if an aggrieved party does not recover when, for his own benefit, he has chosen to carry on an activity that is abnormally sensitive such as raising animals that react to the noise of an explosion by killing each other.[108]

The rule against recovery of pure economic loss may be a crude application of a similar principle. In negligence and strict liability, we have argued, the defendant is liable because he has violated commutative justice. The defendant has profited—in the sense of getting what he wants, or seeking to do so—at the plaintiff's expense. For his own benefit, he has imposed a risk on the plaintiff that he never should have imposed at all or, at least, which exceeds the risk the plaintiff has imposed on him. Nevertheless, a plaintiff may, for his own benefit, hold assets or engage in activities that make him more likely than others to suffer greater harm as a result of the defendant's negligent or abnormally dangerous conduct. If so, part of the plaintiff's loss is due to the extra risk which the defendant imposed on him for the defendant's benefit but part is due to the risks to which the plaintiff exposed himself for his own benefit. If so, commutative justice requires that the plaintiff's recovery be limited in some way.

One limit, albeit a crude one, is to deny the plaintiff recovery for pure economic loss. In Germany, England, and the United States, one consequence is that if the defendant deprives the plaintiff of power by cutting a cable belonging to a third party, the plaintiff cannot recover the profits he lost by ceasing operations.[109] Excavating near someone whose factory will close if I cut his cable is like sharing a flat with the collector of fragile and expensive china. A rule that requires full compensation for harm will, in the end, subsidize his vulnerability at my expense. Of course, in Germany, England, the United States and elsewhere, a defendant who owns fragile and expensive china can recover, absent contributory negligence, against a plaintiff who has destroyed it by conduct which was negligent or for which he is strictly liable. All I can say is that, in principle, he should not be able to recover in full. In awarding damages, the extra risk to which the defendant's conduct exposed the plaintiff should be balanced against the extra risk to which the plaintiff's conduct exposed the

---

[106] Chapter 1 I.   [107] Chapter 4 III A.   [108] Chapter 10 III B.

[109] *Spartan Steel & Alloys Ltd* v. *Martin & Co (Contractors) Ltd*, [1973] 1 QB 27 (CA); *Byrd* v. *English*, 43 SE 419 (Ga 1902); BGH, 9 Dec. 1958, EBGHZ 29, 65.

defendant, as courts actually do when they award damages according to a rule of comparative negligence. That they will not do so in the case of harm to the excessively valuable and vulnerable china is due, in my view, to the practical difficulty of determining how excessively valuable and vulnerable an asset really is compared with others that might have been injured, and also to the fact that such physical assets are usually insured for amounts well in excess of what the typical plaintiff is able to pay.

If, for these reasons, a court is unwilling to consider the value and vulnerability of the physical assets the defendant has injured, we can see an argument for and against denying recovery for pure economic loss. The argument for doing so is that the value and vulnerability of the profits the plaintiff seeks to make can vary a great deal more among individuals than the value and vulnerability of the physical assets the defendant may endanger. As Jane Stapleton has noted, the amount of profits a plaintiff may lose is less predictable. '[E]ach plaintiff is in the best position to foresee the likely extent of his or her profits while the defendant will often be unable even to guess at it . . .'.[110] On the other hand, there is considerable variation in the value and vulnerability of physical assets. It is not surprising that some jurisdictions do not draw this distinction.

This rationale also explains why, in two types of cases, a plaintiff has recovered for pure economic loss even in jurisdictions where he cannot do so as a general rule. In one type of case, the defendant, usually for a fee and invariably as part of his business, prepared information for a third party which he knew would be used by the plaintiff to make an important decision. When the information is inaccurate due to the plaintiff's carelessness, the defendant has sometimes recovered. In England, the plaintiff recovered in *Hedley Byrne & Co., Ltd.* v. *Heller & Partners, Ltd.* The defendant had negligently misinformed him as to the financial responsibility of a third party with whom the plaintiff wished to do business.[111] In the United States, according to the *Second Restatement of Torts*, liability for negligently providing misinformation will be imposed only if the defendant belongs to 'a limited group of persons for whose benefit and guidance' information is supplied.[112] Thus, in *White* v. *Guarente*, defendant accountants were held liable for negligently failing to discover and disclose that the general partners had withdrawn their own funds from a limited partnership in violation of the partnership agreement. The court stressed that the accountants had 'assum[ed] . . . a duty to audit and prepare carefully for the benefit of those in the fixed, definable and contemplated group': the limited partners.[113] The court contrasted the case with *Ultramares Corp.* v. *Touch*, where relief had been denied when the accountants 'knew the balance sheet [they prepared] would be shown to banks, creditors, stockholders, purchasers and sellers [but] did not know it would be shown to the plaintiff in particular'.[114] Similarly, in *Credit Alliance Corp.* v. *Andersen & Co.*, the court decided two companion cases. In both, lenders sought to hold accountants

---

[110] Jane Stapleton, 'Duty of Care and Economic Loss: A Wider Agenda', *L. Quar. Rev.*. 107 (1991), 249 at 255, citing Harvey Perlman, 'Interference with Contract and other Economic Expectancies: A Clash of Tort and Contract Doctrine', *U. Chi. L. Rev.* 49 (1982), 61 at 70–2; Robert Rabin, 'Tort Recovery for Negligently Inflicted Economic Loss: A Reassessment', *Stan. L Rev.* 37 (1985),1513 at 1534.

[111] [1964] AC 465 (HL).   [112] *Restatement (Second) of Torts*, § 552 (1965).

[113] 372 NE 315 (NY 1977).   [114] 174 NE 441 (NY 1934).

liable for negligence in preparing financial statements on which they had relied. In the first case (*Credit Alliance*) the court dismissed the action because, although Smith, the lender, had relied on the statement, the accountants had not been 'employed to prepare the reports with the Smith loan in mind'. In the second (*European American Bank & Trust* v. *Strauhs & Kaye*), the court permitted the action because the accounting firm 'was well aware that a primary if not the exclusive, end and aim of auditing its client, Majestic Electro, was to provide EAB [the lender] with the financial information it required'.[115]

In Germany, a bank recovered from a credit report company which had negligently prepared a financial statement for an enterprise to which, as the defendant knew, the bank was contemplating a loan.[116] Similarly, a company that negligently prepared a report on the advisability of investment in a certain hotel was held liable to the private investors to whom its report was circulated.[117] Admittedly, the Germans are reluctant to speak of this liability as one imposed in tort. That would seem to defy the limitations of their Civil Code. It is equally hard to say that liability to a third party is based on contract. Consequently, German courts have produced such strange explanations as this one: 'It is . . . irrelevant whether the parties giving and receiving information intended to establish contractual relations. It is enough that the party giving information to the one receiving it has, by preparing and sending the information, entered into a relationship that ought to be regarded as contractual as a matter of good faith and therefore should be determined to be contractual.'[118]

Nevertheless, as some commentators have noted, often, in German, English and American law, the question of liability turns on how definite the plaintiff's identity is at the time the defendant prepares the information.[119] It hardly matters what label the German courts feel they must pin on relief if they are drawing much the same distinction.

From the standpoint of our rationale, moreover, this distinction makes sense. When financial information is prepared for the benefit of whoever might be interested, the extent to which a person may be hurt, and the likelihood that he will be, will vary greatly from one potential user of the information to the next. If the preparer were liable, those who will be hurt the most if the information is negligently prepared impose a greater risk on the defendant than others, a risk for which they pay nothing in addition. If the information is prepared for the benefit of a particular individual or a definite or limited group, it is much clearer who may be hurt, how much and with what likelihood. The preparer can receive compensation in proportion to his risk of liability by charging an amount in proportion to his extra risk to the third party who is paying him to prepare the information. The third party can then pass the cost on to the potential plaintiffs. Each plaintiff is not like the one who has damaged someone's fragile and valuable china but like someone the china collector has paid, directly or through an intermediary, to advise him how to protect his china.

---

[115] 483 NE2d 110 (NY 1985). See also *Bily* v. *Arthur Young & Co.*, 834 P2d 745 (Cal 1992).

[116] OLG, Munich, 13 July 1956, BB 1956, 866.   [117] BGH, 12 Feb. 1979, NJW 1979, 1595.

[118] OLG, Munich, 13 July 1956, BB 1956, 866.

[119] For a good discussion of this and other less feasible distinctions, see Basil S. Markesinis and Hannes Unberath, *A Comparative Introduction to the German Law of Tort* (Oxford, 2002), 294–300.

In another type of case, plaintiff's economic loss was not a lost profit but the cost actually incurred in making substitute arrangements after the defendant physically harms property the plaintiff was using. In an Australian case, *Caltex Oil Ltd.* v. *The Dredge Willemstad*,[120] an oil company recovered the extra cost of transporting oil around Botany Bay when a dredger broke an underwater pipeline it had been using. In a Canadian case, *Norsk Pacific Steamship Company Ltd.* v. *Canadian National Railway Co.*,[121] a railroad company recovered the costs incurred in rerouting traffic after plaintiff's barge damaged a bridge over the Fraser River owned by a third party. Here, unlike the cable cutting cases, the plaintiffs were not recovering for an item such as lost profits which could vary enormously among users of the cable. The plaintiffs were recovering the cost of substitute transportation which would be roughly the same for anyone transporting the same volume of products through the pipeline or over the bridge.

Conversely, in France, where supposedly the plaintiff can recover for pure economic harm, courts have sometimes found it necessary to impose a limit. In one case, the plaintiff was a partnership whose 'president-general director' was injured in an accident for which the defendant was responsible. The plaintiff sued to recover for the financial harm that it had suffered because the injured man was unable to consummate deals which were then under negotiation on behalf of the partnership.[122] In another case, the plaintiff had loaned money to a husband and wife who were both killed in an accident for which defendant was responsible. Plaintiff could not recover the debt from their estate because it was insufficient, nor from the heirs of the couple, as would otherwise be permitted under French law, since they had renounced the inheritance, as they had the right to do.[123] In both cases, the court denied recovery. Admittedly, it did not do so on the grounds that purely economic losses were not recoverable. In the first case, the court claimed that the loss was 'hypothetical' and had not been established. In the second case, the court held that the causal relationship between the accident and the loss was 'indirect', and that the plaintiff could have protected itself by insisting that the injured party buy life insurance. One doubts that the court was really concerned about the causal relationship between dying and inability to pay a debt or that it believed plaintiffs in general are obligated to insure against the consequences of defendants' negligence. The plaintiff was trying to recover for financial consequences to third parties that could vary enormously from one defendant to the next. Even a jurisdiction that claims not to limit liability could be concerned about the extent of it in such a case.

If we are right, then, the underlying principle is rather clear: one person should not have to subsidize another's vulnerability. The difficulty is that there is no easy way to translate that principle into practice.

---

[120] (1976–7) 136 CLR 529.   [121] [1992] 1 SCR 1021.
[122] Cass., 2e ch. civ., 12 June 1987, JCP 1987.IV.286.
[123] Cass., 2e ch. civ., 21 Feb. 1979, JCP 1979.IV.145.

PART IV
CONTRACTS

Contracts

This time, the differences in structure between the common law and the civil law will be summarized briefly and then described in more detail in each chapter. As we will see, there has been a convergence. As we will also see, nothing would seem less likely given the origins of Roman law and common law.

The Roman jurists, as has often been noted, had many rules to govern particular types of contracts but no general theory of what a contract was or why it was enforceable. They knew that one could only be bound to a contract by giving one's consent. But whether one was bound by giving one's consent depended on the type of contract one wished to enter into. Some were binding upon consent. Others were enforceable only when an object loaned, pledged, or deposited was delivered, or only after one side had performed, or only upon the completion of a formality. Nor did they have a theory of what constituted consent. One obscure text listed various types of mistakes that were obstacles to consent, but it was buried in a title dealing with sales.

Writers in the Aristotelian tradition, and notably the late scholastics, reorganized Roman law even more thoroughly than the law of torts. They discussed whether promises were binding in principle, and decided that they were. The Roman rules about which contracts were binding when were dismissed as matters of Roman positive law, and eventually, by legislation or judicial decision, most of them vanished. The late scholastics developed a theory based on Aristotelian ideas of voluntary action of when a contract was void for mistake and when relief should be given for changed circumstances. They distinguished two basic types of contracts: contracts to make a gift, which were intended to enrich the other party, and were acts of the Aristotelian virtue of liberality; and contracts to exchange, which were voluntary acts of commutative justice requiring equality so that at the moment of the transaction, neither party was enriched at the other's expense. They impressed Roman rules into service to ensure that contracts of gift were made with adequate deliberation and contracts of exchange were equal. In the one case, the rule was that a promise of gift was enforceable only if the promisor completed a formality called *insinuatio*. In the case of exchange, the rule gave a remedy to one who had sold his land for over half the just price—a rule which the medieval jurists had generalized to protect buyers as well as sellers and parties to any similar transactions. They interpreted the implied terms of a contract—terms which the Romans had said belonged to a contract as a matter of good faith—as terms that preserved equality.

Much of this structure was preserved by the northern natural lawyers of the 17th and 18th centuries, although it is not clear how much they understood of the Aristotelian ideas on which it had originally been founded. In civil law, the break came with the rise of the 'will theories' of the 19th century. The innovation of the will theorists was not the idea that a party enters into a contract by expressing the will to be bound. The Romans had said as much. Their innovation was to try to develop a systematic theory of contract in which, so far as possible, every rule was to be traced back to the will of the parties. Aristotelian theories of voluntary action or of equality no longer made sense to them, although they did retain the rule that promises of gift required a formality.

Common law developed differently. Before the 19th century, with the exception of a few pages in Blackstone, the common lawyers did not think in terms of contracts, let alone in terms of contract theory. They thought in terms of writs or forms of action. One could sue on a promise made under seal by bringing a writ of covenant. Otherwise, one could sue in assumpsit but then the promise had to have 'consideration'. 'Promise' or 'consideration' were not terms that the pre-19th century common lawyers systematically explored. They had no theory of how mistake or changed circumstances could affect the existence or the content of a promise. They had no coherent concept of consideration. Contracts of exchange had consideration, but so did some gratuitous bailments and promises to prospective sons-in-law.

In the 19th century, the common law of contract was remodeled by drawing heavily on the ideas of civil law jurists. 'Consideration' was redefined so that it could be identified with bargain or exchange. Thus the structure of common law came to parallel that of civil law. There were promises of gift which were enforceable by completing a formality (in this case, the seal required by the writ of covenant). There were promises of bargain or exchange which did not require a formality. Moreover, as with their civilian contemporaries, the will of the parties became, as A. W. B. Simpson has said, a sort of *Grundnorm* from which as many rules as possible were to be inferred.[1]

Some have claimed that the rise of the will theories was due to the economic needs of the 19th century or the entrepreneurial class. Some have thought that they were borrowings from philosophies in which will played a dominant role, although the conceptions of will in the philosophies then fashionable were as different as those of Bentham, Kant, and Hegel. My own view is that economic changes had little to do with the rise of the will theories, and that most of the jurists were ignoring the philosophers so far as they could. The jurists never arrived at a coherent philosophical conception of will. The built upon that idea, in my view, because whatever it might mean, it seemed one of the few concepts left that seemed safe once Aristotelian ideas about voluntary action or equality in exchange had been jettisoned.

Be that as it may, the will theories are now out of fashion in both common law and civil law jurisdictions because there is too much they did not explain. The will theorists did not explain why the will itself should be binding. They merely observed that contracts are binding and defined them in terms of the will. Lacking a coherent conception of the will, they never gave a coherent account of why relief is given for mistake or whether it should be given for changed circumstances. They never adequately explained, if all that matters is will, why promises to make gifts should require a special formality. They never explained why sometimes the parties are bound to so-called 'implied terms' which they did not will and, increasingly, are not bound to blatantly unfair terms which they did will.

These are the problems we will discuss in the following chapters.

---

[1] A. W. B. Simpson, 'Innovation in Nineteenth Century Contract Law', *L. Quart. Rev.* 91 (1975), 247 at 266.

13

Promises

Although the 19th century will theorists ignored the question of why promises or expressions of will are binding, the question was reopened in the 20th century. The answers that the writers gave centuries ago are of help in resolving it. We will examine this question, and then turn to a modern one which the earlier writers never considered: whether a party could be bound without a promise as a result of what we would call preliminary negotiations.

I. The Binding Force of a Promise

A. The Reopening of the Debate in the 20th Century

In what has been described as the most important law review article written in the United States, Lon Fuller and William Perdue discussed what they called 'expectation damages', which was the amount necessary to put the promisee in the position in which he would have been had the promisor performed. They claimed that it would be odd to speak of damages for breaking a promise as 'compensation for an injury' because then 'we "compensate" the plaintiff by giving him something he never had'.[1] They argued:

In passing from compensation for change of position to compensation for loss of expectancy, we pass, to use Aristotle's terms... from the realm of corrective justice... The law no longer seeks merely to heal a disturbed status quo but to bring into being a new situation. It ceases to act defensively, restoratively, and assumes a more active role.[2]

They concluded that protection of the promisee who had relied is the most easily intelligible objective the law might have. Nevertheless, they found other reasons why a promise should be enforced to its full extent. The promisee might have relied by foregoing the opportunity to contract on similar terms with someone else. If so, then an award of expectation damages in effect compensates him for this foregone opportunity. Moreover, it may be harder for the promisee to prove the amount of his reliance damages in court than the amount of his expectation damages. If so, then an award of expectation damages will both discourage the promisor from breaking promises on which the promisee has relied, and encourage the promisee to rely even if he knows he cannot prove his reliance damages.[3]

---

[1] Lon L. Fuller and William R. Perdue, 'The Reliance Interest in Contract Damages', *Yale L. J.* 46 (1936), 52 at 52–3.   [2] ibid. 56.

[3] ibid. 60–2.

The distinction between expectation and reliance damages was familiar to Fuller and Perdue from the German Civil Code, which drew a similar distinction between a party's *negatives* and *positives Interesse*.[4] In the 20th century, however, it was novel to argue that while a party should recover his reliance interest, which represented the amount he had been harmed, a special explanation was needed why he could recover his expectation interest.

Yet the argument was not entirely novel. One like it had been made by Tomasso di Vio, better known as Cajetan, in the 16th century, and rejected by most of the late scholastics and early natural lawyers. The argument arose because jurists were theorizing, for the first time, about whether all promises should be enforceable to their full extent and attempting to resolve the question by applying Aristotelian principles. To understand the argument, and why they rejected it, we must first describe the Roman law they inherited. We will then examine Cajetan's argument and see that it was rejected for good reason.

B. The 16th and 17th Century Debate

1. Prelude: Roman law

As mentioned, the Romans had a law of particular contracts, not a general law of contract.[5] Different contracts were formed in different ways. For a long time, medieval and early modern jurists tried to be faithful to the Roman rules while working out a series of practical exceptions.

Some contracts were formed by using a formality. The most general formality was *stipulatio*, which was originally an oral question and answer. The oral formality was thus replaced for practical purposes by a written formality. In medieval and early modern times, the accepted way to complete the formality, and the only safe way, was to go before a notary.[6] As mentioned earlier, a promise to give above a certain

---

[4] Under the Code the normal remedy for breach of contract protects what Fuller and Perdue called the 'expectation interest' although the plaintiff can sometimes recover what they termed his 'reliance interest'. In principle, the plaintiff can demand specific performance (§ 249), but if performance is no longer possible (§ 280) or no longer of use to the other party (§ 286), he must pay the amount the other party has lost through 'non-fulfillment' (*Nichterfüllung*). If the breach of contract consists precisely in making performance impossible or delaying until it is no longer of use, the same measure of damages is provided by §§ 325 and 326 respectively. That is the amount necessary to put him, as far as money can do so, where he would have been had performance taken place. In certain circumstances—for example, when a party avoids a contract on the grounds of mistake—only what Fuller and Perdue called the reliance interest is protected: the disappointed party can recover only for 'damage . . . he has sustained by relying upon the validity' of the contract (§ 122). And then he can recover only an amount that doesn't exceed 'the interest that the other party . . . has in its [its] validity . . .'. Also, only the *negatives Interesse* can be recovered from an agent who unwittingly but falsely holds himself out as acting with authority (§ 179), and from one who knew or should have known that a contract was impossible at the time when it was entered into (§ 307). An attentive reader, especially one familiar with German law, can discover from n. 4 of their article that Fuller and Perdue knew that their distinction was not original: 'The German Civil Code limits relief on contract in certain situations to the "negative" (i.e. reliance interest.)', citing a German commentary to § 122, the section of the Code just cited.

[5] W. W. Buckland, Arnold D. McNair, and F. H. Lawson, *Roman Law and Common Law* (Cambridge, 1952), 265; Helmut Coing, *Europäisches Privatrecht* 1 (Munich, 1985), 398; Alan Watson, *The Law of the Ancient Romans* (Dallas, 1970), 58.

[6] Reinhard Zimmermann, *The Law of Obligations: Roman Foundations of the Civil Law Tradition* (Cape Town, 1990), 547.

amount required another formality: *insinuatio* or registration before a court. Other contracts were formed informally. Some were binding as soon as the parties consented. Justinian's *Institutes* mentioned sale, lease, partnership, and mandate, which was a gratuitous agency.[7] Others were binding when an object was delivered. Justinian's *Institutes* mentioned gratuitous loans of the object for consumption or use, pledges and deposits.[8]

Contracts outside these recognized types were 'innominate'. An example was barter. Initially, they were unenforceable. Eventually, a party who had performed could either force the other party to do so or demand back his own performance. But the rule remained that when neither side had performed his own part of an innominate contract, no action lay on the 'naked pact'.[9]

The eventual disappearance of the Roman system was probably not due to its practical disadvantages. It may have functioned quite well. Parties to a sale or lease usually wish to lock in the advantage of a certain rent or price. A partner or an agent needs to know he can conduct business on the basis of the agreement. But in other transactions, the parties' need to bind themselves in advance is less clear. And if they wished to be bound, they could make a *stipulatio*. Admittedly, the notarial formality in the Middle Ages was more cumbrous than the original oral question and answer.[10] But according to Bartolus, the Roman refusal to enforce innominate contracts had few practical consequences since they were routinely notarized.[11] Molina in the 16th century repeated Bartolus' remark.[12]

Nor did the Roman system survive so long because jurists were ignorant of the moral principle that promises should be kept or of the legal one that contracts owe their force to the consent of the parties. The medieval canon lawyers had recognized that breaking promise was wrongful. They allowed the promisee an action on a broken promise before a canon law court.[13] The Roman civilians did not disagree in principle. By conflating a Roman text that said all contracts require consent[14] with others that spoke of a *ius gentium*, a law 'established among all men by natural reason',[15] they concluded that consent to any contract creates an obligation under the *ius gentium* although not one that the civil law would enforce.[16] Medieval civilians could deny an action while agreeing with the canonists that promises should be kept[17] just as the

---

[7] I. 3.13.22–6.   [8] I. 3.14.

[9] *See generally* W. W. Buckland, *Manual of Roman Private Law* (Cambridge, 1953), 247–71; Max Kaser, *Das Römische Privatrecht* 1 (Munich, 1971), 438–9.

[10] Zimmermann argues that, because of its technical requirements, even the written formality of Justinian required the help of professionals: the *tabelliones*. Hence the need to extend the range of enforceable contracts. Zimmermann, *Law of Obligations*, 547–8.

[11] Bartolus de Saxoferrato, *Commentaria Corpus Iuris Civilis* in *Omnia quae extant opera* (Venice, 1615), to C. 4.6.2.   [12] Ludovicus Molina, *De iustitia et iure tractatus* (Venice, 1614), disp. 255.

[13] Jules Roussier, *Le Fondement de l'obligation contractuelle dans le droit classique de l'église* (Paris, 1933), 20–94, 177–216.   [14] Dig. 2.14.1.3.

[15] I. 1.2.1; Dig. 1.1.9.

[16] e.g. Accursius, *Glossa ordinaria* (Venice, 1581), to I. 3.14 pr. to *necessitate*; Iacobus de Ravanis, *Super Institutionibus Commentaria* to I. 3.14.1, nos. 3, 9 (published under the name of Bartolus de Saxoferrato in *Omnia quae extant opera* (Venice, 1615) (on the authorship see Eduard Maurits Meijers, *Etudes d'histoire du droit*, 3 *Le droit romain au moyen âge* (Leiden, 1959), 68–9); Petrus de Bellapertica, *Lectura Institutionum* (Lyon, 1536), to I. 1.2.1, nos. 30–1.

[17] Guido Astuti, 'I principii fondamentali dei contratti nella storia del diritto italiano', *Annali di storia del diritto* 1 (1957), 13–42, 34–7.

ancient Romans themselves could do so while placing a high moral value on fidelity to promises.

Nevertheless, they had difficulty explaining why there should be no action. Jacobus de Ravanis said in the late 13th century: 'If a layman were to ask the reason for the difference it could not be given for it is merely positive law. And if you ask why the law was so established, the reason can be said to be that the contract of sale is more frequent than that of barter.'[18]

2. The reorganization of the late scholastics and the debate over the binding force of promises

As mentioned, Aristotle described transactions such as sale and lease as acts of 'voluntary commutative justice'. The parties exchanged resources voluntarily. The transaction was just when the value of what each party gave equaled that of what he received.[19] Elsewhere, he described giving resources to enrich another person as the act of another virtue: liberality. Liberality did not simply mean giving money away. According to Aristotle, it meant giving 'to the right people, the right amounts, and at the right time, with all the other qualifications that accompany right giving'.[20] Thomas Aquinas,[21] followed by the late scholastics,[22] classified various transactions recognized in Roman law as either acts of voluntary commutative justice, or acts of another Aristotelian virtue, liberality. The late scholastics were helped by the fact that the 14th century jurist Baldus had already identified liberality and the receipt of something in exchange as the two *causae* or legitimate reasons why the parties would enter into a contract or the law would enforce one. As I have discussed elsewhere,[23] in drawing this distinction, Baldus seems to have drawn on Aristotle and Aquinas.

This distinction cut across the categories into which the Roman law had divided contracts. The late scholastics dismissed the Roman rules that governed when a contract was binding as matters of Roman positive law, established, doubtless, for some good pragmatic reason, but lacking a basis in principle. The stage was then set to argue which promises, in principle, ought to be binding.

---

[18] Iacobus de Ravanis, *Lectura Super Codice* to C. 4.64.3 (published under the name of Petrus de Bellapertica, Paris, 1519) (photographic reproduction, *Opera Iuridica Rariora* 1 (Bologna, 1967) (on the authorship, see Meijers, *Etudes*, 72–7)). In the 14th century, Bartolus and Baldus developed an explanation that was less simplistic but not much better. Bartolus said that by the *ius gentium* itself, and not merely by Roman positive law, some contracts are binding upon consent and others are not. The reason is a difference in 'name'. Contracts such as sale are binding on consent because they take their name from an act a party performs by agreeing. I can sell you my house today by so agreeing even if I do not put you in possession until next month. Contracts such as deposit are not binding on consent because they take their name from an act a party performs by delivering. I cannot say I am depositing an object with you unless I am actually depositing it right now. Bartolus de Saxoferrato, *Commentaria* to Dig. 2.14.7, no. 2. His student Baldus not only accepted this explanation but concluded that innominate contracts were unenforceable even in canon law. Baldus de Ubalis, *Commentaria Corpus Iuris Civilis* (Venice, 1577), to C. 2.3.27.

[19] Aristotle, *Nicomachean Ethics* V.iv 1130ᵇ.   [20] ibid. IV.i, 1119ᵇ–1120ª.

[21] Thomas Aquinas, *Summa theologiae* II-II, q. 1, a. 3.

[22] Domenicus Soto, *De iustitia et iure libri decem* (Salamanca, 1553), lib. 3, q. 5, a. 1; Molina, *De iustitia et iure*, disp. 252; Leonardus Lessius, *De iustitia et iure, ceterisque virtutibus cardinalibus libri quatuor* (Paris, 1628), lib. 2, cap. 17, dub. 1.

[23] James Gordley, *The Philosophical Origins of Modern Contract Doctrine* (Oxford, 1991), 49–57.

Tomasso di Vio, better known as Cajetan, argued that a person promised a gift could not in justice demand that the promise be kept. Certainly, the promisor acted wrongly by breaking his promise. But making a gift is a matter of liberality, not of commutative justice. The object of commutative justice is to preserve each party's share of resources. The refusal to perform leaves the disappointed party no worse off than if the promise had never been made.[24] Cajetan concluded that the promisee could only claim that the promisor acted unjustly toward him if he had become worse off by changing his position in reliance on the promise.[25] He thus anticipated Fuller and Perdue's argument that: '[i]n passing from compensation for change of position to compensation for loss of expectancy, we pass, to use Aristotle's terms...from the realm of corrective justice...'. Admittedly, they were discussing promises in general while Cajetan was discussing promises of gifts. But Cajetan's critic Leonard Lessius pointed out that the argument applied equally well to all promises. One might break a promise of exchange and leave the promisee no worse off than he was before. Granted, the obligation was 'the more perfect one of equality' but why was the promise enforceable when the promisee had not changed his position?[26]

The leading late scholastics disagreed with Cajetan. Molina pointed out that if the donor had given something away and delivered it to the donee, it would belong to the donee. Under the Roman law in force in much of Europe at the time, the donor could not then take it back unless the donee was guilty of gross ingratitude.[27] But there is nothing magical about the moment of delivery. In principle, Molina argued, the donor ought to be able to transfer the right to a thing, or the right to claim it, in advance of delivery. If he did, then depriving him of that right by failing to perform violates commutative justice.[28]

Lessius agreed that the question was one of intent, but he claimed: 'to promise is not merely to affirm that one will give or do something but beyond that to obligate oneself to another, and consequently to grant that person the right to require it'.[29] By this definition, all promises conferred a right on the promisee and were therefore actionable as a matter of commutative justice. Grotius agreed with Molina, and later writers such as Pufendorf and Barbeyrac agreed with Grotius, although they were not always careful to distinguish Molina's position from that of Lessius.[30]

3. The modern debate

Molina and Lessius were assuming, without argument, that if the parties so intended, the promisor should be able to confer a right on the promisee to demand performance.

---

[24] Cajetan (Tomasso di Vio), *Commentaria* to Thomas Aquinas, *Summa theologica* (Padua, 1698), II-II, Q. 88, a. 1; Q. 113, a. 1.   [25] ibid. to II-II, Q. 88, a. 1; Q. 113, a. 1.

[26] Lessius, *De iustitia et iure*, lib. 2, cap. 18, dub. 2.

[27] The rule is described ibid. lib. 2, cap. 18, dub. 8 no. 52, and Molina, *De iustitia et iure*, disps. 272, 281.

[28] Molina, *De iustitia et iure*, disp. 262.

[29] Lessius, *De iustitia et iure*, lib. 2, cap. 18, dub. 8 no. 52.

[30] Hugo Grotius, *De iure belli ac pacis libri tres* (B. J. A. de Kanter-van Hetting Tromp, ed., Leiden, 1939), II.xi.1.3–4; Pufendorf, *De iure naturae et gentium libri octo* (Amsterdam, 1688), III.v.5–7; Jean Barbeyrac, *Le Droit de la guerre et de la paix de Hugues Grotius*, n. 2 to II.xi.1; n. 1 to II.xi.3 (Amsterdam, 1729); Jean Barbeyrac, *Le Droit de la nature et des gens...par le baron de Pufendorf*, n. 10 to III.v.9 (Amsterdam, 1734).

Later we will discuss whether that assumption is correct. If so, however, then they found a fallacy in Cajetan's argument. Cajetan assumed that the promisee did not acquire a right to the performance at the time the promise was made. If he did, the promisor who failed to perform would be depriving him of something to which he was already entitled. Fuller and Perdue were making the same assumption. Otherwise, they could not have concluded that expectation of damages compensate the plaintiff by 'by giving him something he never had'. They therefore concluded, like Cajetan, that protection of the promisee who had relied is the most easily intelligible objective the law might have.

Just as Fuller and Perdue took the position of Cajetan, modern jurists such as Daniel Friedmann, Peter Benson, Randy Barnett, and Stephen Smith have taken a position like that of Molina and Lessius: the promisee does have a right to the performance which he was promised.[31] The question then, as Smith and Richard Craswell have observed, is why he should have such a right.[32] As Craswell noted, unless we can give a reason, we are assuming our conclusion.[33] Craswell rejected this conclusion because he could not find a reason. Fuller and Perdue themselves considered the possibility that 'the law' might be recognizing that the promisee has something like a property right in his 'expectancy'. According to them, to say the purpose of the law is to protect that right is to go in a circle because it is the law that confers that right.[34] And this, indeed, is a problem with the argument of the late scholastics and the northern natural lawyers. They said that the promisor could, if he wished, confer a right to the performance on the promisee at the time that the contract was made. But they did not explain why he should be able to do so.

T. M. Scanlon and Stephen Smith have tried to give an explanation. According to Scanlon, the promisor is bound to perform if he meant to give the promisee 'assurance' that he would.[35] The reason the promisee wants this 'assurance' is not simply to avoid unease about how things will be in the future. The promisee 'want[s] these things actually to be the case'.[36] But that seems to be much like saying that the promisee has the right to performance because that is what he wants and what the promisor means to give him. Indeed, for Scanlon, if the promisee has received an 'assurance', it immediately follows that he has such a right.[37] That does seem to assume the conclusion.

Drawing on Joseph Raz, Smith has suggested a different reason. Raz argued, like Fuller and Perdue, that failure to perform does not, in and of itself, harm the promisee. Therefore, to require him to perform would violate the 'harm principle', which holds

---

[31] Daniel Friedmann, 'The Performance Interest in Contract Damages', *L. Quar. Rev.* 111 (1995), 628; Peter Benson, 'The Unity of Contract Law', in Peter Benson, ed., *A Theory of Contract Law: New Essays* (Cambridge, 2001), 118 at 127; Peter Benson, 'Contract' in Dennis Patterson, ed., *A Companion to the Philosophy of Law and Legal Theory* (Cambridge, Mass., 1996), 24 at 42; Randy E. Barnett, 'A Consent Theory of Contract', *Colum. L. Rev.* 86 (1986), 269 at 304; Stephen Smith, 'Towards a Theory of Contract', in Jeremy Horder, ed., *Oxford Essays in Jurisprudence Fourth Series* (Oxford, 2000), 107 at 126.

[32] Richard Craswell, 'Against Fuller and Perdue', *U. Chi. L. Rev.* 67 (2000), 99 at 123–4; Smith, 'Theory of Contract', 126.   [33] ibid. 124.

[34] Fuller and Perdue, 'Reliance Interest', 218.

[35] T. M. Scanlon, 'Promises and Contracts', in Benson, *Theory of Contract Law*, 86 at 93.

[36] ibid. 95.   [37] ibid. 97.

that 'the only proper purpose for imposing legal obligations on individuals is to prevent harm'.[38] For Raz, the reason the law should require him to perform is not to vindicate the rights of the promisee, but to prevent the 'institutional harm' that results from the 'erosion or debasement of the practice of undertaking voluntary obligations'.[39] Like Cajetan, and like Fuller and Perdue, he assumed that the promisee does not acquire a right to performance when the promise is made.

Smith took that argument a step further. According to Smith, the practice of undertaking voluntary obligations is 'intrinsically valuable', and could not be created if it were understood that promises could sometimes be broken.[40] It permits one to create 'close relationships' or 'special relationships' with another.[41] Therefore, the promisee has a right to the performance he was promised.

In this analysis, to say a promise creates a 'close' or 'special' relationship seems to mean little more than that the promisee can require performance, and that it is valuable for some unspecified reason that he should. That comes close to tautology. Moreover, this explanation seems to assume that promises will lose their value unless the promisee has such a right. On the contrary, Eisenberg observed of donative promises that sometimes the very recognition of a legal right in the promisee is incompatible with the relationship of love and trust that led the promisor to promise.[42] Moreover, one cannot simply assume that a commercial relationship loses its value if the promisee has the right to recover only reliance damages for a change in his position.

Scanlon and Smith were looking for a reason why any promisee should invariably acquire a right to performance. It would be better to ask why he would sometimes want such a right and why the promisor might wish him to have it. If there is a reason which the law should respect, then, in these cases, the law should recognize such a right. If we wish, we can then confine the word 'promise' to cases in which the law does recognize that right, or we can use it more generally to refer to any assurance made by the 'promisor'. It will merely be a matter of terminology.

When the matter is put that way, the question of why the promisee is sometimes entitled to performance becomes much less mysterious since surely there are good reasons why the parties would want him to have such a right. In the case of a gift, the promisor could have at least three good reasons for wishing to confer it. First, he may rightly believe that his present decision to make the gift is more likely to be a good one than a future decision not to make it. His present decision is generous and sensible, he may believe, and the future decision is more likely to reflect greed than good sense. Second, he may rightly believe that conferring a right on the promisee is more consistent with the kind of relationship he wants with him. Eisenberg has noted that to confer such a right may be inconsistent with a relationship of love and trust between the parties.[43] But the converse may be true. Parents might give their adult children a house or bonds rather than merely letting them live in a house or endorsing

---

[38] Joseph Raz, 'Promises in Morality and Law', *Harv. L. Rev.* 95 (1982), 916 at 934.   [39] ibid. 937.

[40] Smith, 'Theory of Contract', 127–8.

[41] Stephen A. Smith, *Contract Theory* (Oxford, 2004), 74–8.

[42] Melvin A. Eisenberg, 'The Theory of Contracts', in Benson, *Theory of Contract Law*, 206 at 230.

[43] ibid.

over interest payments seriatim because they want the children to be independent rather than always beholden to them. Sometimes parents can effectuate such a purpose only if the law permits them to create a right in the children which does not depend on whether the parents have changed their mind or the children have relied. Third, though less likely,[44] the promisor might know the promisee does not trust him to perform absent a legal obligation and might wish to set his mind at rest.

In an exchange, as Melvin Eisenberg has noted, the promisee might want the right to require performance, or a sum reflecting the value to him of performance, in order to lock in a favorable bargain.[45] He might want to do so for three reasons, each of which the law should respect. First, he might regard the performance he is to receive as unique, as one he is not likely to receive elsewhere at the same price. Second, even if the performance is not unique, he might wish to lock in a price for fear of receiving a less favorable price if he waits or shops around. Third, there might be some uncertainty about the characteristics of the performance in the minds of the parties. The parties might wish to agree on a price that discounts that uncertainty. In the end, one party will have paid either more or less than he would if the truth had been known in advance, but each is willing to take his chances. Such an arrangement requires that the loser cannot renege if he happens to lose.

The reasons we have just given why a promise should be enforced correspond to Aristotelian ideas of why the law would regard certain promises as worthy of enforcement. Donative promises should be enforced when they are likely to move wealth from those who acknowledge they have too much to those who have too little. Promises to exchange should be enforced when the value of the performances exchanged is fair, at least in the way that a fair bet is fair. In later chapters, we will see that one can best explain the way the law enforces donative promises and promises of exchange on these principles.

---

[44] This motive is less likely, in my view, because people are less likely to commit themselves to make gifts to those whom they believe do not trust them. Moreover, when they do so, the reason may not be a desire to relieve the promisee's anxiety but concern for their own self-esteem. If a promisor like Diamond Jim Brady announced through a bull-horn that he wants to give a car to every student enrolled at the University of California, he might want to be able to commit himself so that his promise will not look like an empty gesture. In *Dougherty* v. *Salt*, 125 NE 94 (NY 1919), an aunt signed a note to give her nephew money because she was goaded into it by a sister who accused her of wanting to 'take it out in talk'. (The court held the written promise lacked consideration.) Consequently, when the promisor commits himself because he knows the promisee distrusts his word, it is hard for a court to be sure whether his promise was made for a good reason or not.

Nevertheless, for members of the law and economics movement, the motive of relieving the promisee from anxiety is often assumed to be the only reason or at least the standard one for wanting a promise of gift to be binding. When they say that the promisor's motive is the well-being of the promisee, they usually mean that the promisor wants to get the promisee more of what the promisee wants. If the promisee doubts that the promisor will follow through, then his level of well-being will be less, according to Richard Posner, because he will discount the value of the performance by the probability it will be kept, and according to Steven Shavell, because he will be unable to change position in reliance in ways that make him better off. Therefore, if the promisee has these doubts, the promisor will have to promise a larger sum to bring him to the same level of welfare. Richard Posner, 'Gratuitous Promises in Economics and Law', *J. Leg. Stud.* 6 (1977), 411; Steven Shavell, 'An Economic Analysis of Altruism and Deferred Gifts', *J. Leg. Stud.* 20 (1991), 401. This explanation assumes that the donor's motive is to increase the donee's 'welfare', and that he conceives of welfare as an economist does: as enhancing a person's ability to get whatever he wants.

[45] Eisenberg, 'Theory of Contracts', 279.

First, however, we will consider whether a promise is necessary at all for the parties to be bound. Some modern jurists have claimed that it is not.

II. Obligations Without a Promise? The Problem of Preliminary Negotiations

Before Rudolph von Ihering wrote an famous article in 1861 on 'fault in contracting' or *culpa in contrahendo*,[46] jurists had reached a general agreement on the standard grounds for recovery: one could sue for disturbance of property or possession or for violation of obligations in tort, contract, and unjust enrichment. Ihering argued that the commission of a fault in the process of contracting was a distinct source of liability. That was the origin of the doctrine, now accepted in many civil law jurisdictions, that the parties to a contract have a duty to negotiate in good faith,[47] which is distinct from contract, tort or unjust enrichment. I believe that these statements are misleading. In my view, Allan Farnsworth showed why in an article in 1987. He claimed that American law does not need to recognize a duty to negotiate in good faith because the cases which warrant relief can be subsumed under the traditional categories of promise, tort and unjust enrichment.[48] I believe that the same is true in other legal systems which consequently should not recognize a duty to negotiate in good faith or *culpa in contrahendo* as a distinct source of obligation. Ewoud Hondius rightly concluded in his General Report to a comparative study that, aside from some caveats that do not matter here, 'I would underwrite [Farnsworth's] opinion'.[49]

Ihering tried to show, on the basis of Roman legal texts and theoretical considerations, that *culpa in contrahendo* was, indeed, a distinct source of obligations. His principal texts dealt with the problem of parties who agree to buy or sell an object that is *extra commercium* in the sense that its ownership cannot be transferred to a private party. Examples are a free man, an object belonging to the public such as a stadium, or property that was sacred, such as a temple or land on which someone was buried. The Roman jurists deemed such a sale to be invalid. Suppose, however, the buyer was ignorant that the object could not be bought. Several texts—of which the historical roots and original significance are controversial[50]—said that one who bought in ignorance had an action *ex empto* against the seller, that is, an action on the contract even though, under general principles, the contract ought to be invalid.[51] Had he been denied an action *ex empto*, then he could still have brought a *condictio* to recover

---

[46] *Jahrbücher für die Dogmatik des heutigen römischen und deutschen Privatrechts* 4 (1861), 1.

[47] François Terré, Philippe Simler, and Yves Lequette, *Droit civil: Les obligations* (7th edn., Paris, 1999), no. 177; BGH, 10 July 1970, NJW 1970, 1840, 1841; Italian Civil Code (*Codice civile*), art. 1337.

[48] E. Allan Farnsworth, 'Precontractual Liability and Preliminary Agreements: Fair Dealing and Failed Negotiations', *Colum. L. Rev.* 87 (1987), 217.

[49] Ewoud Hondius, 'General Report', in E. Hondius, ed., *Precontractual Liability: Reports to the XIIIth Congress International Academy of Comparative Law Montreal, Canada, 18–24 August 1990* (Boston, 1991), 3 at 27.

[50] J. A. C. Thomas, 'The Sale of *Res Extra Commercium*', *Current Legal Problems* 29 (1976), 136; Peter Stein, *Fault in the Formation of Contract in Roman Law and Scots Law* (Edinburgh, 1958), 61–83.

[51] Dig. 11.7.8.1; Dig. 18.1.62.1; I. 3.23.5.

the purchase price because the contract was invalid. If he could prove the seller had committed fraud by trying to sell an object *extra commercium*, he would also have an action *de dolo* for whatever other damages he had suffered. In an action *ex empto*, however, the buyer could recover for the seller's lack of good faith just as he could if a contract had actually been formed. That meant, according to Ihering, that he could recover for *culpa* or negligence. W. W. Buckland later explained why he thought Ihering was right. While a negligent action might not necessarily be done in bad faith, it would be bad faith not to pay for its consequences.[52]

One consequence of this analysis was an important insight: the parties' efforts to contract can influence their obligations to each other even if neither party's claim is based on the conclusion of a contract. Ihering's immediate conclusion, however, was that a party could be liable for *culpa* or negligence in contracting neither because he had a contractual obligation to use due care nor because of an obligation to do so in tort. Ihering believed he did not have an obligation in tort because, as we have seen, according to Ihering, defendant was not liable in tort for any harm his negligence had caused the plaintiff but only for certain types of harm such as damage to person or property.[53] Modern legal systems that have adopted this principle express it by saying that the negligent defendant is not liable for pure economic loss. That principle was Ihering's reason for believing that he was not just interpreting Roman texts but explaining the theoretical structure of the law of obligations. If the plaintiff should recover for *culpa* when no contract has been formed, and if this recovery cannot be based on tort, then there must be a source of obligations distinct from either contract or tort.

We have already criticized Ihering's view that in principle a negligent defendant should not be liable in tort for pure economic loss. As we will soon see, in certain cases, he should be liable in tort for negligent conduct in process of contracting.

First, however, it is important to see that even if Ihering were right about liability for negligent conduct, his conclusion would have little to do with these situations in which modern legal systems give relief for what they call *culpa in contrahendo*. The relief the courts give usually does not depend on a finding that the defendant acted negligently. Alan Farnsworth describes three familiar principles on which relief could be given in American courts which do not acknowledge a doctrine of *culpa in contrahendo* or a duty of good faith in negotiations. He suggests rightly that these principles can explain the relief most often given in jurisdictions in which this doctrine and duty are acknowledged. None of his principles requires proof of negligence. The first is that a party may have been unjustly enriched by receiving information or some other benefit during negotiations. The second is that he might have deceived the other party, for example, as to his intentions or as to his power to conclude a contract. The third is that he might explicitly or implicitly have made some promise as to how he would conduct himself in the future. These grounds for recovery are perfectly straightforward. They merely apply to pre-contractual negotiations such basic principles as that no one is to be unjustly enriched, other people are not to be deceived and

---

[52] W. W. Buckland, 'Culpa and Bona Fides', *L. Quart. Rev.* 48 (1932), 217 at 229; see Stein, *Fault*, 83.
[53] Chapter 12 I B 1.

promises are to be kept. It is true that in these cases, the plaintiff would not have suffered the harm that he did if the parties had reached agreement on a final contract. But it is misleading to say that the defendant is liable for breaking off negotiations. There is no need to invent special doctrines to explain his liability.

As an example of recovery based on unjust enrichment, Farnsworth cites *Hill* v. *Waxberg*.[54] Hill asked Waxberg, a contractor, to help prepare for the construction of a building on Hill's property. It was understood that if the Federal Housing Authority would finance the project, Hill would give Waxberg the building contract. After Waxberg had put in considerable work and FHA financing was obtained, Hill and Waxberg were unable to agree on a contract and Hill hired another contractor. Waxberg nevertheless recovered for 'the value of the benefit that was acquired' by Hill. Similarly, in England, the plaintiff invented a new kind of carpet grip, and the defendant used the idea after negotiations in England broke down. An English court granted recovery for what it called 'breach of confidence'.[55] In *William Lacey (Hounslow), Ltd.* v. *Davis*,[56] a builder went to a vast amount of work at the request of a landowner preparing estimates as to the amount he would receive from the War Damage Commission for rebuilding the landowner's premises. As a result of his estimates, the landowner received a substantially increased amount. He then hired another builder, disappointing the one who had prepared the estimates in the expectation of being repaid for his efforts by receiving the contract. The court granted recovery in 'quasi-contract'. Similarly, in France, a party who has been enriched at the other's expense has sometimes been held liable, supposedly for breaking off negotiations. A court granted recovery when a commercial agent who wished to retire surrendered his *carte de représentation*. This card had a commercial value, and both parties understood that he was to be compensated for surrendering it. Nevertheless, the defendant refused to agree upon a price, and the plaintiff failed to recover in contract because there could be no contract without a price. The court allowed him to recover for 'tortious rupture of contractual negotiations'. It would be more straightforward to say that he recovered because he received something of value from the plaintiff without paying for it. Similarly, French courts have allowed recovery when the defendant used information imparted to him during negotiations.[57] Under similar circumstances, German courts have allowed recovery for unjust enrichment without feeling the need to speak of pre-contractual liability.

Farnsworth's second principle is that one party may be liable because he has deceived the other during negotiations. His example is *Markov* v. *ABC Transfer & Storage Co.*,[58] in which the lessor of a warehouse assured his lessee that he intended to renew the lease while secretly negotiating to sell the warehouse. When the warehouse was sold and the lessee told to leave, the lessee recovered because the assurance to renew had been fraudulently made because the lessor had no intention of keeping it. Farnsworth notes that any negotiation implies a serious intent to reach agreement, and that a party who negotiates without that intent should be liable for fraud.[59] So

---

[54] 237 F2d 936 (9th Cir 1956), cited E. Allan Farnsworth, *Contracts* (3rd edn., New York, 1999), 199–200.   [55] *Seager* v. *Copydex Ltd.*, [1969] 2 All ER 718.
[56] [1957] 2 All ER 712 (QB).   [57] Cass. com., 3 Oct. 1978, D. 1980.55.
[58] 457 P2d 535 (Wash 1969), cited Farnsworth, *Contract*, 200–1.   [59] Farnsworth, *Contracts*, 201.

should a party who misrepresents his authority to enter into a transaction.[60] English authorities have suggested that a party might be liable in misrepresentation for statements made during pre-contractual negotiations.[61] Similarly, some cases of pre-contractual liability in continental systems could be decided straightforwardly on the grounds of deceit. In France, a defendant was held liable when it continued negotiations to sell its stock to plaintiff even after it had already sold the stock to a third party, thereby harming plaintiff's business interests.[62] In Germany, a defendant was held liable for knowingly acting beyond his authority to contract.[63]

Farnsworth's third principle is that a party may be liable for a promise made during negotiations even if this promise is not equivalent to the final contract toward which the parties are negotiating. His example is the well-known American case of *Hoffman v. Red Owl Stores*.[64]

There Red Owl promised a franchise to Hoffman if he took certain steps to gain experience. They assured him that the $18,000 he had to invest would be sufficient. In response, Hoffman sold his bakery, moved to another town and bought a small grocery store, each time on the assurances of Red Owl. Negotiations broke down when Red Owl demanded a much larger financial investment. Some American jurists have claimed that the underlying principle is that one cannot 'scuttle contractual negotiations with impunity when the other party has been induced to rely to his detriment on the prospect that the negotiations will succeed'.[65] Farnsworth points out that the case is one in which Red Owl broke a specific promise. If the terms of the promised franchise are too indefinite for a court to ascertain, and its profits too uncertain for a court to award, the court can at least award Hoffman the damages he suffered because Red Owl broke its promise.

In England, as Hondius has noted,[66] an obstacle to liability in such a case is the doctrine of consideration: a promise given during negotiations would not be enforceable unless something were promised or given in return. That was not a problem in *Red Owl* where the court granted recovery under the American doctrine of promissory estoppel: all that is necessary is a promise, and reliance on the promise. In England, use of the doctrine of promissory estoppel in this way is supposed to be impossible since it can ground a defense but not an action. In my view, if English doctrines are an obstacle to recovery in such a case, the fault is with these doctrines. As I will describe in a later chapter, several scholars have recognized that the application of the doctrine of consideration in a business context is a crude way of ensuring fairness. Promises which bind only one side often are unfair. But, as I will point out, they are not unfair when, as in *Red Owl*, one party needs a commitment from the other in order to make studies or tests or arrange financing that will indicate the value of a transaction or make it feasible. American courts have solved this problem in a number of ways, only one of

[60] Farnsworth, *Contracts*, 201.

[61] D. K. Allen, 'England', in E. Hondius, ed., *Precontractual Liability*, 125 at 127–9.

[62] Cour d'appel, Paris, 13 May 1988, RTD 1989, 736.

[63] BGH, 20 June 1952, 6 EBGHZ 330.

[64] 133 NW2d 267 (Wis 1965), cited Farnsworth, *Contracts*, 202–3.

[65] Robert Summers, ' "Good Faith" in General Contract Law and the Sales Provisions of the Uniform Commercial Code', *Va. L. Rev.* 54 (1968), 190 at 225.   [66] Hondius, 'General Report', 5–6.

which is the doctrine of promissory estoppel. An Australian court solved it in *Walton Stores (Interstate) Ltd.* v. *Maher*.[67] There, the parties were negotiating an agreement in which the owner of land would demolish a building on it, construct a new one and lease it to the other party. He told the other party that he needed to begin the work immediately to meet the proposed deadline and sought and received their assurance that a contract would be forthcoming. He was given relief although he had to exercise considerable imagination to explain why, consistent with English law, this assurance created an 'estoppel' that could support an action absent a binding contract supported by consideration. In my view, rather than twisting old doctrines or inventing new ones to reach such results, one should do so on the grounds that under such circumstances, a one-sided promise is fair.

Similarly, in France and Germany, plaintiffs have recovered for breach of contractual negotiations when defendants have assured them that a contract is sure to arise, at least provided certain conditions are met. For example, in one French case, the defendant said that he would buy the plaintiff's premises if certain physical changes were made. He was held liable when, after the plaintiff made the changes, the buyer refused to go forward.[68] In another case, when a lease could be assigned only with the lessor's consent, the lessor assured the prospective assignee during negotiations that he would be acceptable. When he tried to retract that assurance, he was held liable for fault in breaking off negotiations.[69] In another case, the prospective buyer said it was willing to buy property but needed a three month delay in order to seek financing. At the end of three months he broke off negotiations but signed an acknowledgment of liability for the seller's costs in immobilizing its property for three months. The lower court held the acknowledgment void for absence of *cause*: the prospective buyer had not owed the seller any money. The *Cour de Cassation* quashed that judgment on the grounds that the prospective buyer might well have believed himself obligated.[70] If so, presumably, it would have been on some implied undertaking to compensate the prospective seller for his costs. In one German case, the defendant agreed that he would provide security out of his own assets if the defendant delivered newsprint to his company. As in *Red Owl*, his promise to provide security was held to be too indefinite to give rise to a binding contract. Nevertheless, because of that promise, he was liable for the newsprint that the defendant did deliver in reliance upon it.[71] There are other cases in which the precise facts cannot be gleaned from the published reports but the defendant was held liable because he expressed his intention to contract or caused the plaintiff to believe that he certainly would do so.[72] In civil as well as common law, any statements that one party makes are taken to mean what a reasonable party in the other's position would have thought that he meant. Very likely, then, we are dealing with cases like *Red Owl* in which the defendant's statement or conduct constituted a promise even if it did not give rise to the final contract toward which the parties were negotiating. If so, then the straightforward reason for holding the defendant liable is that promises should be kept.

---

[67] (1967) 164 CLR 387. [68] Cass., 3e ch. civ., 3 Oct. 1972, Bull. Civ. 1972.III. No. 491, p. 359.
[69] Cass., ch. comm., 13 Feb. 1994, Bull. civ. 1994.IV, no 79, p. 61.
[70] Cass., 1e ch. civ., 19 Jan. 1977, D.S. 1977.J.593. [71] RG, 19 Jan. 1934, ERGZ 143, 219.
[72] BGH, 20 Sept. 1984, EBGHZ 92, 164; BGH, 12 June 1975, NJW 1975, 1774.

The German jurist Canaris believes it is a 'fiction' to claim that relief is granted on the basis of contract law when a party had no intention to be contractually bound.[73] As just mentioned, however, in contract law, a party's statement is taken to mean what a reasonable person in the other party's position would have thought that it meant whether or not that meaning corresponds to the subjective intention of the party making the statement. Thus, it is not a 'fiction' to apply the principles of contract law to hold a party bound when it was reasonable for the other party to think he meant to bind himself. Admittedly, Canaris is right that it would be a fiction to say a party is contractually bound when his statement could not reasonably be taken as a commitment but as the conveyance of information or an indication of his intentions to be bound in the future or a tentative proposal.[74] But as we have seen, if these statements were made deceitfully—or negligently, as we will see later on—then the party who made them should be bound, not on any distinct ground of liability but on general principles of tort.

Farnsworth has a fourth category in which relief should be given which, in my view, is an instance of the third. It is the case in which the parties have explicitly agreed to negotiate in good faith. His example is *Itek Corp.* v. *Chicago Aerial Industries* in which the parties executed a 'letter of intent' providing that they 'shall make every reasonable effort to agree upon and have prepared as quickly as possible a contract . . . embodying the above terms and such other terms and conditions as the parties shall agree upon'.[75] This view is in marked contrast to the that expressed in England by Lord Ackner in *Walford* v. *Miles* who said:

[T]he concept of a duty to carry on negotiations in good faith is inherently repugnant to the adversarial position of the parties when involved in negotiations. Each party to the negotiations is entitled to pursue his (or her) own interest, so long as he avoids making misrepresentations. To advance that interest he must be entitled, if he thinks it appropriate, to threaten to withdraw from further negotiations or to withdraw in fact in the hope that the other party may seek to reopen the negotiations by offering him improved terms.[76]

Lord Ackner would be perfectly correct if the parties had agreed to limit their freedom to break off negotiations in no way at all, or at least in no way a court could determine from what they said to each other and the circumstances in which it was said. Then a party could not be liable, because, so far as a court can determine, he has not violated any obligation. Supposing, however, that a court can determine that a party agreed to limit his freedom, there is no reason why this promise should not be enforced. It is simply another instance in which relief should be given on the standard ground that promises should be kept.

Farnsworth notes that it is hard to find cases of liability that do not fit within his categories even in jurisdictions which recognize liability for *culpa in contrahendo* or a duty to bargain in good faith.[77] None of these categories requires proof of negligence.

---

[73] Claus-Wilhelm Canaris, 'Schutzgesetz—Verkehrspflichten—Schutzpflicten', in Claus-Wilhelm Canaris and Uwe Diederichsen, eds., *Festschrift für Karl Larenz zum 80. Geburtstag* (Munich, 1983), 27 at 93–4; Claus-Wilhelm Canaris, *Die Vertrauenshaftung im deutschen Privatrecht* (Munich, 1971), 425–8.

[74] Canaris, *Vertrauenshaftung*, 425–7.   [75] 248 A2d 625 (Del 1968).

[76] [1992] 2 AC 128 (HL).   [77] Farnsworth, 'Precontractual Liability', 239–40.

As we will see, whether they admit it or not, courts have occasionally allowed recovery for negligence. But the fact that such cases are not the typical ones shows the distance between the modern doctrine of *culpa in contrahendo* and the doctrine developed by Ihering. Ihering was trying to show that a party might be liable for negligence in contracting.

I believe that Ihering was right that a party should be liable for negligence. But Ihering believed that the party was not liable in tort because a negligent defendant cannot be liable for a pure economic loss he has inflicted on the plaintiff. Modern courts that deny recovery for pure economic loss have taken the same view. One German court held the defendant liable for failure for fault in negotiations because 'the needs of commerce require that the negligent party be held liable for the harm caused . . .'. It held that the defendant was not liable in contract, since no final contract had been made,[78] nor in tort, because according to the German Civil Code the defendant is not liable unless the economic loss has been inflicted intentionally. Therefore he imposed liability for misconduct in pre-contractual negotiations on the grounds that it was neither the one nor the other.[79] But as we have seen, there is no reason why, in principle, a party should not be liable in tort for a purely economic loss he has inflicted on the other.[80] If so, the general principles of tort law can explain the situations in which the defendant should be liable.

We must carefully keep in mind, however, what conduct would constitute negligence in pre-contractual negotiations. As we have seen, liability for negligence entails a balancing of two harms: the one the plaintiff is likely to suffer if he takes some measure to protect the defendant and the one which the defendant is likely to suffer if he does not. In the context of pre-contractual negotiations, this duty cannot be construed to mean that the defendant should accept a worse deal so that the plaintiff can have a better one, or (absent any promise to do otherwise), that he cannot break off negotiations simply because a third party has offered a more favorable price. Furthermore, when a party is negotiating, he may pass up other offers or spend money in hopes of reaching a deal. These risks and expenses are in principle no different than any others which a party incurs in making a product which he hopes he can market. There is no reason a party who is unwilling to buy the product should assume a share of these risks merely because he happens to have been negotiating with the party who incurs them. French and German courts themselves have stressed that '[e]ven when the parties find themselves in long and seriously conducted negotiations, either side can object to the conclusion of a contract without for that reason being liable to make compensation for fault in contractual negotiations'.[81] Similarly, a business person 'had no obligation to accept [an] estimate if he found it too high; nor can one see any obligation on his part to communicate . . . the offers of competing firms'.[82]

---

[78] Although earlier, in discussing this case, we argued that because the defendant had agreed to provide security if plaintiff made a delivery of newsprint, he could be held liable simply on the principle that promises should be kept.   [79] RG, 19 Jan. 1934, ERGZ 143, 219.

[80] Chapter 12.   [81] BGH, 22 Feb. 1989, JZ 1991, 199.

[82] Cour d'appel, Pau, 14 Jan. 1969, D.S. 1969.J.716; see Cass., ch. comm., 15 Dec. 1992, RTD (Case comment, Jacques Mestre), 1993, 576–7.

Nevertheless, because negotiation is a cooperative enterprise in which each party's conduct may be a source of danger to the other, each party should take those precautions that are warranted because otherwise his conduct will aggravate the risks to which the other party is exposed. Ihering's example was a negligent communication ordering ten chests of cigars when the buyer wanted to order only one-tenth of a chest. Because of the mistake, no contract is formed for ten chests but the buyer should still have to pay the extra shipping charges.[83] Another example is delay in responding to an offer when the offeree does not need the extra time for some legitimate purpose, such as to consider whether to accept or to seek financing, and the offeror is at risk until a contract is made. In an American case, a farmer applied for hail insurance on 2 July and received no communication from the insurance company until 1 August when his offer was declined. The same day, his crops were ruined by hail. By the terms of the application, if it had been accepted, the farmer would have been insured from—and would have paid premiums from—the date of the application. The court held the insurance company liable for breach of a duty to process the application more rapidly without committing itself as to the doctrinal basis for the duty.[84] Similarly, in a German case, a farmer's wife had applied for insurance, and the insurance company had prepared the policy in a timely fashion. But a local agent of the company delayed delivery of the policy beyond the date at which the offer lapsed. In the meantime, the woman had suffered an accident that the policy would have covered. The German court imposed liability on the company.[85] In these cases, the negligence was in failure to respond in a timely fashion when the delay put the other party at risk.

Some of the cases in which civil law courts have held a party liable for breaking off negotiations involve negligence of a different sort. As noted earlier, if a party were to negotiate with no serious intention of entering into a contract, it should be liable for deceit. But if it were to fail to clarify the likelihood that a contract would result when it knew the other party would be turning down other deals or spending money in reliance, its conduct might be negligent even if it did not amount to deceit. Since the courts speak in general terms about a fault in leading the other party on, it is hard to tell whether we are dealing with a case of negligence or with one of deceit. Either, in other contexts, would be grounds for recovery if we leave aside the rule barring liability for negligent infliction of pure economic loss.

We have seen, then, that one does not need to speak of a duty to negotiate in good faith to account for many cases in which jurisdictions which recognize such a duty have imposed liability for breach of it. One can explain liability by ordinary principles of unjust enrichment, deceit, breach of promise or negligence. I know of only two cases in which it is difficult to explain recovery in any of those ways, and in each, the factual situation was peculiar and might elicit a court's sympathy for reasons that have nothing to do with whether there is a general duty to negotiate in good faith.

One is a French decision in which the plaintiff negotiated with the defendant to purchase a machine that made cement pipe. After the plaintiff had made expenditures traveling to America to see such a machine perform, and just as it seemed a contract

[83] Ihering, '*Culpa in contrahendo*', 16.
[84] *Kukuska* v. *Home Mut. Hail-Tornado* Ins. Co., 235 NW 403 (Wis 1931).
[85] RG, 26 Feb. 1935, ERGZ 147, 103.

might be concluded, the defendant sold the machine to a competitor with a clause in the contract obligating him not to sell a similar machine to anyone in the east of France for two years. The court held the defendant liable for breaking off negotiations 'brutally, unilaterally, and without a legitimate reason . . .'.[86] It seems hard to believe that the result would have been the same if the defendant had only one machine to sell, if he had never even implicitly promised it to the plaintiff and had simply sold to someone else who had offered a higher price. Such a result would be at odds with French case law. So this case is something of a maverick. What might have disturbed the court was that the defendant had been paid, not only to sell a machine, but to guarantee that the seller's competitor could not obtain one like it. The court might have been looking for some way to help the would-be buyer even though it could not identify any specific rule of unfair competition that the seller had infringed.

The other case is a famous one from the Netherlands, *Plas* v. *Valburg*, in which the plaintiff construction firm submitted a proposal to the municipal authorities of a small town to build a swimming pool. Although there was no official bidding, its proposal was judged the best and was agreed to by the mayor and aldermen. Their decision required approval from the city council. It was not approved because, at the initiative of one member of the city council, a rival bid was submitted at a lower price and accepted instead. The highest Dutch court (*Hoge Raad*) ruled in favor of the plaintiff, holding that the process of negotiation is divisible into three stages: an initial one, in which either party can break off negotiations; a middle stage, in which he can do so only if he compensates the other party for expenses incurred; and a final stage in which to break off negotiations at all would be a violation of good faith, and a party who does so is responsible for what a common lawyer would call expectation damages. He is liable, that is, to the same extent that he would be had a final contract been signed.[87]

If one knew the full facts, this case might well fall within one of the categories we have already mentioned. Was there a practice or an implicit understanding that when all bids had been submitted to the major and aldermen, the normal bidding process was closed, and the city council would reject a bid only for extraordinary reasons? If so, then the municipality's conduct amounted to a breach of such an implied promise. Did the competitor make his proposal by taking the plans the plaintiff had already submitted and simply reducing the price? If so, the competitor and the municipality might have been unjustly enriched by appropriating the contractor's work. Then there is the suspicious circumstance that at the last minute, a member of the city council, on his own initiative, intervened to get a contract for a private party with whom he seems to have been personally acquainted. While it is hard to fit that suspicion within a legal category, it does make the plaintiff's case sympathetic. Like the French case, it could have been a maverick in which a court was especially anxious to find some ground for relief.

Nevertheless, while the French case remained a maverick, the Dutch one founded a line of case law to which the *Hoge Raad* still professes to adhere, although it is difficult

---

[86] Cass., ch. comm., 20 Mar. 1972, Bull. civ. 1972.IV, no. 93.
[87] Hoge Raad, 18 June 1982, NJ 1983, 723, described by Jan van Dunné, 'Netherlands', in Hondius, 'Precontractual Liability', at 230–3.

to find a case in which they have actually awarded expectation damages. What is most disturbing about *Plas* v. *Valburg* is not the result, which could be accounted for in various ways, but the doctrine the court espoused. Can it really be true that, absent any of the grounds just discussed, a party could be liable for the other party's expenditures or even for his expectation damages as though a contract had actually been formed? We can see the answer by imagining a case in which each ground we have mentioned is absent. The plaintiff made large expenditures during negotiations which he expected to culminate in a contract. But the defendant was not benefitted or enriched in any way. The defendant did not deceive him by word or conduct: the party making the expenditures was perfectly well aware the other might decide not to contract. The plaintiff could not reasonably have inferred from anything the defendant said or did that he would accept the contract, or accept it if certain conditions were met, or reject it only for certain reasons. The plaintiff's expenditures were not enhanced by any negligent conduct by the defendant either in conveying information or in inciting false hopes. It is hard to see, in such a case, why the defendant should be liable. The plaintiff is in no different position than someone who spent a fortune developing and advertising a product which he thought he could successfully mass market and then discovers no one will buy it. It shouldn't matter that in this case the plaintiff dealt with a particular customer with whom he exchanged information about that customer's needs and the price he might be willing to pay. Perhaps the *Hoge Raad* would say that in such a case, there has been no bad faith in negotiations, and neither the middle stage nor the final stage has been reached. But in that case, to say that there has been no bad faith or that negotiations can be broken off without liability is simply to say that the traditional grounds for relief in private law are absent: there has been no unjust enrichment, deceit, broken promise or negligence. That is not the way the *Hoge Raad* has expressed itself.

Our conclusion, then, is that of Farnsworth. One does not need a doctrine of good faith in pre-contractual negotiations. One simply needs to give relief on traditional grounds which, in my view, should also include negligence. Farnsworth's justification, however, is somewhat different. He speaks of the chilling effect which any wider relief would have on negotiations. People will avoid discussions that could have been profitable for both sides for fear of liability if they break down. My justification is simpler. Absent one of the traditional grounds for liability just discussed, the plaintiff is not the victim of an injustice. No one has violated a commitment to him or wronged him or appropriated anything that belongs to him. Therefore he should be able to hold no one liable for his misadventure.

14

Mistake

I. Mistake as to the Performance Promised

A. Origins: *Error in Substantia*

According to the Roman jurist Ulpian, '[i]t is obvious that there must be consent in a purchase and sale'. He then considered 'whether there is a good sale if there is no mistake as to the identity of the thing (*in corpore*), but there is in regard to its substance (*in substantia*)'. Among his examples were copper sold for gold or lead sold for silver. At one point, he referred to such an error as one in 'essence' (*οὐσία*).[1] It is not at all clear what he meant by these terms.

In the 14th century, Bartolus of Saxoferrato and Baldus degli Ubaldi read an Aristotelian meaning into the words 'substance' and 'essence'. Their interpretation was followed by the late scholastics.

In Aristotelian philosophy, what a thing is depends upon its substantial form or substance as distinguished from its accidents. A human being has one substantial form, that of a rational animal, a plum tree has another substantial form and a lion has another. On account of its substantial form, each thing has a characteristic way in which it behaves. A thing can change 'accidents' such as its height and weight and still be the same kind of thing, but if it loses its substantial form it is no longer a human being, a plum tree, or a lion. A thing's essence is the concept of a thing that one forms in one's mind which corresponds to its substantial form. When one has grasped the essence of a thing, one understands what it is.[2]

It was a short step to the conclusion that a contract was void for an error that went to the substance or essence of the performance contracted for. In Aristotelian terms, a person who made such an error was not getting what he contracted for. Thomas Aquinas concluded that a contract of marriage was void if a party made a mistake that went to the essence of the relationship.[3] As we will see, the medieval jurists Bartolus and Baldus, and then the late scholastics, read this Aristotelian meaning into Ulpian's references to 'substance' and 'essence'.

Thus far, we have been drawing primarily on Aristotle's ideas about distributive and commutative justice. They appeal, in a way that this solution to the problem of mistake does not, to the common sense of most modern people. Most people think that there are better and worse distributions of wealth, and most, I believe, that the

---

[1] Dig. 18.1.9.

[2] For a fuller description of these ideas and their influence on contract law, see James Gordley, *The Philosophical Origins of Modern Contract Doctrine* (Oxford, 1991), 10–29.

[3] *Summa theologiae* Suppl. Q. 41, a. 1.

present distribution is worth defending to the extent it is good and should be changed by a social decision if it is bad, not by each person trying to enrich himself by impoverishing another. I don't see how these beliefs could make sense unless one thought there is a life which is distinctively human, and that he needs certain things to live it well. At that point, we are speaking of a 'substance' or 'essence' or 'nature' of man and consequently a distinctively human way to live, whether we express these ideas in an Aristotelian vocabulary or not.

It seems a leap beyond common sense, though, to start talking about mistakes in the 'essence' or 'substance' of the things for which people contract. Yet these words were used before and after jurists tried to give them an Aristotelian significance. Ulpian himself had no clear idea what these terms meant. Neither did the drafters and judges who used them in modern civil codes or case law. In France, an error warrants relief if it is in substance (*substance*),[4] in Italy, if it is 'essential' (*essenziale*),[5] in Germany, if it is in a characteristic 'regarded in commercial dealings as essential' (*die im Verkehr als wesentlich angesehen werden*).[6] Similar terms were once used by American courts. In the famous case of *Sherwood* v. *Walker*, the court said a contract was void because the error was one in 'substance' rather than 'in some quality or accident'.[7] Similarly, in England, Lord Blackburn said, in dicta, that English law was the same as civil law: relief would be given for an error in 'substance',[8] and this language was quoted favorably by Lord Warrington and Lord Atkin in *Bell* v. *Lever Brothers, Ltd.*[9] Lord Atkin added, in dicta, that a contract is void if the mistake concerned a quality that made the object 'essentially different';[10] Lord Thankerton said the mistake must concern a quality that is 'essential'.[11] Notwithstanding these remarks, as we will see, English courts have been less generous than others in giving relief.

The words 'substance' and 'essence' live on though few jurists can clarify them. I believe that the writers in the Aristotelian tradition can help us to do so. Some evidence that these writers were correct is that their understanding of these terms has been rediscovered and defended, without benefit of Aristotle, by some leading modern jurists such as Jacques Ghestin. To see why these older and contemporary writers may have found a viable solution, it will be helpful first to review the wide range of alternative solutions which, in my view, have failed. In each case, the cause of the failure is that one cannot have a coherent idea of contractual consent without an explanation of 'what' the parties contracted for. Modern approaches have been unable to provide that explanation.

B. The Intractability of the Problem

1. Error in characteristics deemed to be essential in ordinary dealings

The 18th century jurist Robert Pothier said the error must concern 'the quality of the thing that the contracting parties had principally in view and which constitutes the

---

[4] French Civil Code (*Code Civil*), art. 1110.   [5] Italian Civil Code (*Codice Civile*) art. 1428.
[6] German Civil Code (*Bürgerliches Gesetzbuch*) (hereinafter BGB), § 119(2).
[7] 33 NW 919, 923–4 (Mich 1887).
[8] *Kennedy* v. *Panama Royal Mail Co.*, (1867) LR 2, QB 580, 588.   [9] [1932] AC 161, 207, 219.
[10] [1932] AC at 218.   [11] [1932] AC at 235.

substance of the thing'.[12] Borrowing from Pothier, the drafters of the French Civil Code said that to warrant relief, the error must be in 'substance'.[13] The leading 19th century jurists Charles Aubrey and Charles Rau explained such an error in much the same way as Pothier. A party was mistaken as to 'properties which, taken together, determine [a thing's] specific nature and distinguish it according to common notions from things of every other species'.[14] Today, French and Italian jurists refer to this approach as the 'objective theory'[15] although few of them endorse it. A version of it passed into the German Civil Code, which speaks of a characteristic 'regarded in commercial dealings as essential'.[16]

The trouble with this approach is that it depends upon the decision of ordinary people in commercial dealings as to what distinctions amount to a difference in 'essence'. Most people do not spend time on that issue. Even if they did, we need an account of why such a difference is supposed to matter.

2. Error in the determining motive

The leading 19th century jurist François Laurent rejected the approach of Aubry and Rau. He claimed that what mattered was the importance of the quality in question to the parties. If a party would not have contracted if he had known the truth, then he could obtain relief. A similar position was taken by the 19th century German jurist Ferdinand Regelsberger.[17] Some French and Italian jurists take that position today. The error must concern a quality the parties had principally in view,[18] one which led them to contract,[19] one which was the 'determining' motive.[20] French and Italian jurists refer to this approach as the 'subjective theory'.[21] But it does not take much effort to see the problem with it. Any time a party wants to escape from a contract, he has made some mistake absent which he would not have contracted. As we have already seen, nearly all modern jurists agree that an error in motive does not warrant relief. I agree that many errors in motive do not. But often a party would not have contracted but for an error in motive.

3. Mutual mistake

Realizing that the 'subjective theory' goes too far, some French jurists have modified it by requiring, not only that a party would not have contracted had he known the truth,

---

[12] Robert Pothier, *Traité des obligations*, § 18, in *Oeuvres de Pothier* 2 (M. Bugnet, ed., 2nd edn., Paris, 1861), 1.   [13] French Civil Code (*Code civil*), art. 1110.

[14] Charles Aubry and Charles Rau, *Cours de droit civil français* 4 (4th edn., Paris, 1869–71), § 343 bis.

[15] Guy Raymond, *Droit civil* (3rd edn., Paris, 1996), no. 238; Ambroise Colin and Henri Capitant, *Cours élémentaire de droit civil français* (7th edn., Paris, 1932), no. 38; Georges Ripert, Jean Boulanger, and Marcel Planiol, *Traité élémentaire de Planiol* 2 (4th edn., Paris, 1952), no. 199; Rodolfo Sacco and Georgio de Nova, *Il contratto* 1 (Turin, 1993), 384–5.   [16] BGB § 119(2).

[17] Ferdinand Regelsberger, *Pandekten* 1 (Leipzig, 1893), § 142.

[18] Colin and Capitant, *Cours élémentaire* 2, no. 38; Ripert *et al.*, *Traité élémentaire* 2, no. 199.

[19] Colin and Capitant, *Cours élémentaire* 2, no. 38.

[20] ibid. no. 40; Ripert *et al.*, *Traité élémentaire* 2, no. 199; Jacques Mestre, *Obligations et Contrats Speciaux*, *Rév. trim. dr. civil* 88 (1989), 736, 739; Sacco and de Nova, *Contratto* 1, 384–5; Francesco Galgano, *Diritto privato* (10th edn., Paduv, 1999), 276.

[21] Christian Larroumet, *Droit civil 3: Les obligations: Le contrat* (5th edn., Paris, 2003), no. 341; Colin and Capitant, *Cours élémentaire* 2, no. 40; Ripert *et al.*, *Traité élémentaire* 2, no. 199; Sacco and de Nova, *Contratto* 1, 384–5.

but also that both parties know that the characteristic in question was that important.[22] According to the new Dutch Civil Code, relief can be given 'if the other party in entering into the contract has based himself on the same incorrect assumption as the party in error'.[23] Similarly, in Anglo-American law, the traditional rule is that, for relief to be given for a mistake in a characteristic of the performance, the mistake must be mutual in the sense that it must be made by both parties.[24] The endeavor here is to draw a boundary line between errors in motive that do not warrant relief and those errors that do.

French critics have pointed out that mutuality is not a good boundary. Relief should not be given merely because the other party knows about the other party's purposes or believes that the contract will serve them. For example, a sale of land cannot be avoided if both parties knew that the buyer intended to pay for it with money he inherited, and, in fact, he inherited nothing.[25] Anglo-American jurists recognize that the mere fact that a mistake was mutual does not warrant relief. The *Second Restatement of Contracts* requires that the mistake also concern a 'basic assumption' of the parties.[26] But the Anglo-Americans do not explain the relevance of mutuality any better than the French. The *Second Restatement of Contracts* proposes that relief be given when a mistake is unilateral only if the other party had no reason to know of the mistake and enforcement would be 'unconscionable'.[27] There is no requirement that enforcement be unconscionable in the case of a mutual mistake. According to an official Comment, the reason for the difference is that 'if only one party is mistaken, avoidance of the contract will more clearly disappoint the expectations of the other party than if he, too, is mistaken'.[28] I don't see why that should be so. Even if it were so, if one accepted the *Restatement*'s approach, relief should not depend on whether a mistake was mutual or unilateral but on whether a party's expectations were more clearly or less clearly disappointed. Moreover, jurists have traditionally said that relief is given because an error may vitiate consent. Since the consent of both parties is necessary to make a contract, it is not clear why the relief given the party who erred should depend on what the other party happened to know or believe.

4. Error in the manifestation of assent

In the 19th century, the great German jurist Friedrich Karl von Savigny became convinced that if one allowed relief to turn on how important a mistake was to a party, there would be no stopping point. He concluded that the reasons for which a party

---

[22] Raymond, *Droit civil*, no. 236; Christian Larroumet, *Droit civil 3: Les obligations: Le contrat* (5th edn., Paris, 2003), no. 338.   [23] Dutch Civil Code (*Burgerlijk Wetboek*), art. 228(1)(c).

[24] *Restatement (First) of Contracts*, § 503. Allan Farnsworth notes that while that was the traditional view, courts have given relief for unilateral mistake, and not only when a mechanical error was made in compiling a bid, though that is the most frequent case. E. Allan Farnsworth, *Contracts* (New York, 1999), 631, 635. Among his illustrations is a case in which relief was given to a buyer who mistakenly thought the parcel included land belonging to the Forest Service but enclosed by the same fence (*Beatty* v. *Depue*, 103 NW2d 187 (SD 1960)), and one in which relief was given to a seller who mistakenly listed three bags for sale instead of two. *Colvin* v. *Baskett*, 407 SW2d 19 (Tex Civ App 1966).

[25] Paul Esmein, Marcel Planiol, and Georges Ripert, *Traité pratique de droit civil français 6 Obligations* (Paris, 1952), no. 177.   [26] *Restatement (Second) of Contracts* (1981), § 152.

[27] ibid. § 153.   [28] ibid. Comment c to § 153.

contracted were irrelevant. All that mattered was his final decision. Relief should be given only when the final decision which he made mentally did not match the outward expression of this final decision, that is, when the party's will (*Wille*) did not match his declaration (*Erklärung*) of his will.[29] Versions of this approach became widely accepted in Germany,[30] and one eventually passed into the German Civil Code. Section § 119(1) of the Code provides that a person's declaration of will can be avoided when he made an error in its 'content' absent which he would not have made the declaration.

In the United States, Oliver Wendell Holmes took an approach which was actually similar even though he subscribed to an 'objective' theory of contract in which the will of the parties was not supposed to matter. According to the objective theory, the law attached consequences to what they said and did outwardly irrespective of what they willed. Holmes claimed that relief should be given for mistake only if the parties contradicted themselves outwardly. One party might be speaking of one object and the other party of another. Or a party might say he wanted 'these barrels of mackerel' when there was no such object because the barrels contained salt.[31]

The trouble with either Savigny's or Holmes' approach is that it cannot handle classic cases in which relief for mistake is given. For example, copper is sold as gold. Or a party says he wants 'these barrels' thinking they contain mackerel when really they contain salt.

Holmes thought such a party should get relief but he could not explain why. He concluded, in a famous phrase that he used more than once, that 'the distinctions of the law are founded on experience, not on logic'.[32] In other words, Holmes' distinction was not founded on logic.

Savigny's response was to claim that some characteristics are so bound up with a thing's identity that even a party who says he wants 'this ring' has in effect said he wants 'this golden ring'. These were the characteristics by which a thing was classified as a thing of a certain type according to 'conceptions dominant in actual commerce'.[33] A similar approach has been taken in recent times by Werner Flume and Sir Guenter Treitel. Flume rejects the idea that a person who points to a ring or says 'this ring' is merely indicating 'a "something" defined by space and time...' He has a picture (*Vorstellung*) of the object and 'grasps it as having a certain composition'.[34] Treitel believes that '[s]ome particular quality may be so important to [the parties] that they actually use it to *identify* the thing'.[35] Nevertheless, such a solution seemed to many of Savigny's contemporaries to contradict his own principles. If the significance of a characteristic to the parties matters, then we are back to considering the parties' motives. If not, then the significance of the characteristic according to commercially dominant concepts should not matter either. Similarly, Flume's critics have pointed out that one

[29] Friedrich Karl von Savigny, *System des heutigen Römishen Recht* 3 (Berlin, 1840–8), 113.
[30] Gordley, *Philosophical Origins*, 190–6.
[31] Oliver Wendell Holmes, Jr., *The Common Law* (Boston, 1881), 310–11.   [32] ibid. 312.
[33] Savigny, *System* 3, 283.
[34] Werner Flume, *Allgemeiner Teil des Bürgerlichen Gesetzbuchs 2 Das Rechtsgeschäft* (2nd edn., Berlin, 1975), 477. His position was adopted by Dieter Medicus, *Allgemeiner Teil des BGB Ein Lehrbuch* (7th edn., Heidelberg, 1997), no. 770.   [35] Sir Guenter Treitel, *The Law of Contract* (10th edn., London, 1999), 267.

cannot take a party's offer to buy a certain object to be an offer to buy only an object that matches his expectations. Of course, he believes that the milk he is buying is not sour, but that does not mean when he says he wants to buy 'this carton of milk' he means 'this carton of not sour milk'.[36] Moreover, this approach has all the difficulties described earlier of trying to determine which characteristics of an object are supposedly deemed to be essential in commercial dealings. People engaged in commerce do not ordinarily decide what should count as 'essential'.

Other German jurists,[37] among them Bernard Windscheid, concluded that Savigny's solution to the case of gold sold as copper contradicted Savigny's own principles. Windscheid accepted it, *faute de mieux*, as an explanation of the Roman texts which were still in force in parts of 19th century Germany.[38] As we have seen, it passed into § 119(2) of the German Civil Code which gives relief for a mistake concerning characteristics 'regarded in commercial dealings as essential'. In recent times, jurists such as Konrad Larenz have acknowledged, as Windscheid did, that relief for such a mistake is really relief for an error in motive, and therefore is an exception to the general principle that an error in motive doesn't warrant relief.[39] He did not explain why there should be such an exception or how to determine which characteristics are essential in commercial dealings.

5. Error in basic assumption

In the 17th century, Hugo Grotius suggested that the rule governing mistake should be the same as the one governing changed circumstances which we will examine in the next chapter. The question should be whether the 'promise is founded on the presumption of some fact that is really otherwise'.[40] An approach like this has been particularly popular in the United States. Despite his admiration for Holmes, instead of adopting his approach, Samuel Williston said that relief should be given for mistake when a party was mistaken as to a 'fundamental assumption'.[41] A version of this approach passed into the *First*[42] and *Second Restatements of Contracts*. According to the *Second Restatement*, to invalidate a contract, a mistake must concern 'a basic assumption on which the contract was made'.[43] The *Second Restatement* adopts the same

---

[36] Reinhard Bork, *Allgemeiner Teil des Bürgerlichen Gesetzbuchs* (Tübingen, 2001), 315. Similarly, Karl Larenz, *Allgemeiner Teil des deutschen bürgerlichen Rechts* (7th edn., Munich, 1989), 378, argues that the legal problem is what to do when a party is in error. It is not the problem of what to do when the declaration of his will fails to match reality (ibid. 380–1).

[37] e.g. Ernst Bekker, 'Zur Lehre von den Willenserklärung: Einfluss von Zwang und Irrthum', reviewing A. Schliemann, *Die Lehre von Zwange* (1861), in *Kritische Vierteljahresschrift für Gesetzgebung und Rechtswissenschaft* 3 (1861), 180 at 188–9; Achill Renaud, 'Zur Lehre von Einflusse des Irrthums in der Sache auf die Gultigkeit der Kaufverträge mit Rücksicht auf v. Savigny: Der error in substantia', *Arch Civ. Prax.* 28 (1846), 247 at 247–54; M. Hesse, 'Ein Revision der Lehre von Irrthum', *Jherings Jahrbücher* 15 (1877), 62 at 101.

[38] Bernhard Windscheid, *Lehrbuch des Pandektenrechts* (7th edn., Frankfurt-am-Main, 1891), § 76a.

[39] Larenz, *Allgemeiner Teil*, 378–9; Ernst Wolf, *Allgemeiner Teil des bürgerlichen Rechts* (3rd edn., Cologne, 1982), 480.

[40] Hugo Grotius, *De iure belli ac pacis libri tres* (B. J. A. de Kanter-van Ketting Tromp, ed., 1939), II.xi.6.

[41] Samuel Williston and George Thompson, *A Treatise on the Law of Contracts* (New York, 1937), § 1544.   [42] *Restatement (First) of Contracts* (1932), § 502.

[43] *Restatement (Second) of Contracts* (1981), § 152(1).

formulation to describe when relief is given for impracticability.[44] Most recently, this approach has been taken by Melvin Eisenberg. He believes that a shared mistaken tacit assumption that is material justifies giving relief to the adversely affected party.[45]

The difficulty with this approach is to explain what is meant by a basic or a tacit assumption. This phrase could refer to the importance of a belief to the parties.[46] But then we are back to a 'determining motive' test which we have already seen to be inadequate. Anyone who wants to escape from a contract must have been mistaken about something so important that he would not have contracted if he had known the truth. Alternatively, to speak of a mistake in a basic assumption could be to refer to an event in the mind of a party: he took something for granted and acted on it. Eisenberg and Farnsworth use the example of a person who takes it for granted that the floor exists and will support him.[47] But it is hard to see why a person should obtain relief because he took something for granted. Surely, the mere fact that such an assumption was made should not be enough to warrant relief. Many losing contracts are made by people who did not question their assumptions about the durability of the market for mainframe computers, or the capacities of the equipment they bought, or the tastes of the friends for whom they purchased presents. Moreover, the propensity to question one's assumptions varies from one person to the next. It would be odd to deny relief to the timorous and grant it to the sanguine.

According to Eisenberg, such mistakes differ from 'evaluative mistakes', which do not warrant relief. 'Mistaken factual assumptions differ from evaluative mistakes both because they do not concern evaluations of future states of the world and because they are made by an actor who is, by hypothesis, not well-informed'.[48] But then we are no longer talking about a mistaken assumption as a psychological event. We are talking about how well informed a party happened to be about the present state of the world. I have trouble understanding this distinction and why it should matter. One of Eisenberg's examples of an evaluative error is the decision whether to spend a vacation on a cruise or skiing. One of his examples of a mistaken assumption is the case of *Griffith* v. *Brymer*[49] in which the parties contracted for a flat suitable for viewing the coronation procession of King Edward VII not knowing that the king was sick and the procession had been canceled. It seems to me that either of these mistakes could have been made by a well-informed or an ill-informed party depending on what information was available at the time the mistake was made, information which could concern the present or the future.[50] Moreover, it is hard to see why an ill-informed decision warrants relief while a well-informed one does not.

---

[44] ibid. § 261.

[45] Melvin A. Eisenberg, 'Mistake in Contract Law', *Calif. L. Rev.* 91 (2003), 1573 at 1624.

[46] *Restatement (Second) of Contracts*, § 152, Comment b.

[47] Eisenberg, 'Mistake', 1622; Farnsworth, *Contracts*, 624.   [48] Eisenberg, 'Mistake', 63.

[49] [1903] 19 TLR 434 (KB).

[50] Eisenberg also draws a second distinction: 'evaluative mistakes typically concern judgments of the value that a performance will have in a future state of the world'. But here again, I am not sure that is true or why it is significant. In *Krell* v. *Henry*, [1903] 2 KB 740, the facts were the same as in *Griffith* v. *Brymer* except that the parties contracted before the procession was cancelled. The court gave relief. Surely, the explanation of why relief was appropriate in *Krell* must be the same as the explanation in *Griffith*. Moreover, it is hard to see what constitutes a mistake as to a fact in the present as distinguished from a mistake as to the future. Suppose the king was sick when the contract was made in *Krell* but no one knew it yet.

6. Allocation of risk

Yet another approach to the doctrine of mistake, which has also been applied to the doctrine of changed circumstances, is to formulate general principles that describe how the law allocates risks to the parties to a contract. P. S. Atiyah has said, the questions of the law governing mistake, 'are, in the last analysis risk-allocation questions'.[51] The problem that then arises is how to allocate the risk.

For Atiyah, that question seems to be one of interpreting the contract. He does not clearly explain how, by interpretation, one can allocate a risk which, by hypothesis, the parties did not allocate themselves.

For the German jurist Ernst Kramer, the problem is also one of risk allocation. He believes that the party who made the mistake should bear the consequences unless the other party either caused him to err or knew of his error.[52] Although Kramer does not state it expressly, his principle for allocating risk seems to be that a person is responsible for risks that arise from his own conduct even if he is not at fault. Thus the party who errs is responsible for that error, however innocently it was made, unless the other party caused the error to be made or to persist, however innocent that party may have been Similarly, according to the new Dutch Civil Code, relief should be given if the error is 'imputable to information given by the other party'.[53] The trouble with this approach is that it is not clear why this is a sensible way for the law to allocate risk. In contract law, risks are usually allocated according to the intent of the parties. In tort law, they are usually allocated according to fault. When a party is held strictly liable, it is not merely because his conduct created a risk but usually because it created an abnormal risk.[54] Kramer's solution to the problem of mistake thus entails a novel principle of risk allocation, and one that needs a defense.

Partisans of the law and economics movement such as Richard Posner have a clearer principle of risk allocation. The risk should go on the party who is best able to bear it. That is where the parties would have placed the risk had they thought of it themselves.[55] As I have said elsewhere[56] and as will be seen in a later chapter, much can be learned from this approach. But it is not easy to see how to apply it to the problem of mistake. It is one thing to say that if a party consents to a contract, the risks incident to the transaction should fall upon him if he can bear them most easily. It is another to assign risks to someone who can best bear a risk but who, because he was mistaken, may never have consented to do so. The difficulty is exemplified by a hypothetical case put by Posner and expunged from subsequent editions of his casebook. It is based on *Sherwood* v. *Walker*,[57] mentioned earlier, in which a prize breeding cow, presumed

[51] P.S. Atiyah, *An Introduction to the Law of Contract* (5th edn., Oxford, 1995), 227.

[52] Ernst A. Kramer, in Franz Jürgen Säcker, *Münchener Kommentar zum Bürgerlichen Gesetzbuch* (4th edn., Munich, 2001), to § 119, no. 114.   [53] *Burgerlijk Wetboek* 218(1)(a).

[54] See James Gordley, 'Contract and Delict: Toward a Unified Law of Obligations', *Edinburgh L. Rev.* 1 (1997), 345 at 349–52; James Gordley, 'Tort Law in the Aristotelian Tradition', in David Owen, ed., *Philosophical Foundations of Tort Law: A Collection of Essays* (Oxford, 1995), 131 at 151–7.

[55] Richard Posner, *Economic Analysis of Law* (6th edn., New York, 2003), 104–7.

[56] Gordley, 'Contract Law in the Aristotelian Tradition', in Peter Benson, ed., *The Theory of Contract Law: New Essays* (Cambridge, 2001), 265 at 323; James Gordley, 'A Perennial Misstep: From Cajetan to Fuller and Perdue to "Efficient Breach"', *Issues in Legal Scholarship, Symposium: Fuller and Perdue* (2001), 16, http://www.bepress.com/ils/iss1/art4.   [57] 33 NW 919 (Mich 1887).

sterile (according to the majority), was pregnant at the moment of the sale. According to Posner, we should regard the contract as the sale of a cow, and then ask which party could best bear the risk that the cow was fit for breeding or fit only to be sold for beef.[58] The implication of this approach would seem to be that if someone bought 'Bossy', thinking Bossy was a cow, and Bossy turned out to be a horse, we should regard the contract as the sale of an animal, and then ask who could best bear the risk of what sort of animal. Presumably, if 'Bossy' turned out to be a tractor, a sports utility vehicle or a Piper Cub we should say the contract was for the sale of a thing and ask the same question. If we do so, we will not merely be forcing a party to assume the risks ancillary to a contract to which he did consent. He will have to accept a performance to which he never consented if it happens that he is in a better economic position than the other party to face the consequences. That cannot be right.

C. A Solution

1. The late scholastics

As mentioned earlier, the late scholastics may have found a better solution to this problems than any yet described. It was forgotten, but a version of it, without the underlying Aristotelian concepts, has been revived by certain French jurists.

As we have seen, for the late scholastics, one who was wrong about the 'substance' or 'essence' of the performance for which he contracted, in Aristotelian terms, was not getting 'what' he contracted for. As we have seen, Thomas Aquinas concluded that a contract of marriage was void if a party made a mistake that went to the essence of the relationship.[59] Bartolus and Baldus concluded that Ulpian's text was speaking of an error in substance or essence in the Aristotelian sense.[60]

This approach might seem to depend on a metaphysics in which 'what' a thing is depends upon its 'substance' or 'essence', whether it be a lion or a plum tree. From a commercial point of view, however, Bartolus pointed out, however, that what mattered was the substance or essence of an object considered, not on the natural level, but from the standpoint of its suitability for its use. On the natural level, according to Aristotle, the inorganic world was composed of four elements, earth, air, fire and water, each with its own essence. That did not mean that if a party bought land too uneven to farm, there was no mistake in essence since what he received was 'earth':

[O]ne and the same thing is taken in different ways according to a difference in the way it is considered as will now be seen. A field may be considered with regard to its matter, which is earth, and then if a river makes a channel through it, it does not cease to be earth, and so the earth remains something of the same kind. It can also be considered as earth suitable for the driving (*agi*) of animals, that is, earth on which animals are led and can labor, and it is from this use that 'field' (*ager*) receives the name which is proper to it .... Taken in this way it loses its proper form [if the river makes channels through it].[61]

---

[58] Richard Posner, *Economic Analysis of Law* (2nd edn., New York, 1977), 73–4.
[59] *Summa theologiae*, Suppl. Q. 41, a. 1.   [60] *See* Gordley, *Philosophical Origins*, 57–61.
[61] Bartolus de Saxoferrato, *Tractatus de alveo*, § Stricta ratione, nos. 6–7, fo. 141r, in Bartolus de Saxoferrato, *Omnia quae extant opera* 10 (1615).

That approach made good Aristotelian sense. For Aristotle and the scholastics, the essence of a man-made object is determined by its purpose. As Bartolus himself said, man-made things 'take their substantial form from some aptitude which they have toward a certain end for which they were made by their maker'.[62] A house is a building configured so one can live in it.[63] A chair is a piece of furniture configured so one person can sit on it. The field is not a man-made object, but according to Bartolus, it should be regarded the same way. What determines its essence is the purpose to which it is suitable. A field is land suitable for plowing. Lessius called the purpose which determines the 'species' of a thing its 'principal *causa*' or immediate end. An error in this principal *causa* radically vitiates consent. He distinguished it from the 'secondary *causa*' or motive that a person might have for acquiring an object. As we will see, he thought relief should also be given for error in motive but such an error did not vitiate consent.

2. *The formulations of Ghestin and the Mazeauds*

Similarly, some French jurists have said that relief should turn on whether the parties erroneously believed that a performance would be suitable for the purpose envisaged by the person in error. Here they draw a distinction. Sometimes the performance will not serve this purpose for reasons that are peculiar to the person in error while at other times it will not serve for reasons that are general and have to do with the performance itself. Jacques Ghestin, now a leading jurist, explained in a thesis written in 1962:

[a]n error in the suitability of an object [to an end] remains an error in the object. No doubt, the characteristics of the object are evaluated in relation to the end sought by the victim of the error. But this end is never considered independently of the object itself.

As Messieurs Mazeaud and Mazeaud observe, 'from the moment that the thing presents in itself this usefulness or this possibility of utilization which constitutes its substantial quality it matters little that the contracting party cannot use it as he hopes for reasons that are personal and foreign to the contract although another person could have done so. The apartment . . . remains apt for habitation even if the employee who bought it cannot use it because he has been trans-ferred [like] the house which he has bought for his retirement at the time he retires even though he dies first.'[64] In all the cases which we will examine, the inappropriateness of the object for the end pursued is inherent in the object, [and] it does not result from the personal situation of the person in error. The qualities of the object are only appreciated in light of the end pursued, but this end is only considered in relation to the qualities of the object. The two elements are inseparable.'[65]

For Ghestin and the Mazeauds, then, the critical question is, so to speak, the purpose for which an object is bought and sold. An error as to the suitability of the object for this purpose is an error as to the object itself. It is to be distinguished sharply from an error which makes the object suitable for the purposes of a particular buyer as distinguished from buyers in general.

[62] Bartolus de Saxoferrato, *Tractatus de alveo*, no. 3.   [63] ibid. (Bartolus' example).

[64] Henri Mazeaud and Léon Mazeaud, *Leçons de droit civil* 2 (Paris, 1967), no. 166, quoted in Jacques Ghestin, *La Notion d'erreur dans le droit positif actuel* (Paris, 1971), 51. The same solution is given in Henri Mazeaud, Léon Mazeaud, Jean Mazeaud, and François Chabas, *Leçons de droit civil* 2/1 (Paris, 1998), no. 166.   [65] Ghestin, *Erreur*, 51.

3. A rationale

One can distinguish two ways in which, because of a mistake, a performance is unsuitable, not only to the purposes of the party who is to receive it, but to the purposes of parties in general who would otherwise have contracted for such a performance. One way the performance might be unsuitable is that it could not be used to achieve anyone's purposes. For example, in *Griffith* v. *Brymer*,[66] one party rented a flat for a day believed to be suitable for viewing the coronation procession of King Edward VII. Neither party knew that the king was sick and the procession had been canceled. Thus the flat was unsuitable for the purposes of any party renting it for the day. Another way the performance is unsuitable for a purpose is that a person would not use it for that purpose even though to do so would be physically possible. He would use it instead for a different and more valuable purpose. For example, in *Sherwood* v. *Walker*,[67] a cow which would have been worth a great deal if she could be bred was sold on the assumption that she was sterile—or at least, that is how the majority of the court characterized the transaction. The cow was in fact pregnant at the moment of the sale. While it would still be possible to slaughter the cow, no one would have done so.

Either case warrants relief. As mentioned earlier, in the 16th century, Cajetan had asked the question, why a party who failed to keep a promise should be liable if the promisee had not changed his position in reliance on the promise. The majority of the late scholastics, followed by Grotius and Pufendorf, had answered that sometimes the promisor would want to transfer immediately a right to the promisee to require performance. Why, then, would one party want the other to be locked into the deal they have made? As Melvin Eisenberg has noted, he may want to lock in a favorable bargain.[68] That party may be afraid that the other party will renege, no longer wishing to contract or to contract on the same terms.[69] In return for the promisor's agreement to be locked in, the promisee will give something in return: he will contract on terms more favorable to the promisor or agree to be locked in himself.

In discussing the enforceability of promises, we identified three reasons the law should respect why the promisee might want to lock in a favorable bargain. First, he might regard the performance he is to receive as unique, as one he is not likely to receive elsewhere at the same price. Second, even if the performance is not unique, he may wish to lock in a price for fear of receiving a less favorable price if he waits or shops around. Third, there may be some uncertainty about the characteristics of the performance in the minds of the parties. The parties may wish to agree on a price that discounts that uncertainty.[70]

For the moment, we will set this third reason aside and come back to it later. When we consider the first two reasons we can see that neither of them applies to the decision the promisee has made in the situation we are discussing.

If the promisee wished to lock in the right to something he thought was of unique value to himself, the reason would be that he believed some characteristics of that

---

[66] [1903] 19 TLR 434 (KB).   [67] 33 NW 919 (Mich 1887).

[68] Melvin A. Eisenberg, 'The Theory of Contracts', in Benson, ed., *Theory of Contracts*, 223 at 279.

[69] As discussed in Gordley, 'Contract Law in the Aristotelian Tradition', 331–2.

[70] Chapter 13 III B 1.

performance increase its suitability to whatever purpose he is pursuing. In our situation, however, because of a mistake, the performance is not suitable for this purpose. Therefore, these characteristics, even if they do exist, will not increase its suitability.

Moreover, if a party wished to lock in a price, the reason would be fear of receiving a less favorable price later on. The price the parties will agree upon will therefore depend on the price they expect others will offer. What others will offer depends on the suitability of the performance to their purposes. In our situation, because of a mistake, the performance is not suitable for those purposes. Since the contracting parties based their estimate on a use to which the performance could not or would not be put, they could have picked an appropriate price only by coincidence.

As noted earlier, Eisenberg has observed:

a bargain promisor must explicitly or implicitly evaluate: (1) the relation between his own preferences (including his values and his tastes) and the performances due from him and to him under the contract; (2) the expected value to him—that is, the personal, or subjective, value—of those performances; and (3) the expected market, or objective, value of those performances.[71]

To make the first two of these decisions, a party must consider what goal he wants to pursue and how the performances he will give and receive contribute or detract from that goal. To make the third, he must consider what buyers in general will pay for the performance, which will depend on the contribution the performance can make to accomplishing their objectives. If the performance is unsuited both to his objectives and to those of others, both of these decisions are vitiated. Thus, relief should be given for the reason the late scholastics would have given: there was no meaningful consent.

In such cases, modern courts have generally given relief. For example, American courts have done so when land was sold as a housing site and legal regulations kept the buyer from building a house,[72] or as a site for a mobile home park and legal regulations prohibited installation of septic tanks.[73] They have done so when unimproved desert was sold for the cultivation of jojoba, and both parties mistakenly believed there was sufficient water.[74] American and German courts have given relief when land was sold for a building site and legal regulations kept one from building at all.[75] A German court gave relief when a football club paid 40,000 DM for a player not knowing he had been involved in a scandal and could not play.[76] A French court did so when an establishment was sold as a 'clinic' which, because of a servitude, could only be used as a maternity hospital.[77]

England is an exception. The courts enforced a contract for the sale of oats to a horse trainer who mistakenly believed they were old oats, which he could use, rather

[71] Eisenberg, 'Mistake', 1581.

[72] *Rancourt* v. *Verba*, 678 A2d 886 (Vt 1996) (federal and state wetlands restrictions); Cour d'appel, Rouen, 19 Mar. 1968, D.S. 1969.J.211.   [73] *Lang* v. *Koziarz*, 1987 Del Ch LEXIS 466 (1987).

[74] *Renner* v. *Kehl*, 722 P2d 262 (Ariz 1986).

[75] *Gartner* v. *Eikill*, 319 NW2d 397 (Minn 1982); BGH, 11 Feb. 1958, NJW 1958.785 (decided under § 242); OLG Köln, 25 June 1964, MDR 1965, 292 (dicta).   [76] BGH, 13 Jan. 1975, NJW 1976.565.

[77] Cass. civ., 3e ch. civ., 25 May 1972, JCP 1972.II.17249.

than new ones, which he could not.[78] They enforced one for the sale of 300 bales of Calcutta kapok, 'Sree brand', which neither party realized contained cotton and was therefore useless to the buyer.[79] They enforced a contract to buy beans which both parties mistakenly thought were 'fereroles'.[80] Lord Atkin said in dicta that relief should be denied to a party who buys an unfurnished house mistakenly believing it to be inhabitable.[81] The reason is not that the English state the rule differently than anyone else. As we have seen, they ask whether a mistake is substantial or essential. The reason seems to be fear. As Lord Atkin said: 'Nothing is more dangerous than to allow oneself liberty to construct for the parties contracts which they have not in terms made by importing implications which would appear to make the contract more businesslike or more just'.[82] He did not explain why it is not even more dangerous, in cases of doubt, to let a less businesslike and less just construction prevail. Be that as it may, if the results in English cases are based on a fear of meddling rather than a conception of what result is just, it should not trouble us that they contradict the results elsewhere.

D. A Kindred Situation

In the situation just described, the performance is unsuitable both for the purposes of the party who was to receive it and for those of parties in general. Sometimes, however, a performance has characteristics which suit it generically for the purpose for which parties in general would pay for it. Nevertheless, depending on these characteristics, it will be suited to the purposes of one party and not to those of another. That is not because of the peculiar preferences of the parties. That is because it is a generic quality of certain goods that while they answer to a certain purpose, the goods themselves must be different according to the characteristics of any party who uses them. Size 8 shoes will not fit a person who wears size 11. A housing site that suits the plans of one buyer will not suit that of another. A painting that one person likes another may not. Moreover, no one would pay for a quarter acre plot or an imitation Ming vase what he would pay for a 2-acre lot or an original.

Performances such as these may be suitable to one person's purposes and not another for two different reasons. First, independently of the price, the performance that suits one person may not suit another. Even if shoes, or plots of land, or paintings could be bought at the same price, the size 11 does not fit, the configuration of the land may thwart the buyer's building plans, or a painting may not please him. Second, the reason a performance is not suitable is because, if it is appropriately priced, a person will not buy the more expensive one, since he doesn't want to spend so much money, or, alternatively, the less expensive one, since he has the money to spend and wants more than a small parcel or an imitation art work.

In such cases, if the contract is allowed to stand, either or both of two unfortunate consequences will follow. One party may end up with a performance that is not suitable for his purposes: shoes of the wrong size, land with the wrong configuration,

---

[78] *Smith* v. *Hughes*, (1871), LR 2, QB 597.
[79] *Harrison & Jones* v. *Bunten & Lancaster*, (1953) 1 QB 646.   [80] (1953) 2 QB 450.
[81] *Bell* v. *Lever Brothers, Inc.*, [1932] AC 161, 224.   [82] [1932] AC at 226.

an imitation vase. Or one party will pay a price that is inappropriately high or low compared with the price that some party would pay for the land or the vase if both parties knew the truth.

In such cases, the contract should not stand. It may be that the party who is to make the performance contracted in order to lock in what he perceived as a favorable price. As just mentioned, however, the price may be inappropriately high or low because of the error. Here, as before, had the truth been known, the buyer or seller would not have been able to lock in such a price. Earlier, I have explained why, in my view, the law should respect the parties' decision to lock in a price.[83] The risks that the market price will change must be run by someone. By agreeing on a price, the parties allocate that risk. Here, however, if the parties are held to the price on which they agreed, they will be subject to an additional risk—the risk of being mistaken as to what price goods of this sort would command on the market at that time. There is no reason why they should be subject to that additional risk.

In other cases, the price might have been the same if the performance had been sold to a party who was not in error. Size 11 shoes sell at the same price as size 9. The parcel that confounds one party's building plans may suit another's. Works by different artists may be comparably priced. In these cases, it must be admitted that if the contract is invalid, the seller loses the advantage of having locked in a price. We thus face our choice between two unpleasant alternatives: to deprive the seller of the benefit of his bargain or to insist that the buyer take something he cannot use. It would seem that the better alternative is not to enforce the transaction. The seller knows that because of the character of the performance, it will answer to the needs of parties with certain characteristics but not those with others. That risk arises because the performance is not one suitable to the needs of all those who have a certain need. If the purchaser is wrong about his own characteristics which make the performance suitable to him, he should bear the risk. He is in the best position to know, and the seller should not have to run the risk that prices will fall because of the buyer's error. But if the buyer knows his own characteristics correctly, for example his shoe size, then the risk ought to fall on the seller who inadvertently sells him the wrong size shoe. He is in the best position to identify such a mistake, and if it occurs recurrently, to spread the risk across all the buyers who might be injured.

Thus it is not surprising that modern legal systems generally give relief in cases like those described: in which an error concerning a parcel of land thwarts a buyer's plans for it, and in which the parties were in error as to the authenticity or provenance of a jewel, a work of art or a collectable. American courts have given relief when the parties erroneously believed that at least 4 acres of an 18 acre parcel had a right to water for irrigation,[84] when they erroneously believed a parcel of land was large enough to accommodate five 1-acre lots plus an access road,[85] when a parcel's encroachment on federal wetlands created significant restrictions on what one could build,[86] and when the buyer of a 450 foot parcel could not build where he wanted because legal

---

[83] James Gordley, 'Equality in Exchange', *Calif. L. Rev.* 69 (1981), 1587 at 1620–1.
[84] *Lesher* v. *Strid*, 996 P2d 988 (Ore App 2000).   [85] *Murr* v. *Selag*, 747 P2d 1302 (Idaho 1987).
[86] *Shorebuilders, Inc.* v. *Dogwood, Inc.*, 616 F Supp 1004 (D Del 1985).

regulations required a 75 foot setback.[87] French courts have done so when plans to construct a nearby highway made the land they purchased inappropriate for a housing site.[88] German courts have given relief when land is sold as a housing site and the parties do not realize an entrance cannot be built on one of the streets it faces without paying 23,500 RM of street costs,[89] and when a house is sold and the parties do not realize a neighbor could build a multistory structure which blocks the view and turns the access route into a tunnel.[90] English law is less clear. Lord Atkin said by way of dictum that no relief should be given to a party who buys a roadside garage business when the city has already decided to divert nearly all the traffic that passes the garage.[91] But as noted earlier, Lord Atkin himself said that his reluctance to give relief came from a fear of reading into the minds of the parties what he regarded as a just result.

American courts have given relief when violins, sold as a Stradivarius, a Guernarius,[92] and a Bernardel,[93] were imitations, and when a coin, sold as rare, was actually a fake.[94] A French court gave relief when pearls, sold as natural, were in fact cultured,[95] when a statue was sold as Tang dynasty and, in fact, there was no way to determine how old it was,[96] and when two chairs, described as 'marquises' of the Louis XV period were, in fact, 'bergères' 'adroitly reconstructed with pieces from the Louis XV period and following'.[97] A German court gave relief when two Chinese vases, sold as modern, were in fact from the Ming dynasty, and when a painting, sold as Frank Duvenek, was in fact by Wilhelm Leibl.[98]

Again, English law is unclear. Lord Atkin said, by way of dicta, that no relief should be given if one party sells another a work of art which both mistakenly believe to be the work of an Old Master.[99] Indeed, English courts have upheld contracts in which both parties mistakenly believed the painting sold was by Constable[100] or by Munter.[101] The court reached the opposite result when tablecloths and napkins with the arms of Charles I were not the property of that king, as the parties believed, but later copies. The court did so even though the seller had specified in the contract that 'authenticity . . . is not guaranteed'.[102] As mentioned earlier, Lord Atkin himself believed that relief should be denied even in a case where it seemed just. He thought it safer, for some reason, to allow a seemingly unjust result to stand rather than to meddle. It is not surprising that English judges who share this concern reach results which are different than those of judges in other countries and even in England who are less fearful.

---

[87] *Burggraff* v. *Baum*, 1998 Me Super LEXIS 51 (1998) (he also could not use an access road but the court implies that either mistake would warrant relief).

[88] Cour d'appel, Versailles, 30 Mar. 1989, Rev. trim. dr. civ. 1989.739.

[89] OLG Düsseldorf, 28 June 1912, JW 1912, 850.   [90] RG, 31 May 1905, ERGZ 61, 84.

[91] *Bell* v. *Lever Brothers, Ltd*, [1932] AC 161, 224.

[92] *Smith* v. *Zimbalist*, 38 P2d 170 (Cal App 1934) (finding a breach of warranty).

[93] *Bentley* v. *Slavik*, 663 F Supp 736 (SD Ill 1987).

[94] *Beachcomber Coins, Inc.* v. *Boskett*, 400 A2d 78 (NJ Super 1979).

[95] Cass. req., 5 Nov. 1929, D.H. 1929.539.

[96] Cass., 1e ch. civ., 26 Feb.1980, Bull. civ. I, p. 54 no. 66.

[97] Cass., 1e ch. civ., 23 Feb. 1970, JCP 1970.J.16347.   [98] BGH, 8 June 1988, JZ 1989, 41.

[99] *Bell* v. *Lever Brothers, Ltd.*, [1932] AC 161, 224.

[100] *Leaf* v. *Internat'l Galleries*, (1950) 2 KB 86.

[101] *Harlington & Leinster Enterprises* v. *Christopher Hull Fine Art*, (1991) 1 QB 564 (although here, the seller disclaimed any expert knowledge).   [102] *Nicholson & Venn* v. *Smith-Marriott*, (1947) 177 LT 189.

E. Exceptions

Even if the mistake would otherwise warrant relief, courts and scholars have recognized certain exceptional cases in which it will not.

1. Unilateral mistake, culpable mistake

Thus far we have assumed that the error was made by both parties Suppose only one was mistaken. In one sort of case, one party knows that the other is mistaken. For example, suppose the owner of the flat overlooking the route of the procession knew that the procession had been canceled, or the buyer knew that the cow which the seller presumes to be barren is, in fact, pregnant. Such cases raise the problem of duty to disclose which is not under discussion here. I will note in passing, however, that I agree with Melvin Eisenberg and others who have written on this subject that there should be such a duty. In my view, the purpose of contract law is to enable the parties to exchange in a way that is of benefit to them both on terms that are fair in the same way as a fair bet. That purpose is furthered if each party must disclose information that shows that the exchange cannot benefit the other party or is not fair to him. I also agree with Eisenberg and others that there should be an exception if one of the parties has expended money or effort to acquire the information. For example, he buys land that he knows from seismic testing is likely to obtain oil. Or, having been trained as an art historian, he identifies a drawing in a shop as by an Old Master.

Another possibility is that one party does not know that the other is mistaken. For example, the buyer purchases a cow he has discovered to be pregnant by manual inspection not knowing the seller believes her to be barren. Because the cow is less distinguished than the one in *Sherwood* v. *Walker*, the price is not so different as to make the seller's beliefs obvious. Or, for example, a farmer buys nitrites to use as fertilizer not knowing that they are chemically pure and hence more expensive than ordinary nitrites. He agrees to pay the high price because he is using nitrites for fertilizer for the first time and does not know how much they usually cost.

If the parties were contracting to lock in a price, then a court should give relief. A price which is too low or too high because of the one-sided mistake should be treated in the same way as if it were too low or too high because of a two-sided mistake. I believe the court should also give relief even if one of the parties was trying to lock in a performance he thought to be specially advantageous: for example, some unique features of the cow. Admittedly, this purpose will be defeated if he cannot enforce the contract. If our analysis is correct, however, the seller did not give meaningful consent to the price. Therefore, he should not be bound. Suppose that one party wrote a letter offering to buy a house in England for $400,000, and because of an ink smudge on the dollar sign, the owner of the house thought he was offering £400,000. Surely there would be no contract if the owner accepted even though the buyer might have been trying to lock in specially advantageous characteristics of the performance. I don't see why the result should be different if a seller is mistaken about what he is selling.

I must admit, however, that modern legal systems supposedly deal with this problem quite differently. Traditionally, Anglo-American law required that the mistake be mutual. Thus the mistaken party would never get relief. According to some French and Italian jurists, relief will be denied if the mistaken party was at fault for not knowing the truth.[103] German law allows the non-mistaken party to recover for any harm he has suffered by changing his position in reliance.[104] Nevertheless, while jurists state these rules with assurance, the case law is sparse. Nearly all the cases I have found[105] deal with fault of a different kind: the courts refused to come to the aid of a party who did not read the contract he signed[106] or, in some cases, a recorded zoning restriction.[107]

2. Assumption of risk

In the cases we have discussed so far, the party to receive a performance believed at the time he contracted that the performance would answer to his purposes. Suppose, however, that he is unsure. According to the *Second Restatement*, '[a] party bears the risk of a mistake when . . . he is aware, at the time the contract is made, that he has only limited knowledge with respect to the facts to which the mistake relates but treats his limited knowledge as sufficient . . .'.[108] I am not too sure what it means to treat one's knowledge as 'sufficient', but, in my view, sometimes, but only sometimes, a party should be denied relief because he knew of a risk.

As mentioned earlier, there is a third reason the parties might wish to lock in a bargain in addition to the two we have already considered. There may be some uncertainty about the characteristics of the performance in the minds of the parties. The parties may wish to agree on a price that discounts that uncertainty. In the end, one party will have paid either more or less than he would if the truth had been known in advance, but each is willing to take his chances. Such an arrangement requires that the loser cannot renege if he happens to lose.

With these considerations in mind, we can distinguish two kinds of cases. First, there are cases in which the buyer's uncertainty did not seem to affect the price because, while there was uncertainty as to the suitability of the performance for his own purposes, there was no uncertainty as to whether the performance would suit the purposes of others. As long as the contract was one in which the seller was trying to lock in a favorable price—the same price he would have offered others—a court should refuse to give relief. A French court refused to do so when a house was sold to a buyer who wanted to use it both as a house and as a studio for cabinet making. He knew that a servitude on the property permitted only residential use but decided to take his chances.[109] In a similar case, a German court refused relief when the buyer,

---

[103] Raymond, *Droit civil*, no. 237; Larroumet, *Contrat*, no. 355; Sacco and de Nova, *Contratto* 1, 379. Giovanni Iudica, Paolo Zatti, and Vincenzo Ropp, *Il Contratto* (Milan, 2001), 782, take the opposite view. Also, according to the *Second Restatement*, fault does not matter. *Restatement (Second) of Contracts*, § 157.

[104] BGB § 122(1).

[105] An exception may be a French case in which a party who had 'experience with insurance' insured himself twice against the same risk. Cass. civ. 1e ch. civ., 29 June 1959, Bull. civ. I, p. 267, no. 320. I can understand the court's impatience but I believe it should have given him relief.

[106] *Ptacek* v. *Wammes*, 1987 Ohio App LEXIS 5790.

[107] *Hartle* v. *United States*, 22 Cl Ct 843 (1991), but a buyer who inquired about zoning restrictions but did not check the municipal records was held not to be negligent in *Gartner* v. *Eikill*, 319 NW2d 397 (Minn 1982).

[108] *Restatement (Second) of Contracts*, § 154(b).

[109] Cass., 1e ch. civ. 13 June 1967, JCP 1967.II.15290.

hoping to build a vacation home, bought land he knew was zoned to exclude houses.[110] In these cases, the sellers presumably were trying to lock in a price. Moreover, the buyer's uncertainty did not affect the price. The price reflected what others would pay assuming that they, unlike the buyer, would be buying the property for a legally permissible use.

In other cases, however, the uncertainty concerns the use to which any buyer would put the property. Here, in my view, we should distinguish cases in which the parties have, in effect, made a bet as to what the property could be used for from cases in which one party—perhaps negligently—simply failed to check to see if he was mistaken. In cases when a party failed to check, very likely, he thought the risk was too remote to bother. Very likely, then, the risk was not reflected in the price. Such a case is therefore like those discussed earlier in which one party was at fault for making the mistake. It may be that the other party wanted to lock in a price, but if the reason the contract would otherwise be binding is so he could do so, and if the mistake makes that price inappropriate, a court should give relief. The result should be the same here if a party's failure to check on the possibility of mistake makes the price inappropriate.

Some courts have ignored this distinction. One court upheld the sale of what both parties took to be a genuine antique Parker A-1 shotgun which was in fact a fake. The buyer had called a gunsmith who expressed doubts as its authenticity and explained how, by dismantling the gun, he could see if it was genuine. The buyer was unable to dismantle it himself, and the seller would not let him take it to someone who could. The court said he had bought knowing of the risk.[111] Similarly, a court upheld the purchase for $60, at an estate sale, of two oil paintings by a famous artist which the buyer resold for $1,072,000. An appraiser had told personal representatives of the estate that she could appraise personal property but not fine art. The court concluded that they had assumed the risk the art would be by a famous artist.[112]

Other courts have arrived at what I regard as a more reasonable result. One refused to uphold the contract for a home site when the buyer couldn't build the house he planned because a significant portion of it was located on a floodplain. The lower court had denied relief on the grounds that he should have hired an engineer.[113] Another court gave relief when a house was sold and neither party knew that the boundary of the property ran under its eaves although both parties were unsure of where the boundary was and the buyer could easily have checked.[114]

In cases like these, the parties have not, in effect, placed a bet on whether the paintings are by a famous artist, the gun is a fake Parker A-1, the house cannot be built on the site or the boundary runs beneath the eaves. Rather, they have neglected a precaution that would have alerted them to these possibilities. There may or may not have been sufficient uncertainty to have warranted the precaution. In either case, the fact that they went ahead without taking the precaution suggests that, very likely,

---

[110] OLG, Rostock, 23 Feb. 1995, NJW-RR 1995, 1105.

[111] *Cydrus v. Houser*, 1999 Ohio App LEXIS 5746.

[112] *Estate of Martha Newman v. Franz*, 12 P3d 238 (Ariz 2000).

[113] 632 NE2d 507 (Ohio 1994).   [114] *Bailey v. Ewing*, 671 P2d 1099 (Idaho 1983).

the price did not reflect these possibilities. Given what we said in discussing fault, the court should have given relief for mistake in all four cases.

In contrast, sometimes the characteristic in question is one which would affect the suitability of the performance to all parties, and the contract is like a bet as to whether the performance has that characteristic or not. It may be like a bet in several different ways.

Sometimes one party believes that a certain test or procedure will reveal whether the performance has some desirable characteristic. The other is either unwilling or unable to perform the test himself. The degree to which the contract price reflects the possibility that it has this desired characteristic depends on the likelihood that it does and the expected expense of the test. If the test is sufficiently expensive and the characteristic sufficiently unlikely, it may not be reflected in the price at all. The contract should still be upheld because the buyer, at least, is betting that the test will be worthwhile, and he should get the benefit if he wins.

Sherwood v. *Walker* may actually have been such a case. The majority thought that the buyer had also assumed the prize breeding cow was barren and had purchased her for beef. Nevertheless, Eisenberg notes that the buyer was a gentleman rancher, not a butcher, and so, very likely, wanted to see if she could be bred. If that was so, I agree with Eisenberg that the contract should have been upheld even though, as Eisenberg suggests, the cow was sold by the pound and so might have been sold at the price of an ordinary beef cow.[115]

In other cases, the parties both entertained a significant doubt as to the characteristics of a performance and the price was presumably adjusted accordingly. Thus one German court upheld the sale of an experimental medical device—an 'ultrasound' apparatus—when the buyer knew it was uncertain what, if any, illnesses it could cure.[116] A French court upheld the sale of a painting which the seller's expert believed to be 'school of Guardi', when the seller, to be on the safe side, had sold at a reduced price and labeled it, correctly, a 'Venetian landscape, genere of Marieschi'.[117] An American court upheld the sale of a rock the seller had found and sold to the buyer, a jeweler, as a specimen. Neither party knew it was an uncut diamond.[118]

In still other cases, the parties themselves have indicated how uncertainty is to be resolved, for example, by saying that property is sold 'as is'. Courts have respected such clauses.[119]

Finally, there are cases in which, so to speak, everyone is or would be mistaken at the time a contract is made. In an American case, a painting was sold as by Bierstadt. The court denied relief when, later, art historians began expressing doubt and experts accepted the view that the painting was by Key.[120] Something similar seems to have happened in a French case. In 1933, a painting was sold as 'attributed to Fragonard'. In the 1980s, after it had been recognized that the painting really was by Fragonard, the seller tried to reclaim it. The court said that 'in 1933, in buying or in selling a work

---

[115] Eisenberg, 'Mistake', at 1634.   [116] BGH, 18 Dec. 1954, EBGHZ 16, 54.

[117] Trib. gr. inst., Paris, 7 May 1975, Gaz. Pal. 1975.   [118] *Wood* v. *Boynton*, 25 NW 42 (Wisc 1885).

[119] e.g. *Lenawee County Board of Health* v. *Messerly*, 331 NW2d 203 (Mich 1982); Cour d'appel, Riom, 10 May 1989, Rev. trim. dr. civ. 1989.740.

[120] *Firestone & Parson, Inc.* v. *Union League of Philadelphia*, 672 F Supp 819 (EDPa 1987), aff'd without opinion, 833 F2d 304 (3rd Cir 1987).

attributed to Fragonard, the contracting parties had accepted the risk as to the authenticity of the work'.[121] The court's opinion may seem conclusory. Had it invalidated the contract, the parties would not have accepted that risk. In that event, however, the result would have been that every time a painting was upgraded, so to speak, in the eyes of experts a chain of contracts would fall like dominos as far back as the available evidence will take one. To avoid that result, courts must say that the buyer and seller, in effect, make a bet as to whether everyone is wrong at the time they contract. If the buyer and seller know that, then price will reflect the risk that everyone is wrong.

3. Found property

There are cases in which one piece of property is found concealed in another. In one American case, a safe was sold with a locked compartment which the seller had not opened. The buyer, who had paid $50 for the safe, found $32,207 in the compartment. The court said the money belonged to the buyer. In my view, cases like these have less to do with the law of contract than with the law governing finders of property.[122] That branch of law deals with a difficult problem discussed earlier: when an object is found, does it belong to the finder or the owner of the land on which it was found? I will merely note here that the find does not prevent the property from being suited to the purpose for which it was sold. One can still use the safe as a safe.[123]

II. Mistake in Motive

A. The Consensus

Thus far we have discussed two situations. In one, because of a mistake, the performance is unsuitable, not only to the purposes of the party who is to receive it, but to the purposes of parties in general who would otherwise have contracted for such a performance. In a second, the performance has characteristics which suit it, generically, for the purpose for which parties in general would pay for it. Nevertheless, depending on these characteristics, it may be suited to the purposes of one party and not to those of another. These are the cases in which, as we have seen, courts have commonly given relief under rules that require that the parties make an error in 'substance'.

There is another situation, however, in which courts and commentators are generally agreed relief should not be given. A party has made what is commonly called an

---

[121] Cass. 1e ch. civ., 24 Mar., 1987, JCP 1989.J.21300.   [122] *See* Chapter 8 II B.

[123] One might think that a sale of land with minerals beneath it cannot be explained in the same way. Often one cannot use the land as a mine and still use it for the purpose that the buyer or anyone else would have had in mind at the time it was sold. In European countries such as France and Germany, the problem of which party has the right to the minerals cannot arise since the state takes title to them. In the United States, they belong to the landowner. The only justification I can think of for the American rule is that one cannot tell how much the owner benefits personally from the original use of the property. A forced sale may therefore undercompensate him. If that is so, however, then the same reason would dictate that he not be deprived of his land by the person who sold it to him because it contains minerals. Another reason is, as in the Bierstadt and Fragonard cases, to avoid invalidating a long chain of contracts stretching back to the earliest identifiable seller.

'error in motive'.[124] Textbook examples are a friend who buys a wedding gift and then learns that the engagement has been broken,[125] a man who buys a new refrigerator and then learns that a family member has just done so or that his wife hates the color,[126] a merchant who orders goods and then discovers that he already has them in stock,[127] a person who contracts for a cruise and later would prefer to go skiing,[128] an employee who rents a vacation house and then finds out he will not be given a vacation,[129] a basketball club which signs on a player and later decides that he is expendable,[130] a licensee of the right to exploit a film who expects it to be a blockbuster when it turns out to be a flop,[131] a person who sells a valuable object falsely believing that he needs the money,[132] and a person who buys property falsely believing he will inherit the money he needs to pay for it.[133] A performance has become unsuitable or less suitable for the purposes of the party who is to receive it. Nevertheless, the performance is no less suitable for the purposes of other parties who would have been willing to pay for it.

Melvin Eisenberg refers to the type of error just discussed as an 'evaluative mistake'. They are 'cases in which a well-informed and capable actor who made a contract comes to believe that his choice to make the contract was mistaken due to a change in his preferences or a change in the subjective or objective value of the performances due under the contract'.[134] He believes that they 'should not provide a basis for relief from a contract'.[135] One reason he gives is that that 'in many cases the risk that a contracting party has made an evaluative mistake is the very risk that the other party has bargained for. In effect, such contracts normally are fair bets...'.[136] Another is that 'the whole point of a promise is to commit yourself to take a given action in the future even if, when the action is due to be taken, all things considered you do not wish to take it'.[137]

Jurists who have considered this problem have agreed on this proposition for most of history. While common lawyers did not consider this problem until the 19th century,[138] civil lawyers have done so since the time of ancient Rome. When Roman jurists described the errors for which a party should obtain relief, none of their examples is what we would call an error in motive.[139] According to the jurists who

---

[124] French law: Mazeaud *et al.*, *Droit civil* 2/1, no. 166; Raymond, *Droit civil*, no. 241; Georges Ripert *et al.*, *Traité élémentaire de Planiol* 2 (4th edn., Paris, 1952), no. 199. Planiol would seem to be an exception if we consider only his statement that courts should give relief for error in motive provided the other party will not suffer a great prejudice (ibid. no. 185). But elsewhere he says that relief should only be given if the mistake concerned a tacit condition of the contract known to both parties (ibid. no. 177). German law: Larenz, *Allgemeiner Teil*, 378; Flume, *Allgemeiner Teil*, 424–5; Italian law: Rosella Filippi in Paolo Cendon, ed., *Codice civile annotato con la giurisprudenza* (Turin, 1996/7), no. 1 to art. 1429; Galgano, *Diritto privato*, 276; Iudica *et al.*, *Contratto*, 783.

[125] Larenz, *Allgemeiner Teil*, 391. *See* Ghestin, *Erreur* (1971), 62 (a father buys a trousseau for his daughter and then the engagement is broken off).   [126] Iudica *et al.*, *Contratto*, 784.

[127] Larenz, *Allgemeiner Teil*, 391.

[128] Eisenberg, 'Mistake', 1582. Eisenberg speaks, not of an error in motive, but of an error in 'evaluation'.   [129] Ghestin, *Erreur*, 62.

[130] Eisenberg, 'Mistake', 1582.   [131] ibid.   [132] Flume, *Allgemeiner Teil*, 425.

[133] Ripert *et al.*, *Traité élémentaire* 2, no. 177; Ghestin, *Erreur*, 62.

[134] Eisenberg, 'Mistake', 1582.   [135] ibid.   [136] ibid. 1583.   [137] ibid.

[138] Gordley, *Philosophical Origins* (1991), 141–6.

[139] Reinhard Zimmermann, *The Law of Obligations: Roman Foundations of the Civilian Tradition* (Cape Town, 1990), 597.

commented on Roman law in the Middle Ages, a party who had made an error in *causa*, which means purpose or motive, could withdraw from a contract only if the error was induced by fraud.[140]

B. A Dissenting View

Nevertheless, in the early 17th century, Leonard Lessius, one of the leading late scholastic jurists, claimed that sometimes an error in motive did warrant relief. In the 17th century, Lessius' conclusion that an error in motive could warrant relief was accepted by the founders of the northern natural law school, Grotius and Pufendorf. We will see that they were right.

Lessius defended this conclusion with an argument that he and his contemporaries had borrowed from Thomas Aquinas. As we will see in the next chapter, Aquinas had used it to explain a doctrine which common lawyers today call changed and unforeseen circumstances and Germans call *Wegfall der Geschäftsgrundlage*. This doctrine had been invented by the medieval canon lawyers and then borrowed by the medieval Roman lawyers. The canon lawyers concluded that in every promise, 'this condition is always understood: if matters remain in the same state'.[141]

In the 13th century, Aquinas had explained this doctrine by drawing on Aristotle's concept of equity. According to Aristotle, since laws are enacted to serve a purpose, circumstances can always arise in which the purpose will be thwarted if one obeys the law.[142] The law maker would not have wished the law to be binding under those circumstances. Aquinas concluded that an oath, vow, or promise is binding only under circumstances in which the promisor would have intended to be bound had these circumstances been called to his attention.[143] The late scholastics adopted this explanation of the doctrine, and the northern natural lawyers borrowed it from them.[144]

Lessius argued that an error in *causa* or motive could warrant relief for the same reason. As Aquinas had said, promises are binding only under the circumstances in which the promisor had intended to be bound. 'The reason', Lessius said, 'is that a promise only has force because of the will and intention of the promisor . . . ; therefore it cannot bind beyond that intention as expressed or as prudently interpreted'.[145] Drawing on Aquinas' analogy, he explained that promises are like laws. However absolute their wording, laws 'do not obligate in those cases in which the legislator expressly or by interpretation wished to except, and a promise is a sort of particular statute which one freely imposes on oneself'.[146] But 'no one intends to abide by a

---

[140] Or more accurately, if he made an error in the *causa finalis remota*. See Gordley, *Philosophical Origins*, 49–57, 65–7.   [141] *Glossa ordinaria* to *Decretum Gratiani* to *furens* to C. 22, q. 2, c. 14.

[142] Aristotle, *Nicomachean Ethics* V. x 1137ª–1137ᵇ.

[143] Thomas Aquinas, *Summa theologiae* II-II, Q. 88, a. 10; Q. 89, a. 9.

[144] Leonardus Lessius, *De iustitia et iure, certerisque virtutibus cardinalis libri quatuor* (Paris, 1628), lib. 2, cap. 18, dub. 10; Hugo Grotius, *De iure belli ac pacis*, II.xvi.25.2; II.xxi.20.2; Samuel Pufendorf, *De iure naturae et gentium libri octo* III.vi.6 (Amsterdam, 1688, III. vi. 6); Jean Barbeyrac, *Le Droit de la nature et des gens . . . par le baron de Pufendorf* (Amsterdam, 1734), n. 3.

[145] Lessius, *De iustitia et iure*, lib. 2, cap. 18, dub. 10.   [146] ibid. lib. 2, cap. 17, dub. 10.

contract in such a way that he cannot withdraw even if he only contracted because of a great error...'.[147]

Lessius concluded that a party who was led to promise a gift by an 'error in motive' should be able to withdraw because the 'normal and tacit intention of the parties is to be regarded'. While acknowledging that in a contract of exchange both parties must consent, he claimed that the most reasonable conclusion is that a promise to exchange can be revoked if the party who made such an error is not at fault and the positions of the parties have not changed (*res... est integra*). If their positions have changed, then that party can still revoke but the other can claim compensation for any damage he has suffered.[148] The views of Grotius and Pufendorf were similar though less precisely expressed. For example, Grotius spoke of an error in the 'unique' motive for contracting without explaining whether he meant more than any motive without which one would not have contracted.[149]

One might think that if Lessius, Grotius and Pufendorf were right, a contract would never be binding beyond what we would call a person's reliance interest. Anyone could withdraw from a contract provided he compensated the other party for any harm he suffered by relying on it. After all, anyone who wishes to withdraw must have made some error absent which he would not have contracted—if only the error of thinking that he wouldn't change his mind. As Eisenberg said, 'the very point of a promise is to commit oneself to take a given action even if, all things considered, one does not wish to take the action at the time it is supposed to be taken'.[150]

Nevertheless, Lessius, Grotius, and Pufendorf rejected the position that executory contracts are not binding beyond a person's reliance interest.[151] As we have seen, that position had been defended in the 16th century by Cajetan, at least when the promise was to make a gift. He argued that the person promised a gift was no worse off if the promise was broken unless he had changed his position in reliance on the promise. Therefore no injustice was done as long as the promisor compensated him for any harm he had suffered by changing his position.[152] Lessius responded that to assume that, absent reliance, the promisee was no worse off when an executory promise was broken was to assume that at the moment the promise was made, the promisee had not acquired a right to the performance. If the parties so intended, the promisor could confer such a right on the promisee at the moment they contracted. If so, failure to perform deprived the promisee of that right.[153]

Lessius' insight, then, was that if the parties so intend, the promisor can give the promisee a right to require performance, not merely a right to compensation for a change in position. Even then, however, the promisor is not bound under circumstances in which the parties would not have wished him to be had they considered those circumstances. Therefore, he is sometimes not bound because of an error in motive.

---

[147] ibid. lib. 2, cap. 17, dub. 5.   [148] ibid.

[149] Grotius, *De iure belli ac pacis*, II.xi.6; Pufendorf, *De iure naturae et gentium* III.vi.6. For a discussion, see Gordley, *Philosophical Origins*, 89–93.   [150] Eisenberg, 'Mistake', 12.

[151] Lessius, *De iustitia et iure*, lib. 2, cap. 18, dub. 2; Grotius, *De belli ac pacis*, II.xi.1, 3–4; Pufendorf, *De iure naturae et gentium*, III.v.5–11.

[152] Cajetan (Tomasso di Vio), *Commentaria* (Patavii, 1698) to Thomas Aquinas, *Summa theologica* II-II, q. 81, a. 8; q. 113, a. 3.   [153] Lessius, *De iustitia et iure*, lib. 2, cap. 18, dub. 2.

C. A Solution

Lessius did not explain why the parties would want to make an arrangement that binds the promisor, not merely to compensate the promisee who relies, but to perform or pay the value of the promised performance. To put the question in modern terminology, why would the contracting parties want an arrangement that protects the expectation interest and not merely the reliance interest of the promisee?

As we have seen, Melvin Eisenberg has identified a reason the parties might want an arrangement which protects the promisee's expectation interest. A party may want to lock in a favorable bargain.[154] In return for the promisor's agreement to be locked in, the promisee will give something in return: he will contract on terms more favorable to the promisor or agree to be locked in himself. A party might want to lock in the bargain, for example, because of the special qualities of the performance he is to receive, or because he wants to lock in what he believes to be a favorable price.

We can now be more specific about the implications of Lessius' approach. We know that the promisee wanted a promise from the promisor. We should determine whether the reason the promisee wanted the promise from the promisor was for one of the reasons such as we have described that the law should respect. If not, he should not be bound beyond the promisee's reliance interest. If there is such a reason, his liability should be commensurate with it.

With these considerations in mind we can see why a court usually will not grant relief to a party who has made an error in motive. Suppose that a promisee wanted to lock in a performance because of its unique qualities. For example, suppose that the buyer of a house wanted to lock the right to the house because of characteristics that make it specially valuable to him. Suppose that the seller had plans to move to a different house and regrets having contracted when his plans fall through. He may also value the unique qualities of the house. Nevertheless, there is no way that a court could tell to whom the house is most valuable. The seller cannot have the right to the house simply because he once owned it. He should not stand in a different position than anyone else who finds it especially attractive. It is not surprising that a court would not give relief. Next, suppose that a promisee wanted to lock in a price. He might be trading on what I have referred to elsewhere as a perfect market in which the price for which a commodity will sell at a given time is known by all potential buyers and sellers. A party who contracted on such a market might discover he has made an error in motive. For example, a farmer who sold a certain quantity of corn to a dealer might acquire more pigs and decide he would rather keep the grain and feed it to them. Or the grain dealer might decide that he cannot afford the corn without overextending his business. If the market price has moved in favor of the party who was mistaken in his motives, that party could withdraw without paying any damages. He will not wish to do so, of course: the farmer could purchase corn elsewhere for less than he is selling the corn he raised, and the dealer could resell at a profit. If the market price has moved against the mistaken party, however, then there are two reasons why he should not be able to withdraw. To allow him to do so is, in effect, to allow him to

---

[154] Melvin A. Eisenberg, 'Theory of Contracts', 279.

renege on a bet he has lost. If markets work as economists say they do, the party who gains if a price moves in his favor could just as easily have lost if they had moved the other way. When parties contract to lock in the price in what I have called a perfect market, they have, in effect, bet on which way the market will move. As we have just seen, if the market moves in favor of the mistaken party, he will not be withdrawing from the contract. He will profit. It would be unfair to allow him to withdraw if the market price moves against him.

In what I have called an imperfect market, neither party is sure of what others will pay for what he is thinking of buying and selling. An example is the housing market, where neither party is sure whether he can get a better deal elsewhere. Once again, however, the promisee has reneged on a bet. In an imperfect market, each party is betting that the price he is offered is better than any he will find if he waits and shops around. If the promisor had realized after the contract was made that he had offered $100,000 less for a house than other people would, he would not have defaulted. He would have resold at a profit. He should not be able to default if he agreed to buy the house for $100,000 more than others will pay for it.

It is not surprising, then, that usually a court will protect the expectation interest of the promisee when the promisor has made an error in motive. For example, an American court did so when a party bought a dredge built for use in trenching in the mistaken belief that it could perform sweep dredging.[155] A French court did so when a buyer bought a fabric sold as 'cloth for furniture' (*tissu d'ameublement*) and found it insufficiently strong to use for clothing.[156] So did a German court when the buyer purchased land to sell it to a particular third party who then refused to buy.[157]

Nevertheless, if our approach is correct, we cannot accept, as a universal proposition, that error in motive does not matter. Eisenberg, as noted earlier, gave two reasons why it should not. The first is perfectly sound. 'Many bargains are motivated by the parties' differing estimates of the objective value of the performances due under the contract. In effect, such contracts normally are fair bets . . .'.[158] As we have noted, that is one of the reasons a promisee might want to lock in what he regards as a favorable price. If he contracted in order to lock in either the price or the value of a unique performance not easily available elsewhere, he should have the benefit of his bargain. But he may not have contracted in advance to lock in either the price or the performance. He may have simply wished to allow time for the goods to be ordered or made or to reserve a place in line. If so, while he should have to compensate a promisee who changed his position, there is no reason he should be compelled to do more. On the other hand, if the promisee did contract to lock in a unique performance or a price, still, the considerations that led to the making of the promise to be made should circumscribe the remedy for its breach. If the promisee contracted for a unique performance not readily available elsewhere, then the promisor should be compelled to perform. If the promisee contracted to lock in a price, the promisor should be compelled to pay him the difference between the contract and the market price. But if the performance is

---

[155] *Anderson Brothers Corp*, v. *O'Meara*, 306 F2d 672 (5th Cir 1962).
[156] Cass. com., 4 July 1973, Bull. civ. IV, no. 238.
[157] BGH, 27 Sept. 1991, NJW-RR 1992.182.   [158] Eisenberg, 'Mistake', 11.

readily available on the market and the contract price and market price are the same, why should the promisor be compelled to perform? Eisenberg's first reason no longer applies. His second reason is that 'the very point of a promise is to commit oneself to take a given action even if, all things considered, one does not wish to take the action at the time it is supposed to be taken'. But if the very point of the promise is to allow the promisee to lock in a given performance or a given price, then the promise does not lose its point as long as the promisee gets this benefit. Moreover, the point of the promise may be to allow the promisee time to obtain goods or to make them or to perform a service without fear that he lose by doing so. If so, the promise does not lose its point as long as he is compensated for any loss he suffers.

Often the proposition that an error in motive does not matter will not affect the result a court reaches. If the promisee has contracted for a unique performance, the promisor will be compelled to perform. If the promisee has contracted to lock in a price, the promisor will have to pay him the difference between market and contract or contract and market price. Unfortunately, courts have said that error in motive does not matter when the promisor's performance was not unique and prices did not change. Even when prices did not change, the promisee can still recover damages if he is a 'lost volume' seller. He would have made an additional sale if the promisor had not defaulted. He could then have ordered an additional product from his supplier and pocketed the difference between the price the manufacturer charges him and the price he charges his customers. He can also recover if he has excess capacity and could have pocketed the difference between the contract price and his variable costs. If the approach we are defending is correct, the cases which allow him to recover were wrongly decided.

An illustration is the American case, *Neri* v. *Retail Marine Corp.*[159] A customer agreed to buy a new boat of a specified model at a certain price from a retail dealer. Before the boat was delivered, he tried to rescind the sale because he needed hospitalization and surgery. Four months after the boat was delivered to the dealer by the manufacturer it was sold to another customer at the same price. The court held that the dealer could recover the difference between the contract price and the costs he had saved (or, as Uniform Commercial Code §2-708(2) puts it, his overhead plus lost profit). The court never considered the customer's motive for trying to rescind.

If the buyer's error in motive did not matter, and the seller was entitled to expectation damages, the case was correctly decided. If the approach we are now considering is correct, however, then we should ask whether promisee wanted the promise for the reasons we have described. This is not a case in which the dealer wished to lock in a unique performance. The customer's performance was to pay money. It may have been a case in which the dealer (and customer) wished to lock in the price. Even so, the price did not change. The boat was resold at the same price. If the purpose of binding the customers was to lock in the price, his liability should be commensurate with that purpose. The dealer should recover the resale minus the contract price, which in this case is zero.

A German example is a case in which the defendant, who was in some unspecified branch of the automobile industry, reserved 22 beds in a hotel for his employees so

---

[159] 285 NE2d 311 (NY 1972).

they could attend the International Automobile Exhibition in September. He made the reservations on 20 January. On 28 January, he notified the hotel that he did not want the rooms because the exhibition had been canceled. The hotel did not succeed in renting the rooms to anyone else. A German appellate court allowed the hotel to recover its lost profits.[160]

It is true that a hotel might wish a reservation to be uncancelable for a reason we have not yet considered but one mentioned by Fuller and Perdue: the difficulty of proving reliance. If a guest cancels shortly before he arrives, the hotel might have been able to give the room to someone else. It would be hard to prove that those who inquired about rooms and were turned away would actually have taken them. That is why most hotels have a policy which allows cancellation a certain number of days in advance but requires full or nearly full payment thereafter. But that consideration doesn't apply here. It is hard to believe the hotel was so fully booked from January 20 to 28 that it turned away anyone. It tried and failed to rent the rooms from then until September. Nor was the hotel trying to lock in some unique performance. It may have been trying to lock in a price, but the price did not change. The hotel sued for lost profits.

Another example is a line of German cases in which a party agrees to borrow money from a bank, and tries to withdraw when the project for which he borrowed it is no longer feasible. German courts have treated the bank like a lost volume seller and held the borrower liable for its lost profits on the loan.[161] Here again, that result is perfectly reasonable if error in motive doesn't matter, and if expectation damages can be recovered for breach of contract. But these are not cases in which the bank was trying to lock in either a unique performance or in which interest rates had changed. If the bank wanted the borrower to be liable for expectation damages, it would not be for any of the reasons we have discussed.

There is, of course, an additional reason that the bank, the hotel or the retail boat dealer might want to recover expectation damages. They might want to make money by charging customers and guests for things that they don't want. That may indeed have been their motive, but it is one the law should disregard. A basic purpose of contract law is to enable people to get what they do want. The law may sometimes have to compromise this purpose, but that does not mean that the law should assist a party in thwarting this purpose.

---

[160] OLG Braunschweig, 31 July 1975, NJW 1976, 570. Similarly, in Arizona, a resort recovered against a manufacturer who had reserved 190 rooms for a convention of representatives of dealerships, and then cancelled it because 20 percent of the dealerships were afraid to travel during the first Gulf War. *7200 Scotsdale Road General Partners* v. *Kuhn Farm Machinery, Inc.*, 909 P2d 408 (Ariz 1995). It was a strange case since the court seemed to think it relevant that their fears were exaggerated. The court may have been influenced by a provision in the contract charging the manufacturer if fewer people came than he expected.

[161] BGH, 2 Nov. 1989, NJW 1990, 981 (borrower tries to withdraw because he can't raise the additional money needed for his project); BGH, 12 Mar. 1991, NJW 1991, 1817 (borrower's plan to purchase property falls through); BGH, 12 Dec. 1985, NJW-RR 1986, 467 (decided under § 242) (borrower's plan to build single family homes is canceled when delay leads to increased costs). More recently, the Bundesgerichtshof has held that good faith requires the bank to release the buyer from the contract—thereby allowing him, for example, to remove an encumbrance on his property—but only if he pays seller's lost profit. BGH, 1 July 1997, EBGHZ 136, 161, on which see Andreas Früh, 'Der Anspruch des Darlehensgeber auf Einwilligung in die vorzeitige Darlehensrückzahlung', NJW 1999, 262.

Moreover, if that were the reason for requiring the customer or guest to pay expectation damages, the customer and the guest would never agree to do so if they both had their eyes open. We will use the *Neri* case to illustrate why that is so but the reasoning would be the same in the hotel and bank cases as well. If the dealer and his customer were risk averse, as most people are, the dealer could not offer the customer a price reduction sufficient to induce him to agree to pay expectation damages under the circumstances of the *Neri* case. It would amount to a gamble on whether some random event such as a medical problem would make the performance worth less to the customer than what he agreed to pay. Risk averse people won't gamble unless the odds of winning are tilted in their favor. They will not bet $10,000 on a coin flip unless they are offered more than $10,000 if they win. In the case we are imagining, the customer would not agree to pay expectation damages unless he is offered more than the amount of the damages discounted by the probability that he will have to pay. Since the dealer is also risk averse, he will never offer that much.

That is so, I believe, even if the dealer were a monopolist who controlled the retail sale of every boat his customers could buy. Imagine the buyer indicating that he would pay $15,000 for a certain boat, and the dealer responding that he could have his choice: he could buy the boat for $15,000 or they would flip a coin and, depending on the outcome, he would buy the boat for either $17,000 or $13,000. Because the customer is risk averse, he would take the first choice and pay $15,000. To induce him to accept the second, the dealer would have to change the terms in his favor: for example, to $16,500 or $13,500 depending on the coin flip. But those terms would not interest a risk averse dealer.

If the dealer were not a monopolist, it would be still easier to see how parties with their eyes open would write the contract. We can imagine a customer negotiating with two boat dealers to see where he can get the best terms. Imagine that there is an express term in the contract that requires him to pay expectation damages even if he cancels before there has been any reliance and when prices have not changed. He offers the dealer some amount—$500—for the removal of that clause, and the first dealer indicates his willingness to agree. He then asks the second dealer if he will offer a better deal, and the second says he will take out the clause for $400. If the process continues, they will bid the price of removing that clause down to zero.

If this analysis is right, then error in motive does matter, and a generally accepted rule of contract law is wrong. Because the rule is generally accepted, it is not surprising to find that courts often follow it. But because it is wrong, it is not surprising to find that sometimes, guided by their own intuitions about justice, courts give relief for error in motive without admitting that they do so. A German court gave relief for what we call frustration of purpose when a travel agency booked rooms in a hotel and later canceled. The court noted that travel agencies often have to book rooms before they are sure they have customers.[162] In France, a husband and wife each bought theater tickets to the same performance, neither knowing that the other was doing so. The court held that the theater had to return the price of one set of tickets.[163] In

---

[162] BGH, 24 Nov. 1976, NJW 1977, 385, 386.
[163] Trib. comm. Sene, 2 Apr. 1943, Gaz. Pal. 1943.2.81.

another French case, a court gave relief when a person bought insurance not realizing that his deceased mother had already insured him.[164] In an American case, a contractor hired a subcontractor to furnish concrete barriers for a highway project. The court gave relief for frustration of purpose when the government reworked the project so that it no longer included barriers.[165] In a similar case, the court gave relief when a project was reworked so it no longer required the painting and finishing that the subcontractor had been hired to do.[166]

In another American case, a father agreed to pay for karate lessons for his son. His son's doctor then determined that the boy could not take them. A clause in the contract said that the lessons could not be canceled. The court said that it would have given relief for frustration of purpose absent that clause.[167] The court might have gone further and asked why the non-cancellation clause was put in the agreement. It might have been for the legitimate reason that reliance damages would be hard to prove: for example, perhaps the course might not have been offered if fewer people signed up. Or it might have been for what we have seen is not a legitimate purpose: to charge people for what they don't want. Still, absent the clause, the boy's father would not have had to pay.

Other cases involve the status of long-term contracts when one of the parties is no longer doing business and no longer needs what the other was to supply. In one German case, a man had a long-term contract to buy chinchillas for breeding purposes. The seller was also to provide him with ongoing advice on their rearing. The buyer died. The court gave relief for frustration of purpose, noting that his wife and minor children would neither be able to carry on the business nor to resell the chinchillas.[168] In a well-known American case, a hotel entered into a three year contract with a golf club for hotel guests to use the golf course and the hotel to pay the club a monthly fee plus their green fees. The hotel burned down. The court held it was an implied condition of the contract that there would be guests.[169]

---

[164] Cass. req., 6 June 1932, D.H. 1932.396.

[165] *Chase Precast Concrete Corp.* v. *John J. Paonessa Co.*, 566 NE2d 603 (Mass 1991).

[166] *A. T. Switzer Company, Appellant* v. *Midwestern Construction Company of Missouri*, 670 SW2d 69 (Mo Appl 1984). [167] *Jewell* v. *Sports, USA, Inc.*, 19 Va Cir 19 (1989).

[168] OLG Frankfurt, 15 Oct. 1973, MDR 1974, 401. Although, in another case, in which a hotel had agreed to buy at least a certain quantity of beer from a brewery every year, the contract was enforced even though the hotel had ceased operating, K stands to buy beer from brewery stands even if hotel owner/buyer ceases operations (decided under BGB § 242), BGH, 27 Feb. 1985, NJW 1985.2693.

[169] *La Cumbre Golf & Country Club* v. *Santa Barbara Hotel Co.*, 271 P 476 (1928).

15

Impossibility and Unexpected Circumstances

The doctrine of impossibility goes back to Roman law. Traditionally, it denies enforcement to some but not all contracts in which performance is impossible. The doctrine of changed circumstances, in contrast, was developed by the medieval canon lawyers. As traditionally formulated, it provides that a promisor is not liable under certain circumstances under which he would not have been willing to commit himself had he anticipated them.

The Roman and canon lawyers formulated these doctrines but did not attempt to explain them. As before the late scholastics tried to explain them both with ideas taken from Aristotle. In my view, their attempt to explain the doctrine of impossibility was a failure, largely because they were trying to explain a legal doctrine which sometimes excused a promisor in moralistic terms which implied he always should be excused. Attempts to explain the doctrine since then have been equally unsuccessful. Thus our account of impossibility will be one of a doctrine that failed.

Jurists have also found the doctrine of changed circumstances difficult to explain. Most of the 19th century civil lawyers rejected it entirely. Yet, with the notable exception of France, most major legal systems will now give relief. This time, as we will see, the late scholastics and northern natural lawyers found a good explanation of the doctrine, one so good that it can explain the relief that the law gives for impossibility as well.

I. The Doctrine of Impossibility

Before turning to the doctrine of changed circumstances, we will see how traditional explanations of the impossibility doctrine failed, and how the doctrine could have been better rationalized. We will then consider the doctrine of changed circumstances more closely and see how it can explain more than when the law gives relief for impossibility.

A. Origins

A famous Roman text contained the maxim, 'there is no obligation to the impossible'.[1] A number of texts excuse a party when performance was impossible at the time the

[1] Dig. 50.17.185.

contract was made. All of them concern two types of contracts, sale and *stipulatio*.[2] For example, a sale is not valid if the object sold never existed or had perished prior to the sale.[3] It is also true that if a party's performance became impossible after the contract was made, he was excused provided he was not at fault. But one cannot conclude that, in Roman law, a party was excused if his performance was or became impossible and he was not at fault in the ordinary sense. According to one text, if his performance was initially impossible, a party cannot escape liabiliy if performance is merely beyond his own power. It must be beyond anyone's power.[4] As later commentators put it, impossibility must be 'objective' or 'absolute', not 'subjective' or 'personal'. If a party's performance became impossible, he could not escape merely because he was not at fault in the ordinary sense of the word. One who borrowed property gratuitously for his own use is liable if he failed to exercise the most scrupulous diligence (*exactissima diligentia*).[5] He is not liable if the property is destroyed by invading enemies or bands of robbers.[6] The puzzle is why a party should be liable for failing to be 'more diligent than the diligent'.[7] Many modern scholars believe that in classical Roman law, he was liable for *custodia*, which meant neither negligence nor strict liability. A person liable for *custodia* was liable even though he used proper care for a loss that the use of proper care would typically prevent. He was not liable for *vis maior*, that is, for accidents that no one could have prevented.[8] The medieval jurists classified this kind of 'fault' as *culpa levissima*—most light fault. From there, one ascended through *culpa levis*, *culpa lata*, and *culpa latior* to dolus or intentional wrongdoing, the correct definition of each degree remaining a matter of continual argument.[9]

The medieval canon lawyers, however, turned impossibility and fault into basic principles of moral responsibility which the late scholastics then defended on Aristotelian principles. The canonists concluded, after some initial hesitation, that one could not be morally obligated to do the impossible. Gratian had said that when every alternative course of action is sinful, one must choose the lesser sin.[10] In some of the cases he was discussing, the seemingly lesser sin was to break a promise: after promising to keep a friend's secret, one learns he is planning a murder.[11] If Gratian were right, a person might find it impossible not to sin since every possible course of action is sinful. Later canonists rejected his position. By definition, one is morally obligated not to commit a sin. One could not, they argued, be obligated to do the impossible.[12] If a person in these circumstances should reveal the friend's secret, then to do so is not sinful.

The canon lawyers also concluded that a person who was at fault because he failed to use due care was not only morally guilty[13] but morally obligated to make compensation

---

[2] Reinhard Zimmermann, *The Law of Obligations Roman Foundations of the Civilian Tradition* (Cape Town, 1990), 687.   [3] Dig. 18.1.15. pr.; Dig. 18.1.57.

[4] Dig. 45.1.137.   [5] Dig. 44.7.1.4.   [6] Dig. 13.6.18.pr.

[7] Zimmermann, *Law of Obligations*, 192.   [8] ibid. 192–7.

[9] e.g. Bartolus de Saxoferrato, *Commentaria Corpus Iuris Civilis* to D. 16.3.32, nos. 13, 16, 26, 27, in *Omnia quae extant opera* (Venice, 1615).

[10] Gratian, *Decretum* (Venice, 1595), *dicta Gratiani ante*, D. 13 c. 1.   [11] ibid. D. 13, cc. 1–2.

[12] *Glossa ordinaria* to ibid. to *dicta Gratiani ante*, D. 13, c. 1.

[13] Gratian, *Decretum*, D. 50, cc. 49–50; *Decretales Gregorii ix* 5.10.7–13 in *Corpus iuris canonici* 2 (E. Friedberg, ed., Leipzig, 1876); Bernardus Papiensis, *Summa Decretalium* (Laspeyres, ed., Graz, 1956),

for any harm he had caused.[14] Since the canon lawyers were concerned with moral responsibility, it is not surprising that they concluded that a person can be morally responsible only when he could have acted otherwise and was at fault for failing to do so. Therefore, he was not liable for the impossible. Nevertheless, their conclusions about moral responsibility were now in tension with the Roman limitations on civil liability.

In the 13th century, Thomas Aquinas used Aristotle's theory of human responsibility to explain the conclusions of the canonists. Choice was an act of will, and one could only choose what was possible.[15] A promise to do the impossible was not binding.[16]

Once impossibility and fault had been interpreted as principles of moral responsibility, it was difficult to harmonize them with the Roman rules. A struggle now began in which the Roman rules were never displaced by Aristotelian principles—as were the rules governing contract formation—nor explained by them—as were the rules governing relief for mistake and unfairness. The late scholastics and the natural lawyers sometimes ignored the Roman rules, sometimes rejected them and sometimes tolerated the inconsistency.

The late scholastics borrowed the conclusion that one cannot be obligated to keep an impossible promise.[17] They never explained how to reconcile this maxim with the Roman rules. Pufendorf claimed that the seller was never liable for failing to do the impossible but, if he were at fault in making the promise, the buyer could recover any loss suffered.[18] He had achieved consistency but only by sacrificing the Roman texts.

In discussing fault, the late scholastics admitted that they could not reconcile their moral philosophy with Roman law. In moral philosophy and theology, they said, fault means sin,[19] a deviation of the will from right reason and the law of God.[20] For the Roman lawyers, it means 'the omission of some sort of diligence from which something disadvantageous happens',[21] a 'deviation from that which is good and that could be provided for by human diligence'.[22]

Lessius and Molina concluded that the jurists were describing Roman positive law, not natural law. By natural law, one could only be liable for failure to use the care that

---

lib. 5, tit. 10, §§ 5–6; Raimondus de Pennaforte, *Summa de Paenitentia* (Ochoa and Diez, eds., Rome. 1976), lib. 2, tit. 1, § 3. See Stephen Kuttner, *Kanonistische Schuldlehre von Gratian bis auf die Dekretalen Gregors IX* (Vatican City, 1935), 213–27.

[14] *Glossa ordinaria* to *Decretales Gregorii ix* (Venice, 1595), 5.36.5, *Casus* to *non custovit*; to *reddet*; to 5.36.6 to *voluntarie*; to 5.36.9.   [15] Thomas Aquinas, *Summa theologiae* I-II Q. 13, a. 5, ad 1.

[16] ibid. II-II, Q. 88, a. 2 (vow to do the impossible not binding); Q. 89, a. 7 (oath to do the impossible not binding).

[17] Cajetan (Tomasso di Vio), *Commentaria* to Thomas Aquinas, *Summa theologica* (Padua, 1698), to II-II, q. 113, a. 1; Domenicus Soto, *De iustitia et iure libri decem* (Salamanca, 1551), lib. 8, q. 2, a. 1; Ludovicus Molina, *De iustitia et iure tractatus* (Venice, 1614), disp. 271, no. 1; Leonardus Lessius, *De iustitia et iure, ceterisque virtutibus cardinalis libri quatuor* (Paris, 1628), lib. 2, cap. 10, dub. 10, no. 70.

[18] Samuel Pufendorf, *De iure naturae et gentium libri octo* (Amsterdam, 1688), III.vii.2–3.

[19] Lessius, *De iustitia et iure*, lib. 2, cap. 7, dub. 6.   [20] Molina, *De iustitia et iure*, disp. 293, no. 10.

[21] Lessius, *De iustitia et iure*, lib. 2, cap. 7, dub. 6 (omissio alicuius diligentia, unde sequitur aliquod incommodum).

[22] Molina, *De iustitia et iure*, disp. 293, no. 12 (deviationem ab eo, quod bonum est, quodque per hominis potuit diligentiam provideri). The conclusion that fault had a different meaning in law and in theology had been drawn by earlier writers as well. E.g. Sylvester Priarias, *Summa sylvestrina quae summa summarum merito nuncupatur* (Venice, 1591), v. 'culpa', no. 1.

men of the same condition use.[23] They tried, rather unsuccessfully, to find pragmatic justifications for the Roman rules. According to Lessius, these rules prevented fraud and iniquity by promoting diligence.[24] According to Molina, they discouraged litigation and encouraged people to make contracts that promoted commerce and human society such as loans for use, deposit and lease.[25]

The Roman texts were difficult to explain by any theory. It is difficult to see, for example, why one needs two doctrines, impossibility and fault, and why the first should apply when a performance is impossible from the beginning, and the second when the performance becomes impossible. But there was a deeper reason why the natural law theory could not explain the Roman texts. The natural lawyers had a theory about when a person was at fault in the moral sense. As Zimmermann and Wollschläger have pointed out, such a theory could not explain Roman law because the Romans were really imposing liability absent fault for risks that, in their view, should fall on the promisor.[26] One of the weaknesses of the natural law tradition, as I have noted elsewhere, is that it never succeeded in finding a place for strict liability.[27]

The 19th century jurists thus inherited a body of law in disarray. The principled explanations of the natural lawyers did not seem to explain the Roman law, which was very hard to explain in any case. In France, the textual problems changed with the enactment of the Code, although in a way that made principled solutions still more elusive. In Germany, where the Roman texts remained in force, the jurists developed principled explanations, and then forced the Roman texts to conform to them. In England, Roman law was borrowed in part but then confounded with another doctrine entirely, which concerned implied conditions.

In the late 18th century, Thomasius in Germany and Le Brun in France attacked the traditional view that there were degrees of fault, and that the degree for which a person is liable depended on the contract in question.[28] Speaking for the drafting committee, Bigot-Préameneu denounced the old view as useless and overly subtle.[29] Accordingly, article 1137, paragraph 1 declared that when a person is charged with looking after an object, there would be one standard of care, that of a *bon père de famille*, what we would call a 'reasonable person'.

But the older concept of *culpa levissima*, though rejected by this provision, reappeared elsewhere. Articles 1147–8 cast doubt on whether a party was normally liable for ordinary negligence, as article 1137, paragraph 1 suggested. According to article 1147,

[23] Lessius, *De iustitia et iure*, lib. 2, cap. 7, dub. 6, no. 23; Molina, *De iustitia et iure*, disp. 293, no. 18.

[24] Lessius, *De iustitia et iure*, lib. 2, cap. 7, dub. 8, no. 44.

[25] Molina, *De iustitia et iure*, disp. 293, no. 24.

[26] Zimmermann, *Law of Obligations*, 692–3, 695–7; Wollschläger, 'Die willenstheoretische Unmöglichkeitslehre im aristotelisch-thomistischen Naturrecht', in *Sympotica Franz Wieacker* (Göttingen, 1970), 154–79, at 178.

[27] James Gordley, 'Tort Law in the Aristotelian Tradition', in D. Owen, ed., *Philosophical Foundations of Tort Law: A Collection of Essays* (Oxford, 1995), 131.

[28] Christianus Thomasius, *Dissertatio de usu pratico doctrinae de culparum praestatione in contractibus*, in Christianus Thomasius, *Dissertationum academicorum varii inprimis iuris argumenti* 2 (Halle-on-Saale, 1777), 1006; Le Brun, *Essai sur la prestation des fautes*, printed in *Oeuvres de Pothier annotée en corrélation avec le Code civil et la législation actuelle* 2 (M. Bugnet, ed., 2nd edn., Paris, 1861), 503.

[29] Bigot-Préameneu, 'Exposé des motifs', in *Recueil complet des travaux préparatoires du Code civil* 13 (P. Antoine Fenet, ed., Paris, 1836), 230.

a party is liable 'whenever he does not prove that non-performance resulted from an extrinsic cause (*cause étrangère*) that cannot be imputed to him'. According to article 1148, he was not liable if performance had been hindered by 'irresistible force (*force majeure*) or a chance event (*cas fortuit*)'. For Pothier, from whom the drafters had borrowed, *cas fortuit* and *force majeure* meant *vis maior*, the sort of event that would exonerate even the person liable for *faute la plus légère* or *culpa levissima*.[30] Thus the drafters established two contradictory general rules: one imposing liability for ordinary negligence, and the other for what had traditionally been called *culpa levissima*.

This time, the approach of the French commentators was neither conceptualistic nor based on the will theory. It was confused. Initially, Toullier and Duranton each espoused a clear theory, but neither theory was accepted. Toullier claimed that the Code had, in fact, established only one standard of liability in contract as well as tort: liability for *culpa levissima*.[31] Duranton claimed that the Code had preserved the traditional theory of degrees of fault depending on the type of contract the parties entered into.[32]

The later French commentators rejected both views as incompatible with article 1139, paragraph 1. Their own ideas were much less coherent. With variations, Aubry, Rau, Demolombe, Laurent, and Larombière concluded that the standard of care of article 1137, paragraph 1 was ordinary negligence.[33] Nevertheless, they also agreed that under articles 1147–8, a party escapes only if he proves the sort of event traditionally called *vis maior*.[34] Their lists of such events are like those of the Romans: tempest, earthquake, war and so forth. They then sluffed over the contradiction, usually, by asserting or implying that these standards are always or nearly always the same: there is fault when there is no *force majeure, cas fortuit,* or *cause étrangère*.[35] Demolombe did observe that sometimes a party might not be at fault even though no such event had occurred, but he simply noted that the security of transactions requires that the party be held liable.[36]

Demolombe and Laurent also conflated *vis maior* with impossibility. They explained articles 1147–8 as an application of the principle that no one is liable for the impossible. They endorsed the Roman rule that performance will only be excused when it is objectively impossible or impossible for anyone, not if it is only impossible for the particular party.[37]

---

[30] Robert Pothier, *Traité des obligations*, § 142, in *Oeuvres de Pothier* 2: 1.

[31] Charles Toullier, *Le Droit civil français suivant l'ordre du Code* 6 (Paris, 1824–37), 233–4.

[32] Alexandre Duranton, *Cours de droit français suivant le Code Civil* 10 (3rd edn., Paris, 1834–7), §§ 410–12.

[33] Charles Aubry and Charles Rau, *Cours de droit civil français après la méthode de Zachariae* 4 (4th edn., Paris, 1869–71), § 308, n. 28 (art. 1137, par. 1 sets the general standard; other articles create exceptions that can be extended by analogy to like cases); Charles Demolombe, *Cours de Code Napoléon* 24 (Paris, 1854–82), § 1137 (art. 1137, par. 1 sets the general standard; par. 2 allows the judge to apply it flexibly); François Laurent, *Principes de droit civil français* 16 (3rd edn., Paris, 1869–78), §§ 219, 231 (art. 1137, par. 1 sets the general standard; other articles create exceptions); Léobon Larombière, *Théorie et pratique des obligations ou commentaire des titres III & IV, livre III due Code Napoléon art. 1101 à 1386* 1 (Paris, 1857), 400–1 (art. 1137, par. 1 sets a maximum standard of care; other articles reduce it).

[34] Aubry and Rau, *Cours*, 4 § 308; Demolombe, *Cours*, 24, 549–52; Laurent, *Principes*, 16, § 256–7; Larombière, *Obligations* 1, 541–2.

[35] See Aubry and Rau, *Cours*, 4, § 308; Laurent, *Principes*, 16, § 256; Larombière, *Obligations*, 1, 541–2.

[36] Demolombe, *Cours*, 24, § 550.   [37] ibid. § 549; Laurent, *Cours*, 16, § 255.

Finally, René Demogue found a more consistent solution which is now widely accepted. He distinguished obligations to use proper means (*obligations de moyens*) from obligations to actually attain a certain result (*obligations de résultat*). In the former case, a party was liable for ordinary negligence. In the latter case he was liable unless he could prove *force majeure, cas fortuit*, or *cause étrangère*.[38] The problem then is to explain which obligations fall into each category and why. We will turn to that problem after a look at German and Anglo-American law.

Scorning such pragmatic confusion, the 19th century German conceptualists tried to formulate coherent definitions of impossibility and fault. Unlike the natural lawyers, the Germans did not claim to be developing moral or philosophical explanations of responsibility. They were trying to state clearly the ultimate conceptions on which the law rested. This time, however, their method led them to the same sweeping conclusion as the natural lawyers, with the same unfortunate results. They concluded that it was logically contradictory to say that a person is obligated to make an impossible performance. The obligation to do something presupposes the possibility of doing it.[39]

They faced the same difficulties as the natural lawyers in squaring this conclusion with the Roman texts. They acknowledged that a contract was invalid only for initial objective impossibility,[40] a conclusion that found its way into § 306. But they never found a satisfactory explanation of why it should matter that the performance was impossible from the outset. Ultimately, the German reforms of 2002 abolished the distinction between initial and subsequent impossibility.

Similarly, the German jurists concluded that, logically, fault could only mean failure to use the care that a person could reasonably be expected to use. As Puchta said, liability for any higher degree of care is liability for chance.[41] As Windschied said, it is not liability imposed because one was negligent but liability imposed despite the fact that he was not.[42] Again, the texts seemed to stand in their way. Thibaut and Hasse argued that the Roman texts did not impose liability for what had traditionally been called *culpa levissima*.[43] Eventually, most of the German jurists persuaded themselves that Thibaut and Hasse were right.[44] To reach this conclusion, texts that imposed liability for *custodia* were said to refer merely to the kind of care a person must give, not the degree of care.[45] As mentioned earlier, most modern scholars do not read the texts this way.

---

[38] René Demogue, *Traité des obligations en général* 5 (Paris, 1921–33), § 1237.

[39] Alois Brinz and Philipp Lotmar, *Lehrbuch der Pandekten* 3 (2nd edn., Erlangen, 1892), § 245; Heinrich Dernburg, *Pandekten* 2 (4th edn., Berlin, 1894), § 16; Georg Friedrich Puchta, *Pandekten* (2nd edn., Leipzig, 1844), § 302; Bernhard Windscheid, book review of Theodor Mommsen, I *Kritische Zeitschrift für die gesammte Rechtswissenschaft* 2 (1855), 106–45, 118.

[40] Mommsen 1: 5; Bernhard Windscheid, *Lehrbuch des Pandektenrechts* 2 (7th edn., Frankfurt-am-Main, 1891), § 264.   [41] Puchta, *Pandekten*, § 266.

[42] Windscheid, *Lehrbuch*, 1, § 101.

[43] Anton Thibaut, *System des Pandekten-Rechts* (6th edn., Jena, 1823), § 252; Johann Hasse, *Die Culpa des Römischen Rechts* (2nd edn., Bonn, 1838), § 24; Johann Hasse, 'Essai sur la préstation de fautes par Le Brun', *Zeitschrift für geschichtliche Rechtswissenschaft* 4 (1820), 189–256.

[44] Ludwig Arndts von Arnesburg, *Lehrbuch der Pandekten* (14th edn., Stuttgart, 1889), § 86 n. 3; Brinz and Lotmar, *Lehrbuch*, 2, § 267 n. 26; Karl von Vangerow, *Leitfaden für Pandekten-Vorlesungen* 1 (Marburg, 1847), § 107; Windscheid, *Lehrbuch*, 1, § 101.

[45] Arndts, *Lehrbuch*, § 86; Brinz and Lotmar, *Lehrbuch*, 2, § 267; Puchta, *Pandekten*, § 266; Vangerow, *Pandekten-Vorlesungen*, 1, § 107.

The solution of the jurists passed into the German Civil Code. Before the Code was amended in 2002, initial objective impossibility invalidated a contract while subsequent impossibility excused the promisor only if he was not 'responsible' (§ 275). He was responsible if he acted willfully or negligently (§ 276). Negligence was defined as a failure to use 'ordinary care' (§ 277).

The German reforms of 2002 abolished the distinction between initial and subsequent impossibility.[46] Supposedly, a party was to be liable for fault even after this distinction was abolished. Nevertheless, although the drafters of the Civil Code had used the term 'fault' in its ordinary sense, German courts were unwilling to live with that position even before the reforms of 2002. They have held a party liable because of an event which he could not prevent by ordinary care if the event is one that is normally within a person's control: he is liable, for example, if he failed to perform because he lacked the financial resources to do so,[47] or materials were delivered to him late,[48] or his suppliers failed him.[49] Moreover, the event that prevents performance must be one that the parties would not foresee or take into account at the time the contract was formed.[50] As a result, cases in Germany come out in much the same way as in France, and, as we will see, in England and the United States.[51] The problem remains how to distinguish the cases in which the plaintiff is excused from those in which he is not. As in France, that cannot be done by invoking the principle that no one is liable for the impossible or that a person is only liable for fault.

English law before the 19th century is in dispute. English courts sometimes excused a party who could not perform. They did so, for example, when the performance was illegal,[52] or the party obligated to perform had died,[53] or the object bailed had been destroyed by an 'act of God',[54] or a plague suspended construction work.[55] On the other hand, in the case of *Paradine* v. *Jane*,[56] a lessee was not excused from paying rent when soldiers in the English Civil War made it impossible for him to occupy the property.

[46] Before the reforms of 2002, courts and commentators had already distinguished 'initial impossibility' (*anfängliche Unmöglichkeit*) from 'initial inability' (*anfängliches Unvermögen*). In the case of 'initial inability', the promisor is liable even without fault. The distinction was artificial. It simply allowed courts to circumvent the Code in cases in which it seems reasonable that the promisor should bear the risk of his inability to perform. Konrad Zweigert and Hein Kötz, *Einführung in die Rechtsvergleichung* (3rd edn., Tübingen, 1996), 512.

[47] Volker Emmerich in *Münchener Kommentar Zum Bürgerlichen Gesetzbuch* (3rd edn., Munich. 1995), no. 3 to § 285; Manfred Löwisch in Julius Staudinger, *Kommentar zum Bürgerlichen Gesetzbuch* (12th edn., Berlin, 1999), no. 12 to § 285; Frank Peters in Staudinger, *Kommentar*, no. 13 to § 635.

[48] Battes in Walter Erman, *Handkommentar zum Bürgerlichen Gesetzbuch* (9th edn., Münster, 1993), no. 2 to § 285.   [49] Emmerich in *Münchener Kommentar*, no. 3 to § 285.

[50] Emmerich in *Münchener Kommentar*, no. 3 to § 285; Peters in Staudinger, *Kommentar*, no. 10 to § 635; Herbert Wiedemann, in Hans Theodor Soergel, *Kommentar zum Bürgerlichen Gesetzbuch* (12th edn., Stuttgart, 1990), no. 6 to § 285.

[51] Manfred Löwisch in Staudinger, *Kommentar zum Bürgerlichen Gesetzbuch* (13th edn. 1994), no. 11 to § 282; Peter Schlechtriem, 'Rechtvereinheitlichung in Europa und Schuldrechtreform in Deutschland', *Zeitschrift für Europäisches Privatrecht* 1 (1993), 228–9 .

[52] *Abbott of Westminster* v. *Clerke*, 1 Dy 26b, 28b, 73 Eng Rep 59, 63 (KB 1536).

[53] *Hyde* v. *Dean of Windsor*, Cro Eliz 552, 78 Eng Rep 798 (KB 1597).

[54] *Williams* v. *Hide*, Palm 548 (1624).

[55] H. Rolle, Abridgment 450, Cond. (G), p. 10 (London, 1668).

[56] Aleyn 26, 82 Eng Rep. 897 (KB 1647).

In the 20th century, Williston claimed that *Paradine* v. *Jane* represented the original common law principle—that impossibility was no excuse—and that 19th century cases had made inroads in the principle.[57] Max Rheinstein agreed. He said the principle followed from the 'essence' of assumpsit, and the cases excusing performance were exceptions to that principle.[58] Like Williston, Rheinstein thought that impossibility first became a defense in 1863 in the leading case of *Taylor* v. *Caldwell*, when Judge Blackburn excused the owners of a music hall that had burned down from providing it for a performance.[59] According to Williston and Rheinstein, he took this rule from the civil law.[60]

But it is not clear why we should think assumpsit had an 'essence' from which such a principle follows. Moreover, when courts do seemingly contradictory things, it is odd for an historian to claim he knows which actions reflect the true underlying principle and which are exceptions. The pre-19th century judges themselves did not say that *Paradine* v. *Jane* exemplified the underlying principle. They did not discuss the case. The first reference to it seems to have appeared only in 1802 in the notes of Sargeant Williams.[61] Nor was the case discussed by pre-19th century treatise writers. As we have noted, there were none before Blackstone and Powell, and they do not mention it.

Moreover, it is odd to cite *Paradine* for the proposition that, in principle, impossibility does not excuse performance. As Pollock pointed out, the performance remained possible: the tenant could still pay the rent.[62] The court did not even say that impossibility would never excuse the lessee from performing his obligations. It distinguished obligations expressly undertaken—such as paying rent—from those imposed by law without an express promise—such as to give back the premises without 'waste'. The latter would be excused by a sufficiently uncontrollable event.

In any case, instead of trying to revive this distinction, both before and after *Taylor* v. *Caldwell* was decided, the 19th century treatise writers borrowed continental ideas about impossibility. Powell, W. W. Story, Leake, Pollock, and Williston all said that performance was excused by events that made it absolutely or objectively impossible, but not by those that merely made it impossible for the promisor.[63] In the United States, their view passed into the *First Restatement of Contracts* and is preserved, despite a change of vocabulary, in the *Second Restatement*.[64] Leake and Hammon tried and failed to introduce the distinction between initial and subsequent impossibility.[65]

---

[57] Samuel Williston, *The Law of Contracts* (New York, 1920), § 1931.

[58] Max Rheinstein, *Die Struktur des vertraglichen Schuldverhältnisses im anglo-amerikanischen Recht* (Berlin, 1932), 162.   [59] 3 Best & S 826, 122 Eng Rep 309 (1863).

[60] Williston, *Contracts*, § 1931; Rheinstein, *Struktur*, 175.

[61] He cites it in his note to *Walton* v. *Waterhouse*, 2 Wms Saund 420, 85 Eng. Rep. 1233 (KB 1684).

[62] Sir Frederick Pollock, *Principles of Contract Being a Treatise on the General Principles concerning the Validity of Agreements in the Law of England* (4th edn., London, 1888), 365.

[63] John Powell, *Essay upon the Law of Contracts and Agreements* (London, 1890), *161; William Wentworth Story, *The Law of Contracts Not Under Seal* (Boston, 1851), § 463; S. Martin Leake, *Elements of the Law of Contracts* (London, 1867), § 369; Pollock, *Principles*, 356; Williston, *Contracts* § 1932.

[64] *Restatement (Second) of Contracts* § 261, Comment e.

[65] Leake, *Contracts*, 358–9, 361; Louis Hammon, *General Principles of the Law of Contract* (St Paul, Minn., 1912), § 414.

Nevertheless, Blackburn imposed another requirement that must be met before impossibility would excuse performance. A party would only be excused when 'the contract is not to be construed as a positive contract, but as subject to an implied condition that the parties shall be excused in case, before breach, performance becomes impossible from the perishing of the thing without default of the contractor'.[66] In doing so, he conflated the traditional doctrine of impossibility with a traditional formulation of the doctrine of changed circumstances: that the existence of certain circumstances may be an implied condition of a contract. Shortly, we will see that this doctrine provides a better explanation for the cases in which the law gives relief than the doctrine of impossibility.

Unfortunately, in discussing *Taylor* v. *Caldwell*, Williston made an observation that has become a commonplace.[67] He claimed that common law and civil law take opposite positions: unlike civil law, common law treats any case of non-performance as a breach, regardless of fault, though it admits impossibility as an excuse. Actually, the question in France is which contracts are subject to the *cas fortuit* and *force majeure* provisions of arts. 1347–8, in Germany, of when inability to perform counts as 'fault' in the ordinary sense, and in England and the United States, of when an implied condition that a performance is possible is to be read into a contract. The differences do not reflect a disagreement in policy or principle on which contracts to enforce. As Williston said, and as Zweigert and Kötz now say, the practical results are much the same in both systems.[68] They reflect the historical circumstance that different systems borrowed in different ways from traditional continental rules. In any event, each system faces a similar problem in deciding which contracts should and should not be enforced. This problem cannot be solved by an appeal to the principles that were once thought to explain the impossibility doctrine: that no one is liable for failing to achieve the impossible or for a result for which he was not at fault.

B. The Modern Search for Solutions

Some modern attempts to explain relief for impossibility still seem to rely on the idea that a person should not be liable for a performance which has become impossible through no fault of his own. An example is the rule of the Vienna Convention:

A party is not liable for a failure to perform any of his obligations if he proves that the failure was to an impediment beyond his control and that he could not reasonably be expected to have taken the impediment into account at the time of the conclusion of his contract or to have avoided or overcome it or its consequences.[69]

Does an 'impediment beyond his control' mean an impediment that he could not overcome by reasonable efforts? Does a failure to take the impediment into account when he contracted mean that, by reasonable efforts, he should have done so? If so, it would seem that a party is not liable whenever he was not at fault, a principle which cannot explain the law of any of the legal systems we have discussed.

---

[66] 3 Best & S at 122 (QB).   [67] Williston, *Contracts*, § 1789.
[68] ibid. § 1979; Zweigert and Kötz, *Einführung*, 512–13.
[69] Convention on the International Sale of Goods, art. 79.

Since we are not dealing with a doctrine based on fault, it would seem that we must be dealing with a problem of risk allocation independent of fault. That possibility is suggested by German jurists, who, albeit in the context of changed circumstances, discuss to which party's 'sphere of risk' an event belongs.[70] The trouble is that speaking of spheres of risk is not helpful unless one can explain why a risk should be borne by one party rather than the other.

Such an explanation was attempted by Richard Posner.[71] Posner observed, correctly, that a party can better bear a risk if he can better foresee it, better insure or self-insure against it or better prevent its occurrence. These observations are helpful in other contexts. By themselves, they are not so helpful in explaining the doctrine of impossibility. Suppose that war is declared, and so a shipment cannot be made. That is not the sort of event that is likely to be foreseen by parties who made no provision for it in their contract nor one for which a party can readily buy insurance. There is not likely to be a clear answer to the question which party is engaged in similar transactions. One party is repeatedly shipping and the other repeatedly receiving shipments. That leaves us with one factor: control. It is true that the results in the impossibility cases do seem related to the degree to which a party could have controlled the event that made performance impossible. No private party can control whether war is declared. A party has more control over one's suppliers, one's workers or one's financial condition. But from the standpoint of risk allocation, it would seem that the degree of control matters only because the party in control could have lessened the risk by taking reasonable precautions. In that case, why isn't a party always free from liability if he proves he took reasonable precautions? To put it another way, why isn't a party excused whenever he was not at fault as the late scholastics and natural lawyers claimed he should be? This approach is helpful, then, only if we can answer that question.

Still another explanation is that relief should be given because an unforeseen event overturns the 'equivalence' between what a party gives and what he receives. For example, according to art. 6.2.2 of the Unidroit Principles of International Commercial Contracts, relief is given for 'hardship', and '[t]here is hardship where the occurrence of events fundamentally alters the equilibrium of the contract either because the cost of a party's performance had increased or because the value of the performance a party receives is diminished . . .'. The Unidroit principles immediately add, however, that relief will be given only if 'the risk of the events was not assumed by the disadvantaged party'. As Helmut Köhler has noted, before one can speak of a disruption of equivalence, one has to know which party assumed the risk of the event that occurred.[72] In an insurance contract, nothing could seem more unequal than that a person who paid $2,000 to insure his house should receive $800,000 when it burned down. But the contract was not unequal when it was made. Indeed, the point of it was to transfer a risk to the insurance company. Consequently, to ask whether equivalence in the value of the

---

[70] Helmut Heinrichs in Otto Palandt, *Bürgerliches Gesetzbuch* to § 313, nos. 33, 43 (62nd edn., Munich, 2003); Günter Roth in *Münchener Kommentar* to § 242, no. 745.

[71] Richard A. Posner and Andrew M. Rosenfield, 'Impossibility and Related Doctrines in Contract Law: An Economic Analysis', *J. Leg. Stud.* 6 (1977), 83.

[72] Helmut Köhler, 'Zur ökonomischen Analyse der Regeln über die Geschäftsgrundlage', in Claus Ott and Hans-Bernd Schäfter, eds., *Allokationseffizienz in der Rechtsordnung* (Berlin, 1989), 148 at 152.

performances was disrupted is a helpful question only if we can determine what risks the contract transferred.

Another solution is to ask directly what risks were assumed by the party who failed to perform. According to the Uniform Commercial Code[73] and the *Second Restatement of Contracts*[74] that a party is not bound when the contract was predicated on a 'basic assumption' which was false. To ask on what basic assumptions a contract was based is not much different than asking, as Judge Blackburn did, on what implied conditions it was made. As mentioned earlier, Blackburn was conflating the doctrine of impossibility with another traditional doctrine, that of changed circumstances, an implied condition that the parties will not be bound under certain circumstances which they did not envision. As we will now see, this traditional doctrine does help us understand when the law gives relief for impossibility, and to answer the questions which are raised by the other modern approaches just discussed.

C. Impossibility of Performance as a Problem of Changed Circumstances

Shortly, we will look more closely at the doctrine of changed circumstances.

Here, we only need to note that the doctrine requires us to ask what future events the parties would have intended their agreement to govern. By asking what they would have intended, we are no more trying to read minds than the we are when we ask about the implied terms of their agreement, a problem to be discussed in a later chapter. As we will see, fair-minded parties would have wanted to place the risks and burdens incident to the contract on the party by whom they could most easily be borne.[75]

In the case of impossibility, we must ask then, which of two kinds of arrangements the parties would have chosen: an arrangement in which a party is liable for non-performance only if he is not at fault—that is, his failure to perform is not due to causes for which he could reasonably be held accountable—or an arrangement in which a party will be liable whether he is at fault or not. That is simply another way of asking whether his ability to perform is a tacit condition or term of the contract.

It would seem at first sight that to agree to be held liable even absent fault is to make a bet—equal to the amount of damages one must pay—on an event that lies outside one's control. It seems no different in principle that a clause that allows the amount that one party owes another to turn on a throw of dice. As the economists tell us, however, risk averse parties do not gamble unless the odds are tilted in their favor. Suppose the damages occasioned by non-performance are $100,000 and the odds of failing to perform, despite reasonable efforts to do so, are one in a hundred. The one party would not agree to be held liable unless he were offered more than an extra $1,000, an amount which the other party, who is also risk averse, would never be willing to offer.

It would seem, then, that, to use the terminology of the French, all contracts should be *obligations de moyens* or agreements to use reasonable efforts and none should be *obligations de résultat* which commit a party to achieving a certain result. But that clearly is not the case. On the other hand, as we have seen, the reason is not likely to be

---

[73] UCC, § 2–615.   [74] *Restatement (Second) of Contracts*, § 261.   [75] Chapter 17 III.

one of those that Posner has given why one party is in a better position to bear a risk more cheaply than the other party. Here, we are dealing with risks that, in most cases, neither party can better foresee or insure against. It is true that many of the cases do seem to turn on the degree to which a party can normally control the event in question. No private party can control whether war is declared. He has more control over his suppliers, his workers or his financial condition. But from the standpoint of risk allocation, it would seem that the degree of control matters only because the party in control could have lessened the risk by taking reasonable precautions. In that case, why isn't a party always free from liability if he proves he took reasonable precautions?

The answer, in my view, is that it is often difficult for one party to prove that the other was at fault for failing to take reasonable precautions. How is one to know whether he could not have dealt with more reliable suppliers, cultivated better relations with his workers or kept his financial position viable? It will therefore make more sense if, in such cases, he is held liable simply for failure to perform and charges a bit extra to compensate himself for that possibility. If that is so, if liability without fault is not an explicit condition of the contract, it should be an implicit one.

In such a contract, however, some event may prevent performance in which it is extremely unlikely that the party in question is at fault, either because no one could have taken precautions against such an event or because his own interests gave him every reason to take precautions. If the reason one party assumes liability without fault is simply to avoid the difficulties of proving fault, then his agreement to do so should not apply in cases like these, where fault is not seriously in question. As the late scholastics would have said when they were describing the doctrine of changed circumstances, if the parties agreed only to avoid one sort of difficulty, their agreement should not apply when that difficulty does not arise.

II. The Doctrine of Changed Circumstances

A. Origins

According to the canon lawyers, while it was wrong to break a promise, one could legitimately refuse to perform when circumstances had changed sufficiently. Gratian's *Decretum* contained a passage in which St Augustine, following Cicero, said that one need not keep a promise to return a sword to a person who has become insane.[76] A gloss to the *Decretum* explained that 'this condition is always understood: if matters remain in the same state'.[77] The great medieval jurist, Baldus degli Ubaldi, then read the doctrine into civil law. All promises were subject to such a condition.[78]

Thomas Aquinas used Aristotle's theory of equity to explain why. According to Aristotle, whenever a law is made, particular circumstances may arise in which the law-maker would not want it to be applied. As a matter of 'equity', the law should not be applied in those circumstances. Thomas concluded that similarly, promises are a

---

[76] Gratian, *Decretum*, C. 22, q. 2, c. 14.
[77] *Glossa ordinaria* to Gratian, *Decretum* to *furens* to C. 22, q. 2, c. 14.
[78] Baldus de Ubaldis, *Commentaria Corpus iuris civilis* (Venice, 1557), to Dig. 12.4.8.

kind of law one gives to oneself, and they are not binding in circumstances where the promisor would not have intended to be bound.[79]

Thomas' explanation was adopted by the late scholastics[80] and preserved by the 17th and 18th century natural lawyers. The promisor is not bound if the change of circumstances concerns the 'unique reason' or 'unique cause' for his promise[81] or the 'presumption of some fact' on which his consent was conditioned.[82]

In the 19th century, however, the doctrine of changed circumstances had few defenders. These few explained relief by saying the existence of certain circumstances was a tacit or implied condition of the contract. According to the French jurist Larombière, an 'error in motive' affected the validity of a contract only if the parties so wished, but a judge would determine whether they so wished by examining 'according to the circumstances, if the fact alleged as a motive was taken to be the determining reason (*raison déterminante*) and if the consent depended on its reality'.[83] As we saw earlier, it was very unusual to admit that any kind of error in motive could be grounds for relief. The German jurist Windscheid said that the continuation of certain circumstances could be an 'undeveloped condition' of the contract, 'undeveloped' in the sense that it was not expressly willed by the parties.[84] For most 19th century jurists, the obvious objection to the doctrine was that a tacit or undeveloped condition was one that the parties never consciously willed. They had never thought about the change in circumstances, let alone agreed on what should happen if the change occurred. Thus the doctrine of changed circumstances slumbered during the 19th century.

It continues to do so in France, although, beginning in 1916, the administrative courts have developed a version of it called *imprévision*[85] and we will note some rare occasions where civil courts have given relief by speaking of 'mistake'[86] or 'good faith'[87] though they reject the doctrine of '*imprévision*'.[88]

The drafters of the German Civil Code rejected the doctrine. They intended that the Code provisions governing impossibility be construed narrowly and limited to cases in which performance was literally 'impossible' rather than 'extremely onerous'.[89] They expressly rejected inclusion in the Code of a general *clausula rebus sic stantibus*

---

[79] Thomas Aquinas, *Summa theologiae* II-II, q, 88, a. 10; q. 89, a. 9.

[80] Lessius, *De iustitia et iure*, lib. 2, cap. 17, dub. 10; cap. 18, dub. 10.

[81] Hugo Grotius, *De iure belli ac pacis libri tres* (B. J. A. de Kanter-van Hetting Tromp, ed., 1939), II.xvi.25.2; Jean Barbeyrac, *Le Droit de la nature et des gens...par le Baron Pufendorf, traduit du latin* (Amsterdam, 1734), to n. 3 to III.vi.6; Christian Wolff, *Ius naturae metodo scientifica pertractatum* 3 (Frankfurt-am-Main, 1764), § 504.   [82] Pufendorf, *De jure naturae et gentium* III.vi.6.

[83] Larombière, *Obligations* 1, 282–3.   [84] Windscheid, *Lehrbuch* 1, 75–8.

[85] Cons. d'Etat, 30 Mar. 1916, D. 1916.III.25, S. 1916.III.17.

[86] Cass., 3e ch. civ., 11 Jan. 1995, http://www.legifrance.gouv.fr/ WAspad/Visu?cid = 81099&indice = 166&table = CASS&ligneDeb = 161.

[87] e.g. Cass. comm., 24 Nov. 1998, Bull. civ. 1998.IV. no. 277, p. 232 (supplier of Evian water and Kronenbourg beer must ensure his distributor can maintain competitive prices); Cass. soc., 18 May 1999, Bull. civ. 1999.IV. no. 219, p. 161 (employer cannot hold employee to promise he can be relocated when relocation not feasible due to his wife's pregnancy). I am grateful to Raphael de Lasa for calling these cases to my attention.

[88] e.g Cass. soc., 8 Mar. 1972, D. & S. 1972.J.340; Cass. civ., 6 March 1876, D. 1876.1.193.

[89] *Motive zu dem Entwurfe eines bürgerlichen Gesetzbuches* 2 (Berlin, 1888), 44–6.

provision.[90] Nevertheless, the courts resurrected the doctrine under the pressure of the First World War and the drastic inflation of the 1920s.[91] They gave relief under what is perhaps the Code's most general provision, § 242, which requires that a contract be performed in good faith. This doctrine has since been codified in § 313 of the German Civil Code which gives relief when circumstances which formed the basis (*Grundlage*) of the contract have so changed that the parties would not have contracted had they anticipated them.

The doctrine has been applied by German and Anglo-American courts to situations in which a performance is not impossible but more difficult than expected.[92] As described earlier, many jurists now formulate the doctrine in much the same terms as the late scholastics although they do not explain it in terms of Aristotelian theories of equity: the question is one of which party would have committed himself to bear the risk of a change in circumstances. The difficulty is to find a way of answering this question. As we will now see, when a performance has become more difficult, or markets have changed, it can be answered in much the same way as when a performance has become impossible.

B. Increased Difficulty of Performance

1. *Physical hardship*

American and German courts have given relief when performance is not impossible but is physically more difficult than the parties had imagined. The leading American case is *Mineral Park Land Co.* v. *Howard*,[93] in which a California court excused performance when the defendant had agreed to take the gravel he needed from the plaintiff's land but the costs of doing so proved to be much higher than anticipated because, unknown to the parties, the gravel was under water. Even a French court gave relief for 'mistake' under similar circumstances: rock proved much harder to excavate than an architect's plans had indicated.[94]

These cases are in one way like those of impossibility which we have already considered. In the case of impossibility, we saw that the parties had two alternatives: for the promisor to commit himself to use reasonable efforts or for him to commit himself to bringing about a certain result. The promisee would want him to choose the latter, and pay him extra to do so, when it is difficult to prove fault. But that difficulty, and hence the rationale for the choice, disappears when the promisor clearly could not be at fault.

To deal with the possibility of increased hardship, the parties again have two choices: they may make the contract cost plus, so the burden of increased costs falls on the party to receive a performance, or they may make it fixed price, so the burden falls on the party who is to perform. One reason for entering into a cost plus contract is like that for agreeing to bring about a certain result: a difficulty of proof. In a cost plus

---

[90] ibid. 199.   [91] e.g. RG, 29 Nov. 1921, ERGZ 103, 177; RG, 28 Nov. 1923, ERGZ 107, 78.
[92] *Restatement (Second) of Contracts*, § 261, Cmt. d.   [93] 156 P 458 (Cal 1916).
[94] Cass., 3e ch. civ., 11 Jan. 1995, http://www.legifrance.gouv.fr/WAspad/Visu?cid = 81099&indice = 166&table = CASS&ligneDeb = 161.

contract, it may be very hard to show that the party making the performance used reasonable efforts to keep costs under control. If that is so, one can see why relief is given in cases like *Mineral Park Land Co.* v. *Howard.* The cost in question is one that the excavator could not possibly control. He cannot help it that the gravel is under water or that the costs of excavating it are therefore greatly beyond the amount he expected. The rationale is the same as before: if the parties have made the contract cost plus only to avoid certain difficulties, then that arrangement should not govern circumstances in which these difficulties do not apply.

2. Market changes

Sometimes a contract becomes more difficult or easier to perform because market prices change. Normally, such changes do not call for relief. As discussed earlier, one reason the parties would choose an agreement in which they can claim expectation damages rather than reliance damages is to lock in what they believe to be a favorable price. That is clearly their objective in a forward contract for the delivery of fungible goods readily available on the market. This type of sale was not recognized in Roman law although it was by medieval jurists. Its function is to insure against a change in price: to lock in the current market price in order to avoid getting a less favorable price at the time of delivery. One cannot argue that either of the parties entered into the contract with any other risk in mind than a fluctuation of the market price.

Nevertheless, suppose the market price falls through the floor or goes through the ceiling. German courts sometimes have given relief: for example, when the outbreak of the First World War led to a huge increase in the price of steam[95] or of iron wire.[96] In the United States the answer is unclear. In one famous case the Westinghouse corporation sold nuclear generators and agreed to sell uranium at a fixed price for a fixed term thereafter. The price of uranium soared with the world energy crisis so much that performing its contracts would have bankrupted the company. The case was settled, and so one cannot tell whether an American court would have given relief or not.[97]

If the approach we have taken thus far is correct, relief is sometimes warranted. We have to ask why the parties would have wished to lock in what they consider a favorable price. In *Westinghouse*, the purchasers of the generators expected to buy uranium from Westinghouse to power the generators and sell electricity at a profit. The profit would be equal to its revenues from selling electricity minus its operating costs minus the cost of the capital invested in building the generator minus the amount it pays Westinghouse for the uranium. Suppose, however, that the price of uranium rises so much that the purchasers can make more money by shutting down their generators and reselling the uranium on the open market. I don't see why the purchasers should be entitled to recover more than the profit they would otherwise have made minus the costs they saved by shutting down their generators. To allow them to recover more would be to read the contract as though it had two purposes: (1) to guarantee that a rise in the price of uranium would not cut into the profit the purchasers make by

---

[95] RG, 21 Sept. 1970, RGZ 100, 129.   [96] RG, 29 Nov. 1921, RGZ 103, 177.

[97] They have often refused to give relief when performance became more difficult because of a change in prices. 55 ALR 5th 1 n. 21.

selling electricity, and (2) to allow the purchasers to profit by a rise in the price of uranium so great that they can make a higher profit reselling it. The second purpose is simply to bet on the future price of uranium which is not connected with the purchasers use of uranium. Had the parties thought of the possibility that the price of uranium would go so high, they would not have made such a bet. Risk averse parties do not gamble unless the bet is tilted in their favor. Once again, it is outside the purposes they did have in mind when they contracted.

III. Conclusion

In a previous chapter, we discussed another type of case in which relief is commonly said to be given for changed or unforeseen circumstances: a performance is no longer suitable for the purpose for which it is ordinarily suitable. A paradigm example was the Coronation Cases in which flats were rented at a suitably enhanced price to view a coronation procession which was cancelled. If our analysis of error was correct, relief in this case is not a problem of changed circumstances. It should not matter whether the contract to rent the flat was made before or after the procession was canceled. What should matter is that the performance in question is not suitable for the purpose for which it was sold. Therefore, the usual reasons the parties would wish to lock in a good bargain do not apply.

In this chapter, we have seen that the problem of impossibility is like that of changed circumstances. The problem of changed circumstances is again like one that will be discussed in a later chapter: the problem of implied terms. Terms should be implied so as to put risks and burdens on the parties who can bear them most easily.[98] The question therefore is which party would be best able to bear the risk that a performance is impossible or increasingly difficult. Once we see the reason why, however, we can see that this party should no longer be liable for risks or burdens of impossibility or difficulty of performance which he is not able to bear most easily. An economist might regard that solution as efficient. It is, in any case, fair.

---

[98] Chapter 17 III.

16

Promises to Make a Gift

I. Origins

In the *Nicomachean Ethics*, Aristotle described exchange as a type of commutative justice. While distributive justice secures for each citizen a fair share of whatever wealth and honor the society had to divide, commutative justice preserves the share he has.[1] Thus, according to Aristotle, each party to an exchange must give something equivalent in value to what he receives.[2] As described earlier,[3] in another passage in the *Ethics*, Aristotle discussed the virtue of 'liberality': the liberal person disposes of his money wisely, giving 'to the right people the right amounts and at the right time'.[4] Thomas Aquinas put these ideas together: when one person transfers a thing to another, either it is an act of commutative justice that requires an equivalent or it is an act of liberality.[5]

As already mentioned, the late scholastics built a theory of contract on this ground plan that was then borrowed by the northern natural law school in the 17th century. According to the theory, a party, by expressing his will to be bound, might enter into either of these two basic types of arrangement.[6] Grotius and Pufendorf present elaborate schemes of classification in which they show how the contracts familiar in Roman law can be fitted into these two grand categories.[7] This classification meant more than the tautology that a party either does or does not receive back something in return for what he gives. In a gratuitous contract, the donor ideally is exercising the virtue of liberality. He is giving away wealth in a sensible way. In a contract of exchange, a party must receive, not simply a counterperformance, but one of equivalent value. Writers in the Aristotelian traditions thought that the rules that govern the parties' obligations should depend on which sort of agreement they had entered into. The rules should ensure, so far as practicable, that in the case of an exchange, each party receives an equivalent, and in the case of a gratuitous contract, that the donor behaves sensibly.

Having explained gifts as they did, the late scholastics were comfortable with the Roman law of their day. Their aim seemed to be to encourage a person who promised a gift to do so sensibly. A gift above a certain amount required *insinuatio* or registration

---

[1] Aristotle, *Nicomachean Ethics* V.ii.　　[2] ibid. V.iv–v.　　[3] Chapter 13 I B 2.
[4] Aristotle, *Nicomachean Ethics* V. iv–v.　　[5] Thomas Aquinas, *Summa theologiae* II-II, Q. 61, a. 3.
[6] Domenicus Soto, *De iustitia et iure libri decem* (Salamanca, 1553), lib. 3, q. 5, a.1; Ludovicus Molina, *De iustitia et iure tractatus* (Venice, 1614), disp. 252; Leonardus Lessius, *De iustitia et iure, ceterique virtutibus cardinalis libri quatuor* (Paris, 1628), lib. 2, cap. 17, dub. 1.
[7] Hugo Grotius, *De iure belli ac pacis libri tres* (B. J. A. de Kanter-van Hetting Tromp, ed., 1939), II.xvii.1–7; Samuel Pufendorf, *De iure naturae et gentium libri octo* (Amsterdam, 1688), V.ii.8–10;

with a court.[8] That encouraged deliberation. By early modern times, the jurists had recognized some exceptional cases in which a donative promise was deemed particularly worthy and would be enforced without a formality. Examples are promises to charitable causes (*ad causas pias*),[9] to people on account of their marriage (*ad nuptias vel propter nuptias*).[10] An informal promise of compensation was also enforceable when it was made to someone who had conferred a benefit on the promisor, for example, by rescuing him from robbers (*donatio remuneratoria*).[11] Molina explained that such an informal promise was enforceable because it was not really donative. It was made in return for something received.[12]

II. The Requirement of a Formality

Of these rules, one that has survived everywhere is that promises to make gifts require a formality. Typically, in continental systems, the formality is to subscribe to the promise before a notary.[13] As we have seen, traditionally, in common law, a promise to give could be made binding by making it under seal.[14] No lay person without legal advice is likely to understand the effect of a seal or its prerequisites, and so the effect is much the same as on the continent: to be sure his promise is enforceable, a would-be donor must consult a member of the legal profession. Many American jurisdictions have abolished the formality of the seal. But the result is not that when a would-be donor visits his lawyer, he is told he cannot bind himself to give property away. He is told that he must use a deed of gift or a trust to obtain a result which he cannot through the law of contract.[15] By a deed of gift, he can make an immediate gift of personal property. To do so, he executes a signed document declaring the intention to make a gift, and naming the donor, the donee and the object given. By a trust, he can give away any type of property by declaring that he holds it in trust for the donee.[16] The trust is then irrevocable if he so declares, and the intention to create an irrevocable trust will usually be found even absent such a declaration.[17] While a deed of gift transfers the property right away, a person who wishes the gift to take effect in the future can create the trust at once by specifying that the property is reserved for his own use, or

---

[8] Molina, *De iustitia et iure*, disp. 278, no. 3. On the formality in the 16th century, see Julius Clarus, *Sententiarum receptarum liber quartus* (Venice, 1595), lib. 4, § Donatio, q. 15, no. 3; Antonius Gomez, *Variae resolutiones, iuris civilis, communis, et regii* 2 (Venice, 1759), cap. 4, no. 14.

[9] Molina, *De iustitia et iure*, disp. 279, no. 2; Lessius, *De iustitia et iure*, lib. 2, cap. 18, dub. 13, no. 102. On the exception in the 16th century, see Clarus, *Sententiarium*, lib. 4, § Donatio, q. 17, no. 1; Gomez, *Variae resolutiones*, cap. 4, no. 10.

[10] Molina, *De iustitia et iure*, disp. 279, no. 7. On the exception in the 16th century, see Antonius Gama, *Decisionum Supremi Senatus Lusitaniae Centuriae* 4 (Antwerp, 1622), dec. 348, no. 5.

[11] Molina, *De iustitia et iure*, disp. 279, no. 6. On the exception in the 16th century, see Clarus, *Sententiarum*, lib. 4, § Donatio, q. 2, no. 2; q. 3, no. 1; Gomez, *Variae resolutiones*, cap. 4, no. 10.

[12] Molina, *De iustitia et iure*, disp. 279, no. 6.

[13] e.g. French Civil Code (*Code civil*), art. 931; German Civil Code (*Bürgerlichesgesetzbuch*) [hereinafter BGB], § 518.   [14] Part VI, introduction.

[15] See Lon L. Fuller and Melvin A. Eisenberg, *Basic Contract Law* (7th edn., St Paul, Minn., 2001), 9–10.

[16] 1 Austin W. Scott and William F. Fratcher, *The Law of Trusts* 1 (4th edn., Boston, 1987), § 28, at 310–12 and n. 4.   [17] ibid. § 29, at 315.

that income from the trust is to be paid to himself, for a certain period of time.[18] By using a trust, a person can thus give away anything he presently owns, though not property to be acquired in the future.[19] In practice, a lay person will always have the help of a lawyer to execute a deed of gift or establish a trust, even though there is no requirement that he do so. Consequently, at an operational level, the common law rules on contract and trust provide a safeguard like that of the older and more recent civil law. To make a gift enforceable, the promise must be formalized with the help of a member of the legal profession.

Such rules make sense if the considerations on which the law rests are those that mattered to the late scholastics: that the promisor acts sensibly and that he intends to confer a right to claim performance on the promisee. Although the promisor has to judge for himself whether he is giving sensibly, he is particularly likely to do so if he cannot commit himself on the spot but must seek the help (and may receive the advice) of a legal professional. Moreover, the completion of the formality shows that he wanted the promisee to be able to demand performance as a matter of right.

This explanation presupposes that there are more and less sensible ways of giving away property, and that deliberation helps a person to tell the one from the other. To many people that proposition might seem a matter of common sense. It would be troublesome, however, to economists, who regard preference satisfaction as a good whatever preference is satisfied, and to those who base contract on autonomous choice regardless of what is chosen.

Richard Posner, as well as scholars who are less committed to the law and economics movement,[20] has said that the law is reluctant to enforce a gift because it does not serve the same purpose as an exchange: 'to facilitate the movement, by voluntary exchange, to their most valuable uses'.[21] But if one is to judge matters solely from the standpoint of the preferences of the individual, as Posner wants to do, then whatever a person chooses must be valuable—whether to sell property, to give it away or to destroy it. As Posner has observed elsewhere, such a promise 'would not be made unless it conferred utility on the promisor'.[22] If all that matters is preference satisfaction, why not enforce it?

Posner has proposed another solution. The law is reluctant to enforce a gratuitous promise because the social cost of doing so may exceed the utility the promisor gains by making a binding promise. Social cost includes the administrative costs of enforcement and the cost of making mistakes as to whether the promise was actually made.[23]

---

[18] See ibid. IA, § 57.6, at 188.   [19] ibid. 1, § 30, at 316.

[20] e.g. E. Allan Farnsworth, *Contracts* (New York, 1999), § 2.5 (suggesting that gifts are not productive); Lon L. Fuller, 'Consideration and Form', *Colum. L. Rev.* 41 (1941), 799 at 815 (referring to gifts as a 'sterile transmission'); Edwin W. Patterson, 'An Apology for Consideration', *Colum. L. Rev.* 58 (1958), 929 at 944–6 (preferring bargained-for promises over gifts as useful economic devices). Eisenberg speaks of the absence of independent social interests. The only one he identifies is the redistribution of wealth, and he discounts it because '[e]ven assuming . . . that the redistribution of wealth is an appropriate goal of contract law, the enforcement of donative promises would be a relatively trivial instrument for achieving that end'. Melvin A. Eisenberg, 'Donative Promises', *U. Chi. L. Rev.* 47 (1979), 1, at 4. As the objection indicates, he is not thinking about redistributing wealth to a particularly deserving person or charitable cause, but of achieving a more desirable distribution of wealth among the members of society generally.

[21] Richard A. Posner, *Economic Analysis of Law* (6th edn., New York, 2003), 99.

[22] Richard A. Posner, 'Gratuitous Promises in Economics and Law', *J. Leg. Stud.* 6 (1977), 411 at 412.

[23] ibid. 415.

According to Posner, one would expect courts to enforce promises only when the 'stakes' are high so the administrative cost is worth it, and the promise is well evidenced so the chance of error is low.[24] If Posner were right, however, any well-evidenced donative promise would be enforced when the 'stakes' are as high as in commercial litigation.

Neither can the law be explained by a theory based on autonomy. According to Charles Fried, the purpose of contract law is to give each person's will 'the greatest possible range' consistent with the will of others. Since a person who promises to make a gift has made a choice that is consistent with the freedom of others, by Fried's theory, all gratuitous promises should be enforceable. Indeed, Fried himself has rejected the common law doctrine of consideration as inconsistent with 'the liberal principle that the free arrangements of rational persons should be respected'.[25]

As Fried has admitted, that is not the law. Would anyone want it to be? As it turns out, not even Fried. Gifts, he has observed, should be made 'rationally, deliberately' and should not frustrate the 'legitimate interests of third parties'. Paraphrasing Lon Fuller with approval, he has suggested that one benefit of the doctrine of consideration is to exclude 'the more dubious and meretricious kinds of gifts in which strangers are promised the moon, to the prejudice of a spouse or children'.[26] Apparently, the complaints of the spouse and children become legitimate just at the point when, to paraphrase Aristotle, the promisor gives the wrong amount to the wrong person at the wrong time. Sacrificing consistency to common sense, Fried has reintroduced something like the Aristotelian idea of liberality.

Indeed, jurists generally explain the legal requirements to make a promise of gift enforceable as an attempt to encourage deliberation. There would hardly be a point in doing so, however, unless one believed that some decisions were wise, others foolish and that deliberation increases the chance that a wise decision will be made. If one fully—or blindly—respected the will or preference of the promisor, one would respect the promisor's own decision as to how much deliberation was necessary. Moreover, if one believed that the donor's decision depends simply on his will or preferences, there would be no reason to encourage him to deliberate. The donor does not deliberate in order to discover what he already prefers or wills. He thinks that deliberation will help him decide what is the right thing for him to do. When he makes up his mind, he prefers and wills that course of action because he believes it is right; he does not believe it is right merely because he prefers it or wills it. Courts would not encourage deliberation unless they thought it increased the chance a donor will act rightly. At that point, one is close to the Aristotelian idea of liberality as right gift-giving whether one uses that term or not.

III. Exceptions to the Requirement of a Formality

A. Promises to Give to Charitable Causes

Moreover, modern civil and common law courts have sometimes stretched the law in order to enforce the types of promises that courts in the times of the late scholastics

---

[24] ibid. 415, 426.
[25] Charles Fried, *Contract as Promise* (Cambridge, Mass., 1981), 35.   [26] ibid. 38.

found particularly worthy. French courts have sometimes done so by classifying promises to charities as exchanges on the grounds that the feeling of satisfaction or other intangible benefit the donor experiences is a recompense.[27] German courts have sometimes done so by holding that such a promise is not a gift because it does not enrich the charitable organization itself which is merely an intermediary between the promisor and the ultimate beneficiary.[28] My point here is not that French and German courts generally enforce promises to charities[29] but that they have tried to find ways to do so.

Before the rise of the doctrine of promissory estoppel, American courts used fictions to find consideration for such promises. Consideration was found in commitments of other subscribers to donate money,[30] or in the commitment of a charity to name a fund after the donor,[31] to locate a college in a particular town,[32] or even to use the money for charitable purposes.[33] Under the doctrine of promissory estoppel, such promises are supposed to be enforceable without consideration provided that the promisee has relied on them. Yet, courts have not demanded proof of reliance.[34] In deference to the case law, the *Second Restatement* changed the language of Section 90 to provide that such promises are enforceable 'without proof that the promise induced action or forbearance'.[35] To dispense with proof of reliance is as much a fiction as to pretend a gift is really a bargain.[36]

Again, although the late scholastics did not explain why there should be such an exception, it makes sense from the standpoint of their theory. Promises to charitable causes are more likely to be sensible in that they change the distribution of wealth in a good direction. Thus, some American jurists now acknowledge that such promises are enforced because courts regard them as particularly meritorious.[37] As E. Allan

---

[27] See, e.g. Cass. civ. 1e, July 19, 1894, 1895 D.P. I 125 (calling a promise of land to build a church a 'contract subject to payment' rather than a donation requiring a formality, where promisor could expect benefits to himself and to the community); Trib. civ. de Langres, 15 Mar. 1900, 1900 D.P. II 422 (finding an assignment of right of recovery to three priests not a pure act of liberality because assignor could receive consideration from feelings such as vanity, piety or moral obligation). See also John P. Dawson, *Gifts and Promises* (New Haven, 1980), 84–96 (arguing that French courts treat such contracts as commutative, made for the benefit of third parties and thus enforceable).

[28] See e.g. RG, 7 May 1909, ERGZ 71, 140. See Ferdinand Fromholzer, *Consideration US-amerikanisches Recht im Vergleich zum deutschen* (Tübingen, 1997), 321–8.

[29] Generally, they do not. See James Gordley, ed., *The Enforceability of Promises in European Contract Law* (Cambridge, 2001), 24–8, 43–5.

[30] *Congregation B'nai Sholom* v. *Martin*, 173 NW2d 504, 510 (Mich 1969); *First Presbyterian Church* v. *Dennis*, 161 NW 183, 187–8 (Iowa 1917).

[31] *Allegheny College* v. *National Chautauqua County Bank*, 159 NE 173, 176 (NY 1927).

[32] *Rogers* v. *Galloway Female College*, 44 SW 454, 455 (Ark 1898).

[33] *Nebraska Wesleyan University* v. *Griswold's Estate*, 202 NW 609, 616 (Neb 1925).

[34] John D. Calamari and Joseph M. Perillo, *The Law of Contract* (5th edn., St Paul, Minn., 2003), 261–3; Randy E. Barnett and Mary E. Becker, 'Beyond Reliance: Promissory Estoppel, Contract Formalities and Misregreations', *Hofstra L. Rev.* 15 (1987), 443 at 451–3; Charles L. Knapp, 'Reliance in the Revised Restatement: The Proliferation of Promissory Estoppel', *Colum. L. Rev.* 81 (1981), 52 at 59–60. In a few exceptional cases, however, courts have refused enforcement because the charitable organization did not rely. See *Mount Sinai Hospital* v. *Jordan*, 290 So2d 484, 487 (Fla 1974); *Congregation Kadimah Toras-Moshe* v. *DeLeo*, 540 NE2d 691, 693 (Mass 1989).

[35] *Restatement (Second) of Contracts*, § 90(2) (1979).

[36] See Calamari and Perillo, *Contract*, 279–81.   [37] See ibid. 280; Knapp, 'Reliance', 60.

Farnsworth once noted, their enforcement is 'particularly desirable as a means of allowing decisions about the distribution of wealth to be made at an individual level'.[38] But then we are back to the idea that donative promises should be enforced because they allow people to make sensible changes in the distribution of wealth.

Of course, there are equally deserving promises that the law does not enforce: for example, to give a brilliant acquaintance the cash he needs to finish university; or to give money to family members who are in need. But in contrast to these, the promise to a charitable cause is impersonal. For that reason, the promisor's decision is less likely to be influenced by personal pressure or the emotions of the moment.

Moreover, because promises to charitable causes are impersonal, they are more likely to be meant as legal commitments. As Melvin Eisenberg has observed, often, to enable the promisee to demand performance as a matter of right would be inconsistent with the relationship of trust and affection that led the promisor to make the promise.[39] Moreover, often a donative promise is understood to be subject to conditions which are implicit. If a parent promises his son a new car, neither would expect the promise to be binding if the money were needed to pay for a grandparent's medical operation. Eisenberg has noted how hard it would be for a court to decide to what unexpressed conditions a donative promise is subject.[40] For that reason, the promisor might not want the promisee to have a legal right to performance. In an impersonal situation, however, the promisor is likely to spell out whatever conditions he wishes to attach to the promise because he cannot rely on a promisee who is not a friend or family member and who is not familiar with his affairs to understand intuitively the implied conditions that might attach.

B. Marriage Settlements

As noted earlier, in the time of the late scholastics, another exceptional case in which a formality was not required was a promise to people about to marry (*propter nuptias*). In Germany today, such promises are enforceable under Section 1624 of the German Civil Code.[41] The civil codes of France, Italy, and Spain do not contain such a rule, but one may not be as necessary since the custom of wealthy families has been to make such commitments formally and in writing before a marriage is celebrated.

In common law countries, where such promises are more likely to be made informally, courts have found ways to enforce them. Until the 19th century, courts said that the natural love and affection of a parent for a child was consideration.[42] Then, with the

---

[38] E. Allan Farnsworth and William F. Young, *Cases and Materials on Contracts* 98 (4th edn., Westbury, NY, 1988).

[39] Melvin Eisenberg, 'The Theory of Contracts', in Peter Benson, ed., *The Theory of Contract Law: New Essays* (Cambridge, 2001), 206 at 229–30.

[40] Melvin Aron Eisenberg, 'The World of Contract and the World of Gift', *Calif. L. Rev.* 85 (1997), 821 at 850.

[41] Section 1624 provides: 'That which the father or mother accords to a child towards marriage, or towards obtaining an independent position in life' for founding or preserving the establishment of the position in life' does not count as a gift, and therefore is not subject to a formality, except to the extent it is immoderately large, given the parents' circumstances.

[42] A. W. B. Simpson, *A History of the Common Law of Contract: The Rise of the Action of Assumpsit* (Oxford, 1987), 435–7.

rise of the 'bargain theory' of consideration, the forthcoming marriage was said to be the inducement for the parents' promise. Parents who might have begged their children not to marry were treated as though they had bribed them to do so.[43] The doctrine of promissory estoppel now makes that fiction unnecessary. The promise is supposed to be binding as long as the couple change their position in reliance upon it. But, as in the case of charitable subscriptions, courts do not ask whether the parties actually did so. According to the *Second Restatement*, no proof of reliance is required.[44]

Again, one reason to enforce such promises more readily is that they are likely to be sensible. Moreover, even though the promise is personal, it is more likely that the promisor would want to confer a right to performance on the promisee. Particularly when the couple is promised a large amount of money, the promise was probably made to enable them to establish an independent household in which they could treat resources as their own. If so, to allow them to regard these resources as their own is not inconsistent with a relationship of love and trust. Indeed, the purpose of the promisor is to allow them to do so. Given that purpose, it is much less likely that the promisor wants his promise to be subject to unexpressed conditions.

C. Reliance?

In the United States, the great exception to the rule that a formality is required to make a donative promise enforceable is supposed to be the doctrine of promissory reliance: the promisor is liable if the promisee changed his position to his detriment even though he did not make any commitment to the promisor in return, that is, even if there was no consideration for the promise. This doctrine has a number of functions. One, as we have seen, is to replace the fictions that American courts used to use to find consideration for charitable subscriptions and marriage settlements, albeit at the cost of further fictions. Another is to enforce promises in connection with gratuitous loans and bailments, promises which do not normally enrich one party at another's expense.[45] The Romans handled this problem by simply declaring that gratuitious loans for use or consumption did not require a formality but were binding only upon delivery. Today, many civil law systems do so by allowing one who has made a gratuitous loan to reclaim it if he finds a need for it himself.[46] Cases like these may lack consideration, but there is little need to require the same formality as in a promise to transfer wealth since, normally, one part is not enriched at another's expense. Yet, when Arthur Corbin in collaboration with Samuel Williston fathered the doctrine of promissory estoppel in the *First Restatement of Contracts*, he seems to have had in mind, primarily, these cases of gratuitous loans and bailments.[47] As we will see,

---

[43] Even then, in the famous case of *De Cicco* v. *Schweitzer*, 117 NE 807 (NY 1917), it was hard to arrive at the desired result since the promise was made to a fiancé who, having already engaged himself to marry, was legally obligated to do so. Cardozo ingeniously observed that the affianced couple might still have given up their legal right to dissolve their engagement by mutual consent, 117 NE at 809–10. In effect, the parent's promise was treated as though it were made to induce them to marry should they no longer wish to do so.   [44] *Restatement* (*Second*) *of Contracts*, § 90(2) (1979).

[45] James Gordley, 'Enforcing Promises', *Calif. L. Rev.* 83 (1995), 547 at 584–9.

[46] Gordley, *Enforceability of Promises*, 189–91.   [47] Gordley, 'Enforcing Promises', 565.

another function of the doctrine of promissory reliance, in commercial settings, is to enforce promises that are fair but lack consideration. The doctrine of consideration strikes down all one-sided commitments, yet not all of these are unfair, and the doctrine of reliance is often used to enforce those that are not.[48]

For Samuel Williston, however, the rationale of the doctrine was to enforce donative promises on which the promisee relied to his detriment. He first mentioned it in his commentary on the contracts treatise of Sir Frederick Pollock who had repudiated its application in cases involving marriage settlements. In 1856, in the case of *Hammersley* v. *De Biel*,[49] the court had said the promisor in such a case was bound because he made a 'representation' on which the promisee had 'acted'. Pollock denounced this view as the 'exploded doctrine of making representations good'.[50] He thought promises to persons about to marry had consideration.[51] He could not believe that the mere fact that someone had relied on a promise could serve as a substitute for consideration.

When Samuel Williston edited Pollock's treatise, he claimed that Pollock's view could not be squared with certain American decisions.[52] One was a charitable subscription to give money to a college which had already spent money in reliance on the promise.[53] The other, which now appears in almost every American contracts case-book, was *Ricketts* v. *Scothorn*[54] in which the court required executors to pay a note for $2,000 which the decedent, who died solvent without having changed his mind, had given his granddaughter so that she could quit her job. In his enormously influential treatise published in 1920, Williston suggested that reliance might serve as a substitute for consideration in the cases just mentioned. But, he said, 'at present it is opposed to the great weight of authority'.[55] Nevertheless, only a few years later, with Arthur Corbin's support, Williston wrote the doctrine of promissory reliance into § 90 of the *Restatement of Torts*, with little more authority to back it than that described.[56] It has since been accepted almost universally, although, most often, it has been applied in commercial cases of the kind described earlier.

As I have described elsewhere in more detail,[57] I find the doctrine troublesome. It is not troublesome to dispense with the doctrine of consideration in cases in which one-sided promises are fair. It is not troublesome to dispense with formalities in cases in which the promisor is unlikely to be impoverishing himself at the donor's expense. It is not troublesome to enforce a donative promise where a court can see that a promise was made with deliberation, and where the promise was not subject to implied conditions too difficult to articulate. Indeed, if the donor dies solvent without changing his mind, he, at least, has not claimed that he promised rashly, and any implied conditions as to future events have become irrelevant. But in all these cases, there is no reason reliance should matter. If the reason a court will not enforce an

---

[48] ibid. 590–613. [49] 12 Cl & F 45, 62, 88, 8 Eng Rep 1312, 1320, 1331 (1845).

[50] Sir Frederick Pollock, *Principles of Contract at Law and in Equity* (Gustavus H. Wald and Samuel Williston, eds., 7th English edn., 3rd American edn., Boston, 1906), 649, 650 n. k, 915.

[51] ibid. 915–21. [52] ibid. 650 n. 1.

[53] *Miller* v. *Western College*, 52 NE 432 (Ill 1898) (cited by Williston as *Beatty* v. *Western College*).

[54] 77 NW 365 (Neb 1898).

[55] Samuel Williston, *The Law of Contracts* 1 (Boston, 1920), § 139 at 313.

[56] Gordley, 'Enforcing Promises', 566–7. [57] ibid. 578–82.

informal donative promise is because of doubts as to whether it was the result of due deliberation, shouldn't these doubts have occurred to the promisee, and, if so, shouldn't he have looked for more assurance that the promise was meant seriously? But in that case, where there is evidence of deliberation, the court could conclude that the promise was made deliberately even absent reliance. Again, if as Eisenberg says, some promises are subject to implied conditions too difficult to articulate, how do we know they were met when the promisee relied? How do we know that taking his chances when he relied wasn't itself a risk implied in the arrangement? Should I really expect my uncle to reimburse me for a trip he agreed to pay for, but which I could have easily afforded myself, if, due to unforeseen conditions, he needs an operation or cash to keep his business out of bankruptcy? Again, if the promise was based on a relationship of affection which would be harmed by their legal enforcement, how is his suit for reliance damages consistent with that relationship of affection? In short, where the promisee has good reason to rely, the law would most often have a good reason to enforce a donative promise without reliance.[58]

IV. Conclusion

All of these rules make sense only on the assumption that a person can behave sensibly or foolishly when he gives a gift. As Farnsworth put it, if the law enforced all donative promises, 'what would limit your profligacy?'[59] Once we say, however, that gift-giving can be sensible or foolish, we are back to the Aristotelian idea of liberality whether we use that word or not.

For that reason, modern theories of contract based on preference satisfaction or autonomy cannot explain the law that governs gratuitous promises. Unless they incorporate something like the Aristotelian idea of liberality, all preferences or exercises of autonomy must count the same, not as wise or foolish.

---

[58] ibid. 578–82.
[59] E. Allan Farnsworth, 'Promises to Make Gifts', *Am. J. Comp. L.* 43 (1995), 359 at 364.

17

Promises to Exchange

The other basic type of voluntary arrangement discussed by writers in the Aristotelian tradition was a contract of exchange. For these writers, a contract of exchange did not merely mean that one party received a performance in return for what he gave any more than a donative contract meant that he did not. Just as a donative contract was an act of liberality, a contract was an act of voluntary commutative justice. For it to be fair, the resources the parties exchanged had to be of equal value. This idea was foreign to the will theorists of the 19th century for whom a contract was defined in terms of the will regardless of what the parties willed. It is also foreign to modern law and economics scholars for whom a contract is merely a way in which parties enter into an arrangement which *ex ante* they prefer.

The idea of equality in exchange has often been misunderstood. We will see, however, that if understood properly, it not only explains the relief which courts give when contracts are unfair, but another problem which has puzzled modern jurists and which is the source of the implied terms of a contract.

I. Equality in Exchange

A. The Fairness of the Price

We will see how writers in the Aristotelian tradition conceived of a just price. Then we will see how their approach explains the relief that courts actually give when a price is unfair.

1. The meaning of a fair price

As modern scholars have noted,[1] writers in the Aristotelian tradition thought that normally, unless public authority set a price, the fair price was the market price under competitive conditions. They knew that this price varies from day to day and from region to region. It has puzzled scholars that these writers expected exchange at such a price to preserve equality.

A first step to understanding their viewpoint is to recognize that, like modern economists, they thought that the market price had to fluctuate to reflect factors that they called need, scarcity, and cost. Need meant the value people place on goods. It might

---

[1] John Noonan, *The Scholastic Analysis of Usury* (Cambridge, Mass., 1957), 82–8; Raymond de Roover, 'The Concept of the Just Price and Economic Policy', *J. of Econ. Hist.* 18 (1958), 418; C. Ambrosetti, 'Diritto privato ed economia nella seconda scolastica', in Paolo Grossi, ed., *La seconda scolastica nella formazione del diritto privato moderno* (Milan, 1973), 28.

be quite different than goods' intrinsic worth or usefulness. Scarcity meant the quantity available. Cost meant the labor, expenses and risk entailed in producing them.[2]

These factors are like those that determine supply and demand in modern economic theory. Unlike modern economists, however, these writers did not think of supply and demand as separate schedules that clear at a unique equilibrium price.[3] Their explanation of how the market responds to need, scarcity, and cost was a simpler one. Buyers and sellers simply make a judgment of the price that adequately reflects these factors. The market price is set by the common judgment (*communis aestimatio*). In their view, the common judgment could be wrong. If the public authorities thought it was wrong, they might fix a different price at which everyone must trade. But unless they did so, the just price was the market price, which reflected the judgment of buyers and sellers generally.[4] Monopoly prices were unfair because they reflected, not the common judgment, but the efforts of a small group to get rich.[5]

These writers merely discussed why prices change, not why a fluctuating market price preserves equality. But the fact that they thought this explanation sufficient suggests how they conceived of equality. Prices had to change to reflect need, scarcity, and cost. When and if these fluctuations need not be tolerated, public authority can fix a price. If it does not do so, then the market price preserves equality to the extent feasible. There is no need to tolerate the further inequalities that arise when, as Lessius put it, one party took advantage of the other's 'ignorance' or 'necessity' to sell to him for more than the market price or to buy for less.[6]

Moreover, as Soto observed, a party who gains if prices rise might well have lost. A merchant must bear his losses if 'bad fortune buffets him, for example, because an unexpected abundance of goods mounts up', and he may sell for more if 'fortune smiles on him and later there is an unexpected scarcity of goods'. 'For as the business of buying and selling is subject to fortuitous events of many kinds, merchants ought to bear risks at their own expense, and, on the other hand, they may wait for good fortune.'[7] Similarly, Lessius noted that 'this is the condition of merchants, that as they may gain if they receive goods at small expense, so they lose if the expense was disproportionate or extraordinary'.[8]

As I have argued, these considerations explain why the market price is normally a fair price.[9] If society has an interest in seeing that purchasing power is justly

---

[2] James Gordley, *The Philosophical Origins of Modern Contract Doctrine* (Oxford, 1991), 94–102; Domenicus Soto, *De iustitia et iure libri decem* (Salamanca, 1551), lib. 6, q. 2, a. 3; Ludovicus Molina, *De iustitia et iure tractatus* (Venice, 1614), disp. 348. All of these factors had been mentioned, albeit cryptically, by Thomas Aquinas, *In decem libros ethicorum expositio* (A. Pirotti, ed, Turin, 1934), lib. 5, lec. 9; *Summa theologiae* II-II, Q. 77, a. 3, ad 4. They were discussed by medieval commentators on Aristotle. Odd Langholm, *Price and Value in the Aristotelian Tradition* (Bergen, 1979), 61–143.

[3] Langholm, *Price and Value*, 116.

[4] Soto, *De iustitia et iure*, lib. 6, q. 2, a. 3; Molina, *De iustitia et iure*, disp. 348; Leonardus Lessius, *De iustitia et iure, ceterisque virtutibus cardinalis libri quatuor* (Paris, 1628), lib. 2, cap. 21, dub. 2; Hugo Grotius, *De iure belli ac pacis libri tres* (B. J. A. de Kanter-van Hetting Tromp, ed., 1939), II.xii.14 and 23; Samuel Pufendorf, *De iure naturae et gentium libri octo* (Amsterdam, 1688), V.i.8.

[5] Soto, *De iustitia et iure*, lib. 6, q. 2, a. 3; Lessius, *De iustitia et iure*, lib. 2, cap. 21, dub. 21; Grotius, *De iure belli ac pacis*, II.xii.16.　　　　[6] Lessius, *De iustitia et iure*, lib. 2, cap. 21, dub. 4.

[7] Soto, *De iustitia et iure*, lib. 6, q. 2, a. 3.　　　　[8] Lessius, *De iustitia et iure*, lib. 2, cap. 21, dub. 4.

[9] James Gordley, 'Equality in Exchange', *Calif. L. Rev.* 69 (1981), 1587.

distributed, then it should try to preserve existing distribution or to change it by a social decision. A society committed to distributive justice should be committed to commutative justice. An exchange at the market price preserves this distribution insofar as it is feasible to do so. It is true, of course, that the purchasing power a person commands depends on the market value of the resources he owns. It therefore changes when market prices change. We have already seen, however, that some chance events must be allowed to alter a person's share of purchasing power.[10] One reason is that worse evils might ensue if the society tried to compensate the owner for chance losses. Another is that the very effort to do so might redistribute purchasing power.

So it is with losses caused by changes in market prices. To prevent them, we would have to freeze prices. If we did, we would confront the evils economists describe: unsold goods or queues of buyers. Moreover, if buyers queue up because the market doesn't clear, goods will no longer go to those who are willing to pay the most but to those who are ahead in line. We will thus have redistributed the power to obtain these goods from those who should be able to do so, if the initial distribution was just, to those who happen to queue up first. There are, then, certain changes in the distribution of purchasing power that we cannot prevent. That is not a reason for tolerating others. There is no reason for allowing one party to charge more by taking advantage of another's ignorance of the market price or inability to use the market.

Moreover, as Soto suggested, even though prices may change in the future, the party who loses may well have gained. If he contracts at the market price and markets work as economists say they do, either event will be equally likely. Therefore, a party is not poorer at the moment he contracts although the contract does change the risk that he will be poorer in the future.

Critics of my argument have sometimes missed my point. I am claiming that exchange at the market price preserves (so far as possible) each party's share of purchasing power. Of course, the personal value that each party places on the resources he receives will necessarily be greater than the value he places on the resources he gives. Otherwise he wouldn't exchange. As Aristotle said, the shoemaker does not exchange with another shoemaker but with the house builder.[11] I am not claiming that each party places the same personal value on what he gives and gets,[12] or that each party should place the same personal value on what he receives as the other party does,[13] or that each party should be guaranteed that he will obtain something that he personally values as much as what he gave.[14]

Consequently, I am not claiming that the payment of an amount equal to the market price adequately compensates a person for parting with an object that is personally worth more to him. The point of preserving a person's share of purchasing power is so

[10] Chapter 11.   [11] Aristotle, *Nicomachean Ethics* V.v 1133ª.
[12] At one point Trebilcock seems to think I am. He claims that I could not object 'to an exchange coerced at gunpoint if the values exchanges were equivalent market values'. Michael J. Trebilcock, *Limits of Freedom of Contract* (Cambridge, Mass., 1993), 81. But I agree that the value of goods to the party who buys them should be higher than the market value, that this decision is up to him.
[13] Trebilcock, *The Limits of Freedom of Contract*, 115 ('Gordley's proposal holds that both parties should gain equally').
[14] Hugh Collins, 'Distributive Justice through Contracts', *Current Legal Prob.* 45 (1992), 49 at 63 (who thinks I want to 'prevent transactions which are not Pareto optimal').

that he can acquire things which have greater personal value than what he pays for them. Writers in the Aristotelian tradition recognized that once he has done so, compensation for their loss is measured by their value to him, not their value on the market.[15] Michael Trebilcock has objected that unless a person is allowed to charge more than the market price, he will not sell an object that had a higher personal value to himself, such as a house to which he is attached for 'family, sentimental, historical or locational reasons'.[16] The late scholastics thought he could charge a price that would compensate him for this loss of personal value provided that the other party valued the object for a similar reason, or at least, that the other party was not led thorough his own ignorance to pay more than the amount for which he could acquire an object elsewhere that was equally valuable to him.[17] Otherwise, they said, the seller would suffer a loss. Another way to put it is that, as we have stressed, once purchasing power is fairly distributed, goods are supposed to go to whoever will pay the most. In Trebilcock's case, the owner is that person until he is offered a price at which he is willing to sell. It is like an auction in which the owner is, in effect, bidding more than anyone else until someone offers him an amount he will accept. Whether it is an exception to the rule that normally, the just price is the market price, depends on how one defines the market price. In any event, it is not an exception to the principle we have been discussing.

Trebilcock also objects that, if people must trade at the market price, the incentive will disappear 'to search out undervalued assets with a view to moving them to higher valued uses as reflected in prevailing or evolving markets'.[18] I can't see why. Soto, Lessius and, for that matter, Thomas Aquinas, noted that merchants are free to buy goods where and when they can find them cheaply in hopes of a profit when they resell.

2. *Relief when a price is unfair*

Writers in the Aristotelian tradition used the principle of equality to explain why the Roman law of their day gave relief for what was called *laesio enormis*, a deviation of more than one-half from the market price. Thomas Aquinas explained that, for practical reasons, a remedy was given only when the deviation was large.[19] Before Aristotle's *Ethics* was read in the West, medieval jurists had created this remedy by generalizing a Roman text that gave relief to a person who sold land for less than half the just price.[20] Like the writers in the Aristotelian tradition, the medieval jurists identified the just price with a market price that changed from day to day and region to region.[21] Unlike

---

[15] Soto, *De iustita et iure*, lib. 4, q. 6, a. 5; Molina, *De iustitia et iure*, disp. 315, 724; Lessius, *De iustitia et iure*, lib. 2, cap. 12, dubs. 16, 18; cap. 20, dubs. 10–11. See Grotius, *De iure belli ac pacis*, II.xvii.1–2; Pufendorf, *De iure naturae et gentium*, III.1.3; Jean Barbeyrac, *Le Droit de la nature et des gens... traduit du Latin par Jean Barbeyrac* (5th edn., Amsterdam, 1734), n. 1 to III.i.3.

[16] Trebilcock, *Limits of the Freedom of Contract*, 116.

[17] Molina, *De iustitia et iure*, disp. 351; Lessius, *De iustitia et iure*, lib. 2, cap. 21, dub. 4.

[18] Trebilcock, *Limits of Freedom of Contract*, 81–2.

[19] *Summa theologiae* II-II, Q. 77, a. 1, obj. 1 and ad 1.

[20] Cod. 4.44.2. The text was generalized soon after the rediscovery of Roman law. See *Brachylogus* (Berlin, 1829), III.xii.8; Hugolinus de Presbyteris, *Diversitates sive dissensiones dominorum super toto corpore iure civilis* (G. Haenel, ed., Lipsiae, 1834), § 253.

[21] *Glossa ordinaria* to Dig. 13.4.3 [vulg. 13.4.4] to *varia* (Venice, 1581). As the great medieval jurist Accursius pointed out, one who bought something and later sold it for less than half the purchase price

these writers, they had no theory of why the market price was just. They seem to have identified the just price with the market price simply because otherwise thousands of seemingly normal transactions would be called into question.

Today, many legal scholars are in a position like that of the early medieval jurists. Their legal systems give relief when a price is extremely unjust, and yet they have no theory of how prices can be unjust.

In France, article 1674 of the Civil Code of 1804 preserved a remedy for *lésion* for the sale of land at a low price. That was the only case in which French customary law had traditionally permitted relief.[22] In the 19th and 20th centuries, special statutes were enacted which gave a remedy to those who paid an excessive amount for fertilizer, seeds and fodder,[23] or for a rescue at sea,[24] or after an aviation accident[25] Another statute gave a remedy to those who receive too little when selling artistic or literary property.[26] In other cases, courts have sometimes given relief by declaring the contract was procured by fraud, duress, or mistake even though the victim had neither been told a lie nor threatened, and his only mistake concerned the value of what he bought or sold.[27]

In 19th century Germany, although some local statutes limited relief, the traditional remedy for *laesio enormis* was available wherever Roman law remained in force. At the end of the century, the first draft of the German Civil Code of 1900 abolished relief. But an amendment (now art. 138, par. 2) reinstated a remedy whenever one party obtained a 'disproportionate advantage' by exploiting the difficulties, indiscretion or inexperience of the other party. Since 1936, German courts have been willing to give relief for a violation of 'good morals' (German Civil Code, art. 138, par. 1) if the contract is sufficiently one-sided even if such a weakness were not exploited.[28]

In the United States, the courts of equity traditionally gave relief if a contract was 'unconscionable'. In the 19th century, they claimed to do so, not simply because a bargain was one-sided, but because its one-sidedness was evidence of fraud.[29] Nevertheless, they gave relief where no fraud was alleged. As I have shown elsewhere, they did so quite generously.[30] Today, article 2-203 of the Uniform Commercial Code allows a court to give relief in law or equity when a contract to sell goods is severely unfair. Section 208 of the *Second Restatement of Contracts* provides for similar relief in other types of contracts. American courts have held the price to be unconscionable

---

might not receive a remedy for 'it could be . . . that when the sale of the object to him occurred, it was worth more than when he now sells'. *Glossa ordinaria* to C. 4.44.4 to *auctoritate iudicis*.

[22] Claude de Ferrière, *Dictionnaire de droit et de pratique*, II.v. 'lézion d'outre moité de juste prix' (nouv. edn., Paris, 1769), 135, 137; Honoré Lacombe de Prezel, *Dictionnaire portatif de jurisprudence et de pratique* (Paris, 1763), II.v. 'lézion', 430. [23] Law of 8 July 1907.

[24] Law of 29 April 1916, art. 7. [25] Law of 31 May 1925, art. 57.

[26] Law of 11 Mar. 1957.

[27] Cass. req., 27 Apr. 1887, D.P. 1888.I.263; Cass. req., 27 Jan. 1919, S. 1920.I.198; Cass. civ., 29 Nov. 1968, Gaz. Pal. 1969.J.63; Cour d'appel, Douai, 2 June 1930, Jurisp. de la Cour d'appel de Douai 1930.183; Cour d'appel, Paris, 22 Jan. 1953, Sem. jur. 1953.II.7435.

[28] RG, 13 Mar.1936, ERGZ 150, 1.

[29] A. W. B. Simpson, 'The Horwitz Thesis and the History of Contracts', *Univ. Chi. L. Rev.* 46 (1979), 533 at 569. [30] Gordley, *Philosophical Origins*, 154–8.

when home appliances were sold for over three times their usual retail price[31] and homeowners were charged extravagant amounts for windows and sidewalls.[32]

The English are more conservative. They have given relief where, for example, a woman was not compensated for signing a release of her interests in her house.[33] The judge quoted with favor the requirements set down in a 19th century case:[34] 'What has to be considered is, first, whether the plaintiff is poor and ignorant; second, whether the sale was at a considerable undervalue; and third, whether the vendor had independent advice'. Such cases are rare, and the requirements are stringent. The reason, I believe, is an English preference for hard-edged rules.

Relief when a price is disproportionate is easy to explain in Aristotelian terms. For reasons already given, the market price is normally a fair one. It is hard to explain in any other way. Some American jurists have distinguished 'substantive' from 'procedural' unconscionability. Substantive unconscionability means the terms of the contract are unfair. Procedural unconscionability means that one party was at an unfair disadvantage in protecting himself, as, for example, in the English case in which the seller was 'poor and ignorant' and lacked independent advice. Some scholars have said that relief should be given when a transaction is substantively unfair only if it is procedurally unfair as well.[35] Some have said that the reason relief should be given is because of procedural unfairness, for example, because of a disparity in bargaining power.[36]

It is true that no one will pay more or charge less than the market price if they know what the market price is and are physically able to use the market. If these types of ignorance and necessity count as 'procedural unconscionability', then they will accompany every instance of substantive unfairness. It is also true that, sometimes, a party is less able to protect himself for some additional reason such youth, age, or poor education. A court should pay attention to such disadvantages when there is doubt as to whether a transaction deviated from the market price so severely as to warrant relief. The better able a party is to protect himself, the less likely it is that a severe deviation will happen. Nevertheless, the reason relief is given must be that the terms are substantively unfair. If they were not—if a consumer were paying the retail market price for an appliance—no one would care that a salesman could have taken advantage of him. Indeed, procedural unconscionability seems to mean nothing more than any circumstances that would enable the salesman to charge more than the market price. So we come back to the question of why the market price is normally a fair one. The Aristotelian tradition had an answer.

Posner and Landes have tried to explain relief by speaking about efficiency rather than fairness. Suppose a ship in distress promises a huge amount of money, vastly exceeding the costs of rescue, to the only possible rescuer. Under admiralty law, a ship that rescues the property of a ship in distress can charge only a reasonable amount for

---

[31] *Jones* v. *Star Credit Corp.*, 298 NYS2d 264 (Sup Ct 1969); *Frostifresh* v. *Reynoso*, 274 NYS2d 757 (Sup Ct 1966), *rev'd as to damages*, 281 NYS2d 964 (App 1967).

[32] *American Home Improvement Co.* v. *MacIver*, 201 A2d 886 (NH 1964).

[33] *Cresswell* v. *Potter*, [1978] 1 WLR 255 (Ch).   [34] *Fry* v. *Lane* (1888) 40 ChD. 312.

[35] Richard Craswell, 'Property Rules and Liability Rules in Unconscionability and Related Doctrines', *U. Chi. L. Rev.* 60 (1993), 1 at 17.

[36] W. David Slawson, *Binding Promises: The Late Twentieth Century Reformation of Contract Law* (Princeton, 1996), 23 at 38.

doing so. The reason, according to Posner and Landes, is not that the price is unfair but that otherwise, shipowners would overinvest in safety equipment so that they would not find themselves in need of rescue.[37]

This is one of many instances in which scholars who do economic analysis of law have tried to add credibility to their approach by using it to explain what courts do. We ought to be careful. It is one thing to suggest that a judge saw a particular result was right but did not fully grasp the reason, or that he endorsed a certain principle but did not fully grasp its implications. It is quite another to suggest that his decisions can be 'explained' by principles he is unlikely to have had even vaguely in mind. Such an 'explanation' means that, by complete coincidence, a decision taken for one reason has turned out to be advantageous for another quite different one. If that is all that is meant, one should say so. One cannot explain the American seizure of the Philippines in the Spanish American War by pointing out that it makes a good base for military aircraft.

In any event, if Posner and Landes were right, a court would give relief only when there is some possible safety precaution that a shipowner could have taken to avoid the need for a rescue. That is not the law.

Charles Fried, as we have seen, endorses 'the liberal principle that the free arrangements of rational persons should be respected'.[38] One might think that Fried would condemn the doctrine of unconscionability outright as he does that of consideration. Nevertheless, he concedes that 'some bargains, though they meet all the tests I have set out so far, seem just too hard to enforce'.[39] For example, a rescuer should not be able to charge too much to save the cargo of a disabled ship. The reason, according to Fried, is that a random event has caused the breakdown of what Fried calls a 'functioning social system' or 'political system of social redistribution' within which exchange normally takes place.[40] Might one call it a system of commutative and distributive justice? At that point, instead of talking about 'self-determination' it would be more consistent to acknowledge that while promise-keeping is a virtue, justice is a virtue as well.

Following Hegel, Peter Benson has tried to extract the requirement of equality in exchange from the concept of freedom. The realization of freedom is said to require that the wills of the parties become identical, which they supposedly do in a contract of exchange. Their wills would not be identical, however, unless they were directed to something that is the same, and since that cannot be the resources they exchange, it must be their value.[41] One of my problems, again, is that I don't understand why this sort of reasoning counts as reasoning. Freedom is said to be related to equality, but these concepts are neither related to each other deductively, as concepts are in mathematics,

---

[37] William M. Landes and Richard A. Posner, 'Salvors, Finders, Good Samaritans and Other Rescuers: An Economic Study of Law and Altruism', *J. Leg. Stud.* 7 (1978), 83. The same explanation is given by F. H. Buckley, 'Three Theories of Substantive Fairness', *Hofstra L. Rev.* 19 (1990), 33 at 40–8; F. H. Buckley, *Just Exchange: A Theory of Contract* (London, 2005), 149–51.

[38] Charles Fried, *Contract as Promise: A Theory of Contractual Obligation* (Cambridge, Mass., 1981), 35.

[39] ibid. 109.   [40] ibid. 109–10.

[41] Peter Benson, 'Abstract Right and the Possibility of a Nondistributive Conception of Contract: Hegel and Contemporary Contract Theory', *Cardozo L. Rev.* 10 (1989), 1077 at 1192–3. Weinrib, citing Benson, seems to give a version of this argument when he says that 'equal value is necessary if [the parties] are to count for each other as equals within the transaction'. Ernest J. Weinrib, *The Idea of Private Law* (Cambridge, Mass., 1995), 138.

or functionally, as organs or parts are related to an end as in biology or engineering. But, in any event, it seems impossible to get from equality in value as a concept in the mind of the parties to equality in market value as a criterion of fairness. As Benson himself notes, 'Hegel's justification of a requirement of equivalence in exchange should be viewed as elucidating a postulate that goes to the intelligibility of contractual obligation rather than as establishing a rule that can be applied to particular cases'.[42]

Finally, a few scholars have suggested that contract prices should be substantively fair. Their theories get into difficulties because they do not identify the fair price with the market price.

According to Michael Swygert and Katherine Earle, one party ought not to receive 'almost all of the surplus utility created by the transaction'.[43] It seems intuitively wrong, however, that the fairness of a contract depends on the degree of personal advantage the parties derive from it. A beer might be barely worth the market price to one person and ten times that price to another but it is not unfair that they pay the same.[44] Moreover, the person who saves my life at a small cost to himself would not be receiving 'almost all the surplus utility' if he demanded my life savings in return, but it seems unfair for him to do so.

At one point, Stephen Smith claimed that prices are unfair when they deviate from what a person would normally expect, and so 'harm individuals' abilities to plan and thereby to achieve autonomous, fulfilling lives'.[45] Again, that explanation intuitively seems wrong, and Smith seems to have pulled back from it.[46] To rescue someone at small cost in return for his life savings seems unfair even if he expected a rescuer would charge that much. To sell someone an appliance for three times its retail price seems unfair even if the buyer had no expectations about what such an appliance might cost. Monopoly prices are unfair, but as Smith notes, they may not be unexpected. Moreover, if prices become unexpectedly high on a competitive market, the reason must be that there was an unexpected change in cost of production or in demand or in short-term supply. If the change is in cost, it would be odd to say a producer is acting unfairly because he refuses to sell at a loss. Moreover, his plans have been disrupted as well. If the change is in demand or short-term supply, then someone's plans will have to be disrupted. If prices do not rise, the market will not clear, and the person whose plans must change will the one at the end of a queue.

II. The Fairness of Auxiliary Terms

A. Fairness of Auxiliary Terms and Commutative Justice

For Thomas Aquinas, the late scholastics and natural lawyers, the types of exchanges into which the parties might enter—for example, sale or lease—were all acts of

---

[42] Benson, 'Abstract Right', 1104 n. 168.

[43] Michael I. Swygert and Katherine Earle Yanes, 'A Unified Theory of Justice: The Integration of Fairness into Efficiency', *Wash. L. Rev.* 73 (1998), 249 at 262.

[44] A point made by F. H. Buckley, 'Three Theories of Substantive Fairness', 36.

[45] Stephen A. Smith, 'In Defence of Substantive Fairness', *L. Quar. Rev.* 112 (1996), 138 at 157.

[46] Stephen A. Smith, *Contract Theory* (Oxford, 2004), 356.

commutative justice. The terms appropriate to each type were those that would effectuate the parties' purposes while maintaining equality. An illustration is their explanation of why a seller should be liable for defects in the goods he sold. If he were not liable, the contract would be unequal since the buyer would have paid more than he ought for defective goods.[47] The parties could modify these terms in any way that suited them provided they did not violate equality. According to Molina and Jean Domat (a 17th century French jurist influenced by the natural law school), the seller might disclaim liability for defects if he lowered his price to compensate the buyer for the risk the goods would be defective.[48] Thus, risks and burdens can fall on either party provided the price is to compensate him fairly for bearing them.

In my view, this theory provides the best explanation of the cases in which courts refuse to enforce unfair auxiliary terms. To see why, we must consider the reason such a term might appear in a contract. Here we can learn from the economists. As they tell us, the parties would want to place risks and burdens on whichever party can bear them most easily. As long as a party knew that he was to assume a risk or burden and also knew the cost to himself of bearing it, he would agree to bear it only if the price were adjusted in his favor by at least the amount of his cost. Consequently, if both parties always had this knowledge, the terms would never be unfair. That is so even if the market is non-competitive for roughly the same reason that even a monopolist will put leather upholstery in cars if people are willing to pay more for it than his cost. Suppose the cost to one party of bearing a particular risk or burden is $50, and it is $500 to the other. The parties would place the risk or burden on the first party and compensate him by at least $50. For any lesser amount, he would not agree to bear it. For any greater amount, he would want to do so. An economist would say that this allocation of risks and burdens is 'efficient' because there is no way to change it in return for compensation so as to make both parties better off. The Aristotelian approach explains why it is not only efficient but fair. And indeed, Hugh Beale has noted that the terms that courts regard as fair do tend to be those which are 'efficient' in the sense just described.[49]

Suppose, however, that a party does not know that the contract places a risk or burden on him or does not know the cost he will incur by bearing it. Then, the other party might place it on him without adjusting the price by the amount of his cost. Indeed, we can be sure the other party would not adjust the price by that amount if that party could have borne the risk or burden more cheaply himself. A party who can bear the risk or burden for $50 will not throw it on the party who can bear it for $500 if he has to alter his price by $500.[50]

---

[47] Thomas Aquinas, *Summa theologiae* II-II, Q. 77, a. 2; Molina, *De iustitia et iure*, disp. 353.

[48] Molina, *De iustitia et iure*, disp. 353; Jean Domat, *Les Loix civiles dans leur ordre naturel*, I.iv.2 (Paris, 1713).

[49] Hugh Beale, 'Unfair Contracts in Britain and Europe', *Current Legal Prob.* 42 (1989), 197 at 206.

[50] Note that this argument does not assume that the first party keeps the $50 he has saved by shifting the risk or burden to the other. F. H. Buckley notes, quite correctly, that even if consumers cannot tell whether a term in a contract hurts them, and producers cannot compete by eliminating it, the producers may still compete by lowering prices. If so, they may lower their prices until the gain they make by including that term disappears. Buckley, 'Three Theories of Substantive Fairness', 62. Even so, the term will still place a risk or burden on the other party for which he is not adequately compensated. If the producer had to compensate him adequately, he would prefer to bear the risk or burden himself.

B. The Fairness of Auxiliary Terms in Modern Law

In fact, the terms that modern legal systems have held to be unfair are ones that place risks and burdens on a party who is unlikely to have been compensated for bearing them. Admittedly, it is often difficult for a court to estimate the size of a risk or burden and to determine whether a party has been fairly compensated. Courts tend to give relief in cases in which it is easier to see that he has not been fairly compensated.

1. Specific terms that weigh more heavily on the party who assumes them

Sometimes, a term is so onerous for one party and of so little significance for the other that it is clear by inspection that the advantaged party would not have paid fair compensation for inserting it in the contract. In a well-known American case, a farmer had agreed to sell his tomatoes to a soup manufacturer. If, for any reason, the soup manufacturer rejected the tomatoes, the farmer would not be paid and was forbidden to sell them to anyone else.[51] It is hard to believe that the benefit to the soup manufacturer was greater than the damage to the farmer. Therefore, it is hard to imagine that the soup company compensated the farmer adequately for this hardship.

In other cases, it will be clear that a risk or burden is placed on the wrong party after considering the reasons why a party is better able to assume a risk or burden. He might be able to control the occurrence of some event at lesser cost. Even if he could not have prevented such an event, it might be hard to prove whether he could or not, and thus the cheapest solution might be for him to assume liability and raise his price by an amount that will compensate him for doing so. Even if the event is uncontrollable, he might be able to assume the risk of its occurrence more cheaply because he is better able to estimate its likelihood. If people are risk averse, risks or burdens are smaller when they are easier to estimate. Or he might face the same risk or shoulder the same burden continually. A risk would then be easier to bear because, as in the case of an insurance company or a casino, outcomes are more predictable when the same risk is faced over and over.

If a court can see that, for these reasons, one party is better able to bear a risk or burden, it can conclude that the other party could not have been adequately compensated for assuming it. For example, modern courts have refused to enforce a waiver of the seller's liability for defects in factory new products. In *Henningsen* v. *Bloomfield Motors*,[52] an American court held it was unconscionable for a car manufacturer to disclaim liability for personal injury if the car was defective. According to Uniform Commercial Code § 2-217, disclaimers of liability for personal injuries caused by defects are 'prima facie unconscionable'. Most American states reach the same result today by imposing strict liability in tort for product defects. European courts will reach similar results under a European Community directive governing product defects which was inspired by American law.[53]

In such cases, it hard to see how the consumer can be in a better position to bear the risk than the manufacturer. If the consumer by some reasonable precaution could have

---

[51] *Campbell Soup Co.* v. *Wentz*, 172 F2d 80 (3rd Cir 1948).   [52] 161 A2d 69 (1960).
[53] EC Directive Concerning Liability for Defective Products, 32 ILM 1347, OJ 1985 L 210/28–33, § 1(a).

reduced the risk, he will be held to be comparatively negligent if he fails to do so. But otherwise, the manufacturer would have been in the best position to take any feasible precautions. The problems of proving whether he did can be severe. He will be best able to estimate the size of the risk. Moreover, the manufacturer who is held liable will face the same risk over and over. If, for these reasons, the manufacturer can best bear the risk, it is hard to think that he has reduced his price adequately to compensate consumers for bearing it.

2. Terms allowing one party to control the quantity he buys or sells

Suppose, for example, one party promises to buy (or sell) the other however much he wishes of a certain commodity at a fixed price. If the market price rises (or falls) below that price, he might take advantage of the contract to buy (or sell) an amount that goes far beyond his needs and to resell (or repurchase) an equivalent amount on the market. Nothing could be more advantageous to me, or more unfair to you, than if I could buy any amount of coal I wished at $8 a ton on the market and resell it to you at $10 a ton.

Traditionally, common law jurisdictions would not enforce such an arrangement. The reason, supposedly, was not that it was unfair, but because it lacked consideration. A party who promised to buy (or sell) as much as he wished had not limited his freedom of action, and therefore not given up any legal right. That is still the rule in England.[54] The trouble with this approach is that one can get around it by clever drafting. A party could obtain the same unfair advantage by specifying that he must buy (or sell) some very small quantity. Then he would have given up a legal right, and there would be consideration. Consequently, the American Uniform Commercial Code confronts the problem of fairness head-on. It upholds such a contract with the proviso that the quantity offered or demanded must be 'such actual output or requirements as may occur in good faith'.[55]

In a survey of how various continental jurisdictions would confront the problem of one who bought or sold beyond his own needs, the jurists participating claimed that such a contract would be unenforceable albeit for different reasons: in France and Belgium, because it constituted an 'abuse of right'; in the Netherlands, Austria, Germany and Scotland, because this use of the contract was inconsistent with its proper interpretation, and, as well, in Scotland, the Netherlands, Portugal, and Germany, because it violated 'good faith', and in Italy, because the terms of the contract were too uncertain for enforcement.[56]

3. Options to contract or to terminate

It may also be unfair if one party has an option, either to enter into contractual relations, or to terminate them. He can then speculate at the other party's expense. He could do so if he had, for example, a 30-year option, for which he has paid nothing, to buy the other party's land at a set price; or the right to do so, terminable whenever he wishes. The party with such a power can profit by exercising his option if the market

---

[54] Stephen Smith, 'English Report, Case 8', in James Gordley, ed., *The Enforceability of Promises in European Contract Law* (Cambridge, 2001), 212–13.   [55] UCC § 2-306(1).
[56] Gordley, *Enforceability of Contracts*, 217.

price rises above the contract price and refusing to exercise it if it does not. On the other hand, an option may serve a fair and useful purpose. It may enable the party with the option to undertake other commitments without which this commitment will not be of value, or to perform tests or studies on the advantages of the contract which he would not do unless he had such a commitment. Or the option may be so short term, and the market so stable, that there is little chance of speculation at another's expense.

In common law, traditionally, an option for which nothing was paid would be unenforceable for lack of consideration, whether fair or not. Unless a party pays for the option, he does not give up a legal right. While Simon Smith has said this is still the English rule, he has noted that English courts sometimes 'invent' consideration when it seems fair to do so.[57]

In the United States, courts have managed to uphold seemingly fair arrangements, which amount to an option, in a variety of ways. In *Scott* v. *Moragues Lumber Co.*,[58] one party had promised to charter a ship to the other if he decided to purchase it. The court held there to be consideration because the contract was conditional. In *Mattei* v. *Hopper*,[59] one party agreed to purchase land for a shopping center if he could obtain satisfactory leases. The court held there to be consideration even though it admitted that the condition of satisfaction was subjective so that the buyer could profess himself dissatisfied even though a reasonable person would not have been. In some cases, courts have enforced a promise even though the promisee did not even make a conditional commitment. For example, in *The M.F. Parker*[60] a man bought a ship for $315 after a carpenter had said repairs to the ship would cost $150. Unlike the defendant in *Scott*, he did not commit himself to hire the carpenter if he bought the ship. Nevertheless, when the carpenter later billed him $356 for making these repairs, the court held the carpenter could charge no more than $150. In *Wilson* v. *Spry*,[61] the defendant agreed to hold an offer to sell his land open for 45 days so that the prospective buyer could make a thorough examination of it at significant cost to himself. The court found consideration. For reasons I have explained in detail elsewhere, I don't think that these decisions can be reconciled by the doctrines the courts invoked to explain them. I think that the court was trying to prevent the doctrine of consideration from permitting a fair result.[62]

In these cases, a party wanted an option to see if he could safely commit himself to another contract or to explore the value of his investment. Another case in which an option may be fair is when it is short term and on fair terms in a relatively stable market. Under the doctrine of consideration, even a short-term one-sided commitment is invalid. Sometimes courts found an excuse for not applying the doctrine strictly: for example, the presence of nominal consideration[63] or some slight limitation on the

---

[57] Smith, 'English Report, Case 13', in Gordley, *Enforceability of Promises*, 293–5.
[58] 80 So 394 (Ala 1918).   [59] 330 P2d 625 (Cal 1958).   [60] 88 F 853 (ED Va 1880).
[61] 223 SW 564 (Ark 1920).   [62] Gordley, *Enforceability of Contracts*, 600–2.
[63] e.g. *Real Estate Co.* v. *Rudolph*, 153 A 438 (Pa 1930); *Morrison* v. *Johnson*, 181 NW 945, 946 (Minn 1921) (dicta). The second *Restatement of Contracts*, § 87(1) provides that a written offer can be made irrevocable for nominal consideration if it 'proposes an exchange on fair terms within a reasonable time'.

freedom of the uncommitted party.[64] Otherwise, they had to refuse to enforce the commitment even when it was fair. Once again, the Uniform Commericial Code faces the problem more squarely. A commitment to buy or sell goods is binding among merchants for up to three months if it is made in writing.[65]

In a survey of European law, continental jurists said that their own legal systems would address the problem even more directly. They claimed that if the option price were seriously unfair, and one party took advantage of an abrupt change in the market price, the contract would not be enforced because of the disparity between the contract and market price at the time the option was exercised (France), for failure to exercise good faith (the Netherlands, Italy, and Germany) and because the purpose of the original transaction had been thwarted (Spain).[66] Some arrangements that allow a party a free way in or out of a contract can now be set aside under amendments to the law of European Union countries required by the European Community's Directive on Abusive Contract Terms. For example, under the Directive, a contract is deemed to be unfair if one party is bound while the obligations of the other depend on a condition whose fulfillment depends on that party's will alone.[67] It is unfair if one party alone has an option to terminate.[68] In Germany, an option to terminate is deemed unfair unless the contract states a reason for termination.[69]

4. Modifications of terms already agreed upon

Often it is unfair for one party who has entered into one contract to demand that the other party enter into another granting him better terms than were initially agreed. He may be taking advantage of the other party's change in position or simply reneging on a bet on which way prices will move in the future. Traditionally, in such cases, the common law will hold the new contract unenforceable, supposedly, not for unfairness, but for lack of consideration. The party who promised more received nothing in return for his promise. It is now generally recognized that the doctrine of consideration is too blunt an instrument to deal with this situation. Sometimes a modification can be fair, for example, because circumstances have changed in a way that was not anticipated or because the parties contracted in the expectation that they would make periodic adjustments in the amount of compensation even though the contract does not expressly provide for them. The doctrine of consideration does not enable a court to discriminate between those that are fair and those that are not.

In England, the response of the courts has been curious. In 1991, in *Williams* v. *Roffrey Bros. & Nichols (Contractors) Ltd.*, the court broke with traditional contract by holding that a promise would be upheld, even if the promisor received no legal benefit in return, provided he received a 'practical benefit'.[70] English jurists seem unsure what

---

[64] e.g. *Gurfein* v. *Werbelovsky*, 118 A 32 (Conn 1922) (upholding contract to buy plate glass to be shipped within three months, although the buyer could cancel before shipment, on the grounds that if the seller had shipped immediately, the buyer could not exercise this option).

[65] UCC § 2-205. Even such a short-term commitment can be struck down as unconscionable if it operates unfairly (ibid cmt 4).   [66] Gordley, *Enforceability of Promises*, 298–9.

[67] EC Directive on Unfair Contracts, Directive 93/13 EEC, OJ 1993 L 95/29, Annex 1(c).

[68] ibid. Annex 1(f); see 1(p).

[69] German Civil Code (*Bürgerlichesgesetzbuch*) [hereinafter BGB] § 308(3).

[70] *Williams* v. *Roffrey Bros. & Nichols (Contractors) Ltd.* [1991] 1 QB 1.

is meant by a 'practical benefit'. The *Williams* court did indicate, however, that it would not enforce the new promise if it were the result of a threat of non-performance that amounts to duress. As we will see, this is the typical continental solution to the problem.

In the United States, the modern tendency, reflected in both the Uniform Commercial and and the *Restatement (Second) of Contracts* is to try to discriminate between fair and unfair modifications of pre-existing contractual relations. Both the Code and the *Second Restatement* do not require consideration for what are deemed fair modifications. According to the Code, a modification does not need consideration if it is made in 'good faith'.[71] According to the *Second Restatement*, it does not need consideration provided that they are fair because circumstances have changed.[72] The *Second Restatement* also says that promises do not need consideration if the promisee has changed his position in reliance on the new promise, but that seems yet another attempt to use the concept of reliance to solve a problem it alone cannot address. Surely if A takes advantage of B's situation to demand better terms, and circumstances have not changed, it should not matter that A has spent the extra money he demanded. Thus, it has become possible to consider the fairness of the modification of a contract, but only by abandoning the doctrine of consideration.

In Europe, the law of France seems to be in doubt.[73] According to a recent survey of European jurists, however, the modified promise would not be enforced if there were 'abuse of circumstances', which means taking advantage of the other party's 'state of necessity, dependency, wantonness, abnormal mental condition or inexperience'.[74] In England, as noted, and in Italy, Austria, Germany and Greece, the modification would not be enforced if it was induced by a threat not to perform which amounted to economic duress.[75] In addition, special legislation, much of it passed in response to a directive of the European Community, limits the modifications a court will enforce even if they are provided for in the original contract. In France and Germany, it is deemed unfair for one party to be able to unilaterally alter the performance to be made.[76] In Germany, it is unfair for one party to be able to increase his price within four months.[77] According to the European Directive, it is unfair to allow one party to increase his price unless the other has the right to withdraw from the contract.[78] It is also unfair for one party to have the right to modify the terms except for a good reason which the contract specifies.[79]

5. Penalities for non-performance

In other cases, one can see that a term is unfair because, rather than shift a risk to a party who can better bear it, it amounts to a side bet concerning a risk that the parties are equally able to bear. Risk averse parties do not gamble if they must pay the expected value of a bet. A court could conclude that a party would not insert such a clause in the contract if he had to adjust the price sufficiently to compensate the other party.

---

[71] UCC § 2-209(1), cmt 2.   [72] *Second (Restatement) of Contracts*, § 89 (1979).
[73] Gordley, *Enforceability of Promises*, 236.   [74] ibid. 236–7.   [75] ibid. 236–7.
[76] Decree of 24 Mar. 1978, art. 3; BGB § 308(4); EC Directive on Unfair Contracts 1(k) (unfair to modify characteristics of goods without reason).   [77] BGB § 309(4).
[78] EC Directive on Unfair Contracts 1(l).   [79] ibid. 1(j).

The clearest example is a clause that obligates a party in breach to pay a penalty that exceeds the harm that the other party suffers. The party to receive it would not have inserted such a clause merely to encourage the other party to perform. In fact, he will be better off if the other party fails to do so. Nor would he have inserted it if he had to compensate the other party adequately for the risk of having to pay this extra amount. The expected value of their bet is the extra amount times the probability of breach given the incentives not to breach created by the penalty clause. Since both parties are risk averse, party who risks paying the penalty is not adequately compensated unless he receives more than this expected value, and party who stands to benefit will not insert such a clause if he had to pay that much.

It is understandable, then, that common law courts have traditionally refused to enforce such a clause. A contract can require a party in breach to pay an amount that is a reasonable estimate of the damages the other party will suffer. It cannot require him to pay more.[80] Civil law countries have moved in that direction. In France, a law of 1975 allowed the judge 'to reduce or increase the penalty agreed upon if it is manifestly excessive or derisory' despite any 'contrary stipulation' by the parties.[81] In Germany, contract penalties are void,[82] and terms prescribing the damages to be recovered in the event of breach must correspond to what one would expect in the normal course of events.[83] The European Community directive on abusive terms contains a similar provision.[84]

6. Risks and burdens for which no compensation is paid

In the cases we have examined, a risk was placed upon the party who was less suited to bear it. In still another type of case, a party might have been the best suited, but he was never compensated for the risk placed upon him. A good example is the American case of *Williams v. Walker-Thomas Furniture Co.*[85] A woman made a series of purchases on credit from a store. A clause in the contracts she signed provided that all of her payments would be applied to the debt outstanding on all the items she purchased, so that if she defaulted, all the items could be repossessed by the store. The court held this clause unconscionable. Richard Epstein has pointed out that the clause could have served the useful purpose of providing the store with security for the loans it extended, and security of a kind it could easily verify since it knew which items it had already sold.[86] That is true. But Mrs Williams, it seems, did not receive a markdown of the price to compensate her for the added risk she incurred in order to provide the store with this security. For all that appears, she paid just the price charged people who had not previously bought anything that the store could repossess.

C. Conclusion

It is perfectly true, as modern economists have pointed out, that if both parties had their eyes open, they would place the burdens and risks incident to a contract on the

---

[80] *Restatement (Second) of Contracts*, §§ 355–6 (1979).
[81] Law no. 75-597 of 9 July 1975, art. 1, now French Civil Code (*Code civil*), art. 1152.
[82] BGB § 309(6).   [83] BGB § 309(5).
[84] EC Directive on Unfair Contracts 1(e).   [85] 198 A2d 914 (DC 1964).
[86] Richard A. Epstein, 'Unconscionability: A Critical Reappraisal', *J. Law & Econ.* 18 (1975), 293 at 308–10.

party by whom they could most easily be borne, and that party would insist on increased compensation for bearing them. That result would be fair in the sense in which writers in the Aristotelian tradition understood commutative justice. As we have seen, they thought that a contract should be actuarially fair in the way that a fair bet is fair. A party might waive his right to sue if goods are defective, but if so, he should be compensated for taking that risk by receiving a lower price. If the parties always had their eyes open, then we could conclude that contracts work invariably the way economists expect them to work ideally, or at least, on the average among reasonably farsighted people. But sometimes they do not, as all the cases previously cited indicate. At that point, one party is making a bargain with the odds slanted in his own favor and one to which the other party would not agree if he understood the risks and burdens it requires him to assume. Writers in the Aristotelian tradition regarded such a contract as unfair. So, as we have seen, do modern legal systems.

III. The Implied Terms of a Contract

Writers in the Aristotelian tradition used the principle of equality in exchange to explain, not only why courts sometimes disregard the express terms of a contract because they are unfair, but why they read other terms into the contract when the parties are silent. Much of the Roman law of sales, leases and so forth specified what these terms are. The Aristotelian tradition had an explanation of why these terms should be read in. They were appropriate because they effectuated the purposes of the parties while maintaining equality.[87]

In discussing unfair terms, enough has been said to show how one can analyze whether a term will maintain equality. As the law and economics scholars say, risks and burdens should be placed on the party who can bear them at least cost. The price should then be adjusted to compensate him for bearing them. As we have seen, the contract will be unfair if the party who can bear a risk at least cost succeeds in shifting it to the other party since the party shifting the risk would prefer to bear it himself if he had to compensate the other party fairly.

For the law and economics scholars, the rationale is efficiency. Unless risks and burdens are placed on the party that can bear them most cheaply, it is possible to alter the terms of the contract so as to make both parties better off by reassigning the risk or burden and altering the price. In contrast, from an Aristotelian standpoint, the rationale is fairness: to avoid, so far as feasible, changes in the share of purchasing power that belongs to each party.

The trouble with the economic rationale is that we are speaking of implied terms, terms that the parties did not set for themselves when they contracted but which the court reads in later on. It is true that, if the parties considered the matter, they would place risks and burdens on the party who could bear them most cheaply and then adjust the price to compensate him. But they never did consider the matter. Therefore, it is hard to think that their decision to contract was affected by the way they expected

---

[87] Gordley, *Philosophical Origins*, 105–11.

these risks and burdens to be allocated. Quite possibly, the reason that terms later have to be read in is that these terms cover contingencies that are sufficiently remote that *ex ante* it was not worth the parties' time to decide how to deal with them. If so, then the way these risks and burdens are allocated *ex post* will not affect the value of the contract to the parties *ex ante* or their decision to enter into it. If it does not, then an economist has no reason for caring about what happens *ex post*. *Ex post*, a court's decision to place a risk or burden on one party rather than the other merely affects how much money each party has.[88]

One response might be that sometimes, a matter is sufficiently important to the parties that they would draft their own terms to deal with it. The law can spare them this trouble by providing a set of default rules that are like the ones that they would have drafted for themselves. The law should do so if it can do so at a lower cost than the parties would incur. According to this explanation, the advantage of placing risks and burdens on whoever can bear them the most cheaply is not that it is efficient to do so, but that it is efficient to spare the parties the trouble of doing so in the cases in which they care enough *ex ante* to trouble themselves. If so, the entire law of sales, leases, partnerships and so forth exists for the sake of these people. One wonders how many there are. According to Jay Feinman and Melvin Eisenberg, most people don't know what terms the law will read into their contract.[89] That suggests they are not sufficiently interested *ex ante* to find out in order to adjust their prices to reflect the risks they are assuming. If so, it seems unlikely they would be drafting their own terms if the law provided different ones.

On Aristotelian principles, it is easier to see why the law should place a risk or burden on the party who could bear it most easily. The reason is not to affect the parties' decision whether to contract. It is because the contract is fair when this party assumes the risk and is compensated for doing so. It is true that if the parties have not considered a risk or burden *esc ex ante* they may not have adjusted the price to compensate the party who assumes it. Nevertheless, it may be that, without considering specific risks, they have set a fair price based on their general experience with contracts of that type. They may be trading at a market price that reflects costs for a given type of transaction in the industry, and these costs reflect the risks and burdens each party is assuming. It may be that no adjustment of the price is needed because, as in some of the cases discussed earlier, the risk or burden is insignificant for one party even though it is substantial for the other. Finally, even if the parties did not consider a risk or burden *ex ante*, the fact remains that one party can bear it at a lower cost than the other *ex post*, when the risk materializes or the burden has to be shouldered. If we want to preserve, so far as

---

[88] A response might be that *ex post* one party might be better able to bear a risk or burden than another. To allocate it to the party least able to bear it will necessitate another transaction: one in which the parties agree to transfer the risk to the party better able to do so in return for suitable compensation. One problem with that response is that the party who can best bear a risk or burden *ex post* is not necessarily the one who could best do so *ex ante*. Another problem is that, then, we are merely talking about transactions costs which may be quite small, and considerably smaller than the efforts that courts, attorneys, and scholars have put into developing a law of sales, leases, corporations and so forth.

[89] Jay Feinman, 'The Significance of Contract Theory', *U. Cinn. L. Rev.* 58 (1990), 1283 at 1306; Melvin A. Eisenberg, 'The Theory of Contracts', in Peter Benson, ed., *The Theory of Contract Law: New Essays* (Cambridge, 2001), 223 at 249.

possible, the amount of purchasing power that each party controls, it is better for this party to bear the cost rather than the other party.

With the Aristotelian approach, in part, the justification for reading such terms into the contract is that they are fair. In part, the justification is that these are the terms that the parties themselves would have wished to govern their agreement had their intention been the one the law should respect: to exchange resources but not to alter the share of purchasing power that belongs to each. These justifications were not thought to conflict. Writers in the Aristotelian tradition did not conceive of equality in exchange as a requirement foreign to the will of the parties and imposed on them, so to speak, from the outside. Had one of them wished to enrich the other party at his own expense, he would have made a gift rather than entering into an exchange. As Grotius said, 'Nor is it enough for anyone to say that what the other party has promised more than equality is to be regarded as a gift. For such is not the intention of the contracting parties, and is not to be presumed so, except it appear.'[90] Had one of the parties wanted to enrich himself at the other's expense without the other party's consent, he would have had an intention the law should not respect. That intention should not affect the content of his obligations anymore than an undisclosed intention not to perform.

The implied terms were read into the parties' contract, then, because they effectuated the parties' legitimate purposes, and maintaining equality was regarded as one of these purposes. The parties wanted the implied terms in the sense—though only in the sense—that a person who buys a car wants a camshaft even though he has never heard of one: he wants whatever the car must have to make it do what it is supposed to do.

Writers in the Aristotelian tradition thereby avoided the difficulties of modern theorists who explain contractual obligations by autonomy or consent. The implied terms are obligations to which the parties never consciously consented. As Richard Craswell has pointed out, theories based on autonomy are not useful in explaining what these terms should be. Any set of them seems consistent with the parties' freedom to choose the terms to which they expressly consent.[91] Indeed, Charles Fried seems to concede as much. He claims that because a court reads them into the contract by asking what the parties might have done, or what reasonable people might have done, or what is fair, no one should make 'the futile attempt to bring these cases under the promise principle'.[92] As his critics have noted, his principle therefore cannot explain most of contract law.[93]

To do so, other writers have tried to stretch the idea of autonomy or consent to make it the source of implied terms. Conrad Johnson believes that autonomy merely requires that 'the parties must have a fair opportunity to find out what risks they are accepting'.[94] But to have such an opportunity merely means that the parties could have exercised their autonomy, not that they did.

Randy Barnett has admitted that by his theory, if parties have no subjective intent, then their intentions will be satisfied equally by any default rule. But he believes that

[90] Grotius, *De iure belli ac pacis*, II.xii.2.1.
[91] Craswell, 'Contract Law, Default Rules, and the Philosophy of Promising', 514–29.
[92] Fried, *Contract as Promise*, 60, 61, 63, 69.
[93] Eisenberg, 'Theory of Contracts', 279; C. D. Johnson, 'Idea of Autonomy and the Foundations of Contractual Liberty', *L. & Phil.* 2 (1983), 271 at 300.   [94] Johnson, 'Idea of Autonomy', 300–2.

the parties can have expectations that never come to consciousness. The parties' 'subjective consent' is most likely satisfied by a default rule that conforms to 'commonsense or conventional expectations that likely are part of the tacit assumptions of particular parties'.[95] But the body of law that determines what terms govern a contract is vast. It includes most of the law of leases, sales, partnerships and so forth. As Feinman and Eisenberg have noted, most businessmen are ignorant of it.[96] This body of law may not contradict commonsense expectations, but to say it conforms to them is to imagine that the parties have implausibly precise expectations about matters that they never considered.

David Charny has also admitted that with implied terms, 'the principle of autonomy that requires courts to honor parties, choice is simply not in play'. He believes the court should consult 'other principles of autonomy' such as 'the fair sharing of gains and losses not allocated by prior agreement'.[97] But at that point, the terms are said to be autonomous because they are fair, not because they are chosen autonomously.

With the Aristotelian approach there is no need to pretend the parties know law anymore than the car buyer knows engineering. If the implied terms are a means to purposes which the parties have consciously in mind and which the law respects, then the parties would want them, just as a car buyer would want a camshaft even if he has never heard of one. But the reason for reading in the terms, or including the camshaft, is not to respect the will of the parties on a matter they have never considered. It is to help them achieve an end that they have considered.

IV. The Battle of the Forms as a Problem of Implied Terms[98]

It sometimes happens that one party sends another a proposal for a contract on certain terms and conditions and the other party sends a reply in which he assents but on different terms or conditions. In some jurisdictions, including the United States, England and Germany, it was traditionally held that no contract was formed because the acceptance did not match the offer. Indeed, the acceptance counted as a new offer on different terms which the original offeror might accept or reject. If he sent a new copy of his original document, he had rejected the new offer and reinstated his own. If he began to perform without doing so, he was deemed to have accepted the other party's terms. Because the party to send the last document before performance began obtained a contract on his own terms, this solution was known as the 'last shot fired' rule, or, in Germany, as the *Theorie des letzten Wortes*.

---

[95] Randy E. Barnett, 'The Sound of Silence: Default Rules and Contractual Consent', *Va. L. Rev.* 78 (1992), 821 at 876–7.   [96] Feinman, 'Contract Theory', 1206; Eisenberg, 'Theory of Contracts', 249.

[97] David Charny, 'Hypothetical Bargains: The Normative Structure of Contract Interpretation', *Mich. L. Rev.* 89 (1991), 1815 at 1833.

[98] In writing this section, I have been helped enormously by the work done by Giesela Rühl in a paper written under my sponsorship but containing entirely her own research and ideas. She has published it as 'The Battle of the Forms: Comparative and Economic Observations', *U. Pa. J. Int'l Econ. L.* 14 (2003), 189.

This is still the approach of English law. It was questioned by Lord Denning in *Butler Machine Tool Co, Ltd.* v. *Ex-Cell-O Corp. Ltd.*[99] He argued:

Sometimes the battle is won by the man who fires the last shot. He is the man who puts forward the latest terms and conditions; and if they are not objected to by the other party, he may be taken to have agreed to them. . . . In some cases the battle is won by the man who gets the blow in first. If he offers to sell at a named price on the terms and conditions stated on the back; and the buyer orders the goods purporting to accept the offer—on an order form with his own different terms and conditions on the back: then if the difference is so material that it would affect the price, the buyer ought not to be allowed to take advantage of the difference unless he draws it specifically to the attention of the seller. There are yet other cases where the battle depends on the shots fired on both sides. There is a concluded contract but the forms vary. The terms and conditions of both parties are to be construed together. If they can be reconciled so as to give an harmonious result, all well and good. If the differences are irreconcilable—so that they are mutually contradictory—then the conflicting terms have to be scrapped and replaced by a reasonable implication.

Nevertheless, his view was rejected by the majority of the court in *Butler Machine Tool Co.* and in a number of British decisions since.[100]

In France, there is a dispute among comparative lawyers as to what rule the courts are following. Arthur von Mehren believes that they apply the last shot rule except in rare cases in which a deviation is deemed unessential.[101] Giesela Rühl believes that they follow a 'knock-out' rule in which the conflicting terms are ignored and the contract is interpreted as though it did not contain them.[102] French commentators have said little about the problem.

The disagreement between von Mehren and Rühl seems to be due to the fact that they are looking at different cases. Rühl cites many in which French courts have said that conflicting terms cancel each other out, most of them dealing with a seller's reservation of property rights until he is paid[103] or with choice of jurisdiction.[104] She notes one exception in which the first party prevailed because he had a choice of jurisdiction clause in large letters on the front of his form while the second had his in small type buried among other terms of sale.[105] Von Mehren, in contrast, quotes the case comment to a decision in which there was held to be no contract when the buyer added a condition to his acceptance that he receive a loan from a third party of

---

[99] [1979] 1 WLR 401, 404–5.

[100] *Zambia Steel & Building Supplies Ltd.* v. *James Clark & Eaton, Ltd.* [1986], 2 Lloyd's Rep 225 (arbitration clause); *Muirhead* v. *Industrial Tank Specialties, Ltd.* [1986] QB 507 (clause excluding liability for consequential damages); *O.T.M., Ltd.* v. *Hydranautics* [1981] 2 Lloyd's Rep 211 (choice of law clause).

[101] Arthur von Mehren, 'The "Battle of the Forms": A Comparative View', *Am. J. of Comp. L.* 38 (1990), 265 at 274.   [102] Rühl, 'The Battle of the Forms', 205.

[103] Cass. comm., 25 Oct. 1994, Bull. civ. IV, no. 316, p. 256; Cass. comm, 12 July 1994, Bull. Civ. IV, no. 268, p. 213.

[104] Cass. comm., 20 Nov. 1984, Bull. civ. IV, no. 313, p. 253; Cass. 2e ch. civ. 16 Nov. 1961, D.J.429; Cass. comm., 7 Nov. 1956, Bull. civ. III, no. 280, p. 241; Trib. Comm. Lille, 19 Nov. 1956, D. 1957.Somm.99; Angers, 9 Jan. 1952, D. 1952, J.404.

[105] Cass. comm, 29 Oct. 1964, Gaz. Pal. 1965.Jur.45. She also mentions, as a possible second exception, a case in which the seller's offer reserved title until payment and the buyer's acceptance rejected such a provision. The court gave judgment for the buyer, as it would under the last shot rule, although the reason it gave was that the seller knew of the buyer's reservation. Cass. comm., 11 July 1995, Bull. civ. IV, no. 211, p. 197.

120,000 F.[106] Jean Chevalier, the author of the comment, suggests that von Mehren is right: the court will not recognize a contract when it regards the discrepancy between offer and acceptance as 'essential'.[107] The cases cited by Rühl suggest that very often it will not.

Germany and the United States have both moved from a 'last shot' rule toward a 'knock out' rule but in each case the move has been complicated by the effort to weave around a statute. In Germany, the statute is § 150(2) which provides: 'An acceptance with amplifications, limitations or other alterations is deemed a rejection coupled with a new offer'. With rare exceptions,[108] German courts concluded that no contract was concluded unless the terms of the offer and the acceptance were the same.[109] Therefore, the party to make the last offer prevailed.

In 1973, the German high court for civil matters, the *Bundesgerichtshof*, held that the formation of a contract could be inferred from the parties' behavior despite a variation between offer and acceptance although it left the implications of this inference unclear.[110] It based this decision on the vague requirement of § 242 of the Civil Code that a contract be performed in 'good faith'. In 1980 the *Oberlandesgericht* or Court of Appeal of Cologne drew the conclusion that when the parties' terms are in agreement, they will be accepted, but when they are not, the court will read in the terms that would be implied in such a contract absent such an agreement. It reasoned that one could not infer from the fact that a party began to perform that he accepted the other party's terms. He may merely have wished not to create difficulties—an intention that the other party may have had as well since he did not seek clarification.[111] In 1985, this approach was accepted by the *Bundesgerichtshof.*[112]

In the United States, the statutory obstacle was § 2-207 of the Uniform Commercial Code. Paragraph 1 of that section provides that a 'definite and seasonable acceptance . . . operates as an acceptance even though it states terms additional to or different from those offered or agreed upon, unless the acceptance is expressly made conditional on assent to the additional or different terms'. In some cases, the parties were so far from reaching agreement that courts have held there was no 'definite and seasonable acceptance': for example when the parties have expressly quarreled over whether a sale should be 'as is where is' or FOB (freight on board),[113] or when the offer and acceptance call for the sale of a different number of vehicles.[114] Where there is such an acceptance, however, paragraph 2 provides that, as between merchants, the 'additional' terms become part of the contract unless they are material alternations or unless the offeror objects or has limited acceptance to his own terms. The unfortunate result is that, unless either party has insisted on his own terms, all material variations are resolved in favor of the offeror. While the old common law favored the party who fired the last shot, this solution favors the one who fired first. If the old solution is irrational, the new one seems equally so.

---

[106] Cass. comm., 17 July 1967, Bull. civ., no. 299, p. 286.

[107] Jean Chevalier, Case Comment to Cass. comm., 17 July 1967, Bull. civ., no. 299, p. 286 in Rev. trim. dr. civ. 66 (1968), 707 at 708.

[108] BGH, 24 Mar. 1963, NJW 1248 (1963); BGH, 35 June 1957, BB 728 (1957).

[109] BGH, 17 Sept. 1954, BB 882 (1954).   [110] BGH, 26 Sept. 1973, EBGHZ 61, 282.

[111] Cologne, 19 Mar. 1980, BB 1980, 1237.   [112] BGH, 20 Mar. 1985, NJW 1985, 1838.

[113] *Koehring* v. *Glowacki*, 253 NW2d 64 (Wis 1977).

[114] *Columbia Hyundai, Inc.* v. *Carll Hyundai, Inc.*, 484 SE2d 468 (SC 1997).

Courts have escaped by finding ways to bring contracts within paragraph 3 of § 2-207. It provides that '[c]onduct by both parties which recognizes the existence of a contract' establishes one 'although the writings of the parties do not otherwise establish a contract'. It is difficult to see to what situation this provision could apply. At any rate, if a contract falls within paragraph 3, then its terms are 'those . . . on which the writings of the parties agree, together with any supplementary terms incorporated under any other provisions of this act' (that is, the sales provisions of the Uniform Commercial Code). In order to escape paragraph 2 and apply paragraph 3, courts have seized on the fact that paragraph 2 speaks of 'additional' terms, whereas paragraph 1 provides that a contract can be formed when terms are 'additional . . . or different'. That has been taken to mean that when terms are 'different' rather than 'additional', a court can apply article 3.[115] Whether a court regards a term as 'different' rather than 'additional' seems to depend, not on any real distinction between two kinds of terms, but on whether the court wants to apply paragraph 3. In *Dorton* v. *Collins & Aikman Corp.*,[116] the court applied article 3 even though one of the conflicting terms was implied rather than express. According to paragraph 1, a contract will not arise if 'acceptance is expressly made conditional on assent to the additional or different terms'. Nevertheless, courts have cut off this avenue of escape. In *Diamond Fruit Growers, Inc.* v. *Krack Corp.*,[117] an acceptance included such a clause. The court held that it merely entitled the offeree to refuse to enter into a contract if his terms were not accepted. But if, instead of refusing, he acted as though a contract had been concluded, then he was bound, and on terms prescribed by the rule of paragraph 3.

The 'knock out' rule has also been adopted by article 2.22 of the Unidroit Principles of International Commercial Contracts.

The 'last shot' rule was widely accepted when will theories were popular, and some scholars have suggested that it was an expression of such theories.[118] I have a different view. In the 19th and early 20th centuries, jurists were not only fond of will theories; they also liked rules with hard edges on them. There is a tension in every legal system between rules that are more equitable and those that are more precise. When the 'last shot' rule was adopted, jurists had a definite preference for the more precise. One can still see that preference in many areas of English law, for example, in the reluctance of English courts to adopt general principles of unconscionability and good faith. That is the best explanation of why they cling to the 'last shot' rule.

If one were simply to look at the matter from the standpoint of the parties' will, however, one would have to ask to what terms the parties actually agreed to be bound. P. S. Atiyah has accurately diagnosed the problem. When the parties start to perform, although they have not agreed on a single set of terms, they have in fact agreed on a contract but not on what all the terms of the contract should be.[119] If we wish to enforce what they have agreed upon, we will enforce their contract subject to the terms which can reasonably be implied in it. In this sense, the knock out rule does not contradict the will theory or any other theory by which contracts are entered into by

---

[115] *Gardner Zemke Co.* v. *Dunham Bush, Inc.*, 850 P2d 319 (NM 1993).
[116] 453 F2d 1161 (6th Cir 1972).   [117] 794 F2d 1440 (9th Cir 1986).
[118] von Mehren, 'The Battle of the Forms', 269.
[119] P. S. Atiyah, *An Introduction to the Law of Contract* (5th edn., Oxford, 1995), 69–70.

consent. Indeed, it is a consequence of the principle that the parties are bound to what they assented and to what can be read into their contract on the basis of their assent. Viewed in this way, the 'battle of the forms' is simply the problem of deciding what terms to apply when the parties have contracted without reaching agreement on them.

As the knock out rule is sometimes stated, however, it treats terms as though conflict did not exist. These terms may be evidence of a type of unfairness which the drafter was trying to avoid. Of course, the drafter might have inserted a term simply because he was trying to give his client every possible advantage. But he might have been motivated by a legitimate desire to place risks and burdens on the party by whom they can most easily be borne. A court should ask whether that is true. The fact that the drafter included such a term suggests that it might be. After all, it might be that the default rule which is read into a contract when the parties have made no provision at all might be unfair in the context of a particular contract. By this approach, conflicting terms are neither simply accepted nor simply knocked out. They are considered as suggestions as to what fair terms would be.

A court which takes this approach has moved toward what Giesela Rühl has called a 'best shot rule'. By this approach, the judge would decide which of the conflicting documents contains the best terms. The best terms, in her view, are those that are most efficient. That document will govern in its entirety and the terms of the other proposal will be ignored. Consequently, the parties will have an incentive to draft the best terms.[120] As explained earlier, I believe that the terms that are fair are those that the law and economics scholars call 'efficient': they are the terms that will place risks and burdens on the party best able to bear them. Thus the principal difference between my approach and that of Rühl is that she believes only one of the parties' documents should prevail—the one with the best terms—and the other should be ignored. But that would lead a judge to enforce a term which he believes is somewhat unfair (or inefficient) because his only choice would be to enforce one he believes is still more unfair (or inefficient). It would also lead the parties to gamble on just how far they could deviate from a truly fair (or efficient) term without losing the game to the other side. In short, I think the judge should resolve the battle of the forms just as he would the problem of implied terms: by reading in those which are most fair. Only, he should accept the parties' documents as suggestions as to what these fair terms might be.

V. Offer and Acceptance as a Problem of Commutative Justice in Exchange

The late scholastics and northern natural lawyers discussed the question of whether an offer is binding without an acceptance without reference to the problem of equality in exchange. According to Covarruvias, Molina, and Soto,[121] all offers were binding because all promises were offers, and all promises were binding. By way of exception, promises of exchange were not binding until the other party accepted but that was

---

[120] Rühl, 'The Battle of the Forms', 221–2.

[121] Didacus Covarruvias, *Variarum ex iure pontificio, regio et caesareo Resolutionum* (Lyons, 1568), p. 2, § 2, no. ult., § 4, no. 6; Soto, *De iustitia et iure*, lib. 3, q. 5, art. 3; Molina, *De iustitia et iure*, disp. 263.

because they created a mutual obligation and hence required mutual assent. Lessius disagreed.[122] He thought that the promisor intended the promisor's acceptance to be the sine qua non condition for there to be a binding obligation. Grotius endorsed Lessius' position, and was followed by Pufendorf, Barbeyrac, and Pothier.[123]

The late scholastics spent little time, however, discussing the moment at which consent became effective. Lessius suggested that in the case of an exchange, it was effective at the moment the offeror learned of the acceptance because that is the moment at which the offeror would want to be bound.[124]

The 19th century will theorists agreed that an offer needed an acceptance but for a different reason. They defined contract as a concord of wills, a two-sided juristic act (*Rechtsgeschäft*) or an accepted offer. It followed by definition that an offer required an acceptance for there to be a binding contract. In England and the United States, this argument was made by Kent, William Story, Parsons, Metcalf, Leake, Hammon, and Anson.[125] In France, it was made by Aubry and Rau, Demolombe, Larombière, and Laurent.[126] In Germany, it was made by Brinz, Puchta, and Windscheid.[127]

The trouble was that nothing in the definition suggested at what moment an acceptance would be effective so that an offer could not be effectively revoked. Some jurists argued the acceptance was effective on dispatch; some that it was effective on receipt.

Eventually, in England, the United States, Germany, and France, solutions were worked out pragmatically that had little relationship to any straightforward application of the jurists' theories. What they had in common was that they gave considerable protection to the offeree who tried to accept an offer which, unbeknownst to him, the offeror had already attempted to revoke. In England and the United States, courts had arrived at such a solution before the will theorists had attempted to resolve the problem: offers were effective on receipt but acceptances were effective on dispatch.

---

[122] Lessius, *De iustitia et iure*, lib. 2, cap. 18, dub. 6.

[123] Grotius, *De iure belli ac pacis*, II.xi.14; Pufendorf, *De iure naturae ac gentium*, III.vi.15; Jean Barbeyrac, *Le Droit de la nature et des gens*, no. 10 to III.vi.15; Robert Pothier, *Traité des obligations*, § 4, in *Oeuvres de Pothier* (M. Bugnet, ed., 2nd edn., Paris, 1861).

[124] Lessius, *De iustitia et iure*, lib. 2, cap. 18, dub. 6.

[125] James Kent, *Commentaries on American Law* (2 13th edn., Boston, 1884), *477; William Wentworth Story, *The Law of Contracts Not Under Seal* (Boston, 1851), 370; Theophilus Parsons, *The Law of Contracts* (1 Boston, 1860), *399; Theron Metcalf, *Principles of the Law of Contracts* (New York, 1878), 14; S. Martin Leake, *Elements of the Law of Contracts* (London, 1867), 12; Louis Hammon, *General Principles of the Law of Contract* (St Paul, Minn., 1912), 38; William Anson, *Principles of the English Law of Contract* (A. G. Guest, ed., 26th edn., London, 1984), 13. Pollock was one of the few to point out that contract did not need to be defined that way. The law could make a promise binding without mutual assent as it did in the case of promises made by deed. Sir Frederick Pollock, *Principles of Contract: Being a Treatise on the General Principles concerning the Validity of Agreements in the Law of England* (4th edn., London, 1885), 6–7, 9. Nevertheless, he fell back into the same tautology he had criticized: 'before acceptance there is no agreement, and therefore the proposer cannot be bound to do anything' (ibid. 23).

[126] Charles Aubry and Charles Rau, *Cours de droit civil français après la méthode de Zachariae* (4 4th edn., Paris, 1869–71), § 343; Charles Demolombe, *Cours de Code Napoléon* (24 Paris, 1854–82), § 45; Léobon Larombière, *Théorie et pratique des obligations ou commentaire des titres III & IV, livre III du Code Napoléon art. 1101 à 1386* (1 Paris, 1857), 6–7; François Laurent, *Principes de droit civil français* (15 3rd edn., Paris, 1869–78), §§ 468–9.

[127] Alois Brinz and Philipp Lotmar, *Lehrbuch der Pandekten* (4 2nd edn., Erlangen, 1892), § 571; Georg Friedrich Puchta, *Pandekten* (2nd edn., Leipzig, 1844), § 250; Bernhard Windscheid, *Lehrbuch des Pandektenrechts* (2 7th edn., Frankfurt-am-Main, 1891), §§ 304–5.

An acceptance was held to be effective when mailed in *Adams* v. *Lindsell* in 1818.[128] The effect of this rule was to protect the offeree who now knew he had a contract as soon as he mailed his acceptance. But it was a difficult result for the will theorists to explain. Some made the artificial argument that, by mailing an offer, the offeror had made the post office his agent, and therefore, receipt of the acceptance was receipt by the offeror.[129] Christopher Columbus Langdell claimed that, in theory, a contract could not be made until each party had communicated his will to the other, and therefore the acceptance had to be actually received. The law was simply wrong. He acknowledged 'it has been claimed that the purposes of substantial justice, and the interests of the contracting parties as understood by themselves, will be best served' if acceptances are effective on dispatch. 'The true answer to this argument', he said, 'is that it is irrelevant'.[130]

In Germany, the jurist Ferdinand Regelsberger made a self-conscious attempt to provide the offeree with a similar protection with arguments that contemporary will theorists could accept. He claimed that an offer should be irrevocable even if the promisor did not expressly promise to keep it open since a promise to do so was implied in the offer. This implied promise was itself an offer which the offeree was deemed to accept as soon as he learned of it.[131] As a result, the offeree was protected. His revocation was effective only upon receipt but the offeror could not revoke the offer before receiving it. Again, he knew as soon as his revocation was mailed that he had a contract. This solution was adopted by § 145 of the German Civil Code which provided that offers are irrevocable unless the offeror expressly reserves the right to revoke. Like Regelsberger, the drafters spoke of an implied promise to keep the offer open. Nevertheless, like Regelsberger, they acknowledged that they were trying to protect the offeree, who must be able to count on a contract arising when he on his side makes a timely acceptance of the offer.'[132]

In France, despite decades of argument among jurists, whether a contract has been formed by the acceptance of an offer is regarded as a question of fact to be determined according to the particular circumstances. Yet the result can often be to give the offeree the same kind of protection he is afforded in England, Germany, and the United States.[133] An offeror has been held obligated to give the offeree a reasonable time to consider the offer. For example, an offeree was entitled to accept an offer of employment when 'a delay of only nine days occurred between the receipt by the employee of his offer of employment and its revocation by the employer'.[134]

Today, with the will theories in disfavor, more attention has been paid to the question of why the offeree should be able to know, when he sends his acceptance, that

---

[128] 3 Barn & Ald 681, 106 Eng Rep 250 (1818).

[129] *Household Fire & Carriage Acc. Ins. Co.* v. *Grant*, 4 Ex Div 216 (1879); described in E. Allan Farnsworth, *Contracts* (3rd edn. New York, 1999), § 3.22.

[130] Christopher Columbus Landell, *A Summary of the Law of Contracts* (2nd edn., Boston, 1880), 15, 20–1. [131] Ferdinand Regelsberger, *Die Vorverhandlungen* (1 Weimar, 1868), § 13.

[132] *Motive zu dem Entwurfe eines Bürgerliches Gesetzbuches für das Deutsche Reich* (1 Berlin, 1888), 165–6.

[133] e.g. Cass., ch. soc., 22 Mar. 1972, D.S. 1972.468 (The lower court was correct 'in finding... that this delay [in acceptance by the offeree] did not exceed the time for reflection and response which—in the absence of a fixed time period—the company was required to give [him]).

[134] Cass., ch. soc., 22 Mar. 1972, D.S.1972.468.

the offer has not previously been withdrawn. Beth Eisler believes he should not be: he thereby obtains an 'unexpected and unbargained-for protection'.[135]

Ian Macneil thinks this protection is warranted because the offeror's conduct when he revokes is 'somewhat undesirable'.[136] He does not explain why, if offers are legally revocable, the law should deem it undesirable to revoke them.

Others have said that the offeree, relying on the existence of the contract, should be immediately able to begin performing.[137] But then, it would seem, the offeree should be protected only when he is supposed to perform first and it is desirable that he start right away. Allan Farnsworth has suggested that he may not be able to prove he has relied.[138] But American law requires that he prove reliance in other contexts such as in applying the doctrine of promissory estoppel. And suppose it is clear that he has not relied?

Nevertheless, I believe that the key to the problem is an insight which Farnsworth provides in dealing with the problem of whether a party who has already mailed his acceptance should be bound if, before the offeror receives the acceptance, he notifies the offeror that he has changed his mind and does not wish to accept. Farnsworth and the *Second Restatement of Contracts* take the position that the offeree should be bound by his acceptance as of the moment it is dispatched since otherwise there will be a period of time when the offeror is bound—if the offeree so chooses—but the offeree can escape by revoking his acceptance before it arrives. 'In effect, the offeree has an option contract during that time, and, although, the offeror is bound, the offeree can speculate by watching the market and deciding whether to send an overtaking rejection or withdrawal'.[139] American case law is divided,[140] and it may well be that a court would want to disregard the *Restatement* rule when there is no likelihood that the offeree was speculating at the offeror's expense. But the principle is one which we have seen before: in general, it is unfair for one party to be bound when the other has the opportunity to look for a better deal.

That principle can explain the protection normally accorded the offeree. When the two parties cannot come to an agreement simultaneously, one must wait until he hears from the other. That party is bound *de facto* when the other party is not. He must wait to hear before he can accept another proposition. The question is which way to minimize the unfairness: by placing this burden on the offeror or on the offeree.

The fairest rule is to place the burden on the offeror, whether this is done, as in England and the United States, by holding acceptances effective on dispatch, or as in Germany, by holding offers irrevocable in principle, or in France, by giving the offeree a reasonable time to consider the offer. The reason is that a party does not have to be an offeror unless he chooses. He can indicate his interest in certain terms and ask

---

[135] Beth A. Eisler, 'Default Rules for Contract Formation by Promise and the Need for Revision of the Mailbox Rule', *Ky. L. J.*79 (1990–1), 557 at 566.

[136] Ian R. Macneil, 'Time of Acceptance: Too Many Problems for a Single Rule', *U. Pa. L. Rev.* 112 (1964), 947 at 953.   [137] This explanation is described by Farnsworth, *Contracts*, § 3.22.

[138] ibid.   [139] ibid. *See Restatement (Second) of Contracts*, § 63 cmt. c.

[140] Compare *Morrison v. Theolke*, 155 So2d 889, 905 (Fla Dist Ct App 1963) (holding invalid attempted revocation of mailed acceptance, with *G.C. Casebolt v. United States*, 421 F2d 710, 714 (Ct Cl 1970) (arguing that no contract was formed when the United States retrieved its accceptance of a bid from the mail before delivery).

the other party to make an offer. Even if he makes an offer himself, he can protect himself in many jurisdictions by indicating that the offer will lapse unless the acceptance is actually received by a specified time[141] or in Germany by indicating that his offer is revocable.[142] If the offeror protects himself in none of these ways, it is reasonable to assume that the risk of having to wait for a response is smaller for him than for the offeree. He had the chance to protect himself against this risk and did not take it.

The rules of offer and acceptance are thus a sensible way to minimize the unfairness of leaving one party free while the other is bound or, as the late scholastics would say, of avoiding a violation of commutative justice. Lessius was perfectly correct that the offeror would prefer not to be bound until he hears from the offeree. But someone has to run the risk of waiting to hear. Lessius failed to consider that while an offer is merely a promise, it is a legal act which carries the consequence that it empowers the offeree to make a binding contract. Like other legal acts, it should be subject to rules which promote commutative justice.

[141] *Restatement (Second) of Contracts*, §§ 36(2), 41(1), 60.
[142] BGB § 145.

18

Liability for Breach of Contract

I. Remedies

We saw earlier why the parties may have wished the promisee to have a right to full performance.[1] In those cases, he should be able to demand it. The promisor could have at least three good reasons for binding himself to make a gift. First, he may rightly believe that his present decision to make the gift is more likely to be a good one than a future decision not to make it. His present decision is generous and sensible, he may believe, and the future decision is more likely to reflect greed than good sense. Second, he may rightly believe that conferring a right on the promisee is more consistent with the kind of relationship he wants with him. Eisenberg has noted that to confer such a right may be inconsistent with a relationship of love and trust between the parties.[2] But the converse may be true. Parents might give their adult children a house or bonds rather than merely letting them live in a house or endorsing over interest payments seriatim because they want the children to be independent rather than always beholden to them. Sometimes parents can effectuate such a purpose only if the law permits them to create a right in the children which does not depend on whether the parents have changed their mind or the children have relied. Third, though less likely, the promisor might know the promisee does not trust him to perform absent a legal obligation and may wish to set his mind at rest.

In an exchange, as Melvin Eisenberg has noted, the promisee may want the right to require performance, or a sum reflecting the value to him of performance, in order to lock in a favorable bargain.[3] As we have seen, he might want to do so for three reasons, each of which the law should respect. First, he might regard the performance he is to receive as unique, as one he is not likely to receive elsewhere at the same price. Second, even if the performance is not unique, he may wish to lock in a price for fear of receiving a less favorable price if he waits or shops around. Third, there may be some uncertainty about the characteristics of the performance in the minds of the parties. The parties may wish to agree on a price that discounts that uncertainty. In the end, one party will have paid either more or less than he would if the truth had been known in advance, but each is willing to take his chances. Such an arrangement requires that the loser cannot renege if he happens to lose.

---

[1] Chapter 13 III B 1.

[2] Melvin A. Eisenberg, 'The Theory of Contracts', in Peter Benson, ed., *A Theory of Contract Law: New Essays* (Cambridge, 2001), 206 at 230. [3] Eisenberg, 'Theory of Contracts', 279.

The remedy the promisee should receive should correspond to the guarantee he was given and the reason it was given. It should ensure that he receives the benefits that the parties envisioned he was to obtain from this guarantee. That is a fair result for the reasons we have seen in discussing contracts of gift and exchange.

A law and economics scholar should be the first to doubt it is an efficient result since they regard whatever the parties agree upon as of benefit *ex ante* to the parties. Nevertheless, although Richard Craswell mentions Barnett's claim that by making a promise the promisor is conferring a right on the promisee, that fact alone is not a sufficient justification for enforcing a promise in either of the two economic theories which he presents. According to the first theory, 'promise as performance', 'enforcing a promise is efficient just in case performing the promised action would be efficient'. 'For example, if A has promised to sell her car to B for $6000, this theory rests the efficiency of enforcing A's promise on the efficiency (or likely efficiency) of actually exchanging A's car for B's $6000.'[4] What is missed here is that the initial agreement might be, not merely a car for $6000, but a car and a commitment not to renege in exchange for $6000 and a commitment not to renege. If so, part of the exchange took place (and in that sense was 'performed') at the very moment the agreement was made: a commitment was given for a commitment. Since 'efficiency' is judged *ex ante*, as of the moment it is made, this exchange is 'efficient' even though one party may later regret it, just as 'actually exchanging A's car for B's $6000' is 'efficient', even though one party later regrets having done so. The second theory is concerned with incentives: 'enforcing the promise is efficient just in case the new set of incentives is, on balance, efficient'.[5] But as before, 'efficiency', for an economist, should be judged *ex ante* at the moment of the transaction. If, in return for whatever the promisee is to give, the promisor is content to give the promisee the right to require performance, then the transaction is 'efficient'. It is 'efficient' whether or not each party's judgment that he is better off is based on reflections about who is thereby given an incentive to do what.

Some law and economics scholars, such as Richard Posner, have gone further and spoken of an 'efficient breach' of contract. But if the promisor was content to give the promisee the right to require performance, there can be no such thing as an 'efficient breach', at least as such a breach is usually described. Suppose A agrees to sell something to B for a certain price and then discovers that C will pay much more for it than B ever would, and indeed, more than the expectation damages B will suffer if the contract is breached. According to Posner, it is 'efficient' for A to breach his contract with B, pay B damages sufficient to compensate B, and then sell to C. A and C are better off, and B is no worse off. Admittedly, C could have contacted B and asked him to resell. If C and B did not know of each other's existence, A, for a finder's fee, could have offered to provide the necessary information. But resale, according to Posner, 'would have introduced an additional step, with additional transactions costs'.[6] One can raise questions about the significance of these 'transactions costs'. Posner acknowledges that, if B resells, 'litigation costs would be reduced'. But he expects transaction

    [4] Richard Craswell, 'Two Economic Theories of Enforcing Promises', in Benson, *Theory of Contract Law*, 19, 20.   [5] ibid. 20.
    [6] Richard Posner, *Economic Analysis of Law* (6th edn., New York, 2003), 120.

costs to be 'high...because it would be a bilateral monopoly negotiation'.[7] But if A sells to C there will be a bilateral monopoly negotiation. In the hypothetical case Posner uses to illustrate 'efficient breach', A tamely accepts C's initial offer.[8] But A is no more likely to do so than B. Moreover, it is not clear why a bilateral monopoly negotiation has such high transaction costs, given that the parties have an incentive to minimize them. For purposes of argument, however, I will assume throughout that transaction costs are significant.

We can see the difficulty of speaking of an 'efficient breach' if we ask, as before, whether the parties themselves understood that B would have the right to require performance. If not, A is not in breach since he is entitled to renege. If so, then if A sells to C, he is in breach. But in that case, the breach cannot be 'efficient' since 'efficiency' must be judged *ex ante* as of the moment that A and B contracted, and at that moment, A gave B the right to require performance.

Indeed, the parties would typically want B to have this right whenever goods are unique: for example, an oriental rug, a race horse, or a Fragonard. B may be buying, at least in part, with an eye to resale. Even if he is not, both parties understand that after B takes title, B will have the right to resell. Otherwise, they would provide for A to retain title. Presumably, the reason the contract gives B this right is that it is more valuable to him than it is to A, and sufficiently more valuable to offset whatever extra costs will be incurred if B does the reselling. B may think it more likely that he can resell to someone like C, or resell sooner, or for more money, or B may be better positioned to run that risk. Indeed, if he is buying the object to use it himself, his cost of holding it for possible resale may be almost nothing. Consequently, it is hard to see why B should lose the right to resell if C appears on the scene early on, after the contract is made but before title has passed. For that matter, it is hard to see why it should matter, from the standpoint of efficiency, when title passes. It matters legally: once title passes, there cannot be an 'efficient breach' since A cannot sell to C. Or do we need a doctrine of 'efficient conversion'? But in some legal systems, title passes when the agreement is made, and so A could not sell to C at all. In others it passes when B takes possession. But even in these systems, can it really be that A should be able to sell to C if B bought the object without taking possession, but that A should not if B took possession and then asked A to keep the object for him for one more day?

It is understandable, then, that when goods are unique, common and civil law courts do not allow the promisor to escape by paying expectation damages. They require him to perform. They do so even though the doctrines they apply sound very different. In common law jurisdictions, specific performance is granted, in principle, only if a damage remedy is inadequate.[9] In Germany, in principle, the plaintiff always has the right to insist that the defendant perform although he may sue instead for damages if he wishes.[10] In France, he can only demand damages.[11] Nevertheless, when

---

[7] Richard Posner, *Economic Analysis of Law*, 120.   [8] ibid.

[9] See *Restatement (Second) of Contracts*, § 359(1) (1979).

[10] German Civil Code (*Bürgerlichesgesetzbuch*) [hereinafter BGB], § 241. Section 243 says that he must do so even when the performance is generic goods.

[11] This is said to be the effect of French Civil Code (*Code civil*), art. 1142 ('Toute obligation de faire ou de ne pas faire se résout en dommages et intérêts en cas d'inexécution de la part du débiteur').

goods and services are unique, courts in common law jurisdictions grant specific performance because a damage remedy is inadequate. German courts simply order the defendant to perform. French courts force him to perform by *astreinte*, that is, by threatening to award large damages if he does not.[12] No one allows him to resell the goods to someone else and escape by paying expectation damages. That is appropriate because, as we have seen, when goods are unique, the parties would typically want the seller to be obligated to perform, and not merely to pay expectation damages.

We have been speaking, however, only about unique goods and only then about what is typical. Suppose the parties did want the seller or provider of a service to be able to renege on his obligation to perform as long as he pays expectation damages. Could we then speak of an 'efficient breach'?

I don't think so. If the parties expressly provided that the seller or service provider may renege, then he is not in breach. He is doing what the contract permits.

Suppose they did not do so expressly. Perhaps they would have wished him to be able to do so under certain circumstances which they did not consider. We then have the legal problem we discussed in the previous chapter: what to do when new and unforeseen circumstances arise. As we will see, the doctrine of changed circumstances might sometimes relieve a party of his duty to perform. If so, however, the problem is not one of efficient breach but of changed circumstances. Moreover, the party who does not perform is not in breach. His duty to perform has been discharged.

As we have seen, the problem of changed circumstances is really one of implied terms, and has been addressed in a similar way both by law and economics scholars such as Posner, and by Aquinas and the late scholastics. Aquinas agreed with the medieval canon lawyers[13] that a party need not keep a promise when the circumstances are sufficiently different from those he envisioned. Just as laws are enacted to serve a purpose, and the law should not be followed when this purpose is not served by obeying it, so it is with contracts. This doctrine of relief for 'changed circumstances' was then borrowed and passed on by the natural lawyers,[14] and accepted by many modern legal systems. The approach of modern law and economics scholars is similar. They believe that the task for a court asked to interpret a contract to cover a contingency that the parties did not provide for is to imagine how the parties would have provided for the contingency if they had decided to do so. They would have agreed to put a risk or burden on the party who could bear it most cheaply.

In discussing the doctrines of impossibility and changed circumstances, Posner asks which party would find it easiest to bear the risk associated with these circumstances, for example, because he is in the best position to take precautions or to insure or self-insure against it.[15] Modern scholars such as Posner bring an economic precision to the analysis of what the parties would have done which is very helpful, and much

---

[12] Statutory authorization for this traditional practice was finally provided by the Law of 5 July 1972, now superseded by the Law of 9 July 1991. See generally François Terré, Philippe Simler, and Yves Lequette, *Droit civil: Les Obligations* (7th edn., Paris, 1999), §§ 1023–31.

[13] *Glossa ordinaria* to Gratian, *Decretum* (Venice, 1995), C. 22, q. 2, c. 14.

[14] Albeit with a hiatus in the 19th century. James Gordley, 'Contract in Pre-Commercial Societies and in Western History', chapter 2 of volume VII, *Contracts in General* (ed. Arthur von Mehren) of the *International Encyclopedia of Comparative Law* 31, 36–7 (Tübingen, 1997).

[15] Posner, *Economic Analysis*, 104–10.

appreciated even by people like me who disagree on other matters. But the ultimate question is the same: would the promisor have agreed to be bound under these circumstances had he anticipated them? According to Lessius, that is the same question as whether, had he done so, he would have agreed to give the promisee the right to require performance. If we suppose, then, that if the parties had considered the matter, they would have allowed the seller or service provider to renege while paying expectation damages, then, as Posner says, he should be able to do so. But there is no breach, and the reason is changed circumstances.

Posner has said that one cannot escape his conclusion that some breaches are 'efficient' by simply 'redefining the legal concept of breach of contract so that only inefficient terminations counted as breaches'.[16] His reason is that A should still be liable for B's expectation damages. The function of contract is to place such risks on the party who can most easily bear them. 'The breach of contract corresponds to the event that is insured against' when B entered into the contract.[17] A is therefore the proper one to bear that risk.

It is true that although courts may award damages when they give relief for changed circumstances,[18] they have not awarded expectation damages. It does not follow that they never should. Presumably, they should decide what, if anything, to award in the same way they decide whether to apply the doctrine at all: by asking what the parties would have done had they considered the matter. If, by hypothesis, the parties would have agreed that one of them could renege provided he paid expectation damages, then the court should award expectation damages.[19] If a court has not yet done so, the reason may be that such cases are unlikely to arise.

We can see why they are unlikely to arise by considering cases in which courts discharge obligations without awarding expectation damages: A rents B a theater for a performance, but the theater burns down before the performance is given; A gets laryngitis and cannot perform an engagement to B to sing; A's arm is paralyzed and he cannot personally perform his agreement to redo B's kitchen; A agrees to sell B the tomatoes he grows on a particular plot of farmland and the crop is destroyed; A agrees to sell B wine to be taken from a particular vat and the vat is destroyed. As I noted in the previous chapter,[20] I don't think it matters whether these cases are described as instances of 'impossibility' rather than 'changed circumstances'. Note that in some of these cases, the goods or services in question are unique (the theater, the singer), and in others the goods are fungible or the service could be performed by anyone else. In all of them, however, B does not recover expectation damages. If prices have risen or the delay has put him at a disadvantage in obtaining a substitute performance, he must simply pay more for a theater, a singer, a carpenter, the tomatoes, or the wine. He has lost the benefit of the bargain that he entered into the contract to ensure that he would have.

The reason, it would seem, is that, had the parties considered the matter, they would have wanted to place risks on the person who could best bear them. There is no

---

[16] Posner, *Economic Analysis*, 116.   [17] ibid.

[18] *Restatement (Second) of Contract*, § 272(2) ('the court may grant relief on such terms as justice requires...'). *See* Uniform Commercial Code, § 2–615 cmt. 6.   [19] Chapter 15 II.

[20] Chapter 15.

reason to think that A, in these examples, would be best able to bear every risk that might prevent B from getting what B contracted for. The chance events just described destroy A's ability to perform in the manner in which A contemplated. To make a substitute performance he will now have to perform in a manner which he did not contemplate. There is no reason to think he is better placed than B to bear the risks of doing so: for example, to bear the risk of a rise in the price of theaters, singers, carpenters, tomatoes, or wine. Therefore, B cannot demand to be placed where he would have been had performance been forthcoming. He cannot recover expectation damages.

Most cases of changed circumstances are like these. But one can imagine cases in which it would be appropriate to award expectation damages even if the duty to perform had been discharged. Perhaps the court should have done so in the Westinghouse litigation, described in the last chapter, had the case not been settled before trial.[21] Westinghouse had agreed to provide a continuing supply of uranium at a fixed price to fuel nuclear generators. The price of uranium then skyrocketed due to the Arab oil crisis. In the last chapter, I argued that the result should depend on whether Westinghouse would have to buy at the market price to fulfill its contract, and whether this price was so high that if the uranium were delivered, the buyers would not use it themselves. They would find it more profitable to resell. At the time they contracted, the buyers did not contemplate resale. They were merely seeking to ensure that their generators would run profitably. Indeed, under the circumstances they envisioned, they would have used the fuel and so could not have hoped to resell it. They were not like the buyers of an oriental rug, a race horse, or a Fragonard. Consequently, if these contracts were enforced, the buyers would receive a windfall that has no relation to the security they were seeking, and Westinghouse, if it has to buy the uranium on the market, would suffer a corresponding loss. In effect, this arrangement would amount to a wager. As we saw in the last chapter, we can be fairly confident that the parties would not have wanted to wager. Risk averse people do not.

But Westinghouse should be liable for the profits that the buyers would have made had they used the uranium in their generators. In the cases considered earlier, the party whose obligations were discharged could no longer perform in the manner he contemplated: by providing his own theater or services or tomatoes or wine from his own land or vat. There is no reason to think he would voluntarily have borne, or be the best person to bear, the risk of an increase in the price of houses, halls, services. tomatoes or wine. But in this case, Westinghouse has not lost its ability to insure the profits of generators insofar as they depend on the price of uranium. The contract was made to ensure that these profits would not be eaten up by an increase in the price of uranium. It would seem that, had the parties considered the matter, they would have decided that Westinghouse should be liable for these profits even though it need not deliver. If so, then Westinghouse should have to pay expectation damages. But the reason is changed circumstances, not efficient breach. And indeed, although the

---

[21] See generally Paul L. Joskow, 'Commercial Impossibility, the Uranium Market and the Westinghouse Case', *J. Leg. Stud.* 6 (1977), 119.

possibility that Westinghouse should have had to pay such damages has been widely discussed in the literature, everyone assumes the problem is one of changed circumstances, not of efficient breach.

To say the problem is one of changed circumstances is not to quarrel with Posner over terminology but to disagree over how the problem should be analyzed. One can see why by seeing how he analyzes his own hypothetical case. A seller agreed to deliver 100,000 'custom-ground widgets' for 10 cents apiece for use in the buyer's boiler factory. After he has delivered 10,000 to the buyer, a third party comes to him and 'explains that he desperately needs 25,000 custom-ground widgets at once, since otherwise he will be forced to close his pinola factory at great cost', and offers to pay 15 cents apiece. Seller sells him the widgets, causing the original buyer to lose $1,000 in profits, but making for himself an additional profit of $1,250. The principle supposedly illustrated is that the seller should refuse to perform if he can profit by the resale after paying damages: 'If [a party's profit from breach] would exceed...the expected profit to the other party from completion of the contract, and if damages are limited to the loss of that profit, there will be an incentive to commit a breach. But there should be.'[22]

Analyze the problem as one of changed circumstances, however, and what matters is not simply that the seller can pay damages and resell at a profit. Instead, it is critical that in Posner's case, certain circumstances were unforeseen: when the contract was made, the buyers did not contemplate resale. Indeed, under the circumstances they envisioned, they could not have hoped to resell the widgets which would have been incorporated in their machinery. Consequently, the case is not like the sale of an oriental rug, a race horse, or a Fragonard. We have none of the reasons we had in those cases for thinking the parties would want the buyer to have the right to require performance.

Since the parties did not envision resale, the doctrine of changed circumstances requires us to ask how they would have acted had they done so. In that respect, the case is like Westinghouse. But it is more difficult. Westinghouse, we assumed, would have had to buy the uranium which the owners of generators would then have resold.[23] The windfall for them was a loss for Westinghouse. Under those circumstances, the arrangement was like a wager and therefore one which risk averse parties would not want. In Posner's case, however, neither party suffers a loss. One party or the other must get the windfall, or they must share it. I must admit that I don't know what the parties would have done had they considered this possibility. For that reason, it is hard to make the case for relief for changed circumstances. Posner's conclusion is right only if the parties would have allowed the seller to keep the entire windfall in order to minimize transaction costs. Otherwise he is not placing risks and burdens where the parties themselves would have done, which, in other contexts, he says is the correct approach. But then he has to show that the parties would have let the seller keep the windfall. It seems that they might have done other things, transactions costs or not.

[22] Joskow, *J. Leg. Stud.* 6 (1977), 119.

[23] An assumption which is counter to fact to the extent Westinghouse already owned the uranium or had already bought uranium futures.

Posner's argument looks more plausible than it otherwise might for two reasons that have little to do with the merits. First, the facts of his hypothetical case are rather special. The custom-ground widgets are fungible and yet not readily available on the market. If they were unique, like the oriental rug, race horse, or Fragonard, it would seem intuitively implausible that the seller should not be allowed to resell, and, as we have seen, the intuition is a sound one. If the goods were readily available on the market, like steel or apples or uranium, the unforeseen opportunity to sell at a higher price would have arisen only if the market price rose. But then the problem would have been the very one in Westinghouse. It would immediately be seen as a problem of changed circumstances. On the special facts in Posner's case, it is less implausible to think the seller should resell, and less obvious the problem is one of changed circumstances.

Second, Posner's argument looks more plausible than it otherwise would because he never considers whether one party might have given the other the right to require performance, and consequently, whether that party would have done so if he had envisioned the circumstances which unexpectedly arose later on. If one party did give the other this right, then its transfer must be taken to be efficient just like any other transfer of rights on which the parties agree. But to overlook this possibility is easy. Fuller and Perdue overlooked it. So did Cajetan.

II. Foreseeability as Limit on Liability

There is a rule in many legal systems that the a party who breaches a contract is only liable for damages that he could have foreseen at the time the contract was made. It was adopted in England in the famous case of *Hadley* v. *Baxendale*[24] whence it passed to the United States. It was adopted by the French Civil Code[25] whence it passed to the civil codes of Italy[26] and Spain.[27] It was included in early drafts of the German Civil Code but eliminated from the final draft. It was rejected by the drafters of the new Dutch Civil Code.[28] Nevertheless, partly because of its ubiquity, and partly because of doubts about the German and Dutch solutions, this rule was accepted by the Convention on the International Sale of Goods,[29] the Unidroit Principles,[30] and the Lando Principles of European Law.[31]

I think this rule should be re-examined. There is much about it that should make us suspicious. I would like to examine the causes for suspicion and then suggest an alternative. In large part, the alternative is really a recognition that the rule has often played a valuable role, but not one that depends on whether harm is foreseeable. What should matter is whether the damages are disproportionate to the contract price.

---

[24] [1854] 9 Exch 341.   [25] French Civil Code (*Code civil*), art. 1150.
[26] Italian Civil Code (*Codice civile*), art. 1225.   [27] Spanish Civil Code (*Codigo civil*), art. 1107.
[28] Harriet N. Schelhass, 'Damages and Interest', in Daniel Busch, Ewoud H. Hondius, Hugo J. van Kooten, Harriet N. Schelhass, and Wendy M. Schrama, eds., *The Principles of European Contract Law and Dutch Law: A Commentary* (Nijmegen, 2002), 407–9.   [29] Art. 74.
[30] Art. 7.4.4.   [31] Art. 9.503.

A. Causes for Suspicion

1. *The rationale of the foreseeability rule*

Traditionally, both civil and common lawyers have said that the rule rests on the claim that had the breaching party only known of the damages his breach might cause he would not have contracted at all or would have contracted on different terms. As Roland, Starck, and Boyer say, 'le débiteur ne pas *vouloir* s'engager au-delà de ce qu'il a pu *prévoir*'.[32] Alderson observed in his opinion in *Hadley* v. *Baxendale* that 'had the special circumstances [leading to unforeseen injury] been known, the parties might have specially provided for the breach of contract by special terms, as to the damages in that case'.[33]

That may be. But why assume that the breaching party is willing to be liable for the damages he does foresee unless he agrees to be? Yet, according to French and Italian authorities, foreseeability is all that is necessary.[34] In England and the United States it has occasionally been suggested that the breaching party must have implicitly assented to liability. 'On this view,' Beatson notes, 'the mere communication to a party of the existence of special circumstances is not enough: there must be something to show that the contract was made *on the terms* that the defendant was to be liable for the loss'.[35] But this position is rejected by most English and American authorities including Beatson.

Sometimes, however, it is strange to think that a person is willing to be liable for harm simply because the possibility of it has been communicated to him or to his agent. In *Hadley* v. *Baxendale*, the plaintiff's mill was stopped because the mill shaft broke. The defendant was hired to transport it to be repaired. Suppose the plaintiff had explained exactly what had happened to the clerk who took his order. Are we to conclude the defendant wished to assume liability because its clerk did not object? Similarly, suppose that a farmer purchases lighting equipment for his tractor so that he can use it at night. Because the equipment arrives late, the farmer cannot plant and harvest his farm.[36] Or suppose a steamship company gives the agent of a telegraph company a message to be sent to its own agent in the Phillippines directing him to load extra cargo. Because it is not sent, the steamship company loses the profit it could have made on the cargo.[37] These are the facts of two well-known American cases. In each of them, the court refused to hold the defendant liable, noting, among other things, that the plaintiff might have communicated more information than he did.

---

[32] Henri Roland, Boris Starck, and Laurent Boyer, *Obligations 2 Contrat* (5th edn., Paris, 1995), no. 444. Similarly, Terré *et al.*, *Obligations*, no. 538.   [33] 9 Exch at 354–5.

[34] Terré *et al.*, *Obligations*, nos. 538–9; G. de Christofaro in Giorgio Cian and Alberto Trabucchi, *Commentario Breve al Codice civile* (4th edn., Paduv, 1999), to art. 1225.

[35] J. Beatson, *Anson's Law of Contract* (27th edn., Oxford, 1998), 576.

[36] *Lamkins* v. *Internat'l Harvester Co*, 182 SW2d 203 (Ark 1944). This case was the model for Illustration 18 to § 351 of the *Restatement (Second) of Contacts* (1979). The *Restatement* agreed that the seller should not be liable and explained this result, not in terms of foreseeability, but by 'the absence of an elaborate written contract and the extreme disproportion' between the 'loss of profits' and 'the price'.

[37] *Kerr Steamship Co.* v. *Radio Corp. of America*, 157 NE 140 (NY 1927). In other cases, however, a telegraph company has been held liable on similar facts. E.g. *Fererro* v. *Western Union Tel. Co.*, 9 App DC 455 (1896); *United States Tel. Co.* v. *Wenger*, 55 Pa 262 (1867).

The farmer did not 'bring home' to the seller the fact that he might be liable. The message was in cipher and, in any case, would not have conveyed to the agent the nature of plaintiff's business. But suppose each plaintiff had described the loss he might suffer. Does it follow that because the defendants were silent, they would be willing to be liable for them? If not, why does the rule merely require that these losses be foreseeable?

This same objection can be made, not only to the traditional arguments for the requirement of foreseeability, but to the economic explanations of it that are currently popular in the United States. Supposedly the rule will lead to an 'efficient' outcome. The 'efficient' outcome is one which places risks or burdens on the party who can bear them the most cheaply.

Richard Posner put the case of a photographer who hires a film studio to develop pictures of great value which he took in the Himalayas. If he is afraid the studio may ruin the pictures, he could take a number of precautions at relatively low cost. He could shoot more pictures on more rows of film and develop them at different times rather than in one batch. He will have no incentive to take these precautions if he knows that the film studio must fully compensate him if they are ruined. The foreseeability rule 'induces the party with knowledge of the risk either to take appropriate precautions himself, or, if he believes that the other party might be the more efficient preventer or spreader (insurer) of the loss, to reveal the risk to that party and pay him to assume it'.[38] Posner described *Hadley* v. *Baxendale* as a case in which the miller was 'imprudent' because he had not take the precaution of keeping an extra shaft on hand. 'The court refused to imply a duty on the part of the carrier to guarantee the mill owners against the consequences of their own lack of prudence, though of course if the parties had stipulated for such a guarantee the court would have enforced it. The notice requirement of *Hadley* v. *Baxendale* is designed to assure that such an improbable guarantee really is intended.'[39]

This argument, like the traditional one, assumes that the point of the foreseeability requirement is to allow the film studio or transporter to decide on what terms to contract. The photographer is supposed to inform the film studio of his potential loss only because the studio may be willing to assume liability for it in return for more pay. The miller is supposed to inform the carrier only because the court wants 'assurance' that the carrier did not intend to be liable. But are the carrier or the studio to be liable merely because they have been informed, and the harm is therefore foreseeable, or on the supposition that, having been informed, they agreed, expressly or tacitly, to be liable? If they must expressly or tacitly agree, the rule is no longer one of liability for foreseeable harm. It is liability for harm for which one has agreed to be liable.

The same objection can be made to what is presently the most popular economic explanation of the rule. It was introduced by Ian Ayres and Robert Gertner. They describe the requirement of foreseeability as a 'penalty default' 'information forcing' rule. When the parties do not agree on a term expressly, a 'penalty default' rule forces a term upon them which one of them does want to have in his contract. Normally, a

---

[38] Posner, *Economic Analysis*, 127.
[39] *Evra Corp.* v. *Swiss Bank Corp.*, 673 F2d 951, 957 (7th Cir 1982).

court will try to read terms into a contract that the parties would have chosen for themselves. But it may have a reason to do otherwise. For example, it may believe that a party will be able to decide on such a term more accurately and at less cost than a court. To give him an incentive to do so, it may threaten that if he does not, it will read in a term he dislikes.[40] Or it may do so in order to force him to reveal information. The requirement that damages must be foreseeable to be recoverable will operate as a penalty default rule if it is inconsistent with the terms that fully informed parties would have chosen for themselves. If, in fact, the carrier were the most efficient bearer of the risk of loss, the parties would have wanted him to be liable. If the miller is told that the carrier will not be liable unless the miller informs him of the potential loss, the miller has an incentive, as the best informed party, to inform the carrier. The result will be efficient because, if the carrier is informed, he may be able to take some extra and economically reasonable precaution to prevent the loss.[41]

For Ayres and Gertner, the purpose the rule serves is simply to ensure that the carrier be informed of the loss so that he can take measures to avoid it. But suppose the miller is the party best able to take precautions or to bear the risk of loss. What is to prevent him from shifting the risk to the carrier by informing him? Ayes and Gertner are assuming, presumably, that if the carrier is informed, he will refuse to contract except for more remuneration than the miller would be willing to pay. Thus we are back to the assumption that the carrier will refuse unless he is willing to assume the risk.

2. Origins

One cause for suspicion, then, is the difficulty of finding a rationale for the foreseeability rule. Another is its origins. It grew out of a conjecture about a Roman rule that was not framed in terms of foreseeability but dealt with disproportionately high loss. It may have been adopted in England more out of a concern for disproportionate loss than out of a concern for foreseeability.

The Roman rule provided: 'In all cases which have a certain quantity or nature ... damages are not to exceed twice the quantity; however, in other cases which appear to be uncertain judges are to require that the damages which were truly incurred be paid for'.[42]

There was much dispute in medieval and early modern Europe about what it meant to speak of 'cases which have a certain quantity or nature' or 'cases which appear to be uncertain'. As Reinhard Zimmermann notes, '[g]enerations of lawyers have been mystified by the terms of this poorly drafted enactment'.[43] Nevertheless, the rule did not mention foreseeability.

In the 16th century, however, the French jurist Du Moulin claimed: 'the particular rationale of the limitation in the cases of what is certain is that most likely it was not foreseen or thought that greater damage would be suffered or that there was a

---

[40] Ian Ayres and Robert Gertner, 'Filling Gaps in Incomplete Contracts: An Economic Theory of the Default Rule', *Yale L. J.* 99 (1989), 87–130; 96–7.   [41] ibid. 101.

[42] C. 7.47.1.

[43] Reinhard Zimmermann, *The Law of Obligations: Roman Foundations of the Civilian Tradition* (Cape Town, 1990), 828.

risk beyond the principal object than the principal object itself'.[44] As Zimmermann has noted, the 18th century jurist Pothier 'generalized this idea and detached it from the specific provisions' of the Roman text.[45] According to Pothier, 'the person who owes a performance is only liable for the damages that one could have foreseen at the time of the contract that the party owed a performance would suffer'.[46] The drafters of the French Civil Code took the rule from Pothier. They borrowed a great deal from him, often verbatim and without much reflection. They had little time. Bonaparte had given them a short deadline, and, in fact, they produced their draft in a few months.

We have, then, a rule that was once no more than a conjecture as to why one should not recover damages disproportionate to the contract price: the other party might not have foreseen them. That conjecture became the rule of the French Civil Code largely because it appealed to Pothier. But suppose the conjecture was wrong. Suppose what matters is not whether damages are foreseeable but whether they are disproportionate?

In deciding *Hadley* v. *Baxendale*, the court borrowed its rule from Pothier and the French Civil Code.[47] The circumstances make one wonder whether what really mattered was foreseeability. According to the head note of the case 'the plaintiff told the defendant that the mill was stopped'. Is the headnote wrong, or was the court wrong to say that the loss was unforeseeable? Or did the court use Pothier's rule to reach a result that did not in fact turn on foreseeability?

It is interesting to watch the American *Restatement (Second) of Contracts* try to explain *Hadley* v. *Baxendale*. The *Restatement* accepts the rule that '(d)amages are not recoverable for loss that the party in breach did not have reason to foresee . . . when the contract was made'.[48] Nevertheless, it gives this illustration based on *Hadley*:

A, a private trucker, contracts with B to deliver to B's factory a machine that has just been repaired and, without which B's factory, as A knows, cannot reopen. Delivery is delayed because A's truck breaks down. In an action by B against A for breach of contract the court may, after taking into consideration such factors as the absence of an elaborate written contract and the extreme disproportion between B's loss of profits during the delay and the price of the trucker's services, exclude recovery for loss of profits.[49]

According to this explanation, the judge may deny recovery because the damages are disproportionate. Indeed, this illustration is offered, not as an illustration of the foreeseeability rule, but of an emendation of it in § 351(3) of the *Restatement*:

A court may limit damages for foreseeable loss by excluding recovery for loss of profits, by allowing recovery only for loss incurred in reliance, or otherwise if it concludes that in the circumstances justice so requires in order to avoid disproportionate compensation.

And so it turns out that, in the minds of the American Restaters, *Hadley* itself must be explained, not by the foreseeability, as the court said, but by the need to prevent

---

[44] Carolus Molinaeus, *Tractatus de eo quod interest* (Venice, 1589), no. 60.

[45] Zimmermann, *Law of Obligations*, 829.

[46] Robert Pothier, *Traité des obligations*, no. 160, in *Oeuvres de Pothier* 2 (Bugnet, ed., 2nd edn., Paris, 1861), 497.   [47] Zimmermann, *Law of Obligations*, 830.

[48] *Restatement (Second) of Contracts*, § 351(1).

[49] *Restatement (Second) of Contracts*, § 351, Illus. 17, 18.

recovery of disproportionately high damages. Is it not possible that, whatever the judges who decided *Hadley* said, they had the same concern in mind?

3. Application

One test of good legal rule is the way courts apply it. If they do so straightforwardly, it may be that they are satisfied that the rule produces the right results. If they strain to avoid applying the rule or they make exceptions, very likely, they are finding that some applications of the rule conflict with their sense of justice.

English courts, by and large, have followed the rule laid down in *Hadley* v. *Baxendale* without many qualms. There was a brief revolt. Not long after *Hadley*, an English court suggested that mere foreseeability might not be enough. In *British Columbia etc. Saw Mill Co. Ltd.* v. *Nettleship*,[50] plaintiff's saw mill could not be used because the defendant carrier failed to deliver a case containing parts. Bovill CJ could have merely pointed out that the defendant was unaware that mill would not work without the parts contained in the case. He said, however, that the defendant was only liable for damages 'to which he assented expressly or impliedly by entering the contract'.[51] This suggestion was not taken up in later decisions. In 1949, in *Victoria Laundry (Windsor) Ltd.* v. *Newman Industries Ltd.*,[52] the rule was explained simply in terms of foreseeability. As we will see later on, it was innocuous to do so in that case because the damages were probably not disproportionate. But in 1969, *in Koufos* v. *C. Czarnikow, Ltd.* [*the Heron II*], the House of Lords allowed recovery for a loss suffered selling 3,000 tons of sugar in Basra when the vessel carrying it was delayed nine days and the price of sugar fell in the interval. Presumably, the result would be the same however great the drop in price might be, however volatile the market in question might be, however valuable, and therefore however vulnerable to price fluctuations, the cargo might be per pound or per cubic foot, whether or not the defendant charged simply by weight and bulk or included a premium to cover against price fluctuations. English judges pride themselves on their pragmatism. Yet American, French, and German judges have been more willing to take pragmatic account of the importance of a disproportion in damages despite the rules they are supposedly applying.

In the United States, a suggestion like Bovill's was made by Oliver Wendell Holmes: the defendant is not liable unless one could infer that he tacitly agreed to be.[53] It has been accepted only in Arkansas.[54] Nevertheless, some American courts have been unwilling to award damages on the grounds that they are disproportionate even in cases in which they would seem to be foreseeable. In California, a franchisor was not allowed to recover damages for future royalties from a franchisee. To allow him to do so, the court said, would be unconscionable.[55] A federal court applying federal maritime law refused to allow recovery for loss caused by defects in a ship that the defendant had certified to have no defects.[56] A federal court applying New York law

---

[50] (1868) LR 3 CP 499. [51] (1868) LR 3 CP at 505. [52] (1949) 2 KB 528.

[53] *Globe Refining Co.* v. *Landa Cotton Oil Co.*, 190 US 540, 543 (1903).

[54] *Morrow* v. *First Nat'l Bank*, 550 SW2d 429 (Ark 1977). See E. Allan Farnsworth, *Contracts* (3rd edn., New York, 1999), § 12.14.

[55] *Postal Instant Press, Inc.* v. *Sealy*, 51 Cal Rptr 2d 365, 373 75 (Ct App 1996).

[56] *Sundance Cruises Corp.* v. *American Bureau of Shipping*, 7 F3d 1077, 1084 (2nd Cir 1993).

denied recovery for injury to plaintiff's business caused by defendant's delivery of defective tires.[57] A Michigan court would not allow recovery for profits lost on a steam mill and 'salt block' when the defendant failed to provide boilers on time.[58] An Illinois court would not hold the defendant, who failed to finish building a railroad, liable for the profits lost when the road could not be used.[59] An Alabama court did not allow recovery of lost profits from a defendant who failed to furnish a machine for drying bricks with as much capacity as promised.[60] Pennsylvania courts did not allow a miller to recover profits he lost when the defendant breached a contract to dress stones for his mill[61] or the owner of machinery to recover the profit he would have made had it been returned to him on time.[62] In all of these cases, the courts said that the reason for denying recovery was the disproportion. In all but three of them,[63] the court added that the defendant should not be liable unless he undertook to be liable for the damages which plaintiff sought. More cases could be cited.[64] Those mentioned, however, form a chain stretching back almost to *Hadley* v. *Baxendale*.

It is also worth noting the difficulties that judges have had reaching a sensible result and explaining why it is sensible in terms of foreseeability. Benjamin Cardozo, one of the most illustrious American judges, decided the case described earlier in which the defendant failed to send a telegram directing that cargo be loaded in the Philippines.[65] He held that the telegraph company was not liable because the telegram was in cipher. It was not enough that 'the length and cost of the telegram or the names of the parties would fairly suggest to a reasonable man that business of moment is the subject of the message'.[66] There had to be '[s]omething ... to give warning that the subject of the message is not merely business in general, but business of a known order'. Cardozo did not explain why that must be. He did note that 'the whole doctrine as to the need for notice [has] an air of unreality' since 'neither the clerk who receives the message over the counter nor the operator who transmits it nor any other employee gives or is expected to give any thought to the sense of what he is receiving or transmitting'. Nevertheless, '[t]he doctrine ... has prevailed for years so many that it is tantamount to a rule of property'. Its advantage, he said was that companies have been relieved of liabilities that might otherwise be 'crushing'.[67] He did not explain why they are less crushing, or the companies less worthy of relief, if the clerk could have told from the message that it concerned business 'of a known order'.

In France, courts once held that the defendant must have been able to foresee the cause of the harm but not its extent.[68] Even then, however, a passenger was denied recovery for loss of a suitcase that contained money.[69] Now courts say that there is no

---

[57] *Armstrong Rubber Co.* v. *Griffith*, 43 F2d 689, 691 (2nd Cir 1930).

[58] *McEwen* v. *McKinnon*, 11 NW 828, 830 (Mich 1882).

[59] *Snell* v. *Cottingham*, 72 Ill 161, 170 (1874).

[60] *Moulthrop* v. *Hyett*, 17 So 32, 33–4 (Ala 1895) (adding that damages were remote and speculative).

[61] *Fleming* v. *Beck*, 48 Pa 309, 312 (1864).

[62] *Armstrong & Latta* v. *City of Philadelphia*, 94 A 455, 458 (Pa 1915).

[63] *Postal Instant Press, Armstrong* and *Moulthrop*.

[64] They are summarized in Larry T. Garvin, 'Disproportionality and the Law of Consequential Damages: Default Theory and Cognitive Reality', *Ohio St. L. Jour.* 59 (1998), 339 at 345–60.

[65] *Kerr Steamship Co.* v. *Radio Corp. of America*, 157 NE 140 (NY 1927).   [66] 157 NE at 141.

[67] 157 NE at 142.   [68] Terré *et al.*, *Obligations*, no. 539.

[69] Cour d'appel, Pau, 11 Aug. 1903, D.P. 1904.2.302.

liability unless the amount of harm can be foreseen. A transporter is not liable for the contents if a racehorse dies[70] or the contents of a lost box are unusually valuable.[71] If the amount rather than the cause of harm must be foreseen, we have taken a step toward denying recovery when damages would be disproportionately large. The defendant is still supposed to be liable when damages are disprotionately large and yet foreseen. But sometimes, French courts have avoided that result. When a contractor's employee negligently set fire to plaintiff's chateau with a blow torch, the *Cour de Cassation* said it was unforeseeable that the owner would have to borrow money at interest to fix the damage or that he would lose rentals while it was being fixed.[72]

German law does not limit damages to those which were foreseeable. Preliminary drafts of the German Civil Code contained a version of the foreseeability rule: 'The liability for failure to perform of the person owing performance does not extend to compensation for harm the occurrence of which lay beyond the realm of probability given the awareness of the circumstances which that person had or should have had'.[73] It was deleted because it was thought to be too restrictive.[74] In its place a second paragraph was added to what is now § 254. The first paragraph provides that damages may be reduced if the injured party was at fault. According to paragraph 2, 'This provision also applies if the fault of the injured party consisted of an omission to call to the attention of the party owing performance of which that party neither knew nor should have known . . .'. Foreseeability is supposed to matter, then, only if the plaintiff is at fault for failing to alert the defendant to a possibility of harm which he could not otherwise foresee. Even then, it is not supposed to matter unless the defendant could have prevented the harm had he been alerted.[75]

Nevertheless, sometimes this provision seems to be used in the same way that some American and French courts have used the foreseeability rule: to prevent recovery of disproportionately large damages. In one case,[76] the defendant was to translate a brochure concerning motor cycle parts into Dutch, French, English, Spanish, and Italian. The defendant sought damages on the grounds that brochures it printed were unusable because the translation was faulty. The court said that the plaintiff was at fault for not calling the defendant's attention to the fact that it would print the brochures without having the translation checked. Was that really so unlikely? One suspects that the court's real concern was that: 'the damage that threatened, and which occurred, was forty times as large as the fee for translation'.

In another and well-known case,[77] the plaintiff's agent gave his car keys to the night porter at the hotel where he was staying so that the car could be parked in a nearby

[70] Cass. civ., 3 Aug. 1932, D.H. 1932.572.   [71] Cass. civ., 7 July 1924, D.P. 1927.1.119.

[72] Cass., 1e ch. civ., 11 May 1982, Gaz. Pal. 1982.2.612.

[73] *Protokolle der Kommission für die zweite Lesung des Entwurfs des Bürgerlichen Gesetzbuchs* (Berlin, 1897), § 218, p. 292.

[74] 'Antrag von Enneccerus in der XII. Kommission' no. 134 in Horst Heinrich Jakobs und Werner Schubert, eds., *Die Beratung des Bürgerlichen Gesetzbuchs in systematischer Zusammenstellung der unveröffentlichten Quellen* (Berlin, 1978), 117–18.

[75] Wolfgang Grunsky, in Helmut Heinrichs, *Münchener Kommentar zum Bürgerlichen Gesetzbuch* (3rd edn., Munich, 1994), § 254, no. 41.   [76] OLG, Hamm, 28 Feb. 1989, NJW 1989, 2006.

[77] BGH, 29 Jan. 1969, NJW 1969, 789. For an English translation by Tony Weir, see B. S. Markesinis, W. Lorenz, and G. Dannemann, *The German Law of Obligations* 1 (Oxford, 1997), 320–3.

garage, owned by a third party, and used by the hotel to provide parking for its customers. The agent left a collection of jewelry belonging to the plaintiff in the trunk. Although the agent found the trunk locked the next day, the jewelry had been stolen. The garage owner had given the porter a claim check meant to exclude liability but it was never handed to the agent. The plaintiff sued the hotel. The court remanded for a finding on whether the agent was at fault. According to the court, he might have been if he had failed to tell the hotel about the jewelry. On the other hand, the hotel staff might have already known about it. The staff might also have been at fault for not telling him that the garage owner's exclusion of liability made it risky to leave the jewelry in the trunk. These grounds seem strange. If the trunk was found locked, very likely, the thief was someone with access to the agent's key. Telling the staff about the jewelry might have made the theft more likely. Moreover, it seems odd to think that the exclusion of liability made it significantly more likely that the garage or the hotel employed a thief. As before, the court might have been bothered by the disproportion between the value of the jewelry and the fee for parking the car. I have put variants of this case to German jurists and found them reluctant to decide for the plaintiff even on facts that would seem to exclude the agent's fault. Perhaps the judges of the *Bundesgerichtshof* felt the same way.

These American, French, and German cases may not be typical. It is hardly surprising that most of the time, American, French, and German courts follow the rules supposedly in force in their legal systems. Nevertheless, they indicate that sometimes courts have balked at awarding disproportionate damages. That is a further reason to suspect that disproportion rather than foreseeability should matter.

B. An Alternative: Disproportionality Should Matter

Thus far we have seen that there is no good reason why foreseeability, in itself, should matter. We have also seen that the idea that it did matter was initially a conjecture by Du Moulin as to why disproportion mattered. His idea passed into the French Civil Code largely because it appealed to Pothier. Following Pothier and the Code, the foreseeability rule was accepted in English law in *Hadley* v. *Baxendale*, a case that the American *Second Restatement* explains by disproportionality. Moreover, American, French, and German cases sometimes seem to turn on disproportionality.

Du Moulin may have had it backwards. He thought disproportionality mattered because then losses are likely to be unforeseeable. Unforeseeability mattered because it indicates a lack of consent. Instead, we will argue, lack of foreseeability matters because it leads to disproportionality between the amount of the damages plaintiff claims and the price he was charged. Disproportionality matters because allowing these damages to be recovered is unfair.[78]

---

[78] Garvin, 'Disproportionality' and M. N. Kniffin, 'A Newly Discovered Unconscionability: Unconscionability of Remedy', *Notre Dame L. Rev.* 63 (1988), 247, also believe that disproportionality matters. According to Garvin it does because cognitive psychology shows that people are not as sensitive as they should be to the possibility of large losses. I don't see how, on the basis of this argument, one can tell which party should bear them. Kniffin believes, as I do, that imposing liability for a disproportionately large loss is unfair, although she does not explain unfairness in terms of commutative justice.

I have discussed what it means for a contract to be unfair by drawing on Aristotle's concept of commutative justice.[79] In the Aristotelian tradition, commutative justice requires that in an exchange, the value of what each party gives should equal that of what he receives, thereby preserving each party's share of purchasing power. As we have noted, the idea that parties should exchange at a just price has been often misunderstood. It did not mean that each party personally placed the same value on the goods he gave as on those he received. If they had, the parties would not exchange. They identified the just price with the price on a competitive market[80] which, they knew, fluctuates from day to day and place to place in response to need, scarcity, and cost.[81] Although they believed that neither party became richer or poorer at the moment of the transaction, they knew that either might find himself richer or poorer the next day. The contract was fair in much the same way as a fair bet: the party who lost when prices rose could have won if they had risen.[82] Similarly, a term in a contract may impose a risk on one of the parties which, if it eventuates, will make him poorer. Yet if he is compensated for bearing this risk, he is no poorer at the time of transaction, and the other party no richer, in the way that a person who bets at fair odds is at that moment no poorer or richer.

I think we need something like this older idea of commutative justice to make sense of modern ideas about contractual unfairness. According to the Directive of the European Council on Unfair Terms in Consumer Contracts, 'a contractual term that has not been individually negotiated shall be regarded as unfair if, contrary to the requirement of good faith, it causes a significant imbalance in the parties' rights and obligations . . .'.[83] 'Imbalance' here cannot mean that no risks may be placed on the consumer. What it must mean is that he is compensated for the risks placed on him so that, taking both the risks and the compensation into account, the contract is not imbalanced. To make sense of the Directive, then, we must say that a contract is not imbalanced when it is fair in the same way as a fair bet—each party is compensated for the risks that he bears—and an imbalanced contract is unfair. At that point, we are talking about commutative justice as it was understood in the Aristotelian tradition even if we do not use that expression.

We can now see why, if the damages for which a party may be liable are unforeseeable, a contract will be imbalanced in this sense and therefore unfair. Let us take, as an illustration, the English case of *Victoria Laundry (Windsor) Ltd.* v. *Newman Industries Ltd.*[84] Plaintiffs purchased a large boiler for £2,150 from defendants, who

---

[79] James Gordley, 'Contract Law in the Aristotelian Tradition', in Benson, *Theory of Contract Law,* 265, at 310–26.

[80] As noted by John Noonan, *The Scholastic Analysis of Usury* (Cambridge, Mass., 1957), 82–8; Raymond de Roover, 'The Concept of the Just Price and Economic Policy', *Jour. Econ. Hist.* 18 (1958), 418.

[81] James Gordley, *The Philosophical Origins of Modern Contract Doctrine* (Oxford, 1991), 94–102; Domenicus de Soto, *De iustitia et iure libri decem* (Salamanca, 1553), lib. 6, q. 2, a. 3; Ludovicus Molina, *De iustitia et iure tractatus* (Venice, 1614), disp. 348; all of these factors had been mentioned, albeit cryptically, by Thomas Aquinas, *In decem libros ethicorum expositio* (Angeli Pirotta, ed., Marino, 1934), lib. 5, lec. 9; *Summa theologiae* II-II, Q. 77, a. 3 ad 4. They were discussed by medieval commentators on Aristotle. Odd Langholm, *Price and Value in the Aristotelian Tradition* (Bergen, 1979), 61–143.

[82] Soto, *De iustitia et iure,* lib. 6, q. 2, a. 3.   [83] 93/31/EEC, 5 Apr. 1993, art. 3(1).

[84] (1949) 2 KB 528.

knew that the plaintiffs were launderers and dyers and that they wanted to put the boiler to use in their business in the shortest possible time. When the boiler was delivered late, the plaintiffs recovered for the loss of profits they would have made on their ordinary contracts but not on unusual and highly lucrative dyeing contracts they had entered into with the Ministry of Supply. The court said that the defendants could have foreseen the losses on their ordinary contracts but not those on the highly lucrative ones. Suppose the court was right. As a sensible businessman, knowing that he would be liable for plaintiff's losses on the ordinary contracts, the defendant would have charged a price for the boiler that reflected the risk of liability. Because he could not have foreseen the losses on the highly lucrative contracts with the Minister of Supply, he could not have adjusted their price to reflect plaintiff's potential losses on them. Since the risk of liability for these losses was not reflected in the price that the defendant charged, the contract would be imbalanced and therefore unfair if he were held liable for these losses. What matters, then, is that the losses on the unusually lucrative contracts were disproportionate to the contract price. They were disproportionate, not merely because they were high relative to the price, but because the price was not adjusted to charge for the risk of liability.

This analysis treats the risk of breaching a contract and paying damages as a business risk. As in the case of other risks, a contract is imbalanced and unfair if the party who bears this risk is not compensated for doing so. We are supposing, then, that a party cannot simply eliminate the risk by deciding not to breach the contract. But that is surely true except in the case of a willful breach. In the case of a negligent breach, he cannot altogether eliminate the chance that he or someone for whom he is responsible will act negligently. That is why people insure themselves against the consequences of their own negligence. If the contract creates what, as we have seen, the French call an *obligation de résultat*, the breaching party will be liable for a non-negligent breach even in legal systems in which liability is said to be based on fault. If such risks are costs of doing business, like other risks, the defendant should not have to bear them without compensation.

It is a different matter if the breach is committed with what the French call *dol*. If he did, his breach was intentional and unjustified. He could eliminate the risk of this kind of breach by simply deciding to abide by his contract. There is no reason he should be charging extra in compensation for this risk, and if he did not, there is no more injustice in holding him liable than in holding him liable for deliberately destroying the plaintiff's property, even though the contract price did not compensate him for bearing the risk of doing so. French law, quite sensibly, recognizes an exception to the foreseeability rule: the defendant is liable for unforeseeable damages caused by *dol*.[85] This exception was rejected by the Unidroit Principles but accepted by the Lando Commission.[86] If our approach is correct, the Commission made the better choice.[87]

---

[85] French Civil Code (*Code civil*) art. 1150.   [86] Art. 9: 503.

[87] See James Gordley, 'Responsibility in Crime, Tort and Contract for the Unforeseeable Consequences of an Intentional Wrong: A Once and Future Rule?' in Peter Cane and Jane Stapleton, eds., *The Law of Obligations: Essays in Celebration of John Fleming* (Oxford, 1998), 175 at 198–208.

In a case like *Victoria Laundry*, the defendant's inability to foresee the losses on the highly lucrative contracts mattered because, if the defendant could not foresee them, he could not charge an extra amount to compensate him for the risk that he would be liable for them. It does not follow, however, that merely because the plaintiff had called a risk of loss to the defendant's attention, the defendant should be liable for it, and therefore should have charged extra. Normally, if the parties are sensible, and they both have their eyes open, they will place a risk on the party who can bear it most easily. Courts should do the same when the parties do not specify who is to bear a risk.[88] As Posner has observed, the party who can most easily bear a risk of loss is the one who can most easily prevent the loss or spread the risk of loss. He can most easily spread the risk if he faces it over and over, and can, so to speak, self-insure against it by raising his price on each transaction in which the loss might occur. Suppose, if a manufacturer or seller breaches his contract, every customer will face a similar loss. The manufacturer or seller could normally bear that loss most easily. He can prevent it most easily and spread the risk by raising his prices for every customer. If the loss will be suffered by only one of his customers, however, while he may still be in the best position to prevent it, he is no longer in the best position to spread the risk that it will occur. If a customer calls this loss to his attention, he may, of course, agree to be liable for it in the event of breach and charge a suitably enhanced price. Then, of course, he should be liable. But there is no reason why he should automatically be liable simply because the customer has told him about the loss. He may not be the best party to bear the risk. Moreover, if he does not raise his price, he will not be compensated for bearing the risk. It would be unfair to hold him liable.

Moreover, even though normally the parties would want to place a risk on the party that can best prevent or spread it, they will not always want to do so. This will depend on the costs of identifying the risk and adjusting the price to reflect it. These costs may be low enough to be outbalanced by the advantages of placing the risk on the right party. They are likely to be if the contract is an important one, or if, to perform, the manufacturer or builder or seller must already know a lot about the situation of a particular customer, or if many customers are facing the same loss and they are easy to identify. As Melvin Eisenberg has pointed out, however, one who is selling a large quantity of undifferentiated goods or services to many customers is unlikely to find it worthwhile to adjust his price because one of them may suffer a particularly severe loss if the contract is breached.[89] He is particularly unlikely to do so if the price he is charging is small. For that reason, it would be unreasonable to expect a carrier, a seller of lighting equipment, a telegraph company, or a parking garage to allow its clerks to adjust a price if they are informed that a mill is stopped, a farmer wishes to plow at night or a steamship line needs to take on cargo in the Philippines or the trunk of a car contains jewelry.[90] Pricing such a risk would be difficult, and too costly for a high volume low price operation, even if the seller of the good or service could bear it most easily.

---

[88] Gordley, 'Contract Law in the Aristotelian Tradition', 323–6.
[89] Melvin Eisenberg, 'The Principle of Hadley v. Baxendale', *Calif. L. Rev.* 80 (1992), 563 at 592–3.
[90] As noted by Garvin, 'Disproportionality', 385–6.

As a result, as Eisenberg observes,[91] if sellers were held liable for such risks, very likely, they would not customize their prices for high risk customers. They would raise the price for every customer to cover the losses they expect from a small number of contracts. That would also be unfair. Customers who will suffer a small loss if the contract is breached will have to pay an amount which reflects the risk that others will suffer a large one. If it is unfair for a seller to pay for such a loss when he has not been compensated for bearing it, then it is unfair for this loss to be shifted by raising prices for customers who run no risk of it.

III. Liability for Intentional Breach

A. Problems with the Modern Approach

In a previous chapter, we have argued that the defendant should be responsible in tort for the unforeseen consequences of intentional wrong.[92] In the last section we noted that he should be liable for the consequences of a willful breach of contract, however disproportionate, since he can eliminate the risk by deciding not to breach. As in tort, he should pay for all the consequences of a willful wrong.

Some might think that every intentional breach is wrongful or unjust. By definition, it is a violation of contractual duty. Others, particularly partisans of the efficient breach theory, might think that there is nothing wrong with breaching a contract provided one compensates the other party for the loss he suffers.

Every breach is a violation of contractual duty in the sense that the other party fails to receive something owed him and is entitled to a remedy. But not every breach is culpable, let alone wrongful or unjust. A party who finds it impossible to perform may sometimes be liable even though he failed through no fault of his own. That is so, not only in Anglo-American law, where liability is supposed to be strict, but in continental legal systems that supposedly require that the breaching party be at fault.[93]

Moreover, for a party to breach a contract intentionally may not be unjust or wrongful or even culpable. Any party who could perform but refuses to do so breaches his contract intentionally. But even Daniel Friedmann in his critique of the efficient breach theory does not claim a party should never refuse to perform. For example, according to Friedmann, he should breach if he finds that he can only perform at unexpectedly high cost to himself, and that someone else can make the same performance more cheaply.[94] It would be wasteful for him to perform himself rather than to compensate the other party for any increased expense in obtaining the performance from another. The breaching party may or may not have been at fault for putting himself in such a position. But having found himself in it, his decision not to perform is not culpable.

His conclusion follows from the reasons we have seen in an earlier chapter that a party may wish to commit himself by making a promise. It may be just to guarantee

---

91 Eisenberg, 'Hadley v. Baxendale', 592–3.   92 See Chapter 10 I B.

93 James Gordley, 'Contract in Pre-Commercial Societies and in Western History', §§ 89, 93.

94 Daniel Friedmann, 'The Efficient Breach Fallacy', *J. Legal Stud.* 18 (1989), 1 at 10–11.

that the other party will have a performance at a specific price, regardless how the market may behave. If so, that is what the other party is entitled to have.

Under other circumstances, as pointed out earlier, Friedmann is right, and the party who breaches, in effect, appropriates an asset that belongs to the other party even if he does pay compensation for the loss he causes. As we have seen, the point of the contract is to allow the buyer of a Fragonard to have, not only the unique satisfaction of owning that painting, but the benefits if someone else should choose to pay more. If someone else does, breach by the seller is not efficient, as Posner seems to think, nor, as Friedmann points out, is it just.[95]

The situations in which a breach is unjust or wrongful thus correspond to those described earlier in which an unlawful act is unjust: the perpetrator knows he will be appropriating or harming what belongs to the other party. He should then be liable for all of the consequences for the same reason as before. It should not matter that he intended one sort of harm and inflicted another.

As before, moreover, one can think of cases in which it seems intuitively right that he should be liable for unforeseen and disproportionate harm. Suppose that after A sells a Rubens to B but before he delivers it, B agrees to resell it to a private collector who will pay vastly more for it that anyone including A had imagined. If a thief steals the Rubens before A delivers it, it might be unfair to make A compensate B for the unexpected profit he would have made on resale. But it certainly seems fair to hold A liable for that amount if he helped the thief to steal the painting.

Suppose that the plaintiff owned a Rubens and stored it in defendant's warehouse without telling him, and that the defendant would never have expected such a valuable object to be stored there. Suppose a fire broke out. It might be unfair to make the warehouse owner pay for the painting if it was destroyed because he negligently delayed to call the fire department. It seems perfectly fair to hold him liable if he did not call because he wanted to collect insurance on the warehouse when it burned.

Suppose someone sold penicillin to a children's hospital that was diluted with a seemingly harmless chemical compound. Or suppose he sold a rancher a horse that was infected with a disease that could be expected to infect other horses but not cows. If the seller was merely careless in not learning that the penicillin was diluted or the horse infected, it might be unfair to hold him liable if some children died of a severe allergic reaction or the rancher's cows were infected. It seems fair to hold him liable if, like Harry Lime in Orson Welles' film *The Third Man*, he deliberately diluted the penicillin to cut his costs, knowing that some children would die of disease but not of an allergic reaction. It seems fair to hold him liable for the death of the rancher's cows if he sold the horse knowing it would infect the rancher's horses.

B. An Older Solution

As before, a doctrine was once developed to fit cases like these in which relief seems intuitively right. It was developed in France in the 18th century by Robert Pothier. He

---

[95] Daniel Friedmann, *J. Legal Stud.* 18 (1989), 1–2.

said that a breaching party should be liable only for harm that he could have foreseen at the time he contracted unless his breach constituted an intentional wrong (*dol*). If it did, he should be liable for unforeseeable harm as well. While this rule looks like an application to contract law of the canon law doctrine described earlier, Pothier developed it independently, long after the canon law doctrine described earlier[96] had fallen into disfavor, to explain some notoriously intractable Roman texts.

One text said that if the seller fails to deliver, the buyer will get only damages that 'concern the thing itself' (*circa rem*). If the seller failed to deliver wine, the buyer would not get the profit he could have made by reselling it; if he failed to deliver grain, the buyer could not recover the loss he would have suffered if his slaves starved.[97] Another text said that if the seller sold diseased cattle or unsound timber in ignorance of its condition, the buyer would only be compensated for the extra amount he paid because the parties did not know the truth. If the seller had known, however, the buyer could also recover damages if his other cattle died of contagion or the building he constructed with the timber collapsed.[98]

Pothier explained these cases by using a principle formulated in the 16th century by the French jurist Du Moulin: a party should be liable only for harm he could foresee when he entered into a contract. As we saw, Du Moulin had used this principle to explain another Roman rule that put an upper limit to the damages recoverable for breach of contract. Pothier said that normally, a party should be deemed to foresee only those damages that occur as to the thing purchased itself (*par rapport à la chose même*) and not harm that occurs to other goods because of the lack of that thing (*propter rem ipsam non habitam*). If the seller failed to deliver a horse and the buyer had to pay a higher price for one, he could recover the difference in price but not the rents he was unable to collect from tenants because he did not have a horse. If a lessor leases property he did not own and his lessee is evicted, the lessee could recover for any increase in the rent he must pay elsewhere but not for the business he lost by changing locations or any furniture that is broken in moving.[99] These 'extrinsic damages' could be recovered only if they were foreseen at the time of contracting.[100] Nevertheless, unforeseeable damages could be recovered without limit if the breach constituted an intentional wrong (*dol*). As authority, Pothier cited the Roman text in which a person who knowingly sold defective cattle is liable when the buyer's other cattle are infected.[101] Similarly, he said, one who knowingly sold defective wood must pay for the damages suffered when the house that was built with the wood collapses.[102]

C. Modern Law

One way to test the merits of a rule is to see what happens when a legal system either adopts it or fails to do so. Pothier's rule was adopted in France and Italy and rejected in Germany, England, and the United States. We will examine the consequences.

---

[96] Chapter 10 I B.   [97] Dig. 19.1.21.3.   [98] Dig. 19.1.13.pr.
[99] Robert Pothier, *Traité des obligations*, no. 161, in *Oeuvres de Pothier* 2 (2nd. edn., M. Bugnet, 1861).
[100] ibid. no. 162.   [101] ibid. no. 166.   [102] ibid. nos. 160, 166–7.

1. French and Italian law

The drafters of the French Civil Code adopted Pothier's rule[103] whence it passed to the Italian Civil Code.[104] The defendant is liable only for damages foreseeable when the contract was made unless, as Pothier said, he acted with *dol*, or the Italian equivalent, *dolo*. The French and Italians have experienced some difficulties with the rule but we can see from what has already been said how to resolve them.

One difficulty has been defining *dol* or *dolo*. French and Italian courts have swung between different and inadequate formulas: that the breaching party must want to injure the other party;[105] that he must act in bad faith and knowing he will injure him;[106] that he must breach intentionally.[107] Even when they use the latter, they seem to mean the breach must be in some way wrongful as well as intentional. Yet it has proven difficult to explain in what way it should be wrongful. It was in large part because of that difficulty that the drafters of the Unidroit Principles rejected a provision, contained in the preliminary draft,[108] that the defendant would be liable for damages he could not have foreseen if his breach was 'intentional'. It was pointed out that not all intentional breaches are blameworthy or even undesirable. Nevertheless, we have already seen how this difficulty should be resolved. An intentional breach is wrongful when, for his own ends, the perpetrator appropriates or harms what belongs to the other party.

Some jurists have also objected that the rules governing liability for damages should be the same in contract as in tort law. They have pointed out that the French and Italian Codes do not draw a distinction in tort analogous to this one.[109] If our analysis is correct, however, the problem is with the rules in tort which should look like those the codes have for breach of contract.

2. German law

In Germany in the 19th century, jurists claimed that Pothier's rule was wrong in principle. It was an age of conceptualism. They thought liability should be based on

---

[103] French Civil Code (*Code civil*), art. 1150.   [104] Italian Civil Code (*Codice civile*), art. 1225.

[105] This position was taken in France before 1969. Christian Larroumet, *Droit civil Tome 3 Les Obligations Le Contrat* (5th edn., Paris, 2003), no. 623; Geneviève Viney and Patrice Jourdain, *Traité de droit civil: Les obligations: Les effets de la responsabilité* (2nd edn., Paris, 2001), no. 327.

[106] This seems to have been the position of Italian courts before 1984. See Cass., 16 Jan. 1954, no. 85, Giur. it. 1954.I.1.513.

[107] This seems to be the current view of the Italian and French courts. Italy: Cass., 30 Oct. 1984, no. 5566, Giur. it. 1986.I.1.276 (defendant refused to leave premises he rented even after a court had declared he had no right to remain); France: Cass., 1e ch. civ., 4 Feb. 1969, D. 1969.601, JCP 1969.II.16030 (artist breaches by changing employers); Cass., 1e ch. civ., 22 Oct. 1975, D.1976.151 (same). In these cases, however, the defendant appropriated an asset that belonged to the other: an apartment in the Italian case, and artistic services in the French ones. Moreover, the courts used more circumlocution than one would expect if they merely meant that he must breach intentionally. French jurists recognize that even after these decisions, a breach only constitutes *dol* if it is wrongful although they are not clear when that might be. E.g. Note by Jean Mazeaud to Cass, 1e ch. civ., 22 Oct. 1975, D. 1976.151 at 152; Alain Sériaux, *Droit civil: Droit des obligations* (Paris, 1992), 236; Larroumet, *Contrat*, no. 623. On the dispute among Italian jurists, see Giovanna Visintini, *Trattato breve della responsabilità civile* (Padua, 1996), 575.

[108] Art. 6.4.5 which was replaced by Art. 7.44 of the final version. I argued against the change. *Comments by Professor James Gordley on Articles 7.44 and 7.4.13*, Unidroit, Study L-(WG) WP.2 (1993).

[109] Philippe Malaurie and Laurent Aynès, *Cours de droit civil: Obligations* (Paris, 1985–6), no. 489.

two simple concepts. First, a party should be liable only if he was at fault.[110] Second, the party who was at fault should pay the amount necessary to put the other party where he would have been had the contract not been breached.[111] If both parties were at fault, the damages awarded were to be reduced. These principles were adopted by the drafters of the German Civil Code of 1900.[112]

Nevertheless, German law has accepted these principles without accepting what would seem to be their obvious consequences. According to Section 254, paragraph 2 of the Civil Code, the damages awarded are to be reduced 'even if the fault of the injured party consisted in an omission to call the attention of the obligated party to the danger of an unusually serious injury of which the obligated party neither knew nor ought to have known'. Section 254, paragraph 1 provides that when the injured party was also at fault, the damages should be reduced by an amount that depends 'upon the circumstances and especially upon how far the injury has been caused by one party or the other'. Generally, courts make this determination by asking how dangerous and how culpable the conduct of each party was.[113] Nevertheless, the prevailing opinion is that when the plaintiff's 'fault' was a failure to tell the defendant that damages might be unusually high, he can recover no damages at all.[114] Moreover, according to the prevailing opinion, when one party's culpable action was merely negligent and the other's was intentional, the party who acted intentionally must pay them in full.[115] Consequently, Section 254 functions much like Pothier's rule. If the defendant's breach was culpable and intentional, he is liable for all of the consequences. If it was unintentional, supposedly, he is only liable for harm he should have foreseen, either on the basis of his own knowledge or because of what he was told. The principal difference—which does not concern us here—is that for Pothier, though not under the German Civil Code, the damages are supposed to be foreseeable when the contract was made.

3. Anglo-American law

Anglo-American courts adopted Pothier's approach in part. In *Hadley v. Baxendale*,[116] as we have seen, an English court adopted a rule that English and American courts still

---

[110] Karl Arndts, *Lehrbuch der Pandekten* (14th edn., Stuttgart, 1889), § 86 n. 3; Georg F. Puchta, *Pandekten* (2nd edn., Leipzig, 1844), § 266; Georg F. Puchta, *Vorlesungen über das heutige römische Recht* 2 (2nd edn., Leipzig, 1849), §§ 264–7; Bernhard Windscheid, *Lehrbuch des Pandektenrechts* 1 (7th edn., Frankfurt-am-Main, 1891), § 101; Karl Vangerow, *Leitfaden für Pandekten-Vorlesungen* 1 (Marburg, 1847), § 107. For a dissenting view, see Aloys Brinz, *Lehrbuch der Pandekten* (2nd edn., Erlangen, 1879). See Gordley, 'Contract', §§ 90–2.

[111] Puchta, *Vorlesungen*, 2, § 224; Windscheid, *Lehrbuch*, 2, § 257. For a dissenting view, see Karl Vangerow, *Lehrbuch der Pandekten* 3 (7th edn., Marburg, 1863), § 571, Anm. 3. *See* Zimmermann, *Obligations*, 833–4.

[112] BGB, §§ 249, 254, 275–7.

[113] Larenz and Canaris, *Lehrbuch*, § 31 I e; Grunsky in *Münchener Kommentar* 254, no. 7.

[114] Grunsky in *Münchener Kommentar* to § 254, no. 59. See Helmut Heinrichs in *Palandt Bürgerliches Gesetzbuch* (62nd edn., Munich, 2003), to § 254, no. 51; OLG, Bremen, 20 Nov. 1975, *Versicherungs Recht* (1976), 558 at 560.

[115] Larenz and Canaris, *Lehrbuch*, § 31 I e; Grunsky in *Münchener Kommentar* to § 254, no. 7. See OLG, Munich, 23 Feb. 1990, NJW-RR 1990, 828 at 829 (all the damages on the injured party when the injurer was grossly negligent). See Heinrichs in *Palandt* to § 254, no. 51.   [116] 9 Exch 341.

profess to follow. Supposedly, a party is liable only for damages he could have foreseen at the time of contracting, either because they would follow in the normal course of events, or because he had been told they might occur. Historians are agreed that the court took this rule directly from Pothier.[117] But they did not borrow Pothier's exception for cases in which the defendant's breach constituted an intentional wrong. Perhaps they would have done so if, while Pothier's prestige in the Anglo-American world was still great, a case had arisen in which someone knowingly sold infected cattle or unsound timber. By happenstance, it did not.

Nevertheless, as we have seen, however, the defendant is liable in the United States for all of the consequences of an intentional tort under the doctrine of transferred intent. In some jurisdictions, he is liable for all of the consequences of negligent acts. As a result, whether a defendant is liable for all of the consequences of a breach of contract depends on whether the breach also happens to constitute a tort.

The results can be arbitrary. For example, the defendant has committed an intentional tort as well as a breach of contractual duty if he is a physician who intentionally removes the wrong organ from a patient as part of an unauthorized medical experiment; if he is a lifeguard who intentionally holds a swimmer underwater as a prank; or if he is a caretaker who intentionally lights a fire in order to burn down his employer's house. Supposedly, he is liable for all the harm he does, foreseeable or not. In contrast, a physician, a lifeguard or a caretaker has committed a breach of contract but not an intentional tort if he deliberately refrains from acting and so a patient dies, a swimmer drowns or a fire lit by another burns his employer's house. In principle, he is liable only for damages he might have foreseen at the time the contract was made.

In the case described earlier, the defendant who knowingly sold penicillin diluted with a compound he believes to be harmless might well be liable for committing an intentional tort. He might be liable for battery because he caused an unauthorized 'contact' between the chemical compound and the body of the plaintiff. One American court allowed women undergoing prenatal care to recover for battery when, without their knowledge, they were given a pill containing a drug, DES, as part of an experiment to determine its value in preventing miscarriages.[118] In contrast, the defendant who sold cattle that he knows to be inflected could not be held liable in trespass for all of the consequences because he did not enter the plaintiff's property. At least, that was John Fleming's opinion when I put this hypothetical case to him years ago. It is hard to see any rational ground for such a distinction.

English law does not recognize the doctrine of transferred intent in tort. Nevertheless, in England, in both of the cases just described, the defendant might be liable for committing the tort of deceit. If so, then, as Lord Denning held in *Doyle* v. *Olby*, he would be liable for all of the consequences.[119] In contrast, some

---

[117] See Zimmermann, *Law of Obligations*, 830.

[118] *Mink* v. *University of Chicago*, 460 FSupp 713 (ND Ill. 1978). In this case, the advantage of the action in battery was not that it permitted recovery of unforeseeable damages but that it permitted recovery even though the plaintiffs were unable to prove that they themselves had suffered physical harm from the drug. The harm has been suffered by their unborn children.

[119] *Doyle* v. *Olby*, [1969] 2 All ER 119, 122 (CA). See K. M. Stanton, *The Modern Law of Tort* (London, 1994), 100–1.

American courts have said the harm must be caused 'proximately' by defendant's misrepresentation, an expression that usually excludes the unforeseeable.[120] But perhaps these statements are overly broad. In such cases, however, plaintiff often suffered, not consequential harm caused by the circumstances that had been misrepresented, but harm that had nothing to do with these circumstances. The bonds or stock he purchased would have become valueless even if defendant's representations had been true.[121]

To be liable in deceit, however, the defendant must have misrepresented some fact. He would be liable in England if he lied about whether the penicillin was diluted or the horse was infected.[122] In some American jurisdictions, he would be liable if he knew of such a defect and remained silent. For example, the seller of a house is liable if he does not reveal that it is infested with termites.[123] He must, however, have deceived the other party as to a presently existing fact such as the defective condition of the goods.

His present state of mind counts as such a fact. Consequently, he is liable in deceit if he intends to violate his contractual obligations at the moment he contracts. Simply by contracting, he misrepresented his intentions. But he is not liable in deceit if he made his promise in good faith and then violated it.[124]

The results again can be arbitrary. One who owns a warehouse and rents space in it for storage would be liable in deceit if he lied about whether the warehouse was fireproof or whether it was equipped with an fire alarm that would automatically notify the fire department. He would be liable if he promised to fireproof the warehouse or to install such an alarm or to call the fire department if a fire broke out, intending at the time to break his promise. He could therefore be liable if the Rubens stored by a customer burned. But he might not be liable if he later broke his promise to fireproof the warehouse or to install the alarm or to notify the fire department once a fire had started even if he did so because he wanted the warehouse to burn so he could collect the insurance.

To avoid such anomalies, one might change the law of deceit to treat a later and wrongful decision to breach in the same way as an original intention to do so. One would then have arrived by the back door at the rule that the defendant is liable for all of the consequences of a wrongful breach. The more straightforward approach would be to acknowledge that we need such a rule if we are to avoid such results.

---

[120] e.g. *Boatmen's National Co.* v. *M.W. Elkins & Co.*, 63 F2d 214 (8th Cir 1933). Similarly, courts have sometimes said that the proper measure of damages is the difference between the value of the object as it is and its value had it been as represented. *Waddell* v. *White*, 46 Ariz 420, 108 P2d 565 (1940); *Morrell* v. *Wiley*, 119 Conn 578, 178 A 121 (1935).

[121] *Boatmen's National Co.* v. *M.W. Elkins & Co.*, 63 F2d 214 (8th Cir 1933); *Waddell* v. *White*, 46 Ariz 420, 108 P2d 565 (1940). In other cases, the problem was not whether the damages were foreseeable but whether they could be established with any certainty. e.g. *Morrell* v. *Wiley*, 119 Conn 578, 178 A 121 (1935).

[122] Stanton, *Tort*, 330; R. F. V. Heuston and R.A. Buckley, *Salmond and Heuston on the Law of Torts* (21st edn., London, 1996), 370.

[123] e.g. *Obde* v. *Schlemeyer*, 56 Wash2d 449, 353 P2d 672 (1960) (action lies for failure of seller of house to disclose termite infestation).

[124] England: Stanton, *Tort*, 330; Heuston and Buckley, *Torts*, 371. United States: W. P. Keeton, D. Dobbs, R. Keeton, D. Owen, and W. Prosser, *The Law of Torts* (5th edn., St Paul, Minn., 1984), 763–4.

PART V

UNJUST ENRICHMENT

Unjust Enrichment

This part of the book will deal with the law of unjust enrichment. By that I mean a claim based on the ancient principle that one person should not be enriched at another's expense. Some scholars have claimed that this principle has no meaning. I will try to answer them in the following chapter. Others have claimed there is a 'law of restitution', and it is a mistake to try to explain it by this principle alone.[1] It is certainly true that remedies that defy classification have been attributed to the 'law of restitution', and that all the remedies that have supposedly been granted for unjust enrichment cannot be explained by that principle. The last two chapters of this book will point out why. But our purpose will be to show that unjust enrichment is a coherent principle and a proper ground for relief. I don't think it is helpful to speak about a 'law of restitution', as though it were a coherent entity, when it rests, not on some coherent principle, but on the need in disparate cases to fill the gaps left by other branches of law.

[1] James J. Edelman, 'Unjust Enrichment, Restitution and Wrongs', *Texas L. Rev.* 79 (2001), 1869 at 1870. See generally, Peter Birks, *An Introduction to the Law of Restitution* (Oxford, 1985).

19

The Principle Against Unjustified Enrichment

I. Unjust Enrichment without a Principle Against Unjust Enrichment

A celebrated abstraction is the maxim from the *Digest* that no one should be enriched at another's expense.[1] The late scholastics and then the northern natural lawyers thought that this principle could explain the law of unust enrichment. Since the 19th century, German jurists, in particular, have been trying to bring it down to earth. Windscheid and his contemporaries agreed that this principle is too broad, a 'false abstraction', 'untrue at this level of generality'.[2] The truth was suggested by another Roman maxim which said a person was liable for 'a thing which he has without a just basis (*justa causa*)'.[3] According to Windscheid, a person enriched at another's expense 'has the duty to justify (*herauszugeben*) to the disadvantaged party, why he has become richer'.[4]

That conclusion is expressed by the general principle of § 812(1) of the German Civil Code: 'one who has received something through another's performance or at his expense in some other way without legal basis (*ohne rechtlichen Grund*) is obligated to give it back'. Yet 20th century German jurists have found that statement too broad as well. In 1934, Walter Wilburg claimed that it was impossible to formulate any general rule as to when enrichment is unjustified.[5] Ernst von Caemmerer agreed. It is not true that an enrichment is unjustified when the person enriched has no contractual or statutory claim to be. A person might lose his rights to another by prescription. Or he might renounce a right which is consequently acquired by someone else. Or he might open a tourist hotel in a hitherto unknown village or build a dam, thereby enhancing the value of neighboring properties.[6] Other jurists have pointed out that 'enrichment may be due to the display of particular skills

---

[1] 'Natura aequum est, neminem cum alterius detrimento fieri locupletiorem.' Dig. 12.6.14; Dig. 50.17.206.

[2] Bernhard Windscheid, *Lehrbuch des Pankektenrechts* (7th edn., Düsseldorf, 1891), § 421 n. 1.

[3] 'Nam iure gentium condici puto posse ab his, qui non ex iusta causa p[o]ssident.' D. 25.2.25. 'Constat, id demum posse condici alicui, quod vel non ex iusta causa ad eum pervenit, vel redit ad non iustam causam.' Dig. 12.7.1.3. Both passages are quoted in Windscheid, *Lehrbuch* § 421 n. 1.

[4] Windscheid, *Lehrbuch*, § 421.

[5] Walter Wilburg, *Die Lehre von der ungerechtfertigten Bereicherung nach österreichischem und deutschem Recht* (Graz, 1934), 5–6.

[6] Ernst von Caemmerer, 'Grundprobleme des Bereicherungsrechts', *Gesammelte Schriften*, (Hans G. Leser, 1st edn., Tübingen, 1968), 370 at 374–5.

in (lawful) competitition'.[7] Von Caemmerer concluded that, in many cases, 'third parties are advantaged without a contractual or statutory claim to be. But they are not unjustifiably enriched, and there is no action in unjustified enrichment against them.'[8]

According to von Caemmerer, one could not formulate a general principle but only identify types of cases in which the plaintiff has a cause of action. Building on the work of Wilburg, and without intending to be exhaustive, he described four major ones: (1) the plaintiff rendered the defendant a performance (*Leistung*) which was without a legal basis (*Grund*) in the sense that the purpose the plaintiff was pursuing was not achieved; (2) the defendant made an encroachment (*Eingriff*) on the plaintiff's property; (3) the plaintiff incurred expenses (*Impensen, Aufwendungen*, today, commonly, *Verwendungen*) improving the defendant's property; and (4) the plaintiff paid another's debt and now claims recourse (*Rückgriff*) against the defendant. Today, this typology is widely accepted. It is found in most German textbooks and commentaries.[9]

Whether the plaintiff should recover in the fourth case—in which he sues for the defendant for having paid another's debt—depends on whether the legal system in question regards the plaintiff's payment as absolving the defendant from his own obligation to pay the debt. That is a question we do not need to get into here. In the other three types of cases, however, Anglo-American and French law also give relief, and when they do not, one can explain their reluctance by doubts about how much the plaintiff's expenses were worth to the defendant.

Nevertheless, French and Anglo-American law have been more concerned with particular cases than with abstractions. Only two particular cases are described in the French Civil Code: payment of sums not due (art. 1376) and handling another's affairs (art. 1372). French law has been built by analogy to these. Jurists have occasionally mentioned the principle of unjust enrichment, but they have either dismissed it as a meaningless generalization or espoused it without explaining how it can be tied to the cases in which French law gives relief.

For most of its history, Anglo-American law has been tied to particular cases. It has recognized various restitutionary remedies, each with its own rules, but 'the courts gave no sign of any larger purpose or plan, and any suggestion that the continuities they were creating added up to a "law" of restitution would have been met for decades with disbelief'.[10] In the United States, acknowledgment that there was such a body of law came earlier than in England. In 1937, the American Law Institute published a *Restatement of Restitution* although John Dawson has suggested that it merely 'patched the parts together and gave the subject a name'.[11] The first comprehensive American treatise was only published by George Palmer in 1978.[12] In that year, Lord Diplock insisted emphatically that 'there is no general doctrine of unjust enrichment recognized in English law'; there were merely 'specific remedies in particular cases'.[13]

---

[7] Reinhard Zimmermann, *The Law of Obligations: Roman Foundations: of the Civilian Tradition* (Cape Town, 1990), 889.   [8] Von Caemmerer, 'Grundprobleme', 375.

[9] Zimmermann, *The Law of Obligations*, 890.

[10] John P. Dawson, 'Restitution without Enrichment', *Boston U.L. Rev.* 61 (1981), 563, at 564.

[11] ibid. 564–5.   [12] George E. Palmer, *The Law of Restitution* (Boston, 1978).

[13] *Orakpo* v. *Manson Investments Ltd.* [1978] AC 95, 104 (HL).

Nevertheless, Sir Robert Goff and Gareth Jones had already published a treatise on the English law of restitution which was followed in 1985 by a still more systematic one by Peter Birks.[14] Perhaps impressed at the degree of order that these treatise writers had found in the decided cases, English courts have now recognized a general principle of liability for unjustified enrichment.[15]

In one sense, then, German and Anglo-American law have moved toward each other. Beginning with an abstract principle, the Germans arrived at a typology of cases while, beginning with their case law, the English and Americans have sought a principled explanation. For a long time, the principal argument was, what the principle in question might be. In the last works before his premature death, Peter Birks embraced the continental principle that a remedy should be given because, as continental jurists had said, the defendant had been enriched without reason—*sine causa*.[16] In his previous works, Birks, like other English jurists, identified a series of factors which make it unjust for the defendant to be enriched. In some cases, the defendant has been enriched 'by subtraction' from the plaintiff's assets, and the 'transfer' of wealth is unjust if it was 'non-voluntary' on the part of the plaintiff or 'freely accepted' by the defendant. In other cases, the defendant was enriched by committing a wrong, and the type of wrong explains why the enrichment is unjust.[17]

One reason Birks recanted is that, as he notes himself,[18] Sonja Meier drew his attention to a case in which it was difficult to explain the law by unjust factors such as involuntariness.[19] Payments were made *ultra vires*, by an entity which has no power to authorize them. Birk's paradigm example was the so-called 'swaps cases' in which payments made by local authorities as part of a financing scheme were held to be beyond the local authorities' power.[20] One might, of course, have fit these cases into the older approach by adding 'payments *ultra vires*' to the list of 'unjust factors'. But as Meier pointed out, and Birks realized, the older approach would then lose whatever explanatory power it had.[21] No doubt, whenever anyone is unjustly enriched, one can look backward, discover why the transfer of wealth was made and claim that relief is given because of an 'unjust factor'. But if that amounts to no more than saying that the defendant was enriched for no good reason, then the ultimate reason for giving relief is that, as continental jurists have always said, he was enriched *sine causa*. To try to identify an 'unjust reason' is really no more than to explain how such an event occurred. But the reason for giving relief is that it occurred.

From the standpoint of commutative justice, as we have described it, these two approaches are not as opposed as they might seem. Birks' older approach, and that of English jurists who still follow it, concerns whether a transfer of wealth, which enriches one person at another's expense, is truly voluntary or else whether it involves a wrong. Birks's new approach and that of Meier and the continental jurists, concerns

---

[14] Peter Birks, *An Introduction to the Law of Restitution* (Oxford, 1985).
[15] *Lipkin Gorman* v. *Karpnale Ltd.* [1991] 2 AC 548.
[16] Peter Birks, *Unjust Enrichment* (Oxford, 2003), 87–143.
[17] For a chart, see Birks, *Law of Restitution*, 106.   [18] Birks, *Unust Enrichment*, pp. xv, 119.
[19] Sonja Meier, 'Unjust Factors and Legal Grounds', in David Johnson and Reinhard Zimmermann, eds., *Unjustified Enrichment: Key Issues in Comparative Perspective* (Cambridge, 2002), 37 at 62–5.
[20] *Hazell* v. *Hammersmith & Fulham BC*, [1992] 2 AC 1 (HL).
[21] Meier, 'Unjust Factors', 64–5; Birks, *Unjust Enrichment*, 98.

whether someone has been enriched at another's expense without a reason the law recognizes. Whether enrichment through commission of a wrong is a ground for restitution will be considered later.[22] As we have already seen, however, if the law rests on the principle of commutative justice, the reason it will uphold a voluntary transfer of resources cannot be divorced from the basic principle that no one should be enriched at another's expense. In an exchange, it will permit such a transfer, not simply because it is voluntary, but so that each party can obtain what he needs without enriching the other. In a gift, it will do so, not simply because it is voluntary, but because it is likely that the transferor has made a sensible decision to enrich another. If so, it is odd to ask whether the law gives relief for unjust enrichment because of the involuntariness of the transfer or because of enrichment without a reason the law will recognize. The very reason the law will respect a voluntary transfer is either that no one is enriched, or that someone, with the transferor's consent, should be. That principle, we have argued, determines not only the rules that should govern exchange and gift, but which decisions the law should regard as voluntary in a sense worthy of respect and how the law interprets the scope of these decisions. Ask, as the English traditionally have, what 'just factors' warrant a transfer of resources, and one must ask what factors, including voluntariness, should warrant a transfer if it is true, as we have claimed, that neither party should be enriched at another's expense absent a good reason. Ask, as continental jurists traditionally do, whether a party has been enriched for a reason the law will not recognize, and one must ask when, as we have discussed, the law should recognize voluntariness as such a factor. If we look at the problem in this way, the question of what to do about *ultra vires* transfers, which was central to Birks, is a red herring. Of course one can't give away resources when one has no right to do so. The more basic question, however, is why the law of unjust enrichment will sometimes sustain, and sometimes not, a transfer that a party had the authority to make.

The difficulty that remains, however—whether one speaks, as the English traditionally do, of 'unjust factors', or as Birks and continental jurists do, of enrichment *sine causa*—is what sort of enrichment is unjust or lacks a *causa* the law should recognize. Von Caemmerer thought that the natural law approach was wrong. The late scholastics and the northern natural lawyers thought the principle at stake was that no one should be enriched at another's expense. According to von Caemmerer, 'when it is a question of applying a general clause that is framed in so broad and general a way as the maxim of unjust enrichment' one cannot find 'abstract and general criteria of application'. A jurist, 'like a judge in a system of case law', must identify 'groups of cases and types of claims'.[23] To do so is not merely the first step in the analysis. It is the only way the principle can be made concrete. At least before his recantation, Birks agreed that the 'principle against unjust enrichment' 'should be regarded with suspicion' to the extent that it 'threatens to undo the effort to look downwards to the cases'.[24] 'For as soon as steps are taken to bring it down to earth it begins to say nothing other than that the law ought not to be ignored', that is, that '[t]here are circumstances in which the law does not permit one person to be enriched at the expense of another'.[25] One identifies these circumstances by looking 'downwards to the cases', not by working out the

---

[22] Chapter 21.   [23] Von Caemmerer, 'Grundprobleme', 391.
[24] Birks, *Law of Restitution*, 23.   [25] ibid. 23.

implications of the principle. Neither von Caemmerer nor Birks thought that the principle is meaningless. But, they agreed, one cannot get from the principle to a description of those cases in which the plaintiff should recover.

I believe the late scholastics and the northern natural lawyers were closer to the truth than is usually thought. I will try to show (1) that one really can give a definite meaning to the principle that no one should be enriched at another's expense, (2) that although von Caemmerer devised his categories to make this principle more definite, in fact, one needs that principle to give definiteness to von Caemmerer's categories, and (3) that von Caemmerer's categories are nevertheless useful in focusing attention on the fundamental problems that must be resolved before relief is given.

II. The Principle Against Unjustified Enrichment

As just noted, modern jurists are suspicious of the principle because they have a litany of cases in which it seems not to work.[26] One person seems to be enriched at another's expense, and yet it is clear that he should not recover. These examples, however, rest on a fundamental misreading of the principle. It is taken to mean that no one should benefit as a result of a loss or cost suffered or incurred by another. Of course, that cannot be correct.

To avoid misreading the principle, we should consider what it meant to the late scholastics and northern natural lawyers who used it to explain the law of restitution. Roman law gave relief for specific instances of unjust enrichment, and the *Digest* said that no one should be enriched at another's expense. But as Robert Feenstra has pointed out, the late scholastics were the first to recognize this principle as the foundation of a law of unjustified enrichment coeval with contract and tort. The northern natural lawyers borrowed their conclusions.[27]

---

[26] That, at least, is the most common reason for suspicion. Prof. Gallo is suspicious for another reason. He is 'skeptical about a general remedy for the recovery of unjust enrichment' because '[o]ther factors must also be proven, such as acceptance by the person enriched, or injury to a protected interest, impossibility that the person benefitted could intervene in cases of *negotiorum gestio*, the good faith of the improver, or the presence of an "incontrovertible benefit" '. Paolo Gallo, 'Unjust Enrichment: A Comparative Analysis', *Am. Jour. Comp L.* 40 (1992), 431 at 463. But proof of 'acceptance' or 'incontrovertible benefit' merely goes to the question of whether the benefitted person was truly enriched given the problem of 'subjective devaluation' described later in this essay. Proof of 'injury to a protected interest' goes to whether the benefit was at the plaintiff's expense. To require proof of these matters does not contradict the principle that no one should be enriched at another's expense. It merely goes to show enrichment at another's expense is to be proven. In my view, proof that the person benefitted could intervene in cases of *negotiorum gestio* or of the good faith of the improver goes to a quite distinct issue: how to prevent one party from, in effect, forcing a contract upon another by refusing to seek his consent when it is possible to do so. As we will see in Chapter 21, strictly speaking, that problem is not one of unjustified enrichment.

Still another reason for scepticism is the observation that sometimes the defendant is liable when he is not enriched. See John P. Dawson, 'Erasable Enrichment in German Law', *Boston U. L. Rev.* 61 (1981), 271; John P. Dawson, 'Restitution without Enrichment', *Boston U. L. Rev.* 61 (1981), 563; Gallo, 'Unjust Enrichment', 437. I will show in the next chapter that such cases are not really part of the law of unjust enrichment: for example, what to do when a contract is void but sufficiently voluntary so that certain risks should pass to the defendant.

[27] Robert Feenstra, 'Grotius' Doctrine of Unjust Enrichment as a Source of Obligation: Its Origin and its Influence on Roman-Dutch Law', in *Unjust Enrichment* (E. J. H. Schrage, ed., The Hague, 1995), 197.

The late scholastics explained the principle against unjust enrichment in terms of the concept of commutative justice of Aristotle and Aquinas.[28] Distributive justice gives each citizen a fair share of whatever resources the state has to divide, and commutative justice preserves the share of each citizen. As we have seen,[29] they explained why people should have resources in the first place by drawing on Aristotle's criticism of Plato's opinion that property should be held in common. If it were, Aristotle said, people would quarrel, and some would work little and receive much while others worked much and obtained little.[30] Thomas Aquinas explained that private property was a legitimate institution because it avoided the disadvantages that Aristotle had mentioned.[31] Late scholastics such as Soto, Molina, and Lessius followed Aquinas, and natural lawyers such as Grotius and Pufendorf borrowed from them. While they developed these ideas in different ways, they all said that by nature, or originally, or in principle, all things belong to everyone. The point of establishing private rights to property was to prevent quarrels and to give people an incentive to work and to care for resources.[32] Moreover, all of them concluded that because private property was instituted for this purpose, the owner's rights were not absolute but were limited by the considerations that explained why such rights were instituted. For example, as we have seen,[33] a person in urgent need with no other recourse could lawfully take another's property.[34] Grotius said that there is a right of innocent use: one person can use another's property if he can do so without causing any loss or inconvenience.[35]

It followed that absent necessity or some other exception to the normal rules, commutative justice was violated if one person took or used another's resources for his own benefit. That line of reasoning led the late scholastics to recognize unjustified enrichment as a distinct body of law. Thomas Aquinas had said that a person might violate commutative justice either by interfering with another's property in a wrongful manner (*acceptio rei*) or simply by having what belonged to another (*ipsa res accepta*).[36] The late scholastics examined this last possibility more closely. Suppose he no longer had another's property. He was liable, they said, if he had thereby become richer. They thus recognized unjust enrichment as a distinct ground for relief,[37] and the northern natural lawyers followed them.[38]

We should note the context in which they spoke of unjust enrichment. Resources, from which one party had the exclusive right to benefit, had been used to confer on someone else the very benefit to which the first party had the exclusive right.

[28] Jan Hallebeek, *The Concept of Unjust Enrichment in Late Scholasticism* (Nijmegen, 1996), 47.

[29] Chapter 1 I.   [30] *Politics* II. v.   [31] *Summa theologiae* II-II, Q. 66, a. 2.

[32] Domenicus Soto, *De iustitia et iure libri decem* (Salamanca, 1553), lib. 4, q. 3, a. 1; Ludovicus Molina, *De iustitia et iure tractatus* (Venice, 1614), disp. 20; Leonard Lessius, *De iustitia et iure ceterisque virtutibus cardinalis* (Paris, 1628), lib. 2, cap. 5, dubs. 1–2; Hugo Grotius, *De iure belli ac pacis libri tres* (B. J. A. de Kanter-van Hetting Tromp, ed., 1939), II.ii.2; Samuel Pufendorf, *De iure naturae et gentium libri octo* (Amsterdam, 1688), II.vi.5; IV.iv.4–7.   [33] Chapter 7 I.

[34] Thomas Aquinas, *Summa theologiae*, Q. 66, a. 7; Soto, *De iustitia et iure*, lib. 5, q. 3, a. 4; Molina, *De iustitia et iure*, disp. 20; Lessius, *De iustitia et iure*, lib. 2, cap. 12, dub. 12; Grotius, *De iure belli ac pacis*, II.ii.6–7; Pufendorf, *De iure naturae et gentium*, II.vi.5.   [35] Grotius, *De iure bellis ac pacis*, II.ii.11.

[36] *Summa theologiae* II-II, Q. 62, a. 6.

[37] Molina, *De iustitia et iure*, disp. 718, no. 2; Lessius, *De iustitia et iure*, lib. 2, cap. 14, dub. 1, no. 3. See Halleback, *Unjust Enrichment*, 47–58.

[38] Grotius, *De iure bellis ac pacis*, II.x.5; Pufendorf, *De iure naturae et gentium*, IV.xiii.9.

Commutative justice forbad the second party to keep the benefit. That is a quite different and much more defensible claim than to say that no one should benefit as the result of a loss or cost suffered or incurred by somebody else.

If we keep this original context in mind, we will have much less trouble with the principle against unjustified enrichment. In some of the cases that have troubled modern jurists, a party had no exclusive right to the use of the resources that the other used to enrich himself. Thus, when the principle is understood in the way just described, it does not apply to these cases. An example is the case in which one person is enriched by using his own skills in competition with another who loses business as a result. The skillful competitor has not enriched himself by taking or using resources from which the other party had the exclusive right to benefit. The other party has the right to compete but not the exclusive right to do business with potential customers. As Grotius pointed out, there is a difference between 'the right to one's own', which is 'a legal right properly and strictly so-called', and what Aristotle called 'an aptitude' or 'worthiness' to receive something.[39]

As this example illustrates, to apply the principle, one has to know whether the plaintiff had an exclusive right. The principle itself does not tell us what exclusive rights people have. Nevertheless, the approach of the late scholastics and natural lawyers does suggest how such a question should be answered. According to them, the point of establishing private rights to resources is to prevent people from quarreling about their proper share of common resources and to give them an incentive to work and to care for resources. In general, neither of those purposes is served by immunizing a party against competition from those more skilled.

In other cases that have troubled modern jurists, although one party was enriched, he did not obtain the very benefit to which the owner of the resources had the exclusive right. In von Caemmerer's examples, one party is enriched because he owned property or a business in the vicinity of a tourist hotel or dam constructed by the other. But certainly, while the owner of a hotel or dam does enjoy certain exclusive rights over his property, they do not include a right to any benefit that its existence may happen to cause other people.

Again, taken by itself, the principle against unjustified enrichment does not tell us what exclusive rights to benefit belong to one who owns a hotel or a dam. But again, the approach of the earlier jurists enables us to see how such questions can be answered. Allowing the owner to exact compensation for every benefit that his use of his property for his own benefit may confer upon others would go beyond the purposes for which, in their view, private rights are established. One purpose was to prevent the quarrels that arise from sharing property. When rights are established for that purpose, it does not follow that the right holder is entitled to any benefit his use of his right produces for others. If both my children love to play the piano, I might prevent quarrels by allowing each of them to play it half the time. It would not follow that a child who is playing can charge me or the other child for the pleasure of hearing him. The other purpose is to provide an incentive to work and to care for resources. Again, that objective does not require that the hotel or dam builder be able to charge for every

---

[39] Grotius, *De iure belli ac pacis*, I.i.5,7.

benefit he confers. If the hotel or dam is sufficiently profitable to himself, he needs no further incentive. If it is not, he can negotiate with those who will also benefit and agree to build it only if they contribute to the costs. As economists point out, the incentives will be insufficient only where the normal mechanism of negotiation followed by contract breaks down.

In another case that troubled von Caemmerer, that of abandonment or renunciation of rights, the party who lost resources did not expend them to confer the benefit that the other party received. As we will see in more detail later on, expense is a relative term. It makes sense to say that a benefit was obtained at another party's expense only if the other party's resources were actually expended to produce the benefit in question. In the case of abandonment, the rights were lost without the intention of producing any benefit at all.

Finally, there is the case in which rights are lost by adverse possession or prescription. These are indeed cases in which the very benefits to which one party was once exclusively entitled pass to another but ones we discussed earlier.[40] The existence of such cases merely shows that while the principle that no one should be enriched at another's expense holds generally, it does not hold universally. As the late scholastics and natural lawyers recognized, and for reasons we described earlier, sometimes there will be exceptions.

Again, their approach helps us to understand why there should be exceptions and when they should be recognized. We have seen how they thought that private rights should extend only as far as the purposes for which they were created, and how that approach can explain the loss of rights through necessity or adverse possession. In any case, the owner has not really lost rights if, given the purposes of property law, they were conferred on him conditionally: so that he can use rather than neglect resources which are of use to others. If so, the very considerations that explain why private rights are established explain why, in this instance, they may be lost.

The existence of such exceptions does not mean that the principle that no one should be enriched at another's expense is 'false abstraction', 'untrue at this level of generality', as Windscheid thought. According to him we can only say that a person enriched at another's expense 'has the duty to justify to the disadvantaged party, why he has become richer'. If our argument thus far is correct, then Windscheid was wrong. The principle is a sound one provided we understand it to apply to the kinds of cases that the jurists of the natural law era had in mind: those in which resources from which one person has the exclusive right to draw a benefit were used to confer this very benefit on someone else. In such cases, the second party does not merely have a duty to explain why he has become richer. As a general rule, he owes compensation.

III. Von Caemmerer's Categories

Von Caemmerer devised his typology to give definiteness to a principle which he thought was hopelessly indefinite. Instead, the principle is sufficiently definite that all of his categories can be shown to be instances of it. Indeed, to make most of these

---

[40] Chapter 7 II.

categories definite, one needs to have recourse to the principle and to the general considerations on which it is founded.

The need is most obvious in the case of *Eingriff* or encroachment on another's resources: for example, the defendant consumes the plaintiff's heating oil, believing in good faith that it is his own.[41] This was the type of case that the late scholastics and the northern natural lawyers discussed. One person had come into possession of another's resources, and had used them to procure a benefit to which the other person had the exclusive right. Here, in order to tell if there has been an *Eingriff*, one must be able to determine whether the plaintiff had the exclusive right to the use of the resources in question. As Reinhard Zimmermann has noted, von Cammerer's category of *Eingriff* cannot be applied without asking 'who was entitled to the right with regard to which there was interference'.[42]

It would be hard to answer that question without asking why people have exclusive entitlements to resources. Like the earlier jurists, von Caemmerer believed that the reasons the plaintiff recovers in such cases are implicit in the very establishment of private rights to resources:

The meaning of property law is that the owner is assigned the authority to use, to profit from and to consume the object ('uti, frui, abuti'). The advantage that the encroacher derives from the consumption or use of the object is therefore unjustified. The encroacher must give back to the owner the value that he would in fairness have had to pay had he known how matters were. In this group of cases, the enrichment is considered to be unjustified because it is in contradiction to the purpose pursued by the legal order in the assignment of property.[43]

Wilburg said the same.[44] If they were right, then we must ask what purpose the legal order was pursuing in establishing property rights in order to determine whether the plaintiff had an exclusive entitlement on which the defendant has encroached. We have already seen how the approach of the earlier jurists makes such an inquiry possible. They identified two purposes the legal order is pursuing: to prevent the quarrels that would arise from common ownership of property and to provide an incentive to work and to use resources well. The question then becomes, whether recognizing an exclusive right in the plaintiff is called for by either of these purposes. We have seen in a general way how that question can be answered when we discussed the case of a person injured in competition with a skillful competitor.

In the case of von Caemmerer's other categories, or some of them,[45] such an inquiry seems to be unnecessary. We do not have to ask about the extent of the

---

[41] Von Caemmerer, 'Grundprobleme', 378.   [42] Zimmermann, *The Law of Obligations*, 889–90.

[43] 'Es ist der Sinn des Eigentumsrechts, dem Eigentümer die Befugnis zu Gebrauch, Nutzung und Verbrauch der Sache (das "uti, fruit, abuti") zuzuweisen. Der Vorteil, den der Eingreifer durch Verbrauch oder Gebrauch der Sache erlangt, ist damit ungerechtfertigt. Der Eingreifer muss dem Eigentümer den Wert erstatten, den er bei Kenntnis der Sachlage redlicherweise hätte zahlen müssen. In dieser Fallgruppe wird die Bereicherung also deshalb als ungerechtfertigt angesehen, weil sie im Widerspruch zu dem von der Rechtsordnung mit der Zuweisung des Eigentums verfolgten Zweck steht' Von Caemenerer, Grundproblene, 378.

[44] Wilburg, *Die Lehre von der ungerechtfertigten Bereicherung*, 28.

[45] Although it is beside the point we are now making, Wilburg also thought that a claim for improvements, like a claim for encroachment, also was mandated by the very purpose of establishing property rights. Wilburg, *Die Lehre von der ungerechtfertigten Bereicherung*, 28.

plaintiff's entitlements when he improved defendant's property, thinking it to be his own, or rendered defendant a performance without a legal ground, or discharged defendant's debt. As Zimmermann has noted, when one party has rendered the other a performance, 'the legal requirement of "at the expense" as a further criterion for enrichment liability becomes superfluous . . .'.[46] Wilburg concluded that a claim arising out of a performance has 'nothing to do' with a claim arising out of an encroachment on plaintiff's rights. The performance might concern a *Rechtsgut* like property, but it might not.[47]

Nevertheless, all of von Caemmerer's categories are instances in which resources from which defendant had the exclusive right to draw a benefit were used to confer that very benefit on the plaintiff. True, we do not need to inquire about the extent of the plaintiff's entitlements. But the reason is that the mere fact that the plaintiff conferred the benefit in question shows that it was conferred at the plaintiff's expense. That is so whether he acted to enhance the value of property which he happens to own, or to benefit the defendant or the defendant's creditor.

To see why, consider the following cases. In all of them, plaintiff performs the same physical action. He chops down a tree:

Case 1: The plaintiff chops down the tree simply for exercise or for practice using an axe, with no thought of selling the lumber. Or he chops it down because it interferes with his view. He thinks the tree is on his own land, but in fact it is located on that of the defendant. The defendant is pleased because the tree interfered with his own view and because he can now sell the lumber. (Assume, here and in the cases that follow, that the defendant owns the wood. The plaintiff has not gained title to it by felling the tree.)

Case 2: The plaintiff chops down the tree in order to sell the lumber. As before, he thinks the tree is on his own land when it is actually on that of the defendant. The defendant discovered what the plaintiff was doing only after the tree was felled. He had been intending to pay someone to fell the tree so he could sell the lumber. He now wants to sell it.

Case 3: The facts are as in Case 2 except that the plaintiff knows that the tree is on defendant's land and chops it down because he believes that he has a contract with the defendant to do so. The defendant did want the tree chopped down so he could sell it for lumber. But for one reason or another the contract is void.

Case 4: The facts are as in Case 3 except that the tree is on the land of a third party, the plaintiff falsely believes that he is under contract to chop it down, and by doing so he fulfills the obligation of the defendant who is under a contractual duty to do so.

Cases 2, 3, and 4 fall, respectively, into von Caemmerer's categories of *Verwendungen*, *Leistung ohne Grund* and *Rückgriff*. Case 1 falls into none of these categories, and, indeed, does not seem to warrant relief. The reason is that, as

---

[46] Zimmermann, *The Law of Obligations*, 889.
[47] Wilburg, *Die Lehre von der ungerechtfertigten Bereicherung*, 49–50.

mentioned earlier, 'expense' is a relative term. It makes sense to say that a benefit was obtained at another party's expense only if the other party's resources were actually expended to produce the benefit in question. In Cases 2, 3, and 4, resources from which the plaintiff has the exclusive right to benefit—his labor—were used to confer the very benefit on the defendant to which the plaintiff has the exclusive right. One cannot say so in Case 1. In Case 1, plaintiff's conduct is the same: he chops a tree. Moreover, the defendant benefits: he sells the wood or obtains a better view. But in Case 1, the plaintiff acted in order to obtain some other benefit: exercise, practice, or a better view from his own house.

These cases show that there is a subjective element to the question whether one party has been enriched at the *expense* of another. It has long been recognized that the question, whether a party is *enriched*, has its subjective side. In the examples just given, the defendant was enriched because he wanted the tree felled either to have a better view or to sell the lumber. If it was a beautiful shade tree which he valued far beyond the price of the lumber, he would not have been enriched. This is the problem Peter Birks has referred to as 'subjective devaluation': what one person will pay for, another may not even want.[48] As we can now see, the question of whether enrichment was at someone else's *expense* has a subjective side as well. An expenditure of time or effort or anything else is an 'expense' only by reference to some benefit which it is expended to produce. Only if one person has received that very benefit from another's expenditure has he been enriched at the other's expense.

Thus, while von Caemmerer's other categories do not raise the same question as *Eingriff*, nevertheless, they are also instances of the enrichment of one party at the other party's expense. Moreover, at least in the case of *Verwendungen* or improvements and *Leistung* or performance, these categories cannot be made definite without having recourse to the principle against unjustified enrichment and the considerations underlying it. If that principle were too indefinite to apply, these categories would be too indefinite as well.

To determine whether a case falls under *Verwendungen* or improvements, one has to decide whether an expenditure that benefits another's property constitutes an 'improvement'. That question cannot be answered by simply asking whether the property in question was physically transformed. It can be improved without physical transformation. The plaintiff might fell a tree or build a dam in order to improve the view or the water supply on nearby land that belongs to the defendant but which he falsely believes to belong to himself. The nearby land is improved. It would be hard to see a difference in principle between such a case and one in which he actually built on the nearby land.

But not any expenditure that happens to increase the value of the defendant's land can count as an improvement: for example, the dam, built to increase the value of land which the plaintiff actually does own, might increase that of nearby land owned by the defendant. We have already seen how the principle against unjustified enrichment helps to resolve this problem. The plaintiff should recover only if he incurred the

---

[48] Birks, *Law of Restitution*, 109–14.

expenditure to produce the very benefit which the defendant obtained. As we saw, that is the test of whether the defendant was enriched at the plaintiff's expense. As we can see now, it also enables us to determine whether plaintiff's expenditure counts as an improvement of defendant's property. If the test were indefinite, the concept of an 'improvement' would be indefinite as well.

Moreover, von Caemmerer's category of *Leistung ohne Grund* is definite only if we can determine the meaning of *Grund*. For von Caemmerer, *Leistung* does not simply mean that the plaintiff acted to confer a benefit on the defendant. It also means that the plaintiff acted for a particular kind of reason, one which constitutes a 'legal basis', *Rechtsgrund* or *causa*. 'The legal basis of the performance is a contractual or statutory claim—also a "natural" or "moral" obligation.'[49] Relief is given because of a mistake concerning that reason.

Grund or *causa* thus has a double role to play. On the one hand, it is the motive for the plaintiff's performance, a reason why he wished to confer a benefit on the defendant. He would not wish to do so if he is mistaken about the *Grund* or *causa*. On the other hand, it is a *Rechtsgrund* or legal basis: a reason for the law to respect his motive so that, when there is no such mistake, the defendant is entitled to the benefit in question. The question necessarily arises: when should the law respect his motive? To put it another way, when should the law deem it proper for one person to confer a benefit on another at his own expense? One cannot answer that question without considering what sorts of enrichment are not deemed to be proper. To do so, one has to consider when they would offend the principle against unjust enrichment. Again, one needs to understand the principle in order to bring definiteness to von Caemmerer's categories.

As we have seen, the approach of the late scholastics and northern natural lawyers suggests how the principle might be understood. They thought that there were two good reasons or *causae* why one party might confer a benefit on the other. As we have seen,[50] one was liberality: he wished the recipient to benefit at his own expense. The other was voluntary commutative justice: he wished to receive, as of right, something else in exchange for what he gave.[51] Liberality did not simply mean giving wealth away but giving it 'to the right people, the right amounts, and at the right time'.[52] Thus, an act of liberality did enrich one party at the other's expense but, if the party who incurred the expense had acted sensibly, that party ought to be enriched. Commutative justice meant, not merely that each party received something in return for what he gave, but that each received something equivalent in value to what he gave.[53] Thus, the principle against unjust enrichment was not really violated because neither party was enriched. While these ideas about liberality and commutative justice have fallen out of fashion, we have seen they can be of help in understanding modern law. They can help understanding the law of unjustified enrichment by suggesting what should count as the *Grund* of a *Leistung* and why. For present purposes, however, we merely need to note that von Cammerer's category is not definite without an

---

[49] Von Caemmerer, 'Grundprobleme'.   [50] Chapter II B 1.

[51] Soto, *De iustitia et iure*, lib. 3, q. 5, a. 1; Molina, *De iustitia et iure*, disp. 252; Lessius, *De iustitia et iure*, lib. 2. cap. 17, dub. 1.   [52] *Nicomachean Ethics* IV.i 1119^{b}–1120^{a}.

[53] *Nicomachean Ethics* V.ii 1130^{b}–1131^{a}.

account of what should constitute a *Grund*. Any account should explain why plaintiff cannot reclaim his performance when there was a *Grund* for making it. That would mean explaining why, in such cases, the principle against unjust enrichment should not apply.

IV. The Value of von Caemmerer's Typology

We can now see why von Caemmerer's typology is valuable. The reason is not that the principle against unjustified enrichment is hopelessly vague. As we have just seen, his categories are instances in which that principle is applicable. Indeed, one needs the principle in order to give definiteness to his categories. His typology is valuable precisely because it does identify the different ways in which one person can be unjustly enriched at another's expense.

It is also valuable because, as we have seen, each category corresponds to a fundamental question that must be answered to determine whether the plaintiff should recover.[54] In the case of an *Eingriff* or encroachment, the fundamental question, as Zimmermann said, is 'who was entitled to the right with regard to which there was interference', or as we would put it, whether the defendant used the plaintiff's resources to procure a benefit to which the plaintiff was exclusively entitled. In the case of *Verwendungen* or improvements, the fundamental question is whether an expenditure that benefits another's property constitutes an enrichment of the property owner at the expense of the party making the expenditure. As we have seen, it does to the extent that the expenditure was incurred for the sake of that very benefit. In the case of *Leistung ohne Grund*, the fundamental question is what constitutes a *Grund*: a reason why one party would want to confer a benefit on the other and the law would respect his decision to do so. In the case of *Rückgriff*, there is also a distinct and fundamental question that must be answered, although one we will not discuss since it lies beyond the scope of this book: whether the plaintiff's performance has the legal effect of discharging the defendant's obligation. If it does not, the defendant is not enriched. Von Caemmerer's typology is valuable because it keeps these questions distinct: there is a separate category corresponding to each of them.

V. Conclusion

Whatever its merits, von Caemmerer's typology is one of the most successful attempts to date to explain when courts actually give relief. Whether partially or wholly successful, it would be strange if they could succeed at all if the principle against unjustified enrichment were so vague as to be meaningless. If it were, there would be

---

[54] That is not to say one cannot improve on his typology. It is to say that his categories ought to figure in any improved typology.

no underlying reason for relief to be appropriate in one class of cases rather than another. Indeed, it is almost mystical to think that an entire body of law could be founded on a principle that was really so indefinite. We have seen, however, that the principle did have meaning to those who first described unjustified enrichment as a distinct body of law. By recapturing its significance to them, we can better understand our modern law.

20

Restitution Without Enrichment?

In German law,[1] American law[2] and, more recently, English law, it is a defense to an action for unjust enrichment that the defendant is no longer enriched.[3] Nevertheless, many German scholars want to limit this defense. My former teacher, John Dawson, thought it leads to senseless results in Germany[4] which American courts avoid only by refusing to apply it. In the United States, he said, 'we would not as in Germany, conceive of enrichment as a variable that can be recovered only as long as it lasts'.[5]

I do not like to quarrel with Dawson, but this time he may have been mistaken. At any rate, I don't think this defense leads to senseless results as long as we confine it to its original scope, using it to resolve the problems it was originally meant to resolve.

I. Origins

We can see what these problems are if we examine the origins of this defense. The drafters of the German Civil Code took it from the 19th century Pandektists, Windscheid, and Savigny. Savigny seems to have taken it from members of the 17th and 18th century natural law school such as Grotius and Pufendorf, who took it in turn from the late scholastics of the 16th and 17th centuries. As we have seen, they had been discussing the implications of Aristotle's concept of commutative justice as it had been interpreted by Thomas Aquinas, and their efforts produced the modern idea of unjust enrichment as a separate body of law coeval with contract and tort.

Commutative justice is supposed to preserve each person's share of resources. As we have seen,[6] Thomas Aquinas explained that when one person had acquired or interfered with another's property, he might be liable for two different reasons. First, he might be liable because of the way in which he did so (*acceptio rei*): he might have acted wrongfully, against the owner's will, in which case he was liable whether or not he still had the property; or he might have acted with the owner's consent, in which case whether he was liable depended on the kind of voluntary agreement

---

[1] German Civil Code (*Bürgerlichesgesetzbuch*) [hereinafter BGB], § 118(3).
[2] *Restatement of the Law of Restitution, Quasi Contracts and Constructive Trusts* (1937), § 142.
[3] *Lipkin Gorman* v. *Karpnale Ltd.* [1991] 2 AC 548.
[4] John P. Dawson, 'Erasable Enrichment in German Law', *Boston U.L. Rev.* 61 (1981), 271–314.
[5] John P. Dawson, 'Restitution without Enrichment', *Boston U.L. Rev.* 61 (1981), 563 at 564.
[6] Chapter 19 II.

they had made.[7] Second, he might be liable merely because he had another's property, regardless of how he had come by it (*ipsa res accepta*). According to Aquinas, commutative justice required that he give it back.[8]

In this last case, according to the late scholastics, and then Grotius and Pufendorf, a person who no longer has another's property should still be liable if he has become richer by having once had it.[9] Such a person is liable only to the extent that he is still enriched. Thus he is not liable if he consumed another's property[10] or gave it away except to the extent that he saved money he would otherwise have spent. He is not liable if he bought and then resold another's property except if he made a profit.[11]

As we can now see, they reached this conclusion by first setting aside every other reason that the plaintiff might recover until all that is left is the defendant's enrichment by means of the plaintiff's resources. It is a defense that the defendant is no longer enriched, but only if he no longer has the plaintiff's property, and is not liable because of the way he had initially acquired it, whether wrongfully or with the plaintiff's consent. In this chapter, we will see that the doctrine is correct provided that it is confined to its original scope. It should be applied when the only reason the plaintiff should recover is that he has been enriched out of defendant's resources.

II. Cases Outside the Proper Scope of the Doctrine

The trouble in Germany arose, I believe, by oversimplifying this approach: by thinking that a plaintiff who can neither find his property in the defendant's hands, nor recover in tort or contract, must recover in unjust enrichment, and, if so, can recover only to the extent that the defendant is enriched. German courts did so because of the structure of their Code. They supposed that the plaintiff must make out his claim under BGB §§ 812 ff., which governs unjust enrichment, unless he can reclaim property that belongs to him by an action under BGB § 985, the modern version of the Roman *vindicatio*, or recover in tort or recover in contract. At that point, they either had to live with the consequences of the doctrine of *Wegfall der Bereicherung*—the defense that the defendant is no longer enriched—or invent some excuse for not applying it. But could it not be that the reasons for allowing the plaintiff to reclaim his property from a bona fide purchaser in good faith extend beyond the case governed by § 985

---

[7] *Summa theologiae* II-II, Q. 62, a. 6. According to Aquinas, if the transaction was purely for the benefit of the person who received the property—for example, a gratuitous loan—then compensation is due even if the property has been lost; if it was purely for the benefit of the owner—for example, a deposit—then compensation is not due except if the loss was caused by grave fault.   [8] ibid. II-II, Q. 62, a. 6.

[9] Ludovicus Molina, *De iustitia et iure tractatus* (Venice, 1614), disp. 718, no. 2; Leonard Lessius, *De iustitia et iure ceterisque virtutibus cardinalis* (Paris, 1628), lib. 2, cap. 14, dub 1, no. 3; Hugo Grotius, *De iure belli ac pacis libri tres* (B. J. A de Kanter-van Hetting Tromp, ed., 1939), II.x.2.1; Samuel Pufendorf, *De iure naturae ac gentium libri octo* (Amsterdam, 1688), IV.xiii.6.

[10] Lessius, *De iustitia et iure*, lib. 2, cap. 14, dub. 1, no. 5 ('For example, if he spent ten gold pieces of another's property and only saved five of his own because he would only have consumed five otherwise, he is only liable for five because he appears to have become richer only to that extent'); Grotius, *De iure belli ac pacis* II.x.5; Pufendorf, *De iure naturae ac gentium* IV.xiii.9.

[11] Molina, *De iustitia et iure*, disp. 718, no. 2, disp. 721, no. 6; Lessius, *De iustitia et iure*, lib. 2, cap. 14, dub. 1, no. 4; Grotius, *De iure belli ac pacis*, II.x.8; Pufendorf, *De iure naturae ac gentium*, IV.xiii.8.

in which the purchaser still has the property? Could it not matter whether the one party wronged or injured the other even if the plaintiff's action is not in tort? Could it not matter that a party did consent even if he did not enter into an enforceable contract? Questions like these seem to threaten the overall order of this book, which, thus far, has divided legal questions neatly into property, tort, contract, and unjust enrichment. But if one is to take a functional approach, one must recognize that some solutions make sense given the purposes of the legal system even if they don't fit neatly in these categories. If that is so, then the oversimplification leads in the wrong direction. In the law of unjust enrichment, it seems that there cannot be an action unless the defendant is enriched. But one might decide, for reasons extraneous to the law of unjust enrichment, what is the responsibility of a bona fide purchaser, or of a person who commits a wrong or injury, or of a person who makes a voluntary decision even if it does not result in an enforceable contract.

A. The Bona Fide Purchaser

In Germany as elsewhere, an owner can reclaim his stolen car from a bona fide purchaser. The reason, we now recognize, is not simply that the thief had no title to give. It concerns the buyer's ability to protect himself by dealing with someone who is reputable or at least amenable to a lawsuit. It may be that for the same reason, the owner should recover from a bona fide purchaser who has resold the car. If so, all one needs to say to justify this result is that the bona fide purchaser can still sue whoever originally sold the car to him. German courts, however, say the remedy lies in unjust enrichment, and then explain away the requirement that the defendant be enriched by claiming that the money he paid the thief was not causally related to his enrichment.[12] As Dawson has pointed out, that claim is inconsistent with the loose approach they take to causation in other cases.[13] As Werner Lorenz has observed, it is not helpful because it obscures the reason the plaintiff is allowed to recover, which has nothing to do with whether the defendant is enriched.[14]

B. Wrong or Injury

Suppose, next, that one of the parties committed a wrong or injury. We will examine four types of cases: (i) the defendant wrongfully induced the plaintiff to contract, (ii) the defendant exploited the plaintiff's need or ignorance to contract on unfairly advantageous terms, (iii) the defendant wrongfully appropriated a benefit that he should have obtained by contract, and (iv) one party injured the other by disavowing the contract after he had changed his position in reliance upon it, and yet the party committing the injury is not at fault because he is a minor, an insane person or otherwise incompetent.

[12] Bundesgerichtshof, EBGHZ 14, 7, 9–10 (1954); EBGHZ 9, 333, 335–6 (1953); EBGHZ 55, 176, 180 (1971) (two bulls sold to butcher who cut them up, thereby acquiring title).

[13] As noted by Dawson, 'Erasable Enrichment', 294.

[14] Werner Lorenz in Julius von Staudinger, *Kommentar zum Bürgerlichen Gesetzbuch mit Einführungsgesetz und Nebengesetzen* (13th edn., Berlin, 1994), no. 38 to BGB § 818.

1. *Wrongfully inducing the other party to contract*

Suppose the defendant fraudulently induced the plaintiff to buy a car, and that the car has been destroyed. Lord Denning once said in a fraud case,[15] as I have said earlier in this book,[16] that a person who commits an intentional wrong should be liable for its unforeseen consequences. If so, then the reason the plaintiff should recover the purchase price is because the defendant committed a wrong, not because he was enriched. German courts have reached this result by saying that the remedy is in unjust enrichment, but then creating an exception to the requirement that the defendant be enriched. Rather than entering by one door only to exit by another, it would be better to say that the remedy is not one for unjust enrichment.

2. *Unfair terms*

In another type of case, the wrong was to obtain unfair terms by exploiting the plaintiff's ignorance or necessity. The plaintiff cannot then claim that, but for the wrong, he would not have contracted at all. He would have done so but on better terms. The appropriate remedy, as we have seen, would be to enforce the contract but on fair terms, which, in fact, is done in the United States.[17] If this result were thought to be too hard on a defendant who might not have contracted at all on such terms, he could be given the option to reject these terms and rescind the contract. That, in fact, was done under the *ius commune* when a remedy was given for *laesio enormis* or gross disparity in price.[18] German courts face the difficulty that BGB § 138 prescribes only one remedy when a contract is one-sided: the contract is void. Consequently, they apply the law of unjust enrichment to return the parties, so far as possible, to their original position. In one case, a seller had been forced by his necessity to sell at too low a price, and the buyer had resold at a profit. The seller later became insolvent. The court awarded the seller the difference between the resale price and the initial purchase price.[19] Supposedly, that was the amount by which the buyer had been enriched. Dawson believes that the seller should recover the initial purchase price and that the buyer should have to line up with the seller's other creditors to recover anything at all.[20] If, as I have suggested, the seller should merely recover the difference between a fair price and the unfair purchase price, then both approaches are wrong. One source of the difficulty is the rigidity of BGB § 138. But another is the assumption of both the German court and Dawson that the problem is one of unjust enrichment rather than of devising a remedy for a certain type of wrong.

3. *Wrongful appropriation of a benefit which one should have obtained by contract*

In another type of case, the wrong was knowingly to appropriate something instead of obtaining it by contract. Here, German courts not only do not apply the doctrine of

---

[15] *Doyle* v. *Olby* (1969) 2 All ER 199, 122 (CA).   [16] Chapter 10 I B.

[17] UCC, § 2–302. See *Jones* v. *Star Credit Corp.*, 298 NYS2d 264 (Sup Ct 1969); *Frostifresh* v. *Reynoso*, 274 NYS2d 757 (Sup Ct 1966), rev'd as to damages, 281 NYS2d 964 (App 1967); *American Home Improvement Co.* v. *MacIver*, 201 A2d 886 (NH, 1964).

[18] James Gordley, 'Just Price', *The New Palgrave Dictionary of Economics and the Law* 2 (P. Newman, ed., London, 1998), 410.   [19] RG, JW 1915, 918, 919.

[20] Dawson, 'Erasable Enrichment', 290 (at least, that seems to be what he means: he says the seller should get 'direct recovery').

Wegfall but they do not even require that the defendant ever have been enriched. In a famous case, the defendant managed to take a trip to New York (and back again, when he was refused entry) without paying the plaintiff airline for his ticket. The court required him to pay even though he was not enriched by that amount.[21] When a railroad put more traffic across plaintiff's land than its right-of-way permitted, the court required it to pay the amount it would have had to pay had it acquired the right in the normal way. The railroad was not allowed to say that it would not have done so, had it expected to pay that amount.[22] A motorcycle manufacturer that used a picture, taken without his consent, of a well-known actor in its advertising, was made to pay the license fee that would usually be paid a celebrity.[23] American courts have reached similar results by holding that a contract has been formed. According to the *Second Restatement of Contracts*, the offeree's 'silence and inaction operate as an acceptance' where he 'takes the benefit of offered services with reasonable opportunity to reject them and reason to know that they were offered with the expectation of compensation'.[24] For example, one who reads newspapers delivered to him without his request is deemed to have bought them even if he clearly did not intend to do so.[25] In such cases, to say a contract was formed is a fiction since the defendant did not consent. Nevertheless, they are not cases of unjust enrichment in the ordinary sense since it does not matter whether the defendant was enriched or enriched by the purchase price. He is liable because he wrongfully attempted to appropriate a benefit instead of contracting for it. He is not allowed to better his position by refusing to contract.[26]

4. Injury caused by an incompetent party

A related question is what to do when an incompetent party has injured someone by entering into a contract with a person who changes his position in reliance on it. The competent party cannot ask a court to enforce the contract and thereby protect his right to the bargain that he has made. He has not made a valid bargain because the incompetent party cannot give consent. Nevertheless, should he be able to recover any loss he has suffered from the incompetent party? The question is like the one in tort law about whether insane people or minors should have to pay for the physical damage that they do.[27] The answer is not obvious. On the one hand, they are not at fault. On the other, because of their condition, they have caused someone else a loss. Not surprisingly, different legal systems have given different answers.

In the United States and Germany, however, the problem is approached as one of unjust enrichment. Yet, this approach has not prevented American and German courts from protecting, albeit only partially, a party who has suffered a loss by contracting with an incompetent. In the United States, sometimes the contract is enforced, and when it is not, the right of the incompetent to recover for unjust enrichment is conditioned on the return of whatever benefits he received.[28] In Germany, protection was traditionally given by applying the so-called Saldo theory. The claims in unjust enrichment of each party are aggregated so that the defendant may deduct

---

[21] BGH, 1 July 1971, NJW 1971, 609.   [22] RG, 20 Dec. 1919, ERGZ 97, 310 (1919).
[23] BGH, 8 May 1956, EBGHZ 20, 345 (1956).   [24] *Restatement (Second) of Contracts*, § 69 (1981).
[25] *Austin* v. *Burge*, 137 SW 618 (Mo App 1911).   [26] Chapter 21 II.   [27] Chapter 10 II B.
[28] Dawson, 'Erasable Enrichment', 298 n. 91.

the value of whatever he gave the plaintiff from the value of whatever the plaintiff had given him. For example, in one case in which the doctrine was first applied, the incompetent party, who was supervising the construction of a building, purchased steel girders in his own name. They were incorporated into the building which later was seized and sold to satisfy the demands of creditors. After he died, his heirs sued to recover the purchase price in just enrichment. They recovered an insignificant amount because the court allowed the defendant to deduct the value of the girders.[29] Dawson pointed out that if one wants an incompetent person to bear a loss that he occasioned, this is hardly a logical way to do so.[30] The competent party is protected only when he is a defendant. He is protected if the incompetent party seeks money damages but not if title to a movable has not passed, and the incompetent part recovers it by self-help or without suing in unjust enrichment to do so. Dawson also claimed that to give even this limited protection was inconsistent with the doctrine of *Wegfall* since the disappearance of the plaintiff's enrichment—for example, by the incorporation of the girders in the building—is ignored.[31] He is quite right that the real question is whether the competent party should be protected against the loss that the incompetent one would otherwise cause him. But then the real basis for liability is not that the incompetent has been enriched but rather that the competent should be protected. Since it does not matter whether the incompetent was enriched, there is no reason why the doctrine of *Wegfall* or loss of enrichment should apply.

C. Consent

A contract may be void, and yet one of the parties may still have made a decision voluntarily which should affect his rights. We will examine (i) the decision to enter into a contract which turns out to be void, and (ii) the decision to employ a third party whose actions have prejudiced the other party to the void contract.

1. The decision to enter into a contract that proves to be void

Suppose that the defendant has received the plaintiff's property voluntarily, even though the transaction is not an enforceable contract: for example, he buys plaintiff's goods but the contract is void for defect in form. Suppose that these goods are now valueless because they were destroyed or because they were specially made for the defendant, who does not want them any more. If the contract is void, it follows that neither party can claim the benefit of his bargain. It does not follow that the transaction must be regarded as involuntary for all purposes. It might be that the risks should still fall where they do whenever resources are exchanged voluntarily. If the goods are destroyed by chance, the risk falls on the buyer; if they are destroyed because they were defective when delivered, the risk falls on the seller; if they were specially made to the buyer's order, the risk falls on him that neither he nor anyone else will want them. If so, then, these results are appropriate because the reason

---

[29] J. A. Gruchot, *Beiträge zur Erläuterung des deutsches Rechts* 55, 963 (Reichsgericht 1911).
[30] Dawson, 'Erasable Enrichment', 299.   [31] ibid. 298.

for declaring the contract void does not extend to all the consequences a voluntary transaction normally carries with it. Once again, they have nothing to do with whether the defendant is enriched.

Again, German courts arrive at these results but to do so, they find a way around the requirement that the defendant must be enriched. If the goods were destroyed by chance after delivery, German courts again apply the Saldo theory. The claims of buyer and seller in unjust enrichment are aggregated so that the seller returns the purchase price less the value of the car he had delivered and which the buyer is unable to return to him. Thus, while the risk of destruction falls on the buyer, the seller does not receive the benefit of his bargain, as he would if the contract were enforceable. If the goods are worthless because they were defective, the Saldo theory has been construed to allow the buyer to recover the purchase price,[32] an explanation that German authors regard as artificial even though they approve of the result.[33] In one case, where goods were specially made to the buyer's order and were worthless, the seller was allowed to deliver them and keep the purchase price.[34] Having done so, supposedly, he was no longer enriched.

Nevertheless, since courts have to bob and weave to come to the right result, it is not surprising that, in some of the cases to which Dawson objected, they came to the wrong one. In one case, for example, the defendant employed the plaintiff to drill a hole on his land to the depth of 800 meters. Plaintiff could not even recover his costs, because, the court said, the hole was worthless, and therefore the defendant had not been unjustly enriched.[35] Although the case is an old one, Dawson argued that there is no logical escape from this result under German law.[36] There isn't if we imagine that the defendant is liable solely because he has been enriched. We should say instead that even if the contract is void, those who order holes to be dug should bear the normal risks of doing so.

Moreover, it is worth noting that American courts have sometimes made the same mistake, not by asking whether enrichment has disappeared, but by asking whether the defendant was ever enriched at all. In one case, the defendant had contracted for the plaintiff to carve and erect a stone monument. The contract was unenforceable. The plaintiff was allowed to recover in unjust enrichment for having dug a hole for the monument but not for the work he had done carving the stone, supposedly because the hole benefitted the defendant but the carving did not since it had not been finished and the stone had not been erected.[37] According to the approach I am suggesting, he should have recovered for both since what matters is that the defendant voluntarily agreed for him to build the monument.

Those familiar with the German literature will have noticed that this approach is like that of Werner Flume. He believed that a person who had voluntarily decided to contract should not escape the normal consequences simply because the contract was

---

[32] RG, 20 Dec. 1918, ERGZ 94, 253, 255 (1918).   [33] Lorenz to § 831, no. 46.
[34] RG, 11 Oct. 1927, ERGZ 118, 185, 188 (1927). Here, the machines had not yet been delivered, and so the court did not apply the Saldo theory; rather, it allowed the manufacturer to transfer the machines to the buyer in satisfaction of his claim for unjust enrichment.   [35] RG, 1910, JW 1911, 756.
[36] Dawson, 'Erasable Enrichment', 312–13.   [37] *Dowling* v. *McKenny*, 124 Mass 478 (1878).

unenforceable.[38] But Flume rested this conclusion on a claim about causation. He tried to distinguish between events the defendant himself had caused and those that were caused by the receipt of the plaintiff's asset.[39] Consequently, he had to say, for example, that if the defendant gave away property he believed he had received as a gift, the cause was the receipt of the property rather than the defendant's decision to give it away.[40] That seems forced. Moreover, Flume spent the bulk of his article arguing that the defense of *Wegfall der Bereicherung* was an ill-advised 19th century innovation. Thus his solution seems to be an attempt to domesticate a defense he disliked. In my view, the defense is perfectly sound provided we remember that from its very origins, it was meant to apply only when the plaintiff's claim was based simply on the fact that the defendant was enriched.

Although Dawson liked Flume's article, he said, 'I know of no way that an American approach could make use of this peculiar formula, which enforces promises ("commitments") made in contracts found to be void'.[41] In fact, it is the best description of what American and English courts do. If, under a void contract, the seller altered a house at the buyer's request, he recovers the reasonable value of the alterations even if they lower its market value.[42] If the defendant contracted for the plaintiff's services as an architect, he pays the value of these services even if he never uses the plaintiff's plans.[43] If the defendant contracted for the plaintiff's services marketing his products, he pays their value whether or not they were successful.[44] In a famous early English case, a publisher who commissioned a book and then decided before it was written not to publish it had to pay the author for a manuscript that was never completed.[45] Dawson himself says that in such cases, the 'responsibilities and risks continue to be those assigned by or inherent in the contract itself . . .'.[46] That comes close to saying that it doesn't matter if defendant was enriched when he voluntarily decided to acquire plaintiff's resources.

In that respect, voluntary acquisition differs from what Peter Birks calls 'free acceptance'. For Birks, the defendant's 'free acceptance' of a performance, knowing plaintiff expected to be paid, proves that the defendant was enriched by the amount that he expected the plaintiff to charge.[47] But the defendant is often liable for that amount even if, in retrospect, he can show he wasn't enriched, as when he commissions

---

[38] 'Wen jemand mit seinem Willen einen gegenseitigen Vertrag schliesst, so fällt er damit—auch wenn der Vertrag nichtig ist—die vermögensmässige Entscheidung, dass er statt des Vermögenswerts seiner Gegenleistung die ihm zu erbringende Leistung haben will. Die Konsequenzen dieser Entscheidung muss er tragen, denn er ist es, der die Entscheidung gefällt hat.' Werner Flume, 'Der Wegfall der Bereicherung in der Entwicklung vom römischen zum geltenden Recht', in *Festschrift für Hans Niedermeyer* (Göttingen, 1953), 103 at 165.   [39] ibid. 154.

[40] 'Zwar ist der Empfänger des Erwerbs sine causa in diesen Fällen auch durch sein Verhalten ursächlich für die Vermögensminderung geworden. Das Verhalten des Empfängers wurder aber ursächlich bestimmt durch den Erwerb sine causa' (ibid. 158).   [41] Dawson, 'Erasable Enrichment', 303 n. 110.

[42] *Dearns* v. *Andree*, 139 A 695 (Conn 1928).

[43] e.g. *Barnes* v. *Lozoff*, 123 NW2d 543 (1963); *Parrish* v. *Tahtaras*, 318 P2d 642 (1957); *Sterling* v. *Marshall*, 54 A2d 353 (DC 1947).

[44] *Fabian* v. *Wasatch Orchard Co.*, 125 P 860 (Utah 1912). I mention these cases because Palmer regards them as typical. George E. Palmer, *The Law of Restitution* 2 (Boston, 1978), § 16.3.

[45] *Planché* v. *Colburn* (1831), 8 Bing 14, cited with approval, Birks, *Law of Restitution*, 232.

[46] Dawson, 'Restitution without Enrichment', 584.   [47] Birks, *Law of Restitution*, 114–16.

architectural drawings that he later decides not to use, or, as Birks notes, when he does not receive the performance he commissioned, as in the case of the publisher.[48] In such cases, the defendant should be liable because it does not matter whether he was enriched or not.

2. *The decision to employ a person whose actions prejudice the other party*

Closely related are cases in which the loss is due to the conduct of a third party whom the defendant hired, or to the fact that this party is insolvent or cannot be sued. Here, the defendant's decision to hire this party was voluntary, whether his contract with the plaintiff was voluntary or not. That decision should carry its normal consequence: the loss falls on the defendant. When the plaintiff paid money to the defendant's agent who then embezzled it, the defendant has sometimes escaped liability on the grounds that he was not enriched,[49] although, in one case, the court avoided this result by noting that he could sue his admittedly judgment-proof agent.[50] As Dawson notes, he should be liable. In one American case, a railroad that negligently overpaid a contractor recovered the entire amount although, because of the error, the contractor had passed on some of the money by overpaying his subcontractors who subsequently disappeared.[51] Dawson agrees with the result, and believes it shows that the doctrine of *Wegfall* is wrong.[52] But all one needs to say is that the contractor's decision to hire the subcontractors was voluntary, and it should carry its normal consequences when the subcontractors disappear.

Indeed, sometimes German courts have used the doctrine of *Wegfall* to reach an appropriate result. In one case, the buyer of meat paid the defendant's agent, believing with good reason that the agent was in fact the seller. The agent became insolvent, and the contract was declared void for mistake as to the identity of the parties. When the owner sued the buyer in unjust enrichment, the court allowed him to deduct the money he paid to the agent.[53] Dawson objected,[54] but this is precisely the result that should be reached if the hiring of the agent is to have its normal consequence.

III. Cases Within the Proper Scope of the Doctrine

Sometimes, then, we should not be troubled that the defendant is not enriched. He may have purchased plaintiff's goods from a third party, committed a wrong, or voluntarily accepted plaintiff's performance, or voluntarily hired a third party for whom he should be responsible. In other cases, however, the plaintiff has done none of these things, and we should resist the temptation to allow the plaintiff to recover. In one American case, the plaintiff delivered a carload of coal to the wrong party, the defendant, who

---

[48] ibid. 232.
[49] See RG, 5 Apr. 1932, Höchstrichterliche Rechtsprechung 1933, no. 1843; RG, 4 Mar. 1907, ERGZ 65, 292, 297–8.   [50] JW 1929, 791 (OLG Frankfurt am. Main 1929).
[51] *Houston & T.C. Ry.* v. *Hughes*, 133 SW 731 (Tex Civ App 1911).
[52] Dawson, 'Restitution without Enrichment', 573.
[53] RG, 20 Jan. 1920, ERGZ 98, 64; *accord*, BGH, 14 Mar. 1974, NJW 1132.
[54] Dawson, 'Erasable Enrichment', 291.

consumed it. Its market value was $6.85 a ton but the defendant had a contract with another supplier to buy coal at $3.40 a ton. Quite properly, the plaintiff was allowed to recover only $3.40 a ton, the amount the defendant had saved.[55] Dawson agreed this case is different, because, he said, a mistake like this 'carries one beyond the realm of contract, even the illusion of contract ...'.[56] To put it another way, the defendant never decided to acquire coal at such a price, and so it mattered, to this court, whether he was actually enriched. Yet Dawson is not sure the defendant should only have had to pay the lower price.[57] Why? What reason could there be for him to owe the plaintiff money except that he was enriched?

Indeed, I do not see why the defendant who has not been enriched should pay even if his role was a more active one than simply to burn the coal the plaintiff delivered. In a celebrated American case, the defendant hired the plaintiff to build him a Turkish bathhouse. Due to an architect's error, the defendant expected to pay about $23,000, which was approximately what the bathhouse added to the value of his land, and the defendant expected to charge about $33,000, which was approximately the fair value of the work. The court allowed the plaintiff to recover the higher figure.[58] Dawson liked the result and noted that it would not have been reached under German law.[59] He did not like the result[60] in a German case in which the an officer, who was immune from suit, seized and sold goods to satisfy a judgment that belonged to the plaintiff rather than the judgment debtor. When the plaintiff sued the judgment creditor, who had received the proceeds, the creditor was allowed to deduct the costs of the judicial sale.[61] Nor did Dawson like the result[62] in another German case in which the lessee of plaintiff's land, without authority to do so, agreed to sell defendant a right of way so he could build a private railway leading from his industrial plant to the *autobahn*. When the owner sued for unjust enrichment, the defendant was allowed to set off its expenses constructing and maintaining the railway.[63] The results would be different in the United States, Dawson claimed, where American courts have not applied the defense of change of position unless the defendant altered his position after being enriched. I agree with the way German law would resolve all of these cases. I don't see why the defendant should be held for more than he ever agreed to pay unless he was enriched by that amount.

Dawson's favorite example of the good sense of the common law is the rule that the innocent converter who takes and sells another's property is liable for its value even if he sells it for less.[64] I do not see the wisdom of this solution. It seems to be a relic of an age in which justice was done in a rough and ready fashion by writs, in this case, lumping people together as innocent converters without sorting through the differences in their circumstances and asking whether they should matter.

Dawson agrees that the defendant should have a defense of change of position when he lost all or part of the amount by which he was enriched by acting in reliance

[55] *Michigan Central R.R.* v. *State*, 155 NE 50 (Ind 1927).
[56] Dawson, 'Restitution without Enrichment', 598.   [57] ibid.
[58] *Vickery* v. *Ritchie*, 88 NE 835 (Mass. 1909).
[59] Dawson, 'Restitution without Enrichment', 594, 597.
[60] Dawson, 'Erasable Enrichment', 252.   [61] BGH, 28 Apr. 1960, EBGHZ 32, 240.
[62] Dawson, 'Erasable Enrichment', 293.   [63] RG, 28 Apr. 1960, JW 1932, 1044.
[64] Palmer, *Law of Restitution*, § 2.2. For example, in *Felder* v. *Reeth*, 34 F2d 744 (9th Cir 1929), the defendant was liable for $3,000, the value of the chattel he converted, even though he sold it for $550.

on a belief induced by the plaintiff's conduct. Indeed, he believes that in American law, 'the purpose of reimbursing loss through reliance will explain the defense of change of position'.[65] Consequently, he has a quite different reason than I do for believing that the plaintiff should recover the value of services performed under a void contract whether or not they enriched the defendant. My reason is that the defendant voluntarily decided that these services should be performed for him. Dawson's reason is that the plaintiff relied on defendant's statements. He also has a different reason for believing that the defendant should be able to deduct expenses he incurred only because he believed that he could keep some benefit which the plaintiff conferred upon him.[66] My reason is that, having spent this money only in that belief, defendant was not enriched by the full amount of the benefit. Dawson's reason is that the defendant relied on a belief induced by the plaintiff's conduct in conferring the benefit. In the cases just mentioned over which we disagree, according to Dawson, the defendant should not have the defense of change of position, even though the enrichment disappeared, because he did not rely on a belief that the plaintiff's conduct had induced.

I do not see why reliance should matter. The reason, for Dawson, is not that the plaintiff foresaw that the defendant might rely. Dawson says that he should be liable even if the reliance could not have been foreseen.[67] The reason cannot be that the plaintiff was at fault for the conduct that induced the reliance. Nor can it be that the plaintiff consented that the defendant's services be performed even though the contract was void. Reliance matters for Dawson even if the plaintiff was not at fault and did not consent.

Dawson seems to think that the ultimate principle at stake, and the principle that is violated by the defense of *Wegfall* in Germany, is that risks should be assigned to the party who is the proper one to bear them.[68] Does this mean that we should analyze who that party is and place the risks on him? Not according to Dawson. He is critical, and rightly so, of German jurists such as Wilburg and Flessner who take that approach. They think that when a loss must fall on either the plaintiff or the defendant, the law must consider which of the two is the appropriate person to bear it. Flessner wants to assign liability by asking about spheres of risk, the ability to bear burdens and the purposes of allocating them, and the causal connections between activities and losses.[69] By this approach, it would seem that a feather could tip the balance.[70] As Dawson notes, it leads into a 'maze' in which one soon becomes 'lost and bewildered'.[71] In a similar vein, Flume asked what Wilburg could possibly mean by assigning liability to conduct that is 'contrary to commerce (*verkehrswidrig*)—contrary to commercial usage or expectation?—although it is neither culpable nor contrary to law'.[72] Dawson's test is admittedly less difficult to apply: the defense of change of circumstances is available only if the defendant relied on a belief induced by plaintiff's conduct. But Dawson does not explain how this test is related to the ultimate question which

---

[65] Dawson, 'Restitution without Enrichment', 569.   [66] ibid. 574–5.   [67] ibid. 569.

[68] This suggestion seems to me to be implicit in his criticisms of the German doctrine. See Dawson, 'Erasable Enrichment', 292, 293, 298, 303; Dawson, 'Restitution without Enrichment', 574, 584, 596, 599.

[69] Axel Flessner, *Wegfall der Bereicherung* (Berlin, 1978), 112, 162.

[70] ibid. 94; Walter Wilburg, *Die Lehre von der ungerechtfertigen Bereicherung* (1934), 18–21, 143–4.

[71] Dawson, 'Erasable Enrichment', 305.   [72] Flume, 'Wegfall', 151.

Dawson, like Wilburg and Flessner, seems to think is decisive: which is the appropriate party to bear a risk? Among parties who are equally innocent, neither of whom has decided that a risk should be taken, it is hard to see how that question could be answered.

It is, indeed, unfortunate if an innocent plaintiff has suffered a loss. According to an ancient principle, however, before he can shift it to the defendant he must to give some reason why the defendant should bear it instead. If the only reason is that the defendant has become richer through the use of his resources, then, it would seem, his claim should fail if the defendant has not become richer.

21

Remedies in Restitution

I. Remedies for Deriving Benefits to which Another is Entitled

As we have seen, Roman law recognized particular cases of what we now call unjust enrichment.[1] But historically, the idea that there is a general law of unjust enrichment, coeval with contract and tort, originated in the 16th century when a group of jurists known to historians as the 'late scholastics' considered the implications of Aristotle's idea of commutative justice.

As we have seen, these earlier jurists followed Thomas Aquinas. He observed that, as a matter of commutative justice, a person who had another's property might be liable for two different reasons: because of the way in which he initially acquired it (*acceptio rei*) or simply because he still has it (*ipsa res acceptae*).[2] The way in which he acquired it might have been wrongful, in which case he was liable even if he no longer had the property. It might have been rightful and with the owner's consent, in which case whether he was liable depended on the type of agreement he had with the owner. In contrast, a person who still has another's property is not liable because of the way he initially acquired it. Commutative justice requires him to give it back simply because it belongs to someone else.[3]

The late scholastics, followed by Grotius and Pufendorf, took the argument in this last case a step further. According to them, a person who once had another's property, however he might have acquired it, should be liable if he has become richer by means of it.[4] As Robert Feenstra has pointed out, they thus recognized a general principle of liability for unjust enrichment for the first time.[5] For them, the rationale was that one who owns property should have the right to the wealth that is generated by that property.

Modern scholars have drawn a similar distinction. For Ernest Weinrib, for example, the owner has the right to a gain that the defendant made by misappropriating his

---

[1] Reinhard Zimmermann, *The Law of Obligations: Roman Foundations of the Civilian Tradition* (Cape Town, 1990), 838–57. [2] *Summa theologiae* II-II, Q. 62, a. 6.

[3] See Chapter 19 II.

[4] Ludovicus Molina, *De iustitia et iure tractatus* (Venice, 1614), disp. 718, no. 2; Leonard Lessius, *De iustitia et iure ceterisque virtutibus cardinalis* (Paris, 1628), lib. 2, cap. 14, dub. 1, no. 3; Hugo Grotius, *De iure bellis ac pacis libri tres* (B. J. A. de Kanter-van Hetting Tromp, ed., 1939), II.x.5; Samuel Pufendorf, *De iure naturae et gentium libri octo* (Amsterdam, 1688), IV.xiii.9.

[5] Robert Feenstra, 'L'influence de la scolastique espagnole sur Grotius en droit privé: quelques expériences dans des questions de fond et de forme, concernant notamment les doctrines de l'erreur et de l'enrichissement sans cause', in Robert Feenstra, *Fata iuris Romani* (Leyden, 1974), 338.

property because this right is the logical correlative of the owner's right to gain from its use. He has the right to recover if the defendant harmed him because it is the logical correlative of his right not be harmed.[6] But the question is why should the law recognize these two kinds of rights.

We have to distinguish these two kinds of rights to make sense of the law of unjust enrichment. The plaintiff can recover restitutionary damages when the defendant appropriates his land or chattels, violates his patent or copyright, or puts his name or image to a commercial use. He generally cannot when he is the victim of battery, negligence, nuisance, or defamation even if the defendant has profited. Modern treatise writers agree that the distinction is fundamental. They nevertheless find it perplexing since it is not clear why the law treats these rights differently or how they are to be distinguished.[7] To resolve those problems, one has to ask what purpose is served by drawing the distinction.

As we have seen,[8] Aristotle considered the purpose of recognizing rights to private property when he criticized the theory of his teacher Plato that property should be held in common. If it were, Aristotle said, people would quarrel, and some would work little and receive much while others worked much and received little.[9] Thomas Aquinas explained that private property was a legitimate institution because it avoided the disadvantages that Aristotle had mentioned.[10] Nevertheless, Aristotle and Aquinas also believed that the end of external things was to meet human needs.[11] Aquinas concluded that the owner's rights were not absolute but limited by the considerations that explained the institution of rights to private property. For example, a person in urgent need with no other recourse could lawfully take another's property.[12]

Late scholastics such as Soto, Molina, and Lessius followed Aquinas, and natural lawyers such as Grotius and Pufendorf borrowed from them. As we have seen, while they developed these ideas in different ways, they all said that by nature, or originally, or in principle, all things belong to everyone. They all describe private ownership as instituted to overcome the disadvantages of common ownership, usually the ones mentioned by Aristotle and Aquinas.[13]

In the Aristotelian tradition, then, rights to private property are a solution to the problems of allocating resources and of providing incentives to produce and care for them. When resources are shared, quarrels arise easily because there is no clear answer to the question when one person has had his share or taken his turn. Incentives to

---

[6] Ernest J. Weinrib, 'Restitutionary Damages as Corrective Justice', vol. 1, *Theoretical Inquiries in Law* (*Online edn.*): No. 1, Article 1 (2000), 12, http://www.bepress.com/til/default/vol1/iss1/art1.

[7] As George Palmer puts it, when the plaintiff recovers for unjust enrichment, the defendant's gain must have been 'the product of the legally protected interest that was invaded'. George E. Palmer, *The Law of Restitution* 1 (Boston, 1978), § 2.10. The tort in question, Peter Birks says, must have 'the purpose of preventing disapproved modes of enrichment'. Peter Birks, *An Introduction to the Law of Restitution* (Oxford, 1985), 328. The question thus arises, when a gain is the product of a protected legal interest, or when a tort has the purpose of preventing enrichment.   [8] Chapter 1 I.

[9] Politics II.v.   [10] *Summa theologiae* II-II, Q. 66, a. 2.

[11] *Politics* I.viii, cited in *Summa theologiae* II-II, Q. 66, a. 1.

[12] *Summa theologiae*, Q. 66, a. 7. See Chapter 7 I.

[13] Domenicus Soto, *De iustitia et iure libri decem*, lib. 4, q. 3, a. 1 (Salamanca, 1553); Molina, *De iustitia et iure*, disp. 20; Lessius, *De iustitia et iure*, lib. 2, cap. 5, dubs. 1–2; Grotius, *De iure belli ac pacis*, II.ii.2; Pufendorf, *De iure naturae et gentium* II.vi.5; IV.iv.4–7.

produce or care for resources are weak. This explanation is like that of modern economists only more general: private property has these advantages but it is not, by definition, necessary for 'efficient' allocation. In any event, like the economic explanation, it explains property rights in terms of a purpose they serve. Once such rights are recognized, then it does follow that the benefit of using the right belongs to the right-holder and that, accordingly, he is entitled to restitutionary damages if someone else appropriates that benefit. But the purpose served by recognizing such rights ultimately explains why it should be so.

When we keep in mind the purpose of creating property-like rights, we can see both how it is possible and why it is sometimes difficult to distinguish them from mere rights to be free from interference by others. Property-like rights cannot be created without recognizing the right of the proprietor to be free from certain forms of interference. A private right to farmland or to living space would not be a private right if others could uproot the owner's crop or move into his home. The point of having a private right to living space may be to avoid interferences with one's own privacy and activities. Such rights would be worth much less if the owners were not also protected against intermittent trespass and the side-effects of their neighbors' activities. One might think that a property-like right is nothing more than an aggregation of rights against interference.

One cannot see the difference by making a formal analysis of the concepts of 'property' and 'interference'. One has to think about the purposes for which rights are created. Recognition of the rights against interference is necessary to constitute a property right and to make it valuable. Nevertheless, the purpose of creating the property right, in the Aristotelian tradition at least, is to solve the problems of allocating benefits and giving people incentives to produce them. Consequently, it is one thing for the defendant merely to interfere with the rights of an owner that are established so that the owner can derive a benefit. It is another thing for him to appropriate the benefit that these rights are established to allow the owner to obtain. That is so even though the same act can constitute both an appropriation of the benefit and an interference with these rights. One who uproots his neighbor's crop to plant his own both interferes with his neighbor's farming and also appropriates the benefit that goes with owning farmland. One who moves into another's house may invade his privacy or disturb his activities but, in any case, appropriates the benefit that goes with private living space. In contrast, those who commit negligence or nuisance damage the owner's property or interfere with his ability to benefit from it. But they do not appropriate the very benefit which the owner has the right to derive from his property and which the law of negligence and nuisance are designed to protect. It is somewhat misleading to speak of rights against interference as opposed to property-like rights. It would be better to speak of mere interferences as opposed to acts of appropriation.[14]

Borderline cases are a good example of why, to make sense of the law of restitution, one must think in terms of the purposes for which property rights are recognized. Take trespass. In *Phillips* v. *Homfray*,[15] the court denied the plaintiff's claim for way leave rent when defendant used underground passageways to remove his own minerals.

---

[14] See Chapter 7 I B.   [15] [1883] 24 ChD 439 (CA).

For Weinrib, the case is wrong. 'The key to the recovery of gain-based damages is that the defendant has dealt with the plaintiff's property.'[16] The defendant is liable for violating the proprietor's exclusive right to deal with the thing owned. For Weinrib, it seems to follow from the concept of a property right that the plaintiff has an exclusive right to use the underground passageways and therefore to gain-based damages if anyone else uses them.

I do not think it even follows from the concept of property rights that the owner has an exclusive right to use them. Establishing that proposition requires an argument, and one based on the reasons for recognizing property rights. Grotius, as we have seen, thought that there should be a right of innocent use: in view of the purposes for which private property rights are established, one person should be able to use another's property in ways that cause no loss or inconvenience. While modern law does not recognize such a right, at least in general terms, it will not allow an owner to complain of certain physical entries on his property that cannot cause him loss or inconvenience. He cannot complain about entry by radio or television waves unless they interfere with his own reception. He cannot complain about high flying aircraft.[17] By analogy, it has been held that he cannot complain about a sewer underneath his property at a depth of 150 feet.[18] It would seem, then, that the only reason he can complain about people coming on his property is that their presence may interfere with his privacy or his own activities. If so, it would seem that whether he can complain about use of the underground passageways should depend on whether there is sufficient potential for interference to treat the case like an ordinary entry on land rather than like an overflight.

Supposing that he can do so, however, one who commits a mere trespass hardly seems to have appropriated the benefit of owning the property. The rule against trespassing seems to be like the rules against interference which are designed to make the owner's right more valuable. Moreover, it is a second-order rule, since it does not forbid an interference but rather conduct that may on occasion lead to an interference. If so, it would seem that, as in the case of nuisance, an owner should not get damages that go beyond the harm or interference he has suffered.

This conclusion is reinforced by our intuitions—partially reflected in the law—about how much it would be fair to charge for an easement allowing another person to do what otherwise would be nuisance or trespass. I think that most people would think that a fair price would be based on the inconvenience the landowner would suffer rather than the gain that the other party would reap. Suppose that a farmer will suffer from the presence of a nearby cement plant. Most people would agree that the plant should compensate him for the smoke it makes. I don't think many people would want a farmer with land worth $25,000 to be able to demand half the profits of a multi-million dollar cement plant if the plant could not function without making the smoke.[19] I think that many jurists would agree that by committing the nuisance,

---

[16] Weinrib, 'Restitutionary Damages', 15–26.

[17] *Smith* v. *New England Aircraft Co.*, 170 NE 385 (Mass 1929); *United States* v. *Causby*, 328 US 256 (1946) (dicta).

[18] *Boehringer* v. *Montalto*, 254 NYS 276, 277 (1931) ('By analogy [to airspace] the title of an owner of the soil will not be extended to a depth beyond which the owner cannot reasonably make use thereof').

[19] See Chapter 4 II B.

the cement company has violated the right of the farmer to be free from interference rather than a property-like right. Suppose, then, that a gold mine could not operate without laying a pipe to get water through a strip of land along a nearby river. Most people would have the same intuition as in the case of the cement plant: the mine owner should compensate the owner of land for the interference caused by laying the pipe. I don't think many people would like it if the owner could demand half the profits of the mine. In contrast, no one would object if a farmer sold his land to a developer at a price that reflects its value as a housing development.

Admittedly, in the case of the cement plant and the gold mine, the landowner could not obtain such a high price unless he had a monopoly in the sense that the plant or mine owner must deal with him and him only. Most people would find monopoly prices intuitively wrong even if the owner were selling the land itself. Suppose, for example, the owner of a house knew that a developer had acquired every parcel on the block except his own and must acquire every parcel to build an office or apartment building. Legally, the owner could hold out for a large slice of the developer's profits. Nevertheless, I think that most people would find that result objectionable. That insight is reflected in the law of eminent domain. If the state takes the last parcel to acquire the entire block for a public purpose, it does not need to pay the price the owner could demand from a private party by threatening to hold out. It only pays the value of the parcel 'between willing buyers and sellers'. That would not be the law if we thought that the hold-out price reflected the fair value of the land. When the law allows the owner to demand the hold-out value from a private party, rather than granting that party a private right of eminent domain, the reason, presumably, is not a belief that the price is fair but a reluctance to force the owner to sell at a price set by a court. It is hard to tell what the land is worth to the owner personally. Perhaps it is worth more than the price a court would set.

Still, when the owner sells the cement plant or the gold mine an easement to make smoke or to lay a pipe, the reason most people would object to the high price is not only that he is exploiting a monopoly. It seems objectionable for him to charge a high price because the easement is of value to the plant or mine owner, of such value that the plant or mine cannot operate without it. Indeed, even in the United States, where property rights are taken to extremes not known in other countries, the law will often not allow him to charge so much. In the celebrated case of *Boomer* v. *Atlantic Cement Co.*,[20] an American court allowed a cement plant to stay and pay damages. It did not issue an injunction which, in effect, would require the plant to pay the owner's price for an easement in order to stay open. Statutes in some American states allow mine owners, homeowners or farmers to condemn the right to lay pipes or utility lines across adjoining property.[21] Such statutes were upheld by the United States Supreme Court even in the era when it regarded private property rights as sacrosanct.[22] Other American states

---

[20] 257 NE2d 870 (NY 1970). See W. Page Keeton, Dan B. Dobbs, Robert E. Keeton, and David G. Owen, *Prosser and Keeton on the Law of Torts* (5th edn., St Paul, Minn., 1984), 630–2, 637–41. See Chapter 4 II B.

[21] John P. Dwyer and Peter S. Menell, *Property Law and Policy: A Comparative Institutional Perspective* (Westbury, NY, 1998), 739.

[22] *Clark* v. *Nash*, 198 US 361 (1905) (owner of farm can condemn right of way for irrigation ditch); *Strickley* v. *Highland Boy Gold Mining Co.*, 200 US 527 (1906) (mine owner can condemn right of way for aerial bucket line).

help such a landowner by judicially developed rules that provide for implied easements and easements by necessity.[23] It is easier for the law to force an easement upon a landowner, as in these cases, than for it to accept a private right to acquire possession by eminent domain because the easement merely requires the landowner to put up with interference. When the law does so, it usually requires compensation but the compensation reflects the extent of the interference, not the value of the easement to the party who acquires it.

These considerations suggest that one who commits a mere trespass, like one who commits a nuisance, violates a right that is designed to protect property rights against interference but that he does not appropriate the very benefit which property rights confer exclusively on the owner. Should we therefore conclude that the damages for trespass should be limited to compensation for the interference, if any, which has occurred?

There is an argument for awarding more extensive damages. Sometimes, one party will gain more by violating another's property rights than he will lose if he has to pay for the interference. What should be done if he merely goes ahead, violates the owner's rights and then proposes to pay compensation afterward? If he should not be able to do so, then the law must make him pay more than compensatory damages.

Whether he should be allowed to go ahead and merely pay compensation afterward is not an easy question to answer. If he is required to obtain the owner's permission first, then the owner may charge him a price that reflects how much he needs the easement. To do so would be unfair. But it might also be unfair merely to award compensatory damages afterward since then, in effect, the owner may be forced to sell his rights for less than they were worth to him. The amount the court awards as compensatory damages will be no more than a guess as to what they were worth.[24] It is not surprising that solutions to this problem vary. In the case of nuisance, as we have seen, some jurisdictions allow the perpetrator merely to pay damages.[25] In the case of easements for pipes, wires and rights of way, some allow him to condemn an easement. But in jurisdictions which reject these solutions, what should the remedy be?

There is no elegant answer. In nuisance, English law rejects the result in *Boomer* v. *Atlantic Cement* on the grounds that to give damages in lieu of an injunction amounts to a forced sale of a landowner's rights.[26] But then if a valuable enterprise could not function without emitting smoke, a court would have two unpleasant alternatives. It could issue an injunction which would allow the plaintiff to skim off a large part of its value. Or it could take the value of the enterprise into account in determining whether the activity was a nuisance, thereby depriving the landowner of any remedy.

[23] *The American Law of Property: A Treatise on the Law of Property in the United States* (Boston, 1952), §§ 8.31–8.43.

[24] Our objection is that it is unjust to force the owner to part with the right for less than he would sell it. An economist would merely say the result is inefficient. Guido Calabresi and A. Douglas Melamed, 'Property Rules, Liability Rules, and Inalienability: One View of the Cathedral', *Harv. L. Rev.* 85 (1972), 1089 at 1106–7.   [25] Chapter 4 II B.

[26] See *Elliott* v. *Islington Borough* [1991] 10 EG 145; *Munro* v. *Southern Dairies* [1955] VLR 332; *Miller* v. *Jackson* [1977] QB 966; W. V. H. Rogers, *Winfield and Jolowicz on Tort* (14th edn., London, 1994); Simon F. Deakin, Angus Johnston, and Basil Markesinis, *Tort Law* (5th edn., Oxford, 2003), 483, 484–5.

In my view, the 'restitutionary' damages an English court awarded in the case of *Wrotham Park Estates Ltd.* v. *Parkside Homes, Ltd.*[27] can best be understood as another way to deal with this kind of problem. The defendant had built houses in violation of a covenant that ran for the benefit of plaintiff's land. Although a covenant is established by a private agreement, its purpose is like the rules against trespass or nuisance: to protect the plaintiff's land from interference—in this case, from interference by neighboring buildings. The court awarded such damages as, it said, 'might reasonably have been demanded by plaintiff' had the defendant sought his permission in advance. It estimated this amount at 5 percent of the defendant's profits.

Damages in this amount are not compensatory. They do not reflect merely the extent of the interference with plaintiff's view, light and air, which, the court noted, was minimal. But, strictly speaking, they are not restitutionary either. They do not give the plaintiff the entire benefit that the defendant reaped by violating the covenant. Nor do they give him the amount that he could have charged the defendant for releasing the covenant if the defendant had no alternative but to forego building or to accept the plaintiff's price. That amount might have been well over 5 percent.[28] Nor are the damages punitive. Punitive damages are supposed to deter the defendant. To do so they must be high enough to ensure that he cannot profit by non-compliance. In this case, if the defendant could not have proceeded without plaintiff's permission, plaintiff might have charged much more.

Instead, these damages are a pragmatic attempt to deal with the problem that the defendant went ahead and violated plaintiff's rights even though, as the court notes, plaintiff had served notice of its rights and served a writ seeking an injunction before any substantial construction had taken place. The court refused to grant an injunction, supposedly because it would be wasteful to tear down the houses and to do so would aggravate a housing shortage. But since, as the court notes, the interference with the plaintiff was minimal, it is strange to think he would have insisted that the injunction be enforced rather than simply selling his rights to the defendant in return for a large share of the profit. The court's decision must be understood as an attempt to avoid that result. Yet the court disliked allowing the developer to come out ahead by violating plaintiff's rights and paying damages afterward. '[T]he fact that these houses will remain', the court insisted, 'does not spell out a charter entitling others to despoil adjacent areas of land in breach of valid restrictions imposed by conveyances. A developer who tries that course may be in for a rude awakening.' Or he may not if, as here, he need only pay 5 percent of his profits.

Inelegant as this solution may appear, however, it is a quite sensible way to deal with the alternatives of a forced sale or a hold-up. The developer is not allowed to escape by paying compensatory damages. He is encouraged to ask permission first and faces

---

[27] (1974) 1 WLR 798.

[28] Nor did plaintiff receive the amount he would have charged if we could imagine that somehow he did not enjoy a monopoly position. Admittedly such a case is hard to imagine. As a thought experiment, however, we can picture a builder who has a choice of many comparable sites, each subject to a restrictive covenant held by a nearby landowner. If these landowners were to bid competitively, the price for a release would fall to an amount slightly higher than the sum that would compensate for the interference. It would not reflect the builder's profits, and certainly not include 5 percent of them, any more than the long-run price of steel reflects the automotive industry's profits rather than the steel industry's costs.

the possibility of a 'rude awakening' if he does not. Yet since the damages may be only the amount that a court thinks 'might reasonably have been demanded by plaintiff', the landowner has to be careful about what he charges. Such damages, strictly speaking, are neither compensatory nor restitutionary nor punitive. They are 'you-are-encouraged-to-contract-instead' damages.

In a case like *Phillips* v. *Homfray*, the case for awarding such damages is less strong. The interference with the landowner was minimal. Consequently, if he is forced, in effect, to sell his rights, the damages are likely to compensate him adequately for the interference. Moreover, since use of the underground passageways was by far the most economical way for the defendant to remove minerals, if the defendant were required to ask permission in advance, the landowner could charge an exorbitant price based on his difficulty moving them in any other way. A court might well conclude that this is the sort of case in which the defendant who does not ask permission in advance should only pay compensatory damages later.[29]

If our analysis is correct, however, any rule a court applies must take account of two purposes which are in tension: to avoid a forced sale and to prevent a sale at an exorbitant price. These purposes must be understood in terms of others: the price might be exorbitant because the right in question is merely one against interference; rights against interference are established to protect the owner's own use of his property; his exclusive right to this use is protected to allocate the benefits among people who want them and provides an incentive to produce them. The law is not incoherent because it must be understood in terms of purposes, even when all of these purposes cannot be perfectly accommodated. It has a teleological or functional coherence, like

[29] I am suggesting that these distinctions can explain the difference in the measure of damages in *Phillips* and *Wrotham Park Estates* but not that English courts would take express account of these distinctions. Indeed, English courts seem to think that the measure of damages should be the same in all trespass cases although that belief has not kept them from reaching sensible results. In cases in which a trespasser lived on residential property—thereby appropriating the benefits of private living space, an owner has recovered the amount for which the property would normally rent without having to prove he would have rented it to another. *Swordheath Properties, Ltd.* v. *Tabet* [1979] 1 WLR 285; *Ministry of Defence* v. *Ashman* [1993] 2 EGLR 102 (although, here, the Ministry recovered rent but less than the market rent when an RAF officer's wife stayed on in subsidized housing after her husband had left her; one judge cited *Phillips* but the reason seems to have been either that the property was not normally rented for its market value or that she had no choice given the shortage of housing). Similarly, a dock company recovered the fee for a berth from a trespasser who docked his 'pontoon' without permission even though the dock was closed and so the berth would not have been let to another. *Penarth Dock Engineering Co., Ltd.* v. *Pounds* [1963] 1 Lloyd's Rep 359 (Denning, MR, described this fee as the amount the defendant would have to pay for a berth elsewhere). In my view these cases are consistent with a refusal to give restitutionary damages in cases such as *Phillips* where the trespasser did not appropriate the very benefit that ownership is supposed to confer on the owner. Nevertheless, it must be admitted that in most of the cases usually cited to show that *Phillips* may still be good law, the courts had some other reason for wanting to avoid restitutionary damages. *In Polly Peck International plc* [1997] 2 BCLC 630, the defendant had sold interests in its subsidiaries, which allegedly had appropriated plaintiff's hotel properties. While the court cited *Phillips*, it also noted that the defendant had profited, if at all, only by charging more for its interests, and if it did, then the buyer had not discounted for the rights to the hotels which still, allegedly, were held by the plaintiff. In *Morris* v. *Tarrant* [1971] 2 QB 143, the court cited *Phillips* but noted that the defendant was not in the normal sense a trespasser. He had lived with his wife in a home she owned and continued to do so after ordering her out because of her association with another man. Similarly, as described earlier, in *Ministry of Defence* v. *Ashman*, *Phillips* was cited although restitutionary damages were awarded that fell short of full market rental value.

the organs of the body or the parts of a machine. The purposes are not extraneous but explain its structure.

II. Remedies for Willful Wrongdoing

Thus far we have been concerned with a question on which earlier and more modern jurists agree: why, in principle, gain-based damages are awarded. We can now turn to one on which they disagree: the significance of the distinction between innocent and willful wrongdoing. According to Weinrib, for example, whether the defendant acted willfully or innocently can affect whether he was unjustly enriched. If the defendant mined the plaintiff's gold, knowing that it belongs to the plaintiff, he must give back the value of the gold without deducting the expenses of mining it. He need not deduct his expenses if he mined it innocently. The reason is that his claim for the expenses is 'normatively incoherent':[30] it 'asserts what the severance as wilful trespass denied, that the defendant regards the interaction with the plaintiff as governed by the parties' rights'.[31] If the defendant profits by violating his fiduciary duty to the plaintiff, the plaintiff should recover that profit, even if he could not have made it himself, because he had an 'entitlement' to the duty. The 'gains can be regarded as the material embodiment of the breach of duty—what the fiduciary has, as it were, sold out the duty for...'.[32] If the defendant is a thug paid to beat up the plaintiff, the plaintiff has a right to the fee charged by the thug. While the plaintiff's physical integrity is not ordinarily a resource that defendant can appropriate, it should be so regarded when the defendant 'treated the plaintiff's bodily integrity as an item that [he] was in effect selling for a price'.[33]

In contrast, for the late scholastics and the natural lawyers, the defendant's guilt or innocence did not go to whether he was enriched at the plaintiff's expense. According to Molina, one who had to disgorge the profits he made by using another's property could deduct his expenses even if he had acted in bad faith.[34] According to Lessius and Grotius, a person who took money to commit an unjust act could keep the money even though, as a matter of justice, he had no right to it.[35] As Lessius noted, others, such as Soto and Cajetan, thought that in certain cases he could not: for example, a judge could not keep a bribe. But they thought he had to give the money to a charitable cause or, perhaps, return it to the party who had paid it.[36] No one claimed that he owed the money to the victim on the grounds that he was unjustly enriched at the victim's expense.

---

[30] Weinberg, 'Restitutionary Damages', 29.   [31] ibid.   [32] ibid. 33.   [33] ibid. 34.

[34] Molina, *De iustitia et iure*, disp. 725, no. 3.

[35] Lessius, *De iustitia et iure*, lib. 2, cap. 1, dub. 6, nos. 52, 56; Grotius, *De iure belli ac pacis*, II.x.12.

[36] Tomasso di Vio (Cajetan), *Commentaria* to Thomas Aquinas, *Summa theologiae* (Patavii, 1698) to II-II, Q. 32, a. 7; Soto, *De iustitia et iure*, lib. 4, q. 7, a. 1, ad. 2, cited in Lessius, *De iustitia et iure*, lib. 2, cap. 1, dub. 6, nos. 54, 61. Cajetan and Soto are following Thomas Aquinas, *Summa theologiae* to II-II, Q. 32, a. 7; Q. 62, a. 5, ad. 2 who said that in cases such as simony, 'something is wrongfully acquired which the person who acquired it cannot retain but nevertheless is not owed to the person from whom it was acquired'. It should be given in alms.

This disagreement, again, seems to reflect the difference between a purposive or teleological approach and what Weinrib calls a formal analysis. For the late scholastics and natural lawyers, as for Weinrib, the paradigm case in which the plaintiff can obtain gain-based damages is the misappropriation of a property right. For these earlier jurists, however, the reason the defendant must pay is that he has taken a gain that belongs to the owner exclusively. The reason that owners have such exclusive rights is to remedy the disadvantages of common ownership. The purpose of preserving such an exclusive right is not served by prohibiting the willful gold miner from deducting his expenses or requiring the thug to disgorge his fee. The law is not recognizing or preserving a person's right to have his gold mined for free or to charge people for beating him up.

For Weinrib, however, the misappropriation of a property right is a paradigm case, not because of what the law is trying to accomplish, but because the defendant's wrongfulness is embodied in the gain he has derived. The gain is 'the materialization of a possibility—the opportunity to gain—that rightfully belonged to the plaintiff'. Therefore it 'take[s] on the normative quality of wrongfulness'.[37] '[T]he significance of the wrongfulness is not merely that it produces the gain, but that it survives into the gain and informs it.'[38] What does it mean, however, for wrongfulness to survive into a gain? Or to inform it? For Weinrib, it would seem, the answer is not to be found by asking about purposes. His goal is logical coherence. But is the answer to be found by logical deduction from concepts of 'gain', 'survival', and 'wrongfulness'? If not, what sort of coherence can there be which is neither functional, like the kind known to biologists and engineers, nor deductive, like that known to mathematicians? How do we know when we have found it?[39]

Weinrib's explanation in the examples just mentioned is that the defendant is somehow being held to the logical implications of his conduct. By mining the plaintiff's gold, the defendant has asserted, in effect, that his relationship with the plaintiff is not governed by the parties' rights, and therefore he cannot claim the right to deduct his expenses. By treating the loyalty to which the plaintiff is entitled, or the plaintiff's bodily integrity, as something that can be sold, the dishonest fiduciary or the thug is liable for the selling price just as if he had sold plaintiff's property. In my view, however, the impression that some logical relationship is involved is due to the way in which Weinrib characterizes the defendant's conduct and the law's response to it. These characterizations do not follow logically from what the defendant did even though they are chosen to give that impression. Granted, the gold mining defendant knew he was violating plaintiff's rights. It does not logically follow that the law should disregard the defendant's rights. Even if it did, it would not follow that the law should disregard only one of his rights: the right to deduct his expenses in computing the amount by which he has been unjustifiably enriched. Granted, the dishonest fiduciary and the thug made money by violating plaintiff's rights. It does not logically follow that they 'sold' anything belonging to the plaintiff, and even if it did, it would not follow that what they 'sold' is therefore a property-like right for which the plaintiff can claim gain-based damages. These characterizations are metaphors. When they are

---

[37] Weinrib, 'Restitutionary Damages', 8.   [38] ibid.   [39] Chapter 1 II B 2 a.

taken as more than that, they become formal fallacies. The dishonest fiduciary and the thug take money for depriving plaintiff of something to which he is entitled; so does one who sells another's property; therefore they violated a property-like right. All cats die; Socrates is dead; therefore Socrates is a cat.

Moreover, if one is entitled to proceed in this way, it is hard to see where to stop. Why doesn't everyone who gains by intentionally violating another's rights have to disgorge the gain? One could argue, as before, that because they violated the plaintiff's rights, they cannot claim a right to the gain; or that the gain is the price for which they have sold the plaintiff's rights. But at that point, all rights, when intentionally violated, would become property-like rights. One could not explain the cases described earlier in which the law does not require one who violates another's rights to disgorge the entire gain. One could not explain why one who commits a nuisance and thereby saves the cost of some expensive smoke or noise prevention equipment can keep the profit. Perhaps one who commits battery in a fit of rage would have to pay an amount that corresponds to the satisfaction of his passions if it exceeds the harm he does. Indeed, it is hard to stop with intentional violations of rights. As Weinrib observes in a footnote, perhaps 'a negligent defendant who failed to take precautions . . . out of a calculation that the cost of precautions would be less than the cost of liability could be assessed the amount saved'. That amount was a gain he made 'in an advertent disregard of plaintiff's rights'.[40] And suppose that the defendant failed to take precautions even though he expected the precautions to cost less than his liability but that, by chance, the liability turned out to be less because the plaintiff was injured only slightly. By the same logic, it would seem that he should pay the cost saved by not taking the precautions. Suppose then, that the cost of liability is zero because he exposed the plaintiff to a risk in 'advertent disregard' of his rights but happened not to injure him. It would seem that he should still pay.

If that is truly the implication of Weinrib's theory, then it is subject to an objection which, as we have seen, Jules Coleman once raised to the very effort to understand law in terms of corrective or commutative justice.[41] If corrective justice is supposed to restore each party to his former position, he argued, then the defendant must be deprived of any gain he has made whether or not he has caused plaintiff a loss. But the law does not attempt to do so.[42] The answer to the objection is that the law should not try. As Thomas Aquinas said of corrective justice, '[t]he chief end . . . is not that he who has more than his due may cease to have it, but that he who has less than his due may be compensated'.[43] Thus the defendant did not have to pay if the plaintiff was not harmed: for example, if the plaintiff's use was unimpaired, as when the defendant took a light from the plaintiff's candle,[44] or if the plaintiff had already been compensated by another tortfeasor.[45]

We should conclude, as the late scholastics and natural lawyers did, that whether defendant's conduct was intentionally wrongful does not go to the question of

---

[40] Weinrib, 'Restitutionary Damages', 8.   [41] Chapter 10 I A.

[42] Jules L. Coleman, 'Property, Wrongfulness and the Duty to Compensate', *Chicago-Kent L. Rev.* 63 (1987), 451 at 461–2. Coleman now has 'given up the view that corrective justice has anything at all to do with wrongful gains'. Jules L. Coleman, *Risks and Wrongs* (1992), 369.

[43] *Summa theologiae* II-II, Q. 62, a. 6, ad 2.   [44] ibid. Q. 62, a. 3.   [45] ibid. Q. 62, a. 7, ad. 2.

whether he deprived the plaintiff of a property-like right. But it does not follow that whether the defendant committed an intentional wrong is irrelevant. In discussing trespass and nuisance, we saw one reason why it might matter. The law might prefer that the defendant buy an easement rather than choose to commit trespass or nuisance and pay compensation afterwards. The defendant will have that choice if the law merely awards compensatory damages. Strictly speaking, however, one cannot describe damages awarded for this reason as either compensatory or restitutionary or punitive. They are 'you-are-encouraged-to-contract-instead' damages. In any event, in such cases, it matters whether the defendant acted intentionally. If he did not know he was violating plaintiff's rights, he did not choose to go ahead instead of making a contract.

Similarly, if the defendant knew he was mining plaintiff's gold, it might be wrong to award him the full value of the work as distinguished from his out-of-pocket costs. To do so would be to allow him to force the plaintiff to hire him to mine the gold. This case is a bit different than those just considered because the defendant has no legitimate reason to go ahead and mine rather than making a contract first. In the cases of nuisance and trespass, he might go ahead in fear that if he asks first he will be held up. In any event, the damages should be similar: an amount that leaves the defendant somewhat worse off than if he had entered into a fair contract with the plaintiff, and generous enough so that the plaintiff is sure to be as well off as if the defendant had not intervened. Again, strictly speaking, the damages are neither compensatory nor restitutionary nor punitive. They are 'you-should-have-contracted-instead-damages', a close relative of 'you-are-encouraged-to-make-a-contract-instead' damages.

The same considerations come into play if the plaintiff offers some benefit contractually which the defendant appropriated without entering into a contract. In a German case described earlier, the defendant managed to take a trip to New York (and back again, when he was refused entry) without paying the plaintiff airline for his ticket. The court made him pay its purchase price.[46] The damages were not really compensatory since they did not correspond to the harm the airline suffered. It did not suffer any since there were empty seats on the plane. Neither, strictly speaking, were they restitutionary since they did not correspond to the amount the defendant had gained by taking the trip. He was sent back immediately, and even if he had stayed in New York, the trip might have been worth less to him than the price of the ticket. Nor are the damages merely punitive. They are not based on the degree of the defendant's culpability or the need to deter people from stowing away on airplanes. They answer to the intuition that when the plaintiff knows that the defendant has offered something for a price, if he takes it, he owes the price to the defendant. The same principle seems to be operating in American cases that hold that a contract is formed by an assertion of dominion over an article offered for sale. According to the *Second Restatement of Contracts*, the offeree's 'silence and inaction operate as an acceptance' where he 'takes the benefit of offered services with reasonable opportunity to reject them and reason to know that they were offered with the expectation of compensation'.[47] For example, one who reads newspapers delivered to him without his request is deemed to have bought them even if he clearly did not intend to do so.[48] If a contract requires mutual assent, it is a fiction

---

[46] BGH, NJW 1971, 609.   [47] *Restatement (Second) of Contracts* (1981), § 69.
[48] *Austin v. Burge*, 137 SW 618 (Mo App 1911).

to say that a contract was formed in these cases. It seems better to say that while the case is one in unjust enrichment, the damages are not restitutionary, since, as in the case of the airplane, the defendant's gain may have been less than the price. They are, again, 'you-should-have-contracted-instead' damages although this time measured by the price the plaintiff had already asked. In any event, as before, it matters whether the defendant's conduct was intentionally wrongful in that he knew he was appropriating something offered for a price.

Another reason why intentional wrongdoing might matter is illustrated by a conclusion of Lessius: if the defendant learns that he has something belonging to the plaintiff and fails to return it, he is liable for its value if it is destroyed. But the reason, he said, was because of the wrongful way in which he held possession, not because of any profit he made.[49] Similarly, the German Civil Code provides that a person who knows he is not entitled to another's property cannot defend on the grounds that his position has changed so that he is no longer enriched.[50] In my view, that result illustrates a more general principle, discussed earlier,[51] that a person who commits an intentional wrong—here, not returning plaintiff's property—is liable even for the unforeseeable consequences—here, its chance destruction. Earlier, I have explained why I think that principle is right as a matter of corrective or commutative justice. Here, all that needs to be noted is that the damages in such a case are not gain-based. They compensate the plaintiff for a harm he suffered because the defendant did not return his property as he should have.

These considerations do not explain why a defendant who mines plaintiff's gold cannot deduct his expenses, why a dishonest fiduciary must disgorge a profit his principal could never have obtained or why a thug should pay plaintiff money taken for beating him up. Nevertheless, these cases seem out of the mainstream of the law of unjust enrichment, particularly when we take account of the law of other countries. The rule that the willful converter cannot deduct expenses incurred in improving the plaintiff's property is a peculiarity of the common law of conversion. The law of conversion took shape at a time when justice was done in a rough and ready fashion according to which writ the plaintiff had brought and with little thought about the principles on which he should recover. The extreme protection of the fiduciary relationship is also peculiar to the common law. Moreover, in the bulk of the cases, a dishonest fiduciary has been forced to disgorge a profit that the principal might have obtained for himself.[52] The remaining cases seem to me, at best, efforts at prophylaxis, which is how they are explained by Birks, and at worst, overly zealous overreactions. Then there is the thug. This case has never been decided. It is a hypothetical put by Birks. He cites in support cases in which courts have awarded punitive damages.[53]

[49] Lessius, *De iustitia et iure*, lib. 2, cap. 14, dub. 1, no. 2.
[50] German Civil Code (*Bürgerlichesgesetzbuch*) [hereinafter BGB] §§ 818(3), 819.
[51] Chapter 10 I B.   [52] Birks, *Restitution*, 339.
[53] ibid. 327, citing *Rookes* v. *Barnard* [1964] AC 1129; *Cassell & Co. Ltd.* v. *Broome* [1972] AC 1027.

Index

Lightning Source UK Ltd.
Milton Keynes UK
25 March 2010

151817UK00002B/6/P